D1560618

THE HP-UX
SYSTEM ADMINISTRATION
HANDBOOK AND TOOLKIT

ISBN 0-13-905571-1

9 780139 055713

90000

Hewlett-Packard Professional Books

Atchison	Object-Oriented Test & Measurement Software Development in C++
Blinn	Portable Shell Programming: An Extensive Collection of Bourne Shell Examples
Blommers	Practical Planning for Network Growth
Caruso	Power Programming in HP OpenView: Developing CMIS Applications
Cook	Building Enterprise Information Architectures
Costa	Planning and Designing High Speed Networks Using 100VG-AnyLAN, Second Edition
Crane	A Simplified Approach to Image Processing: Classical and Modern Techniques
Day	The Color Scanning Handbook: Your Guide to Hewlett-Packard ScanJet Color Scanners
Fernandez	Configuring the Common Desktop Environment
Fristrup	USENET: Netnews for Everyone
Fristrup	The Essential Web Surfer Survival Guide
Grady	Practical Software Metrics for Project Management and Process Improvement
Grosvenor, Ichiro, O'Brien	Mainframe Downsizing to Upsize Your Business: IT-Preneuring
Gunn	A Guide to NetWare® for UNIX®
Helsel	Graphical Programming: A Tutorial for HP VEE
Helsel	Visual Programming with HP VEE, Second Edition
Holman, Lund	Instant JavaScript
Kane	PA-RISC 2.0 Architecture
Knouse	Practical DCE Programming
Lee	The ISDN Consultant: A Stress-Free Guide to High-Speed Communications
Lewis	The Art & Science of Smalltalk
Lund	Integrating UNIX® and PC Network Operating Systems
Madell	Disk and File Management Tasks on HP-UX
Mahoney	High-Mix Low-Volume Manufacturing
Malan, Letsinger, Coleman	Object-Oriented Development at Work: Fusion in the Real World
McFarland	X Windows on the World: Developing Internationalized Software with X, Motif®, and CDE
McMinds/Whitty	Writing Your Own OSF/Motif Widgets
Norton, DiPasquale	Thread Time: The Multithreaded Programming Guide
Orzessek, Sommer	Digital Video: An Introduction to Digital Video Services in Broadband Networks
Phaal	LAN Traffic Management
Pipkin	Halting the Hacker: A Practical Guide to Computer Security
Poniatowski	The HP-UX System Administrator's "How To" Book
Poniatowski	HP-UX 10.x System Administration "How To" Book
Poniatowski	Learning the HP-UX Operating System
Poniatowski	The Windows NT and HP-UX System Administrator's "How To" Book
Poniatowski	The HP-UX System Administration Handbook and Toolkit
Ryan	Distributed Object Technology: Concepts and Applications
Thomas	Cable Television Proof-of-Performance: A Practical Guide to Cable TV Compliance Measurements Using a Spectrum Analyzer
Weygant	Clusters for High Availability: A Primer of HP-UX Solutions
Witte	Electronic Test Instruments
Yawn, Stachnick, Sellars	The Legacy Continues: Using the HP 3000 with HP-UX and Windows NT

Hewlett-Packard Professional Books

MORE BOOKS FROM MARTY PONIATOWSKI

The HP-UX System Administrator's "How To" Book

◆

HP-UX 10.x System Administration "How To" Book

◆

Learning the HP-UX Operating System

◆

The Windows NT and HP-UX System Administrator's "How To" Book

THE HP-UX
SYSTEM ADMINISTRATION
HANDBOOK AND TOOLKIT

Marty Poniatowski

http://www.hp.com/go/retailbooks

To join a Prentice Hall PTR Internet
mailing list, point to:
http://www.prenhall.com/mail_lists/

Prentice Hall PTR
Upper Saddle River, NJ 07458

Library of Congress Cataloging-in-Publication Data

Poniatowski, Marty.
    The HP-UX system administration handbook and toolkit / Marty
Poniatowski.
        p. cm.
    Includes index.
    ISBN 0-13-905571-1 (pbk. : alk. paper)
    1. HP-UX.   2. Operating systems (Computers)   I. Title.
QA76.76.063P648   1997
005.4'469--dc21   97-36113
                                       CIP

Editorial/production supervision: *Patti Guerrieri*
Cover design director: *Jerry Votta*
Cover designer: *Talar Agasyan*
Manufacturing manager: *Alexis R. Heydt*
Marketing manager: *Miles Williams*
Acquisitions editor: *Bernard Goodwin*
Editorial assistant: *Diane Spina*
Manager, Hewlett-Packard Press: *Patricia Pekary*

©1998 by Hewlett-Packard Company

Published by Prentice Hall PTR
Prentice-Hall, Inc.
A Simon & Schuster Company
Upper Saddle River, NJ 07458

Prentice Hall books are widely used by corporations and government agencies
for training, marketing, and resale.

The publisher offers discounts on this book when ordered in bulk quantities.
For more information, contact: Corporate Sales Department, Phone: 800-382-3419;
Fax: 201-236-7141; E-mail: corpsales@prenhall.com; or write: Prentice Hall PTR,
Corp. Sales Dept., One Lake Street, Upper Saddle River, NJ 07458.

Printed in the United States of America
10 9 8 7 6 5 4 3 2 1

ISBN   0-13-905571-1

Prentice-Hall International (UK) Limited, *London*
Prentice-Hall of Australia Pty. Limited, *Sydney*
Prentice-Hall Canada Inc., *Toronto*
Prentice-Hall Hispanoamericana, S.A., *Mexico*
Prentice-Hall of India Private Limited, *New Delhi*
Prentice-Hall of Japan, Inc., *Tokyo*
Simon & Schuster Asia Pte. Ltd., *Singapore*
Editora Prentice-Hall do Brasil, Ltda., *Rio de Janeiro*

PREFACE

Welcome to *HP-UX System Administration Handbook & Toolkit*. This book starts out with the basics and then proceeds to cover the details of HP-UX system administration. It is sometimes said that "The devil is in the details..." and I certainly believe that is true when working with operating systems. In this book I cover many HP-UX topics in detail that you won't find in any other book. For instance, I cover HP-UX system auditing by discussing the aspects of your system that you should regularly audit and provide several concise audit scripts that you can run on your system on a regular basis.

As the HP-UX system administration functions you perform become more advanced, you may also find it helpful to have at your disposal tools that can assist you. You may find, for instance, that as you load many applications on your system that you need to address performance issues. You may also find that you need to enhance interoperability between HP-UX and other operating systems such as Windows NT. That is why I have included two CD-ROMs that contain a lot of useful loaner software. CD-ROM #1 contains all of the latest HP-UX performance tools. CD-ROM #2 contains some of the HP-UX and Windows NT interoperabilty software covered in Chapter 9 from Hummingbird Ltd. such as X Windows and NFS software for Windows NT. This CD-ROM also contains several audit programs which you can build on to create a suite of custom audit programs for your systems.

There is also a four-panel quick reference card included in the book to help you with the following "must know" topics of HP-UX system administration:

- Logical Volume Manager (LVM)

- Building an HP-UX kernel

- Software Distributor HP-UX (SD-UX)

- System Administration Manager (SAM)

I selected these four topics because every HP-UX system administrator needs to know them. In fact, that is one of the objectives of all of my books - to cover the topics every system administrator needs to know.

Along with carefully selecting the topics that are covered in the book, I also have a unique approach to writing this book. You can view this book as a "translation" of HP-UX system administration. What I have done with this and my other HP-UX books is to translate HP-UX system administration into an understandable form. This translation includes a blueprint from which you can work, many tips and recommendations from my experience working with HP-UX, as well as what I have learned working with many HP-UX system administrators over the years.

My translation is a loose one. What I mean by this is that HP-UX system administration can't be translated literally like a programming language. There are guidelines in system administration, but there is too little structure in system administration for me to provide you with a literal translation. No matter how detailed a training course or manual, they always leave out some of the specific tasks you'll need to perform. Instead of getting mired down in excruciating detail, I'll provide the common denominator of information every HP-UX system administrator needs to know. I'll provide you with all the essential information you need so you'll be able to take on new and unforeseen system administration challenges with a good knowledge base.

The blueprint I provide consists of many things; among them is a setup flowchart. As I describe the specific steps in the flowchart, I'll also provide pertinent background information. This means that as you learn how to perform a specific system administration function, I'll also provide background that will help you understand why you are performing it and what is taking place on your system.

This sometimes means that I'll be describing a procedure and use a command or procedure covered earlier. As a result of this you may see the same command and corresponding output more than once in this book. I do this because it saves you the time and confusion of trying to flip back to where you originally saw the command. As an example of this I use the **sysdef** and **ioscan** commands in both the section on building a kernel and the section on device files. The **ioscan** and **sysdef** examples appear in both places. Both the kernel building and device file sections are in Chapter 1. Device files and building a kernel are both confusing topics and I don't wish to compound the difficulty of understanding these by making you turn pages looking for the spot where a command was explained earlier. I sometimes include the same command and procedure in different chapters as well.

You may very well find that you'll need additional resources as your system administration challenges increase. No matter what anyone tells you, there is no one resource that can answer everything you need to know about HP-UX system administration. Just when you think you know everything there is to know about HP-UX system administration you'll be asked to do something you've never dreamed of before. That's why I'm not trying to be all things to all people with this book. I cover what everyone needs to know and leave topics in specific areas to other people. You may need training courses, manuals, other books, or consulting services to complete some projects. In any case, I'll bet that every topic in this book would be worthwhile for every HP-UX system administrator to know. *HP-UX System Administration Handbook & Toolkit* covers tasks all system administrators need to perform: It shows you how to perform each task, tells why you are doing it, and how it is affecting your system. Much of the knowledge I have gained has come from the fine HP-UX manual set, HP Education Center courses, and the concise online manual pages. Some of the

procedures in the book are based on those in the HP-UX manual set and
some of the command summaries in the book are based on the on-line manual pages. I am grateful for all of the hard work my HP associates have put
into both the manual set and the on-line manual pages. If you plan to perform detailed system administration work, you'll want to have a complete
set of HP-UX manuals.

Speaking of examples, I sometimes use a workstation (Series 700) and
sometimes a server (Series 800) in the examples. When it is required, I use
both a workstation and server to show the differences. Sometimes I use the
term workstation instead of Series 700 and sometimes server system
instead of Series 800. In general though I use Series 700 and Series 800.

HP-UX System Administration Handbook & Toolkit is comprised of the following chapters:

- Chapter 1: Setting Up Your HP-UX System
- Chapter 2: HP-UX File System and Related Commands
- Chapter 3: Networking
- Chapter 4: System Administration Manager (SAM)
- Chapter 5: The Art of System Administration
- Chapter 6: Common Desktop Environment (CDE)
- Chapter 7: Shell Programming for System Administrators
- Chapter 8: HP-UX System Auditing
- Chapter 9: HP-UX and Windows NT Interoperability Topics
- Chapter 10: The vi Editor

Covered in these chapters is everything you need to get started and work through advanced topics in HP-UX system administration.

Software Supplied with This Book

There are two CD-ROMs that accompany this book. Information on the suppliers of this software, order forms, and other such material are supplied on the CD-ROMs. Here is a brief description of the contents of each of the two CD-ROMs.

CD-ROM #1   This CD-ROM contains extensive trial performance software for HP-UX, Sun, AIX, and NCR. This is a full suite of software including: HP GlancePlus; HP Measureware Agent; and HP PerfView. Most of the software on this CD-ROM will run for a 60-day trial period, after which you can use the information on the CD-ROM to buy a permanent license for the software. Every HP-UX installation should run some of the performance software on this CD-ROM in order to monitor system performance as well as tune the system. There is no better way to determine the software that best suits the needs of your environment than to test the software for 60 days and make your own determinations.

CD-ROM #2   This CD-ROM has on it several pieces of useful software. The first is a suite of software from Hummingbird Communications, Ltd. This software is covered in the Windows NT and HP-UX interoperability chapter of this book and includes

X Windows and NFS products. This software runs on Windows NT.

Other software on this CD-ROM includes audit programs and examples of running audit programs. These audit programs will run on most HP-UX systems with minor changes. HP-UX system auditing is covered in a chapter of the book and there are many useful audit scripts that you can customize and use on your system.

There is also detailed background information on HP OpenStudio, not the OpenStudio application software. This is a software product covered in the interoperability chapter that supports software development on both Windows NT and HP-UX.

The software and information included on the CD-ROMs is very useful in HP-UX installations. No installation should be without some performance tools. With Windows NT and HP-UX coexisting in more and more installations I think it is important to know what interoperability tools exist, such as those from Hummingbird, and test them to determine which are best suited to enhance the interoperability in your environment. I also think you will find the custom audit scripts on the CD-ROM to be useful. I have made changes to these and run them on several HP-UX systems over the last few months.

Please don't hesitate to contact the vendors that have offered to put their software on the CD-ROMs. I'm sure they'll be happy to hear from you.

An Overview of My HP-UX Books

This is my fifth book covering the HP-UX operating system. The primary difference in the books is the audience for whom the book is written. For instance, this book, *The HP-UX System Administration Handbook & Toolkit*, covers only the HP-UX operating system and goes into great detail. *Windows NT and HP-UX System Administrator's "How To" Book* covers both the Windows NT and HP-UX operating systems for system administrators at an introductory level. The following brief descriptions, starting with my newest book, provide an overview of each book and the audience intended. All of my books have been published by Prentice Hall PTR.

HP-UX System Administration Handbook & Toolkit

(ISBN 0-13-905571-1)

This is the most detailed of my system administration books. In this book I cover many HP-UX topics in detail which you will not find covered in any other source. I cover HP-UX system auditing, for instance, by discussing aspects of your system that should be regularly audited **and** providing several audit scripts you can use. There are two CD-ROMs included with this book and a four-panel quick reference card. This book, along with the next book described, *Windows NT and HP-UX System Administrator's "How To" Book*, are meant to be companion books in the sense that the greatest coverage of both HP-UX and Windows NT topics is achieved by having both books. The topics covered in both books combined with the software supplied with this book will put you well on your way to achieving HP-UX, Windows NT, and interoperability expertise.

Windows NT and HP-UX System Administrator's "How To" Book
(ISBN 0-13-861709-0)

> This book covers both the Windows NT and HP-UX operating systems. It is intended for system administrators who are new to one or both of these operating systems. There is a chapter devoted to each system administration topic for both Windows NT and HP-UX. In addition, there are five chapters covering Windows NT and HP-UX system interoperability topics such as networking, software development, X windows, and so on.

Learning the HP-UX Operating System

(ISBN 0-13-258534-0)

> This book is useful for anyone new to the HP-UX operating system, including users, system administrators, operators, and so on. This book covers all of the topics new users need to get started quickly, including the most often used commands, a thorough discussion of the vi editor, shell programming, and so on.

HP-UX 10.x System Administrator's "How To" Book

(ISBN 0-13-125873-7)

> This book covers system administration specifically for the HP-UX 10.x operating system release. It is for new system administrators who need to get up and running quickly. This book

starts with the first task of loading the HP-UX operating system on both servers and workstations. It then progresses through all of the topics new system administrators need to know such as networking, the System Administration Manager (SAM), performance analysis, managing the Common Desktop Environment (CDE), and other useful topics.

The HP-UX System Administrator's "How To" Book

(ISBN 0-13-099821-4)

This book covers system administration specifically for the HP-UX 9.x operating system release. This book covers all of the same topics as *HP-UX 10.x System Administrator's "How To" Book* for HP-UX 9.x.

All of my books are written from the point of view of a system administrator or user of HP-UX, not from the point of view of a super HP-UX expert. This is because I work with users and system administrators every day so I know what topics are important to you. The auditing chapter in this book, for instance, is useful to system administrators in every HP-UX installation. This is not a mainstream topic in the sense that custom shell programs are required to perform a thorough audit. I have worked in hundreds of different HP-UX installations so I know what the common topics of interest are when auditing a system. There are not many authors who can supply you with this kind of practical information.

Because I have seen Windows NT and HP-UX systems working together in many of the installations in which I work, I thought it would be useful to introduce system administrators to both operating systems as well as some interoperability products that can make the two operating systems work together more smoothly.

I hope you find this and my other books useful and that they make your installation more successful and smoother running. That is the reason I write these books.

Conventions Used in the Book

I don't use a lot of complex notations in the book. Here are a few simple conventions I've used to make the examples clear and the text easy to follow:

$ and #
: The HP-UX command prompt. Every command issued in the book is preceded by one of these prompts.

italics
: Italics is used primarily in Chapter 4 when referring to functional areas and menu picks in the System Administration Manager (SAM).

bold and " "
: Bold text is the information you would type, such as the command you issue after a prompt or the information you type when running a script. Sometimes information you would type is also referred to in the text explaining it and the typed information may appear in quotes.

<----
: When selections have to be made, this indicates the one chosen for the purposes of the example.

One additional convention is that used for command formats. I don't use command formats more than I have to because I could never do as thorough a job describing commands as the HP-UX manual pages. The manual pages go into detail on all HP-UX commands. Here is the format I will use when I cover commands:

```
form 1      command [option(s)]  [arg(s)]
form 2      command [option(s)]  [arg(s)]
form n      command [option(s)]  [arg(s)]
```

I try not to get carried away with detail when covering a command but there are sometimes many components that must be covered in order to understand a command. Here is a brief description of the components listed above:

form # -There are sometimes many forms of a command. If there is more than one form of a command that requires explanation, then I will show more than one form.

command - The name of the executable.

option(s) - Several options may appear across a command line.

cmd_arg(s) - Command arguments such as path name.

There are two releases of the HP-UX operating system used throughout this book. The vast majority of the book focuses on release 10.x of HP-UX. HP-UX 10.x refers to release 10.0 and later "dot" revisions of HP-UX 10.

There are some references in the book to HP-UX 9.x. The file system layout changed dramatically going from HP-UX 9.x to HP-UX 10.x so I do still include some references to HP-UX 9.x for long-time HP-UX users.

Acknowledgments

There were too many people involved in helping me with this book to list them all. I have decided to formally thank those who wrote sections of the book and those who took time to review it. I'm still not sure if it takes more time to write something or review something that has been written to ensure it is correct. Aside from the reviewers and those who wrote sections of the book, I must thank my manager, Fran Ioppolo. Fran supported me in every way possible while I was writing this book.

A group that requires special thanks is my family who put up with a workstation on our kitchen table for the year I was writing this book and for putting up with the many late nights I spent at customer sites and HP offices working on the book.

Dick Watts

Dick is a Senior Vice President of Hewlett-Packard Company and General Manager of the Computer Systems Organization (CSO). Dick acted as the executive sponsor of the book. His support was invaluable in helping get the resources necessary to complete this book.

The Author - Marty Poniatowski

Marty has been a Technical Consultant with Hewlett Packard for ten years in the New York area. He has worked with hundreds of Hewlett Packard customers in many industries including on-line services, financial, and manufacturing.

Marty has been widely published in computer industry trade publications. He has published over 50 articles on various computer-related topics. In addition to this book, he is the author of four other Prentice Hall books: *Windows NT and HP-UX System Administrator's "How To" Book* (1997); *Learning the HP-UX Operating System* (1996); *HP-UX 10.x System Administrator's "How To" Book* (1995); and *The HP-UX System Administrator's "How To" Book* (1993).

Marty holds an M.S. in Information Systems from Polytechnic University (Brooklyn, NY), an M.S. in Management Engineering from the

University of Bridgeport (Bridgeport, CT), and a B.S. in Electrical Engineering from Roger Williams University (Bristol, RI).

Tom Dolan

Tom Dolan is a Senior Technical Consultant with Hewlett Packard in the New York area. He is an expert in many areas including: HP OpenView IT/O and IT/A; several programming languages; client/server development; shell programming; HP-UX system administration; and many others.

Tom contributed all of the material related to HP-UX system audits. He is an expert in every facit of HP-UX system and network managment. When there are no HP or third-party applications to meet the specific needs of his HP-UX clients, then Tom designs the solution himself as he did with his suite of HP-UX audit programs. Tom was gracious enough to contribute several HP-UX audit modules that are on the CD-ROM that accompanies this book.

Charlie Fernandez

Charlie has been working in the graphical user interface area for the last ten years, first as a technical writer for HP X Window System documentation, then as a product manager for HP VUE, multimedia, and collaboration, and most recently as the Strategic Planner for desktop, multimedia, and collaboration.

He wrote *Configuring the Common Desktop Environment* published by Prentice Hall. Charlie's book is a practical guide to understanding and working with all CDE files to tailor the CDE desktop to your end-user environment needs. Charlie's book is a requirement if you're going to be doing any work with CDE.

Reviewers

I'm not sure what makes someone agree to review a book. You don't get the glory of a contributing author but it is just as much work. I would like to thank the many people who devoted a substantial amount of time to reviewing this book to ensure I included the topics important to new system administrators and covered those topics accurately.

Special thanks goes to Donna Kelly of Hewlett Packard in Roseville, CA. Donna performed a careful technical review of the entire manuscript. Donna has extensive experience with many operating systems including HP-UX, Windows NT, MPE, and AS/400.

Other reviewers of the manuscript I would like to thank are: Brian Beckwith of Dow Jones & Company; Suneal Verma of Hummingbird Communications; Eric Roseme of Hewlett Packard; Jerry Duggan of Hewlett Packard; and David Fahrland of Hewlett Packard.

I would like to thank Tammy Heiserman and her lab group in Fort Collins, CO for not only reviewing the book but also hosting me in their lab to shore up the weak areas of the book and improve the book in general. I am eternally indebted to all of Tammy's group for their support: Doug Drees (who organized all of the reviews and meetings), Edgar Circenis, Mark Rolfs, Jim Darling, Bill Gates, Ermei Jia, Scott Warren, Debbie Stephens, Arpana Das-Caro, and Aland Adams (the original organizer of my visit).

Others who reviewed sections of the book are: Larry Schwarcz and John Mendonca of HP Cupertino, CA; Dave Glover of HP Roseville, CA; Dave Brink of the New York Metro Education Center; Diana Danelo of the HP Rockville, MD Education Center; Ricardo Villafana-Pino, Alison Popowicz, and Nadine Odet of HP Grenoble, France; Thomas Goetzl of HP Boeblingen, Germany; and many others.

CHAPTER 1

Setting Up
Your HP-UX System

You are going to have a great time setting up your HP-UX system(s). I know you are because I have set up hundreds and hundreds of systems and my customers always enjoy it. Why? Because you think it's going to be one thing - pain and misery, and it turns out to be another - smooth, easy, and a great learning experience.

The systems I have helped set up have come in all shapes and sizes. They range from a network of hundreds of low-end desktop systems to massive data center systems with thousands of users. In the distributed environment, networking is more of an issue; in the data center environment, disk management is more of an issue. In either case, though, HP-UX is HP-UX and what you know about one system applies to the other. This is what I am hoping you get from this book: **the common denominator of HP-UX system administration knowledge that applies to all systems**.

I am in a good position to help you with this knowledge. I have been setting up HP-UX systems since they were introduced. Before that I set up other UNIX systems. This means that although I haven't learned much else, I *really* know UNIX systems. In addition, I have a short memory so I write down most things that work. The result is this book and my other HP-UX books.

To help you understand the tasks you will have to perform, I have included a flowchart for setting up HP-UX systems. One of the most intimidating aspects to setting up a new system is that there are so many tasks to perform, it is easy to get lost in the detail. Figure 1-2 helps put in perspective the tasks to be performed and the sequence of performing them. I hope this helps make your setup more manageable.

The nature of learning HP-UX system administration is that in addition to the specific steps to be performed there is also some background information you need to know. What I have done is include the background in the appropriate setup step. This way you're not reading background information for the sake of reading background information. Instead, you're reading background information that applies to a specific setup step. An example of this is providing background information about the program used to load software and background on the HP-UX 10.x file system under the setup step called "Install HP-UX 10.x." You need to know about the software installation program in order to load software and you should also know the file system layout when you load software. It, therefore, makes sense to put this background information under this step of the setup flowchart.

Although I can't include every possible step you might need to perform, I have included the steps common to most installations. If a step is irrelevant to your site, you can skip it. Based on the many installations I have performed, I think I have discovered the common denominator of most installations. In any event, you can use this flowchart as an effective step-by-step approach to getting your system(s) up and running.

SAM

Many of the steps you'll see in the flowchart are simple procedures you can perform with the System Administration Manager (SAM). SAM is an HP-UX system administrator's best friend. I have devoted all of Chapter 3 to SAM because, except for initial system setup, you can perform most of your **routine** system administration functions with SAM. As a preview, here are the **major** headings under the SAM main menu:

- Accounts for Users and Groups

- Auditing and Security

- Backup and Recovery

- Disks and File Systems

- Kernel Configuration

- Networking and Communications

- Peripheral Devices

- Printers and Plotters

- Process Management

- Routine Tasks

- Run SAM on Remote Systems

- Software Management

- Time

Figure 1-1 shows the graphical user interface of SAM through which you could select any of the areas (there is also a terminal user interface for SAM if you do not have a graphics display).

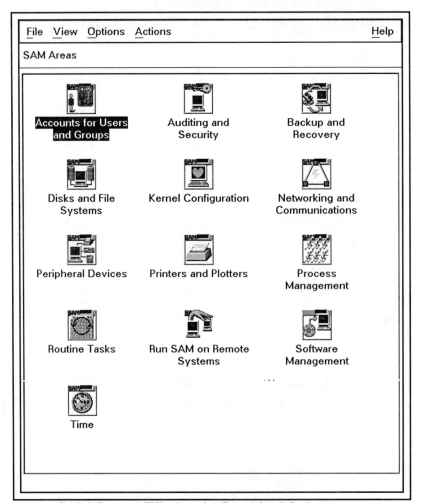

Figure 1-1 SAM Startup Window in Graphics Mode

You select one of these headings, such as *Accounts for Users and Groups*, and SAM walks you through the process of adding users, deleting users, and so on. Because SAM does a great job with the routine system administration functions it helps you perform, I won't spend a lot of time with these tasks in the flowcharts. I will cover the tasks you can do with SAM at a cursory level and refer you to Chapter 3 for more detail. I will discuss all of the non-SAM topics in detail. Although I recommend you use SAM because it makes system administration so much easier, I also suggest you understand what SAM is doing so you can attack system problems intelligently. If, for instance, you allow SAM to configure your networking and you don't know what has occurred in the background, you won't know where to begin troubleshooting a problem if one should arise.

Server vs. Workstation Implementation

Although one of the most important advancements in HP-UX 10.x is the convergence of workstation (Series 700) and servers (Series 800) functionality, there are still some minor differences between the two. When I come across one of these differences while covering a topic, I will point it out. Because the differences are minor, I'm not going to devote a lot of space to covering them. There are, however, a few differences worth mentioning here.

When covering the **ioscan** command, for instance, I will provide both Series 700 and Series 800 examples. Because of the difference in hardware between the Series 700 and Series 800, you see somewhat different results when you run this command. This, however, is true even among the Series 700 systems and Series 800 systems for different models.

The Series 700 has an option for "Desktop HP-UX" that does not exist on the Series 800. This is for client/server applications that run only on the Series 700 that require a scaled down HP-UX.

Another area where I spend some time pointing out the differences between the Series 700 and Series 800 is when installing software. When installing software you may see one Boot program on one system and a different sequence on another system. This is true even within the Series 700 and Series 800 families. When I cover installing software, I show two different Boot possibilities depending on how old your Series 700 is. When covering such differences, I have decided to cover them to the extent necessary, that is, share with you the more important points and not get dragged down into excruciating detail in differences. You will see a variety of systems used in the examples throughout the book. Keep in mind that although there may indeed be differences among models, the procedures are very similar for different models.

Your knowledge of the Series 700 is directly applicable to the Series 800 and vice versa. I have seen many system administrators move from a workstation environment to a data center environment and vice versa with very little difficulty. You will almost certainly need to learn new applications if you choose to make such a switch. You may, for instance, go from scientific and engineering applications to database or other commercial applications if you make a switch from workstations to the data center. For the most part, though, you can take comfort in knowing that your HP-UX knowledge is directly applicable to both environments.

If you are currently using HP-UX 9.x then you may find moving to HP-UX 10.x easy. You should obtain the kit that provides analysis and conversion tools from HP before you make the move. This will help you perform a smooth migration.

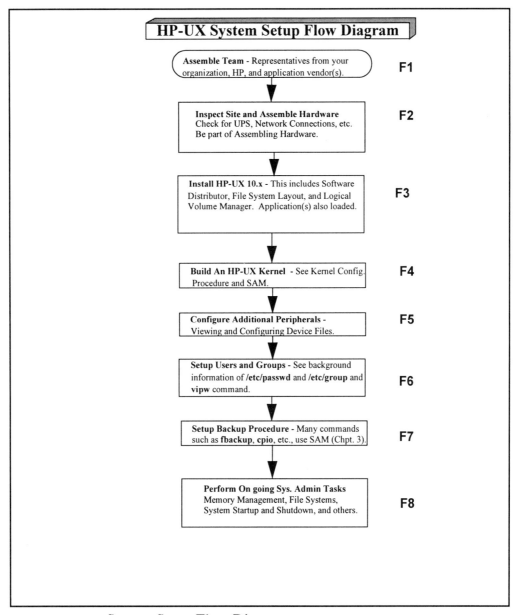

HP-UX System Setup Flow Diagram

Assemble Team - Representatives from your organization, HP, and application vendor(s).   **F1**

Inspect Site and Assemble Hardware
Check for UPS, Network Connections, etc.
Be part of Assembling Hardware.   **F2**

Install HP-UX 10.x - This includes Software
Distributor, File System Layout, and Logical
Volume Manager. Application(s) also loaded.   **F3**

Build An HP-UX Kernel - See Kernel Config.
Procedure and SAM.   **F4**

Configure Additional Peripherals -
Viewing and Configuring Device Files.   **F5**

Setup Users and Groups - See background
information of **/etc/passwd** and **/etc/group** and
vipw command.   **F6**

Setup Backup Procedure - Many commands
such as **fbackup**, **cpio**, etc., use SAM (Chpt. 3).   **F7**

Perform On going Sys. Admin Tasks
Memory Management, File Systems,
System Startup and Shutdown, and others.   **F8**

Figure 1-2   System Setup Flow Diagram

Using the Setup Flowchart

The goal is to get the system up and running as soon as possible, doing as little rework as possible after users are on the system. Although you might plan to have the system exclusively for setup-related work for a few weeks after it is delivered, you will probably find users are eager to get on the system. This usually means the setup gets compromised in the interest of getting users on the system. If possible, don't let this happen to you. Although the setup flowchart looks straightforward and gives you the impression you can get your system going step by step, there are invariably some steps you'll have to redo. This will, of course, affect any users who jump on the system before you have had a chance to complete the set-up and do adequate testing.

This simplified setup flow diagram in Figure 1-2 can be of great value to you for three reasons:

1. It gives you an overview of the tasks you'll need to perform.

2. It serves as a checklist as you complete activities.

3. It serves as a basis for your own custom flowchart, which includes your application installation procedures.

Although system administration books and manuals abound with information about how to perform a particular setup step such as adding users or performing backups, I have never seen a set-up flowchart like the one in this chapter that encompasses HP-UX systems. I encourage you to copy this flowchart and edit it to reflect the process at your site.

This flowchart is by no means complete. This flowchart acts as a good common denominator. You may need to perform additional tasks, but virtually every new HP-UX installation involves the tasks shown in the flowchart.

The following sections cover the steps shown in the flowchart.

Assemble Team (F1)

What a fascinating process I have found this to be. When you consider the number of team members who might be required for a large, distributed project, this might seem to be an impossible task. I have found the converse to be true. In general, I have found application vendors, consultants, hardware vendors, customer representatives, and others involved in a project happy to have the opportunity to carefully plan a project and devote resources to ensure its success.

I think those of us involved in technology know the importance of both planning and working together as a team. I am often pleasantly surprised at how well planning can proceed when the right group of people are brought together. Although you are in the best position to determine who should be part of the team, I will list a few of my suggestions here.

- Within your organization you have a variety of people interested in the project including application developers; system administrators; managers responsible for the installation; help desk representatives; users, and others who you may want to consider making part of your team.

- Hewlett Packard may have a number of representatives involved in making your installation successful including a sales representative, consultants in the Professional Services Organization; support people in the System Support Organization; and others.

- You may have several application vendors who will play a part in your project. If these representatives can be made part of your team rather than just software suppliers, you may find that you'll encounter fewer unforeseen problems such as software incompatibility, and when you do encounter problems, you may get a better response.

- You may have other consultants who fill a void within your organization. If they are part of the team, they may have prior experience they can share with the group that may be valuable.

You may have others you wish to be part of the team. As long as you have a team made up of people important to the project, you will know who is responsible for what and may end up with a smoother running project.

Inspect Site and Assemble Hardware (F2)

The systems used in the examples throughout this book were delivered with owner's manuals that included illustrated steps for setting up the system. There isn't really much to assembling the hardware. Just unpack the boxes, connect the cables, and power up. The manual for the Series 800 Model K460 used in some of the examples went into some detail about the environment for the system, but in general there isn't much to setting up one of the smaller systems.

A large T600 or V class system, on the other hand, may require a lot of work to assemble. For a modest fee, the HP System Support Organization (SSO) will perform the hardware setup for you. I normally recommend my customers do this for a number of reasons. First, if you don't have a lot of experience with HP, you will meet your Customer Engineer (CE). Although HP equipment is highly reliable, you may need to see your CE for possible future hardware problems, so it makes sense to become acquainted with him or her. Secondly, it may be comforting to have a CE set up the system, tell you "it's working great," and give you some tips. Finally, the CE will take down all the serial numbers of the equipment and verify that all your hardware support is in order. It's good to take care of this when the system is set up and to ensure there won't be a delay when you need service.

The really important part of this step is what you do *before* you set up the equipment. I always recommend that the CE perform a site inspection to verify that your physical environment can accommodate the system(s) you have ordered. In the case of the systems used in the examples in this book, which operate in a standard office environment, you wouldn't think there is a lot to inspect. A trained eye, however, can uncover hidden problems. The most common of these is lack of sufficient power. Even though these systems consume a modest amount of power, some offices aren't wired for more than an adding machine and calculator charger! There is no greater disappointment than setting up your system only to find you have insufficient power to run it. Your CE can point out all such potential problems.

Consider all of the material you think you'll need to get your systems up and running. Here is a checklist of items I recommend my customers review.

Hardware Configuration

Cabling   LAN cable (twisted pair, thin net, etc.) of the length you require. Don't measure distance "as the crow flies." Remember that if your office is not prewired, you'll have to run wires up the wall, across the ceiling, and back down the wall to go from office to office.

Media Attachment Unit   MAU to attach cable to the connector on the back of the computer. An example is attaching twisted pair cable to the AUI connector on the back of the computer. HP workstations come with both a thin net connector and AUI. Order the system with the interface you want so you don't have to mess with this when you connect your systems.

Power   Make sure you have sufficient power and power outlets. Many offices already have PCs in them so you want to make sure you have enough power and outlets in the office. If your Series 800 system is going in a computer room, you will be pleasantly surprised by how little space it consumes compared to the dinosaurs for which computer rooms were originally designed.

Software Configuration

System Names   Think about system names. The most common delay I encounter when installing systems is waiting for users to select the names of their systems. It doesn't matter what theme you choose for system names. Just be sure you, the administrator, are happy with the theme. Some good system names are colors, planets, and sports teams. Choose a theme that can accommodate additional systems later.

Addresses   Have IP addresses ready. If you don't now use IP addresses, HP can provide you with class C addresses. Ask your HP Technical Consultant (TC) how to obtain these addresses from HP. Please don't make up IP addresses. Since you will be using the Internet, you will want to use registered IP addresses.

Network Diagram Since I recommend having your HP TC assist you with the installation on a consulting basis, I also recommend you ask your TC to give a rundown on what he or she will do to get your systems running. I normally produce a flowchart. A formal document isn't necessary, but it will be helpful to you to understand your TC's plan. TCs do this kind of work every day and can install your system quickly, but you won't know what he or she is doing unless you're involved.

Order Documentation

As part of preparing for your system you also want to consider your documentation needs when you buy your system. There is very little documentation delivered with either a new Series 800 or Series 700 unit; however, there are many manuals you can order with your system. The documentation is well organized into sets of manuals covering related topics. There is an extensive HP-UX 10.x documentation set. Be sure to order the documentation sets you need, such as system administration, programming reference, CDE, etc. when ordering your system. You can also order the manual set on CD-ROM.

Install HP-UX 10.x (F3)

Installing HP-UX means building an initial "bare-bones" HP-UX 10.x system and later building your complete full-function HP-UX system. The initial system is loaded from the HP-UX Install media for both the Series 700 and Series 800 or from another system on the network for the Series 700 (not covered here). The full function system is loaded from the Core OS media and Applications media or from another system on the network.

IMPORTANT NOTE

Before you begin loading software you may want to consider reviewing Chapter 2. Chapter 2 covers all aspects of the HP-UX file system including commonly used commands and an example of reconfiguring a file system. You'll want to look at Chapter 2 before you get too far with your system to familiarize yourself with the HP-UX file system.

You can have your system delivered with instant ignition, which means HP-UX has been loaded on your system and you'll only have to add to it the software you need. I'll cover the complete installation process for both a Series 700 and Series 800 from CD-ROM so you can see the process start to finish. If you have instant ignition on your system, you may need to install additional software on your system in the future or use some of the techniques described in this section to load additional software on your system.

The K4xx server systems I have worked with that were delivered with instant ignition did not have the **/SD_CDROM** directory which is used in the examples in this chapter to load software. Although I don't cover instant ignition much in this chapter, you may have your systems delivered with instant ignition and choose to not reinstall the operating system. If you have instant ignition and wish to load software using the directory **/SD_CDROM**, you may have to create **/SD_CDROM**.

The Install media that you use to install HP-UX 10.x on the Series 700 and Series 800 is self-contained; that is, it has on it everything you need for the initial installation. I will use CD-ROM media for the installation process for both the Series 700 and Series 800. Later versions of HP-UX have both installation and core operating system software on the same CD-ROM.

Before you start installing anything, make sure your configuration is a supported HP-UX 10.x configuration. If your system is not supported for HP-UX 10.x, you are taking a risk by installing it. There are a number of generic requirements that must be met, such as a minimum of 16 MBytes of RAM and 400 MBytes of disk space for a standalone workstation. In addition, you want to make sure your processor is one of the supported devices for HP-UX 10.x

Loading HP-UX 10.x Software on Series 700

In order to install HP-UX software, place the HP-UX 10.x Install media into the device from which you want to install. In the upcoming example I am using a CD-ROM. Be sure to insert the CD-ROM Install media before you begin the installation. When you boot an older Series 700 unit and hit the ESCAPE key before it autoboots, a screen appears that looks something like Figure 1-3.

```
Selecting a system to boot.
To stop selection process, press and hold the ESCAPE key.

Selection process stopped.

Searching for Potential Boot Devices.
To terminate search, press and hold the ESCAPE key

Device Selection    Device Path    Device Type
-------------------------------------------------------------

P0                  scsi.6.0       HP      C2235
P1                  scsi.3.0       TOSHIBA CD-ROM XM-3301TA
P2                  scsi.0.0       TEAC    FC-1       HF    07


b)    Boot from specified device
s)    Search for bootable devices
a)    Enter Boot Administration mode
x)    Exit and continue boot sequence

Select from menu: BOOT P1
```

Figure 1-3 Booting a Series 700 Example #1

What is shown in this Figure 1-3 (Example #1) are the bootable devices found. Some workstations may show the menu of boot commands instead of the potential boot devices as shown in Figure 1-4 (Example #2).

```
---------------------------------------------------------------
Command                               Description
-------                               -----------
Auto [boot|search] [on|off]           Display or set auto flag

Boot [pri|alt|scsi.addr] [isl]        Boot from primary,alt or SCSI

Boot lan[.lan_addr][install][isl]     Boot from LAN

Chassis [on|off]                      Enable chassis codes

Diagnostic [on|off]                   Enable/disable diag boot mode

Fastboot [on|off]                     Display or set fast boot flag

Help                                  Display the command menu

Information                           Display system information

LanAddress                            Display LAN station addresses

Monitor [type]                        Select monitor type

Path [pri|alt] [lan.id|SCSI.addr]     Change boot path

Pim [hpmc|toc|lpmc]                   Display PIM info

Search [ipl] [scsi|lan [install]]     Display potential boot devices

Secure [on|off]                       Display or set security mode
---------------------------------------------------------------
BOOT_ADMIN>
```

Figure 1-4 Booting a Series 700 Example #2

If this is the case with your system, the **SEARCH** command will show the bootable devices presented in Figure 1-5. This is the result of searching on a B132L system.

```
BOOT_ADMIN> SEARCH

Searching for potential boot device.
This may take several minutes

To discontinue, press ESCAPE.


   Path Number      Device Path              Device Type
   -----------      ----------------         -----------
   P0               FWSCSI.6.0               SEAGATE ST34371W
   P1               SESCSI.3.0               HP C1533A
   P2               SESCSI.2.0               TOSHIBA CD-ROM


BOOT_ADMIN> BOOT SESCSI.2.0
```

Figure 1-5 Series 700 Boot **SEARCH** Example

This list shows a disk drive on the fast and wide SCSI bus at address 6. There is also a tape drive on the single-ended SCSI bus at address 3 and a CD-ROM at address 2 on this bus. Once the bootable devices have been displayed, you may select an entry from the list. In this case I have the HP-UX 10.X Install and Core O.S. media on CD-ROM so I can boot from P3 with the command **BOOT SESCI.2.0**. With HP-UX 10.20 the installation and core operating system are on the same CD-ROM. You may then be asked if you wish to interact with IPL. If you respond "No" you immediately begin the boot off the CD-ROM. You may then be asked what language you want. In my case the language is "28) PS2_DIN_ITF_US_English." After selecting your language, the options in Figure 1-6 exist.

```
              [    Install HP-UX    ]

              [ Run a Recover Shell ]

              [   Cancel and Reboot ]

              [   Advanced Options  ]


                     [ Help ]
```

Figure 1-6 Installation Options on Series 700 HP-UX 10.x Install Media

From this menu I select *Install HP-UX*. The disks on the system are then listed and you can select from among this group to install HP-UX 10.x. In addition, on a workstation you are given the following two choices for system configuration:

- *Standard LVM configuration*

- *LVM configuration with VxFS (Journaled file system)*

I selected the first choice. I normally select standard LVM for workstations and VxFS for servers. VxFS has many advantages over standard LVM configuration. The most notable of these is a quick recovery time when the system crashes. I recommend using VxFS for because of its many advantages; however, at the time of this writing there are several VxFS patches available. If you install VxFS, you want to check the patch list to see if any of the available patches apply to your installation.

The next information to be entered is information such as primary swap, secondary swap, software language, and so on. You want to consider your primary swap space very carefully. There is a detailed discussion about swap space later in this chapter. For HP-UX 10.x on the workstation used in this example the following default parameters were set, all of which you can modify:

Primary Swap Size	256Mb
Secondary Swap Size	None
Software Selection	CDE Runtime Environment
Software Language	English
Locale Selection	default (C)
File system file name length	Long
/home Configuration	Minimal
Make volatile dirs separate	True
Create /export volume	False

After having accepted these defaults you are then prompted for the mount directory default sizes. You will get different default mount directory sizes depending on the size of the disk you have selected to load HP-UX 10.x onto. The mount directory default sizes in Table 1-1 were configured on my system for a 4 GByte disk.

TABLE 1-1   Mount Directory Default Sizes for 4 GByte Disk

Mount Directory	Size (Mb)	Usage	Disk Group
/	84	HFS	vg00.
/stand	48	HFS	vg00
(swap)	256	swap	vg00
/home	20	HFS	vg00
/opt	252	HFS	vg00
/tmp	32	HFS	vg00
/usr	332	HFS	vg00
/var	160	HFS	vg00

Keep in mind these defaults will vary depending on the size of your disk. You can select Modify Disk/FS Parameters and make disk and file system changes. At this point you can change the parameters associated with a mount directory including its size.

After making the appropriate selections, you reach a point where you are asked if you want to interact with **swinstall**. There is an overview of the Software Distributor-UX product used for installing all HP-UX 10.x software in this chapter. You may want to take a look at this overview to get a feel for the type of functionality Software Distributor offers. The **swinstall** program is the Software Distributor program used to install software. If you decide you want to interact with **swinstall,** you will be asked for codeword information and select from among software to load. If your software is protected, you will have to enter codeword information. If you need a codeword, it should be printed on the CD-ROM certificate you received with your software. This codeword is tied to the ID number of a hardware device on your system.

If you don't want to interact with **swinstall,** the software option you earlier selected, such as the CDE Runtime Environment, will be loaded for you along with the operating system.

Both the installation software and core operating system are on the same CD-ROM for some revisions of HP-UX.

You may have an older version of the operating system in which case after the contents of the Install media have been copied to your system, you will be prompted to insert the Core OS media with a message like the following:

```
                    USER INTERACTION REQUIRED

To complete the installation you must now remove the HP-UX
installation CD and insert the HP-UX Core Operating System CD.

Once this is done, press the <Return> key to continue:
```

When you interact with **swinstall,** you select the desired software to load from the Core OS media. You can mark software to be loaded from the Core OS media and then proceed to load the software. Software "bundles" may be selected and loaded. Software bundles are new to HP-UX 10.x so those of you who have HP-UX 9.x experience may not have heard this term before. Software bundles are a collection of filesets. A software bundle is sort of analogous to a partition in HP-UX 9.x, except a software bundle is more flexible in that a bundle can contain filesets from a variety of different products. If you do not interact with **swinstall,** the installation of the CDE Runtime Environment takes place automatically. The process of loading the software consists of an analysis phase and an installation phase. Analysis may determine that you don't have enough disk space to load the desired software. After successfully completing the analysis phase, you can proceed with the installation. When the installation is complete, you exit **swinstall** and your HP-UX kernel is built.

Series 700 Boot After Installation

When the system comes up after installation, a series of windows appear that allow you to configure your system name, time zone, root password, Internet Protocol (IP) address, subnet mask, and other networking setup (IP address and subnet mask background is provided in Chapter 2). This same information can be entered after your system boots by running **/sbin/set_parms**. This program can be used to set an individual system parameter or all of the system parameters that would be set at boot time.   **/sbin/set_parms** uses one of the arguments in Table 1-2 depending on what you would like to configure.

TABLE 1-2   /sbin/set_parms ARGUMENTS

set_parms Argument	Comments
hostname	Set hostname.

set_parms Argument	Comments
timezone	Set time zone.
date_time	Set date and time.
root_passwd	Set root password.
ip_address	Set Internet Protocol address (see Chapter 2 for networking background).
addl_network	Configure subnet mask, Domain Name System, and Network Information Service.
font_c-s	Use this system as a font server or font client.
initial	Go through the entire question and answer session you would experience at boot time.

If you use the **initial** argument, you'll interact with a variety of dialog boxes asking you for information. The system host name dialog box is shown in the Figure 1-7.

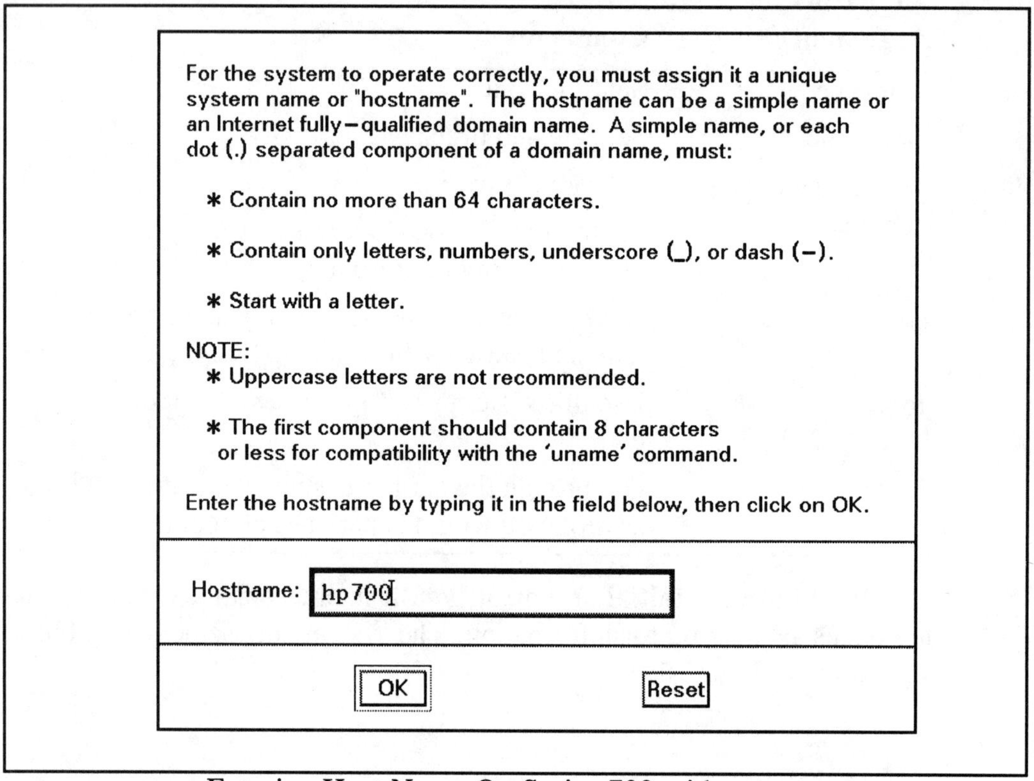

For the system to operate correctly, you must assign it a unique
system name or "hostname". The hostname can be a simple name or
an Internet fully-qualified domain name. A simple name, or each
dot (.) separated component of a domain name, must:

    * Contain no more than 64 characters.

    * Contain only letters, numbers, underscore (_), or dash (-).

    * Start with a letter.

NOTE:
    * Uppercase letters are not recommended.

    * The first component should contain 8 characters
      or less for compatibility with the 'uname' command.

Enter the hostname by typing it in the field below, then click on OK.

Hostname: [hp700]

[OK]   [Reset]

Figure 1-7 Entering Host Name On Series 700 with **set_parms**

You'll then be asked for your time zone and root password. Figure
1-8 shows the dialog box for entering your IP address.

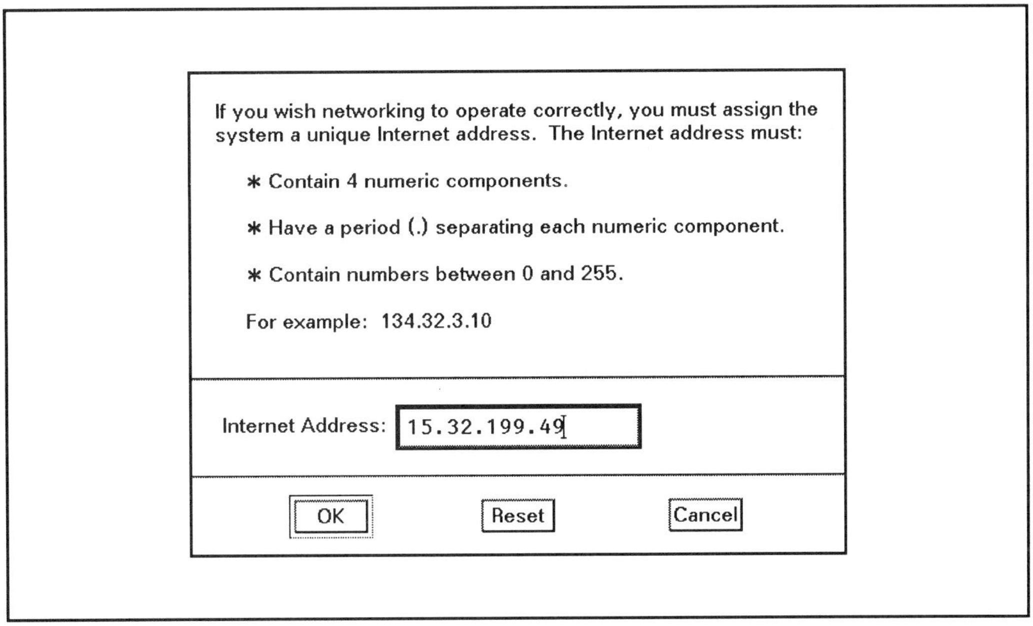

If you wish networking to operate correctly, you must assign the system a unique Internet address. The Internet address must:

✳ Contain 4 numeric components.

✳ Have a period (.) separating each numeric component.

✳ Contain numbers between 0 and 255.

For example: 134.32.3.10

Internet Address: 15.32.199.49

[OK]   [Reset]   [Cancel]

Figure 1-8 Entering IP Address on Series 700 with **set_parms**

You can then configure your subnet mask and other networking configuration.

Please be careful if you configure some of the additional networking parameters (**set_parms addl_netwrk**). Do not configure a system as an NIS client if it hasn't been set-up on the NIS server. I have encountered some interesting problems booting if you configure your system as an NIS client *and* select the option "Wait For NIS Server on Bootup: yes". This means your system will wait forever for the NIS server to respond before the system boot will complete. If you are having problems with your NIS server, you can forget about booting (this is a problem I encountered on a K460 server acting as an NIS client). Your system won't boot and you'll have no way of running **set_parms** to change to "Wait For NIS Server on Bootup: no". I found there are two ways to make this change if your system won't complete the boot process. The first is to shut off the system and boot in single-user state from the ISL prompt with the following command:

```
ISL> hpux -is boot
```

When the system boots, it is in single user mode with a login prompt. If you run **set_parms** and change to "Wait For NIS Server on Bootup: no", you think you have changed this variable to "no" but the file where this is changed (**/etc/rc.config.d/namesvrs**) has not been updated because you are in single user mode and the commands required to make this change are on a logical volume which has not yet been mounted.

After finding out that the change had not been made by running **set_parms,** I decided to manually edit **/etc/rc.config.d/namesvrs** where I could make this change. The logical volume **/usr** is not mounted in single-user mode, however, so there isn't access to the **/usr/bin/vi** editor I wanted to use to make this change. To mount **/usr** I issued the following commands (the **fsck** is required because the system was improperly shutdown earlier):

```
$ fsck /dev/vg00/rlvol6
$ mount /dev/vg00/lvol6 /usr
```

I then edited **/etc/rc.config.d/namesvrs** and changed the variable in this file to WAIT_FOR_NIS_SERVER="FALSE" and proceeded with the boot process. This fixed the problem but not without a lot of monkeying around. This is an area where you must be careful when setting up your system(s).

Loading HP-UX 10.x Software on Series 800

Loading software on a Series 800 is different enough from a Series 700 that I decided to break these up into two different procedures. In this Series 800 example I will use a model K460.

In order to install HP-UX software, place the HP-UX 10.x Install media into the device from which you want to install. In the upcoming example I am using a CD-ROM. Be sure to insert the CD-ROM Install media before you begin the installation. As your Series 800 unit boots, you will see a variety of messages fly by including information about your processors, buses, boot paths, and so on. You are then given some time to hit any key before the system autoboots. If you do this, you'll see the menu shown in Figure 1-9.

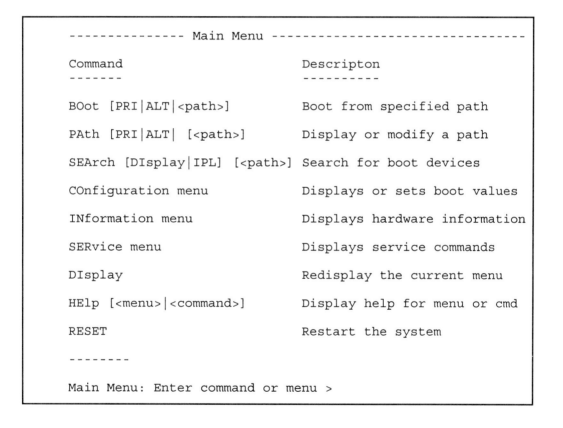

```
-------------- Main Menu --------------------------------

Command                         Descripton
-------                         ----------

BOot [PRI|ALT|<path>]           Boot from specified path

PAth [PRI|ALT| [<path>]         Display or modify a path

SEArch [DIsplay|IPL] [<path>]   Search for boot devices

COnfiguration menu              Displays or sets boot values

INformation menu                Displays hardware information

SERvice menu                    Displays service commands

DIsplay                         Redisplay the current menu

HElp [<menu>|<command>]         Display help for menu or cmd

RESET                           Restart the system

--------

Main Menu: Enter command or menu >
```

Figure 1-9 Booting a Series 800

You can view the bootable devices with the **SEARCH** command as shown in Figure 1-10.

```
Main Menu: Enter command or menu > SEARCH

Searching for potential boot device(s)
This may take several minutes.

To discontinue search, press any key
(termination may not be immediate).

Path Number    Device Path (dec)    Device Type
-----------    -----------------    -----------
P0             10/0.6               Random access media
P1             10/0.5               Random access media
P2             10/4/4.1             Random access media
P3             10/4/4.2             Random access media
P4             10/4/4.3             Random access media
P5             10/4/12.1            Random access media
P6             10/4/12.2            Random access media
P7             10/4/12.3            Random access media
P8             10/12/5.2            Random access media
P9             10/12/5.0            Sequential access media
P10            10/12/6.0            LAN Module


Main Menu: Enter command or menu >
```

Figure 1-10 Series 800 Boot **SEARCH** Example

The information from this screen does not tell us what devices exist at each address. In fact, it is a guess at this point. I doubt people with little HP-UX experience know what such things as "Random access media" are; I know I don't. But since I know I ordered a system with four identical internal disk drives and I have what appear to be four indentical entries at P0, P1, P2, and P3, I assume that none of these is a CD-ROM. I'll guess that my CD-ROM is the next entry which is P8:

```
Main Menu: Enter command or menu > BOOT P8
Interact with IPL (Y or N)?> N
```

This was a lucky guess! This tells me that both hard disk drives and CD-ROMs are random access media to the boot process. I'm sorry to say

I actually cheated here and looked at the inside of the front door of the K460 which listed the devices and their corresponding addresses. Going back to the Series 700 boot examples shown earlier, it was much clearer what devices were present. With the Series 800 it appears the categories of devices are much more broad.

After successfully selecting the CD-ROM, I get the screen in Figure 1-11.

```
┌──────────────────────────────────────────────────────────────┐
│          Welcome to the HP-UX installation process            │
│                                                                │
│                                                                │
│                                                                │
│             [     Install HP-UX     ]                          │
│                                                                │
│             [ Run a Recover Shell ]                            │
│                                                                │
│             [   Cancel and Reboot  ]                           │
│                                                                │
│             [   Advanced Options   ]                           │
│                                                                │
│                                                                │
│                     [ Help ]                                   │
│                                                                │
└──────────────────────────────────────────────────────────────┘
```

Figure 1-11 Installation Options on Series 800 HP-UX 10.x Install Media

From this menu I select *Install HP-UX*. You can install networking at this point or wait until the installation is further along. I normally wait so I can concentrate on the operating system portion at this time and the networking portion when the system boots. The disks on your system are then listed for you to select from. In this case the information in Figure 1-12 is shown for the K460.

```
The installation utility has discovered the following disks
attached to your system. You must select one disk to be your
root disk. When configured, this disk will contain (at least)
the boot area, a root file system and primary swap space.

Hardware                    Product                 Size
Path                        ID                      (Megabytes [Mb] }
-----------------------------------------------------------------------
10/4/4.3.0                  ST15150W                4095
10/4/4.2.0                  ST15150W                4095
10/4/4.1.0                  ST15150W                4095
10/4/12.3.0                 ST15150W                4095
10/4/12.2.0                 ST15150W                4095
10/4/12.1.0                 ST15150W                4095
10/0.6.0                    ST15150W                4095
10/0.5.0                    ST15150W                4095




[  OK  ]                    [ Cancel ]              [ Help ]
   -                           -                       -
```

Figure 1-12 Selecting a Series 800 Disk

In most cases I load the operating system on the internal disk at SCSI address 6 which in this case is 10/0.6.0. After selecting the 4 GByte disk at 10/0.6.0, you're given the following two choices for system configuration:

- *Standard LVM configuration*

- *LVM configuration with VxFS (Journaled file system)*

If you have not reviewed the Logical Volume Manager section of Chapter 2, you will want to do so before you make this selection (LVM is Logical Volume Manager). I am a strong advocate of using Logical Volume Manager whenever possible with both the Series 800 and Series 700. There are many advantages to using Logical Volume Manager and you should be aware of these. Among the many advantages of Logical Volume Manager is that a logical volume may span multiple physical disks.

I selected the journaled file system option and proceeded with the installation.

The next information to be entered is information such as primary swap, secondary swap, software language, and so on. You want to consider your primary swap space very carefully. There is a detailed discussion about swap space later in this chapter. For HP-UX 10.20 the following default parameters were set for a 4 GByte disk, all of which you can modify:

Primary Swap Size	512Mb
Secondary Swap Size	none
Software Selection	CDE Runtime Environment
Software Language	English
Locale setting	default (C)
File system file name length	Long
/home Configuration	Minimal
How many disks in root group	One
Make volatile dirs separate	True
Create export volume	False

Keep in mind that these defaults will vary depending on the size of your disk.

At this point you can load the runtime environment.

The mount directory default sizes shown in Table 1-3 existed for a 4 GByte disk.

TABLE 1-3   Mount Directory Default Sizes for 4 Gbyte Disk

Mount Directory	Size (Mb)	Usage	Disk Group
/	84	VxFS	vg00.
/stand	48	HFS	vg00
(swap)	512	swap	vg00
/home	20	VxFS	vg00
/opt	252	VxFS	vg00
/tmp	32	VxFS	vg00
/usr	332	VxFS	vg00
/var	160	VxFS	vg00

You can select Modify Disk/FS Parameters and make disk and file system changes. At this point you can change the parameters associated with a mount directory including its size. The sizes of logical volumes you select depend on the needs of your environment. Some of the changes I make on a regular bases are to increase /tmp to a minimum of 100 MBytes, /var to a minimum of 300 MBytes, /usr to a minimum of 450 MBytes and /opt to a minimum of 300 MBytes.

After making the appropriate selections, you reach a point where you are asked if you want to interact with **swinstall**. There is an overview of the Software Distributor product used for installing all HP-UX 10.x software in this chapter. You may want to take a look at this overview to get a feel for the type of functionality Software Distributor offers. The **swinstall** program is the Software Distributor program used to install software. If you decide you want to interact with **swinstall,** you will be asked for codeword information and select from among software to load. If your software is protected, you will have to enter codeword information. If you need a codeword, it should be printed on the CD-ROM certificate you received with your software. This codeword is tied to the ID number of a hardware device on your system.

If you don't want to interact with **swinstall,** the software option you earlier selected, such as the Runtime Environment, will be loaded for you.

Beginning with HP-UX 10.20 the installation and core operating system are contained on the same CD-ROM. In earlier releases you are prompted to insert the Core OS media with a message like the following:

```
            USER INTERACTION REQUIRED

To complete the installation you must now remove the HP-UX
installation CD and insert the HP-UX Core Operating System CD.

Once this is done, press the <Return> key to continue:
```

When you interact with **swinstall,** you select the desired software to load from the Core OS media. You can mark software to be loaded from the Core OS media and then proceed to load the software. Software "bundles" may be selected and loaded. Software bundles are new to HP-UX 10.x so those of you who have HP-UX 9.x experience may not have heard this term before. Software bundles are a collection of filesets. A software bundle is sort of analogous to a partition in HP-UX 9.x except a software bundle is more flexible in that a bundle can contain filesets from a variety of different products. If you do not interact with **swinstall,** the installation of the Runtime Environment takes place automatically. The process of loading the software consists of an analysis phase and an installation phase. Analysis may determine that you don't have enough disk space to load the desired software. After successfully completing the analysis phase, you can proceed with the installation. When the installation is complete, you exit **swinstall** and your HP-UX kernel is built.

Series 800 Boot After Installation

When the system comes up after installation, the boot path will be displayed for you. For the K460 used in the example the following message appeared:

```
Boot:
: disc3(10/0.6.0;0)/stand/vmunix
```

Then a series of windows appear that allow you to configure your system name, time zone, root password, Internet Protocol (IP) address, subnet mask, and other networking setup (IP address and subnet mask background is provided in Chapter 3). This same information can be entered after your system boots by running **/sbin/set_parms**. This program can be used to set an individual system parameter or all of the system parameters that would be set at boot time. You give **/sbin/set_parms** one of the arguments in Table 1-4 depending on what you would like to configure.

TABLE 1-4   /sbin/set_parms ARGUMENTS

set_parms Argument	Comments
hostname	Set host name.
timezone	Set time zone.
date_time	Set date and time.
root_passwd	Set root password.
ip_address	Set Internet Protocol address (see Chapter 2 for networking background).
addl_network	Configure subnet mask, Domain Name System, and Network Information Service.
font_c-s	Use this system as a font server or font client.
initial	Go through the entire question and answer session you would experience at boot time.

If you use the **initial** argument, you'll interact with a variety of dialog boxes asking you for information. The dialog box asking your system hostname is shown in Figure 1-13.

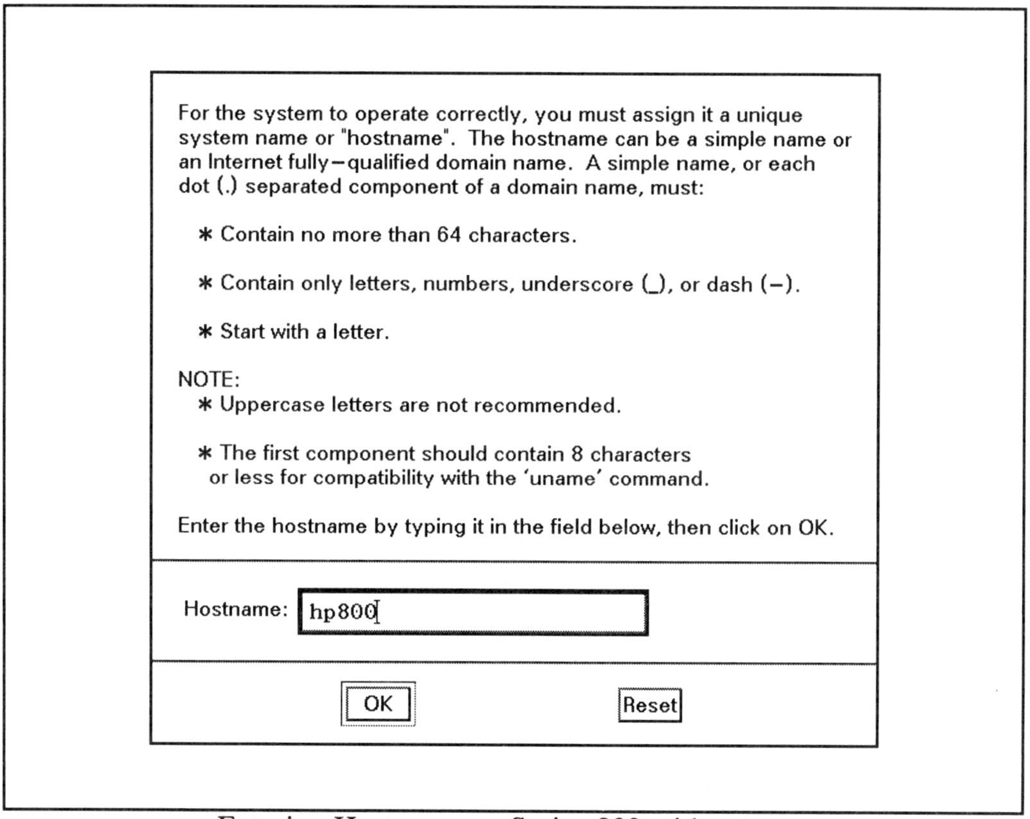

For the system to operate correctly, you must assign it a unique system name or "hostname". The hostname can be a simple name or an Internet fully-qualified domain name. A simple name, or each dot (.) separated component of a domain name, must:

  * Contain no more than 64 characters.

  * Contain only letters, numbers, underscore (_), or dash (−).

  * Start with a letter.

NOTE:
  * Uppercase letters are not recommended.

  * The first component should contain 8 characters or less for compatibility with the 'uname' command.

Enter the hostname by typing it in the field below, then click on OK.

Hostname: | hp800|

| OK | |Reset|

Figure 1-13 Entering Hostname on Series 800 with **set_parms**

You'll then be asked for your time zone and root password. Figure 1-14 shows the dialog box for entering your IP address.

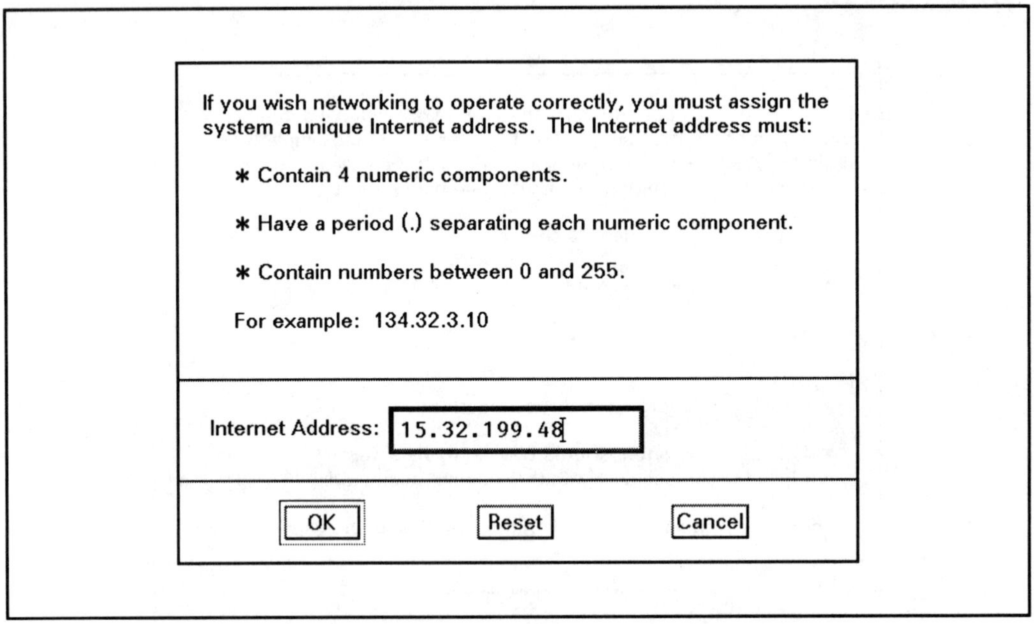

If you wish networking to operate correctly, you must assign the
system a unique Internet address. The Internet address must:

* Contain 4 numeric components.

* Have a period (.) separating each numeric component.

* Contain numbers between 0 and 255.

For example: 134.32.3.10

Internet Address: | 15.32.199.48|

[OK]   [Reset]   [Cancel]

Figure 1-14   Entering IP Address on Series 800 with **set_parms**

You can then configure your subnet mask and other networking configuration.

Please be careful if you configure some of the additional networking
parameters (**set_parms addl_netwrk**). Do not configure a system as an
NIS client if it hasn't been set-up on the NIS server. I have encountered
some interesting problems booting if you configure your system as an
NIS client *and* select the option "Wait For NIS Server on Bootup: yes".
This means your system will wait forever for the NIS server to respond
before the system boot will complete. If you are having problems with
your NIS server, you can forget about booting (this is a problem I
encountered on a K460 server acting as an NIS client). Your system
won't boot and you'll have no way of running **set_parms** to change to
"Wait For NIS Server on Bootup: no". I found there are two ways to
make this change if your system won't complete the boot process. The
first is to shut off the system and boot in single-user state from the ISl
prompt with the following command:

```
ISL> hpux -is boot
```

When the system boots it is in single-user mode with a login prompt. If you run **set_parms** and change to "Wait For NIS Server on Bootup: no", you think you have changed this variable to "no" but the file where this is changed (**/etc/rc.config.d/namesvrs**) has not been updated because you are in single-user mode and the commands required to make this change are on a logical volume which has not yet been mounted.

After finding out that the change had not been made by running **set_parms,** I decided to manually edit **/etc/rc.config.d/namesvrs** where I could make this change. The **/usr** logical volume is not mounted in single-user mode, however, so there isn't access to **/usr/bin/vi**, the editor I wanted to use to make this change. To mount **/usr** I issued the following commands (the **fsck** is required because the system was improperly shutdown earlier):

```
$ fsck /dev/vg00/rlvol6
$ mount /dev/vg00/lvol6 /usr
```

I then edited **/etc/rc.config.d/namesvrs** and changed the variable in this file to WAIT_FOR_NIS_SERVER="FALSE" and proceeded with the boot process. This fixed the problem but not without a lot of monkeying around. This is an area where you must be careful when setting up your system(s).

Installing Software with Software Distributor-HP-UX

Software Distributor-HP-UX (I'll call this Software Distributor throughout the book; HP documentation typically uses SD-UX) is the program used in HP-UX 10.x to perform all tasks related to software management. Software Distributor will be used in an example to install software on a

Series 700 and Series 800 shortly. Software Distributor is a standards-based way to perform software management. It conforms to the Portable Operating System Interface (POSIX) standard for packaging software and utilities related to software managment. The Software Distributor product described in this section comes with your HP-UX system. There is additional functionality you can obtain by buying the OpenView Software Distributor (SD-OV) product. SD-OV provides support for addtional platforms and allows you to "push" software out to target systems. In this section I won't cover SD-OV but will make some comments about SD-OV functionality where appropriate.

Software Distributor can be invoked using the commands described in this section, by using SAM which is covered in Chapter 3, or by installing software for the first time as described earlier in this chapter. Although I don't cover upgrading from HP-UX 9.x to 10.x, you can use Software Distributor to match what is on your HP-UX 9.x system to produce a 10.x system. This is described in detail in the HP-UX upgrade manual part number B2355-90050.

The following are the four phases of software installation performed with Software Distributor:

- Selection - You can select the source and software you wish to load during this phase. In the upcoming example the graphical user interface of Software Distributor is used and you'll see how easy it is to select these. With SD-OV you could also select the target on which you wish to load software - remember the SD-OV "push" capability?

- Analysis- All kinds of checks are performed for you including free disk space; dependencies; compatibility; mounted volumes; and others. Among the very useful outputs of this phase is the amount of space the software you wish to load will consume on each logical volume. This will be shown in the example.

- Load - After you are satisfied with the analysis, you may proceed with loading the software.

- Configuration - It is possible the software you load requires kernel rebuilding and a system reboot. Startup and shutdown scripts may also need to be modified.

There is some terminology associated with Software Distributor that I tend to use somewhat loosely. I have nothing but good things to say about Software Distributor, but I don't tend to conform to the official Software Distributor terminology as much as I should. I tend, for instance, to use the word system a lot which could mean many different things in the Software Distributor world. For instance, Software Distributor uses local host (a system on which Software Distributor is running or software is to be installed or managed by Software Distributor), distribution depot (a directory which is used as a place for software products), and development system (a place where software is prepared for distribution). I will use the word system to mean the system on which we are working in the examples because software is loaded onto the system from CD-ROM.

Here are some of the common software managment-related tasks you can perform with Software Distributor:

Installing and Updating Software (Command Line or GUI)

The **swinstall** command is used to install and update software. The source of the software you are loading can come from a variety of places including a CD-ROM, magnetic tape, or a "depot" directory from which software can be distributed. Using the depot, you can load software into a directory and then install and update software on other nodes from this directory. Software loaded from the CD-ROM with Software Distributor must be loaded onto the local system; this technique is used in the upcoming example. You have a lot of flexibility with SD-OV only when selecting the target system onto which you want to load software and the source from which you will load the software. You can, for instance, load software from a depot which is on another system on your network. This command can be run at the command line or with the graphical user interface.

Copying Software to a Depot (Command Line or GUI)

The **swcopy** command is used to copy software from one depot to another. The depot used in the upcoming examples is a CD-ROM. By setting up depots, you can quickly install or update software to other nodes simultaneously with SD-OV only. This command can be run at the command line or with the graphical user interface.

Removing Software from a System (Command Line or GUI)

The **swremove** command is used to remove software from a system that has had software loaded with Software Distributor. This includes removing installed and configured software from a system or removing software from a depot. This command can be run at the command line or with the graphical user interface.

List Information about Installation Software

The **swlist** command provides information about the depots that exist on a system, the contents of a depot, or information about installed software. Examples of using this command are provided shortly.

Configure Installed Software

The **swconfig** command configures or unconfigures installed software. Configuration of sofware normally takes place as part of **swinstall** but configuration can be deferred until a later time.

Verify Software

The **swverify** command confirms the integrity of installed software or software stored in a depot.

Package Software Install Later *(Local System Only)*

You may want to produce "packages" of software that you can later put on tape or in a depot with the **swpackage** command. This packaged software can then be used as a source for **swinstall** and be managed by other Software Distributor commands.

Control Access to Software Distributor Objects

You may want to apply restricted access to Software Distributor objects such as packaged software. Using the **swacl** command, you can view and change the Access Control List (ACL) for objects.

Modify Information about Loaded Software *(Local System Only)*

The Installed Products Database (IPD) and associated files are used to maintain information about software products you have loaded. **swmodify** can be run at the command line to modify these files.

Register Or Unregister a Depot

A software depot can be registered or unregistered with **swreg**. This means you don't have to remove a depot; if you temporarily don't want it used, you can unregister it.

Manage Jobs (Command Line or GUI, SD-OV Only)

Software Distributor jobs can be viewed and removed with **swjob**. The graphical user interface version of this command can be invoked with **sd** or **swjob -i**.

Software Distributor Example

The example of Software Distributor in this section describes the process of loading software from the CD-ROM to the local system. What I'll show here only begins to scratch the surface of functionality you have with Software Distributor, but, since I want to get you up and running fast, this overview should be helpful. You can load software from a variety of media as well as across the network. The graphical user interface that appears throughout this section makes the process of dealing with software easy. You don't, however, have to use this graphical user inter-

face. You can use the **swinstall** command from the command line specifying source, options, target, etc. I would recommend using the graphical
user interface because this is so much easier. If, however, you like to do
things the "traditional UNIX" way, you can issue the **swinstall** command
with arguments. You can look at the manual page for **swinstall** to understand its arguments and options and use this command from the command
line. The graphical user interface of Software Distributor works with the
sd (this is an SD-OV command and may also be invoked with **swjob -i**),
swcopy, **swremove**, and **swinstall** commands. There is also an interactive terminal user interface for these commands if you don't have a graphics display.

The first step when loading software from CD-ROM is to insert the
media and mount the CD-ROM. The directory **/SD_CDROM** should
already exist on your HP-UX 10.x system. If not, you can create this
directory or use any name you like. You can use SAM to mount the CD-
ROM for you or do this manually. I issued the following commands to
mount a CD-ROM at SCSI address two on a workstation and start Software Distributor:

```
$ mount /dev/dsk/c0t2d0 /SD_CDROM

$ swinstall
```

Software Distributor may look for a software depot on your local
system as a default source location for software. If this is not found,
you'll receive a dialog box in which you can change the source depot
path. In this case I changed the source depot path to the default for a CD-
ROM, **/SD_CDROM**. This is the Selection process described earlier
whereby you select the source and target for software to be loaded. You
can now select the specific software you wish to load.

When the Software Selection Window is opened for you, you can
perform many different operations. To identify software bundles you
wish to load on your system, you can highlight these and *Mark For Install*
from the *Actions* menu as I have done in Figure 1-15 for *The C/ANSI C
Developers Bundle*.

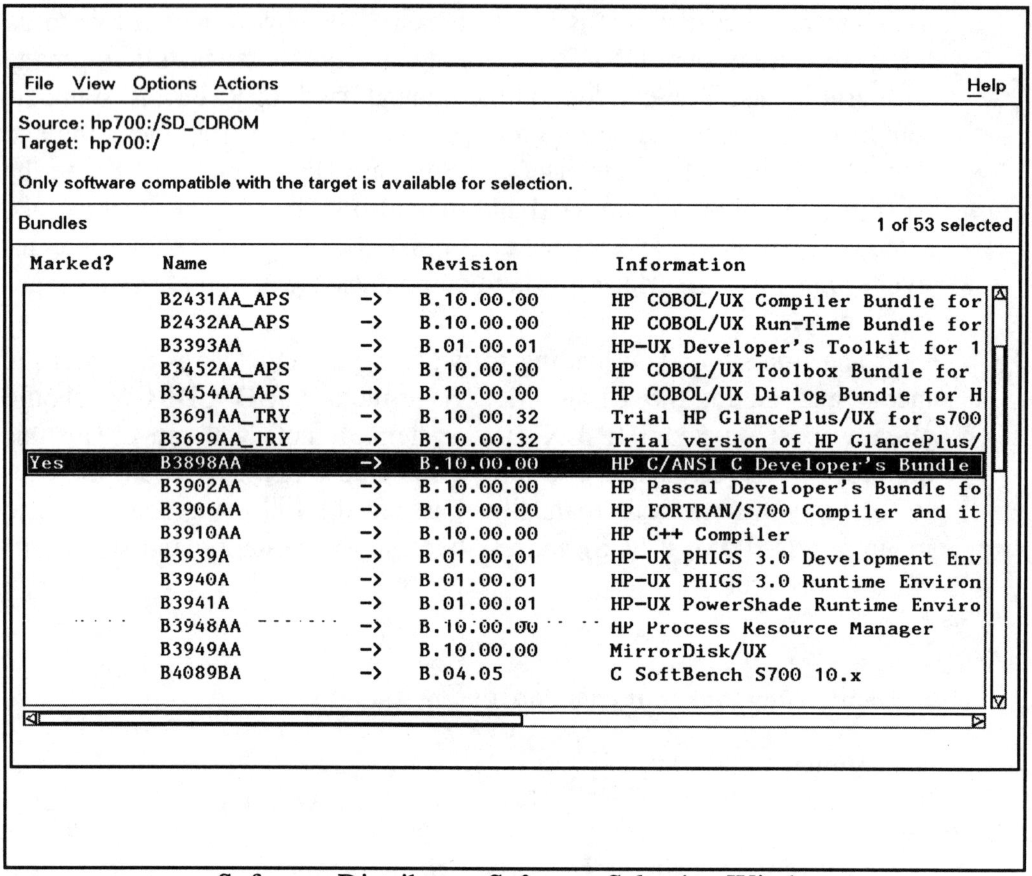

```
┌──────────────────────────────────────────────────────────────────────────┐
│                                                                            │
│  ┌──────────────────────────────────────────────────────────────────────┐│
│  │ File  View  Options  Actions                                     Help  ││
│  ├──────────────────────────────────────────────────────────────────────┤│
│  │ Source: hp700:/SD_CDROM                                               ││
│  │ Target:  hp700:/                                                      ││
│  ├──────────────────────────────────────────────────────────────────────┤│
│  │ Only software compatible with the target is available for selection.  ││
│  ├──────────────────────────────────────────────────────────────────────┤│
│  │ Bundles                                               1 of 53 selected ││
│  ├──────────────────────────────────────────────────────────────────────┤│
│  │ Marked?     Name            Revision       Information                 ││
│  │ ┌──────────────────────────────────────────────────────────────────┐ ││
│  │ │           B2431AA_APS    ->  B.10.00.00   HP COBOL/UX Compiler Bundle for ││
│  │ │           B2432AA_APS    ->  B.10.00.00   HP COBOL/UX Run-Time Bundle for ││
│  │ │           B3393AA        ->  B.01.00.01   HP-UX Developer's Toolkit for 1 ││
│  │ │           B3452AA_APS    ->  B.10.00.00   HP COBOL/UX Toolbox Bundle for  ││
│  │ │           B3454AA_APS    ->  B.10.00.00   HP COBOL/UX Dialog Bundle for H ││
│  │ │           B3691AA_TRY    ->  B.10.00.32   Trial HP GlancePlus/UX for s700 ││
│  │ │           B3699AA_TRY    ->  B.10.00.32   Trial version of HP GlancePlus/ ││
│  │ │ Yes       B3898AA        ->  B.10.00.00   HP C/ANSI C Developer's Bundle  ││
│  │ │           B3902AA        ->  B.10.00.00   HP Pascal Developer's Bundle fo ││
│  │ │           B3906AA        ->  B.10.00.00   HP FORTRAN/S700 Compiler and it ││
│  │ │           B3910AA        ->  B.10.00.00   HP C++ Compiler                 ││
│  │ │           B3939A         ->  B.01.00.01   HP-UX PHIGS 3.0 Development Env  ││
│  │ │           B3940A         ->  B.01.00.01   HP-UX PHIGS 3.0 Runtime Environ ││
│  │ │           B3941A         ->  B.01.00.01   HP-UX PowerShade Runtime Enviro ││
│  │ │           B3948AA        ->  B.10.00.00   HP Process Resource Manager     ││
│  │ │           B3949AA        ->  B.10.00.00   MirrorDisk/UX                   ││
│  │ │           B4089BA        ->  B.04.05      C SoftBench S700 10.x           ││
│  │ └──────────────────────────────────────────────────────────────────┘ ││
│  │                                                                        ││
│  └──────────────────────────────────────────────────────────────────────┘│
│                                                                            │
└──────────────────────────────────────────────────────────────────────────┘
```

Figure 1-15   Software Distributor *Software Selection* Window

A bundle, such as the one selected, may be comprised of products, subproducts, and filesets. You can select *Open Item* from the *Actions* menu if you want to drop down one level to see the subproducts or filesets. Figure 1-16 shows *Open Item* for *C/ANSI C Developers Bundle*.

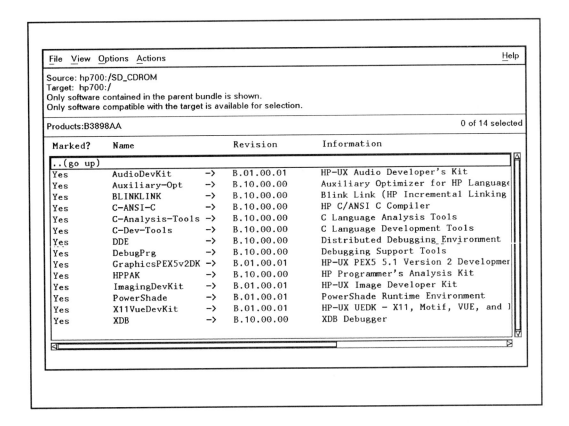

Figure 1-16 Software Distributor *Open Item*

After you have specified items to *Mark For Install,* you can select *Install (analysis)* from the *Actions* menu. Before starting analysis or before loading software, you should select *Show Description Of Software* from the *Actions* menu to see if a system reboot is required (you may have to scroll down the window to see the bottom of the description). You want to know this before you load software so you don't load software that requires a reboot at a time that it is inconvenient to reboot. Figure1-17 is an example *Install Analysis* window for installing *Trial HP Glance-Plus/UX for s700.*

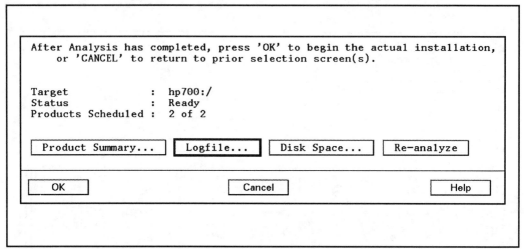

```
After Analysis has completed, press 'OK' to begin the actual installation,
    or 'CANCEL' to return to prior selection screen(s).


Target             :  hp700:/
Status             :  Ready
Products Scheduled :  2 of 2

   Product Summary...    Logfile...    Disk Space...    Re-analyze

   OK                       Cancel                       Help
```

Figure 1-17 Software Distributor *Install Analysis* Window

You can see that there are two products to be loaded in this bundle. Among the many useful pieces of information analysis provides you is a *Logfile* that contains a good review of the analysis and a *Disk Space* window that shows the amount of space that will be consumed by the software you plan to load. Figure 1-18 shows the *Disk Space* window which includes the amount of disk space available on the affected Logical Volumes both before and after the software load takes place.

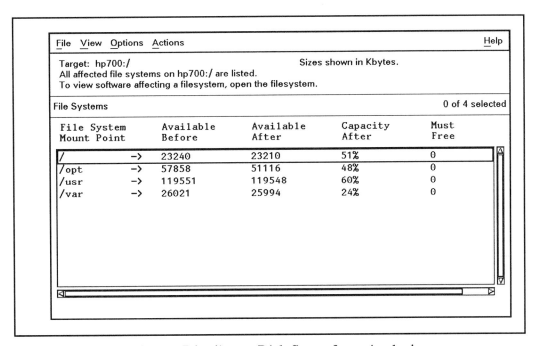

Figure 1-18 Software Distributor *Disk Space* from Analysis

This window is a dream come true for system administrators who have traditionally not had a lot of good information about either the amount of space consumed by the software they are loading or the destination of the software they are loading. You also have menus here that allow you to further investigate the software you're about to load on your system.

After you are satisfied with the analysis information, you may proceed with loading the software by clicking on OK.

There is also a graphical tool for removing software. The **swremove** command can be run interactively or from the command line. Figure 1-19 shows the **swremove** graphical interface, with the first product marked for removal.

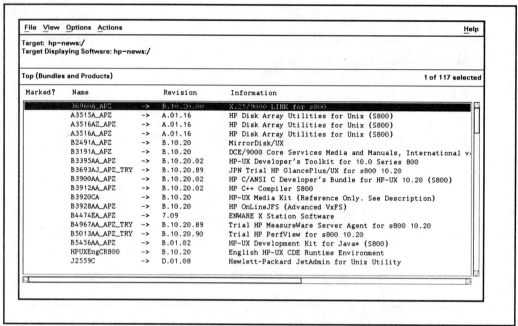

File View Options Actions   Help

Target: hp-news:/
Target Displaying Software: hp-news:/

Top (Bundles and Products)   1 of 117 selected

Marked?   Name   Revision   Information

          36960A_APZ   ->   B.10.20.00   X.25/9000 LINK for s800
          A3515A_APZ   ->   A.01.16   HP Disk Array Utilities for Unix (S800)
          A3516AZ_APZ   ->   A.01.16   HP Disk Array Utilities for Unix (S800)
          A3516A_APZ   ->   A.01.16   HP Disk Array Utilities for Unix (S800)
          B2491A_APZ   ->   B.10.20   MirrorDisk/UX
          B3191A_APZ   ->   B.10.20   DCE/9000 Core Services Media and Manuals, International v
          B3395AA_APZ   ->   B.10.20.02   HP-UX Developer's Toolkit for 10.0 Series 800
          B3693AJ_APZ_TRY   ->   B.10.20.89   JPN Trial HP GlancePlus/UX for s800 10.20
          B3900AA_APZ   ->   B.10.20.02   HP C/ANSI C Developer's Bundle for HP-UX 10.20 (S800)
          B3912AA_APZ   ->   B.10.20.02   HP C++ Compiler S800
          B3920CA   ->   B.10.20   HP-UX Media Kit (Reference Only. See Description)
          B3928AA_APZ   ->   B.10.20   HP OnLineJFS (Advanced VxFS)
          B4474EA_APZ   ->   7.09   ENWARE X Station Software
          B4967AA_APZ_TRY   ->   B.10.20.89   Trial HP MeasureWare Server Agent for s800 10.20
          B5013AA_APZ_TRY   ->   B.10.20.90   Trial HP PerfView for s800 10.20
          B5456AA_APZ   ->   B.01.02   HP-UX Development Kit for Java* (S800)
          HPUXEngCR800   ->   B.10.20   English HP-UX CDE Runtime Environment
          J2559C   ->   D.01.08   Hewlett-Packard JetAdmin for Unix Utility

Figure 1-19 **swremove** with Software Marked for Removal

This interface is nearly identical to the **swinstall** interface and makes
removing software easy.

Software Distributor Background

It is important to have some background on the way software is organized
in Software Distributor. I earlier talked about software bundles in HP-UX
10.x being somewhat analogous to partitions in HP-UX 9.x except that
software bundles are more flexible in that they can contain filesets from a
variety of different products. Figure 1-20 shows the hierarchy of software
bundles.

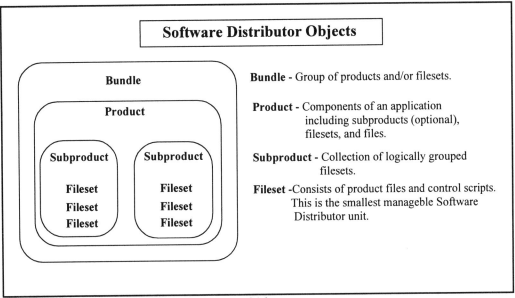

Figure 1-20 Software Distributor Objects

You can look at the bundle in Figure 1-20 as a group of software. This can be products, subproducts, and filesets as shown in the diagram. The concept here is to organize software in such a way that it is easy to manage. The diagram is somewhat oversimplified in that a bundle can contain a whole or partial product. This allows a fileset to be in more than one product.

Listing Software

Although I like the graphical user interface of **swinstall,** you can also issue Software Distributor commands at the command line. One example is the **swlist** command. The **swlist** command is useful for viewing the software you have loaded on your system, the software you have loaded in a depot, or producing a list of depots. A graphical user interface to the **swlist** command is available in SAM. With the **swlist** command you perform many functions including the following:

- List the software you have at the specified level with the **-l** option. I will show several examples of this shortly. The levels you can specify are

  root
  depot
  bundle
  product
  subproduct
  fileset
  file

Levels are delineated by "." so you will see *bundle.[product].[sub-product].[fileset]*. You can get all kinds of useful information out of the **swlist** command and use this for other purposes. Some of the things you can do with **swlist** are

- Display the table of contents from a software source.

- Specify which attributes you wish to see for a level of software such as name, size, revision, etc.

- Create a list of products that can be used as input to other Software Distributor commands such as **swinstall** and **swremove**.

- Get a current list of software and patches applied to your system.

When you run **swlist** with no options, you get a list of the software products installed on your system. Let's try a few **swlist** commands with the "-l" option to view software installed on a system (by default **swlist** will list installed products; you can use the "-s" option to specify a software depot or other source).

The following example shows listing software with no option to the **swlist** command which lists all software on the system.

```
$ swlist

# Initializing...
# Contacting target "system1"...
#
# Target:  system1:/
#
```

```
#
# Bundle(s):
#

   36960A_APZ        B.10.20.00     X.25/9000 LINK for s800
   A3515A_APZ        A.01.16        HP Disk Array Utilities for Unix (S800)
   A3516AZ_APZ       A.01.16        HP Disk Array Utilities for Unix (S800)
   A3516A_APZ        A.01.16        HP Disk Array Utilities for Unix (S800)
   B2491A_APZ        B.10.20        MirrorDisk/UX
   B3191A_APZ        B.10.20        DCE/9000 Core Services Media and Manuals,
                                    International version
   B3395AA_APZ       B.10.20.02     HP-UX Developer's Toolkit for 10.0 Series 800
   B3693AJ_APZ_TRY   B.10.20.89     JPN Trial HP GlancePlus/UX for s800 10.20
   B3900AA_APZ       B.10.20.02     HP C/ANSI C Developer's Bundle for HP-UX 10.20 (S800)
   B3912AA_APZ       B.10.20.02     HP C++ Compiler S800
   B3920CA           B.10.20        HP-UX Media Kit (Reference Only. See Description)
   B3928AA_APZ       B.10.20        HP OnLineJFS (Advanced VxFS)
   B4474EA_APZ       7.09           ENWARE X Station Software
   B4967AA_APZ_TRY   B.10.20.89     Trial HP MeasureWare Server Agent for s800 10.20
   B5013AA_APZ_TRY   B.10.20.90     Trial HP PerfView for s800 10.20
   B5456AA_APZ       B.01.02        HP-UX Development Kit for Java* (S800)
   HPUXEngCR800      B.10.20        English HP-UX CDE Runtime Environment
   J2559C            D.01.08        Hewlett-Packard JetAdmin for Unix Utility
   J2669AA_APZ       A.03.01        LAN Manager 2.2 for HP9000/800
   J2760AA_APZ       B.10.20.01     HP-PB 100Base-T/9000
   Z7240A_APZ        B.02.23        X.25/ACC Bundled Product
#
# Product(s) not contained in a Bundle:
#

   NetWorker         4.2            NetWorker for HP-UX
   PHCO_5400         B.10.00.00.AA  cleanup script removes obsolete patch files
   PHCO_7314         B.10.00.00.AA  ups_mond(1M) cumulative patch
   PHCO_7817         B.10.00.00.AA  fixes LVM maintenance mode HFS fsck error
   PHCO_7891         B.10.00.00.AA  allows mount to turn on hfs-specific options
   PHCO_7892         B.10.00.00.AA  config fails with library table overflow
   PHCO_8008         B.10.00.00.AA  fixes mount problem with outside filesystems
   PHCO_8246         B.10.00.00.AA  for SAM to read terminal control database
   PHCO_8247         B.10.00.00.AA  for SAM to update terminal control database
   PHCO_8353         B.10.00.00.AA  cumulative awk(1) patch
   PHCO_8488         B.10.00.00.AA  lpspool subsystem cumulative patch
   PHCO_8549         B.10.00.00.AA  extendfs_hfs fix for large file systems
   PHCO_8654         B.10.00.00.AA  expreserve(1) patch.
   PHCO_8696         B.10.00.00.AA  fixes expr(1) match operation return value
   PHCO_8820         B.10.00.00.AA  cumulative sar(1) patch.
   PHCO_8892         B.10.00.00.AA  libcurses patch
   PHCO_8893         B.10.00.00.AA  make(1) cumulative patch.
   PHCO_8927         B.10.00.00.AA  stty(1) patch to fix -g option.
   PHCO_8934         B.10.00.00.AA  jfs fscat large offset patch
   PHCO_8935         B.10.00.00.AA  Fix for vxfs volcopy with LFS disks.
   PHCO_9014         B.10.00.00.AA  mkboot patch
   PHCO_9211         B.10.00.00.AA  performance patch for sed.
   PHCO_9213         B.10.00.00.AA  LVM commands cumulative patch
   PHCO_9227         B.10.00.00.AA  POSIX shell cumulative patch
   PHCO_9228         B.10.00.00.AA  Fbackup(1M) Long User or Group Name Patch
   PHCO_9261         B.10.00.00.AA  libc header file cumulative patch
   PHCO_9272         B.10.00.00.AA  patch for grep for performance problems.
   PHCO_9295         B.10.00.00.AA  libcurses library patch
   PHCO_9329         B.10.00.00.AA  csh(1) cumulative patch
   PHCO_9348         B.10.00.00.AA  cron(1M) and at(1) patch
   PHCO_9396         B.10.00.00.AA  Fix for umountable VxFS file systems
   PHCO_9457         B.10.00.00.AA  cut(1) patch to preserve last delimiter
   PHCO_9484         B.10.00.00.AA  ksh(1) cumulative patch
   PHCO_9490         B.10.00.00.AA  ex/vi patch to correct expression anchoring
   PHCO_9543         B.10.00.00.AA  Allows umount to unmount a Stale NFS FS
   PHCO_9559         B.10.00.00.AA  su should not prompt when used by root
   PHCO_9577         B.10.00.00.AA  libc cumulative patch
   PHCO_9597         B.10.00.00.AA  chfn(1) cumulative patch
   PHCO_9598         B.10.00.00.AA  useradd(1M) Cumulative patch
   PHCO_9602         B.10.00.00.AA  chsh(1) cumulative patch
   PHCO_9605         B.10.00.00.AA  cumulative newgrp(1) patch
   PHCO_9608         B.10.00.00.AA  tar padding fix
   PHCO_9626         B.10.00.00.AA  ls(1) Cumulative patch
   PHCO_9641         B.10.00.00.AA  passwd(1) cumulative patch
```

```
PHCO_9895       B.10.00.00.AA   Cumulative SAM Patch 4.
PHKL_10058      B.10.00.00.AA   panic occurs with optical media devices
PHKL_10443      B.10.00.00.AA   SCSI Passthru driver cumulative patch
PHKL_7764       B.10.00.00.AA   Data loss when truncating VxFS (JFS) files
PHKL_7765       B.10.00.00.AA   hpux(1M) for kernels larger than 13 MBytes
PHKL_7900       B.10.00.00.AA   JFS KI, page fault, deadlock, & setuid fixes
PHKL_7952       B.10.00.00.AA   Fix ptrace
PHKL_7968       B.10.00.00.AA   Fix lofs
PHKL_8204       B.10.00.00.AA   Fix for system hang during panic
PHKL_8377       B.10.00.00.AA   Fix vmtrace bug. Release malloc memory.
PHKL_8445       B.10.00.00.AA   fix bad count of blocked processes in vmstat
PHKL_8482       B.10.00.00.AA   JFS (VxFS) performance improvements
PHKL_8656       B.10.00.00.AA   panic with autochanger connected to FW interface
PHKL_8694       B.10.00.00.AA   sys/time.h fix for select(2)/C++ defects
PHKL_8756       B.10.00.00.AA   HSC SCSI tape cumulative patch
PHKL_8923       B.10.00.00.AA   KI change for vasusage performance problem
PHKL_9076       B.10.00.00.AA   MMF performance, large SHMEM, large buffer cache
PHKL_9156       B.10.00.00.AA   NFS Kernel Cumulative Megapatch
PHKL_9271       B.10.00.00.AA   Fix for current path name in proc/thread
PHKL_9274       B.10.00.00.AA   high %sys and switch rate during file locking
PHKL_9307       B.10.00.00.AA   HP-PB SCSI cumulative patch (scsi1/scsi3)
PHKL_9362       B.10.00.00.AA   Fix panic caused by MP race
PHKL_9371       B.10.00.00.AA   Various fixes for unmountable VxFS file systems
PHKL_9373       B.10.00.00.AA   VxFS (JFS) patch for "fsadm -b" and quotas panic
PHKL_9416       B.10.00.00.AA   OnLine JFS (VxFS) cumulative patch
PHKL_9530       B.10.00.00.AA   LVM kernel and pstat cumulative patch
PHKL_9570       B.10.00.00.AA   NFS and VxFS (JFS) cumulative patch
PHKL_9724       B.10.00.00.AA   select() system call performance improvement
PHNE_7109       B.10.00.00.AA   'ifalias' command for IP address aliasing
PHNE_7671       B.10.00.00.AA   fixes telnet(1) binary negotiation problem
PHNE_7864       B.10.00.00.AA   BIND 4.9.3 components
PHNE_7918       B.10.00.00.AA   patch for RCP.
PHNE_8164       B.10.00.00.AA   netTL cummulative patch
PHNE_8310       B.10.00.00.AA   NFS/NIS cumulative megapatch
PHNE_8328       B.10.00.00.AA   cumulative telnetd(1M) patch
PHNE_8702       B.10.00.00.AA   sendmail (1M) patch
PHNE_8807       B.10.00.00.AA   cumulative rlogin/rlogind patch
PHNE_9060       B.10.00.00.AA   Fix a panic in STREAMS
PHNE_9107       B.10.00.00.AA   cumulative ARPA Transport patch
PHNE_9219       B.10.00.00.AA   patch for RDIST.
PHNE_9286       B.10.00.00.AA   2.23 Z7240A ACC X.25 Bundle (HP-PB) Patch
PHNE_9381       B.10.00.00.AA   patch for mailx
PHNE_9438       B.10.00.00.AA   Cumulative Mux and Pty Patch
PHNE_9504       B.10.00.00.AA   arp general patch
PHSS_7725       B.10.00.00.AA   CDE msg cat Aug96 Patch
PHSS_7726       B.10.00.00.AA   CDE Dtterm August 96 patch
PHSS_8583       B.10.00.00.AA   dld.sl(5) cumulative patch
PHSS_8667       B.10.00.00.AA   CDE Runtime Nov96 Patch
PHSS_8668       B.10.00.00.AA   CDE Dev. Env. Nov96 Patch
PHSS_8967       B.10.00.00.AA   LIBCL large file support patch
PHSS_9400       B.10.00.00.AA   ld(1) cumulative patch
PHSS_9627       B.10.00.00.AA   CDE Dtlogin and Dtsession Point Patch
```

Let's now inspect one of the products more carefully to see **swlist** work by specifying different levels. The following example shows listing a specific software package at the *bundle* level.

```
$ swlist -l bundle Z7240A_APZ
```

```
# Initializing...
# Contacting target "system1"...
#
# Target:  system1:/
#

  Z7240A_APZ B.02.23          X.25/ACC Bundled Product
```

This product is a software bundle.

If we run **swlist** to the product level, the following is produced for this software:

```
$ swlist -l product Z7240A_APZ

# Initializing...
# Contacting target "system1"...
#
# Target:  system1:/
#

# Z7240A_APZ B.02.23             X.25/ACC Bundled Product
  Z7240A_APZ.ACCB.02.23          ACC Base Product
  Z7240A_APZ.ACC-X25B.02.23       X.25 - ACC Accessory Product
  Z7240A_APZ.ACC-X25STB.02.23      X.25/ACC - ACC Accessory
                                   Product

      (bundle)      (product)
```

This bundle is comprised of the three products shown in this example. Are there any subproducts of which this software is comprised? The following example will help us determine this.

```
$ swlist -l subproduct Z7240A_APZ

# Initializing...
# Contacting target "system1"...
#
# Target:  system1:/
#
```

```
# Z7240A_APZ         B.02.23           X.25/ACC Bundled Product

# Z7240A_APZ.ACC    B.02.23            ACC Base Product
  Z7240A_APZ.ACC.DevelopmentACC Programmatic Interface
  Z7240A_APZ.ACC.FirmwareACC Base Firmware
  Z7240A_APZ.ACC.ManualsACC Man Pages
  Z7240A_APZ.ACC.RuntimeACC Runtime Software

# Z7240A_APZ.ACC-X25B.02.23           X.25 - ACC Accessory Product
  Z7240A_APZ.ACC-X25.DevelopmentZCOM X.25 Interface Routines
  Z7240A_APZ.ACC-X25.FirmwareX.25 Firmware
  Z7240A_APZ.ACC-X25.ManualsX.25 Man Pages
  Z7240A_APZ.ACC-X25.RuntimeX.25 Runtime Software

# Z7240A_APZ.ACC-X25STB.02.23         X.25/ACC - ACC Accessory Product
  Z7240A_APZ.ACC-X25ST.RuntimeX.25/ACC Runtime Software

     (bundle)      (product)    (subproduct)
```

From this output we can see that the original bundle has three products, each of which has subproducts beneath it. The first two products
each have four subproducts. The last product has only one subproduct
beneath it.

We can now take this process one step further and view the filesets
of which each of the subproducts is comprised. To get the filesets as well
as the bundle, product, and subproduct levels, I issue the **swlist** command
with all levels specified as shown in the following example.

```
$ swlist -l bundle -l product -l subproduct -l fileset Z7240Z_APZ

# Initializing...
# Contacting target "system1"...
#
# Target:  system1:/
#

# Z7240A_APZ         B.02.23           X.25/ACC Bundled Product

# Z7240A_APZ.ACC    B.02.23            ACC Base Product

# Z7240A_APZ.ACC.DevelopmentACC Programmatic Interface
  Z7240A_APZ.ACC.Development.ACC-PRGB.02.23          ACC Programmatic Interface

# Z7240A_APZ.ACC.FirmwareACC Base Firmware
  Z7240A_APZ.ACC.Firmware.ACC-FWB.02.23        ACC Base Firmware

# Z7240A_APZ.ACC.ManualsACC Man Pages
  Z7240A_APZ.ACC.Manuals.ACC-MANB.02.23        ACC Man Pages

# Z7240A_APZ.ACC.RuntimeACC Runtime Software
  Z7240A_APZ.ACC.Runtime.ACC-KRNB.02.23        ACC Driver Software
  Z7240A_APZ.ACC.Runtime.ACC-RUNB.02.23        ACC Runtime Software

# Z7240A_APZ.ACC-X25B.02.23           X.25 - ACC Accessory Product

# Z7240A_APZ.ACC-X25.DevelopmentZCOM X.25 Interface Routines
  Z7240A_APZ.ACC-X25.Development.ACC-X25-PRGB.02.23          ZCOM X.25 Interface Routines

# Z7240A_APZ.ACC-X25.FirmwareX.25 Firmware
  Z7240A_APZ.ACC-X25.Firmware.ACC-X25-FWB.02.23        X.25 Firmware

# Z7240A_APZ.ACC-X25.ManualsX.25 Man Pages
```

```
    Z7240A_APZ.ACC-X25.Manuals.ACC-X25-MANB.02.23        X.25 Man Pages

#   Z7240A_APZ.ACC-X25.RuntimeX.25 Runtime Software
    Z7240A_APZ.ACC-X25.Runtime.ACC-X25-KRNB.02.23        X.25 Driver Software
    Z7240A_APZ.ACC-X25.Runtime.ACC-X25-RUNB.02.23        X.25 Runtime Software

#   Z7240A_APZ.ACC-X25STB.02.23        X.25/ACC - ACC Accessory Product

#   Z7240A_APZ.ACC-X25ST.RuntimeX.25/ACC Runtime Software
    Z7240A_APZ.ACC-X25ST.Runtime.ACC-X25ST-KRNB.02.23     X.25/ACC Driver Software
    Z7240A_APZ.ACC-X25ST.Runtime.ACC-X25ST-RUNB.02.23     X.25/ACC Runtime Software

        (bundle)   (product)   (subproduct) (fileset)
```

With the **swlist** command and the **-l** option, we have worked our way down the hierarchy of this software bundle. Going down to the file level with the **-l** command and all four levels shown produces a long list of files associated with this product.

The other Software Distributor commands listed earlier can also be issued at the command line. You may want to look at the manual pages for these commands as you prepare to do more advanced Software Distributor work than loading software from a CD-ROM or tape.

To system administrators familiar with HP-UX 9.x, this is a different organization of software, but the graphical user interface of **swinstall** combined with the better organization of Software Distributor makes this an advantage of HP-UX 10.x.

Build an HP-UX Kernel (F4)

There are a variety of reasons to build a new HP-UX kernel on your system as well as a variety of ways to build the kernel. I would recommend you use the System Administration Manager (SAM) covered in Chapter 3 to build your kernel. There is, however, no substitute for understanding the process by which you would manually build an HP-UX kernel and, therefore, be more informed when you have SAM do this for you in the future. In this chapter I will discuss various commands related to kernel generation and cover the process by which you would manually create a kernel. As with most other system administration functions in HP-UX 10.x, creating an HP-UX kernel is the same for both a workstation and server system.

You may need to create a new HP-UX kernel in order to add device drivers or subsystems, to tune the kernel to get improved performance, or to change the dump and swap devices.

To begin, let's take a look at an existing kernel running on a Series 700 and Series 800. The **sysdef** command is used to analyze and report tunable parameters of a currently running system. You can specify a specific file to analyze if you don't wish to use the currently running system. The following two listings are **sysdef** outputs from a Series 700 and 800, respectively. These outputs, which reflect the default settings on both systems, are identical.

(on Series 700)

```
$  /usr/sbin/sysdef
```

NAME	VALUE	BOOT	MIN-MAX	UNITS	FLAGS
acctresume	4	-	-100-100		-
acctsuspend	2	-	-100-100		-
allocate_fs_swapmap	0	-	-		-
bufpages	4450	-	0-	Pages	-
create_fastlinks	0	-	-		-
dbc_max_pct	50	-	-		-
dbc_min_pct	5	-	-		-
default_disk_ir	1	-	-		-
dskless_node	0	-	0-1		-
eisa_io_estimate	768	-	-		-
eqmemsize	15	-	-		-
file_pad	10	-	0-		-
fs_async	0	-	0-1		-
hpux_aes_override	0	-	-		-
maxdsiz	16384	-	256-655360	Pages	-
maxfiles	60	-	30-2048		-
maxfiles_lim	1024	-	30-2048		-
maxssiz	2048	-	256-655360	Pages	-
maxswapchunks	256	-	1-16384		-
maxtsiz	16384	-	256-655360	Pages	-
maxuprc	75	-	3-		-
maxvgs	10	-	-		-
msgmap	16711680	-	3-		-
nbuf	2544	-	0-		-
ncallout	292	-	6-		-
ncdnode	150	-	-		-
ndilbuffers	30	-	1-		-
netisr_priority	-1	-	-1-127		-
netmemmax	11227136	-	-		-
nfile	800	-	14-		-
nflocks	200	-	2-		-
ninode	476	-	14-		-
no_lvm_disks	0	-	-		-

```
nproc                276         -        10-                      -
npty                  60         -        1-                       -
nstrpty               60         -        -                        -
nswapdev              10         -        1-25                     -
nswapfs               10         -        1-25                     -
public_shlibs          1         -        -                        -
remote_nfs_swap        0         -        -                        -
rtsched_numpri        32         -        -                        -
sema                   0         -        0-1                      -
semmap           4128768         -        4-                       -
shmem                  0         -        0-1                      -
shmmni               200         -        3-1024                   -
streampipes            0         -        0-                       -
swapmem_on             1         -        -                        -
swchunk             2048         -        2048-16384    kBytes     -
timeslice             10         -        -1-2147483648 Ticks      -
unlockable_mem      1689         -        0-            Pages      -
```

The following is the output from **sysdef** run on a K460 Series 800:

(on Series 800)

$ /usr/sbin/sysdef

NAME	VALUE	BOOT	MIN-MAX	UNITS	FLAGS
acctresume	4	-	-100-100		-
acctsuspend	2	-	-100-100		-
allocate_fs_swapmap	0	-	-		-
bufpages	35653	-	0-	Pages	-
create_fastlinks	0	-	-		-
dbc_max_pct	50	-	-		-
dbc_min_pct	5	-	-		-
default_disk_ir	0	-	-		-
dskless_node	0	-	0-1		-
eisa_io_estimate	768	-	-		-
eqmemsize	23	-	-		-
file_pad	10	-	0-		-
fs_async	0	-	0-1		-
hpux_aes_override	0	-	-		-
maxdsiz	32768	-	256-655360	Pages	-
maxfiles	256	-	30-2048		-
maxfiles_lim	1024	-	30-2048		-
maxssiz	2048	-	256-655360	Pages	-
maxswapchunks	1024	-	1-16384		-
maxtsiz	16384	-	256-655360	Pages	-
maxuprc	312	-	3-		-
maxvgs	10	-	-		-
msgmap	2555904	-	3-		-
nbuf	22044	-	0-		-
ncallout	1070	-	6-		-
ncdnode	150	-	-		-
ndilbuffers	30	-	1-		-
netisr_priority	-1	-	-1-127		-
netmemmax	186941440	-	-		-
nfile	2198	-	14-		-
nflocks	200	-	2-		-
ninode	1446	-	14-		-
no_lvm_disks	0	-	-		-
nproc	1054	-	10-		-

```
npty                        60          -       1-                          -
nstrpty                     60          -       -                           -
nswapdev                    10          -       1-25                        -
nswapfs                     10          -       1-25                        -
public_shlibs                1          -       -                           -
remote_nfs_swap              0          -       -                           -
rtsched_numpri              32          -       -                           -
sema                         0          -       0-1                         -
semmap                 4128768          -       4-                          -
shmem                        0          -       0-1                         -
shmmni                     200          -       3-1024                      -
streampipes                  0          -       0-                          -
swapmem_on                   1          -       -                           -
swchunk                   2048          -       2048-16384      kBytes      -
timeslice                   10          -       -1-2147483648   Ticks       -
unlockable_mem            8192          -       0-              Pages       -
```

In addition to the tunable parameters, you may want to see a report of all the hardware found on your system. The **ioscan** command does this for you. Using **sysdef** and **ioscan,** you can see what your tunable parameters are set to and what hardware exists on your system. You will then know the way your system is set up and can then make changes to your kernel. The following is an **ioscan** output of the same B class Series 700 for which **sysdef** was run. Examples of **ioscan** with and without the **-f** option, which produces a "full" listing, are shown.

(on Series 700)
$ **/usr/sbin/ioscan**

```
H/W Path    Class               Description
================================================
            bc
8           bc                  Pseudo Bus Converter
8/0         unknown             GSC-to-PCI Bus Bridge
8/12        ext_bus             GSC Fast/Wide SCSI Interface
8/12.6      target
8/12.6.0    disk                SEAGATE ST34371W
8/12.7      target
8/12.7.0    ctl                 Initiator
8/16        ba                  Core I/O Adapter
8/16/0      ext_bus             Built-in Parallel Interface
8/16/1      audio               Built-in Audio
8/16/4      tty                 Built-in RS-232C
8/16/5      ext_bus             Built-in SCSI
```

```
8/16/5.2                    target
8/16/5.2.0                    disk        TOSHIBA CD-ROM XM-5401TA
8/16/5.3                    target
8/16/5.3.0                    tape        HP        C1533A
8/16/5.7                    target
8/16/5.7.0                    ctl         Initiator
8/16/6              lan                   Built-in LAN
8/16/7              ps2                   Built-in Keyboard/Mouse
8/20          ba                          Core I/O Adapter
8/20/1              hil                   Built-in HIL
8/20/2              tty                   Built-in RS-232C
8/20/5              ba                    EISA Bus Adapter
8/24          graphics                    Graphics
62            processor                   Processor
63            memory                      Memory
```

$ /usr/sbin/ioscan -f

```
Class      I   H/W Path    Driver      S/W State H/W Type  Description
=========================================================================
bc         0               root        CLAIMED   BUS_NEXUS
bc         1   8           bc          CLAIMED   BUS_NEXUS Pseudo Bus Converter
unknown   -1   8/0                     UNCLAIMED UNKNOWN   GSC-to-PCI Bus Bridge
ext_bus    0   8/12        c720        CLAIMED   INTERFACE GSC Fast/Wide SCSI Interface
target     0   8/12.6      tgt         CLAIMED   DEVICE
disk       0   8/12.6.0    sdisk       CLAIMED   DEVICE    SEAGATE ST34371W
target     1   8/12.7      tgt         CLAIMED   DEVICE
ctl        0   8/12.7.0    sctl        CLAIMED   DEVICE    Initiator
ba         0   8/16        bus_adapter CLAIMED   BUS_NEXUS Core I/O Adapter
ext_bus    2   8/16/0      CentIf      CLAIMED   INTERFACE Built-in Parallel Interface
audio      0   8/16/1      audio       CLAIMED   INTERFACE Built-in Audio
tty        0   8/16/4      asio0       CLAIMED   INTERFACE Built-in RS-232C
ext_bus    1   8/16/5      c720        CLAIMED   INTERFACE Built-in SCSI
target     2   8/16/5.2    tgt         CLAIMED   DEVICE
disk       1   8/16/5.2.0  sdisk       CLAIMED   DEVICE    TOSHIBA CD-ROM XM-5401TA
target     3   8/16/5.3    tgt         CLAIMED   DEVICE
tape       0   8/16/5.3.0  stape       CLAIMED   DEVICE    HP        C1533A
target     4   8/16/5.7    tgt         CLAIMED   DEVICE
ctl        1   8/16/5.7.0  sctl        CLAIMED   DEVICE    Initiator
lan        0   8/16/6      lan2        CLAIMED   INTERFACE Built-in LAN
ps2        0   8/16/7      ps2         CLAIMED   INTERFACE Built-in Keyboard/Mouse
ba         1   8/20        bus_adapter CLAIMED   BUS_NEXUS Core I/O Adapter
hil        0   8/20/1      hil         CLAIMED   INTERFACE Built-in HIL
tty        1   8/20/2      asio0       CLAIMED   INTERFACE Built-in RS-232C
ba         2   8/20/5      eisa        CLAIMED   BUS_NEXUS EISA Bus Adapter
graphics   0   8/24        graph3      CLAIMED   INTERFACE Graphics
processor  0   62          processor   CLAIMED   PROCESSOR Processor
memory     0   63          memory      CLAIMED   MEMORY    Memory
```

The full listing with the **-f** output produces some additional useful information such as the full hardware path, and the software and hardware types.

The following is an **ioscan** output of a Series 800. Examples of the **ioscan** command with and without the **-f** option, and with the **-funC disk** option, which produces a full listing of only usable disk devices, are shown.

(on Series 800)

```
$ /usr/sbin/ioscan

H/W Path       Class             Description
==================================================
               bc
8              bc                I/O Adapter
8/0                ext_bus       GSC add-on Fast/Wide SCSI Interface
8/0.1              target
8/0.1.0                disk      SEAGATE ST34371W
8/0.2              target
8/0.2.0                disk      SEAGATE ST34371W
8/0.3              target
8/0.3.0                disk      SEAGATE ST34371W
8/0.4              target
8/0.4.0                disk      SEAGATE ST34371W
8/0.5              target
8/0.5.0                disk      SEAGATE ST34371W
8/0.6              target
8/0.6.0                disk      SEAGATE ST34371W
8/0.7              target
8/0.7.0                ctl       Initiator
8/0.8              target
8/0.8.0                disk      SEAGATE ST34371W
8/0.9              target
8/0.9.0                disk      SEAGATE ST34371W
8/4                ext_bus       GSC add-on Fast/Wide SCSI Interface
8/4.1              target
8/4.1.0                disk      SEAGATE ST34371W
8/4.2              target
8/4.2.0                disk      SEAGATE ST34371W
8/4.3              target
8/4.3.0                disk      SEAGATE ST34371W
8/4.4              target
8/4.4.0                disk      SEAGATE ST34371W
8/4.5              target
8/4.5.0                disk      SEAGATE ST34371W
8/4.6              target
8/4.6.0                disk      SEAGATE ST34371W
8/4.7              target
8/4.7.0                ctl       Initiator
8/4.8              target
8/4.8.0                disk      SEAGATE ST34371W
8/4.9              target
8/4.9.0                disk      SEAGATE ST34371W
8/8                ext_bus       GSC add-on Fast/Wide SCSI Interface
8/8.3              target
8/8.3.0                disk      SEAGATE ST34371W
8/8.4              target
8/8.4.0                disk      SEAGATE ST34371W
8/8.5              target
8/8.5.0                disk      SEAGATE ST34371W
8/8.6              target
```

```
8/8.6.0              disk         SEAGATE ST34371W
8/8.7                target
8/8.7.0              ctl          Initiator
8/12         ext_bus             GSC add-on Fast/Wide SCSI Interface
8/12.1               target
8/12.1.0             disk         SEAGATE ST34371W
8/12.2               target
8/12.2.0             disk         SEAGATE ST34371W
8/12.3               target
8/12.3.0             disk         SEAGATE ST34371W
8/12.4               target
8/12.4.0             disk         SEAGATE ST34371W
8/12.5               target
8/12.5.0             disk         SEAGATE ST34371W
8/12.6               target
8/12.6.0             disk         SEAGATE ST34371W
8/12.7               target
8/12.7.0             ctl          Initiator
8/12.8               target
8/12.8.0             disk         SEAGATE ST34371W
8/12.9               target
8/12.9.0             disk         SEAGATE ST34371W
10          bc                   I/O Adapter
10/0         ext_bus             GSC built-in Fast/Wide SCSI Interface
10/0.1               target
10/0.1.0             disk         SEAGATE ST34371W
10/0.2               target
10/0.2.0             disk         SEAGATE ST34371W
10/0.3               target
10/0.3.0             disk         SEAGATE ST34371W
10/0.4               target
10/0.4.0             disk         SEAGATE ST34371W
10/0.5               target
10/0.5.0             disk         SEAGATE ST34371W
10/0.6               target
10/0.6.0             disk         SEAGATE ST34371W
10/0.7               target
10/0.7.0             ctl          Initiator
10/4         bc                   Bus Converter
10/4/0               tty          MUX
10/4/4               ext_bus     HP 28696A - Wide SCSI ID=7
10/4/4.1             target
10/4/4.1.0           disk         SEAGATE ST34371W
10/4/4.2             target
10/4/4.2.0           disk         SEAGATE ST34371W
10/4/4.3             target
10/4/4.3.0           disk         SEAGATE ST34371W
10/4/4.4             target
10/4/4.4.0           disk         SEAGATE ST34371W
10/4/4.5             target
10/4/4.5.0           disk         SEAGATE ST34371W
10/4/4.6             target
10/4/4.6.0           disk         SEAGATE ST34371W
10/4/4.8             target
10/4/4.8.0           disk         SEAGATE ST34371W
10/4/4.9             target
10/4/4.9.0           disk         SEAGATE ST34371W
10/4/12              ext_bus     HP 28696A - Wide SCSI ID=7
10/4/12.1            target
10/4/12.1.0          disk         SEAGATE ST34371W
10/4/12.2            target
10/4/12.2.0          disk         SEAGATE ST34371W
10/4/12.3            target
10/4/12.3.0          disk         SEAGATE ST34371W
10/4/12.4            target
10/4/12.4.0          disk         SEAGATE ST34371W
10/4/12.5            target
10/4/12.5.0          disk         SEAGATE ST34371W
10/4/12.6            target
10/4/12.6.0          disk         SEAGATE ST34371W
10/4/12.8            target
10/4/12.8.0          disk         SEAGATE ST34371W
10/4/12.9            target
10/4/12.9.0          disk         SEAGATE ST34371W
10/4/16              nacc         ACC MUX
```

```
10/8               ext_bus          GSC add-on Fast/Wide SCSI Interface
10/8.7                target
10/8.7.0                 ctl        Initiator
10/12              ba               Core I/O Adapter
10/12/0              ext_bus        Built-in Parallel Interface
10/12/5              ext_bus        Built-in SCSI
10/12/5.0               target
10/12/5.0.0                tape     HP      C1533A
10/12/5.2               target
10/12/5.2.0                disk     TOSHIBA CD-ROM XM-5401TA
10/12/5.7               target
10/12/5.7.0                ctl      Initiator
10/12/6              lan            Built-in LAN
10/12/7              ps2            Built-in Keyboard/Mouse
10/16              bc               Bus Converter
10/16/4              ext_bus        HP 28696A - Wide SCSI ID=7
10/16/4.2               target
10/16/4.2.0                tape     Quantum DLT4000
10/16/4.3               target
10/16/4.3.0                tape     Quantum DLT4000
10/16/4.4               target
10/16/4.4.0                tape     Quantum DLT4000
10/16/4.5               target
10/16/4.5.0                tape     Quantum DLT4000
10/16/4.6               target
10/16/4.6.0                spt      HP      C1194F
10/16/12             ext_bus        HP 28696A - Wide SCSI ID=7
10/16/12.1              target
10/16/12.1.0               disk     SEAGATE ST34371W
10/16/12.2              target
10/16/12.2.0               disk     SEAGATE ST34371W
10/16/12.3              target
10/16/12.3.0               disk     SEAGATE ST34371W
10/16/12.4              target
10/16/12.4.0               disk     SEAGATE ST34371W
10/16/12.5              target
10/16/12.5.0               disk     SEAGATE ST34371W
10/16/12.6              target
10/16/12.6.0               disk     SEAGATE ST34371W
10/16/12.8              target
10/16/12.8.0               disk     SEAGATE ST34371W
10/16/12.9              target
10/16/12.9.0               disk     SEAGATE ST34371W
32               processor          Processor
34               processor          Processor
36               processor          Processor
49               memory             Memory
```

$ /usr/sbin/ioscan -f

```
Class       I   H/W Path    Driver    S/W State H/W Type  Description
==========================================================================
bc          0               root      CLAIMED   BUS_NEXUS
bc          1   8           ccio      CLAIMED   BUS_NEXUS I/O Adapter
ext_bus     0   8/0         c720      CLAIMED   INTERFACE GSC add-on Fast/Wide SCSI
Interface
target      0   8/0.1       tgt       CLAIMED   DEVICE
disk        0   8/0.1.0     sdisk     CLAIMED   DEVICE    SEAGATE ST34371W
target      1   8/0.2       tgt       CLAIMED   DEVICE
disk        1   8/0.2.0     sdisk     CLAIMED   DEVICE    SEAGATE ST34371W
target      2   8/0.3       tgt       CLAIMED   DEVICE
disk        2   8/0.3.0     sdisk     CLAIMED   DEVICE    SEAGATE ST34371W
target      3   8/0.4       tgt       CLAIMED   DEVICE
disk        3   8/0.4.0     sdisk     CLAIMED   DEVICE    SEAGATE ST34371W
target      4   8/0.5       tgt       CLAIMED   DEVICE
disk        4   8/0.5.0     sdisk     CLAIMED   DEVICE    SEAGATE ST34371W
target      5   8/0.6       tgt       CLAIMED   DEVICE
disk        5   8/0.6.0     sdisk     CLAIMED   DEVICE    SEAGATE ST34371W
target      6   8/0.7       tgt       CLAIMED   DEVICE
ctl         0   8/0.7.0     sctl      CLAIMED   DEVICE    Initiator
target      7   8/0.8       tgt       CLAIMED   DEVICE
```

```
disk        6   8/0.8.0     sdisk    CLAIMED   DEVICE     SEAGATE ST34371W
target      8   8/0.9       tgt      CLAIMED   DEVICE
disk        7   8/0.9.0     sdisk    CLAIMED   DEVICE     SEAGATE ST34371W
ext_bus     1   8/4         c720     CLAIMED   INTERFACE  GSC add-on Fast/Wide SCSI
Interface
target      9   8/4.1       tgt      CLAIMED   DEVICE
disk        8   8/4.1.0     sdisk    CLAIMED   DEVICE     SEAGATE ST34371W
target      10  8/4.2       tgt      CLAIMED   DEVICE
disk        9   8/4.2.0     sdisk    CLAIMED   DEVICE     SEAGATE ST34371W
target      11  8/4.3       tgt      CLAIMED   DEVICE
disk        10  8/4.3.0     sdisk    CLAIMED   DEVICE     SEAGATE ST34371W
target      12  8/4.4       tgt      CLAIMED   DEVICE
disk        11  8/4.4.0     sdisk    CLAIMED   DEVICE     SEAGATE ST34371W
target      13  8/4.5       tgt      CLAIMED   DEVICE
disk        12  8/4.5.0     sdisk    CLAIMED   DEVICE     SEAGATE ST34371W
target      14  8/4.6       tgt      CLAIMED   DEVICE
disk        13  8/4.6.0     sdisk    CLAIMED   DEVICE     SEAGATE ST34371W
target      15  8/4.7       tgt      CLAIMED   DEVICE
ctl         1   8/4.7.0     sctl     CLAIMED   DEVICE     Initiator
target      16  8/4.8       tgt      CLAIMED   DEVICE
disk        14  8/4.8.0     sdisk    CLAIMED   DEVICE     SEAGATE ST34371W
target      17  8/4.9       tgt      CLAIMED   DEVICE
disk        15  8/4.9.0     sdisk    CLAIMED   DEVICE     SEAGATE ST34371W
ext_bus     2   8/8         c720     CLAIMED   INTERFACE  GSC add-on Fast/Wide SCSI
Interface
target      18  8/8.3       tgt      CLAIMED   DEVICE
disk        16  8/8.3.0     sdisk    CLAIMED   DEVICE     SEAGATE ST34371W
target      19  8/8.4       tgt      CLAIMED   DEVICE
disk        17  8/8.4.0     sdisk    CLAIMED   DEVICE     SEAGATE ST34371W
target      20  8/8.5       tgt      CLAIMED   DEVICE
disk        18  8/8.5.0     sdisk    CLAIMED   DEVICE     SEAGATE ST34371W
target      21  8/8.6       tgt      CLAIMED   DEVICE
disk        19  8/8.6.0     sdisk    CLAIMED   DEVICE     SEAGATE ST34371W
target      22  8/8.7       tgt      CLAIMED   DEVICE
ctl         2   8/8.7.0     sctl     CLAIMED   DEVICE     Initiator
ext_bus     3   8/12        c720     CLAIMED   INTERFACE  GSC add-on Fast/Wide SCSI
Interface
target      23  8/12.1      tgt      CLAIMED   DEVICE
disk        20  8/12.1.0    sdisk    CLAIMED   DEVICE     SEAGATE ST34371W
target      24  8/12.2      tgt      CLAIMED   DEVICE
disk        58  8/12.2.0    sdisk    CLAIMED   DEVICE     SEAGATE ST34371W
target      25  8/12.3      tgt      CLAIMED   DEVICE
disk        21  8/12.3.0    sdisk    CLAIMED   DEVICE     SEAGATE ST34371W
target      26  8/12.4      tgt      CLAIMED   DEVICE
disk        22  8/12.4.0    sdisk    CLAIMED   DEVICE     SEAGATE ST34371W
target      27  8/12.5      tgt      CLAIMED   DEVICE
disk        23  8/12.5.0    sdisk    CLAIMED   DEVICE     SEAGATE ST34371W
target      28  8/12.6      tgt      CLAIMED   DEVICE
disk        24  8/12.6.0    sdisk    CLAIMED   DEVICE     SEAGATE ST34371W
target      29  8/12.7      tgt      CLAIMED   DEVICE
ctl         3   8/12.7.0    sctl     CLAIMED   DEVICE     Initiator
target      30  8/12.8      tgt      CLAIMED   DEVICE
disk        25  8/12.8.0    sdisk    CLAIMED   DEVICE     SEAGATE ST34371W
target      31  8/12.9      tgt      CLAIMED   DEVICE
disk        26  8/12.9.0    sdisk    CLAIMED   DEVICE     SEAGATE ST34371W
bc          2   10          ccio     CLAIMED   BUS_NEXUS  I/O Adapter
ext_bus     4   10/0        c720     CLAIMED   INTERFACE  GSC built-in Fast/Wide SCSI
Interface
target      32  10/0.1      tgt      CLAIMED   DEVICE
disk        27  10/0.1.0    sdisk    CLAIMED   DEVICE     SEAGATE ST34371W
target      33  10/0.2      tgt      CLAIMED   DEVICE
disk        28  10/0.2.0    sdisk    CLAIMED   DEVICE     SEAGATE ST34371W
target      34  10/0.3      tgt      CLAIMED   DEVICE
disk        29  10/0.3.0    sdisk    CLAIMED   DEVICE     SEAGATE ST34371W
target      35  10/0.4      tgt      CLAIMED   DEVICE
disk        30  10/0.4.0    sdisk    CLAIMED   DEVICE     SEAGATE ST34371W
target      36  10/0.5      tgt      CLAIMED   DEVICE
disk        31  10/0.5.0    sdisk    CLAIMED   DEVICE     SEAGATE ST34371W
target      37  10/0.6      tgt      CLAIMED   DEVICE
disk        32  10/0.6.0    sdisk    CLAIMED   DEVICE     SEAGATE ST34371W
target      54  10/0.7      tgt      CLAIMED   DEVICE
ctl         4   10/0.7.0    sctl     CLAIMED   DEVICE     Initiator
bc          3   10/4        bc       CLAIMED   BUS_NEXUS  Bus Converter
tty         0   10/4/0      mux2     CLAIMED   INTERFACE  MUX
ext_bus     5   10/4/4      scsi3    CLAIMED   INTERFACE  HP 28696A - Wide SCSI ID=7
```

```
target      38  10/4/4.1       target         CLAIMED   DEVICE
disk        33  10/4/4.1.0     disc3          CLAIMED   DEVICE     SEAGATE ST34371W
target      39  10/4/4.2       target         CLAIMED   DEVICE
disk        34  10/4/4.2.0     disc3          CLAIMED   DEVICE     SEAGATE ST34371W
target      40  10/4/4.3       target         CLAIMED   DEVICE
disk        35  10/4/4.3.0     disc3          CLAIMED   DEVICE     SEAGATE ST34371W
target      41  10/4/4.4       target         CLAIMED   DEVICE
disk        36  10/4/4.4.0     disc3          CLAIMED   DEVICE     SEAGATE ST34371W
target      42  10/4/4.5       target         CLAIMED   DEVICE
disk        37  10/4/4.5.0     disc3          CLAIMED   DEVICE     SEAGATE ST34371W
target      43  10/4/4.6       target         CLAIMED   DEVICE
disk        38  10/4/4.6.0     disc3          CLAIMED   DEVICE     SEAGATE ST34371W
target      44  10/4/4.8       target         CLAIMED   DEVICE
disk        39  10/4/4.8.0     disc3          CLAIMED   DEVICE     SEAGATE ST34371W
target      45  10/4/4.9       target         CLAIMED   DEVICE
disk        40  10/4/4.9.0     disc3          CLAIMED   DEVICE     SEAGATE ST34371W
ext_bus      6  10/4/12        scsi3          CLAIMED   INTERFACE HP 28696A - Wide SCSI ID=7
target      46  10/4/12.1      target         CLAIMED   DEVICE
disk        41  10/4/12.1.0    disc3          CLAIMED   DEVICE     SEAGATE ST34371W
target      47  10/4/12.2      target         CLAIMED   DEVICE
disk        42  10/4/12.2.0    disc3          CLAIMED   DEVICE     SEAGATE ST34371W
target      48  10/4/12.3      target         CLAIMED   DEVICE
disk        43  10/4/12.3.0    disc3          CLAIMED   DEVICE     SEAGATE ST34371W
target      49  10/4/12.4      target         CLAIMED   DEVICE
disk        44  10/4/12.4.0    disc3          CLAIMED   DEVICE     SEAGATE ST34371W
target      50  10/4/12.5      target         CLAIMED   DEVICE
disk        45  10/4/12.5.0    disc3          CLAIMED   DEVICE     SEAGATE ST34371W
target      51  10/4/12.6      target         CLAIMED   DEVICE
disk        46  10/4/12.6.0    disc3          CLAIMED   DEVICE     SEAGATE ST34371W
target      52  10/4/12.8      target         CLAIMED   DEVICE
disk        47  10/4/12.8.0    disc3          CLAIMED   DEVICE     SEAGATE ST34371W
target      53  10/4/12.9      target         CLAIMED   DEVICE
disk        48  10/4/12.9.0    disc3          CLAIMED   DEVICE     SEAGATE ST34371W
nacc         0  10/4/16        nacc0          CLAIMED   INTERFACE ACC MUX
ext_bus      7  10/8           c720           CLAIMED   INTERFACE GSC add-on Fast/Wide SCSI
Interface
target      55  10/8.7         tgt            CLAIMED   DEVICE
ctl          5  10/8.7.0       sctl           CLAIMED   DEVICE     Initiator
ba           0  10/12          bus_adapter CLAIMED   BUS_NEXUS Core I/O Adapter
ext_bus      9  10/12/0        CentIf      CLAIMED   INTERFACE Built-in Parallel Interface
ext_bus      8  10/12/5        c720           CLAIMED   INTERFACE Built-in SCSI
target      56  10/12/5.0      tgt            CLAIMED   DEVICE
tape         0  10/12/5.0.0    stape          CLAIMED   DEVICE     HP       C1533A
target      57  10/12/5.2      tgt            CLAIMED   DEVICE
disk        49  10/12/5.2.0    sdisk          CLAIMED   DEVICE     TOSHIBA CD-ROM XM-5401TA
target      66  10/12/5.7      tgt            CLAIMED   DEVICE
ctl          6  10/12/5.7.0    sctl           CLAIMED   DEVICE     Initiator
lan          0  10/12/6        lan2           CLAIMED   INTERFACE Built-in LAN
ps2          0  10/12/7        ps2            CLAIMED   INTERFACE Built-in Keyboard/Mouse
bc           4  10/16          bc             CLAIMED   BUS_NEXUS Bus Converter
ext_bus     10  10/16/4        scsi3          CLAIMED   INTERFACE HP 28696A - Wide SCSI ID=7
target      67  10/16/4.2      target         CLAIMED   DEVICE
tape         3  10/16/4.2.0    tape2          CLAIMED   DEVICE     Quantum DLT4000
target      68  10/16/4.3      target         CLAIMED   DEVICE
tape         4  10/16/4.3.0    tape2          CLAIMED   DEVICE     Quantum DLT4000
target      69  10/16/4.4      target         CLAIMED   DEVICE
tape         5  10/16/4.4.0    tape2          CLAIMED   DEVICE     Quantum DLT4000
target      70  10/16/4.5      target         CLAIMED   DEVICE
tape         6  10/16/4.5.0    tape2          CLAIMED   DEVICE     Quantum DLT4000
target      71  10/16/4.6      target         CLAIMED   DEVICE
spt          0  10/16/4.6.0    spt            CLAIMED   DEVICE     HP       C1194F
ext_bus     11  10/16/12       scsi3          CLAIMED   INTERFACE HP 28696A - Wide SCSI ID=7
target      58  10/16/12.1     target         CLAIMED   DEVICE
disk        50  10/16/12.1.0   disc3          CLAIMED   DEVICE     SEAGATE ST34371W
target      59  10/16/12.2     target         CLAIMED   DEVICE
disk        51  10/16/12.2.0   disc3          CLAIMED   DEVICE     SEAGATE ST34371W
target      60  10/16/12.3     target         CLAIMED   DEVICE
disk        52  10/16/12.3.0   disc3          CLAIMED   DEVICE     SEAGATE ST34371W
target      61  10/16/12.4     target         CLAIMED   DEVICE
disk        53  10/16/12.4.0   disc3          CLAIMED   DEVICE     SEAGATE ST34371W
target      62  10/16/12.5     target         CLAIMED   DEVICE
disk        54  10/16/12.5.0   disc3          CLAIMED   DEVICE     SEAGATE ST34371W
target      63  10/16/12.6     target         CLAIMED   DEVICE
disk        55  10/16/12.6.0   disc3          CLAIMED   DEVICE     SEAGATE ST34371W
target      64  10/16/12.8     target         CLAIMED   DEVICE
```

```
disk        56  10/16/12.8.0  disc3      CLAIMED    DEVICE     SEAGATE ST34371W
target      65  10/16/12.9    target     CLAIMED    DEVICE
disk        57  10/16/12.9.0  disc3      CLAIMED    DEVICE     SEAGATE ST34371W
processor    0  32            processor  CLAIMED    PROCESSOR  Processor
processor    1  34            processor  CLAIMED    PROCESSOR  Processor
processor    2  36            processor  CLAIMED    PROCESSOR  Processor
memory       0  49            memory     CLAIMED    MEMORY     Memory
```

$ /usr/sbin/ioscan -funC disk

```
Class    I  H/W Path    Driver     S/W State H/W Type  Description
========================================================================
disk     0  8/0.1.0     sdisk      CLAIMED    DEVICE     SEAGATE ST34371W
                        /dev/dsk/c0t1d0   /dev/rdsk/c0t1d0
disk     1  8/0.2.0     sdisk      CLAIMED    DEVICE     SEAGATE ST34371W
                        /dev/dsk/c0t2d0   /dev/rdsk/c0t2d0
disk     2  8/0.3.0     sdisk      CLAIMED    DEVICE     SEAGATE ST34371W
                        /dev/dsk/c0t3d0   /dev/rdsk/c0t3d0
disk     3  8/0.4.0     sdisk      CLAIMED    DEVICE     SEAGATE ST34371W
                        /dev/dsk/c0t4d0   /dev/rdsk/c0t4d0
disk     4  8/0.5.0     sdisk      CLAIMED    DEVICE     SEAGATE ST34371W
                        /dev/dsk/c0t5d0   /dev/rdsk/c0t5d0
disk     5  8/0.6.0     sdisk      CLAIMED    DEVICE     SEAGATE ST34371W
                        /dev/dsk/c0t6d0   /dev/rdsk/c0t6d0
disk     6  8/0.8.0     sdisk      CLAIMED    DEVICE     SEAGATE ST34371W
                        /dev/dsk/c0t8d0   /dev/rdsk/c0t8d0
disk     7  8/0.9.0     sdisk      CLAIMED    DEVICE     SEAGATE ST34371W
                        /dev/dsk/c0t9d0   /dev/rdsk/c0t9d0
disk     8  8/4.1.0     sdisk      CLAIMED    DEVICE     SEAGATE ST34371W
                        /dev/dsk/c1t1d0   /dev/rdsk/c1t1d0
disk     9  8/4.2.0     sdisk      CLAIMED    DEVICE     SEAGATE ST34371W
                        /dev/dsk/c1t2d0   /dev/rdsk/c1t2d0
disk    10  8/4.3.0     sdisk      CLAIMED    DEVICE     SEAGATE ST34371W
                        /dev/dsk/c1t3d0   /dev/rdsk/c1t3d0
disk    11  8/4.4.0     sdisk      CLAIMED    DEVICE     SEAGATE ST34371W
                        /dev/dsk/c1t4d0   /dev/rdsk/c1t4d0
disk    12  8/4.5.0     sdisk      CLAIMED    DEVICE     SEAGATE ST34371W
                        /dev/dsk/c1t5d0   /dev/rdsk/c1t5d0
disk    13  8/4.6.0     sdisk      CLAIMED    DEVICE     SEAGATE ST34371W
                        /dev/dsk/c1t6d0   /dev/rdsk/c1t6d0
disk    14  8/4.8.0     sdisk      CLAIMED    DEVICE     SEAGATE ST34371W
                        /dev/dsk/c1t8d0   /dev/rdsk/c1t8d0
disk    15  8/4.9.0     sdisk      CLAIMED    DEVICE     SEAGATE ST34371W
                        /dev/dsk/c1t9d0   /dev/rdsk/c1t9d0
disk    16  8/8.3.0     sdisk      CLAIMED    DEVICE     SEAGATE ST34371W
                        /dev/dsk/c2t3d0   /dev/rdsk/c2t3d0
disk    17  8/8.4.0     sdisk      CLAIMED    DEVICE     SEAGATE ST34371W
                        /dev/dsk/c2t4d0   /dev/rdsk/c2t4d0
disk    18  8/8.5.0     sdisk      CLAIMED    DEVICE     SEAGATE ST34371W
                        /dev/dsk/c2t5d0   /dev/rdsk/c2t5d0
disk    19  8/8.6.0     sdisk      CLAIMED    DEVICE     SEAGATE ST34371W
                        /dev/dsk/c2t6d0   /dev/rdsk/c2t6d0
disk    20  8/12.1.0    sdisk      CLAIMED    DEVICE     SEAGATE ST34371W
                        /dev/dsk/c3t1d0   /dev/rdsk/c3t1d0
disk    58  8/12.2.0    sdisk      CLAIMED    DEVICE     SEAGATE ST34371W
                        /dev/dsk/c3t2d0   /dev/rdsk/c3t2d0
disk    21  8/12.3.0    sdisk      CLAIMED    DEVICE     SEAGATE ST34371W
                        /dev/dsk/c3t3d0   /dev/rdsk/c3t3d0
disk    22  8/12.4.0    sdisk      CLAIMED    DEVICE     SEAGATE ST34371W
                        /dev/dsk/c3t4d0   /dev/rdsk/c3t4d0
disk    23  8/12.5.0    sdisk      CLAIMED    DEVICE     SEAGATE ST34371W
                        /dev/dsk/c3t5d0   /dev/rdsk/c3t5d0
disk    24  8/12.6.0    sdisk      CLAIMED    DEVICE     SEAGATE ST34371W
                        /dev/dsk/c3t6d0   /dev/rdsk/c3t6d0
disk    25  8/12.8.0    sdisk      CLAIMED    DEVICE     SEAGATE ST34371W
                        /dev/dsk/c3t8d0   /dev/rdsk/c3t8d0
disk    26  8/12.9.0    sdisk      CLAIMED    DEVICE     SEAGATE ST34371W
                        /dev/dsk/c3t9d0   /dev/rdsk/c3t9d0
disk    27  10/0.1.0    sdisk      CLAIMED    DEVICE     SEAGATE ST34371W
                        /dev/dsk/c4t1d0   /dev/rdsk/c4t1d0
disk    28  10/0.2.0    sdisk      CLAIMED    DEVICE     SEAGATE ST34371W
                        /dev/dsk/c4t2d0   /dev/rdsk/c4t2d0
```

```
disk    29  10/0.3.0      sdisk    CLAIMED   DEVICE     SEAGATE ST34371W
                          /dev/dsk/c4t3d0    /dev/rdsk/c4t3d0
disk    30  10/0.4.0      sdisk    CLAIMED   DEVICE     SEAGATE ST34371W
                          /dev/dsk/c4t4d0    /dev/rdsk/c4t4d0
disk    31  10/0.5.0      sdisk    CLAIMED   DEVICE     SEAGATE ST34371W
                          /dev/dsk/c4t5d0    /dev/rdsk/c4t5d0
disk    32  10/0.6.0      sdisk    CLAIMED   DEVICE     SEAGATE ST34371W
                          /dev/dsk/c4t6d0    /dev/rdsk/c4t6d0
disk    33  10/4/4.1.0    disc3    CLAIMED   DEVICE     SEAGATE ST34371W
                          /dev/dsk/c5t1d0    /dev/rdsk/c5t1d0
disk    34  10/4/4.2.0    disc3    CLAIMED   DEVICE     SEAGATE ST34371W
                          /dev/dsk/c5t2d0    /dev/rdsk/c5t2d0
disk    35  10/4/4.3.0    disc3    CLAIMED   DEVICE     SEAGATE ST34371W
                          /dev/dsk/c5t3d0    /dev/rdsk/c5t3d0
disk    36  10/4/4.4.0    disc3    CLAIMED   DEVICE     SEAGATE ST34371W
                          /dev/dsk/c5t4d0    /dev/rdsk/c5t4d0
disk    37  10/4/4.5.0    disc3    CLAIMED   DEVICE     SEAGATE ST34371W
                          /dev/dsk/c5t5d0    /dev/rdsk/c5t5d0
disk    38  10/4/4.6.0    disc3    CLAIMED   DEVICE     SEAGATE ST34371W
                          /dev/dsk/c5t6d0    /dev/rdsk/c5t6d0
disk    39  10/4/4.8.0    disc3    CLAIMED   DEVICE     SEAGATE ST34371W
                          /dev/dsk/c5t8d0    /dev/rdsk/c5t8d0
disk    40  10/4/4.9.0    disc3    CLAIMED   DEVICE     SEAGATE ST34371W
                          /dev/dsk/c5t9d0    /dev/rdsk/c5t9d0
disk    41  10/4/12.1.0   disc3    CLAIMED   DEVICE     SEAGATE ST34371W
                          /dev/dsk/c6t1d0    /dev/rdsk/c6t1d0
disk    42  10/4/12.2.0   disc3    CLAIMED   DEVICE     SEAGATE ST34371W
                          /dev/dsk/c6t2d0    /dev/rdsk/c6t2d0
disk    43  10/4/12.3.0   disc3    CLAIMED   DEVICE     SEAGATE ST34371W
                          /dev/dsk/c6t3d0    /dev/rdsk/c6t3d0
disk    44  10/4/12.4.0   disc3    CLAIMED   DEVICE     SEAGATE ST34371W
                          /dev/dsk/c6t4d0    /dev/rdsk/c6t4d0
disk    45  10/4/12.5.0   disc3    CLAIMED   DEVICE     SEAGATE ST34371W
                          /dev/dsk/c6t5d0    /dev/rdsk/c6t5d0
disk    46  10/4/12.6.0   disc3    CLAIMED   DEVICE     SEAGATE ST34371W
                          /dev/dsk/c6t6d0    /dev/rdsk/c6t6d0
disk    47  10/4/12.8.0   disc3    CLAIMED   DEVICE     SEAGATE ST34371W
                          /dev/dsk/c6t8d0    /dev/rdsk/c6t8d0
disk    48  10/4/12.9.0   disc3    CLAIMED   DEVICE     SEAGATE ST34371W
                          /dev/dsk/c6t9d0    /dev/rdsk/c6t9d0
disk    49  10/12/5.2.0   sdisk    CLAIMED   DEVICE     TOSHIBA CD-ROM XM-5401TA
                          /dev/dsk/c8t2d0    /dev/rdsk/c8t2d0
disk    50  10/16/12.1.0  disc3    CLAIMED   DEVICE     SEAGATE ST34371W
                          /dev/dsk/c11t1d0   /dev/rdsk/c11t1d0
disk    51  10/16/12.2.0  disc3    CLAIMED   DEVICE     SEAGATE ST34371W
                          /dev/dsk/c11t2d0   /dev/rdsk/c11t2d0
disk    52  10/16/12.3.0  disc3    CLAIMED   DEVICE     SEAGATE ST34371W
                          /dev/dsk/c11t3d0   /dev/rdsk/c11t3d0
disk    53  10/16/12.4.0  disc3    CLAIMED   DEVICE     SEAGATE ST34371W
                          /dev/dsk/c11t4d0   /dev/rdsk/c11t4d0
disk    54  10/16/12.5.0  disc3    CLAIMED   DEVICE     SEAGATE ST34371W
                          /dev/dsk/c11t5d0   /dev/rdsk/c11t5d0
disk    55  10/16/12.6.0  disc3    CLAIMED   DEVICE     SEAGATE ST34371W
                          /dev/dsk/c11t6d0   /dev/rdsk/c11t6d0
disk    56  10/16/12.8.0  disc3    CLAIMED   DEVICE     SEAGATE ST34371W
                          /dev/dsk/c11t8d0   /dev/rdsk/c11t8d0
disk    57  10/16/12.9.0  disc3    CLAIMED   DEVICE     SEAGATE ST34371W
                          /dev/dsk/c11t9d0   /dev/rdsk/c11t9d0
```

Again the full listing with the **-f** output produces some additional useful information such as the full hardware path, and the software and hardware types. The **-funC disk** option produces information related to usable disk on the system. In configurations with a substantial amount of disk space, such as the system used in the example with a lot of HP high availability disks, it is useful to have a listing of the disks only for your system notebook, as well as a full listing of all devices.

The file **/stand/vmunix** is the currently running kernel. Here is a long listing of the directory **/stand** on the Series 800 which shows the file **/stand/vmunix**:

```
$ ll  /stand

-rw-r--r--  1 root    sys         190 Jul 12 18:09 bootconf
drwxr-xr-x  2 root    root       1024 Jul 12 18:37 build
-rw-r--r--  1 root    root        684 Jul 12 18:05 ioconfig
-rw-r--r--  1 root    sys          82 Jul 12 18:31 kernrel
drwxr-xr-x  2 root    root       8192 Jul 12 16:32 lost+found
-rw-r--r--  1 root    sys         609 Jul 12 18:15 system
-rwxr-xr-x  1 root    root    6938348 Jul 12 18:37 vmunix
```

In order to make a change to the kernel, we would change to the directory **/stand/build** (**cd /stand/build**) where all work in creating a new kernel is performed and issue the **system_prep** command as shown below:

```
$ /usr/lbin/sysadm/system_prep  -s  system
```

Some more advanced changes I made to a kernel when performing a benchmark were to modify many of the parameters in the system file.
The default **/stand/build/system** looked like the following:

```
*************************************
* Generic system file for new computers
*************************************
*
* Drivers/Subsystems
ccio
c720
sctl
sdisk
mux2
CentIf
stape
ps2
```

```
cdfs
vxbase
lvm
lv
hpstreams
clone
strlog
sad
echo
sc
timod
tirdwr
pipedev
pipemod
ffs
lan2
dlpi
inet
uipc
nm
ni
tpiso
inet_cots
inet_clts
netdiag1
ldterm
ptem
pts
ptm
pckt
nfs
diag0
fddi
vxadv
dump lvol
nstrpty60
maxswapchunks 512
```

The modifications I made to the **/stand/build/system** file in order to run the benchmark are shown in the following file:

```
* Drivers and Subsystems
```

```
CentIf
CharDrv
asp
asyncdsk
c720
ccio
cdfs
clone
core
diag0
dlpi
echo
ffs
hpstreams
inet
inet_clts
inet_cots
klog
lan2
lasi
ldterm
lv
lvm
mux2
netdiag1
netman
nfs
ni
pa
pckt
pfail
pipedev
pipemod
ps2
ptem
ptm
pts
sad
sc
sctl
sdisk
sio
stape
```

```
strlog
strpty_included
timod
tirdwr
tpiso
uipc
vxadv
vxbase
wsio



* Kernel Device info

fddi
dump lvol



* Tunable parameters

create_fastlinks 1
dbc_min_pct      2
default_disk_ir 1
fs_async         1
max_async_ports 256
maxdsiz          0X040000000
maxfiles         100
maxssiz          0X017777F77
maxswapchunks    16384
maxtsiz          0X040000000
maxuprc          3500
maxvgs           20
msgmni           1024
msgseg           4092
msgssz           16
msgtql           1024
nfile            60500
nflocks          2000
ninode
ninode(((NPROC+16+MAXUSERS)+32+(2*NPTY)+
                   (10*NUM_CLIENTS))+56800)

nproc            3504
nstrpty          60
o_sync_is_o_dsync 1
```

```
semmni              3500
semmns              3500
semmnu              3500
semume              50
shmmax              0X40000000
```

We can now proceed to edit the file **/stand/build/system** and make the desired changes to the kernel, including adding a driver or subsystem such as cdfs for CD-ROM file system, or the more advanced changes I showed in the earlier **system** file associated with the benchmark.

With the desired changes having been made to the **system** file, we can create the new kernel which will be called **/stand/build/vmunix_test** with the command shown below:

```
$ mk_kernel  -s  system
```

At this point the new kernel exists in the **/stand/build** directory and can be moved to the **/stand** directory. I would first recommend moving the existing kernel (**/stand/vmunix**) to a backup file name and then moving the new kernel to the **/stand** directory as shown below:

```
$ mv  /stand/vmunix    /stand/vmunix.prev

$ mv  /stand/build/vmunix_test    /stand/vmunix
```

You can now shut down the system and automatically boot off the new kernel.

In HP-UX 10.x you may want to rebuild the kernel for dynamic buffer cache. You can, for instance, specify a buffer cache boundry using *dbc_min_pct* as a lower boundry and *dbc_max_pct* as an upper boundry.

Figure 1-21 summarizes the process of building a new kernel in HP-UX 10.x.

Step	Comments
1) run **sysdef** and **ioscan -f**	Analyze and report tunable parameters of currently running kernel.
2) perform long listing of **/stand** directory	The file **vmunix** is the existing kernel and **system** is used to build a new kernel.
3) **cd /stand/build**	This is the directory where the new kernel will be built.
4) **/usr/lbin/sysadm/system_prep -s system**	This extracts the **system** file from the currently running kernel.
5) edit **system** file and make desired changes	Takes place in the **/stand/build** directory.
6) **mk_kernel -s system**	Makes a new kernel in the **/stand/build** directory called **vmunix_test**. **conf.c**, **conf.o**, and **config.mk** are also produced.
7) **mv /stand/system /stand/system.prev** **mv /stand/build/system /stand/system**	Save the existing **system** file as **/stand/system.prev** and copy the new **system** file in **/stand/build/system** to **/stand/system**.
8) **mv /stand/vmunix /stand/vmunix.prev** **mv /stand/build/vmunix_test /stand/vmunix**	Save the existing **vmunix** file as **/stand/vmunix.prev** and copy the new kernel in **/stand/build** to **/stand/vmunix**.
9) **cd /** **shutdown -h 0**	Change directory to / and shut down the system so it comes up with the new kernel.

Figure 1-21 Creating a Kernel in HP-UX 10.x

Configure Additional Peripherals (F5)

As you progress through the installation flow, you reach a point where it makes sense to add the additional peripherals that are part of your system. A typical installation will have terminals, printers, a tape drive, a CD-ROM drive, etc. Some devices are "standard," meaning they are HP products or third-party products officially supported by HP. You have to be careful here, though, because what may seem as if it should work may not work after all and may not be supported. There is almost always a way to get things working eventually, but beware of devices you may be adding that aren't supported and may cause you trouble.

As you add additional peripherals to your system you will either have to add device files manually or use SAM to create them for you. Most all devices you add can be added through SAM. I find adding peripherals to be much like setting up networking; that is, I almost always use SAM but I find it important to know what is going on in the background. As an example, you could add a printer to your system using SAM and never know what has been done to support the new printer. In the event the printer does not work for some reason, you really can't begin troubleshooting the problem without an understanding of device files.

I touched on device files in the file system section but did not want to go into too much detail. Here is the rest of the story on device files.

All About Device Files in HP-UX 10.x

What could be more confusing in the UNIX world than device files? Fortunately, HP-UX device files for the Series 700 and Series 800 are nearly identical, so if you learn one, it applies to the other. There were many more differences in device files in HP-UX 9.x. In this section I'll cover

- The structure of device files.

- Some commands associated with helping you work with device files.

- Some examples of creating device files.

A device file provides the HP-UX kernel with important information about a specific device. The HP-UX kernel needs to know a lot about a device before input/output operations can be performed. With HP-UX 10.x the device file naming convention is the same for workstations and server systems. Device files are in the **/dev** directory. There may also be a subdirectory under **/dev** used to further categorize the device files. An example of a subdirectory would be **/dev/dsk** where disk device files are usually located and **/dev/rmt** where tape drive device files are located. Figure 1-22 shows the HP-UX 10.x device file naming convention.

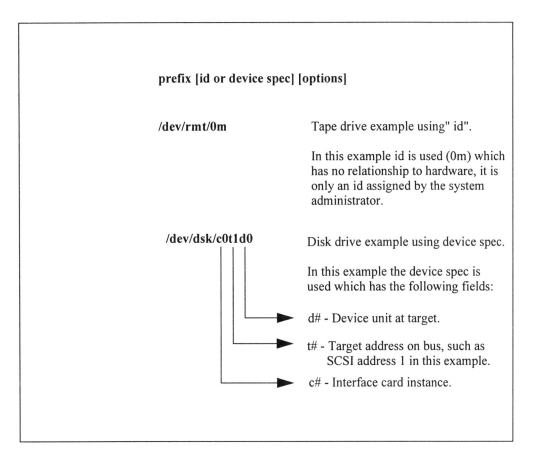

prefix [id or device spec] [options]

/dev/rmt/0m   Tape drive example using" id".

In this example id is used (0m) which has no relationship to hardware, it is only an id assigned by the system administrator.

/dev/dsk/c0t1d0   Disk drive example using device spec.

In this example the device spec is used which has the following fields:

d# - Device unit at target.

t# - Target address on bus, such as SCSI address 1 in this example.

c# - Interface card instance.

Figure 1-22 HP-UX 10.x Device File Naming Convention

There are a number of commands you use as you go about creating device files. The **ioscan** command is the first of these. This command was covered under "Building a Kernel in HP-UX 10.x," but I'll go over this again and provide the same **ioscan** examples for the Series 700 and Series 800 shown earlier so you don't have to flip back to the earlier section. The following is an **ioscan** output of the same Series 700 for which **sysdef** was run when describing how a kernel is created. (Using **-f** with **ioscan** would have created a full listing; you should try it with and without **-f**.)

(on Series 700)

```
$ /usr/sbin/ioscan
```

```
H/W Path      Class                 Description
==================================================
              bc
8             bc                    Pseudo Bus Converter
8/0               unknown           GSC-to-PCI Bus Bridge
8/12              ext_bus           GSC Fast/Wide SCSI Interface
8/12.6                target
8/12.6.0              disk          SEAGATE ST34371W
8/12.7                target
8/12.7.0              ctl           Initiator
8/16          ba                    Core I/O Adapter
8/16/0            ext_bus           Built-in Parallel Interface
8/16/1            audio             Built-in Audio
8/16/4            tty               Built-in RS-232C
8/16/5            ext_bus           Built-in SCSI
8/16/5.2              target
8/16/5.2.0               disk       TOSHIBA CD-ROM XM-5401TA
8/16/5.3              target
8/16/5.3.0               tape       HP          C1533A
8/16/5.7              target
8/16/5.7.0               ctl        Initiator
8/16/6            lan               Built-in LAN
8/16/7            ps2               Built-in Keyboard/Mouse
8/20          ba                    Core I/O Adapter
8/20/1            hil               Built-in HIL
8/20/2            tty               Built-in RS-232C
8/20/5            ba                EISA Bus Adapter
8/24          graphics              Graphics
62            processor             Processor
63            memory                Memory
```

The following is an **ioscan** output of the same Series 800 for which **sysdef** was run when describing how a kernel is created. (Using **-f** would have created a full listing; you should try with and without **-f**.) Note the three processors shown in this output.

(on Series 800)
```
$ /usr/sbin/ioscan
```

```
H/W Path      Class               Description
=================================================
              bc
8             bc                  I/O Adapter
8/0           ext_bus             GSC add-on Fast/Wide SCSI Interface
8/0.1             target
8/0.1.0           disk            SEAGATE ST34371W
8/0.2             target
8/0.2.0           disk            SEAGATE ST34371W
8/0.3             target
8/0.3.0           disk            SEAGATE ST34371W
8/0.4             target
8/0.4.0           disk            SEAGATE ST34371W
8/0.5             target
8/0.5.0           disk            SEAGATE ST34371W
8/0.6             target
8/0.6.0           disk            SEAGATE ST34371W
8/0.7             target
8/0.7.0           ctl             Initiator
8/0.8             target
8/0.8.0           disk            SEAGATE ST34371W
8/0.9             target
8/0.9.0           disk            SEAGATE ST34371W
8/4           ext_bus             GSC add-on Fast/Wide SCSI Interface
8/4.1             target
8/4.1.0           disk            SEAGATE ST34371W
8/4.2             target
8/4.2.0           disk            SEAGATE ST34371W
8/4.3             target
8/4.3.0           disk            SEAGATE ST34371W
8/4.4             target
8/4.4.0           disk            SEAGATE ST34371W
8/4.5             target
8/4.5.0           disk            SEAGATE ST34371W
8/4.6             target
8/4.6.0           disk            SEAGATE ST34371W
8/4.7             target
8/4.7.0           ctl             Initiator
8/4.8             target
8/4.8.0           disk            SEAGATE ST34371W
8/4.9             target
8/4.9.0           disk            SEAGATE ST34371W
8/8           ext_bus             GSC add-on Fast/Wide SCSI Interface
8/8.3             target
8/8.3.0           disk            SEAGATE ST34371W
8/8.4             target
8/8.4.0           disk            SEAGATE ST34371W
8/8.5             target
8/8.5.0           disk            SEAGATE ST34371W
8/8.6             target
8/8.6.0           disk            SEAGATE ST34371W
8/8.7             target
8/8.7.0           ctl             Initiator
8/12          ext_bus             GSC add-on Fast/Wide SCSI Interface
8/12.1            target
8/12.1.0          disk            SEAGATE ST34371W
8/12.2            target
8/12.2.0          disk            SEAGATE ST34371W
8/12.3            target
8/12.3.0          disk            SEAGATE ST34371W
8/12.4            target
8/12.4.0          disk            SEAGATE ST34371W
8/12.5            target
8/12.5.0          disk            SEAGATE ST34371W
8/12.6            target
8/12.6.0          disk            SEAGATE ST34371W
8/12.7            target
8/12.7.0          ctl             Initiator
8/12.8            target
```

```
8/12.8.0                disk        SEAGATE ST34371W
8/12.9               target
8/12.9.0                disk        SEAGATE ST34371W
10            bc                    I/O Adapter
10/0              ext_bus           GSC built-in Fast/Wide SCSI Interface
10/0.1               target
10/0.1.0                disk        SEAGATE ST34371W
10/0.2               target
10/0.2.0                disk        SEAGATE ST34371W
10/0.3               target
10/0.3.0                disk        SEAGATE ST34371W
10/0.4               target
10/0.4.0                disk        SEAGATE ST34371W
10/0.5               target
10/0.5.0                disk        SEAGATE ST34371W
10/0.6               target
10/0.6.0                disk        SEAGATE ST34371W
10/0.7               target
10/0.7.0                ctl         Initiator
10/4          bc                    Bus Converter
10/4/0            tty               MUX
10/4/4            ext_bus           HP 28696A - Wide SCSI ID=7
10/4/4.1             target
10/4/4.1.0              disk        SEAGATE ST34371W
10/4/4.2             target
10/4/4.2.0              disk        SEAGATE ST34371W
10/4/4.3             target
10/4/4.3.0              disk        SEAGATE ST34371W
10/4/4.4             target
10/4/4.4.0              disk        SEAGATE ST34371W
10/4/4.5             target
10/4/4.5.0              disk        SEAGATE ST34371W
10/4/4.6             target
10/4/4.6.0              disk        SEAGATE ST34371W
10/4/4.8             target
10/4/4.8.0              disk        SEAGATE ST34371W
10/4/4.9             target
10/4/4.9.0              disk        SEAGATE ST34371W
10/4/12           ext_bus           HP 28696A - Wide SCSI ID=7
10/4/12.1            target
10/4/12.1.0             disk        SEAGATE ST34371W
10/4/12.2            target
10/4/12.2.0             disk        SEAGATE ST34371W
10/4/12.3            target
10/4/12.3.0             disk        SEAGATE ST34371W
10/4/12.4            target
10/4/12.4.0             disk        SEAGATE ST34371W
10/4/12.5            target
10/4/12.5.0             disk        SEAGATE ST34371W
10/4/12.6            target
10/4/12.6.0             disk        SEAGATE ST34371W
10/4/12.8            target
10/4/12.8.0             disk        SEAGATE ST34371W
10/4/12.9            target
10/4/12.9.0             disk        SEAGATE ST34371W
10/4/16           nacc              ACC MUX
10/8              ext_bus           GSC add-on Fast/Wide SCSI Interface
10/8.7               target
10/8.7.0                ctl         Initiator
10/12         ba                    Core I/O Adapter
10/12/0           ext_bus           Built-in Parallel Interface
10/12/5           ext_bus           Built-in SCSI
10/12/5.0            target
10/12/5.0.0            tape         HP       C1533A
10/12/5.2            target
10/12/5.2.0             disk        TOSHIBA CD-ROM XM-5401TA
10/12/5.7            target
10/12/5.7.0             ctl         Initiator
10/12/6           lan               Built-in LAN
10/12/7           ps2               Built-in Keyboard/Mouse
10/16         bc                    Bus Converter
10/16/4           ext_bus           HP 28696A - Wide SCSI ID=7
10/16/4.2            target
10/16/4.2.0            tape         Quantum DLT4000
10/16/4.3            target
```

```
10/16/4.3.0              tape        Quantum DLT4000
10/16/4.4                target
10/16/4.4.0              tape        Quantum DLT4000
10/16/4.5                target
10/16/4.5.0              tape        Quantum DLT4000
10/16/4.6                target
10/16/4.6.0              spt         HP      C1194F
10/16/12        ext_bus              HP 28696A - Wide SCSI ID=7
10/16/12.1               target
10/16/12.1.0             disk        SEAGATE ST34371W
10/16/12.2               target
10/16/12.2.0             disk        SEAGATE ST34371W
10/16/12.3               target
10/16/12.3.0             disk        SEAGATE ST34371W
10/16/12.4               target
10/16/12.4.0             disk        SEAGATE ST34371W
10/16/12.5               target
10/16/12.5.0             disk        SEAGATE ST34371W
10/16/12.6               target
10/16/12.6.0             disk        SEAGATE ST34371W
10/16/12.8               target
10/16/12.8.0             disk        SEAGATE ST34371W
10/16/12.9               target
10/16/12.9.0             disk        SEAGATE ST34371W
32              processor            Processor
34              processor            Processor
36              processor            Processor
49              memory               Memory
```

The next command that helps you when creating device files is **lsdev**. **lsdev** lists all of the drivers configured into your system. When adding a device file, you need to have the driver for the device you use configured into the system. If it is not configured into the system, you can use SAM to configure it or use the manual kernel configuration process covered earlier in this chapter. There is a column for the major number for a character device and block device, the driver name, and class of the driver. Here is an example of running **lsdev** on the same Series 700 **ioscan** was run on:

(on Series 700)
```
$ /usr/sbin/lsdev
```

Character	Block	Driver	Class
0	-1	cn	pseudo
1	-1	ansio0	tty
3	-1	mm	pseudo
16	-1	ptym	ptym
17	-1	ptys	ptys
46	-1	netdiag1	unknown
52	-1	lan2	lan
56	-1	ni	unknown

```
  60        -1        netman    unknown
  64        64        lv        lvm
  66        -1        audio     audio
  69        -1        dev_config pseudo
  72        -1        clone     pseudo
  73        -1        strlog    pseudo
  74        -1        sad       pseudo
 112        24        pflop     floppy
 116        -1        echo      pseudo
 119        -1        dlpi      pseudo
 122        -1        inet_cots unknown
 122        -1        inet_cots unknown
 156        -1        ptm       strptym
 157        -1        ptm       strptys
 159        -1        ps2       ps2
 164        -1        pipedev   unknown
 168        -1        beep      graf_pseudo
 174        -1        framebuf  graf_pseudo
 188        31        sdisk     disk
 189        -1        klog      pseudo
 203        -1        sctl      pseudo
 205        -1        stape     tape
 207        -1        sy        pseudo
 216        -1        CentIF    ext_bus
 227        -1        kepd      pseudo
 229        -1        ite       graf_pseudo
```

Here is an example of running **lsdev** on the same Series 800 **ioscan** was run on.

(on Series 800)
$ **/usr/sbin/lsdev**

```
Character    Block      Driver     Class
   0         -1        cn        pseudo
   3         -1        mm        pseudo
  16         -1        ptym      ptym
  17         -1        ptys      ptys
  28         -1        diag0     diag
  46         -1        netdiag1  unknown
  52         -1        lan2      lan
  56         -1        ni        unknown
  60         -1        netman    unknown
  64         64        lv        lvm
  69         -1        dev_config pseudo
  72         -1        clone     pseudo
  73         -1        strlog    pseudo
```

```
    74            -1          sad           pseudo
   116            -1          echo          pseudo
   119            -1          dlpi          pseudo
   122            -1          inet_cots     unknown
   122            -1          inet_cots     unknown
   136            -1          lpr0          unknown
   156            -1          ptm           strptym
   157            -1          ptm           strptys
   159            -1          ps2           ps2
   164            -1          pipedev       unknown
   168            -1          beep          graf_pseudo
   188            31          sdisk         disk
   189            -1          klog          pseudo
   193            -1          mux2          tty
   203            -1          sctl          pseudo
   205            -1          stape         tape
   207            -1          sy            pseudo
   216            -1          CentIF        ext_bus
   227            -1          kepd          pseudo
```

From these two **lsdev** outputs you can observe some minor differences in the devices. The Series 700, for instance, has such classes as audio and floppy and the Series 800 has a multiplexer.

You can use **ioscan** to show you the device files for a particular peripheral. Going back to the Series 800 that had four disks and a CD-ROM attached to it, you could issue the following **ioscan** command to see the device files associated with *disk*:

(on Series 800)

```
$ /usr/sbin/ioscan -fn -C disk

Class  I  H/W Path      Driver  S/W State  H/W Type   Description
=================================================================
disk   0 10/0.3.0       sdisk   CLAIMED    DEVICE      HP C2490WD
                        /dev/dsk/c0t3d0   /dev/rdsk/c0t3d0

disk   1 10/0.4.0       sdisk   CLAIMED    DEVICE      HP C2490WD
                        /dev/dsk/c0t4d0   /dev/rdsk/c0t4d0

disk   2 10/0.5.0       sdisk   CLAIMED    DEVICE      HP C2490WD
                        /dev/dsk/c0t5d0   /dev/rdsk/c0t5d0
```

```
disk   3 10/0.6.0      sdisk   CLAIMED      DEVICE      HP C2490WD
                       /dev/dsk/c0t6d0   /dev/rdsk/c0t6d0

disk   3 10/12/5/2/0 sdisk   CLAIMED      DEVICE      CD-ROM
                       /dev/dsk/c1t2d0   /dev/rdsk/c1t2d0
```

You can see from this **ioscan** all of the devices files associated with *disk* including the CD-ROM. All disks on the system are shown in this output because I did not use the **-u** option, which would have shown only usable disks.

You could find out more information about one of these devices with the **diskinfo** command and the character device you want to know more about as shown below (using the "-v" option for verbose provides more detailed information).

```
$ diskinfo /dev/rdsk/c0t5d0

SCSI describe of /dev/rdsk/c0t5d0
          vendor: HP
      product id: C2490WD
            type: direct access
            size: 2082636 bytes
 bytes per sector: 512
```

Before we construct a device file, let's view two existing device files on the Series 700 and see where some of this information appears. The first long listing is that of the tape drive and the second is the disk, both of which are on the Series 700 in the earlier listing.

(on Series 700)
```
$ ll /dev/rmt/0m

crw-rw-rw- 2 bin bin 205 0x003000 Feb 12 03:00 /dev/rmt/0m
```

(on Series 700)
```
$ ll /dev/dsk/c0t1d0

brw-r----- 1 root sys 31 0x001000 Feb 12 03:01 /dev/dsk/c0t1d0
```

The tape drive device file shows a major number of 205 corresponding to that shown for the *character* device driver *stape* from **lsdev**. The disk drive device file shows a major number of 31 corresponding to the *block* device driver *sdisk* from **lsdev**. Since the tape drive requires only a character device file and there is no major number for a block stape device, as indicated by the "-1" in the block column of **lsdev**, this is the only device file that exists for the tape drive. The disk, on the other hand, may be used as either block device or character device (also referred to as the raw device). Therefore, we should see a character device file with a major number of 188 as shown in **ioscan** for sdisk.

(on Series 700)

```
$ ll /dev/rdsk/c0t0d0

crw-r----- 1 root sys 188 0x001000 Feb 12 03:01 /dev/rdsk/c0t1d0
```

We can now create a device file for a second tape drive, this time at SCSI address 2, and a disk device file for a disk drive at SCSI address 5 using the **mksf** command. You can run **mksf** two different ways. The first form of **mksf** requires you to include less specific information such as the minor number. The second form requires you to include more of this specific information. Some of these arguments relate only to the specific form of **mksf** you use.

-d	Use the device driver specified. A list of device drivers is obtained with the **lsdev** command.
-C	The device specified belongs to this class. The class is also obtained with the **lsdev** command.

-H	Use the hardware path specified. Hardware paths are obtained with the **ioscan** command.
-m	The minor number of the device is supplied.
-r	Create a character, also known as a raw, device file
-v	Use verbose output which prints the name of each special file as it is created.

We could now create a *block* device file for a disk at SCSI address 5 using the following **mksf** comand:

(on Series 700)

```
$ /sbin/mksf -v -C disk -m 0x005000 /dev/dsk/c0t5d0
        making /dev/dsk/c0t5d0 b 31 0x005000
```

Similarly, we could now create a *character* device file for a disk at SCSI address 5 using form two of **mksf**:

(on Series 700)

```
$ /sbin/mksf -v -r -C disk -m 0x005000 /dev/dsk/c0t5d0
        making /dev/rdsk/c0t5d0 c 188 0x005000
```

The "-v" option used in these examples prints out each device file as it is created. If you wanted to add a second tape drive at SCSI address 2 to your system in addition to the existing tape drive (/**dev/rmt/0m**), you might use the following **mksf** command:

(on Series 700)

```
$ /sbin/mksf   -v -C tape -m 0x002000 /dev/rmt/1m

      making /dev/rmt/1m c 205 0x002000
```

Character devices are automatically produced for these tape drives since no block device drivers are shown using the **lsdev** command as indicated by a -1 in the "Block" column.

An Example of Adding a Peripheral

One common use for many of the commands and procedures related to building a kernel and device files are required when you connect a new device to your system. Many new devices are introduced before any automatic configuration tools are in place. Let's take a look at some of the steps required to configure a Digital Linear Tape (DLT) on a K class system when it was first introduced. The tape drive to be configured holds 48 tapes and has four drives.

The process of configuring the DLT consists of the following steps:

- Configure the necessary driver statements into the kernel and reboot the system.

• Gather device file information and create the device file for a DLT component.

• Test the DLT.

The SCSI pass through driver (*spt*) is required for DLT operation. Before beginning this operation I familiarized myself with *spt* by viewing the **scsi_pt** manual page as well as looking at the many *spt* entries in LaserROM. Generic SCSI commands can be sent to the device controlled with this driver. This driver needs to be configured into the kernel for the DLT to operate. To view what is configured in the existing kernel you would run **system_prep** in order to create a **system** file that reflects the current kernel configuration. By creating and viewing the file that reflects the currently running kernel we can determine if we need to add the *spt* driver for the DLT. This work should take place in the **/stand/build** directory as shown below.

```
# cd /stand/build
# system_prep -s system
```

You can then view the **system** file just created to see if indeed there are any *spt* drivers configured into the kernel.

```
# more system | grep spt
spt
#
```

In this case the *spt* driver has been configured into the kernel. However, not only does there need to be a line in the system file for *spt*, we also need a line that attaches the *spt* driver to the DLT device. I added the second of the two following lines in the **system** file under the "drivers" area in order to link the *spt* driver to the path of the DLT.

```
spt
driver 10/16/4.6.0 spt
```

The path of the DLT device of 10/16/4.6.0 was determined by running **ioscan**. This device came up with a class of "unknown" for the device with this path, as shown in the following **ioscan** output, but it should have been *spt*. We will get to creating the device file with the class *spt* shortly, however, it is sufficient to know at this time that the DLT device at this path was "unknown."

```
10/16/4.6.0   unknown   HP    C1194F
```

The driver statement mapping the DLT hardware to *spt* will override any standard SCSI driver also mapped to the device.

After insuring both of the *spt* lines are in the **system** file you reconfigure the kernel with the following command.

```
# mk_kernel -s /stand/build/system
```

This creates the file **vmunix_test**. You can now view the pass through driver and its revision with the following command.

```
# what ./vmunix_test | grep scsi_pt
```

You would then go through the process described in the earlier figure for moving the old files to those with a **.prev** extension and moving the new **system** and **vmunix** files into place. A reboot is required for the new kernel to take effect.

There are also many device files associated with the DLT. Some have been automatically created and others have not. The device earlier identified as that which the *spt* will use was at the location 10/16/4.6.0. This device came up as unknown but we want this to have a class of *spt*. We'll use the **mknod** command to produce the device file. We first need to get some information about *spt* with the **lsdev** command.

```
# lsdev -d spt
Character      Block      Driver      Class
    138          -1        spt          spt
```

This tells us that the major number for *spt* is 138. With the other information we have we are now able to run the following **mknod** command for the device as shown below. The "a" in the minor number comes from the "10" in the interface ("I") column for "ext_bus" of the **ioscan** output. The "6" in the minor number comes from the SCSI ID of the "spt" entry of the **ioscan** output. The "0" after the "6" in the minor number comes from the LUN of the "spt" in the **ioscan** output. The last two "0s" in the minor number are reserved fields. The numbers used to create the minor number appear bold in the upcoming **ioscan** output shown after the **mknod** command.

```
# mknod /dev/sjid1u1 c 138 0x0a6000
```

Running **ioscan -f** now produces a list of components related to the DLT. The following listing shows the components related to the DLT only.

```
Class      I   H/W Path     Driver    S/W State H/W Type  Description
===================================================================
ext_bus   10   10/16/4       scsi3     CLAIMED    INTERFACE HP 28696A      <------
target    67   10/16/4.2     target    CLAIMED    DEVICE
tape       3   10/16/4.2.0   tape2     CLAIMED    DEVICE    Quantum DLT4000
target    68   10/16/4.3     target    CLAIMED    DEVICE
tape       4   10/16/4.3.0   tape2     CLAIMED    DEVICE    Quantum DLT4000
target    69   10/16/4.4     target    CLAIMED    DEVICE
tape       5   10/16/4.4.0   tape2     CLAIMED    DEVICE    Quantum DLT4000
target    70   10/16/4.5     target    CLAIMED    DEVICE
tape       6   10/16/4.5.0   tape2     CLAIMED    DEVICE    Quantum DLT4000
target    71   10/16/4.6     target    CLAIMED    DEVICE
spt        0   10/16/4.6.0   spt       CLAIMED    DEVICE    HP      C1194F <-----
```

Included in this list are the four disks internal to the DLT and the *spt* device that earlier came up "unknown."

In addition we can look at the tape devices associated with the DLT that were automatically created under **/dev/rmt** as shown in the following listing:

```
crw-rw-rw-   2 bin      bin      212 0x0a2000 Mar 24 15:20 3m
crw-rw-rw-   2 bin      bin      212 0x0a2080 Apr 24 10:47 3mb
crw-rw-rw-   2 bin      bin      212 0x0a2040 Mar 24 09:28 3mn
crw-rw-rw-   2 bin      bin      212 0x0a20c0 Apr 24 13:15 3mnb
crw-rw-rw-   2 bin      bin      212 0x0a3000 Mar 24 09:28 4m
crw-rw-rw-   2 bin      bin      212 0x0a3080 Apr 24 10:44 4mb
crw-rw-rw-   2 bin      bin      212 0x0a3040 Mar 24 09:28 4mn
crw-rw-rw-   2 bin      bin      212 0x0a30c0 Apr 24 11:04 4mnb
crw-rw-rw-   2 bin      bin      212 0x0a4000 Apr 24 10:32 5m
crw-rw-rw-   2 bin      bin      212 0x0a4080 Apr 24 10:41 5mb
crw-rw-rw-   2 bin      bin      212 0x0a4040 Mar 24 09:28 5mn
crw-rw-rw-   2 bin      bin      212 0x0a40c0 Apr 24 11:06 5mnb
crw-rw-rw-   2 bin      bin      212 0x0a5000 Apr 24 10:35 6m
crw-rw-rw-   2 bin      bin      212 0x0a5080 Apr 24 10:39 6mb
crw-rw-rw-   2 bin      bin      212 0x0a5040 Mar 24 09:28 6mn
crw-rw-rw-   2 bin      bin      212 0x0a50c0 Apr 24 12:47 6mnb
crw-rw-rw-   2 bin      bin      212 0x0a2000 Mar 24 15:20 c10t2d0BEST
crw-rw-rw-   2 bin      bin      212 0x0a2080 Apr 24 10:47 c10t2d0BESTb
crw-rw-rw-   2 bin      bin      212 0x0a2040 Mar 24 09:28 c10t2d0BESTn
crw-rw-rw-   2 bin      bin      212 0x0a20c0 Apr 24 13:15 c10t2d0BESTnb
crw-rw-rw-   2 bin      bin      212 0x0a3000 Mar 24 09:28 c10t3d0BEST
crw-rw-rw-   2 bin      bin      212 0x0a3080 Apr 24 10:44 c10t3d0BESTb
crw-rw-rw-   2 bin      bin      212 0x0a3040 Mar 24 09:28 c10t3d0BESTn
crw-rw-rw-   2 bin      bin      212 0x0a30c0 Apr 24 11:04 c10t3d0BESTnb
crw-rw-rw-   2 bin      bin      212 0x0a4000 Apr 24 10:32 c10t4d0BEST
crw-rw-rw-   2 bin      bin      212 0x0a4080 Apr 24 10:41 c10t4d0BESTb
crw-rw-rw-   2 bin      bin      212 0x0a4040 Mar 24 09:28 c10t4d0BESTn
crw-rw-rw-   2 bin      bin      212 0x0a40c0 Apr 24 11:06 c10t4d0BESTnb
crw-rw-rw-   2 bin      bin      212 0x0a5000 Apr 24 10:35 c10t5d0BEST
crw-rw-rw-   2 bin      bin      212 0x0a5080 Apr 24 10:39 c10t5d0BESTb
crw-rw-rw-   2 bin      bin      212 0x0a5040 Mar 24 09:28 c10t5d0BESTn
crw-rw-rw-   2 bin      bin      212 0x0a50c0 Apr 24 12:47 c10t5d0BESTnb
crw-rw-rw-   2 bin      bin      205 0x080000 Mar 19 09:33 c8t0d0BEST
crw-rw-rw-   2 bin      bin      205 0x080080 Mar 19 09:33 c8t0d0BESTb
crw-rw-rw-   2 bin      bin      205 0x080040 Mar 19 09:33 c8t0d0BESTn
crw-rw-rw-   2 bin      bin      205 0x0800c0 Mar 19 09:33 c8t0d0BESTnb
crw-r--r--   1 bin      bin      205 0xffffffe Mar 19 09:33 stape_config
crw-r--r--   1 bin      bin      212 0xffffffe Mar 24 09:28 tape2_config
```

There are both complex names for some of the drives and more descriptive names. A simple test of the device would be to use **tar** to write a file to one of the devices.

```
# tar -cvf /dev/rmt/6mb /home
```

All files were reported written to this device and I used **tar -tvf /dev/rmt/6m** to produce a table of contents of the tape.

Although you probably won't need to perform any of this manual configuration for the DLT, you may need to perform a similar process for new devices on your system. These commands are useful to know and use so when you need to configure devices on your system, you can check your existing configuration and make the necessary changes.

Set Up Users and Groups (F6)

As you may have guessed by now, performing system administration functions on your HP-UX system is easy; it's the planning that takes time and effort. Setting up users and groups is no exception. Thanks to SAM, doing just about anything with users and groups is simple.

There is one exception to this easy setup: Common Desktop Environment (CDE) customization. SAM doesn't really help with CDE customization and it can be quite tricky to modify one's CDE setup manually. I have most of Chapter 6 to assist you with CDE customization.

You need to make a few basic decisions about users. Where should user's data be located? Who needs to access data from whom, thereby defining "groups" of users? What kind of particular startup is required by users and applications? Is there a shell that your users will prefer? Then there is the subject of CDE customization covered in Chapter 6.

You will want to put some thought into these important user-related questions. I spend a lot of time working with my customers rearranging user data for several reasons. It doesn't fit on a whole disk (this is one reason I strongly recommend using Logical Volume Manager), users can't freely access one another's data, or even worse, users *can* access one another's data too freely.

We will consider these questions, but first, let's look at the basic steps to adding a user, whether you do this manually or rely on SAM. Here is a list of activities:

- Select a user name to add

- Select a user ID number

- Select a group for the user

- Create an **/etc/passwd** entry (in HP-UX 10.x you can specify such options as minimum and maximum times between password changes)

- Assign a user password

- Select and create a home directory for user

- Select shell the user will run (I strongly recommend the default POSIX shell)

- Place startup files in user's home directory

- Test the user account

This may seem like a lot of work, but there is nothing to it if you run SAM and answer the questions. Most of what you do is entered in the file **/etc/passwd** where information about all users is stored. You can make all of these entries to the **/etc/passwd** file with the **/usr/sbin/vipw** command. Figure 1-23 is a sample **/etc/passwd** entry.

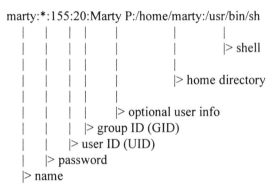

```
marty:*:155:20:Marty P:/home/marty:/usr/bin/sh
   |   |  | |    |          |          |
   |   |  | |    |          |          |> shell
   |   |  | |    |          |
   |   |  | |    |          |> home directory
   |   |  | |    |
   |   |  | |    |> optional user info
   |   |  | |> group ID (GID)
   |   |  |> user ID (UID)
   |   |> password
   |> name
```

Figure 1-23   Sample **/etc/passwd** Entry

Here is a description of each of these fields:

name.   The user name you assign. This name should be easy for the user and other users on the system to remember. When sending electronic mail or copying files from one user to another, the easier it is to remember the user name, the better. If a user has a user name on another system and it is an easy name for others to remember, you may want to assign the same user name on your HP-UX system. Some systems don't permit nice, easy user names, so you may want to break the tie with the old system and start using sensible, easy-to-remember user names on your HP-UX system. Remember, there is no security tied to the user name; security is handled through the user's password and the file permissions.

password.   This is the user's password in encrypted form. If an asterisk appears in this field, the account can't be used. If it is empty, the user has no password assigned and can log in by typing only his or her user name. I strongly recommend each user have a password which he or she changes periodically. Every system has different security needs, but at a minimum every user on every system should have a password. Some features of a good password are

- A minimum of six characters that should include special characters such as slash, dot, asterisk, etc.

- No words should be used for a password.

- Don't make the password personal such as name, address, favorite sports team, etc.

- Don't use something easy to type such as 123456, or qwerty.

- Some people say misspelled words are acceptable, but I don't recommend using them. Spell check programs that match misspelled words to correctly spelled words can be used to guess at words that might be misspelled for a password.

- A password generator that produces unintelligible passwords works the best.

user ID (UID).   The identification number of the user. Every user on your system should have a unique UID. There are no conventions for UIDs. SAM will assign a UID for you when you add users, but you can always change this. I would recommend you reserve UIDs less than 100 for system-level users.

group ID (GID).   The identification number of the group. The members of the group, and their GID, are in the **/etc/group** file. You can change the GID assigned if you don't like it, but you may also have to change the GID of many files. As a user creates a file, their UID is assigned to the file as well as the GID. This means if you change the GID well after users of the same group have created many files and directories, you may have to change the GID of all these. I usually save GIDs less than 10 for system groups.

optional user info.   In this space you can make entries, such as the user's phone number or full name. SAM asks you for this information when you create a user. You can leave this blank, but if you manage a system or network with many users you may want to add the user's full name and extension so if you need to get in touch with him or her, you'll have the information at your fingertips.

home directory.   The home directory defines the default location for all the users' files and directories. This is the present working directory at the time of login.

shell.   This is the startup program the user will run at the time of login. The shell is really a command interpreter for all of the commands the user issues from the command line. I recommend using the default POSIX shell (**/usr/bin/sh**), but there are also three traditional popular shells in the HP-UX environment: C shell (**/usr/bin/csh**); Bourne shell (**/usr/old/bin/sh**); and Korn shell (**/usr/bin/ksh**). Shell programming for the system administrator is covered in Chapter 6.

Assigning Users to Groups

After defining all user-related information, you need to consider groups. Groups are often overlooked in the HP-UX environment until the system administrator finds that all his or her users are in the very same group, even though from an organizational standpoint they are in different groups. Before I cover the groups in general, let's look at a file belonging to a user and the way access is defined for a file:

```
$ ll
-rwxr-x--x   1 marty      users      120 Jul 26 10:20 sort
```

For every file on the system HP-UX supports three classes of access:

- User access (u). Access granted to the owner of the file
- Group access (g). Access granted to members of the same group as the owner of the file
- Other access (o). Access granted to everyone else

These access rights are defined by the position of r (read), write (w), and execute (x) when the long listing command is issued. For the long listing (**ll**) above, you see the following permissions in Table 1-5.

TABLE 1-5   LONG LISTING PERMISSIONS

Access	User Access	Group Access	Other
Read	r	r	-
Write	w	-	-
Execute	x	x	x

You can see that access rights are arranged in groups of three. There are three groups of permissions with three access levels each. The owner, in this case marty, is allowed read, write, and execute permissions on the file. Anyone in the group users is permitted read and execute access to the file. Others are permitted only execute access of the file.

These permissions are important to consider as you arrange your users into groups. If several users require access to the same files, then you will want to put those users in the same group. The trade-off here is that you can give all users within a group rwx access to files, but then you run the risk of several users editing a file without other users knowing it, thereby causing confusion. On the other hand, you can make several copies of a file so each user has his or her personal copy, but then you have multiple versions of a file. If possible, assign users to groups based on their work.

When you run SAM and specify the groups to which each user belongs, the file /etc/group is updated. The /etc/group file contains the group name, encrypted password, group ID, and list of users in the group. Here is an example of an /etc/group file:

```
root::0:root
other::1:root, hpdb
bin::2:root,bin
sys::3:root,uucp
adm::4:root,adm
daemon::5:root,daemon
mail::6:root
lp::7:root,lp
tty::10:
nuucp::11:nuucp
military::25:jhunt,tdolan,vdallesandro
commercial::30:ccascone,jperwinc,devers
nogroup:*:-2:
```

This /etc/group file shows two different groups of users. Although all users run the same application, a desktop publishing tool, some work on documents of "commercial" products while others work on only "military" documents. It made sense for the system administrator to create two groups, one for commercial document preparation and the other for military document preparation. All members of a group know what documents are current and respect one another's work and its importance. You will have few problems among group members who know what each other are doing and will find these members don't delete files that shouldn't be deleted. If you put all users into one group, however, you may find that you spend more time restoring files because users in this broader group don't find files that are owned by other members of their group to be important. Users can change group with the newgrp command.

Another important entry in the /etc/passwd file is the location of his or her home directory. You have to select a location for the user's "home" directory in the file system where the user's files will be stored. With some of the advanced networking technology that exists, such as NFS, the user's home directory does not even have to be on a disk that is physically connected to the computer he or she is using! The traditional place to locate a user's home directory on an HP-UX system is the **/home** directory in HP-UX 10.x and **/users** in HP-UX 9.x.

The **/home** directory is typically the most dynamic in terms of growth. Users create and delete files in their home directory on a regular basis. This means you have to do more planning related to your user area than in more static areas, such as the root file system and application areas. You would typically load HP-UX and your applications and then perform relatively few accesses to these in terms of adding and deleting files and directories. The user area is continuously updated, making it more difficult to maintain.

Setup Backup Procedure (F7)

The best way to manage backups in HP-UX is through SAM. Backup with SAM is covered in Chapter 4. SAM uses the commands **fbackup** and **frecover** to perform backups and restore data. The reason SAM is the best way to specify backups in HP-UX is that it prompts you for all the relevant information related to backups. There are, however, a variety of commands you can use to back up your system, some of which I'll give an overview of shortly. SAM helps you manage both *Automated Backups* and *Interactive Backup and Recovery*. There are also some advanced backup programs you can procure from both HP and third parties. In general, I find the capabilities of **fbackup** and **frecover** are sufficient for new HP-UX installations. If, however, you have a highly distributed environment or need to back up large amounts of data to several devices simultaneously, you may want to consider a more advanced product. Here are some of the more important factors related to backup and recovery you should know about.

To begin with, let's consider why you perform backups. A backup is a means of recovering from any system-related problem. System-related problems range from a disk hardware problem that ruins every byte of data on your disk, to a user who accidentally deletes a file he or she really needs. The disk hardware problem is a worst-case scenario. You will need an entire (full) backup of your system performed regularly in order to recover from this. The minor problem that your user has created can be recovered from with regular incremental backups. This means you need to perform full system backups regularly and incremental backups as often as possible. Depending on the amount of disk space you have and the backup device you have, you may be in the comfortable position of performing backups as often as you want. Assuming you have the backup device, what is the full and incremental backup technique you should employ? I am a strong advocate of performing a full backup, then performing incremental backups of every file that has changed since the **last full backup**. This means that to recover from a completely "hosed" (a technical term meaning destroyed) system, you need your full backup tape and only one incremental tape. If, for instance, you performed a full backup on Sunday and an incremental backup on Monday through Friday, you would need to load only Sunday's full backup tape and Friday's incremental backup tape to completely restore your system. **fbackup** supports this scheme.

SAM can handle all of the options to the **fbackup** command for you, such as whether this is a full or incremental backup, but it is worthwhile to know what is taking place with **fbackup**. Here is an explanation of the **fbackup** command and *some* of its options:

/usr/sbin/fbackup -f device [-0-9] [-u] [-i path] [-e path] [-g graph]

-f device	The tape drive for the backup, such as **/dev/rmt/ 0m** for your local tape drive.
[-0-9]	This is the level of backup. If you run a full backup on Sunday at level 0, then you would run an incremental backup at level 1 the other days of the week. An incremental backup will back up all information changed since a backup was made at a lower level. You could back up at 0 on Sunday, 1 on Monday, 2 on Tuesday, and so on. This would mean, however, that to recover your system you would need to load Sunday's tape, Monday's tape, Tuesday's tape, etc. to fully recover.

[-u]	This updates the database of past backups so it contains such information as the backup level, time of the beginning and end of the backup session, and the graph file (described shortly) used for the backup session.
[-i path]	Specified path is to be included in the backup. This can be issued any number of times.
[-e path]	This excludes the path from the backup. This may be specified any number of times.
[-g graph]	The graph file contains the list of files and directories to be included or excluded from the backup.

Although **fbackup** is quite thorough and easy to use, it does not have embedded in it the day and time at which full and incremental backups will be run. You have to make a **cron** entry to run **fbackup** automatically. SAM will make a **cron** entry for you, thereby running **fbackup** whenever you like.

Since SAM runs the **fbackup** for you, there really isn't much more you have to know about **fbackup**. There are, however, many other backup programs that are widely used in the UNIX world that you should be aware of. Some of these may prove important to you because they are widely used in exchanging information between UNIX systems of different manufacturers. They can also be used for backup purposes, but I recommend using **fbackup** through SAM. Keep in mind that **fbackup** runs under HP-UX only so you can restore only to an HP-UX system. Here is brief overview of some other backup methods.

tar	**tar** is the most popular backup utility. You will find that many applications are shipped on tar tapes. This is the most widely used format for exchanging data with other UNIX users. **tar** is the oldest UNIX backup method and therefore runs on all UNIX systems. You can also append files to the end of a **tar** tape, which you can't do with **fbackup**. When sending files to another UNIX

user, I would strongly recommend **tar**. **tar** is as slow as dirt, so you won't want to use it for your full or incremental backups. One highly desirable aspect of **tar** is that when you load files onto a tape with **tar** and then restore them onto another system, the original users and groups are retained. For instance, to back up all files belonging to frank and load them onto another system, you would use the following commands:

$ cd /home/frank

$ tar -cvf /dev/rmt/0m 'ls'   (grav around ls)

You could then load all frank's files on another system even if the user frank and his group don't yet exist on that system.

cpio   **cpio** is also portable and easy to use like **tar**. In addition, **cpio** is much faster than **tar**. Not as fast as **fbackup**, but much faster than **tar**.

dd   This is a bit-for-bit copy. It is not smart in the sense that it does not copy files and ownerships; it just copies bits. You could not, therefore, select only a file off a **dd** tape as you could with **fbackup**, **tar**, or **cpio**.

dump   **dump** is similar to **fbackup**. If you use **fbackup** on HP-UX, you will see much similarity when you use **dump**. **dump** provides the same level backup scheme as **fbackup** and creates **/var/adm/dumpdates** which lists the last time a file system was backed up.

Examples of Remote Backup Using cpio, tar, and fbackup

Let's now go back to the DLT we configured earlier in this chapter and use it to show how some of these backup commands could be used to back up a system across the network. In the following examples the DLT is attached to system1 and we are going to back up the **/usr1/patches** directory on system2. Relative path names are used for some examples and absolute path names in others. Keep in mind that files are on system1 but the DLT is on system2 and backups and restores are taking place to and from the DLT.

cpio Backup and Restore Example

The following is an example of backing up on the DLT using **cpio**. The three commands used in this backup are **find**, **cpio**, and **dd**. The following shows an example of running a backup.

```
# cd /usr1/patches
# find . -depth -xdev | cpio -ovxcB 2> /tmp/index | remsh
     system1 -l root "cat - | dd of=/dev/rmt/1m obs=5k"

40636+8 records in
4064+0 records out
```

The files that are part of the backup are not shown, however; they are contained in the **/tmp/index** file.

This **find** command takes place from the current directory down as indicated by the ".". The "-depth" indicates that all entries in a directory will be acted on before the directory itself. The "-xdev" is used to prevent a mount point from being crossed that is below the starting point.

The output of the **find** command is then piped to **cpio**. In this case **cpio** is used to create an archive. The "-o" is used to read standard input, in this case the output of the **find** command, and copy the files to standard output. The "-v" option prints a list of file names as they are processed. The "-x" option saves device special files. The "-B" option blocks output at 5120 blocks per record. The "2" following the list of **cpio** options send standard error to the file **/tmp/index**. You may want to take a look at the manual page for the shell you are using. "1" is standard output and "2" is standard error. Rather than have these print to the screen, you can redirect them to a file as I have done with standard error in this command line. The file **/tmp/index** is used as the index file for the backup. Standard error is also written to this file. The output of **cpio** is then piped to the **remsh** command on the next line.

The **remsh** command is run on system1 (remember that we are backing up information on system2 to the DLT attached to system1) as the user root. The **dd** command is used to write the files to the DLT with a block size of 5K.

To restore the files to their original location we would issue the following commands. Again, there is a long list of options to the **cpio** command.

```
# cd /usr1/patches
# remsh system1 -l root dd if=/dev/rmt/1m bs=5k |
                    cpio -icvdxumB

PHKL_8756.depot
PHKL_8756.text
PHKL_9307.depot
PHKL_9307.text
PHKL_9416.depot
PHKL_9416.text
PHSS_7930.depot
PHSS_7930.text
cpio.restore
cpio.save
fbackup.save
frecover.restore
tar.restore
tar.save
PHCO_9228
```

```
PHCO_9895
PHKL_10058
PHKL_8055
PHKL_8656
PHKL_8756
PHKL_9307
PHKL_9416
PHNE_9107
PHSS_7930
```

In this case we run a **remsh** on system1 with the output of **dd** piped to **cpio** in order to restore the files.

tar Backup and Restore Example

To back up using **tar** across the network you would issue the following command:

```
# cd /usr1/patches
# tar cvf - . | remsh system1 -l root "cat - |
                    dd of=/dev/rmt/1m bs=10k"

a ./PHKL_8756.depot 480 blocks
a ./PHKL_8756.text 15 blocks
a ./PHKL_9307.depot 660 blocks
a ./PHKL_9307.text 13 blocks
a ./PHKL_9416.depot 140 blocks
a ./PHKL_9416.text 14 blocks
a ./PHSS_7930.depot 5120 blocks
a ./PHSS_7930.text 297 blocks
a ./cpio.restore 1 blocks
a ./cpio.save 1 blocks
a ./fbackup.save 1 blocks
a ./frecover.restore 1 blocks
a ./tar.restore 1 blocks
a ./tar.save 1 blocks
a ./PHCO_9228 1124 blocks
a ./PHCO_9895 10286 blocks
a ./PHKL_10058 207 blocks
a ./PHKL_8055 165 blocks
a ./PHKL_8656 122 blocks
a ./PHKL_8756 367 blocks
a ./PHKL_9307 541 blocks
```

```
a ./PHKL_9416 104 blocks
a ./PHNE_9107 720 blocks
a ./PHSS_7930 20264 blocks
0+6255 records in
0+6255 records out
```

In this case the file names are displayed as they are stored because there is no **/tmp/index** file specified to include the list of files that are part of the backup.

No **find** command is required in this case because we provide the list of files to be backed up as part of **tar**. The "cvf" options to **tar** do the following: create a new archive; produce a verbose output which in this case is our list of files to back up; and use the next argument as the name of the archive instead of the default which is **/dev/rmt/0m**.

This output is then piped to system1 where a **dd** takes place to the DLT.

To restore the files to their original location we would issue the following command:

```
# cd /usr1/patches
# remsh system1 -l root dd if=/dev/rmt/1m bs=10k | tar xvf -

x ./PHKL_8756.depot, 245760 bytes, 480 tape blocks
x ./PHKL_8756.text, 7464 bytes, 15 tape blocks
x ./PHKL_9307.depot, 337920 bytes, 660 tape blocks
x ./PHKL_9307.text, 6332 bytes, 13 tape blocks
x ./PHKL_9416.depot, 71680 bytes, 140 tape blocks
x ./PHKL_9416.text, 6887 bytes, 14 tape blocks
x ./PHSS_7930.depot, 2621062 bytes, 5120 tape blocks
x ./PHSS_7930.text, 151962 bytes, 297 tape blocks
x ./cpio.restore, 77 bytes, 1 tape blocks
x ./cpio.save, 107 bytes, 1 tape blocks
x ./fbackup.save, 38 bytes, 1 tape blocks
x ./frecover.restore, 52 bytes, 1 tape blocks
x ./tar.restore, 74 bytes, 1 tape blocks
x ./tar.save, 70 bytes, 1 tape blocks
x ./PHCO_9228, 575283 bytes, 1124 tape blocks
x ./PHCO_9895, 5265981 bytes, 10286 tape blocks
x ./PHKL_10058, 105778 bytes, 207 tape blocks
```

```
x ./PHKL_8055, 84265 bytes, 165 tape blocks
x ./PHKL_8656, 62111 bytes, 122 tape blocks
x ./PHKL_8756, 187840 bytes, 367 tape blocks
x ./PHKL_9307, 276989 bytes, 541 tape blocks
x ./PHKL_9416, 53136 bytes, 104 tape blocks
x ./PHNE_9107, 368594 bytes, 720 tape blocks
x ./PHSS_7930, 10374875 bytes, 20264 tape blocks
0+6255 records in
0+6255 records out
```

In this case a **remsh** is run on system1 to use **dd** to restore the files. The "x" option used with **tar** extracts files from the tape.

fbackup Backup and Restore Example

To back up using **fbackup** across the network you would issue the following command. In this case I have used the absolute path name rather than the relative path name as in the other examples.

```
# fbackup -f system1:/dev/rmt/1m -v -i /usr1/patches

fbackup(1004): session begins on Fri May 23 12:18:07
fbackup(3309): unable to read a volume header
fbackup(3024): writing volume 1 to the output
file system1:dev/rmt/0m
     1: /
     2: /usr1
     3: /usr1/patches
     4: /usr1/patches/PHCO_9228
     5: /usr1/patches/PHCO_9895
     6: /usr1/patches/PHKL_10058
     7: /usr1/patches/PHKL_8055
     8: /usr1/patches/PHKL_8656
     9: /usr1/patches/PHKL_8756
    10: /usr1/patches/PHKL_8756.depot
    11: /usr1/patches/PHKL_8756.text
    12: /usr1/patches/PHKL_9307
    13: /usr1/patches/PHKL_9307.depot
    14: /usr1/patches/PHKL_9307.text
    15: /usr1/patches/PHKL_9416
```

```
16: /usr1/patches/PHKL_9416.depot
17: /usr1/patches/PHKL_9416.text
18: /usr1/patches/PHNE_9107
19: /usr1/patches/PHSS_7930
20: /usr1/patches/PHSS_7930.depot
21: /usr1/patches/PHSS_7930.text
22: /usr1/patches/cpio.restore
23: /usr1/patches/cpio.save
24: /usr1/patches/fbackup.save
25: /usr1/patches/frecover.restore
26: /usr1/patches/tar.restore
27: /usr1/patches/tar.save
fbackup(1005): run time: 62 seconds
```

You can see that **fbackup** has much of the functionality of the other commands built into it. The "-f" option to **fbackup** allows you to specify any device for the output file. In this case we are actually writing to the DLT on a remote system. The "-v" option is to run in verbose mode. The "-i" option specifies the tree to be included in the backup.

To restore the files to their original location we would issue the following command:

```
# frecover -r -o -vf system1:/dev/rmt/1m

-rw-r-----      root      sys     /usr1/patches/PHCO_9228
-rw-r-----      root      sys     /usr1/patches/PHCO_9895
-rw-r-----      root      sys     /usr1/patches/PHKL_10058
-rw-r-----      root      sys     /usr1/patches/PHKL_8055
-rw-r-----      root      sys     /usr1/patches/PHKL_8656
-rw-r-----      root      sys     /usr1/patches/PHKL_8756
-rw-r--r--      root      sys     /usr1/patches/PHKL_8756.depot
-rw-r--r--      root      sys     /usr1/patches/PHKL_8756.text
-rw-r-----      root      sys     /usr1/patches/PHKL_9307
-rw-r--r--      root      sys     /usr1/patches/PHKL_9307.depot
-rw-r--r--      root      sys     /usr1/patches/PHKL_9307.text
-rw-r-----      root      sys     /usr1/patches/PHKL_9416
-rw-r--r--      root      sys     /usr1/patches/PHKL_9416.depot
-rw-r--r--      root      sys     /usr1/patches/PHKL_9416.text
-rw-r-----      root      sys     /usr1/patches/PHNE_9107
-rw-r-----      root      sys     /usr1/patches/PHSS_7930
-rw-r--r--      root      sys     /usr1/patches/PHSS_7930.depot
-rw-r--r--      root      sys     /usr1/patches/PHSS_7930.text
-rwxrwxrwx      root      sys     /usr1/patches/cpio.restore
```

```
-rwxrwxrwx        root      sys      /usr1/patches/cpio.save
-rwxrwxrwx        root      sys      /usr1/patches/fbackup.save
-rwxrwxrwx        root      sys      /usr1/patches/frecover.restore
-rwxrwxrwx        root      sys      /usr1/patches/tar.restore
-rwxrwxrwx        root      sys      /usr1/patches/tar.save
```

The **frecover** command is similar to **fbackup**. The "-r" option is used to read the media and recover the files. The "-v" option specifies verbose output. The "-f" option is used to specify the device from which the recovery will take place. In this example I have used the "-o" option for overwrite. By default, a file that exists will not be overwritten by the **frecover** command unless the "-o" option is used.

Perform Ongoing System Administration Tasks (F8)

A system administrator's job is never done. This is good news if you need to keep making a living for a few more years. There are enough ongoing tasks and new technologies that will be introduced into your environment to keep you busy.

Many of my fastest paced customers find new technology to implement every month! Some of this technology is unproven and some of it you would not normally think would work well together. There are, however, business needs forcing many companies, possibly your company, to continue to press ahead with such technology. A lot of the burden of making this new technology work and maintaining it will be your job. Although you don't need to pay overly close attention to the way your system is being used, I do have some recommendations:

- Monitor overall system resource utilization, including
  - CPU
  - Disk (file system usage)
  - Networking
  - Swap space

- Devise a thorough backup strategy that you have 100 percent confidence in. This means that you test it out by restoring select files, and then restoring your entire system. The backup commands I covered earlier are only commands, not a strategy. You have to be confident that any or all of your data can be restored whenever necessary.

- Keep printers and plotters running

- Have a network map that you keep current. Change the network configuration to keep collisions low and tune the network whenever necessary.

- Update applications with new releases and, if possible, have a test system on which you can test new releases of HP-UX and applications.

- Update HP-UX on the test system if this is available.

- Keep a book of all hardware and software and be sure to update these whenever you change the configuration of a system.

- Keep a record of the kernel configuration of all your systems and be sure to update this whenever you rebuild a kernel.

- Record the patches you apply to each system.

- Make a detailed list of the logical volumes on all your systems.

- Audit your system on a regular basis.

As the system administrator, you can't rely on HP to handle your system and HP-UX-related issues and on the application vendor to handle your application-related issues. There are just too many system dependencies. Congratulations, this is your job.

Among the most important ongoing tasks you can perform is to regularly audit your HP-UX system. Chapter 8 provides an overview of some areas of system you want to focus on as part of a system audit.

One of the ongoing tasks to perform on your system is patch management. Beginning with HP-UX 10.20 patch management became much easier due to the distribution of the "Extension Software" CD-ROM. This CD-ROM includes patches categorized in the following way.

- General-Release Patches - These are related to core HP-UX and apply to most all HP-UX systems.

- Critical Patches - These patches fix problems that could result in serious system problems such as data corruption and loss.

- Hardware-Enablement Patches - These patches allow you to use the latest hardware and included here are hardware drivers.

The patches on the Extension Software CD-ROM are organized by operating system release and architecture. You mount the CD-ROM and use **swinstall** as you normally would and specify the source and target. The source would be the full path of the patch directory on the CD-ROM. The following example shows the source path for HP-UX 10.20 General-Release Patches for the Series 800.

```
/UPDATE_CDROM/10.X/800/10.20/XSW800GR1020
```

There are also useful **README** files on the CD-ROM that explain the process of using the Extension Software. One of the README files covers the Extension Software in general, including installing the software. Other files describe the specific details of patches such as critical patches for the Series 800. These files have the ".lst" appendix.

The following is an example of the ".lst" file for critical Series 800 patches.

```
EXTSW Hardware Enablement and Critical Bundle for s800 Release
10.20 rev 32
#########################################################

Content List
@@@@@@@@@@@@@@@@@@@@@@@@@@@@@

+-----------+-------------------------------------------------
| Patch ID  | Description
```

```
+-----------+--------------------------------------------------------
| PHCO_9213 | LVM commands cumulative patch
| PHCO_9396 | fsck_vxfs(1M) fix for umountable file system
| PHCO_9770 | 10.10-20 AutoRAID Manager (ARM) software
| PHKL_7764 | Data loss when truncating VxFS (JFS) files
| PHKL_8118 | tape driver patch
| PHKL_8507 | GSC SCSI tape driver cumulatve patch
| PHKL_9307 | HP-PB SCSI cumulative patch (scsi1/scsi3)
| PHKL_9366 | data corruption on PA-8000 based systems
| PHKL_9371 | Fixes for unmountable VxFS (JFS) file systems
| PHKL_9530 | LVM kernel and pstat cumulative patch
+-----------+--------------------------------------------------------


Disk Space Usage
@@@@@@@@@@@@@@@@@@@@@@@@@@@@@@@@@@@@@@@


+-------------------+---------------------------------------
| Increase (Kbytes) | File System
+-------------------+---------------------------------------
|               147 | /usr
|                72 | /tmp
|              3173 | /var
|                 0 | /
+-------------------+---------------------------------------
```

Before you install any patches using Extension Software on your system, you want to make sure you carefully review the patch documentation to make certain the patch applies to your system and you know the potential impact of the patch on your system, such as the amount of disk space required.

Memory Management

What is swap? HP-UX system administrators spend a lot of time worrying about swap. It must be very important. Swap is one part of the overall HP-UX memory management scheme, one of three parts to be exact. As any student of computer science will tell you, computers have three types of memory: cache memory, Random Access Memory (RAM), and disk memory. These are listed in order of their speed; that is, cache is much faster than RAM, which is much faster than disk.

Cache Memory

The HP Precision Architecture chip set is configured with both data and instruction cache, which, I might add, is used very efficiently. You must rely on the operating system to use cache efficiently, since you have very little control over this. If you need information from memory and it is loaded in cache (probably because you recently accessed this information or accessed some information which is located close to what you now want), it will take very little time to get the information out of cache memory. This access, called a cache "hit," is instantaneous for all practical purposes. One of the reasons cache memory is so fast is that it is usually physically on the same chip with the processor. If it were possible to put large amounts of cache on-chip with the processor, this would obviate the need for RAM and disk. This, however, is not currently possible, so efficient use of memory is a key to good overall system performance.

Checking Available RAM

Your system spells out to you what RAM is available. **/sbin/dmesg** gives you the amount of "physical" memory installed on the system, as shown below for a 64-MByte system:

Physical: 65536 Kbytes

Don't get too excited when you see this number because it is not all "available" memory. Available memory is what is left over after some memory is reserved for kernel code and data structures. You'll also see the available memory, in this case approximately 54 MBytes, with **/sbin/ dmesg**:

available: 55336 Kbytes

Some of the available memory can also be "lockable." Lockable memory is that which can be devoted to frequently accessed programs and data. The programs and data that lock memory for execution will remain memory resident and run faster. You will also see the amount of lockable memory, in this case approximately 44 MBytes, at the time of system startup:

lockable: 45228

/sbin/dmesg shows you these values, and a summary of system-related messages. You should issue this command on your system to see what it supplies you.

The following is an example of having run **dmesg** on a K460 with three processors and 2 GBytes of RAM. The last lines of the output summarize the memory on the system.

```
$ dmesg

Apr 11 14:53
vuseg=a2ef000
  inet_clts:ok  inet_cots:ok 8 ccio
8/0 c720
8/0.1 tgt
8/0.1.0 sdisk
8/0.2 tgt
8/0.2.0 sdisk
8/0.3 tgt
8/0.3.0 sdisk
8/0.4 tgt
8/0.4.0 sdisk
8/0.5 tgt
8/0.5.0 sdisk
8/0.6 tgt
8/0.6.0 sdisk
8/0.7 tgt
8/0.7.0 sctl
8/0.8 tgt
8/0.8.0 sdisk
8/0.9 tgt
8/0.9.0 sdisk
8/4 c720
8/4.1 tgt
8/4.1.0 sdisk
8/4.2 tgt
8/4.2.0 sdisk
8/4.3 tgt
```

```
8/4.3.0 sdisk
8/4.4 tgt
8/4.4.0 sdisk
8/4.5 tgt
8/4.5.0 sdisk
8/4.6 tgt
8/4.6.0 sdisk
8/4.7 tgt
8/4.7.0 sctl
8/4.8 tgt
8/4.8.0 sdisk
8/4.9 tgt
8/4.9.0 sdisk
8/8 c720
8/8.3 tgt
8/8.3.0 sdisk
8/8.4 tgt
8/8.4.0 sdisk
8/8.5 tgt
8/8.5.0 sdisk
8/8.6 tgt
8/8.6.0 sdisk
8/8.7 tgt
8/8.7.0 sctl
8/12 c720
8/12.1 tgt
8/12.1.0 sdisk
8/12.2 tgt
8/12.2.0 sdisk
8/12.3 tgt
8/12.3.0 sdisk
8/12.4 tgt
8/12.4.0 sdisk
8/12.5 tgt
8/12.5.0 sdisk
8/12.6 tgt
8/12.6.0 sdisk
8/12.7 tgt
8/12.7.0 sctl
8/12.8 tgt
8/12.8.0 sdisk
8/12.9 tgt
8/12.9.0 sdisk
10 ccio
10/0 c720
10/0.1 tgt
10/0.1.0 sdisk
10/0.2 tgt
10/0.2.0 sdisk
10/0.3 tgt
10/0.3.0 sdisk
10/0.4 tgt
10/0.4.0 sdisk
10/0.5 tgt
10/0.5.0 sdisk
10/0.6 tgt
10/0.6.0 sdisk
10/0.7 tgt
10/0.7.0 sctl
10/4 bc
10/4/0 mux2
10/4/4 scsi3
10/4/4.1 target
10/4/4.1.0 disc3
10/4/4.2 target
10/4/4.2.0 disc3
10/4/4.3 target
10/4/4.3.0 disc3
10/4/4.4 target
10/4/4.4.0 disc3
10/4/4.5 target
10/4/4.5.0 disc3
10/4/4.6 target
10/4/4.6.0 disc3
10/4/4.8 target
```

```
10/4/4.8.0 disc3
10/4/4.9 target
10/4/4.9.0 disc3
10/4/12 scsi3
10/4/12.1 target
10/4/12.1.0 disc3
10/4/12.2 target
10/4/12.2.0 disc3
10/4/12.3 target
10/4/12.3.0 disc3
10/4/12.4 target
10/4/12.4.0 disc3
10/4/12.5 target
10/4/12.5.0 disc3
10/4/12.6 target
10/4/12.6.0 disc3
10/4/12.8 target
10/4/12.8.0 disc3
10/4/12.9 target
10/4/12.9.0 disc3
10/4/16 nacc0
10/8 c720
10/8.7 tgt
10/8.7.0 sctl
10/12 bus_adapter
10/12/5 c720
10/12/5.0 tgt
10/12/5.0.0 stape
10/12/5.2 tgt
10/12/5.2.0 sdisk
10/12/5.7 tgt
10/12/5.7.0 sctl
10/12/6 lan2
10/12/0 CentIf
ps2_readbyte_timeout: no byte after 500 uSec
ps2_readbyte_timeout: no byte after 500 uSec
10/12/7 ps2
10/16 bc
10/16/4 scsi3
10/16/4.2 target
10/16/4.2.0 tape2
10/16/4.3 target
10/16/4.3.0 tape2
10/16/4.4 target
10/16/4.4.0 tape2
10/16/4.5 target
10/16/4.5.0 tape2
10/16/4.6 target
10/16/4.6.0 spt
10/16/12 scsi3
10/16/12.1 target
10/16/12.1.0 disc3
10/16/12.2 target
10/16/12.2.0 disc3
10/16/12.3 target
10/16/12.3.0 disc3
10/16/12.4 target
10/16/12.4.0 disc3
10/16/12.5 target
10/16/12.5.0 disc3
10/16/12.6 target
10/16/12.6.0 disc3
10/16/12.8 target
10/16/12.8.0 disc3
10/16/12.9 target
10/16/12.9.0 disc3
32 processor
34 processor
36 processor
49 memory
Networking memory for fragment reassembly is restricted to 186941440 bytes
Logical volume 64, 0x3 configured as ROOT
Logical volume 64, 0x2 configured as SWAP
Logical volume 64, 0x2 configured as DUMP
     Swap device table:  (start & size given in 512-byte blocks)
```

```
        entry 0 - major is 64, minor is 0x2; start = 0, size = 2048000
WARNING: Insufficient space on dump device to save full crashdump.
    Only 1048576000 of 2147484672 bytes will be saved.
    Dump device table:  (start & size given in 1-Kbyte blocks)
        entry 0 - major is 31, minor is 0x46000; start = 52064, size = 1024000
netisr real-time priority reset to 100
Starting the STREAMS daemons.
    9245XB HP-UX (B.10.20) #1: Sun Jun  9 06:31:19 PDT 1996

Memory Information:
    physical page size = 4096 bytes, logical page size = 4096 bytes
    Physical: 2097152 Kbytes, lockable: 1573196 Kbytes, available: 1806588 Kbytes
```

Managing Cache and RAM

If the information you need is not in cache memory but in RAM, then the access will take longer. The speed of all memory is increasing and RAM speed is increasing at a particularly rapid rate. You have a lot of control over the way in which RAM is used. First, you can decide how much RAM is configured into your system. The entire HP product line, both workstations and server systems, support more RAM than you will need in the system. RAM, at the time of this writing, is inexpensive and is going down in price. RAM is not a good area in which to cut corners in the configuration of your system. Secondly, you can use whatever RAM you have configured efficiently. One example of this is when configuring an efficient HP-UX kernel. The HP-UX kernel is always loaded in RAM. This means if it is 1 or 2 MBytes too big for your needs, then this is 1 or 2 MBytes you don't have for other purposes. If you need to access some information in RAM, it will take roughly one order of magnitude longer to access than if it were in cache.

Virtual Memory

If your system had only cache and, say 64 MBytes of RAM, then you would be able to have user processes that consumed only about 64 MBytes of physical memory. With memory management, you can have user processes that far exceed the size of physical memory by using virtual memory. Virtual memory allows you to load into RAM only parts of a process while keeping the balance on disk. You move blocks of data back and forth between memory and disk in pages.

Swap

Swap is used to extend the size of memory, that is, reserve an area on the disk to act as an extension to RAM. When the load on the system is high, swap space is used for part or all of processes for which there is not space available in physical memory. HP-UX handles all this swapping for you with the **vhand**, **statdaemon**, and **swapper** processes. You want to make sure you have more than enough swap space reserved on your disk so this memory management can take place without running out of swap space.

There are three types of swap space: primary swap, secondary swap, and file system swap. These are described next.

Primary swap   Swap that is available at boot. Primary swap is located on the same disk as the root file system. If there is a problem with this primary swap, you may have a hard time getting the system to boot.

Secondary swap Swap that is located on a disk other than the root disk.

File system swap

This is a file system that supports both files and data structures as well as swapping.

Don't labor too much over the amount of swap to configure. Your primary applications will define the amount of swap required. Most of the applications I've worked with make clear the maximum amount of swap required for the application. If you are running several applications, add together the swap required for each application if they are going to be running simultaneously.

System Startup and Shutdown

Startup and shutdown for HP-UX 10.x are based on a mechanism that separates startup scripts from configuration information. In order to modify the way your system starts or stops, you don't have to modify scripts, which in general is considered somewhat risky; you can instead modify configuration variables. The startup and shutdown sequence is based on an industry standard that is similar to many other UNIX-based systems, so your knowledge on HP-UX applies to many other systems. If you have experience with HP-UX 9.x, you will find this new startup and shutdown structure much different (and improved).

Startup and shutdown are going to become increasingly more important to you as your system administration work becomes more sophisticated. As you load and customize more applications, you will need more startup and shutdown knowledge. What I'll do in this section is give you an overview of startup and shutdown and the commands you can use to shut down your system.

There are the following components in the startup and shutdown model:

Execution Scripts - Execution scripts read variables from configuration variable scripts and run through the startup or shutdown sequence. These scripts are located in **/sbin/init.d**.

Configuration Variable Scripts - These are the files you would modify to set variables that are used to enable or disable a subsystem or perform some other function at the time of system startup or shutdown. These are located in **/etc/rc.config.d**.

Link Files -   These files are used to control the order in which scripts execute. These are actually links to execution scripts to be executed when moving from one run level to another. These files are located in the directory for the appropriate run level such as **/sbin/rc0.d** for run level zero, **/sbin/rc1.d** for run level 1, and so on.

Sequencer Script - This script invokes execution scripts based on run-level transition. This script is **/sbin/rc**.

Figure 1-24 shows the directory structure for startup and shutdown scripts.

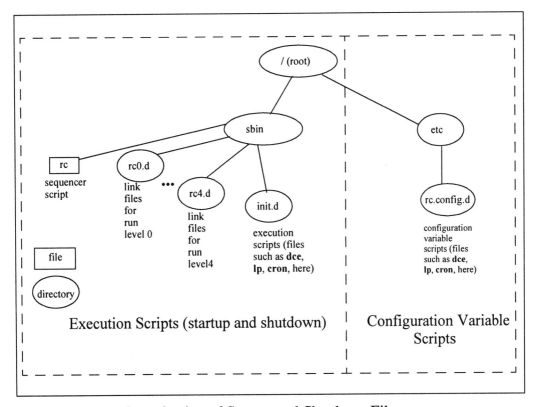

Figure 1-24 Organization of Startup and Shutdown Files

Execution scripts perform startup and shutdown tasks. **/sbin/rc** invokes the execution script, with the appropriate start or stop arguments, and you can view the appropriate start or stop messages on the console. The messages you see will have one of the three following values:

OK   This indicates that the execution script started or shut down properly.

FAIL   A problem occurred at startup or shutdown.

N/A   The script was not configured to start.

In order to start up a subsystem, you would simply edit the appropriate configuration file in **/etc/rc.config.d**. An example showing **/etc/rc.config.d/audio** is shown with the **AUDIO_SERVER** variable set to **1**.

```
#    ********** File:  /etc/rc.config.d/audio **************
# Audio server configuration.  See audio(5)
#
# AUDIO_SER:         Set to 1 to start audio server daemon
#

AUDIO_SERVER=1
```

This results in the following message being shown at the time the system boots:

```
Start audio server daemon .........................[ OK ]
```

And this message at the time the system is shut down:

```
Stopping audio server daemon ......................OK
```

Run levels have been mentioned several times in this discussion. Both the startup and shutdown scripts described here as well as the **/etc/inittab** file depend on run levels. In HP-UX 10.x the following run levels exist:

0	Halted run level.
s	Run level s, also known as single-user mode, is used to ensure no one else is on the system so you can proceed with system administration tasks.
1	Run level 1 starts various basic processes.
2	Run level 2 allows users to access the system. This is also known as multi-user mode.
3	Run level 3 is for exporting NFS file systems.
4	Run level 4 starts the HP Visual User Environment (HP VUE).
5 and 6	Not currently used.

/etc/inittab is also used to define a variety of processes that will be run and is used by **/sbin/init**. The **/sbin/init** process ID is 1. It is the first process started on your system and it has no parent. The **init** process looks at **/etc/inittab** to determine the run level of the system.

Entries in the **/etc/inittab** file have the following format:

id:run state:action:process

id:	The name of the entry. The id is up to four characters long and must be unique in the file. If the line in **/etc/inittab** is preceded by a "#", the entry is treated as a comment.
run state:	Specifies the run level at which the command is executed. More than one run level can be speci-

	fied. The command is executed for every run level specified.
action:	Defines which of 11 actions will be taken with this process. The 11 choices for action are initdefault; sysinit; boot; bootwait; wait; respawn; once; powerfail; powerwait; ondemand; off.
process	The shell command to be run if the run level and/or action field so indicates.

Here is an example of an **/etc/inittab** entry:

```
vue :4:respawn:/usr/vue/bin/vuerc

   |   |    |              |
   |   |    |              |> process
   |   |    |> action
   |   |> run state
   |> id
```

This is in the **/etc/inittab** file as opposed to being defined as a startup script because HP VUE may be killed and have to be restarted whenever it dies even if there is *not* a change in run level. **respawn** starts a process if it does not exist and restarts the process when it dies.

Another example is the first line from **/etc/inittab**:

```
init:4:initdefault:
```

The default run level of the system is defined as 4. You can change the run level interactively by executing **init** and specifying a run level as shown below:

```
$ init s
```

This command switches the system to single-user mode.

The basics of system startup and shutdown described here are important to understand. You will be starting up and shutting down your system and possibly even modifying some of the files described here. Please take a close look at the startup and shutdown files before you begin to modify these.

Now lets take a look at the commands you can issue to shut down your system.

System Shutdown

What does it mean to shut down the system? Well, in its simplest form, a shutdown of the system simply means issuing the **/sbin/shutdown** command. The **shutdown** command is used to terminate all processing. It has many options including the following:

-r   Automatically reboots the system, that is, brings it down and brings it up.

-h   Halts the system completely.

-y   Completes the shutdown without asking you any of the questions it would normally ask.

grace   Specifies the number of seconds you wish to wait before the system is shut down in order to give your users time to save files, quit applications, and log out.

Here are some of the things your system does when you issue the **shutdown** command:

- Checks to see if the user who executed shutdown does indeed have permission to execute the command.

- Changes the working directory to root (/).

- Sets *PATH* to **/usr/bin/:/usr/sbin:/sbin**.

- Updates all superblocks.

- Informs the users that a **shutdown** has been issued and asks them to log out.

- **/sbin/rc,** which does such things as unmount file systems and other tasks, is run.

- **/sbin/reboot** is run if the **-h** or **-r** options were used.

So, to halt the system you would type

```
$ shutdown -h
```

You may then be asked if you want to type a message to users informing them of the impending system shutdown. After you type the message, it is immediately sent to all users. After the specified time elapses, the system begins the shutdown process. Once you receive a message that the system is halted, you can power off all your system components.

To shut down the system in two minutes without being asked any questions, type

```
$ shutdown -h -y 120
```

If the system is already in single-user mode or you like to live dangerously, you can execute **/usr/sbin/reboot**. I strongly suggest you issue **shutdown** which we'll call **reboot**. The **reboot** command terminates all processes and then halts or reboots the system. **reboot** has many options including the following:

-h	Shut down the system and halt the CPU.
-r	Shut down the system and automatically reboot.

-n	Do not sync the disks before reboot or halt.
-s	Sync the disks before reboot or halt (this is default).
-q	This is a quick reboot. No messages are sent and all processes are terminated.
-t time	Specify the time to bring down the system. Type either now or +number where number is the seconds in which to reboot or hour:min where hour:min is the time at which to reboot.
-m mesg	Sends the message specified to all terminals.

Again, I recommend using the **shutdown** command, not **reboot**. You may, however, want to go into single-user mode with **shutdown**, perform some task such as a backup, and then reboot the system to return it to its original state.

CHAPTER 2

The HP-UX File System and Related Commands

Introduction

A thorough understanding of the HP-UX file system is essential to performing system administation. In this chapter I'll cover the following topics:

- HP-UX File Types - This section describes the different types of files in HP-UX and using the **file** command to determine the file type.

- File System Layout - You need to know the layout of the file system including important directories and their contents.

- Logical Volume Manager (LVM) - You will probably be using LVM to manange the data on your system. I provide LVM background in this section.

- Example of Using LVM to Reconfigure Disks - I included an example of a complex disk reconfiguration performed on a real system to show how many LVM commands are used. Although this disk reconfiguration does not apply to your system(s) it is a good example of using LVM commands.

• Some Additional File System Commands.

HP-UX File Types

There are a variety of different file types on an HP-UX system. A file is a means by which information is stored on an HP-UX system. The commands you issue, the applications you use, the data you store, and the devices you access such as printers and keyboard are all contained in files. This is one of the aspects of HP-UX that makes it both simple and complex, simple because you know everything out there is a file, complex because the contents of a file could be anything ranging from simple data you can read, to a device file that is created by your system administrator with a unique set of commands.

Every file on the system has a file name. The operating system takes care of all file system related tasks; you just need to know the name of the file and how to use it. The file types we will look at are.

- Text Files

- Data Files

- Source Code Files

- Executable Files

- Shell Programs

- Links

- Device Files

Text Files

What could be simpler than a file that contains characters, just like the ones you're now reading in this chapter? These ASCII characters are letters and numerals that represent the work you perform. If, for instance, you use an HP-UX editor to create an electronic mail message or a letter, you are creating a text file in most cases. Here is an example of part of a text file:

```
 *                                                                 *
   *                                                             *
     *                    HP LaserROM/UX                       *
       *                     README File                      *
         ***********************************************
```

```
This version of HP LaserROM/UX can only be installed and run
on HP-UX Operating System Release 10.x or better.

The graphical user interface of HP LaserROM/UX requires the X
Window System version 11, Release 5 or later.
```

This text file is easy to read, has no data or other information in it, and can easily be modified.

Data Files

A file that contains data used by one of your applications is a data file. If you use a sophisticated desktop publishing tool such as FrameMaker®

to write a book, you create data files that FrameMaker uses. These data files contain data, which you can usually read, and formatting information, which you can sometimes read but is usually hidden from you. If your HP-UX installation uses a database program, then you may have data files which you can partially read.

Source Code File

A source code file is a text file that contains information related to a programming language such as C, C++, Pascal, Fortran, and so on. When a programmer develops a source code file, they create a file that conforms to the naming convention of the program language being used, such as adding a ".c" to the end of the file if creating a C program.

The following is an example of a C source code file:

```
/* this is K & R sort program */

# include <stdio.h>
# include <stdlib.h>

        int N;
        int v[1000000];        /* v is array to be sorted */
        int left = 0;          /* left pointer */
        int right;
        int swapcount, comparecount = 0;
                               /* count swaps and compares*/
         int i, j, t;
        char print;
        char pr_incr_sorts;


main()

{
    printf("Enter number of numbers to sort : ");
    scanf("%10d", &N);                 /* 10d used for a BIG input */
    printf ("\n");                         /* select type of input to sort */

    printf("Enter rand(1), in-order(2), or reverse order (3)    sort : ");
    scanf("%2d", &type);
    printf ("\n");                      /* select type of input to sort */

    if (type == 3)
                for (i=0; i<N; ++i)      /* random        */
                    v[i] = (N - i);

    else if (type == 2)
```

```
              for (i=0; i<N; ++i)
                  v[i]= (i + 1);          /* in order      */
      else if (type == 1)
              for (i=0; i<N; ++i)
                  v[i]=rand();            /* reverse order */
      fflush(stdin);
      printf("Do you want to see the numbers before sorting (y or n)? : ");
      scanf("%c", &print);
      printf ("\n");                      /* View unsorted numbers?  */
      if (print == 'y')
        {
              printf ("\n");
          for (i=0; i<N; ++i)
              printf("a[%2d]= %2d\n", i, v[i]);
              printf ("\n");
        }


      fflush(stdin);
      printf("Do you want to see the array at each step as it sorts? (y or n)? : ");
      scanf("%c", &pr_incr_sorts);
      printf ("\n");                      /* View incremental sorts?  */


        right = N-1;                      /* right pointer          */

                qsort(v, left, right);




      {
          fflush(stdin);
          printf ("Here is the sorted list of %2d items\n", N);
              printf ("\n");
          for (i=0; i<N; ++i)
              printf ("%2d\n ", v[i]);
              printf ("\n");
              printf ("\n");               /* print sorted list       */
                  }
                      printf ("number of swaps = %2d\n ", swapcount);
                      printf ("number of compares = %2d\n ", comparecount);
      }

/* qsort function */

          void qsort( v, left, right)
                      int v[], left, right;
      {
                  int i, last;
                  if (left > right)
                   return;

                  swap(v, left, (left + right)/2);
                  last = left;
                  for (i=left+1; i <= right; i++)
                  {
                     comparecount = ++comparecount;
                       if (v[i] < v[left])
                     swap(v, ++last, i);
                     }
                  swap(v, left, last);
                  qsort(v, left, last-1);
                  qsort(v, last+1, right);
                  }

              /* swap function  */


              swap(v, i, j)
                 int v[], i, j;
```

```
                              {int temp;
                                 swapcount = swapcount++;
                                 temp = v[i];
                                 v[i] = v[j];
                                 v[j] = temp;


             if (pr_incr_sorts == 'y')
               {
                              printf("Incremental sort of array = ");
                   printf ("\n");
                   for (i=0; i<N; ++i)
                      printf("a[%2d]= %2d\n", i, v[i]);
                      printf ("\n");
               }
        }
```

Executable Files

Executable files are compiled programs that can be run. You can't read executable files and you'll typically get a bunch of errors, unreadable characters, and beeps from your HP-UX system when you try to look at one of these. It is also possible you will lose your screen settings and cause other problems.

You don't have to go far in HP-UX to find executable files; they are everywhere. Many of the HP-UX commands you issue are executable files that you can't read. In addition, if you are developing programs on your system, you are creating your own executables.

Here is an example of what you see if you attempt to send an executable to the screen:

```
unknown/etc/ttytyperunknown<@=>|<@=>|:unknown<@=>
callocLINESCOLUMNSunknownPackaged for
argbad aftger%3
parmnumber missing <@=>|<@=>|:
@ @ 3### @@@A:2TTO|>@#<|2X00R
EraseKillOOPS<@=>|<@=>|:
<@=>|<@=>|:
<@=>|<@=>|:<@=>|ATOO<@=>|:<@=>|<@=>|:<@=>|<@=>|:<@=>|<@=>|:
```

Shell Programs

A shell program is both a file you can run to perform a task and a file that you can read. So yes, even though you can run this file because it is executable, you can also read it. I'm going to describe shell programming in more detail in an upcoming chapter.

I consider shell programming to be an important skill for every user to have. I'll spend some time going over the basics of shell programming. Some of the background I'm about to cover relating to file types and permissions is important when it comes to shell programming, so this is important information for you to understand.

Here is an example of part of a shell program from an old startup file:

```
# Check if login script contains non-comment to "VUE"
# If it does, assume it's VUE safe, and set VUESOURCEPROFILE
# to true.

if [ "${SHELL:-}" -a -d "${HOME:-}; then
 case ${SHELL##*/} in
  sh | ksh ) shellprofile="$HOME/.profile" ;;
       csh ) shellprofile="$HOME/.login" ;;
         * ) shellprofile="" ;;

 esac
 if [[ -r "$shellprofile"]] ; then
   [ 'grep -c '^[^#:].*VUE' $shellprofile' !=0 ] &&
     VUERESOURCEPROFILE="true"
 fi
fi

# Place customization code beyond this point.

PATH="$PATH:/usr/local/bin:/usr/sbin:$HOME:."
export PATH

mesg y

umask 022
```

The shell program is text you can read and modify if indeed you have permissions to do so. In addition to programming information, shell programs contain comments indicated by lines beginning with a #.

Links

A link is a pointer to a file stored elsewhere on the system. Instead of having two or more copies of a file on your system, you can link to a file that already exists on your system.

One particularly useful way links have been used in HP-UX is related to new releases of the operating system. The locations of files sometimes change going from one release to another, and rather than learn all the new locations, there are links produced from the old location to the new one. When you run a command using the old location, the link points to the new location.

Links are also useful for centralizing files. If a set of identical files has to be updated often, it is easier to link to a central file and update it rather than have to update several copies of the file in several different locations.

Device Files

Device files, sometimes called device special files, contain information about the hardware connected to your system. Devices on your system can often be accessed with different device files. A disk, for instance, can be accessed with either a block device file or a character device file. There is extensive coverage of device files in this book.

There are other types of files on your system as well, but for the purposes of getting started with HP-UX, the file types I describe supply sufficient background to get you started.

The file Command

The **file** command is used to determine the file type. This command is useful because the name of a file does not always indicate its file type. The following examples perform a long listing of a file to provide some background information on the file, and then the **file** command is run to show the file type.

Text File

(Described by the **file** command as ascii text.)

```
# ll  .mosaic-global-history
-rw-r--r--  1 201      users       587 Dec 22  1996 .mosaic-global-history
# file  .mosaic-global-history
.mosaic-global-history: ascii text
#
```

Data File

(Described by the file command as data.)

```
# ll Static.dat
-rw-r--r--  1 201      users    235874 Aug 26  1997 Static.dat
# file Static.dat
Static.dat:     data
#
```

Source Code File

(Described by the file command as c program text.)

```
# ll krsort.c
-rwxrwxrwx   1 201       users       3234 Nov 16  1996 krsort.c
# file krsort.c
krsort.c:        c program text
#
```

Executable File

(Described by the file command as shared executable.)

```
# ll krsort
-rwxr-xr-x   1 201       users       34592 Nov 16  1996 krsort
# file krsort
krsort:          PA-RISC1.1 shared executable dynamically linked -not stripped
#
```

Shell Program

(Described by the file command as commands text.)

```
# ll llsum
-rwxrwxrwx   1 root      sys         1267 Feb 23  1997 llsum
# file llsum
llsum:           commands text
#
```

Link

(The link is not referenced by the file command, this is shown as a shared executable dynamically linked. The reference to dynamically linked does not mean this is a link.)

```
# ll /usr/bin/ar
lr-xr-xr-t   1 root      sys            15 Mar 23  1997 ar -> /usr/ccs/bin/ar
# file /usr/bin/ar
/usr/bin/ar:          s800 shared executable dynamically linked
#
```

Block Device File

(Described by the file command as block special.)

```
# ll /dev/dsk/c0t1d0
brw-r--r--   1 bin      sys        31 0x001000 Apr 17  1997 /dev/dsk/c0t1d0
# file /dev/dsk/c0t1d0
/dev/dsk/c0t1d0:       block special (31/4096)
#
```

Character Device File

(Described by the file command as character special.)

```
# ll /dev/rdsk/c0t1d0
crw-r-----  1 root      sys       188 0x001000 Mar 23  1997 /dev/rdsk/c0t1d0
# file /dev/rdsk/c0t1d0
/dev/rdsk/c0t1d0:     character special (188/4096)
#
```

File System Layout

One of the biggest improvements in going from HP-UX 9.x to 10.x is the file system layout. The 10.x file system layout is derived from the OSF/1 layout which is based on the AT&T SVR4 layout. Before I begin my description let me say that changes to the file system layout mean directory changes, not physical changes to the file system format.

Before I get into the layout of the file system you should know that there are different types of file systems. This is important to know for several reasons, including the fact that many HP-UX commands allow you to specify the option "-F" followed by the file system type. Some of the commands that support this new option are **dcopy**, **fsck**, **mksf**, **mount**, **newfs**, and others. Here is a brief description of four file system types supported by HP-UX:

- High Performance File System (HFS) is HP's version of the UNIX File System. This is the most common file system and the one used in most of the examples.

- CD-ROM File System (CDFS) is used when you mount a CD-ROM. A CD-ROM is read-only so you can't write to it.

- Network File System (NFS) is a way of accessing files on other systems on the network from your local system. An NFS mounted file system looks as though it is local to your system even though it is located on another system. NFS is covered in this chapter.

- Loopback File System (LOFS) allows you to have the same file system in multiple places.

- VxFs is an extent-based Journal File System that supports fast file system recovery and on-line features such as backup.

I will include information about the HP-UX 10.x file system layout, the HP-UX 9.x file system layout, and various comparisons of the two. It is important for me to include information on the 10.x file system layout, the 9.x file system layout, and a comparison because I'm sure many of you have experience with HP-UX 9.x. If you are new to HP-UX and don't care about the history of HP-UX, then please don't feel obligated to read the 9.x file system and comparison information. If, however, you think you may indeed need to work on a 9.x system at some point, you may find the 9.x and comparison information helpful. Some of the finest HP documentation produced is in the form of white papers; much of the material in this section is from a white paper I read on HP-UX 10.x long before its introduction in 1995. Some of these excellent white papers may be found in the **/usr/share/doc** directory.

You'll be very happy to read that all of the file-system-related information in this section applies to both HP 9000 Series 800 and Series 700 systems. This means that you can take the information in this section and apply it to all HP 9000 systems.

HP-UX 10.x File System Layout

Figure 2-1 is a high-level depiction of the HP-UX 10.x file system.

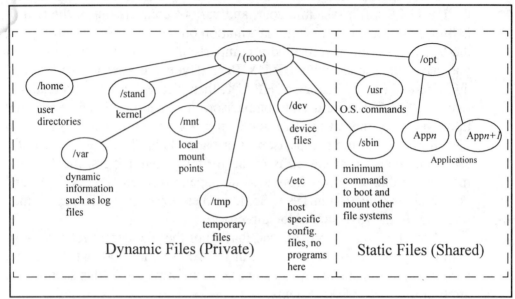

Figure 2-1 HP-UX 10.x File System Layout

Here are some of the more important features of the 10.x file system layout:

- Files and directories are organized by category. The two most obvious categories that appear in Figure 2-1 are static vs.dynamic files. There are also other categories such as executable, configuration, data files, etc. From a system administration perspective, this file system layout is easy to manage. The static files are also labeled shared because other hosts on the network may share these. The directories **/usr**, **/sbin**, and **/opt** are shared directories. When **/opt** is shared, the subdirectories of **/opt** should be mounted and not **/opt**.

- The operating system and applications are kept separate from one another. For those of us who have loaded many applications over the years, this is a technique we have been practicing because of its benefits. Application vendors don't care where there applications are loaded; that is up to you. But as a system administrator it is highly desirable to keep applications separate from the operating system so you don't inadvertently have application files overwriting operating system files. In addition, if your applications are loaded in a separate area, they are "modular," meaning you can add, remove, and modify them without affecting the operating system or other applications. Applications are kept in the **/opt** directory.

- Intrasystem files are kept in a separate area from intersystem, or network accessable, files. As a system administrator you can now be selective when specifying what files and directories other systems will have access to. **/usr** and **/sbin** are shared operating system directories. There is no host-specific information in these two directories. **/etc** is used to hold the host specific configuration files.

- Executable files are kept separate from system configuration files so that the executables may be shared among hosts. Having the configuration files separate from the programs that use them also means that updates to the operating system won't affect the configuration files.

I'll provide descriptions of some of the most important directories for HP-UX 10.x. Some of these look much different than what you may have been accustomed to with HP-UX 9.x. Later I include a description of the 9.x directories in case you need this to manage 9.x system.

Here are descriptions of some important 10.x directories.

/	This is the root directory which is the base of the file system's hierarchical tree structure. A directory is logically viewed as being part of /. Regardless of the disk on which a directory or logical volume is stored, it is logically viewed as a part of the root hierarchy.
/dev	Contains host-specific device files just as in HP-UX 9.x.

/etc	Contains host-specific system and application configuration files. The information in this directory is important to the operation of the system and is of a permanent nature. There are also additional configuration directories below /etc. This is a big change from 9.x where there were several commands, log files, the "rc" startup scripts, and many other files not related to system configuration. There are two /etc subdirectories of particular interest:

/etc/rc.config.d contains configuration data files for startup and shutdown programs.

/etc/opt contains host-specific application configuration data.

/export	This is used for diskless file sharing only. Servers export root directories for networked clients.
/home	Users' home directories are located here. In 9.x **/users** was the typical location for home directories. Since the data stored in user's home directories will be modified often, you can expect this directory to grow in size.
/lost + found	This is the lost files directory. Here you will find files that are in use but are not associated with a directory. These files typically become "lost" as a result of a system crash which caused the link between the physical information on the disk and the logical directory to be severed. The program **fsck**, which is run at the time of boot and interactively by you if you wish, finds these files and places them in the **lost + found** directory.

/mnt   This directory is reserved as a mount point for
                    local file systems. You can either mount directly
                    to **/mnt** or have **/mnt** subdirectories as mount
                    points such as **/mnt1**, **/mnt2**, **/mnt3**, etc.

/net   Name reserved as mount points for remote file
                    systems.

/opt   The directory under which applications are
                    installed. As system administrators, we have
                    always used our best judgement to install appli-
                    cations in a sensible directory in the past. As a
                    rule, application vendors never specified a par-
                    ticular location for their applications to be
                    installed. Now, with **/opt**, we have a standard
                    directory under which applications should be
                    installed. This is an organizational improvement
                    for system administrators because we can now
                    expect applications to be loaded under **/opt** and
                    the application name.

/sbin   Contains commands and scripts used to boot,
                    shut down, and fix file system mounting prob-
                    lems. **/sbin** is available when a system boots
                    because it contains commands required to bring
                    up a system.

/stand   Contains kernel configuration and binary files
                    that are required to bring up a system. Two sig-
                    nificant files contained in this directory are the
                    system and **vmunix** (kernel) files.

/tmp   This is a free-for-all directory where any user
                    can *temporarily* store files. Because of the loose
                    nature of this directory, it should not be used to
                    store anything important, and users should know
                    that whatever they have stored in **/tmp** can be
                    deleted without notice. In 10.x, application
                    working files should go in **/var/tmp** or **/var/opt/
                    appname**, not in **/tmp**.

/usr   Most of the HP-UX operating system is con-
                    tained in **/usr**. Included in this directory are
                    commands, libraries, and documentation. There
                    are a limited number of subdirectories that can
                    appear in **/usr**. Here is a list of **/usr** subdirecto-
                    ries:

                    /usr/bin - Common utilities and applications are
                    stored here.

                    /usr/ccs - Tools and libraries used to generate C
                    programs are stored here.

                    /usr/conf - Static directory containing the shar-
                    able kernel build environment.

                    /usr/contrib - Contributed software directory;
                    this is the same as HP-UX 9.x

                    /usr/include - Contains header files; this is the
                    same as HP-UX 9.x.

                    /usr/lib - Contains libraries and machine depen-
                    dent databases. Much of what was in **/lib** in 9.x
                    is in **/usr/lib** in HP-UX 10.x.

                    /usr/newconfig - Contains default operating sys-
                    tem data files such as those found in **/etc/new-
                    config** in HP-UX 10.x, although the directory
                    structure of **/usr/newconfig** is different than that
                    of **/etc/newconfig**.

/usr/old - Old files from an operating system update will be stored here.

/usr/sbin - System administration commands are in this directory including many that had been in /etc in HP-UX 9.x.

/usr/share - Contains files that are architecture independent and can be shared.

/usr/share/man - Directory for manual pages.

/var   Holds files that are primarily temporary. Files such as log files which are frequently deleted and modified are stored here. Think of this as a directory of "variable" size. Files that an application or command create at runtime should be placed in this directory including log and spool files. There may, however, be some applications which store state information in **/var**. Be careful if you delete files from this directory in order to free up disk space.

/var/adm - Directory for adminstrative files, log files, and databases such as kernel crash dumps will be stored here.

/var/adm/crash - Kernel crash dumps will be placed here.

/var/adm/sw - Software Distributor log files, etc.

/usr/var/cron - Log files for **cron**.

/var/mail - Incoming mail messages are kept here.

/var/opt - Application runtime files, such as log files, for applications mounted in **/opt** will be stored in **/var/opt** under the application name.

/var/spool -Spool files, such as those in **/usr/ spool** in HP-UX 10.x, are stored here.

Figure 2-2 is a window showing the top-level file system with the **sbin** directory selected.

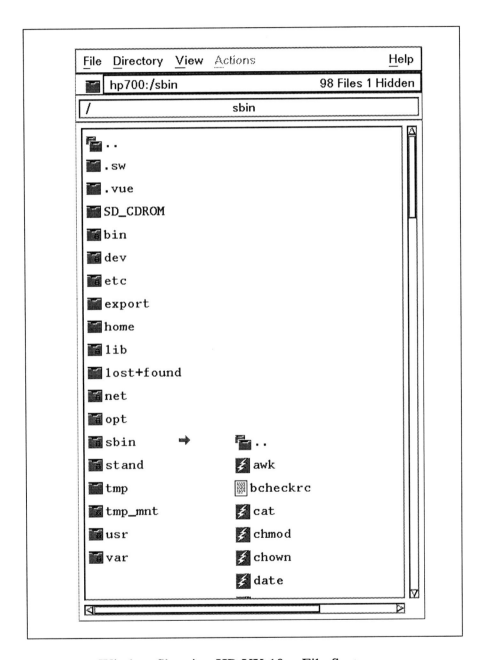

Figure 2-2 Window Showing HP-UX 10.x File System

HP-UX 9.x File System Layout

Here are descriptions of some of the most important directories at the / level for HP-UX 9.x. I included this as a comparison for those of you who have used 9.x or will have to maintain 9.x systems.

/	This is the root directory which is the base of the file system's hierarchical tree structure. A directory is logically viewed as being part of /. If, for instance, you had a second disk, mounted under the **/applications** directory, then the mount directory is **/applications**. This means that even though the **/applications** directory is **physically** contained on the second disk, it is logically viewed as just another directory under /. This is part of the beauty of the HP-UX file system structure: Everything is logical and easy to visualize from a logical standpoint. You, as the system administrator, must understand the physical point of view as well; however, one of your objectives is to make the logical organization of the system as easy to work with as possible. The **/applications** directory was physically on the second disk of the Series 700, but if a user wanted to access the **/applications** directory, he or she would simply type "**cd /applications**". The beauty of the logical file system is further enhanced by some networking technology, including NFS in which the file systems of **other** computers look as though they are locally attached.
/bin	This directory holds most of the executable programs which are part of HP-UX. Other HP-UX

commands are located in **/usr/bin** and other sub-directories.

/dev   This is the device directory which contains special files known as device files. Device files make a connection between a piece of hardware and the file system. Every time you wish to use a piece of hardware such as disk drive, printer, terminal, modem, etc., the device file is used. A great deal of your system administration effort will involve device files. When you wish to add a printer to your system, for instance, you will have to create a device file as part of the process of adding the printer. SAM will handle most of the device files you'll need to create; however, there will always be some issues related to device files you'll need to handle.

/etc   This directory contains most of the administration commands you'll execute as well as administration and configuration files. You will spend a lot more time in this directory executing commands and modifying files than will your users.

/lib   This directory contains library files such as those related to your programming languages and windowing environment.

/lost+found   This is the lost files directory. Here you will find files that are in use but are not associated with a directory. These files typically become "lost" as a result of a system crash which caused the link between the physical information on the disk and the logical directory to be severed. The program

fsck, which is run at the time of boot and interactively by you if you wish, finds these files and
places them in the lost+found directory on the
disk partition on which they were found. Each
disk partition has a /lost+found directory.

/users   This is typically the directory where HP-UX user
                    home directories are located. This tends to be the
                    most dynamic directory on your system because
                    you are always adding and deleting users, and
                    users themselves are adding and deleting files
                    and directories.

/usr   This directory typically contains your applica-
                    tions and several HP-UX programs, such as files
                    related to printing, plotting, and mail.

/tmp   This is a free-for-all directory where any user
                    can temporarily store files. Because of the loose
                    nature of this directory, it should not be used to
                    store anything important, and users should know
                    that whatever they have stored in /tmp can be
                    deleted without notice.

Locating Files

There are clearly many differences between the HP-UX 10.x and 9.x file
ystem layouts. If you haven't worked with HP-UX 9.x, then the HP-UX
10.x file system layout is your baseline. If, however, you are somewhat
experienced with HP-UX 9.x or you will need to support both HP-UX

10.x and 9.x systems, there are a variety of commands that can assist you. The **fnlookup** command allows you to type in an HP-UX 10.x file name and get the corresponding HP-UX 9.x file name or type in an HP-UX 9.x file name and get the corresponding HP-UX 10.x file name. For instance, /**bin** in HP-UX 9.x is now /**usr/bin** in HP-UX 10.x. You could use **fnlookup** with the "-o" option and old file name to give you the new file name. You could use **fnlookup** with the "-n" option and the new file name to give you the old file name.

I loaded the partition called 10-PREPARATION on my HP-UX 9.x system with the **update** program. Among the tools loaded for me on the 9.x system was the **fnlookup** command. Some examples of using the fnlookup command on my 9.x system are shown below.

The old directory name /**bin** is now /**usr/bin** in HP-UX 10.x:

```
$ /upgrade/bin/fnlookup -o /bin
/usr/bin
```

The new directory name /**usr/bin** was /**bin** in HP-UX 9.x:

```
$ /upgrade/bin/fnlookup -n /usr/bin
/bin/posix
/bin
/usr/bin
```

In addition to providing the **fnlookup** command, the designers of HP-UX 10.x took other measures to make the file system layout change from HP-UX 10.x to 9.x much easier. Chapter 7 covers links that were established between the old shell program locations and new locations. For instance, the new POSIX shell (/**usr/bin/sh**), which is a superset of the Bourne shell (/**bin/sh**), has the same inode number as shown below:

```
$ ll -i /usr/bin/sh

  603 -r-xr-xr-x 2 bin bin 405504 Dec 12 03:00 /usr/bin/sh
```

```
$ ll -i /bin/sh

   603 -r-xr-xr-x 2 bin bin 405504 Dec 12 03:00 /bin/sh
```

You can still use the old Bourne shell by specifying the path **/usr/old/bin/sh**, but since the new POSIX shell is a superset of the Bourne shell, the designers of HP-UX 10.x provided this link.

There are also many "transitional" links provided in HP-UX 10.x. Here are examples of some of the transitional links that are in place denoted by the sticky bit set with a "t":

```
$ ll /bin

   lr-xr-xr-xt 1 root sys 8 Feb 7 13:39 /bin -> /usr/bin
```

```
$ ll /lib

   lr-xr-xr-xt 1 root sys 8 Feb 7 13:39 /lib -> /usr/lib
```

```
$ ll /bin/make

    lr-xr-xr-xt 1 root sys 17 Feb 7 13:39 /bin/make ->
/usr/ccs/bin/make
```

```
$ ll /etc/checklist

   lr-xr-xr-xT 1 root sys 10 Feb 7 13:39 /etc/checklist ->
/etc/fstab
```

These transitional links are installed and removed with the **tlinstall** and **tlremove** commands, respectively. The links shown above were all installed on my system as part of a standard HP-UX 10.0 installation.

Logical Volume Manager Background

Logical Volume Manager is a disk management subsystem that allows you to manage physical disks as logical volumes. This means that a file system can span multiple physical disks. You can view Logical Volume Manager as a flexible way of defining boundaries of disk space that are independent of one another. Not only can you specify the size of a logical volume, but you can also change its size if the need arises. This is a great advancement over dedicating a disk to a file system or having fixed-size partitions on a disk. Logical volumes can hold file systems, raw data, or swap space. You can now specify a logical volume to be any size you wish, have logical volumes that span multiple physical disks, and then change the size of the logical volume if you need to!

So, what do you need to know in order to set up Logical Volume Manager and realize all these great benefits? First you need to know the terminology, and second you need to know Logical Volume Manager commands. As with many other system administration tasks you can use SAM to set up Logical Volume Manager for you. I recommend you use SAM to set up Logical Volume Manager on your system(s). But, as usual, I recommend you read this overview and at least understand the basics of Logical Volume Manager before you use SAM to set up Logical Volume Manager on your system. The SAM chapter has an example of using SAM to create logical volumes. After reading this section you may want to take a quick look at that example.

Logical Volume Manager Terms

The following terms are used when working with Logical Volume Manager. This is only some of the terminology associated with Logical Volume Manager, but it is enough for you to get started with Logical Volume Manager. You can work with Logical Volume Manager without knowing all of these terms if you use SAM. It is a good idea, however, to read the following brief overview of these terms if you plan to use Logical Volume Manager so you have some idea of what SAM is doing for you.

Volume   A volume is a device used for file system, swap,
                      or raw data. Without Logical Volume Manager
                      a volume would be either a disk partition or an
                      entire disk drive.

Physical Volume A disk that has been initalized for use by Logical
                      Volume Manager. An entire disk must be initial-
                      ized if it is to be used by Logical Volume Man-
                      ger; that is, you can't initialize only part of a
                      disk for Logical Volume Manager use and the
                      rest for fixed partitioning.

Volume Group   A volume group is a collection of logical vol-
                      umes that are managed by Logical Volume Man-
                      ager. You would typically define which disks on
                      your system are going to be used by Logical Vol-
                      ume Manager and then define how you wish to
                      group these into volume groups. Each individual
                      disk may be a volume group, or more than one
                      disk may form a volume group. At this point
                      you have created a pool of disk space called a
                      volume group. A disk can belong to only one
                      volume group. A volume group may span multi-
                      ple physical disks.

Logical Volume This is space that is defined within a volume
                      group. A volume group is divided up into logical
                      volumes. This is like a disk partition, which is of
                      a fixed size, but you have the flexibility to
                      change its size. A logical volume is contained
                      within a volume group, but the volume group
                      may span multiple physical disks. You can have

a logical volume which is bigger than a single disk.

Physical Extent   A set of contiguous disk blocks on a physical volume. If you define a disk to be a physical volume then the contiguous blocks within that disk form a physical extent. Logical Volume Manager uses the physical extent as the unit for allocating disk space to logical volumes. If you use a small physical extent size such as 1 MByte, then you have a fine granularity for defining logical volumes. If you use a large physical extent size such as 256 MBytes, then you have a coarse granularity for defining logical volumes.

Logical Extents   A logical volume is a set of logical extents. Logical extents and physical extents are the same size within a volume group. Although logical and physical extents are the same size, this doesn't mean that two logical extents will map to two contiguous physical extents. It may be that you have two logical extents that end up being mapped to physical extents on different disks!

Mirroring   Logical volumes can be mirrored one or more times creating an identical image of the logical volume. This means a logical extent can map to more than one physical extent if mirrored.

Figure 2-3 grapically depicts some of the logical volume terms I just covered. In this diagram it is clear that logical extents are not mapped to contiguous physical extents because some of the physical extents are not used.

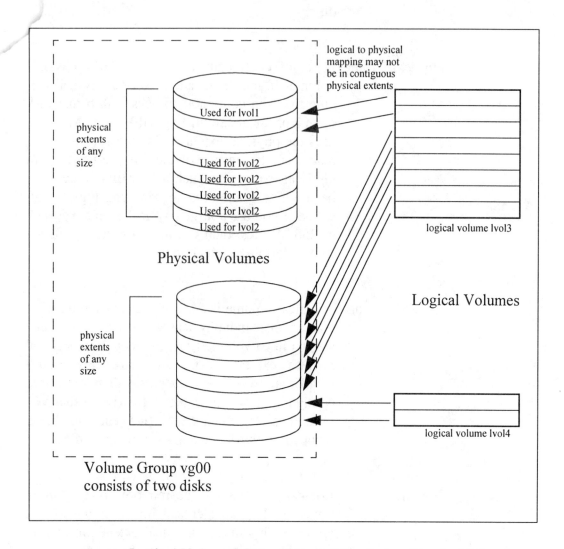

Figure 2-3 Logical Volume Manager Partial Logical to Physical Mapping

In addition to the setup of your logical volumes, you may have an environment where you wish to mirror some of these logical volumes. SAM can be used to set up disk mirroring for you. You must first, however, decide the characteristics of your mirroring. There is a mirroring policy called "strict." You define one of the following three strict policies when you create the logical volume using the following options:

n   This is not a strict allocation policy, meaning that mirrored copies of a logical extent can share the same physical volume. This means that your original data and mirrored data may indeed be on the same physical disk. If you encounter a disk mechanism problem of some type, you may lose both your original and mirrored data.

y   Yes, this is a strict allocation policy meaning that mirrored copies of a logical extent may not share the same physical volume. This is safer than allowing mirrored copies of data to share the same physical volume. If you have a problem with a disk in this scenario you are guaranteed that your original data is on a different physical disk from your mirrored data. Original data and mirrored data are always part of the same volume group even if you want them on different physical volumes.

g   Mirrored data will not be on the same Physical Volume Group (PVG) as the original data. This is called a PVG strict allocation policy.

The strict allocation policy depends on your environment. Most installations that employ mirroring buy sufficient disk to mirror all data. In an environment such as this I would create two volume groups, one for the original data and one for the mirrored data, and use the "strict -g" option when creating logical volumes so that the original data is on one volume group and the mirrored data on the other.

Logical Volume Manager Commands

The following are definitions of some of the more common Logical Volume Commands. Many of these commands are found in the log file SAM

creates when setting up logical volumes for you. I am giving a description
of these commands here so that when you see them you'll have an idea of
what each command is used for. Although these are not all of the Logical
Volume Manager commands, these are the ones I use most often and are
the commands you should have knowledge of when using Logical Volume
Manager. The commands are broken down in logical volume (lv) commands, physical volume (pv) commands, and volume group (vg) commands. All of these commands are found in the manual pages. Some of
the commands such as **lvdisplay**, **pvdisplay**, and **vgdisplay** were issued
so you could see examples of these. The following output of **bdf** will be
helpful to you when you view the output of Logical Volume Manager
commands that are issued. The output of **bdf** shows several logical volumes mounted (lvol1, lvol3, lvol4, lvol5, lvol6, lvol7), all of which are in
volume group vg00 (see **bdf** command overview in this chapter).

$ **bdf**

Filesystem	kbytes	used	avail	%used	Mounted on
/dev/vg00/lvol1	47829	18428	24618	43%	/
/dev/vg00/lvol7	34541	8673	22413	28%	/var
/dev/vg00/lvol6	299157	149449	119792	56%	/usr
/dev/vg00/lvol5	23013	48	20663	0%	/tmp
/dev/vg00/lvol4	99669	32514	57188	36%	/opt
/dev/vg00/lvol3	19861	9	17865	0%	/home
/dev/dsk/c0t6d0	802212	552120	169870	76%	/mnt/9.x

Logical Volume Commands

lvcreate   This command is used to create a new logical
                     volume. A logical volume is created within a

volume group. A logical volume may span multiple disks but must exist within a volume group. SAM will execute this command for you when you create a logical volume using SAM. There are many options for this command and two that you would often use are -L to define the size of the logical volume and -n to define the name of the logical volume.

lvchange

This command is used to change the logical volume in some way. For example, you may wish to change the permission on a logical volume to read-write (w) or to read (r) with the **-p** option. Or you may want to change the strict policy (described under the **lvcreate** command) to strict (y), not to strict (n), or to PVG strict (g).

lvdisplay

This command shows the status and characteristics of every logical volume that you specify. If you use the verbose (-v) option of this command, you get a lot of useful data in many categories including those in the paragraphs below

Information about the way in which the logical volumes are set up such as the physical volume on which the logical extents appear; the number of logical extents on a physical volume; and the number of physical extents on the physical volume.

Detailed information for logical extents including the logical extent number and some information about the physical volume and physical extent for the logical extent.

The following is an example of **lvdisplay** for the first of the logical volumes (lvol1) shown in the earlier **bdf** example:

```
$   lvdisplay -v /dev/vg00/lvol1

--- Logical volumes ---
LV Name                 /dev/vg00/lvol1
VG Name                 /dev/vg00
LV Permission           read/write
LV Status               available/syncd
Mirror copies           0
Consistency Recovery    MWC
Schedule                parallel
LV Size (Mbytes)        48
Current LE              12
Allocated PE            12
Stripes                 0
Stripe Size (Kbytes)    0
Bad block               off
Allocation              strict/contiguous

   --- Distribution of logical volume ---
   PV Name              LE on PV    PE on PV
   /dev/dsk/c0t1d0      12          12

   --- Logical extents ---
   LE    PV1                   PE1     Status 1
   0000 /dev/dsk/c0t1d0        0000    current
   0001 /dev/dsk/c0t1d0        0001    current
   0002 /dev/dsk/c0t1d0        0002    current
   0003 /dev/dsk/c0t1d0        0003    current
   0004 /dev/dsk/c0t1d0        0004    current
   0005 /dev/dsk/c0t1d0        0005    current
   0006 /dev/dsk/c0t1d0        0006    current
   0007 /dev/dsk/c0t1d0        0007    current
   0008 /dev/dsk/c0t1d0        0008    current
   0009 /dev/dsk/c0t1d0        0009    current
   0010 /dev/dsk/c0t1d0        0010    current
   0011 /dev/dsk/c0t1d0        0011    current
```

Although most of what is shown in this example is self-explanatory, there are some entries that require explanation. The size of the logical volume is 48 MBytes which consists of 12 Logical Extents (LEs) and 12 Physical Extents (PEs). This means that each physical extent is 4 MBytes in size   (4 MBytes x 12 extents = 48 MBytes) which we can verify when we display the characteristics of the physical volume in an upcoming example. At the bottom of this listing you can see the mapping of logical extents onto physical extents. In this case there is a direct mapping between logical extents 0000 - 0011 and physical extents 0000 - 0011.

lvextend

This command is used to increase the number of physical extents allocated to a logical volume for a variety of reasons. We sometimes underestimate the size required for a logical volume and with this command you can easily correct this. You may want to extend a logical volume to increase the number of mirrored copies (using the -m option), to increase the size of the logical volume (using the -L option), or to increase the number of logical extents (using the -l option).

lvlnboot

Use this to set up a logical volume to be a root, primary swap, or dump volume (this can be undone with **lvrmboot**).

lvsplit & **lvmerge**

These commands are used to split and merge logical volumes repectively. If you have a mirrored logical volume, **lvsplit** will split this into two logical volumes. **lvmerge** merges two logical volumes of the same size, increasing the number of mirrored copies.

lvmmigrate

This command prepares a root file system in a partition for migration to a logical volume. You would use this if you had a partition to convert to a logical volume.

lvreduce   Use this to decrease the number of physical extents allocated to a logical volume. When creating logical volumes, we sometimes overestimate the size of the logical volume. This command can be used to set the number of mirrored copies (with the -m option), decrease the number of logical extents (with the -l option), or decrease the size of the logical volume (with the -L option).

lvremove   After closing logical volumes, you can use this command to remove logical volumes from a volume group.

lvrmboot   Use this if you don't want a logical volume to be root, primary swap, or a dump device (this is the converse of the **lvlnboot** command).

lvsync   There are times when mirrored data in a logical volume becomes "stale" or out of date. **lvsync** is used to synchronize the physical extents in a logical volume.

Physical Volume Commands

pvchange   This command is used to change the physical volume in some way. For example, you may wish to allow additional physical extents to be added to the physical volume if this is not permitted, or prohibit additional physical extents from being added to the physical volume if indeed this is allowed.

pvcreate
This command is used to create a physical volume that will be part of a volume group. Remember that a volume group may consist of several physical volumes. The physical volumes are the disks on your system.

pvdisplay
This command shows information about the physical volumes you specify. You can get a lot of information about the logical to physical mapping with this command if you use the (-v) for verbose option. With "-v," **pvdisplay** will show you the mapping of logical to physical extents for the physical volumes specified.

You will get a lot of other useful data from this command such as the name of the physical volume; name of the volume group to which the physical volume belongs; the status of the physical volume; the size of physical extents on the physical volume; the total number of physical extents; and the number of free physical extents.

The following is a partial example of running **pvdisplay**:

```
$  pvdisplay -v /dev/dsk/c0t6d0

--- Physical volumes ---
PV Name                /dev/dsk/c0t1d0
VG Name                /dev/vg00
PV Status              available
Allocatable            yes
VGDA                   2
Cur LV                 7
```

```
PE Size (Mbytes)          4
Total PE                  157
Free PE                   8
Allocated PE              149
Stale PE                  0

     --- Distribution of physical volume ---
     LV Name              LE of LV       PE for LV
     /dev/vg00/lvol1      12             12
     /dev/vg00/lvol2      17             17
     /dev/vg00/lvol6      75             75
     /dev/vg00/lvol7      9              9
     /dev/vg00/lvol4      25             25
     /dev/vg00/lvol5      6              6
     /dev/vg00/lvol3      5              5

     --- Physical extents ---
     PE    Status   LV                       LE
     0000  current  /dev/vg00/lvol1          0000
     0001  current  /dev/vg00/lvol1          0001
     0002  current  /dev/vg00/lvol1          0002
     0003  current  /dev/vg00/lvol1          0003
     0004  current  /dev/vg00/lvol1          0004
     0005  current  /dev/vg00/lvol1          0005
     0006  current  /dev/vg00/lvol1          0006
     0007  current  /dev/vg00/lvol1          0007
     0008  current  /dev/vg00/lvol1          0008
     0009  current  /dev/vg00/lvol1          0009
     0010  current  /dev/vg00/lvol1          0010
     0011  current  /dev/vg00/lvol1          0011
     0012  current  /dev/vg00/lvol2          0000
     0013  current  /dev/vg00/lvol2          0001
     0014  current  /dev/vg00/lvol2          0002
     0015  current  /dev/vg00/lvol2          0003
     0016  current  /dev/vg00/lvol2          0004
     0017  current  /dev/vg00/lvol2          0005
     0018  current  /dev/vg00/lvol2          0006
     0019  current  /dev/vg00/lvol2          0007
     0020  current  /dev/vg00/lvol2          0008
     0021  current  /dev/vg00/lvol2          0009
     0022  current  /dev/vg00/lvol2          0010
     0023  current  /dev/vg00/lvol2          0011
     0024  current  /dev/vg00/lvol3          0000
     0025  current  /dev/vg00/lvol3          0001
     0026  current  /dev/vg00/lvol3          0002
     0027  current  /dev/vg00/lvol3          0003
     0028  current  /dev/vg00/lvol3          0004
     0029  current  /dev/vg00/lvol4          0000
     0030  current  /dev/vg00/lvol4          0001
     0031  current  /dev/vg00/lvol4          0002
     0032  current  /dev/vg00/lvol4          0003
     0033  current  /dev/vg00/lvol4          0004
```

```
0034 current  /dev/vg00/lvol4    0005
0035 current  /dev/vg00/lvol4    0006



          .
          .
          .
0156 free                        0000
```

From this listing you can see that lvol1, which is roughly 48 MBytes, has many more physical extents assigned to it than lvol3, which is roughly 20 MBytes.

pvmove You can move physical extents from one physical volume to other physical volumes with this command. By specifying the source physical volume and one or more destination physical volumes, you can spread data around to the physical volumes you wish with this command.

Volume Group Commands

vgcfgbackup This command is used to save the configuration information for a volume group. Remember that a volume group is made up of one or more physical volumes.

vgcfgrestore This command is used to restore the configuration information for a volume group.

vgchange   This command makes a volume group active or inactive. With the "-a" option, you can deactivate (-a n) a volume group or activate (-a y) a volume group.

vgcreate   You can create a volume group and specify all of its parameters with this command. You specify a volume group name and all of the associated parameters for the volume group when creating it.

vgdisplay   Displays all information related to the volume group if you use the verbose (-v) option including volume group name; the status of the volume group; the maximum, current, and open logical volumes in the volume group; the maximum, current, and active physical volumes in the volume group; and physical extent related information.

                      The following is an example of using **vgdisplay** for the volume group vg00:

```
$ vgdisplay /dev/vg00

--- Volume groups ---
VG Name                /dev/vg00
VG Write Access        read/write
VG Status              available
Max LV                 255
Cur LV                 7
Open LV                7
Max PV                 16
Cur PV                 1
Act PV                 1
Max PE per PV          2000
VGDA                   2
PE Size (Mbytes)       4
Total PE               157
Alloc PE               149
Free PE                8
Total PVG              0
```

vgexport   This command removes a logical volume group from the system but does not modify the logical volume information on the physical volumes. These physical volumes can then be imported to another system using **vgimport**.

vgextend   Physical volumes can be added to a volume group with this command by specifying the physical volume to be added to the volume group.

vgimport   This command can be used to import a physical volume to another system.

vgreduce   The size of a volume group can be reduced with this command by specifying which physical volume(s) to remove from a volume group.

vgremove   A volume group definition can be completely removed from the system with this command.

vgscan   In the event of a catastrophe of some type, you can use this command to scan your system in an effort to rebuild the **/etc/lvmtab** file.

vgsync   There are times when mirrored data in a volume group becomes "stale" or out of date. **vgsync** is used to synchronize the physical extents in each mirrored logical volume in the volume group.

Reconfiguring Some Disks - An Example of Using Some Logical Volume Commands

I have always advised in my books and articles to take great care when you first set up disks on your HP-UX systems to make sure the disk layout you select is one you can live with for a long time. No matter how careful you are, however, you often need to perform some logical volume reconfiguration. It is much more difficult to make changes to an existing logical volume layout than it is to set up your system right when it is first installed. This section describes the steps performed to make some changes to the dump and mirror on an existing system.

This is not a procedure you should follow. It is an example of some advanced Logical Volume Manager (LVM) commands used to reconfigure some disks on a specific system. It is a good procedure for illustrating how several LVM commands can be used.

Why Change?

Figure 2-4 shows the original configuration of disks on a system and the updated configuration we wish to implement.

The overall objective here is to move the 4 GByte disk used as the mirror of the root disk to a different SCSI channel and to install a 2 GByte dump device on the same SCSI channel as the root disk.

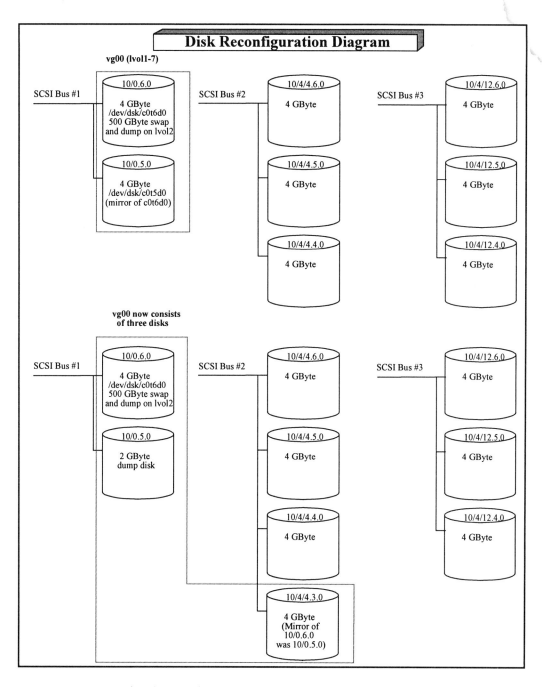

Figure 2-4 Disk Reconfiguration Diagram

The procedure consists of several parts. The first is to obtain a snap-shot of the system before any reconfigurations. This serves two purposes. The first is to have documentation of the original system configuration that can be included in the system administration notebook. Should any questions arise in the future as to the original configuration and changes made to it, the original configuration will be in the system administration notebook. The second purpose of having this information is to have all of the relevant information about the configuration available as you proceed with the reconfiguration process.

The second part of the procedure is to shut down the system and install the new 2 GByte disk and move the 4 GByte disk.

The next part of the procedure is to perform the system administration reconfiguration of the dump and mirror.

Figures 2-5, 2-6, and 2-7 show a flowchart showing the procedure we'll follow throughout this section. The step numbers in the upcoming procedure correspond to the step numbers shown in these figures. Let's now proceed beginning with the snapshot of the system.

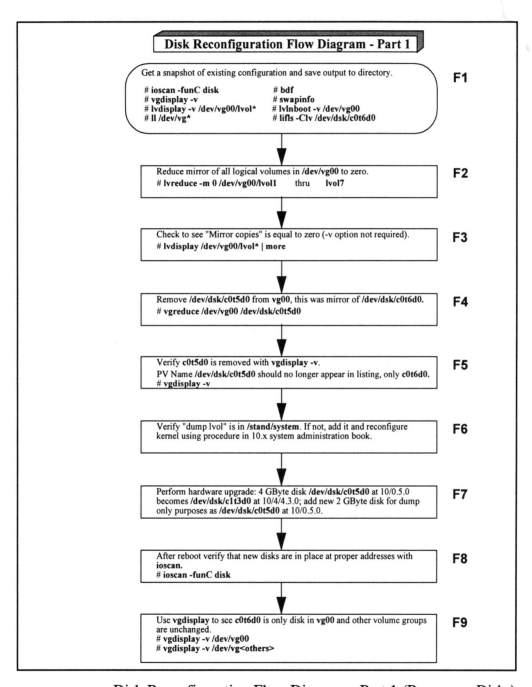

Disk Reconfiguration Flow Diagram - Part 1

Get a snapshot of existing configuration and save output to directory.   **F1**
ioscan -funC disk   # **bdf**
vgdisplay -v   # **swapinfo**
lvdisplay -v /dev/vg00/lvol★   # **lvlnboot -v /dev/vg00**
ll /dev/vg★   # **lifls -Clv /dev/dsk/c0t6d0**

Reduce mirror of all logical volumes in **/dev/vg00** to zero.   **F2**
lvreduce -m 0 /dev/vg00/lvol1   thru   **lvol7**

Check to see "Mirror copies" is equal to zero (-v option not required).   **F3**
lvdisplay /dev/vg00/lvol★ | more

Remove **/dev/dsk/c0t5d0** from **vg00**, this was mirror of **/dev/dsk/c0t6d0**.   **F4**
vgreduce /dev/vg00 /dev/dsk/c0t5d0

Verify **c0t5d0** is removed with **vgdisplay -v**.   **F5**
PV Name **/dev/dsk/c0t5d0** should no longer appear in listing, only **c0t6d0**.
vgdisplay -v

Verify "dump lvol" is in **/stand/system**. If not, add it and reconfigure   **F6**
kernel using procedure in 10.x system administration book.

Perform hardware upgrade: 4 GByte disk **/dev/dsk/c0t5d0** at 10/0.5.0   **F7**
becomes **/dev/dsk/c1t3d0** at 10/4/4.3.0; add new 2 GByte disk for dump
only purposes as **/dev/dsk/c0t5d0** at 10/0.5.0.

After reboot verify that new disks are in place at proper addresses with   **F8**
ioscan.
ioscan -funC disk

Usc **vgdisplay** to sec **c0t6d0** is only disk in **vg00** and other volume groups   **F9**
are unchanged.
vgdisplay -v /dev/vg00
vgdisplay -v /dev/vg<others>

Figure 2-5 Disk Reconfiguration Flow Diagram - Part 1 (Rearrange Disks)

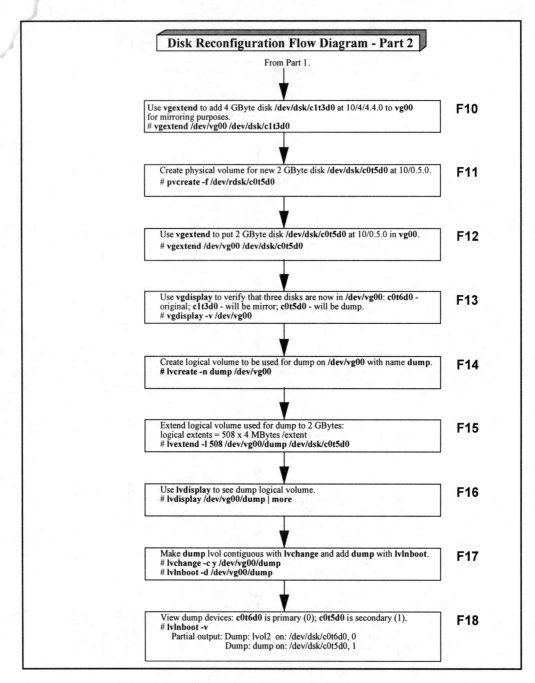

Disk Reconfiguration Flow Diagram - Part 2

From Part 1.

Use **vgextend** to add 4 GByte disk **/dev/dsk/c1t3d0** at 10/4/4.4.0 to **vg00** for mirroring purposes.
vgextend /dev/vg00 /dev/dsk/c1t3d0   **F10**

Create physical volume for new 2 GByte disk **/dev/dsk/c0t5d0** at 10/0.5.0.
pvcreate -f /dev/rdsk/c0t5d0   **F11**

Use **vgextend** to put 2 GByte disk **/dev/dsk/c0t5d0** at 10/0.5.0 in **vg00**.
vgextend /dev/vg00 /dev/dsk/c0t5d0   **F12**

Use **vgdisplay** to verify that three disks are now in **/dev/vg00**: c0t6d0 - original; **c1t3d0** - will be mirror; **c0t5d0** - will be dump.
vgdisplay -v /dev/vg00   **F13**

Create logical volume to be used for dump on **/dev/vg00** with name **dump**.
lvcreate -n dump /dev/vg00   **F14**

Extend logical volume used for dump to 2 GBytes:
logical extents = 508 x 4 MBytes /extent
lvextend -l 508 /dev/vg00/dump /dev/dsk/c0t5d0   **F15**

Use **lvdisplay** to see dump logical volume.
lvdisplay /dev/vg00/dump | more   **F16**

Make **dump** lvol contiguous with **lvchange** and add **dump** with **lvlnboot**.
lvchange -c y /dev/vg00/dump
lvlnboot -d /dev/vg00/dump   **F17**

View dump devices: **c0t6d0** is primary (0); **c0t5d0** is secondary (1).
lvlnboot -v
    Partial output: Dump: lvol2 on: /dev/dsk/c0t6d0, 0
                    Dump: dump on: /dev/dsk/c0t5d0, 1   **F18**

Figure 2-6   Disk Reconfiguration Flow Diagram - Part 2 (Set Up Dump)

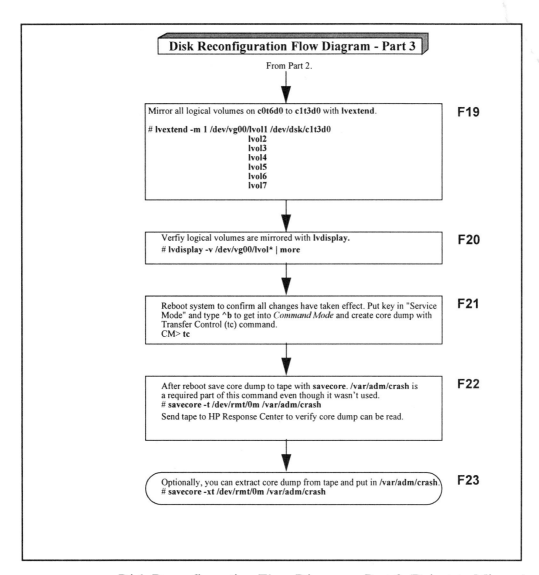

Disk Reconfiguration Flow Diagram - Part 3

From Part 2.

Mirror all logical volumes on **c0t6d0** to **c1t3d0** with **lvextend**.

lvextend -m 1 /dev/vg00/lvol1 /dev/dsk/c1t3d0
                         lvol2
                         lvol3
                         lvol4
                         lvol5
                         lvol6
                         lvol7

F19

Verfiy logical volumes are mirrored with **lvdisplay**.
lvdisplay -v /dev/vg00/lvol* | more

F20

Reboot system to confirm all changes have taken effect. Put key in "Service Mode" and type ^**b** to get into *Command Mode* and create core dump with Transfer Control (tc) command.
CM> **tc**

F21

After reboot save core dump to tape with **savecore**. **/var/adm/crash** is a required part of this command even though it wasn't used.
savecore -t /dev/rmt/0m /var/adm/crash
Send tape to HP Response Center to verify core dump can be read.

F22

Optionally, you can extract core dump from tape and put in **/var/adm/crash**.
savecore -xt /dev/rmt/0m /var/adm/crash

F23

Figure 2-7 Disk Reconfiguration Flow Diagram - Part 3 (Reinstate Mirrors)

F1

First let's run **ioscan** to see the disks on the system.

```
$ /usr/sbin/ioscan -funC disk
```

```
Class     I  H/W Path      Driver     S/W State  H/W Type  Description
=======================================================================
disk      2  10/0.5.0      sdisk      CLAIMED    DEVICE    SEAGATE ST15150W
                /dev/dsk/c0t5d0    /dev/rdsk/c0t5d0
disk      3  10/0.6.0      sdisk      CLAIMED    DEVICE    SEAGATE ST15150W
                /dev/dsk/c0t6d0    /dev/rdsk/c0t6d0
disk      6  10/4/4.4.0    sdisk      CLAIMED    DEVICE    SEAGATE ST15150W
                /dev/dsk/c1t4d0    /dev/rdsk/c1t4d0
disk      7  10/4/4.5.0    sdisk      CLAIMED    DEVICE    SEAGATE ST15150W
                /dev/dsk/c1t5d0    /dev/rdsk/c1t5d0
disk      8  10/4/4.6.0    sdisk      CLAIMED    DEVICE    SEAGATE ST15150W
                /dev/dsk/c1t6d0    /dev/rdsk/c1t6d0
disk      9  10/4/12.4.0   sdisk      CLAIMED    DEVICE    SEAGATE ST15150W
                /dev/dsk/c2t4d0    /dev/rdsk/c2t4d0
disk     10  10/4/12.5.0   sdisk      CLAIMED    DEVICE    SEAGATE ST15150W
                /dev/dsk/c2t5d0    /dev/rdsk/c2t5d0
disk     11  10/4/12.6.0   sdisk      CLAIMED    DEVICE    SEAGATE ST15150W
                /dev/dsk/c2t6d0    /dev/rdsk/c2t6d0
disk      5  10/12/5.2.0   sdisk      CLAIMED    DEVICE    TOSHIBA CD-ROM XM-5401TA
                /dev/dsk/c3t2d0    /dev/rdsk/c3t2d0
```

Note that the disks in this configuration correspond to those on the top of Figure 2-4. We haven't yet looked at the logical volume information related to these disks, only their physical addresses.

F1

Next run **vgdisplay** to see the volume groups. **lvol2** on **vg00** is the dump logical volume we are going to move to a separate 2 GByte disk. We don't yet know if **lvol1-7** on **vg00** are all mirrored.

```
# vgdisplay -v
 --- Volume groups ---
VG Name              /dev/vg00
VG Write Access      read/write
VG Status            available
Max LV               255
Cur LV               7
Open LV              7
Max PV               16
Cur PV               2
```

```
Act PV                  2
Max PE per PV           1023
VGDA                    4
PE Size (Mbytes)        4
Total PE                2046
Alloc PE                688
Free PE                 1358
Total PVG               0

    --- Logical volumes ---
LV Name                 /dev/vg00/lvol1
LV Status               available/syncd
LV Size (Mbytes)        92
Current LE              23
Allocated PE            46
Used PV                 2

LV Name                 /dev/vg00/lvol2
LV Status               available/syncd
LV Size (Mbytes)        500
Current LE              125
Allocated PE            250
Used PV                 2

LV Name                 /dev/vg00/lvol3
LV Status               available/syncd
LV Size (Mbytes)        20
Current LE              5
Allocated PE            10
Used PV                 2

LV Name                 /dev/vg00/lvol4
LV Status               available/syncd
LV Size (Mbytes)        252
Current LE              63
Allocated PE            126
Used PV                 2

LV Name                 /dev/vg00/lvol5
LV Status               available/syncd
LV Size (Mbytes)        32
Current LE              8
Allocated PE            16
Used PV                 2

LV Name                 /dev/vg00/lvol6
LV Status               available/syncd
LV Size (Mbytes)        320
Current LE              80
Allocated PE            160
Used PV                 2
LV Name                 /dev/vg00/lvol7
LV Status               available/syncd
LV Size (Mbytes)        160
Current LE              40
Allocated PE            80
Used PV                 2

    --- Physical volumes ---
PV Name                 /dev/dsk/c0t6d0
PV Status               available
Total PE                1023
Free PE                 679

PV Name                 /dev/dsk/c0t5d0
PV Status               available
Total PE                1023
Free PE                 679
```

F1

View detailed logical volume information with **lvdisplay**. Note that all of these logical volumes are mirrored and that each has "current" status. Only **lvol1** and **lvol2** are shown in the listing. **lvol3** through **lvol7** are not shown.

```
# lvdisplay -v /dev/vg00/lvol*
 --- Logical volumes ---
LV Name                 /dev/vg00/lvol1
VG Name                 /dev/vg00
LV Permission           read/write
LV Status               available/syncd
Mirror copies           1
Consistency Recovery    MWC
Schedule                parallel
LV Size (Mbytes)        92
Current LE              23
Allocated PE            46
Stripes                 0
Stripe Size (Kbytes)    0
Bad block               off
Allocation              strict/contiguous

 --- Distribution of logical volume ---
PV Name             LE on PV  PE on PV
/dev/dsk/c0t6d0     23        23
/dev/dsk/c0t5d0     23        23


 --- Logical extents ---
LE    PV1                  PE1   Status 1 PV2               PE2   Status 2
0000 /dev/dsk/c0t6d0      0000  current  /dev/dsk/c0t5d0   0000  current
0001 /dev/dsk/c0t6d0      0001  current  /dev/dsk/c0t5d0   0001  current
0002 /dev/dsk/c0t6d0      0002  current  /dev/dsk/c0t5d0   0002  current
0003 /dev/dsk/c0t6d0      0003  current  /dev/dsk/c0t5d0   0003  current
0004 /dev/dsk/c0t6d0      0004  current  /dev/dsk/c0t5d0   0004  current
0005 /dev/dsk/c0t6d0      0005  current  /dev/dsk/c0t5d0   0005  current
0006 /dev/dsk/c0t6d0      0006  current  /dev/dsk/c0t5d0   0006  current
0007 /dev/dsk/c0t6d0      0007  current  /dev/dsk/c0t5d0   0007  current
0008 /dev/dsk/c0t6d0      0008  current  /dev/dsk/c0t5d0   0008  current
0009 /dev/dsk/c0t6d0      0009  current  /dev/dsk/c0t5d0   0009  current
0010 /dev/dsk/c0t6d0      0010  current  /dev/dsk/c0t5d0   0010  current
0011 /dev/dsk/c0t6d0      0011  current  /dev/dsk/c0t5d0   0011  current
0012 /dev/dsk/c0t6d0      0012  current  /dev/dsk/c0t5d0   0012  current
0013 /dev/dsk/c0t6d0      0013  current  /dev/dsk/c0t5d0   0013  current
0014 /dev/dsk/c0t6d0      0014  current  /dev/dsk/c0t5d0   0014  current
0015 /dev/dsk/c0t6d0      0015  current  /dev/dsk/c0t5d0   0015  current
0016 /dev/dsk/c0t6d0      0016  current  /dev/dsk/c0t5d0   0016  current
0017 /dev/dsk/c0t6d0      0017  current  /dev/dsk/c0t5d0   0017  current
0018 /dev/dsk/c0t6d0      0018  current  /dev/dsk/c0t5d0   0018  current
0019 /dev/dsk/c0t6d0      0019  current  /dev/dsk/c0t5d0   0019  current
0020 /dev/dsk/c0t6d0      0020  current  /dev/dsk/c0t5d0   0020  current
0021 /dev/dsk/c0t6d0      0021  current  /dev/dsk/c0t5d0   0021  current
0022 /dev/dsk/c0t6d0      0022  current  /dev/dsk/c0t5d0   0022  current

LV Name                 /dev/vg00/lvol2
VG Name                 /dev/vg00
LV Permission           read/write
LV Status               available/syncd
Mirror copies           1
Consistency Recovery    MWC
Schedule                parallel
LV Size (Mbytes)        500
```

```
Current LE              125
Allocated PE            250
Stripes                 0
Stripe Size (Kbytes)    0
Bad block               off
Allocation              strict/contiguous

--- Distribution of logical volume ---

PV Name            LE on PV  PE on PV
/dev/dsk/c0t6d0    125       125
/dev/dsk/c0t5d0    125       125

--- Logical extents ---

LE    PV1                PE1   Status 1  PV2               PE2   Status 2

0000 /dev/dsk/c0t6d0    0023  current   /dev/dsk/c0t5d0   0023  current
0001 /dev/dsk/c0t6d0    0024  current   /dev/dsk/c0t5d0   0024  current
0002 /dev/dsk/c0t6d0    0025  current   /dev/dsk/c0t5d0   0025  current
0003 /dev/dsk/c0t6d0    0026  current   /dev/dsk/c0t5d0   0026  current
0004 /dev/dsk/c0t6d0    0027  current   /dev/dsk/c0t5d0   0027  current
0005 /dev/dsk/c0t6d0    0028  current   /dev/dsk/c0t5d0   0028  current
0006 /dev/dsk/c0t6d0    0029  current   /dev/dsk/c0t5d0   0029  current
0007 /dev/dsk/c0t6d0    0030  current   /dev/dsk/c0t5d0   0030  current
0008 /dev/dsk/c0t6d0    0031  current   /dev/dsk/c0t5d0   0031  current
0009 /dev/dsk/c0t6d0    0032  current   /dev/dsk/c0t5d0   0032  current
0010 /dev/dsk/c0t6d0    0033  current   /dev/dsk/c0t5d0   0033  current
0011 /dev/dsk/c0t6d0    0034  current   /dev/dsk/c0t5d0   0034  current
0012 /dev/dsk/c0t6d0    0035  current   /dev/dsk/c0t5d0   0035  current
0013 /dev/dsk/c0t6d0    0036  current   /dev/dsk/c0t5d0   0036  current
                          .
                          .
                          .
0111 /dev/dsk/c0t6d0    0134  current   /dev/dsk/c0t5d0   0134  current
0112 /dev/dsk/c0t6d0    0135  current   /dev/dsk/c0t5d0   0135  current
0113 /dev/dsk/c0t6d0    0136  current   /dev/dsk/c0t5d0   0136  current
0114 /dev/dsk/c0t6d0    0137  current   /dev/dsk/c0t5d0   0137  current
0115 /dev/dsk/c0t6d0    0138  current   /dev/dsk/c0t5d0   0138  current
0116 /dev/dsk/c0t6d0    0139  current   /dev/dsk/c0t5d0   0139  current
0117 /dev/dsk/c0t6d0    0140  current   /dev/dsk/c0t5d0   0140  current
0118 /dev/dsk/c0t6d0    0141  current   /dev/dsk/c0t5d0   0141  current
0119 /dev/dsk/c0t6d0    0142  current   /dev/dsk/c0t5d0   0142  current
0120 /dev/dsk/c0t6d0    0143  current   /dev/dsk/c0t5d0   0143  current
0121 /dev/dsk/c0t6d0    0144  current   /dev/dsk/c0t5d0   0144  current
0122 /dev/dsk/c0t6d0    0145  current   /dev/dsk/c0t5d0   0145  current
0123 /dev/dsk/c0t6d0    0146  current   /dev/dsk/c0t5d0   0146  current
0124 /dev/dsk/c0t6d0    0147  current   /dev/dsk/c0t5d0   0147  current
```

F1

Next view **/dev/vg00** to have a record of the logical volumes.

```
# ll /dev/vg00

/dev/vg00:
total 0
crw-r--r--  1 root    sys    64 0x000000 May 29 04:44 group
brw-r-----  1 root    sys    64 0x000001 May 29 04:44 lvol1
brw-r-----  1 root    sys    64 0x000002 Jul  9 17:10 lvol2
brw-r-----  1 root    sys    64 0x000003 May 29 04:44 lvol3
brw-r-----  1 root    sys    64 0x000004 May 29 04:44 lvol4
brw-r-----  1 root    sys    64 0x000005 May 29 04:44 lvol5
brw-r-----  1 root    sys    64 0x000006 May 29 04:44 lvol6
brw-r-----  1 root    sys    64 0x000007 May 29 04:44 lvol7
crw-r-----  1 root    sys    64 0x000001 May 29 04:44 rlvol1
```

```
crw-r-----   1 root      sys        64 0x000002 Jul  9 17:10 rlvol2
crw-r-----   1 root      sys        64 0x000003 May 29 04:44 rlvol3
crw-r-----   1 root      sys        64 0x000004 May 29 04:44 rlvol4
crw-r-----   1 root      sys        64 0x000005 May 29 04:44 rlvol5
crw-r-----   1 root      sys        64 0x000006 May 29 04:44 rlvol6
crw-r-----   1 root      sys        64 0x000007 May 29 04:44 rlvol7
```

F1

Next view **/dev/vg_nw** and any other volume groups.

```
# ll /dev/vg_nw

/dev/vg_nw:
total 0
crw-rw-rw-   1 root      sys        64 0x010000 Jul  9 12:03 group
brw-r-----   1 root      sys        64 0x010003 Jul  9 13:01 lv_nwbackup
brw-r-----   1 root      sys        64 0x010004 Jul  9 13:01 lv_nwlog
brw-r-----   1 root      sys        64 0x010002 Jul  9 12:54 lv_nwsys
brw-r-----   1 root      sys        64 0x010001 Jul  9 12:53 lv_nwtext
crw-r-----   1 root      sys        64 0x010003 Jul  9 13:01 rlv_nwbackup
crw-r-----   1 root      sys        64 0x010004 Jul  9 13:01 rlv_nwlog
crw-r-----   1 root      sys        64 0x010002 Jul  9 12:55 rlv_nwsys
crw-r-----   1 root      sys        64 0x010001 Jul  9 12:54 rlv_nwtext
```

F1

Next view the file systems with **bdf**. Notice that **lvol2** is not shown because this is swap and dump device.

```
# bdf
Filesystem               kbytes     used    avail %used Mounted on
/dev/vg00/lvol1           91669    31889    50613   39% /
/dev/vg00/lvol7          159509    83630    59928   58% /var
/dev/vg00/lvol6          319125   197912    89300   69%
/usr /dev/vg00/lvol5      31829    11323    17323   40% /tmp
/dev/vg00/lvol4          251285    67854   158302   30% /opt
/dev/vg_nw/lv_nwtext    4099465  2070905  1618613   56% /nwtext
/dev/vg_nw/lv_nwsys     4099465  1063909  2625609   29% /nwsys
/dev/vg_nw/lv_nwlog       99669    17313    72389   19% /nwlog
/dev/vg_nw/lv_nwbackup  2552537   377388  1919895   16% /nwbackup
/dev/vg00/lvol3           19861     2191    15683   12% /home
```

F1

Next run **swapinfo** to see that **lvol2** is the only swap device.

```
# swapinfo
              Kb        Kb        Kb   PCT  START/     Kb
TYPE        AVAIL     USED     FREE   USED  LIMIT  RESERVE  PRI  NAME
dev        512000        0   512000    0%      0        -    1  /dev/vg00/lvol2
reserve         -   512000  -512000
memory    1670828  1474704   196124   88%
```

F1

Next look at the boot information with **lvlnboot**. **lvol2** on **vg00** is the dump device.

```
# lvlnboot -v /dev/vg00
Boot Definitions for Volume Group /dev/vg00:
Physical Volumes belonging in Root Volume Group:
        /dev/dsk/c0t6d0 (10/0.6.0) -- Boot Disk
        /dev/dsk/c0t5d0 (10/0.5.0) -- Boot Disk
Root: lvol1         on: /dev/dsk/c0t6d0
                        /dev/dsk/c0t5d0
Swap: lvol2         on: /dev/dsk/c0t6d0
                        /dev/dsk/c0t5d0
Dump: lvol2         on: /dev/dsk/c0t6d0, 0
```

F1

Look at boot area with **lifls**.

```
#lifls -Clv /dev/dsk/c0t6d0

volume ISL10 data size 7984 directory size 8 94/11/04 15:46:53
filename    type     start   size   implement  created
============================================================
ODE         -12960   584     496    0          95/05/19 13:36:50
MAPFILE     -12277   1080    32     0          95/05/19 13:36:50
SYSLIB      -12280   1112    224    0          95/05/19 13:36:50
CONFIGDATA  -12278   1336    62     0          95/05/19 13:36:50
SLMOD       -12276   1400    70     0          95/05/19 13:36:50
SLDEV       -12276   1472    68     0          95/05/19 13:36:50
SLDRIVERS   -12276   1544    244    0          95/05/19 13:36:50
MAPPER      -12279   1792    93     0          95/05/19 13:36:51
IOTEST      -12279   1888    150    0          95/05/19 13:36:51
PERFVER     -12279   2040    80     0          95/05/19 13:36:51
PVCU        -12801   2120    64     0          95/05/19 13:36:51
SSINFO      -12286   2184    1      0          96/09/16 09:04:01
ISL         -12800   2192    240    0          94/11/04 15:46:53
AUTO        -12289   2432    1      0          94/11/04 15:46:53
HPUX        -12928   2440    800    0          94/11/04 15:46:54
LABEL       BIN      3240    8      0          96/05/29 01:49:55
```

F2

After all of the appropriate information has been saved for the existing configuration, we can begin the reconfiguration. First we break the mirror with **lvreduce** and the **-m** option.

```
# lvreduce -m 0 /dev/vg00/lvol1
Logical volume "/dev/vg00/lvol1" has been successfully reduced.
Volume Group configuration for /dev/vg00 has been saved in /etc/lvmconf/vg00.conf
# lvreduce -m 0 /dev/vg00/lvol2
Logical volume "/dev/vg00/lvol2" has been successfully reduced.
Volume Group configuration for /dev/vg00 has been saved in /etc/lvmconf/vg00.conf
# lvreduce -m 0 /dev/vg00/lvol3
Logical volume "/dev/vg00/lvol3" has been successfully reduced.
Volume Group configuration for /dev/vg00 has been saved in /etc/lvmconf/vg00.conf
# lvreduce -m 0 /dev/vg00/lvol4
Logical volume "/dev/vg00/lvol4" has been successfully reduced.
Volume Group configuration for /dev/vg00 has been saved in /etc/lvmconf/vg00.conf
# lvreduce -m 0 /dev/vg00/lvol5
Logical volume "/dev/vg00/lvol5" has been successfully reduced.
Volume Group configuration for /dev/vg00 has been saved in /etc/lvmconf/vg00.conf
# lvreduce -m 0 /dev/vg00/lvol6
Logical volume "/dev/vg00/lvol6" has been successfully reduced.
Volume Group configuration for /dev/vg00 has been saved in /etc/lvmconf/vg00.conf
# lvreduce -m 0 /dev/vg00/lvol7
Logical volume "/dev/vg00/lvol7" has been successfully reduced.
Volume Group configuration for /dev/vg00 has been saved in /etc/lvmconf/vg00.conf
```

You can type each command or make a file with the **lvreduce** commands in it and run the file. You can call the file **/tmp/reduce** with the following entries:

```
lvreduce -m 0 /dev/vg00/lvol1
lvreduce -m 0 /dev/vg00/lvol2
lvreduce -m 0 /dev/vg00/lvol3
lvreduce -m 0 /dev/vg00/lvol4
lvreduce -m 0 /dev/vg00/lvol5
lvreduce -m 0 /dev/vg00/lvol6
lvreduce -m 0 /dev/vg00/lvol7
```

After you create this file, change it to executable and then run with the following two commands.

```
# chmod 555 /tmp/reduce
# /tmp/reduce
```

You will then see all of the output of having run the **lvreduce** commands.

F3

Check to see mirroring of **lvol1-7** has been reduced with **lvdisplay**. Look to see that mirrored copies are equal to 0. Only **lvol1** through **lvol3** are shown in this listing.

```
# lvdisplay -v /dev/vg00/lvol* | more

--- Logical volumes ---
LV Name                  /dev/vg00/lvol1
VG Name                  /dev/vg00
LV Permission            read/write
LV Status                available/syncd
Mirror copies            0
Consistency Recovery     MWC
Schedule                 parallel
LV Size (Mbytes)         92
Current LE               23
Allocated PE             23
Stripes                  0
Stripe Size (Kbytes)     0
Bad block                off
Allocation               strict/contiguous

LV Name                  /dev/vg00/lvol2
VG Name                  /dev/vg00
LV Permission            read/write
LV Status                available/syncd
Mirror copies            0
Consistency Recovery     MWC
Schedule                 parallel
LV Size (Mbytes)         500
Current LE               125
Allocated PE             125
Stripes                  0
Stripe Size (Kbytes)     0
Bad block                off
Allocation               strict/contiguous

LV Name                  /dev/vg00/lvol3
VG Name                  /dev/vg00
LV Permission            read/write
LV Status                available/syncd
Mirror copies            0
Consistency Recovery     MWC
Schedule                 parallel
LV Size (Mbytes)         20
Current LE               5
Allocated PE             5
Stripes                  0
Stripe Size (Kbytes)     0
Bad block                on
Allocation               strict
```

F4

Now remove **c0t5d0** from **vg00** with **vgreduce**. Since there is no mirroring in place, this will work. This disk will be put on a different SCSI controller and again used for mirroring later in the procedure.

```
# vgreduce /dev/vg00 /dev/dsk/c0t5d0
Volume group "/dev/vg00" has been successfully reduced.
Volume Group configuration for /dev/vg00 has been saved in /etc/lvmconf/vg00.conf
```

F5

At this point **c0t5d0** is not longer in **vg00**. Verify that "PV Name" **c0t5d0** is no longer in **vg00** with **vgdisplay**.

```
# vgdisplay -v
```

There should be no **c0t5d0** in **vg00**.

F6

Verify that "dump lvol" is in **/stand/system**. If not, add "dump vol" and reconfigure kernel. See kernel rebuild procedure in Chapter 1.

F7

Now the hardware upgrade takes place. The system is shut down, disk drives are added and moved, and the system is rebooted. The 4 GByte disk **/dev/dsk/c0t5d0** becomes **/dev/dsk/c1t3d0** at address 10/4/4.3.0 and a new 2 GByte disk is introduced as 10/0.5.0 with the device name **/dev/dsk/c0t5d0**. The second half of Figure 2-4 depicts this change.

F8

The first activity to perform after the hardware upgrade is to view the new disks with **ioscan**. There is now a 2 GByte disk at 10/0.5.0 and a 4 GByte disk at 10/4/4.3.0.

```
# ioscan -funC disk
Class     I  H/W Path     Driver       S/W State H/W Type  Description
=====================================================================
disk      2  10/0.5.0     sdisk        CLAIMED   DEVICE SEAGATE      ST32550W
                          /dev/dsk/c0t5d0   /dev/rdsk/c0t5d0
disk      3  10/0.6.0     sdisk        CLAIMED   DEVICE    SEAGATE ST15150W
                          /dev/dsk/c0t6d0   /dev/rdsk/c0t6d0
disk     12  10/4/4.3.0   disc3        CLAIMED   DEVICE    SEAGATE ST15150W
                          /dev/dsk/c1t3d0        /dev/rdsk/c1t3d0
                          /dev/floppy/c1t3d0     /dev/rfloppy/c1t3d0
disk      6  10/4/4.4.0   disc3        CLAIMED   DEVICE    SEAGATE ST15150W
                          /dev/dsk/c1t4d0        /dev/rdsk/c1t4d0
                          /dev/floppy/c1t4d0     /dev/rfloppy/c1t4d0
disk      7  10/4/4.5.0   disc3        CLAIMED   DEVICE    SEAGATE ST15150W
                          /dev/dsk/c1t5d0        /dev/rdsk/c1t5d0
                          /dev/floppy/c1t5d0     /dev/rfloppy/c1t5d0
disk      8  10/4/4.6.0   disc3        CLAIMED   DEVICE    SEAGATE ST15150W
                          /dev/dsk/c1t6d0        /dev/rdsk/c1t6d0
                          /dev/floppy/c1t6d0     /dev/rfloppy/c1t6d0
disk      9  10/4/12.4.0  disc3        CLAIMED   DEVICE    SEAGATE ST15150W
                          /dev/dsk/c2t4d0        /dev/rdsk/c2t4d0
                          /dev/floppy/c2t4d0     /dev/rfloppy/c2t4d0
disk     10  10/4/12.5.0  disc3        CLAIMED   DEVICE    SEAGATE ST15150W
                          /dev/dsk/c2t5d0        /dev/rdsk/c2t5d0
                          /dev/floppy/c2t5d0     /dev/rfloppy/c2t5d0
disk     11  10/4/12.6.0  disc3        CLAIMED   DEVICE    SEAGATE ST15150W
                          /dev/dsk/c2t6d0        /dev/rdsk/c2t6d0
                          /dev/floppy/c2t6d0     /dev/rfloppy/c2t6d0
disk      5  10/12/5.2.0  sdisk        CLAIMED   DEVICE    TOSHIBA CD-ROM XM-5401TA
                          /dev/dsk/c3t2d0   /dev/rdsk/c3t2d0
```

F9

Now we run **vgdisplay** to see new volume group information. Only **c0t6d0** is in **vg00** and no mirroring is yet configured. The other volume groups have remained the same. Only **lvol1** through **lvol3** are shown.

```
# vgdisplay -v /dev/vg00

--- Volume groups ---
VG Name                 /dev/vg00
VG Write Access         read/write
```

```
VG Status                available
Max LV                   255
Cur LV                   7
Open LV                  7
Max PV                   16
Cur PV                   1
Act PV                   1
Max PE per PV            1023
VGDA                     2
PE Size (Mbytes)         4
Total PE                 1023
Alloc PE                 344
Free PE                  679
Total PVG                0

--- Logical volumes ---
LV Name                  /dev/vg00/lvol1
LV Status                available/syncd
LV Size (Mbytes)         92
Current LE               23
Allocated PE             23
Used PV                  1

LV Name                  /dev/vg00/lvol2
LV Status                available/syncd
LV Size (Mbytes)         500
Current LE               125
Allocated PE             125
Used PV                  1

LV Name                  /dev/vg00/lvol3
LV Status                available/syncd
LV Size (Mbytes)         20
Current LE               5
Allocated PE             5
Used PV                  1
```

(F9 continued)

Only the first three logical volumes in **/dev/vg_nw** are shown.

```
# vgdisplay -v /dev/vg_nw
VG Name                  /dev/vg_nw
VG Write Access          read/write
VG Status                available
Max LV                   255
Cur LV                   4
Open LV                  4
Max PV                   16
Cur PV                   6
Act PV                   6
Max PE per PV            1023
VGDA                     12
PE Size (Mbytes)         4
Total PE                 6138
Alloc PE                 5416
Free PE                  722
Total PVG                2
   --- Logical volumes ---
LV Name                  /dev/vg_nw/lv_nwtext
LV Status                available/syncd
LV Size (Mbytes)         4092
Current LE               1023
Allocated PE             2046
Used PV                  2
```

```
LV Name             /dev/vg_nw/lv_nwsys
LV Status           available/syncd
LV Size (Mbytes)    4092
Current LE          1023
Allocated PE        2046
Used PV             2

LV Name             /dev/vg_nw/lv_nwbackup
LV Status           available/syncd
LV Size (Mbytes)    2548
Current LE          637
Allocated PE        1274
Used PV             2
```

F10

Use **vgextend** to add the 4 GByte disk to **vg00** for mirroring (you may also have to run **pvcreate** here too).

```
# vgextend /dev/vg00 /dev/dsk/c1t3d0
Volume group "/dev/vg00" has been successfully extended. Volume Group configuration for
/dev/vg00 has been saved in /etc/lvmconf/vg00.conf
```

F11

Now we can create the new 2 GByte disk and add it to **vg00** using the two following commands: **pvcreate** (F11) to create the physical volume and **vgextend** (F12) to extend the volume group.

```
# pvcreate -f /dev/rdsk/c0t5d0
Physical volume "/dev/rdsk/c0t5d0" has been successfully created.
```

F12

```
# vgextend /dev/vg00 /dev/dsk/c0t5d0
Volume group "/dev/vg00" has been successfully extended.
Volume Group configuration for /dev/vg00 has been saved in /etc/lvmconf/vg00.conf
```

F13

We can check to see that these two disks have indeed been added to **vg00** with **vgdisplay**. Only **lvol1** through **lvol3** are shown. The end of the display is the significant part of the listing showing three physical volumes.

```
# vgdisplay -v /dev/vg00

   --- Volume groups ---
VG Name                     /dev/vg00
VG Write Access             read/write
VG Status                   available
Max LV                      255
Cur LV                      7
Open LV                     7
Max PV                      16
Cur PV                      3
Act PV                      3
Max PE per PV               1023
VGDA                        6
PE Size (Mbytes)            4
Total PE                    2554
Alloc PE                    344
Free PE                     2210
Total PVG                   0

--- Logical volumes ---

LV Name                     /dev/vg00/lvol1
LV Status                   available/syncd
LV Size (Mbytes)            92
Current LE                  23
Allocated PE                23
Used PV                     1

LV Name                     /dev/vg00/lvol2
LV Status                   available/syncd
LV Size (Mbytes)            500
Current LE                  125
Allocated PE                125
Used PV                     1

LV Name                     /dev/vg00/lvol3
LV Status                   available/syncd
LV Size (Mbytes)            20
Current LE                  5
Allocated PE                5
Used PV                     1

                    .
                    .
                    .

--- Physical volumes ---

PV Name                     /dev/dsk/c0t6d0
PV Status                   available
```

```
Total PE             1023
Free PE              679

PV Name              /dev/dsk/c1t3d0
PV Status            available
Total PE             1023
Free PE              1023

PV Name              /dev/dsk/c0t5d0
PV Status            available
Total PE             508
Free PE              508
```

F14

We can now create the dump logical volume in **vg00** with **lvcreate** (F14), extend it to 2 GBytes with **lvextend** (F15), and view it with **lvdisplay** (F16).

```
# lvcreate -n dump  /dev/vg00
Logical volume "/dev/vg00/dump" has been successfully created with character device
"/dev/vg00/rdump".
Volume Group configuration for /dev/vg00 has been saved in /etc/lvmconf/vg00.conf
```

F15

```
# lvextend -l 508 /dev/vg00/dump /dev/dsk/c0t5d0
Logical volume "/dev/vg00/dump" has been successfully extended.
Volume Group configuration for /dev/vg00 has been saved in /etc/lvmconf/vg00.conf
```

F16

```
# lvdisplay /dev/vg00/dump | more

--- Logical volumes ---
LV Name               /dev/vg00/dump
VG Name               /dev/vg00
LV Permission         read/write
LV Status             available/syncd
Mirror copies         0
Consistency Recovery  MWC
Schedule              parallel
LV Size (Mbytes)      2032
Current LE            508
Allocated PE          508
Stripes               0
Stripe Size (Kbytes)  0
Bad block             on
Allocation            strict
```

```
--- Distribution of logical volume ---
PV Name               LE on PV  PE on PV
/dev/dsk/c0t5d0       508       508
                                 .
                                 .
                                 .
```

F17

In order to make **/dev/vg00/dump** the dump device we must first make it contiguous with **lvchange** and then make it a dump device with **lvlnboot**.

```
# lvchange -C y /dev/vg00/dump
```

```
# lvlnboot -d /dev/vg00/dump
```

F18

View dump devices.

```
# lvlnboot -v | more
Boot Definitions for Volume Group /dev/vg00:
Physical Volumes belonging in Root Volume Group:
            /dev/dsk/c0t6d0 (10/0.6.0) -- Boot Disk
            /dev/dsk/c1t3d0 (10/4/4.3.0) -- Boot Disk
            /dev/dsk/c0t5d0 (10/0.5.0)
Root: lvol1       on:       /dev/dsk/c0t6d0
Swap: lvol2       on:       /dev/dsk/c0t6d0
Dump: lvol2       on:       /dev/dsk/c0t6d0, 0
Dump: dump        on:       /dev/dsk/c0t5d0, 1
```

This may not be what we want. The primary dump device, as indicated by the "0" is **/dev/dsk/c0t6d0** and the secondary dump device, indicated by the "1," is **/dev/dsk/c0t5d0**. We can optionally redo this. Let's proceed with mirroring the lvols on **/dev/vg00** and come back to dump devices.

F19

Let's now extend all of the volumes in **vg00** for one mirror using **lvextend**.

```
# lvextend -m 1 /dev/vg00/lvol1 /dev/dsk/c1t3d0
The newly allocated mirrors are now being synchronized.
This operation will take some time. Please wait ....
Logical volume "/dev/vg00/lvol1" has been successfully extended.
Volume Group configuration for /dev/vg00 has been saved in /etc/lvmconf/vg00.conf
```

Put the following in **/tmp/mirror** and run. **lvol1** was extended earlier; **lvol2** is swap and doesn't need to be extended:

```
lvextend -m 1 /dev/vg00/lvol3 /dev/dsk/c1t3d0
lvextend -m 1 /dev/vg00/lvol4 /dev/dsk/c1t3d0
lvextend -m 1 /dev/vg00/lvol5 /dev/dsk/c1t3d0
lvextend -m 1 /dev/vg00/lvol6 /dev/dsk/c1t3d0
lvextend -m 1 /dev/vg00/lvol7 /dev/dsk/c1t3d0

The newly allocated mirrors are now being synchronized.
This operation will take some time.
Please wait .... Logical volume "/dev/vg00/lvol2" has been successfully extended.
Volume Group configuration for /dev/vg00 has been saved in /etc/lvmconf/vg00.conf
        .
        .
        .
```

F20

Let's now verify the mirroring is in place with **lvdisplay** (only **lvol1** and **lvol2** are shown).

```
# lvdsisplay -v /dev/vg00/lvol* | more

--- Logical volumes ---
LV Name                /dev/vg00/lvol1
VG Name                /dev/vg00
LV Permission          read/write
LV Status              available/syncd
Mirror copies          1
Consistency Recovery   MWC
Schedule               parallel
LV Size (Mbytes)       92
Current LE             23
Allocated PE           46
Stripes                0
Stripe Size (Kbytes)   0
Bad block              off
Allocation             strict/contiguous
```

```
--- Distribution of logical volume ---
PV Name            LE on PV  PE on PV
/dev/dsk/c0t6d0      23        23
/dev/dsk/c1t3d0      23        23

--- Logical extents ---
LE    PV1              PE1   Status 1  PV2              PE2   Status 2
0000  /dev/dsk/c0t6d0  0000  current   /dev/dsk/c1t3d0  0000  current
0001  /dev/dsk/c0t6d0  0001  current   /dev/dsk/c1t3d0  0001  current
0002  /dev/dsk/c0t6d0  0002  current   /dev/dsk/c1t3d0  0002  current
0003  /dev/dsk/c0t6d0  0003  current   /dev/dsk/c1t3d0  0003  current
                         .
                         .
                         .
```

You can see from this listing that **c0t6d0** is mirrored on **c1t3d0**.

F21

Reboot the system to confirm all changes have taken effect.

After reboot, do the following to create a dump. The key must be in the "Service" position for **^b** to work (you must be on a server for this to work).

Use **^b** to get **CM>** prompt.

Use **tc** command at **CM>** prompt to create core dump

F22

The system will automatically reboot after core dump. Use the following command to save core dump to tape. The **/var/adm/crash** file name is required even though the core dump is in the dump logical volume and not in the **/var/adm/crash** directory.

```
# savecore -t /dev/rmt/0m /var/adm/crash
```

F23

Then use **savecore -xt** and directory name to extract core dump. If you do not have room for the core dump, or you want a more thorough check, you can place a call and ask the HP Response Center to verify the **savecore** to tape has worked.

```
# savecore -xt /dev/rmt/0m /var/adm/crash
```

The core dump space requirements is calculated from the end of dump back toward the front. For this reason about roughly 1.5 GBytes is written to the **dump** logical volume and then roughly 600 MBytes are written to **lvol2**.

Optional Procedure to Exchange Dump Priorities

This procedure removes all boot definitions, including swap and dump, from **/dev/vg00** with **lvrmboot** and replaces them with **lvlnboot**. This needs to be done because **lvol2** is the primary dump logical volume (0) and dump is the secondary dump logical volume (1).

You must reboot in order for these changes to take affect. Figure 2-8 shows the steps required to complete this optional procedure.

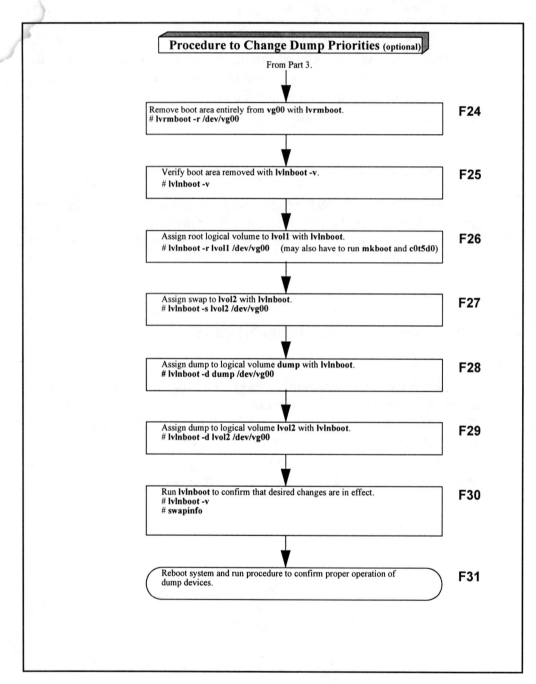

Figure 2-8   Procedure to Change Dump Priorities (Optional)

F24

Remove boot area entirely from **vg00** with **lvrmboot**.

```
# lvrmboot -r /dev/vg00
```

F25

Verify boot area removed with **lvlnboot.**

```
# lvlnboot -v
Boot Definitions for Volume Group /dev/vg00: The Boot Data Area is empty.
```

F26

Assign root logical volume to **lvol1** on **/dev/vg00** with **lvlnboot**.

```
# lvlnboot -r lvol1 /dev/vg00
```

F27

Assign swap to **lvol2** on **/dev/vg00**.

```
# lvlnboot -s lvol2 /dev/vg00

# swapinfo
            Kb        Kb      Kb     PCT   START/      Kb
TYPE      AVAIL     USED    FREE    USED   LIMIT RESERVE  PRI  NAME
dev      512000        0  512000     0%       0       -    1  /dev/vg00/lvol2
reserve       -    23144  -23144
memory  1671008    27324 1643684     2%
```

F28

Assign dump to logical volume **dump** on **/dev/vg00**.

```
# lvlnboot -d dump /dev/vg00
```

F29

Assign secondary dump device as **lvol2** (primary swap) on **lvol2**.

```
# lvlnboot -d lvol2 /dev/vg00
```

F30

Run **lvlnboot** to confirm that dump and swap are properly configured with priority "0" on 2 GByte disk **c0t5d0** and "1" on **c0t6d0**.

```
# lvlnboot -v       # after adding lvol2 as secondary dump

Boot Definitions for Volume Group /dev/vg00:
Physical Volumes belonging in Root Volume Group:
                    /dev/dsk/c0t6d0  (10/0.6.0) -- Boot Disk
                    /dev/dsk/c1t3d0  (10/4/4.3.0) -- Boot Disk
                    /dev/dsk/c0t5d0  (10/0.5.0)
Root: lvol1         on:      /dev/dsk/c0t6d0
                             /dev/dsk/c1t3d0
Swap: lvol2         on:      /dev/dsk/c0t6d0
                             /dev/dsk/c1t3d0
Dump: dump          on:      /dev/dsk/c0t5d0, 0
Dump: dump          on:      /dev/dsk/c0t6d0, 1
```

F31

Reboot system and run steps 21-23 to confirm proper operation of
dump devices.

Although this procedure to reconfigure disks is for a specific system
it is useful for illustrating the many LVM commands required to perform
such tasks. LVM, and disk management in general, are the areas I find
consumes the most system administration time in mature HP-UX installations. There are many commands used in this procedure for which there
is no way to "back out," so use caution whenever using LVM commands.

Some Additional File System Related Commands

Viewing File Systems with bdf

You can manually view the file systems you have mounted with the **bdf** command. **bdf** provides the following output:

File system	Block device file system name. In the following example there are several logical volumes shown.
KBytes	Number of KBytes of total disk space on the file system.
used	The number of used KBytes on the file system.
avail	The number of available KBytes on the file system.
%used	The percentage of total available disk space that is used on the file system.
Mounted on	The directory name the file system is mounted on.
iused	Number of inodes in use (only if you use the -i option with **bdf**).
ifree	Number of free inodes (only if you use the -i option with **bdf**).
%iuse	Percent of inodes in use (only if you use the -i option with **bdf**).

Here is an example of **bdf** that is also used under Logical Volume Manager in this chapter:

$ /usr/bin/bdf

File system	kbytes	used	avail	%used	Mounted on
/dev/vg00/lvol1	47829	18428	24618	43%	/
/dev/vg00/lvol7	34541	8673	22413	28%	/var
/dev/vg00/lvol6	299157	149449	119792	56%	/usr
/dev/vg00/lvol5	23013	48	20663	0%	/tmp
/dev/vg00/lvol4	99669	32514	57188	36%	/opt
/dev/vg00/lvol3	19861	9	17865	0%	/home
/dev/dsk/c0t6d0	802212	552120	169870	76%	/mnt/9.x

File System Maintenance with fsck

fsck is a program used for file system maintenance on HP-UX systems. **fsck** checks file system consistency and can make many "lifesaving" repairs to a corrupt file system. **fsck** can be run with several options including the following:

-F   This option allows you to specify the file system type (see explanation of file system types earlier in this chapter). If you do not specify a file system type, then the **/etc/fstab** file will be used to determine the file system type. See **fstab** description in this section.

-m   This is a sanity check of the file system. If you run this, you'll be told if your file system is OK or not. I

did the following to check lvol3 which is mounted as
/home:

```
$ umount /home
$ fsck -m /dev/vg00/lvol3

fsck: sanity check,/dev/vg00/lvol3 okay
```

-y   **fsck** will ask questions if run in interactive mode and
            the **-y** option causes a "yes" response to all questions
            asked by **fsck**. Don't use this! If you have a serious
            problem with your file system, data will probably
            have to be removed and the **-y** indicates that the
            response to every question, including removing data,
            will be yes.

-n   The response to all questions asked by **fsck** will be
            "no." Don't use this either. If your file system is in
            bad shape, you may have to respond "yes" to some
            questions in order to repair the file system. All "no"
            responses will not do the job.

Since your system runs **fsck** on any file systems that were not
marked as clean at the time you shut down the system, you can rest
assured that when your system boots, any disks that were not properly
shut down will be checked. It is a good idea to run **fsck** interactively on a
periodic basis just so you can see firsthand that all of your file systems are
in good working order.

Should **fsck** find a problem with a directory or file, it places these in
the **lost+found** directory which is at the top level of each file system. If a
file or directory appears in **lost+found**, you may be able to identify the
file or directory by examining it and move it back to its original location.
You can use the **file**, **what**, and **strings** commands on a file to obtain
more information about a file to help identify its origin.

How are file system problems created? The most common cause for
a file system problem is improper shutdown of the system. The informa-

tion written to file systems is first written to a buffer cache in memory. It is later written to the disk with the **sync** command by unmounting the disk, or through the normal use of filling the buffer and writing it to the disk. If you walk up to a system and shut off the power, you will surely end up with a file system problem. Data in the buffer that was not synced to the disk will be lost. The file system will not be marked as properly shut down and **fsck** will be run when the system boots.

Proper shutdown of the system is described in this chapter. Although **fsck** is a useful utility that has been known to work miracles on occasion, you don't want to take any unnecessary risks with your file systems so be sure to properly shut down your system.

A sudden loss of power can also cause an unproper system shut down.

The **/etc/fstab** file mentioned earlier is used by **fsck** to determine the sequence of the file system check if it is required at the time of boot. The sequence of entries in **/etc/fstab** is important if there is not a "pass number" for any of the entries. Here is an example of the **/etc/fstab** file:

```
# System /etc/fstab file. Static information about the file
# systems. See fstab(4) and sam(1m) for further details.

/dev/vg00/lvol1  /              hfs   defaults   0        1
/dev/vg00/lvol3  /home          hfs   defaults   0        2
/dev/vg00/lvol1  /opt           hfs   defaults   0        2
/dev/vg00/lvol1  /tmp           hfs   defaults   0        2
/dev/vg00/lvol1  /usr           hfs   defaults   0        2
/dev/vg00/lvol1  /var           hfs   defaults   0        2
/dev/dsk/c0tt6d0 /tmp/mnt9.x    hfs   rw, suid   0        2

      |              |            |         |        |         |

      |              |            |         |        |         |

      v              v            v         v        v         v
```

device special file	directory	type	options	backup frequency	pass #

device special file

> This is the device block file, such as **/dev/vg00/ lvol1** in the example.

directory

> Name of the directory under which the device special file is mounted.

type

> Can be one of several types including:
> cdfs (local CD-ROM file system)
> hfs (high-performance local file system)
> nfs (network file system)
> vxfs
> swap
> swapfs

options

> Several options are available including those shown in the example.

backup frequency

> Used by backup utilities in the future.

pass #

> Used by **fsck** to determine order in which file system checks (**fsck**) will take place. If the same pass number is specified for two hfs file systems, then these will be checked in parallel with **fsck - p**.

comment

> Anything you want, as long as it's preceded by a #.

For those of you who worked with HP-UX 9.x, you will notice the similarity between the **/etc/checklist** file (used in HP-UX 9.x) and the **/etc/fstab** file (used in HP-UX 10.x). There is a transitional link between the **/etc/checklist** file and the **/etc/fstab** file. This was shown earlier in the chapter and I include it again here:

```
$ ll /etc/checklist

   lr-xr-xr-xT 1 root sys 10 Feb 7 13:39 /etc/checklist  -> /etc/fstab
```

Initialize with mediainit

Another command you should be aware of is **mediainit**. When you use SAM to set up disks for you, the **mediainit** command may be run.

Here are some of the options of **mediainit**:

-v	This is the verbose option. **mediainit** normally just prints error messages to the screen. You can get continuous feedback on what **mediainit** is doing with the -v option.
-i interleave	Allows you to specify the interleave factor, which is the relationship between sequential logical and physical records. **mediainit** will provide this if one is not specified.
-f format	The format option allows you to specify format options for devices such as floppy disks which support different format options. This is not required for hard disks.

pathname   The character device file to be used for **medi-ainit**.

newfs is used to create a new file system. **newfs** calls the **mksf** command. **newfs** builds a file system of the type you specify (this is one of the commands that uses the "-F" option so you can specify the file system type).

CHAPTER 3

Networking

Networking is the aspect of system administration that varies the most from installation to installation. Some installations, such as highly centralized and isolated systems which have only ASCII terminals connected to the system, require the system administrator to pay very little attention to networking. Other installations, such as highly distributed environments in which there are thousands of systems connected to a network that may span many geographic sites, may require the system administrator to pay a great deal of attention to networking. In this scenario the amount of time a system administrator devotes to networking may exceed the amount of time spent on all other system administration functions combined! Rather than ignore networking altogether, as the first system administrator might, or cover all aspects of network administration, as the second system administrator may require, I will cover in this chapter the aspects of network administration that most new system administrators care about. This is based on my experience working in a variety of new HP-UX installations. In the event that you require more networking background than I cover in this chapter, I would recommend the following book as an excellent source of networking information - *UNIX Networks* by Bruce H. Hunter and Karen Bradford Hunter (Prentice Hall, ISBN 0-13-08987-1). In addition, if you are going to be setting up any serious networking, the HP manual *Installing and Administering Internet Services* (part number b1030-90000) will be very helpful to you.

In this chapter I'll provide both background and setup information on many networking topics. Most of what I'll cover falls under the "Internet Services" umbrella in HP terminology. This includes ARPA and Berkeley Services. Here is a list of topics I'll cover:

- Some general UNIX networking background
- Internet Protocol (IP) addressing (classes A, B, and C)
- Subnet mask
- ARPA Services
- Berkeley commands
- Host name mapping
- Network File System (NFS) background
- HP-UX networking commands
- Some examples

UNIX Networking

Connecting to other machines is an important part of every HP-UX network. This means connecting to both other UNIX machines as well as non-UNIX machines. The machines must be physically connected to one another as well as functionally connected to one another so you can perform such tasks as transferring files and logging in to other systems. Many commands exist on your HP-UX system which provide you with the functionality to log in and transfer files between systems. These are known as the ARPA commands **telnet** and **ftp**.

The **telnet** command allows remote logins in a heterogenous environment. From your HP-UX system, for instance, you can **telnet** to non-HP-UX systems and log in to the system. After login on the remote system, you need to have an understanding of the operating system running on that system. If you need to connect to a different computer for only the purpose of transferring files to and from the system, then you can use **ftp**. This command allows you to transfer files between any two systems without having an understanding of the operating system running on the remote system.

These commands are somewhat primitive compared to the commands that can be issued between UNIX systems. To UNIX systems, networking is not an afterthought that needs to be added on to the system. The **ftp** and **telnet** commands come with your HP-UX system as well as more advanced commands and functionality you can use to communicate between your HP-UX system and other UNIX systems. These more advanced commands, known as Berkeley commands, allow you to perform many commands remotely such as copying files and directories and logging in. This functionality continues to increase to a point where you are working with files that can be stored on any system on the network and your access to these files is transparent to you with the Network File System (NFS).

Before I cover the setup required on your HP-UX system to achieve the level of network functionality you require, we'll take a look at some of the basics of UNIX networking.

What Is All This Ethernet, IEEE802.3, TCP/IP Stuff Anyway?

In order to understand how the networking on your HP-UX system works, you first need to understand the components of your network that exist on your HP-UX system. There are seven layers of network functionality that exist on your HP-UX system as shown in Figure 3-1. I'll cover the bottom four layers at a cursory level so you can see how each plays a part in the operation of your network and therefore be more informed when you configure and troubleshoot networking on your HP-UX system. The top layers are the ones that most HP-UX system administrators spend time working with because they are closest to the functionality you can relate to. The bottom layers are, however, also important to understand at some level so you can perform any configuration necessary to improve the network performance of your system which will have a major impact on the overall performance of your system.

Layer Number	Layer Name	Data Form	Comments
7	Application		User applications here.
6	Presentation		Applications prepared.
5	Session		Applications prepared.
4	Transport	Packet	Port to port transportation handled by TCP
3	Network	Datagram	Internet Protocol (IP) handles routing by either going directly to the destination or default router.
2	Link	Frame	Data encapsulated in Ethernet or IEEE 802.3 with source and destination addresses.
1	Physical		Physical connection between systems. Usually thinnet or twisted pair.

Figure 3-1 ISO/OSI Network Layer Functions

I'll start reviewing Figure 3-1 at the bottom with layer 1 and describe each of the four bottom layers. This is the International Standards Organization Open Systems Interconnection (ISO/OSI) model. It is helpful to visualizing the way in which networking layers interact.

Physical Layer

The beginning is the physical interconnect between the systems on your network. Without the **physical layer** you can't communicate between systems and all of the great functionality you would like to implement will not be possible. The physical layer converts the data you would like to transmit to the analog signals that travel along the wire (I'll assume for now that whatever physical layer you have in place uses wires). The information traveling into a network interface is taken off the wire and prepared for use by the next layer.

Link Layer

In order to connect to other systems local to your system, you use the link layer which is able to establish a connection to all the other systems on your local segment. This is the layer where you have either IEEE 802.3 or Ethernet. Your HP-UX system supports both of these "encapsulation" methods. This is called encapsulation because your data is put in one of these two forms (either IEEE 802.3 or Ethernet). Data is transferred at the link layer in frames (just another name for data) with the source and destination addresses and some other information attached. You might think that because there are two different encapsulation methods that they must be much different. This, however, is not the case. IEEE 802.3 and Ethernet are nearly identical. This is the reason your HP-UX system can handle both types of encapsulation. So with the bottom two layers you have a physical connection between your systems and data that is encapsulated into one of two formats with a source and destination address attached. Figure 3-2 lists the components of an **Ethernet** encapsulation and makes comments about IEEE802.3 encapsulation where appropriate.

destination address	6 bytes	address data is sent to
source address	6 bytes	address data is sent from
type	2 bytes	this is the "length count" in 802.3
data	46-1500 bytes	38-1492 bytes for 802.3; the difference in these two data sizes (MTU) can be seen with the **ifconfig** command
crc	4 bytes	checksum to detect errors

Figure 3-2 Ethernet Encapsulation

One interesting item to note is the difference in the maximum data size between IEEE 802.3 and Ethernet of 1492 and 1500 bytes, respectively. This is the Maximum Transfer Unit (MTU). The **ifconfig** command covered shortly displays the MTU for your interface. The data in Ethernet is called a *frame* (the re-encapsulation of data at the next layer up is called a *datagram* in IP, and encapsulation at two levels up is called a *packet* for TCP).

Keep in mind that Ethernet and IEEE 802.3 will run on the same physical connection, but there are indeed differences between the two encapsulation methods. With your HP-UX systems you won't have to spend much, if any, time setting up your network interface for encapsulation.

Network Layer

Next we work up to the third layer which is the network layer. This layer on UNIX systems is synonymous with Internet Protocol (IP). Data at this layer is called *datagrams*. This is the layer which handles the routing of data around the network. Data that gets routed with IP sometimes encounters an error of some type which is reported back to the source system with an Internet Control Message Protocol (ICMP) message. We will see some ICMP messages shortly. **ifconfig** and **netstat** are two HP-UX commands that are used to configure this routing that I'll cover shortly.

Unfortunately, the information IP uses does not conveniently fit inside an Ethernet frame so you end up with fragmented data. This is really re-encapsulation of the data so you end up with a lot of inefficiency as you work your way up the layers.

IP handles routing in a simple fashion. If data is sent to a destination connected directly to your system, then the data is sent directly to that system. If, on the other hand, the destination is not connected directly to your system, the data is sent to the default router. The default router then has the responsibility to handle getting the data to its destination. This routing can be a little tricky to understand so I'll cover it in detail shortly.

Transport Layer

This layer can be viewed as one level up from the network layer because it communicates with *ports*. TCP is the most common protocol found at this level and it forms packets which are sent from port to port. The port used by a program is defined in **/etc/services** along with the protocol (such as TCP). These ports are used by network programs such as **telnet**, **rlogin**, **ftp**, and so on. You can see that these programs, associated with ports, are the highest level we have covered while analyzing the layer diagram. **/etc/services** will be covered in more detail shortly.

Internet Protocol (IP) Addressing

The Internet Protocol address (IP address) is either a class "A," "B," or "C" address (there are also class "D" and "E" addresses I will not cover). A class "A" network supports many more nodes per network than either a class "B" or "C" network. IP addresses consist of four fields. The purpose of breaking down the IP address into four fields is to define a node (or host) address and a network address. Figure 3-3 summarizes the relationships between the classes and addresses.

Address Class	Networks	Nodes per Network	Bits Defining Network	Bits Defining Nodes per Network
A	a few	the most	8 bits	24 bits
B	many	many	16 bits	16 bits
C	the most	a few	24 bits	8 bits
Reserved	-	-	-	-

Figure 3-3 Comparison of Internet Protocol (IP) Addresses

These bit patterns are significant in that the number of bits defines the ranges of networks and nodes in each class. For instance, a class A address uses 8 bits to define networks and a class C address uses 24 bits to define networks. A class A address therefore supports fewer networks than a class C address. A class A address, however, supports many more nodes per network than a class C address. Taking these relationships one step further, we can now view the specific parameters associated with these address classes in Figure 3-4.

Figure 3-4   Address Classes

Address Class	Networks Supported	Nodes per Network	Address Range		
A	127	16777215	0.0.0.1	-	127.255.255.254
B	16383	65535	128.0.0.1	-	191.255.255.254
C	2097157	255	192.0.0.1	-	223.255.254.254
Reserved	-	-	224.0.0.0	-	255.255.255.255

Looking at the 32-bit address in binary form, you can see how to determine the class of an address:

Class "A"

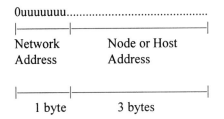

net.host.host.host

A class "A" address has the first bit set to 0. You can see how so many nodes per network can be supported with all of the bits devoted to the node or host address. The first bit of a class A address is 0 and the remaining 7 bits of the network portion are used to define the network. There are then a total of 3 bytes devoted to defining the nodes with a network.

Figure 3-4   Address Classes (Continued)

Class "B"   10uuuuuuuuuuuuuu...........................

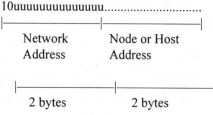

Network   Node or Host
Address   Address

2 bytes   2 bytes

net.net.host.host

A class "B" address has the first bit set to a 1 and
the second bit to a 0. There are more networks
supported here than with a class A address, but
fewer nodes per network. With a class B address
there are 2 bytes devoted to the network portion of
the address and 2 bytes devoted to the node portion of the address.

Class "C"   110uuuuuuuuuuuuuuuuuuuuuuu...............

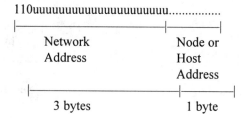

Network   Node or
Address   Host
                  Address

3 bytes   1 byte

net.net.net.host

A class "C" address has the first bit and second bit
set to 1 and the third bit is 0. The greatest number of
networks and fewest number of nodes per network
are associated with a class C address. With a class C
address there are 3 bytes devoted to the network
and 1 byte devoted to the nodes within a network.

These addresses are used in various setup files that will be covered shortly when the **/etc/hosts** file is described. Every interface on your network must have a unique IP address. Systems that have two network interfaces must have two unique IP addresses. If you are about to setup your network for the first time, your HP Technical Consultant can help you obtain your IP addresses. You will need these addresses before you can perform any of the setup steps covered later.

Let's now switch to the high level and look at some networking functionality and then come back to some of the details of configuring networking on HP-UX.

Using Networking

The ISO/OSI model is helpful for visualizing the way in which the networking layers interact. The model does not, however, tell you how to use the networking. This is really your goal. Before you perform any configuration you need to know how networking is used and then you can perform the appropriate configuration. Two widely used networking services that are worth taking a look at as you set up your system are ARPA and NFS.

The first networking product to configure on your system is HP 9000 ARPA Services - what I have been calling ARPA. ARPA is a combination of "ARPA Services" and "Berkeley Services." ARPA Services supports communications among systems running different operating systems, and Berkeley Services supports UNIX systems. The following is a list of the most common commands. Although there are many programs which can be run under each of these services, the following are the most commonly used ones in the HP-UX world. In some cases there are examples that show how these commands are used. For all of the examples the local host is **system1** and the remote host is **system2**.

ARPA Services (Communication among Systems with Different OS)

File Transfer Protocol (ftp) Transfer files, or multiple files, from one system to another. This is often used when transferring files between an HP-UX workstation and a personal computer or VAX, etc. The following example shows copying the file **/tmp/krsort.c** from system2 (remote host) to the local directory on system1 (local host).

	comments
$ ftp system2	Issue ftp command
Connected to system2.	
system2 FTP server (Version 16.2) ready.	
Name (system2:root): root	Log in to system2
Password required for root.	
Password:	Enter password
User root logged in.	
Remote system type is UNIX.	
Using binary mode to transfer files.	
ftp> **cd /tmp**	**cd** to **/tmp** on system2
CWD command successful	
ftp> **get krsort.c**	Get krsort.c file
PORT command successful	
Opening BINARY mode data connection for **krsort.c**	
Transfer complete.	
2896 bytes received in 0.08 seconds	
ftp> **bye**	Exit ftp
Goodbye.	
$	

In this example both systems are running HP-UX; however, the commands you issue through **ftp** are operating system independent. The **cd** for change directory and **get** commands used above work for any operating system on which **ftp** is running. If you become familiar with just a few **ftp** commands, you may find that transferring information in a heterogeneous networking environment is not difficult.

Chances are that you will be using your HP-UX system(s) in a heterogenous environment and may therefore use **ftp** to copy files and directories from one system to another. Since **ftp** is so widely used, I'll describe some of the more commonly used **ftp** commands.

ascii	Set the type of file transferred to ASCII. This means you will be transferring an ASCII file from one system to another. This is the default so you don't have to set it. Example: **ascii**
binary	Set the type of file transferred to binary. This means you'll be transferring a binary file from one system to another. If, for instance, you want to have a directory on your HP-UX system which will hold applications that you will copy to non-HP-UX systems, then you will want to use binary transfer. Example: **binary**
cd	Change to the specified directory on the remote host. Example: **cd /tmp**
dir	List the contents of a directory on the remote system to the screen or to a file on the local system if you specify a local file name.

get   Copy the specified remote file to the specified local file. If you don't specify a local file name, then the remote file name will be used.

lcd   Change to the specified directory on the local host.

Example: **lcd /tmp**

ls   List the contents of a directory on the remote system to the screen or to a file on the local system if you specify a local file name.

mget   Copy multiple files from the remote host to the local host.

Example: **mget *.c**

put   Copy the specified local file to the specified remote file. If you don't specify a remote file name, then the local file name will be used.

Example: **put test.c**

mput   Copy multiple files from the local host to the remote host.

Example: **mput *.c**

system   Show the type of operating system running on the remote host.

Example: **system**

bye/quit   Close the connection to the remote host.

                        Example: **bye**

There are other **ftp** commands in addition to those I have covered here. If you need more information on these commands or wish to review additional **ftp** commands, the HP-UX manual pages for **ftp** will be helpful.

telnet   Used for communication with another host using the telnet protocol. Telnet is an alternative to using **rlogin** described later. The following example show how to establish a telnet connection with the remote host system2.

	comments
$ telnet system2	
Connected to system2.	Telnet to system2
HP-UX system2	
login: **root**	Log in as root on system2
password:	Enter password
Welcome to system2.	
$	HP-UX prompt on system2

Domain Name System

                        This is commonly used to support communication among systems on a large network such as the Internet. I am not going to cover this but the *Installing and Administering Internet Services* manual thoroughly covers this topic.

Berkeley Commands (Communication between UNIX Systems)

Remote Copy (rcp)

> This program is used to copy files and directories from one UNIX system to another. To copy /tmp/krsort.c from system1 to system2 you could do the following:

$ rcp   system2:/tmp/krsort.c /tmp/krsort.c

You need to configure some networking files to get this level of functionality. In this example the user who issues the command is considered "equivalent" on both systems and has permission to copy files from one system to the other with **rcp**. (These will be described shortly.)

Remote login (rlogin)

> Supports login to a remote UNIX system. To remotely log in to system2 from system1 you would do the following:

$ rlogin system2

password:

Welcome to system2

$

If a password is requested when the user issues the **rlogin** command, the users are not equivalent on the two systems. If no password is requested, then the users are indeed equivalent.

Remote shell (remsh)

With the **remsh** command you can sit on one HP-UX system and issue a command to be run remotely on a different HP-UX system and have the results displayed locally. In this case a **remsh** is issued to show a long listing of / **tmp/krsort.c**. The command is run on system2 but the result is displayed on system1 where the command was typed:

$ remsh system2 ll /tmp/krsort.c

-rwxrwxrwx 1 root sys 2896 Sept 1 10:54 /tmp/krsort.c

$

In this case the users on system1 and system2 must be equivalent or permission will be denied to issue this command.

Remote who (rwho)

Find out who is logged in on a remote UNIX system. Here is the output of issuing **rwho**:

$ rwho

```
root      system1:ttyu0    Sept 1 19:21
root      system2:console  Sept 1 13:17
tomd      system2:ttyp2    Sept 1 13:05
 |           |        |         |       | > time of login
 |           |        |         | > day of login
 |           |        |
 |           |        | > terminal line
 |           | > machine name
 |
 | > user name
```

For **rwho** to work, the **rwho** daemon (**rwhod**) must be running.

Host Name Mapping

Your most important decision related to networking is how you will
implement host name mapping in ARPA. There are three techniques for
host name mapping:

- Berkeley Internet Named Domain (BIND)

- Network Information Service (NIS)

- HP-UX file **/etc/hosts**

The most common and simplest way to implement host name
mapping is with **/etc/hosts**, so I'll cover that technique here. Keep in
mind that there are networking manuals devoted to many networking
topics including NFS, ARPA, and others. These manuals serve as
good reference material if you need to know more about networking
than is covered here.

/etc/hosts

This file contains information about the other systems you are connected
to. It contains the Internet address of each system, the system name, and
any aliases for the system name. If you modify your **/etc/hosts** file to
contain the names of the systems on your network, you have provided the
basis for **rlogin** to another system. There is an important distinction here
that confuses many new HP-UX administrators. Although you can now
rlogin to other UNIX systems, you cannot yet **rcp** or **remsh** to another
system. Don't worry though; adding **remsh** and **rcp** functionality is easy
and I'll show you this next. Here is an example **/etc/hosts** file:

127.0.0.1	localhost	loopback
15.32.199.42	a4410827	
15.32.199.28	a4410tu8	
15.32.199.7	a4410922	
15.32.199.21	a4410tu1	
15.32.199.22	a4410tu2	
15.32.199.62	a4410730	
15.32.199.63	hpxterm1	
15.32.199.64	a4410rd1	
15.32.199.62	a4410750	hp1

This file is in the following format:

< internet_address >   < official_hostname >   < alias >

The Internet Protocol address (IP address) is either a class "A," "B," or "C" address. A class "A" network supports many more nodes per network than either a class "B" or "C" network. The purpose of breaking down the IP address into four fields is to define a node (or host) address and a network address. The figures earlier presented describe these classes in detail.

Assuming the above **/etc/hosts** file contains class "C" addresses, the rightmost field is the host or node address and other three fields comprise the network address.

You could use either the official_hostname or alias from the **/etc/ hosts** file when issuing one of the ARPA or Berkeley commands described earlier. For instance, either of the following ARPA commands will work:

$ telnet a4410750

or

$ telnet hp1

Similarly, either of the following Berkeley commands will work:

$ **rlogin a4410750**

or

$ **rlogin hp1**

Subnet Mask

Your HP-UX system uses the subnet mask to determine if an IP datagram
is for a host on its own subnet, a host on a different subnet but the same
network, or a host on a different network. Using subnets you can have
some hosts on one subnet and other hosts on a different subnet. The subnets can be separated by routers or other networking electronics that connect the subnets.

To perform routing, the only aspects of an address that your router
uses are the net and subnet. The subnet mask is used to mask the host part
of the address. Because you can setup network addresses in such a way
that you are the only one who knows which part of the address is the host,
subnet, and network, you use the subnet mask to make your system aware
of the bits of your IP address that are for the host and which are for the
subnet.

In its simplest form what you are really doing with subnet masking is
defining what portion of your IP address defines the host, and what part
defines the network. One of the most confusing aspects of working with
subnet masks is that most books will show the subnet masks in Figure 3-5
as the most common.

Address Class	Decimal	Hex
A	255.0.0.0	0xff000000
B	255.255.0.0	0xffff0000
C	255.255.255.0	0xffffff00

Figure 3-5 Subnet Masks

This, however, assumes you are devoting as many bits as possible to the network and as many bits as possible to the host and no subnets are used. Figure 3-6 shows an example of using subnetting with a class B address.

Address Class	Class B		
host IP address	152.128.	12.	1
breakdown	network	subnet	hostid
number of bits	16 bits	8 bits	8 bits
subnet mask in decimal	255.255.	255.	0
subnet mask in hexadecimal	0xffffff00		
Example of different host on same subnet	152.128.	12.	2
Example of host on different subnet	152.128.	13.	1

Figure 3-6 Class B IP Address and Subnet Mask Example

In this figure the first two bytes of the subnet mask (255.255) define the network, the third byte (255) defines the subnet, and the fourth byte (0) is devoted to the host ID. Although this subnet mask for a class B address did not appear in the earlier default subnet mask figure, the subnet mask of 255.255.255.0 is widely used in class B networks to support subnetting.

How does your HP-UX system perform the comparison using the subnet mask of 255.255.255.0 to determine that 152.128.12.1 and 152.128.13.1 are on different subnets? Figure 3-7 shows this comparison.

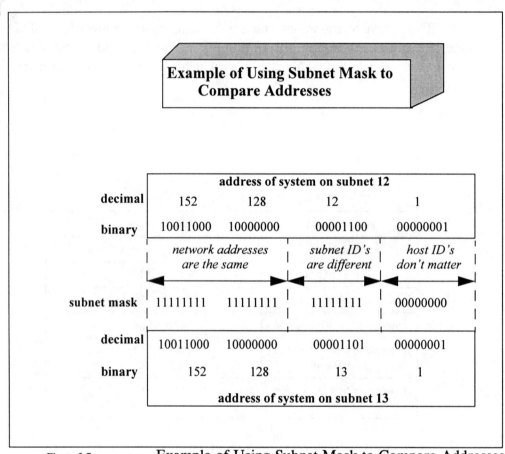

**Example of Using Subnet Mask to
Compare Addresses**

	address of system on subnet 12			
decimal	152	128	12	1
binary	10011000	10000000	00001100	00000001
	network addresses are the same		*subnet ID's are different*	*host ID's don't matter*
subnet mask	11111111	11111111	11111111	00000000
decimal	10011000	10000000	00001101	00000001
binary	152	128	13	1
	address of system on subnet 13			

Figure 3-7   Example of Using Subnet Mask to Compare Addresses

Figure 3-8 shows these two systems on the different subnets.

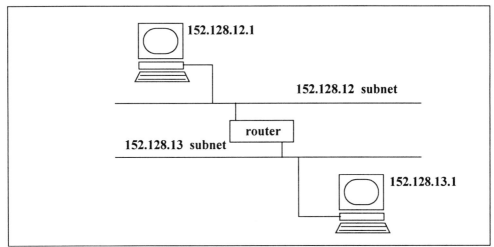

Figure 3-8   Class B Systems on Different Subnets

You don't have to use the 8-bit boundaries to delineate the network, subnet, and host ID fields. If, for instance, you wanted to use part of the subnet field for the host ID, you could do so. A good reason for this would be to accommodate future expandability. You might want subnets 12, 13, 14, and 15 to be part of the same subnet today and make these into separate subnets in the future. Figure 3-9 shows this.

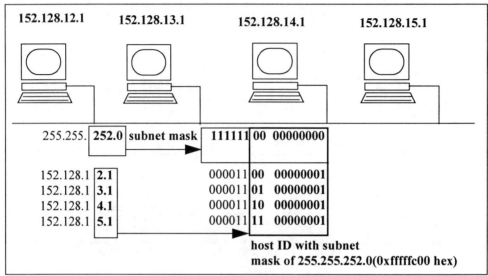

Figure 3-9   Future Expandability Using Subnet Mask

These systems are connected to the same subnet even though part of
the third byte, normally associated with the subnet, is used for the host
ID. In the future, the subnet mask could be changed to 255.255.255.0 and
have four separate subnets of 12, 13, 14, 15. This would require putting
routers in place to route to these separate subnets.

/etc/hosts.equiv

If you don't want users to have to issue a password when they **rlogin**
to a remote system, you can set up equivalent hosts by editing this
file. If you have many hosts on your network that you wish to be
accessed by the same users, then you will want to create this file. The
login names must be the same on both the local and remote systems
for **/etc/hosts.equiv** to allow the user to bypass entering a password.
You can either list all of the equivalent hosts in **/etc/hosts.equiv** or
you can list the host and user name you wish to be equivalent. Users
can now use **rcp** and **remsh** because they are equivalent users on these

systems. I usually just enter all of the host names on the network. Here is an example of **/etc/hosts.equiv**:

```
a4410730
a4410tu1
a4410tu2
hpxterm1
a4410827
a4410750
```

Keep in mind the potential security risks of using **/etc/ hosts.equiv**. If a user can log in to a remote system without a password, you have reduced the overall level of security on your network. Even though your users may find it convenient to not have to enter a password when logging into a remote system, you have given every user in **/etc/hosts.equiv** access to the entire network. If you could ensure that all of the permissions on all the files and directories on all systems were properly set up, then you wouldn't care who had access to what system. In the real HP-UX world, however, permissions are sometimes not what they are supposed to be. Users have a strong tendency to "browse around," invariably stumbling upon a file they want to copy which they really shouldn't have access to.

/.rhosts

This file is the **/etc/hosts.equiv** for superuser. If you log in as root, you will want to have this file configured with exactly the same information as **/etc/hosts.equiv**. If you do this, however, you have compounded your network security risk by allowing superuser on any system to log in to a remote system without a root password. If you are the undisputed ruler of your network and you're 100 percent certain there are no security holes, then you may want to set up **/.rhosts** so you don't have to issue a password when you log in remotely to a system as superuser. From a security standpoint, however, you should know this is frowned upon.

Now that you have made the appropriate entries in **/etc/hosts**, **/etc/hosts.equiv**, and **/.rhosts**, you can use the ARPA Services commands **ftp** and **telnet** as well as the Berkeley commands **rcp**, **rlogin**, **remsh**, and **rwho**.

I have described the process of setting up the appropriate files to get the most commonly used ARPA Services up and running. Virtually every HP-UX system administrator will use the functionality I have described here. It may be that you require additional ARPA functionality such as BIND. You will want to refer to the *HP-UX Networking Manuals* if you need to configure your networking beyond what I have covered here.

Network File System (NFS)

NFS allows you to mount disks on remote systems so they appear as though they are local to your system. Similarly, NFS allows remote systems to mount your local disk so it looks as though it is local to the remote system. Configuring NFS to achieve this functionality is simple. You have to perform four activities to get NFS going on your system:

1. Start NFS.

2. Specify whether your system will be an NFS Client, NFS Server, or both.

3. Specify which of your local file systems can be mounted by remote systems.

4. Specify the remote disks you want to mount and view as if they were local to your system.

As with ARPA, there are other aspects to NFS you could enable, but I will again cover what I know to be the NFS functionality that nearly every HP-UX installation uses.

So far I have been using NFS terminology loosely. Here are definitions of some of the more important NFS terms.

Node   A computer system that is attached to or is part of a computer network.

Client   A node that requests data or services from other nodes (servers).

Server   A node that provides data or services to other nodes (clients) on the network.

File System   A disk partition or logical volume.

Export   Make a file system available for mounting on remote nodes using NFS.

Mount   To access a remote file system using NFS.

Mount Point   The name of a directory on which the NFS file system is mounted.

Import   To mount a remote file system.

SAM is the best way to enable NFS. Among other things, SAM updates the **/etc/rc.config.d/nfsconf** file. This configuration file contains NFS information such as whether or not your system is an NFS client, an NFS server, and starts the daemon called **/usr/sbin/rpc.mountd**.

mountd is a remote procedure call server that handles file system mount requests. Here are some of the variables SAM may change for you:

```
NFS_CLIENT=1
NFS_SERVER=1
AUTOMOUNT=1
START_MOUNTD=1
```

You may want to take a look at this file for a good explanation of these and the other variables in this file. The automount variable, for instance, will mount remote file systems only when you make a request to them.

If your system is going to be an NFS server and you will be exporting file systems, SAM will create the **/etc/exports** and **/etc/xtab** files which specify the file systems to be exported. These files have in them the directory exported and options such as "ro" for read only, and "anon" which handles requests from anonymous users. If "anon" is equal to 65535, then anonymous users are denied access.

The following is an example **/etc/exports** file in which **/opt/app1** is exported to everyone but anonymous users, and **/opt/app2** is exported only to the system named system2:

```
/opt/app1    -anon=65534
/opt/app2    -access=system2
```

You may need to run **/usr/sbin/exportfs -a** if you add a file system to export.

Remote file systems to be mounted locally are put in **/etc/fstab** by SAM. Here is an example of an entry in **/etc/fstab** of a remote file system that is mounted locally. The remote directory **/opt/app3** on system2 is mounted locally under **/opt/app3**:

```
system2:/opt/app3    /opt/app3    nfs    rw,suid    0    0
```

You can use the **showmount** command to show all remote systems (clients) that have mounted a local file system. **showmount** is useful for determining the file systems that are most often mounted by clients with NFS. The output of **showmount** is particularly easy to read because it lists the host name and the directory which was mounted by the client. There are the three following options to the **showmount** command:

-**a** prints output in the format "name:directory".

-**d** lists all of the local directories that have been remotely mounted by clients.

-**e** prints a list of exported file systems.

Other Networking Commands and Setup

Setting up networking is usually straightforward. Should you encounter a problem, however, it is helpful to have an understanding of some networking commands that can be life savers. In addition, there can be some tricky aspects to networking setup if you have some networking hardware that your HP-UX systems must interface to routers, gateways, bridges, etc. I'll give an example of one such case, connecting an HP-UX system to a router. At the same time I'll cover some of the most handy networking commands as part of this description.

Consider Figure 3-10 in which an HP-UX system is connected directly to a router.

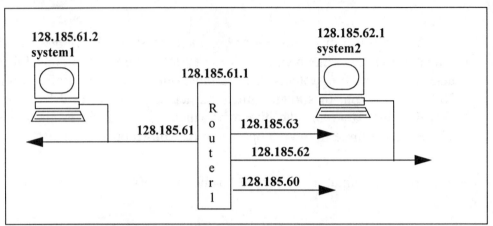

Figure 3-10 HP-UX System and Router Example

Here we have an HP-UX system connected to segment 128.185.61. This is a class "B" Internet address with subnetting enabled.

The **/etc/hosts** file needs to have in it the HP-UX system with node ID 2, the router, and any other systems on this segment or segments on the other side of the router.

If the router is properly configured, we should be able to seamlessly connect to systems on segments 60, 62, and 63 from 61. The router should be configured to allow our system to connect to systems on other segments (60, 62, and 63) by going through the router. There was some unforeseen configuration required to make this simple network operate seamlessly. In this case there was a problem getting system1 to connect to systems on the other side of the router on 60, 62, and 63. Before discussing the additional configuration that needed to be done, I'll first show the **/etc/hosts** file and then use some very useful HP-UX commands that show the state of the network. Here is the **/etc/hosts** file showing just the HP-UX system and router:

$ cat /etc/hosts

```
127.0.0.1    localhosts loopback
128.185.61.1  router1      # router
128.185.61.2  system1      # HP-UX system on 61
128.185.62.1  system2      # HP-UX system on 62
```

This host file is simple and allows system1 to connect to router1 and system2. The connection from system1 to system2 takes place by going through the router.

ping

How do I know I have a connection between system1 and the router and the other systems on the other side of the router? I use the **ping** command. **ping** is a simple command that sends an ICMP echo packet to the host you specify once per second. You may recall that ICMP was covered earlier under the network, or third layer. **ping** stands for Packet InterNet Groper. Here is how I know that system1 is connected to router1:

$ ping router1

PING router1: 64 byte packets
64 bytes from 128.185.61.2: icmp_seq=0. time=0. ms
64 bytes from 128.185.61.2: icmp_seq=1. time=0. ms
64 bytes from 128.185.61.2: icmp_seq=2. time=0. ms

Each line of output here represents a response that was returned from the device that was pinged. This means that the device responded. You will continue to get this response indefinitely and have to type ^c (control c) to terminate the **ping**. If no output is produced, as shown below, then there is no response and you may have a problem between your system and the device you are checking the connection to.

$ ping system2

PING router1: 64 byte packets

You would see this message and that is as far as you would get. A ^c will kill the **ping** and you'll see that some number of packets were sent and none were received. I did indeed get this response when issuing the **ping** command so I know there is a problem with the connection between system1 and router1.

ping should be used only for testing purposes such as manual fault isolation because it generates a substantial amount of network traffic. You would not want to use **ping** on an ongoing basis such as in a script that is running continuously.

A nice variation of **ping** that I use is to specify a packet size of 4096 bytes, rather than the default of 64 bytes shown in the previous examples, and count the number of times **ping** will transmit before terminating, rather than having to type ^c to terminate **ping**. The following example shows this:

$ ping router1 4096 5

PING router1: 64 byte packets
4096 bytes from 128.185.51.2: icmp_seq=0. time=8. ms
4096 bytes from 128.185.51.2: icmp_seq=1. time=8. ms
4096 bytes from 128.185.51.2: icmp_seq=2. time=9. ms
4096 bytes from 128.185.51.2: icmp_seq=3. time=8. ms
4096 bytes from 128.185.51.2: icmp_seq=4. time=8. ms

Notice that the time required to transmit and receive a response, the round-trip time, is substantially longer than with only 64 bytes transmitted. I usually find that the round-trip time for 64 bytes is 0 ms, although this depends on a number of factors, including network topology and network traffic.

lanscan

lanscan is used to get Local Area Network (LAN) device configuration status. An example is shown below.

$ lanscan (HP-UX 10.x)

Hardware Path	Station Address	Crd In#	Hardwr State	Net-Interface Name	Unit State	NM ID	MAC Type	HP DLPI Support	Mjr Num
2/0/2	0x080009353626	0	UP	lan0	UP	4	ETHER	Yes	52

lanscan provides a good summary of the state and configuration of your network interfaces. In this case there is one LAN card configured in the system. You would receive a line for each LAN card that is configured into your system (many systems have two identical LAN cards or one IEEE 802.3 card and one IEEE 802.5, or token ring, card). Here is a brief description of the **lanscan** headings in the order they appear above:

- Series 700 or 800 hardware path.
- The station address, which is sometimes known as the LAN or Ethernet address.
- Card interface number in 10.x only.
- The hardware state of the device which should be "UP."
- The name of the network interface.
- The network management ID.
- MAC type in the 10.x output.
- The logical unit (lu) of the device (present in 9.x version only).
- Whether or not DLPI is supported in 10.x output.
- Major number of driver for LAN interface.

Using the "-v" option produces additional information.

netstat

From the earlier description of the subnet mask, you can see that routing from one host to another can be configured in a variety of ways. The path that information takes in getting from one host to another depends on routing.

You can obtain information related to routing with the **netstat** command. The **-r** option to **netstat** shows the routing tables, which you usually want to know, and the **-n** option can be used to print network addresses as numbers rather than as names. With the **-v** option you get additional information related to routing such as subnet mask. In the following examples **netstat** is issued with the **-r** option (this will be used when describing the **netstat** output), the **-rn** options, and the **-rnv** options so you can compare the two outputs.

```
# netstat -r

Routing tables
Destination      Gateway        Flags   Refs        Use  Interface  Pmtu PmtuTime
localhost        localhost      UH         0        465  lo0        4608
system1          localhost      UH         2     837711  lo0        4608
default          wellfleet      UG        12    1051826  lan0       1500
169.200.112      system1        U             751821954  lan0       1500
```

```
# netstat -rn

Routing tables
Destination      Gateway          Flags  Refs        Use  Interface  Pmtu PmtuTime
127.0.0.1        127.0.0.1        UH        0        465  lo0        4608
169.200.112.1    127.0.0.1        UH        2     837735  lo0        4608
default          169.200.112.250  UG       12    1051827  lan0       1500
169.200.112.0    169.200.112.1    U            751821991  lan0       1500
```

```
# netstat -rnv

Routing tables
Dest/Netmask    Gateway         Flags  Refs      Use  Interface  Pmtu PmtuTime
127.0.0.1/255.255.255.255
                127.0.0.1       UH        0      465  lo0        4608
169.200.112.1/255.255.255.255
                127.0.0.1       UH        1   837756  lo0        4608
default/0.0.0.0 169.200.112.250 UG       14  1051834  lan0       1500
169.200.112.0/255.255.255.0
                169.200.112.1   U        751822050  lan0         1500
```

With **netstat** there is some information provided about the router which is the middle entry. The **-r** option shows information about routing, but there are many other useful options to this command. Of particular interest in this output is "Flags," which defines the type of routing that takes place. Here are descriptions of the most common flags from the HP-UX manual pages:

1 = U	Route to a *network* via a gateway that is the local host itself.
3 = UG	Route to a *network* via a gateway that is the remote host.
5 = UH	Route to a *host* via a gateway which is the local host itself.
7 = UGH	Route to a *host* via a remote gateway which is a host.

The first line is for the local host or loopback interface called **lo0** at address 127.0.0.1 (you can see this address in the **netstat -rn** example). The UH flags indicate the destination address is the local host itself. This class A address allows a client and server on the same host to communicate with one another with TCP/IP. A datagram sent to the loopback interface won't go out onto the network; it will simply go through the loopback.

The second line is for the default route. This entry says send packets to router1 if a more specific route can't be found. In this case the router has a UG under Flags. Some routers are configured with a U; others, such as the one in this example, with a UG. I've found that I usually end up determining through trial and error whether a U or UG is required. If there is a U in Flags and I am unable to ping a system on the other side of a router, a UG usually fixes the problem.

The third line is for the system's network interface **lan0**. This means to use this network interface for packets to be sent to 169.200.112.

There are also two forms of **netstat** that I use to obtain network statistics as opposed to routing information. The first is **netstat -i** which shows the state of interfaces that are autoconfigured. Since I am most often interested in getting a summary of lan0, I issue this command. Although **netstat -i** gives a good rundown of lan0, such as the network it is on, its name and so on.

The following diagram shows the output of **netstat -i**:

```
# netstat -i

Name  Mtu   Network      Address           Ipkts Ierrs   Opkts Oerrs  Coll
ni0*  0     none         none                  0     0       0     0     0
ni1*  0     none         none                  0     0       0     0     0
lo0   4608  loopback     127.0.0.1           232     0     232     0     0
lan0  1500  169.200.112  169.200.112.2   3589746     2   45630     0   104
```

Here is a description of the nine fields in the **netstat** example:

Name   The name of your network interface (Name), in this case "lan0."

MTU   The "maximum transmission unit" which is the maximum packet size sent by the interface card.

Network   The network address of the LAN to which the interface card is connected (169.200).

Address   The host name of your system. This is the symbolic name of your system as it appears in the file /etc/**hosts**.

Start of statistical information:

Ipkts   The number of packets received by the interface card, in this case lan0.

Ierrs
: The number of errors detected on incoming packets by the interface card.

Opkts
: The number of packets transmitted by the interface card.

Oerrs
: The number of errors detected during the transmission of packets by the interface card.

Collis
: The number of collisions (Collis) that resulted from packet traffic.

netstat provides cumulative data since the node was last powered up; you might have a long elapsed time over which data was accumulated. If you are interested in seeing useful statistical information, you can use **netstat** with different options. You can also specify an interval to report statistics. I usually ignore the first entry since it shows all data since the system was last powered up. This means the data includes non-prime hours when the system was idle. I prefer to view data at the time the system is working its hardest. This following **netstat** example provides network interface information every 5 seconds.

```
# netstat -I lan0 5
(lan0) -> input          output         (Total) -> input          output
    packets  errs  packets  errs colls      packets  errs  packets  errs colls
    3590505    2    45714    0   104        3590737    2    45946    0    104
        134    0        5    0     0            134    0        5    0      0
        174    0        0    0     0            174    0        0    0      0
        210    0       13    0     0            210    0       13    0      0
        165    0        0    0     0            165    0        0    0      0
        169    0        0    0     0            169    0        0    0      0
        193    0        0    0     0            193    0        0    0      0
        261    0        7    0     0            261    0        7    0      0
        142    0        8    0     0            142    0        8    0      0
        118    0        0    0     0            118    0        0    0      0
        143    0        0    0     0            143    0        0    0      0
        149    0        0    0     0            149    0        0    0      0
```

With this example you get multiple outputs of what is taking place on the LAN interface. As I mentioned earlier, you may want to ignore the first output since it includes information over a long time period. This may include a time when your network was idle and therefore the data is not important to you.

You can specifiy the network interface on which you want statistics reported by using **-I interface**; in the case of the example it was **-I lan0**. An interval of five seconds was also used in this example.

lanadmin and landiag

lanadmin is a new command for HP-UX 10.x that is used to perform local area network administration. **lanadmin** is the same program as **landiag**; both have a menu-driven interface which allows you to perform such tasks as display LAN statistics and reset the LAN interface.

route

The information displayed with **netstat** are the routing tables for your system. Some are automatically created with the **ifconfig** command when your system is booted or the network interface is initialized. Routes to networks and hosts that are not directly connected to your system are entered with the **route** command.

You can make routing changes on the fly, as I did to change the Flags from U to UG:

$ /usr/sbin/route add default 128.185.61.1 3

First is the **route** command. Second we specify we wish to add a route; the other option is to delete a route. Third, we specify the destination, in this case the default. This could be a specific host name, a network name, an IP address, or default which signifies the wildcard gateway route which is shown in our example. Fourth is the gateway through which the destination is reached. In the above example the IP address was used but this could also be a host name. The 3 corresponds to the count which is used to specify whether the gateway is the local host or a remote gateway. If the gateway is the local host, then a count of 0 is used. If the gateway is a remote host, which is the case in the example, a count of >0 is used. This will correspond to UG for Flags. This manually changed the network routing table by adding a default route with the appropriate Flags.

Before issuing **/usr/sbin/route** with the **add** option, you can first use the **delete** option to remove the existing default route which is not working.

ifconfig

The **ifconfig** command provides additional information on a LAN interface. The following example provides the configuration of a network interface:

$ /etc/ifconfig lan0
lan0:   flages=863<UP,BROADCAST,NOTRAILERS,RUNNING>
           inet 128.185.61.2 netmask ffff0000 broadcast 128.185.61.255

From this example we can quickly see that the interface is up, it has an address of 128.185.61.2, and a netmask of ffff0000.

You can use **ifconfig** to get the status of a network interface as I have done here to assign an address to a network interface, or to configure network interface parameters. The network address you have will fall into classes such as "A," "B," or "C" as mentioned earlier. You want to be sure you know the class of your network before you start configuring your LAN interface. This example is a class "B" network so the netmask is defined as ffff0000 (typical for a class "B" address) as opposed to ffffff00 which is typical for a class "C" network. The netmask is used to determine how much of the address to reserve for subdividing the network into smaller networks. The netmask can be represented in hex, as shown above, or in decimal format as in the **/etc/hosts** file. Here is the **ifconfig** command I issued to configure the interface:

$ /etc/ifconfig lan0 inet 128.185.61.2 netmask 255.255.0.0

- The 255.255.0.0 corresponds to the hex ffff000 shown earlier for the class "B" subnet mask.

- lan0 is the interface being configured.

- inet is the address family, which is currently the only one supported.

- 128.185.61.2 is the address of the LAN interface for system1.

- netmask shows how to subdivide the network

- 255.255.0.0 is the same as ffff0000 which is the netmask for a class "B" address.

I have made good use of **netstat, lanscan, ping,** and **ifconfig** to help get the status of the network. **ifconfig, route,** and **/etc/hosts** are used to configure the network should you identify changes you need to make. The subnet examples show how flexible you can be when configuring your network for both your current and future needs. In simple networks you may not need to use many of these commands, or complex subnetting. In complex networks, or at times when you encounter configuration difficulties, you may have to make extensive use of these commands. In either case, network planning is an important part of setting up HP-UX systems.

CHAPTER 4

System Administration Manager (SAM)

SAM Overview

SAM is a program you can use that automates performing various system administration tasks. I would like to go on record right now and suggest you use System Administration Manager (SAM) for performing routine system administration tasks. You'll talk to UNIX experts who say that any tool that automates system administration tasks is doing things behind your back and is therefore "evil." Don't believe them. SAM is a tool developed by HP-UX gurus who know as much about UNIX as anyone. I have met and worked with some of these people and they have labored long and hard to give you and me a tool that *helps* us do our job and doesn't hinder us from doing it. Does this mean that you blindly use SAM? Of course not. If you have no idea how TCP/IP works, then you shouldn't have SAM perform networking configuration for you. Similarly, you wouldn't want SAM to add users to your system without knowing what files will be updated. On the other hand, there is no reason to do this manually if SAM can do this for you. Let SAM help you perform your job better and don't feel guilty about it.

Four features of SAM that make it particularly useful:

1. It provides a central point from which system administration tasks can be performed. This includes both the built-in tasks that come with SAM as well as those you can add into the SAM menu hierarchy. You can run SAM on a remote system and display it locally so you do truly have a central point of control.

2. It provides an easy way to perform tasks which are difficult in that you would have to perform many steps. SAM performs these steps for you.

3. It provides a summary of what your system currently looks like for any of the categories of administration tasks you wish to perform. If you want to do something with the disks on your system, SAM first lists the disks you currently have connected. If you want to play with a printer, SAM first lists all your printers and plotters for you. This cuts down on mistakes by putting your current configuration right in front of you.

4. You can assign non-root users to perform some of the system administration functions in SAM. If, for instance, you feel comfortable assigning one of your associates to manage users, you can give them permission to perform user-related tasks and give another user permission to perform backups, and so on.

There are some tasks SAM can't perform for you. SAM does most routine tasks for you, but troubleshooting a problem is not considered routine. Troubleshooting a problem gives you a chance to show off and to hone your system administration skills.

When SAM is performing routine tasks for you, it isn't doing anything you couldn't do yourself by issuing a series of HP-UX commands. SAM provides a simple user interface that allows you to perform tasks by selecting menu items and entering pertinent information essential to performing the task.

Running and Using SAM as Superuser

To run SAM, log in as root and type

$ sam

This will invoke SAM. If you have a graphics display, SAM will run with the Motif interface. If you have a character-based display, SAM will run in character mode. You have nearly all the same functionality in both modes, but the Motif environment is much more pleasant to use.

If you have a graphics display and SAM does not come up in a Motif window, you probably don't have your DISPLAY variable set for root.

Type the following to set the DISPLAY variable for default POSIX, Korn, and Bourne shells:

$ DISPLAY=system_name:0.0
$ export DISPLAY

Just substitute the name of your computer for *system_name*. This can be set in your local **.profile** file.

Type the following to set the DISPLAY variable for C shell:

 # setenv DISPLAY system_name:0.0

Again you would substitute the name of your computer for system_name. This would typically be done in your **.login** file.

Figure 4-1 shows the System Administration Manager running in graphics mode. This is the top-level window of the hierarchical SAM environment called the Functional Area Launcher (FAL). The 13 categories or areas of management shown are the default functional areas managed by SAM. You can select one of these functional areas and be placed in a subarea. Because SAM is hierarchical, you may find yourself working your way down through several levels of the hierarchy before you reach the desired level. I'll cover each of these categories or areas in this chapter.

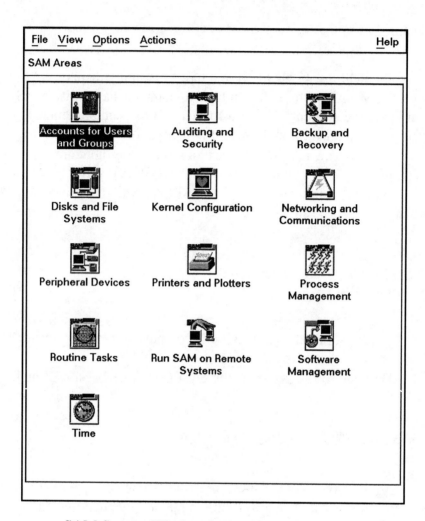

Figure 4-1 SAM Startup Window in Graphics Mode

In addition to selecting a functional area, you can select from the pull-down menu bar across the top of the SAM window. I will indicate selections made in SAM and keyboard keys in this chapter with italics. The five selections are *File, View, Options, Actions,* and *Help*. The title line shown in the figure reads *SAM Areas*. If you're running Restricted SAM Builder, you will also see a status line with the message "Privileges for user: <username>". As you progress down the hierarchy the title line will change to reflect your level in the SAM hierarchy. You can move into one of the areas shown, such as *Backup and Recovery*, by double-clicking the left mouse button on this functional area. You move back up the hierarchy by selecting the *Actions-Close Level* menu pick.

You don't need a graphics display to run SAM. You have access to nearly all the same functionality on a text terminal as you do on a graphics terminal. Figure 4-2 is SAM running in character mode with the same 13 functional areas you have in graphics mode.

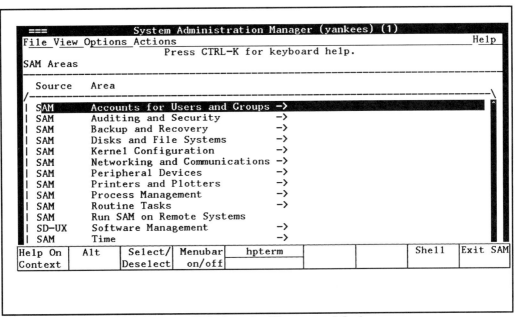

Figure 4-2 SAM Startup Window in Character Mode

The View menu can be used in character mode to tailor the information desired, filter out some entries, or search for particular entries.

Because you don't have a mouse on a text terminal, you use the keyboard to make selections. The point and click method of using SAM when in graphics mode is highly preferable to using the keyboard; however, the same structure to the functional areas exists in both environments. When you see an item in reverse video on the text terminal (such as *Accounts*

For Users and Groups in Figure 4-2), you know you have that item selected. After having selected *Accounts For Users and Groups* as shown in the Figure 4-2, you would then use the *tab* key (or *F4*) to get to the menu bar, use the < - -> keys to select the desired menu, and use the *space bar* to display the menu. This is where having a mouse to make your selections is highly desirable. Figure 4-3 shows a menu bar selection for both a text and graphic display. In both cases the *Actions* menu of *Disks and File Systems* has been selected.

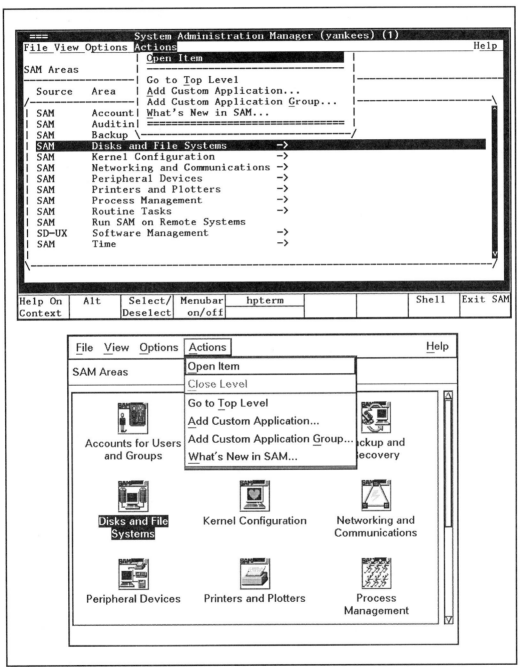

Figure 4-3 SAM Menu Selection for Text and Graphics Displays

Of particular interest on the pull-down menu are *Add Custom Application* and *Add Custom Application Group*. When you use *Add Custom Application Group*, you are prompted for the *Label* and optional *Help File* for the group. After you enter this information, a new icon appears, if you have a graphics display, with the name of your application group. You can then go into this application group and *Add Custom Applications*. This means that you can customize SAM to meet your specific administration needs by adding functionality to SAM. After you familiarize yourself with the aspects of system administration SAM can help you with, you'll want to test adding your own application to SAM. Adding a simple application like opening a log file or issuing the **/bin/find** command will take you only seconds to create.

Running Restricted SAM Builder

SAM can be configured to provide a subset of its overall functionality to specified users such as operators. You may, for instance, wish to give a user the ability to start a backup but not the ability to manage disks and file systems. With the Restricted SAM Builder you have control of the functional areas specified users have access to.

You can specify areas within SAM that specific users can have access to. You may have users to whom you would like to give access to backup and restore, or managing users, or handling the print spooler. Invoking SAM with the "-r" option will allow you to select a user to whom you want to give access to a SAM area and then select the specific area(s) you want to enable that user to have access to. You can also give a user partial access to some areas such as providing access to backup and recovery but not providing access to handling automated backups. As you progress through the detailed descriptions of SAM areas in this chapter, you'll want to think about which of these areas may be appropriate for some of your users to have access to.

When specifying the functionality you wish to give a user, you invoke SAM with the "-r" option initiating a Restricted SAM Builder session. After you have setup a user with specific functionality, you can then invoke SAM with both the "-r" and "-f" options with the login name of a user you wish to test. The functionality of the user can be tested using these two options along with the login name.

Initially Setting User Privileges

When you invoke SAM with the "-r" option, you are first asked to select the user to whom you want to assign privileges. You will then be shown a list of default privileges for a new restricted SAM user. Figure 4-4 shows the default privileges SAM recommends for a new restricted user. Note that custom SAM functional areas are disabled by default.

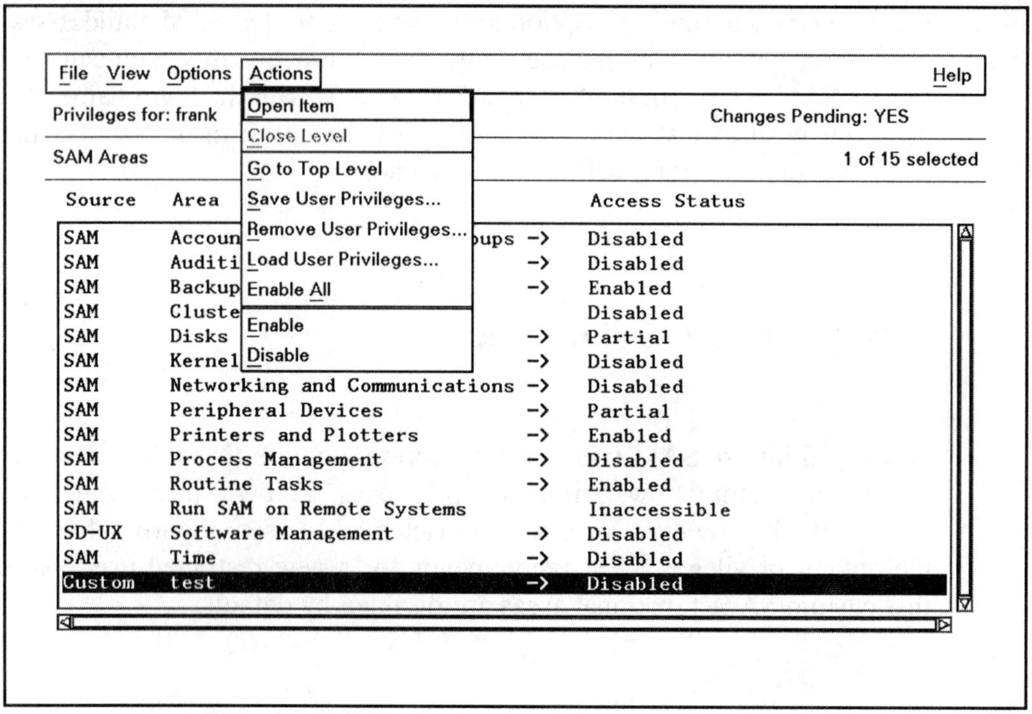

```
  File  View  Options  Actions                                           Help
 Privileges for: frank   Open Item                      Changes Pending: YES
                         ──────────
 SAM Areas               Close Level                          1 of 15 selected
                         Go to Top Level
   Source    Area        Save User Privileges...         Access Status

  SAM       Accoun ─Remove User Privileges...─ups ->   Disabled
  SAM       Auditi Load User Privileges...          ->   Disabled
  SAM       Backup Enable All                        ->   Enabled
  SAM       Cluste ──────────                              Disabled
  SAM       Disks  Enable                            ->   Partial
  SAM       Kernel Disable                           ->   Disabled
  SAM       Networking and Communications            ->   Disabled
  SAM       Peripheral Devices                       ->   Partial
  SAM       Printers and Plotters                    ->   Enabled
  SAM       Process Management                       ->   Disabled
  SAM       Routine Tasks                            ->   Enabled
  SAM       Run SAM on Remote Systems                     Inaccessible
  SD-UX     Software Management                      ->   Disabled
  SAM       Time                                     ->   Disabled
  Custom    test                                     ->   Disabled
```

Figure 4-4   Restricted SAM Builder Screen

You can select from the *Actions* shown in the figure to control access
to functional areas. Of particular interest is the ability to save the privileges which you may later use as a template for other users with *Load
User Privileges* from the *Actions* menu.

Verify Restricted Access

After having selected the appropriate privileges for a user by invoking
SAM with the "- r" option, you can then use the "-f" option and login
name to test the privileges for a user. The command shown below can be
used to test user frank's privileges:

$ sam -r -f frank

When the user invokes SAM, they see only the functional areas to which they have been given access. They can then proceed to perform tasks under one of these functional areas.

Accounts for Users and Groups

In Chapter 1 I explained the information that is associated with each user and group. There is an entry in the **/etc/passwd** file for each user and an entry in **/etc/group** for each group. To save you the trouble of flipping back to Chapter 1, Figure 4-5 is an example of a user entry from **/etc/passwd** and Figure 4-6 is an example of a group entry from **/etc/group.**

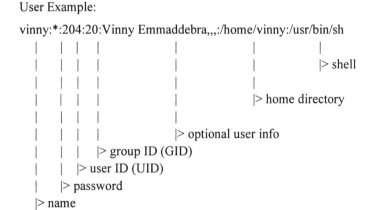

User Example:

vinny:*:204:20:Vinny Emmaddebra,,,:/home/vinny:/usr/bin/sh

Figure 4-5 Sample **/etc/passwd** Entry

Group Example:

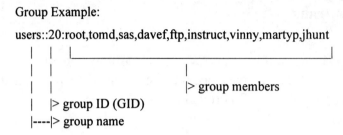

Figure 4-6   Sample **/etc/group** Entry

The *Accounts for Users and Groups* top-level SAM category or area has beneath it only two picks: *Groups* and *Users*. The menu hierarchy for "Users and Groups" is shown in the Figure 4-7.

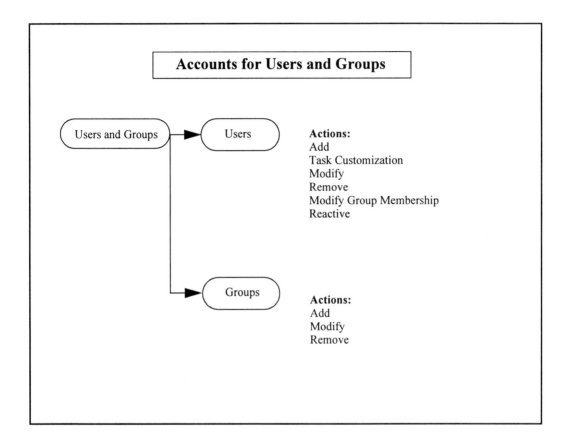

Figure 4-7   Accounts for Users and Groups

When you select *Accounts for Users and Groups* and then *Users* from the
SAM menu, you are provided with a list of all the users on your system.
Table 4-1 is a partial list of users provided by SAM for my system:

Login Name	User ID (UID)	Real Name	Primary Group	Office Phone	Office Location
root	0		sys		
daemon	1		daemon		

Login Name	User ID (UID)	Real Name	Primary Group	Office Phone	Office Location
bin	2		bin		
adm	4		adm		
uucp	5		sys		
lp	9		lp		
vinny	204	Vinny D.	users	Internal 5611	Stmfd
marty	219	Marty P.	users	Internal 5613	Stmfd
tftp	510	Trivial FTP user	other		
sas	205		users		

TABLE 4-1   LIST OF USERS

Adding a User

SAM is ideal for performing administration tasks related to users and groups. These are routine tasks that are not complex but require you to edit the **/etc/passwd** and **/etc/group** files, make directories, and copy default files, all of which SAM performs for you. Finally, take a minute to check what SAM has done for you, especially if you modify an existing user or group.

To add an additional user, you would select *Add* from the *Actions* menu under *Users* and then fill in the information as shown in Figure 4-8.

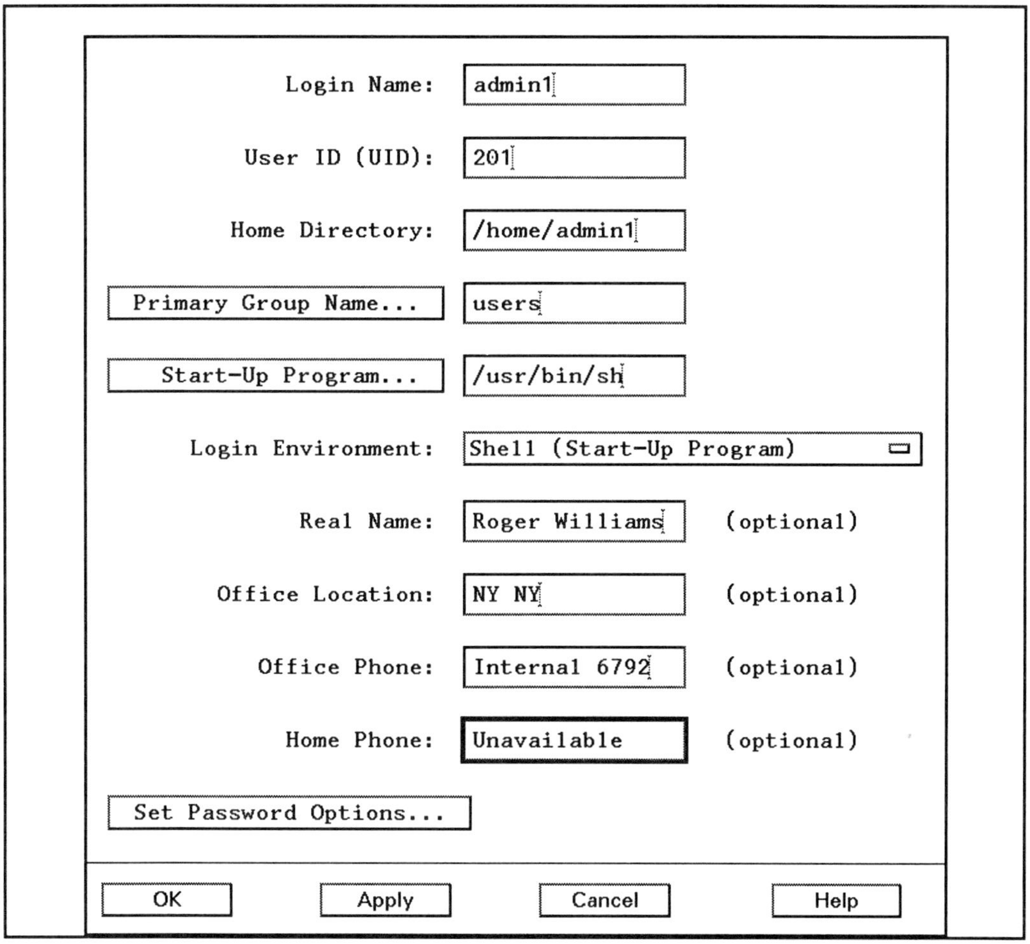

```
                Login Name:   [admin1]

             User ID (UID):   [201]

           Home Directory:   [/home/admin1]

    [ Primary Group Name... ]  [users]

    [ Start-Up Program... ]   [/usr/bin/sh]

        Login Environment:   [Shell (Start-Up Program)      ▭]

                Real Name:   [Roger Williams]   (optional)

          Office Location:   [NY NY]           (optional)

            Office Phone:   [Internal 6792]   (optional)

             Home Phone:   [Unavailable]     (optional)

    [ Set Password Options... ]


    [     OK     ]   [   Apply   ]   [   Cancel   ]   [   Help   ]
```

Figure 4-8 Example of Adding a New User

There are some restrictions when entering this information. For instance, a comma and colon are not permitted in the Office Location field. When I tried to enter a comma, SAM informed me this was not permitted.

As a result of adding user admin1, the following **/etc/passwd** entry was made. (Notice there is no entry for password; please make sure you always enter a password on your system.)

admin1::201:20:Roger Williams,NY NY,Internal 6792,Unavailable:/ home/admin1:/usr/bin/sh

Adding this user gives us an opportunity to look at one of the best features of SAM - the ability to review what took place when this user was added with the "SAM Log Viewer" as shown in Figure 4-9.

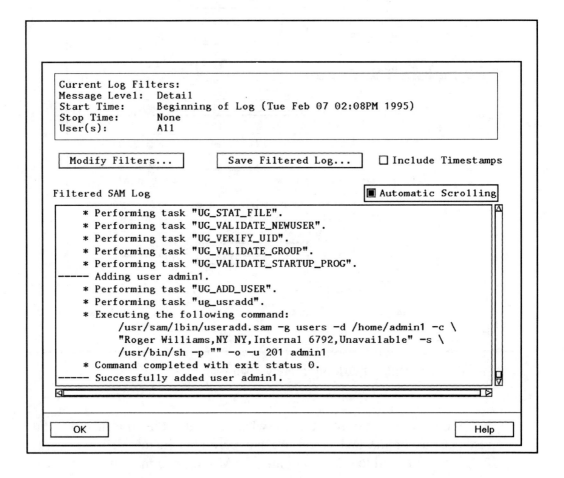

Figure 4-9   SAM Log Viewer for Adding a User

The log file is viewed by selecting *View SAM Log* from the *Actions* menu bar.

The scroll bar on the right-hand side of the SAM Log Viewer allows you to scroll to any point in the log file. We are viewing only the part of the log file that pertains to adding the user Roger Williams. You can select the level of detail you wish to view with the log file. The four levels are *Summary, Detail, Verbose,* and *Commands Only.* The level shown in Figure 4-9 is *Detail.* I like this level because you can see what has taken place without getting mired down in too much detail.

Adding a Group

Adding an additional group is similar to adding a new user. To add an additional group, you would select *Add* from the *Actions* menu under *Groups.* Figure 4-10 shows the Add a New Group window.

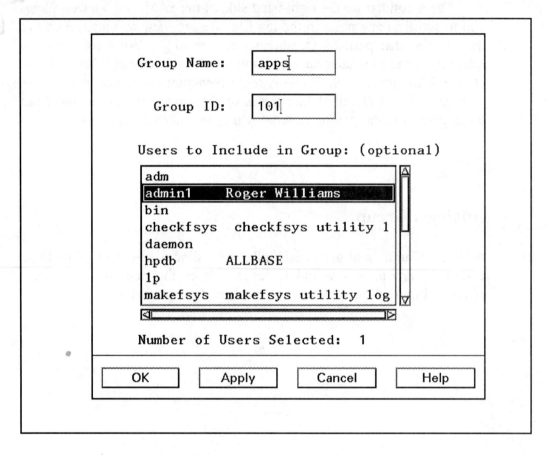

Figure 4-10 Example of Adding a New Group

In this example I added a new group called "apps" with a group ID of 101 and into that group I added the user admin1.

Auditing and Security

Under *Auditing and Security* you manage the security of your system. This is becoming an increasingly important aspect of system management. Some installations care very little about security because of well-known, limited groups of users who will access a system. Other installations, such as those connected to the Internet, may go to great pains to make their systems into fortresses with fire walls, checking each and every user who attempts to access a system. I suggest you take a close look at all of the ramifications of security, and specifically a trusted system, before you enable security. You'll want to review the "Managing System Security" chapter of the *HP-UX System Administration Tasks Manual*. Although SAM makes creating and maintaining a trusted system easy, there are a lot of files created for security management that take place under the umbrella of auditing and security. Among the modifications that will be made to your system, should you choose to convert to a trusted system, is the **/etc/rc.config.d/auditing** file that will be updated by SAM. In addition, passwords in the **/etc/passwd** file will be replaced with "*" and the encrypted passwords will be moved to a password database. All users are also given audit ID numbers. Figure 4-11 shows the hierarchy of Auditing and Security.

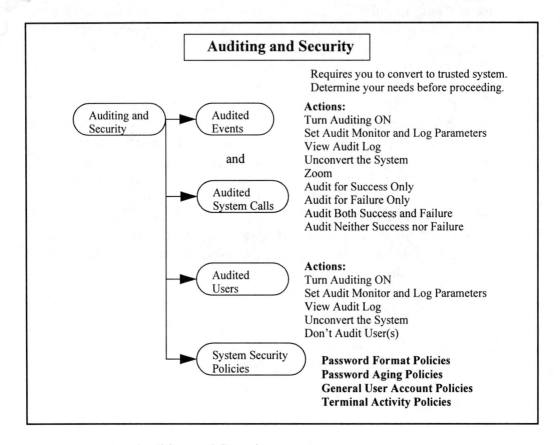

Figure 4-11　Auditing and Security

One choice to observe in this figure is an *Actions* menu choice to *Unconvert the System*. This means to reverse the trusted system environment. I have tried this on various systems and it seems to work fine, but you should have a good idea of what a trusted system can do for and to you before you make the conversion.

I hope I have given you a reasonably good overview of auditing and security because in order to investigate it yourself, you must first convert to a trusted system. Before you do this, please read this section to get an idea of the functionality this will provide and then convert to a trusted system if you think there is adequate benefit.

Audited Events and Audited System Calls

Under *Audited Events* you can select the particular events you wish to analyze and detect which may cause security breaches. Under *Audited System Calls* you can monitor system calls. This is a function of the trusted system which you must convert to in order to perform auditing. You may have in mind particular events and system calls that are most vital to your system's security that you wish to audit and not bother with the balance. There are a number of events and system calls that you may wish to keep track of for security reasons.Figure 4-12 shows the *Audited Events* window with the *Actions* menu shown as well.

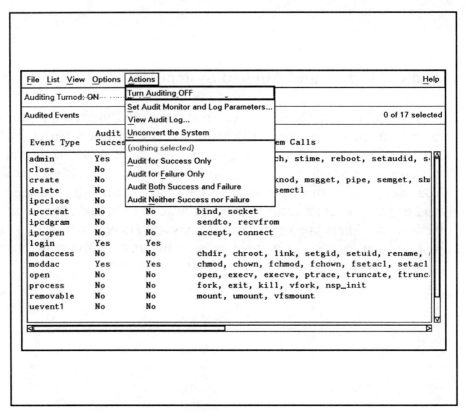

Figure 4-12 *Audited Events* Window

Auditing these events gives you a detailed report of the event. The same is true of system calls. Notice from the *Actions* menu that you have many options for the conditions you do and don't want to monitor. SAM uses the auditing commands of HP-UX such as **audsys**, **audusr**, **audevent**, **audomon**, and **audisp** to perform auditing.

Audited Users

Under *Audited Users* you can use the *Actions* menu to turn auditing on and off for specific users. Since the audit log files, which you can also control and view through the *Actions* menu, get big very fast, you may want to select specific users to monitor to better understand the type of user audit information that is created.

System Security Policies

The most important part of HP-UX security are the policies you put in place. If, for instance, you choose to audit each and every system call but don't impose any restrictions on user passwords, then you are potentially opening up your system to any user. You would be much better off restricting users and not worrying so much about what they're doing. Being proactive is more important in security than being reactive.

You have several options for passwords under *Password Format Policies* shown in Figure 4-13.

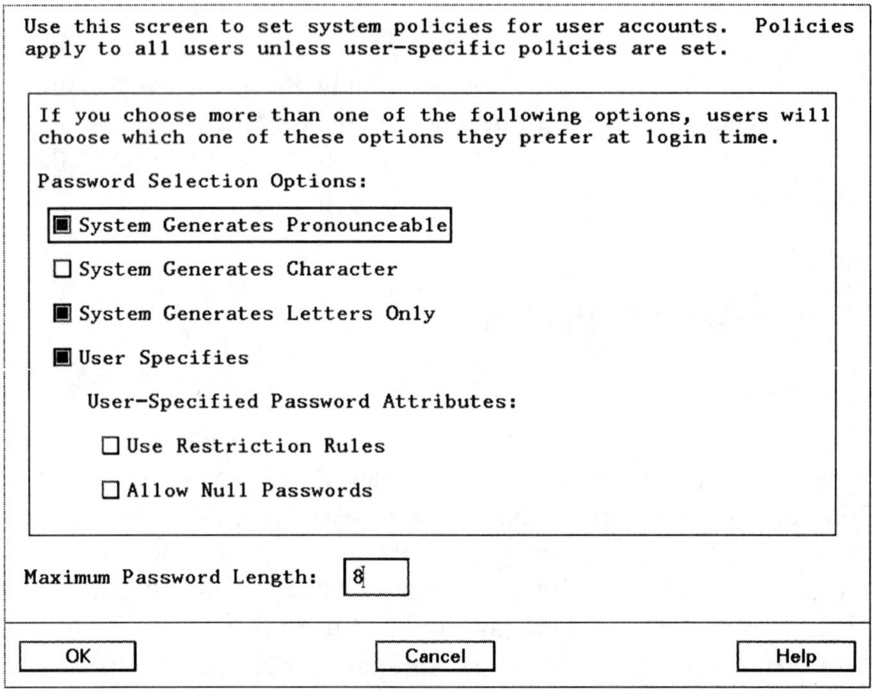

```
Use this screen to set system policies for user accounts.  Policies
apply to all users unless user-specific policies are set.

  If you choose more than one of the following options, users will
  choose which one of these options they prefer at login time.

  Password Selection Options:

  ■ System Generates Pronounceable

  □ System Generates Character

  ■ System Generates Letters Only

  ■ User Specifies

    User-Specified Password Attributes:

      □ Use Restriction Rules

      □ Allow Null Passwords


Maximum Password Length:   8


   OK                    Cancel                    Help
```

Figure 4-13 *Password Format Policies* Window

Password Aging Policies, when enabled, allows you to select.

- Time between Password Changes
- Password Expiration Time
- Password Expiration Warning Time
- Password Life Time
- Expire All User Passwords Immediately

General User Account Policies, when enabled, allows you to specify the time in which an account will become inactive and lock it. In addition, you can specify the number of unsuccessful login tries that are permitted.

Terminal Security Policies allows you to set

- Unsuccessful Login Tries Allowed
- Delay between Login Tries
- Login Timeout Value in seconds

Backup and Recovery

The most important activities you'll perform as a system administrator are system backup and recovery. The SAM team put a lot of thought into giving you all the options you need to ensure the integrity of your system through backup and recovery. Figure 4-14 shows the hierarchy of the "Backup and Recovery" SAM menu.

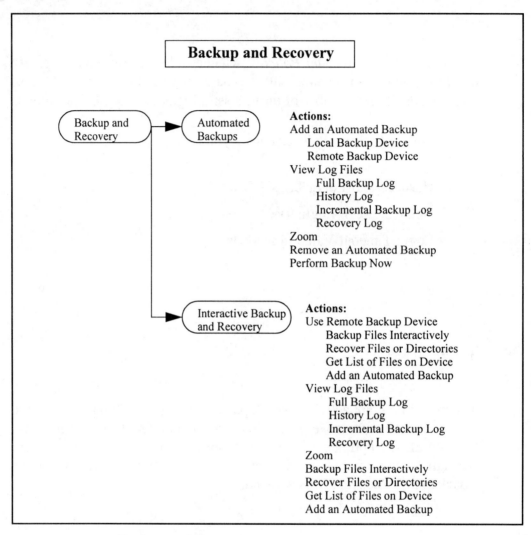

Backup and Recovery

Backup and Recovery → Automated Backups

Actions:
Add an Automated Backup
    Local Backup Device
    Remote Backup Device
View Log Files
    Full Backup Log
    History Log
    Incremental Backup Log
    Recovery Log
Zoom
Remove an Automated Backup
Perform Backup Now

Interactive Backup and Recovery

Actions:
Use Remote Backup Device
    Backup Files Interactively
    Recover Files or Directories
    Get List of Files on Device
    Add an Automated Backup
View Log Files
    Full Backup Log
    History Log
    Incremental Backup Log
    Recovery Log
Zoom
Backup Files Interactively
Recover Files or Directories
Get List of Files on Device
Add an Automated Backup

Figure 4-14   Backup and Recovery

Scheduling a Backup

The first step is to enter the *Automated Backups* subarea. You won't see any automated backups appear in the list until you have specified one.

Using the *Actions* menu and selecting *Add an Automated Backup,* you can specify all the information about your automated backup. When you select *Add an Automated Backup,* you have to specify whether your backup will be to a local or remote backup device. You will have to enter information pertaining to the backup scope, backup device, backup time, and additional parameters.

Select Backup Scope

You can view the backup scope as the files that will be included and excluded from the backup. This can include Network File System (NFS) mounted file systems as well. Figure 4-15 shows the window used to specify files to be included and excluded from the backup.

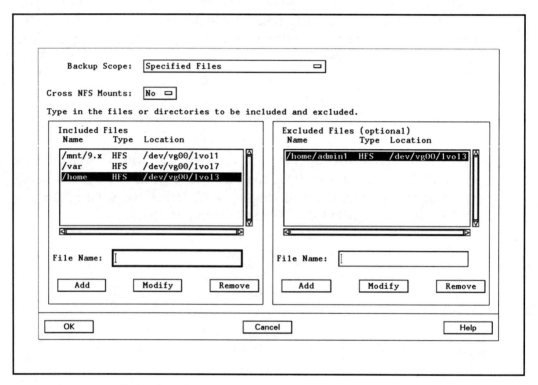

Figure 4-15 Selecting the Backup Scope

In the selections shown in Figure 4-15 there are three directories specified under included files. You can specify entire directories or individual files to be included or excluded from the backup. Although I want **/home** to be included in the backup, I don't want the home directory of **admin1**, the user we earlier created, to be included in the backup.

Instead of *Specified Files* as shown above, I could have selected *Local File Systems Only,* in which case all local file systems would have appeared in the *Included Files* list. If I had specified *All File Systems,* then all local file systems and NFS file systems (this will include **/net** by default) would have appeared in the list.

Select Backup Device

If you plan to back up to a local backup device, then those attached to your system will be listed and you select the desired device from the list.

If you plan to use a remote backup device, then you will be asked to specify the remote system name and device file.

Select Backup Time

As with the backup scope, you are provided with a window in which you can enter all of the information about backup time for both full and incremental backups as shown in Figure 4-16. If *Incremental Backup* is *Enabled,* then you must provide all pertinent information about both the full and incremental backup as shown in the figure.

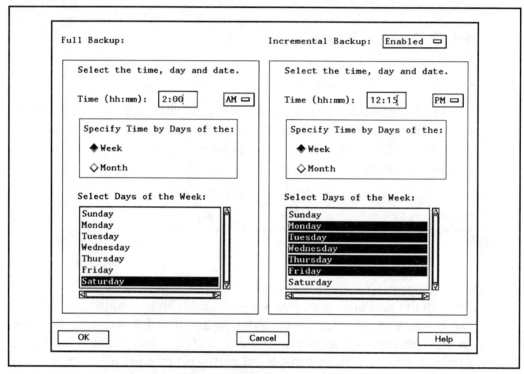

Figure 4-16 Selecting the Backup Time

A key point to keep in mind here is that the incremental backup that SAM creates for you includes files that have been changed *since the last full backup*. This means that you need only the full backup and last incremental backup to recover your system; that is, you do not need to restore the full backup and each incremental backup.

Set Additional Parameters

You can also specify additional parameters such as whether or not to create an index log, which I strongly suggest you do, and to whom to mail the results of the backup. We can now view the **crontab** entry SAM has made for root for these backups. The **crontab** file is used to schedule jobs that are automatically executed by **cron**. **crontab** files are in the **/var/ spool/cron/crontabs** directory. **cron** is a program that runs other programs at the specified time. **cron** reads files that specify the operation to be performed and the date and time it is to be performed. Since we want to perform backups on a regular basis, SAM will activate **cron**.

The format of entries in the **crontab** file are as follows:

minute   hour   monthday   month   weekday   user name   command

minute - the minute of the hour, from 0-59
hour - the hour of the day, from 0-23
monthday - the day of the month, from 1-31
month - the month of the year, from 1-12
weekday - the day of the week, from 0 (Sunday) - 6 (Saturday)
user name - the user who will run the command if necessary
          (not used in example)
command - specifies the command line or script file to run

You have many options in the **crontab** for specifying the *minute, hour, monthday, month,* and *weekday* to perform a task. You could list one entry in a field and then a space, several entries in any field separated by a comma, two entries separated by a dash indicating a range, or an asterisk, which corresponds to all possible entries for the field.

To list the contents of the **crontab** file you would issue the following command. The output of this command is the **crontab** file created for the user root in the SAM backup example.

```
$ crontab -l

00 2 * * 6 /usr/sam/lbin/br_backup DAT FULL Y /dev/rmt/0m /etc/sam/br/
graphDCAa02410 root Y 1 N > /tmp/SAM_br_msgs 2>&1 #sambackup

15 12 * * 1-5 /usr/sam/lbin/br_backup DAT PART Y /dev/rmt/0m /etc/sam/
br/graphDCAa02410 root Y 1 N > /tmp/SAM_br_msgs 2>&1 #sambackup
```

Although these seem to be excruciatingly long lines, they do indeed conform to the format of the **crontab** file. The first entry is the full backup; the second entry is the incremental backup. In the first entry the *minute* is 00; in the second entry the *minute* is 15. In the first entry the *hour* is 2; in the second entry the *hour* is 12. In both entries the *monthday* and *month* are all legal values (*), meaning every *monthday* and *month*. In the first entry the *weekday* is 6 for Saturday (0 is Sunday); in the second entry the *weekdays* are 1-5 or Monday through Friday. The optional *user name* is not specified in either example. And finally, the SAM backup command (**/usr/sam/lbin/br_backup**) and its long list of associated information is provided.

minute	hour	monthday	month	weekday	user name	command
00	12	all	all	6	n/a	br_backup
15	12	all	all	1-5	n/a	br_backup

The *graph* file that is used by **/usr/sam/lbin/br_backup** is a list of files to be included and excluded from the backup. The following is the contents of the graph file **/etc/sam/br/graphDCAa02410** that was created for the full and incremental backups:

> i /mnt/9.x
>
> i /var
>
> i /home
>
> e /home/admin1

Lines that start with an "i" are files and directories to be included in the backup and those starting with an "e" will be excluded from the backup.

You will see various crontab **commands** when you use the *SAM Log Viewer* to see what SAM has done for you to create the **crontab** files. For instance, if you change your backup plan, SAM will remove the old crontab file with the command

```
$ crontab -r
```

This will remove the **crontab** file for the user from the **/var/spool/ cron/crontabs** directory.

To place a file in the **crontab** directory you would simply issue the **crontab** command and the name of the **crontab** file:

```
$ crontab crontabfile
```

You can schedule cron jobs using SAM. The section in this chapter covering *Process Management* has a subsection called *Scheduling Cron Jobs*.

Interactive Backup and Recovery

The *Interactive Backup and Recovery* subarea is used to perform a backup interactively or restore information that was part of an earlier backup. When you enter this area, you are asked to select a backup device from a list that is produced in the same way you are asked to select a backup device when you first enter the **Automated Backups** subarea.

After selecting a device from the list, you may select an item from the *Actions* menu shown earlier. If you decide to use *Backup Files Interactively,* you are again provided a window in which you can specify files to be included and excluded from the backup. You are asked to *Select Backup Scope, Specify Tape Device Options*, and *Set Additional Parame-*

ters. You are not, however, asked to *Select Backup Time* since the backup is taking place interactively.

The steps in this area will vary depending on the tape devices you have selected.

The log file **/var/sam/log/br_log** reports on the backup. The index files can be reviewed from the *Actions* menu. These are stored in the **/var/sam/log** directory. The following shows the very top and bottom of an index file that is 800 KBytes in size:

```
#   1 /
#   1 /.profile
#   1 /.rhosts
#   1 /.sh_history
#   1 /.sw
#   1 /.sw/sessions
#   1 /.sw/sessions/swinstall.last
#   1 /.sw/sessions/swlist.last
#   1 /.sw/sessions/swmodify.last
#   1 /.sw/sessions/swreg.last
#   1 /.vue
#   1 /.vue/.trashinfo
#   1 /.vue/Desktop
#   1 /.vue/Desktop/Five                    TOP
#   1 /.vue/Desktop/Four
#   1 /.vue/Desktop/One
#   1 /.vue/Desktop/Six
#   1 /.vue/Desktop/Three

                    .
                    .
                    .

#   1 /var/uucp/.Log/uucico
#   1 /var/uucp/.Log/uucp
#   1 /var/uucp/.Log/uux
#   1 /var/uucp/.Log/uuxqt
#   1 /var/uucp/.Old
#   1 /var/uucp/.Status
#   1 /var/vue                              BOTTOM
#   1 /var/vue/Xerrors
#   1 /var/vue/Xpid
#   1 /var/vue/recserv.langconfig
#   1 /var/yp
#   1 /var/yp/Makefile
#   1 /var/yp/binding
#   1 /var/yp/securenets
```

```
#   1  /var/yp/secureservers
#   1  /var/yp/updaters
#   1  /var/yp/ypmake
#   1  /var/yp/ypxfr_1perday
#   1  /var/yp/ypxfr_1perhour
#   1  /var/yp/ypxfr_2perday
```

Performing a Restore

A full or incremental backup, however, is only as good as the files it restores. To retrieve a file from the backup tape, you supply information in three areas: *Select Recovery Scope; Specify Tape Device Options*; and *Set Additional Parameters*. The device options you specify will depend on the tape device you are using.

Select Recovery Scope allows you to either enter a file name that contains the files to be recovered or manually list the files to be included in the recovery. You can optionally list files to be excluded from the recovery as well.

A list of tape device files is provided in *Specify Tape Device Options* from which you can select the tape device. In this step you may select the tape device file; in other cases you might make selections such as a magneto-optical surface or have nothing to select at all.

Under *Set Additional Parameters* you can select any of the following options:

Overwrite Newer Files

Preserve Original File Ownership

Recover Files Using Full Path Name

Place Files in Non-Root Directory

After you make all of the desired selections, the recovery operation begins. If a file has been inadvertently deleted and you wish to restore it from the recovery tape, you would select the *Preserve Original File Ownership* and *Recover Files Using Full Path Name* options. You will receive status of the recovery as it takes place and may also *View Recovery Log,* from the *Actions* menu after the recovery has completed. If you *View Recovery Log,* you will receive a window which provides the name of the index log and the name of the files recovered:

```
Recovery Log (/var/sam/log/br_index.rec)

-rw-r--r--  admin1  users  /home/admin1/fortran/makefile
```

Disks and File Systems

Disks and File Systems helps you manage disk devices, file systems, logical volumes, swap, and volume groups (you may also manage HP disk arrays through SAM if you have these installed on your system). There is no reason to manually work with these since SAM does such a good job of managing these for you. Figure 4-17 shows the hierarchy of *Disks and File Systems*.

Figure 4-17 Disks and File Systems

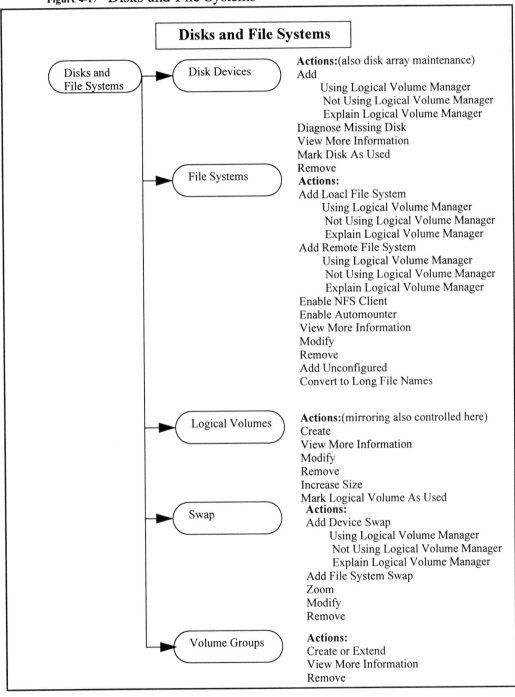

Disk Devices

When you enter this subarea, SAM shows you the disk devices connected to your system. Figure 4-18 shows a listing of the disks for a Series 800 unit (this is the same system used in several examples in Chapter 1).

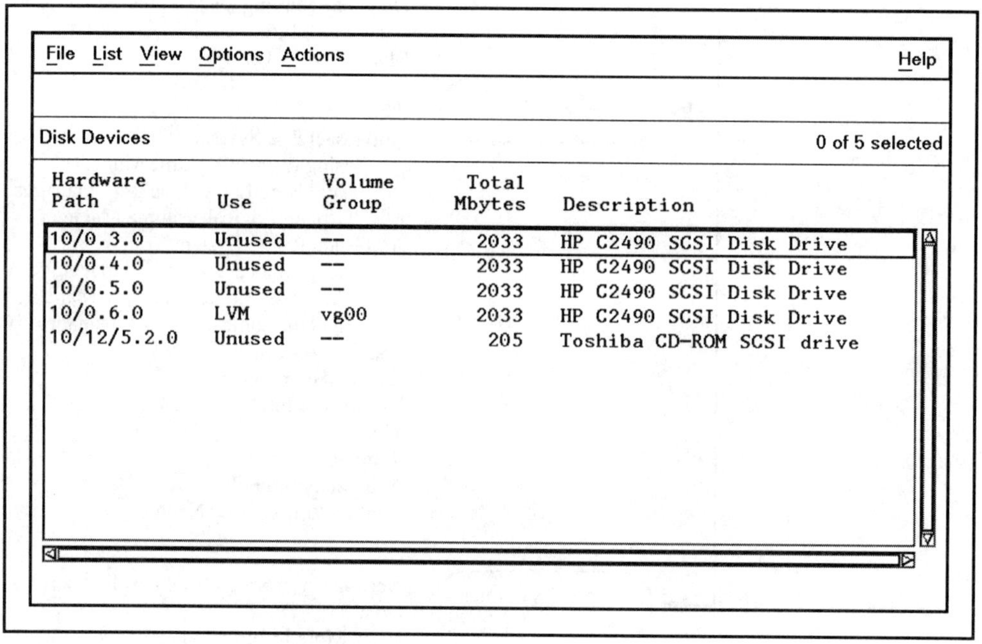

```
 File  List  View  Options  Actions                                        Help

 Disk Devices                                                       0 of 5 selected

   Hardware              Volume        Total
   Path         Use      Group         Mbytes    Description
  ┌─────────────────────────────────────────────────────────────────────────┐
  │10/0.3.0      Unused   --            2033      HP  C2490  SCSI  Disk Drive  │▲
  │10/0.4.0      Unused   --            2033      HP  C2490  SCSI  Disk Drive  │
  │10/0.5.0      Unused   --            2033      HP  C2490  SCSI  Disk Drive  │
  │10/0.6.0      LVM      vg00          2033      HP  C2490  SCSI  Disk Drive  │
  │10/12/5.2.0   Unused   --            205       Toshiba CD-ROM SCSI drive    │
  │                                                                           │
  │                                                                           │▼
  └─────────────────────────────────────────────────────────────────────────┘
  ◁                                                                          ▷
```

Figure 4-18 *Disk Devices* Window

The first four entries are the Fast/Wide 2 GByte SCSI disks in the system. Only the disk at SCSI address 6 is in use at this time. The last entry is the CD-ROM. The following **ioscan** command from Chapter 1 shows these disk devices:

(on Series 800)
```
$ /usr/sbin/ioscan -fn -C disk

Class  I  H/W Path      Driver  S/W State  H/W Type   Description
================================================================
disk   0 10/0.3.0       sdisk   CLAIMED    DEVICE        HP C2490WD
                        /dev/dsk/c0t3d0  /dev/rdsk/c0t3d0

disk   1 10/0.4.0       sdisk   CLAIMED    DEVICE        HP C2490WD
                        /dev/dsk/c0t4d0  /dev/rdsk/c0t4d0

disk   2 10/0.5.0       sdisk   CLAIMED    DEVICE        HP C2490WD
                        /dev/dsk/c0t5d0  /dev/rdsk/c0t5d0

disk   3 10/0.6.0       sdisk   CLAIMED    DEVICE        HP C2490WD
                        /dev/dsk/c0t6d0  /dev/rdsk/c0t6d0

disk   3 10/12/5/2/0 sdisk  CLAIMED    DEVICE         CD-ROM
                        /dev/dsk/c1t2d0  /dev/rdsk/c1t2d0
```

You can see from this **ioscan** all of the device files associated with disks including the CD-ROM. Using SAM to view and manipulate these devices is easier and clearer than typing such commands as **ioscan**. This doesn't mean you don't have to know the **ioscan** command or that it is not useful, but SAM certainly makes viewing your system a lot easier. We can now add one of the unused disks in SAM by selecting *Add* from the *Actions* menu. Using Logical Volume Manager we can create a new volume group or select the volume group we wish to add the new disk to. We would then select the new logical volumes we wanted on the volume group or extend the size of existing logical volumes. Other information such as the mount directory and size of the logical volume would be entered.

Another common disk device that you may configure through SAM is Redundant Arrays of Inexpensive Disks (RAID). RAID from HP can be configured directly through SAM under Disk Devices. These devices have a Storage Control Processor (SP) and disk which can be configured in a variety of ways. Using SAM you can specify the RAID level, and which disks will bind to which SPs.

After the RAID has been configured, you can access it as you would any other disks by specifying logical volumes and so on.

File Systems

File Systems shows the *Mount Directory*, *Type* of file system, and *Source Device or Remote Directory*. Figure 4-19 shows the information you see when you enter *File Systems* for the Series 800 used in earlier examples.

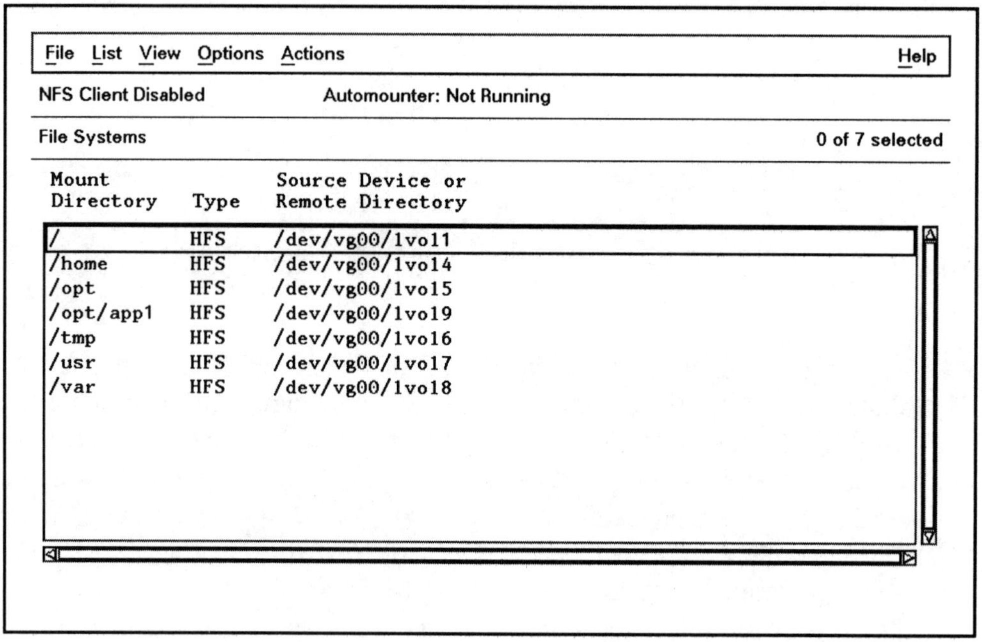

```
 File  List  View  Options  Actions                              Help

 NFS Client Disabled              Automounter: Not Running

 File Systems                                              0 of 7 selected

 Mount                    Source Device or
 Directory      Type      Remote Directory
 /              HFS       /dev/vg00/1vol1
 /home          HFS       /dev/vg00/1vol4
 /opt           HFS       /dev/vg00/1vol5
 /opt/app1      HFS       /dev/vg00/1vol9
 /tmp           HFS       /dev/vg00/1vol6
 /usr           HFS       /dev/vg00/1vol7
 /var           HFS       /dev/vg00/1vol8
```

Figure 4-19 *File Systems* Window

At this level you could perform such tasks as *Add Local File System, Add Remote File System*, and others from the *Actions* menu.

There are several types of file systems that may be listed under the Type column. The most common are

Auto-Indirect   Directory containing auto-mountable remote NFS file systems. You may see the **/net** directory here if you have auto-mounter running.

Auto-Mount   Auto-mountable remote NFS file system.

CDFS   CD-ROM file system if it is currently mounted.
                    If, for instance, you have a CD-ROM mounted
                    as **/SD_CDROM**, you will see this as type
                    CDFS in the list.

HFS   Local HFS file system. These are local HFS file
                    systems that are part of your system.

NFS   Remote NFS file system that is currently
                    mounted.

LOFS   Loopback file system that allows you to have the
                    same file system in multiple places.

VxFS   Extent-based Journal File System that supports
                    fast file system recovery and on-line features
                    such as backup.

Logical Volumes

You can perform several functions related to logical volume manipulation
in SAM. Such tasks as *Create, Modify, Remove,* and *Increase Size* can be
performed in SAM. Figure 4-20 shows increasing the size of lvol4
(/home) from 20 MBytes to 500 MBytes.

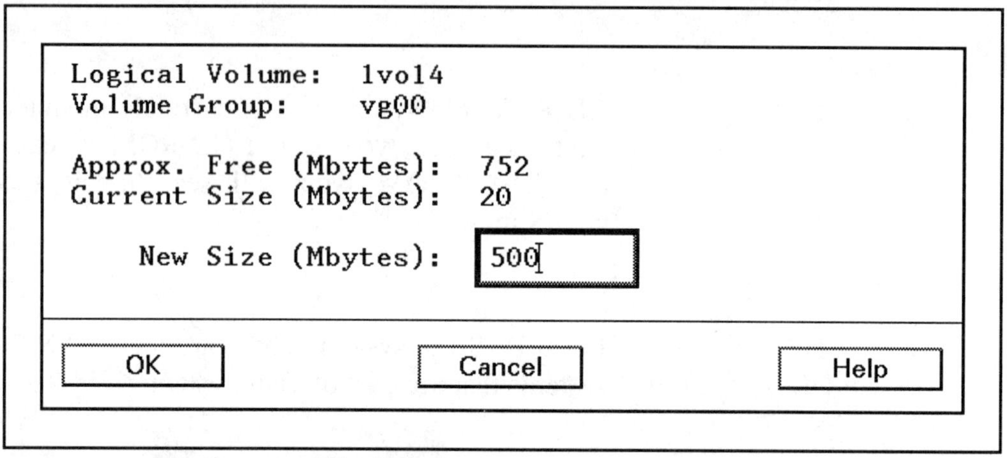

```
Logical Volume:    lvol4
Volume Group:      vg00

Approx. Free (Mbytes):    752
Current Size (Mbytes):    20

    New Size (Mbytes):   500


  OK              Cancel              Help
```

Figure 4-20 *Increase Size* Window

SAM will only increase the size of the logical volume if it can be unmounted. Viewing the log file after this task has been completed shows SAM ran such commands as **/sbin/lvextend** and **/sbin/extendfs** to extend the size of the logical volume and file system, and **/usr/sbin/umount** and **/usr/sbin/mount** to unmount and mount the file system.

Increasing the Size of a Logical Volume in SAM

SAM may create a unique set of problems when you attempt to increase the size of a logical volume. Problems may be encountered increasing the size of a logical volume if it can't be unmounted. If, for instance, you wanted to increase the size of the **/opt** logical volume, it would first have to be unmounted by SAM. If SAM can't umount **/opt,** you will receive a message from SAM indicating the device is busy. You can go into single-user state but you will have to have some logical volumes mounted in order to get SAM to run such as **/usr** and **/var.** You would then bring the system up to the appropriate run level when you have completed your work. This works for directories such as **/opt** which SAM does not need in order to run.

Alternatively, you could exit SAM and kill any processes accessing the logical volume you wish to extend the size of and then manually unmount that logical volume. You could then use SAM to increase the size of the logical volume. This also works for **/opt**.

Swap

Both device swap and file system swap are listed when you enter *Swap*. Listed for you are the *Device File/Mount Directory, Type, Mbytes Available*, and *Enabled*. You can get more information about an item by highlighting it and selecting *Zoom* from the *Actions* menu.

Volume Groups

Listed for you when you enter volume groups are *Name, Mbytes Available, Physical Volumes*, and *Logical Volumes*. If you have an unused disk on your sytem, you can extend an existing volume group or create a new volume group.

Kernel Configuration

Your HP-UX kernel is a vitally important part of your HP-UX system that is often overlooked by HP-UX administrators. Perhaps this is because administrators are reluctant to tinker with such a critical and sensitive part of their system. Your HP-UX kernel, however, can have a big impact on system performance, so you want to be sure you know how it is configured. This doesn't mean you have to make a lot of experimental changes, but you should know how your kernel is currently configured so you can assess the possible impact that changes to the kernel may have on your system.

SAM allows you to view and modify the four basic elements of your HP-UX kernel. There is a great deal of confusion among new HP-UX system administrators regarding these four elements. Before I get into the details of each of these four areas, I'll first give you a brief description of each.

- *Configurable Parameters* - These are parameters that have a *value* associated with them. When you change the value, there is a strong possibility you will affect the performance of your system. An example of a *Configurable Parameter* is **nfile** which is the maximum number of open files on the system.

- *Drivers* - Drivers are used to control the hardware on your system. You have a driver called **CentIF** for the parallel interface on your system, one called **sdisk** for your SCSI disks, and so on.

- *Dump Devices* - A dump device is used to store the contents of main memory in the event that a serious kernel problem is encountered. If no dump device is configured, then the contents of main memory are saved on the primary swap device. A dump device is different than a swap device.

- *Subsystems* - A subsystem is different from a driver. A subsystem is an area of functionality or support on your system such as **CD-ROM/9000** which is CD-ROM file system support, **LVM** which is Logical Volume Manager support, and so on.

When you go into one of the four subareas described above, the configuration of your system for the respective subarea is listed for you. The first thing you should do when entering *Kernel Configuration* is to go into each of the subareas and review the list of information about your system in each.

In *Kernel Configuration* there is a *current* kernel and *pending* kernel. The *current* kernel is the one you are now running and the *pending* kernel is the one for which you are making changes.

Figure 4-21 shows the SAM menu hierarchy for *Kernel Configuration*.

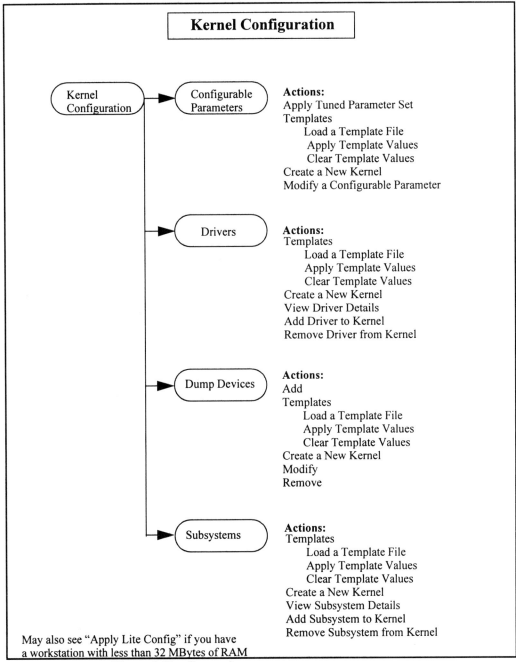

Kernel Configuration

Kernel Configuration → Configurable Parameters

Actions:
Apply Tuned Parameter Set
Templates
    Load a Template File
    Apply Template Values
    Clear Template Values
Create a New Kernel
Modify a Configurable Parameter

Drivers

Actions:
Templates
    Load a Template File
    Apply Template Values
    Clear Template Values
Create a New Kernel
View Driver Details
Add Driver to Kernel
Remove Driver from Kernel

Dump Devices

Actions:
Add
Templates
    Load a Template File
    Apply Template Values
    Clear Template Values
Create a New Kernel
Modify
Remove

Subsystems

Actions:
Templates
    Load a Template File
    Apply Template Values
    Clear Template Values
Create a New Kernel
View Subsystem Details
Add Subsystem to Kernel
Remove Subsystem from Kernel

May also see "Apply Lite Config" if you have
a workstation with less than 32 MBytes of RAM

Figure 4-21 Kernel Configuration

Configurable Parameters

Selecting *Configurable Parameters* lists all of your configurable kernel parameters. For each configurable parameter the following information is listed:

- Name - Name of the parameter.
- Current Value - Value of parameter in **/stand/vmunix**.
- Pending Value - Value of parameter in kernel to be built.
- Description - A few words describing parameter.

You can then take a number of *Actions* including the following:

Apply Tuned Parameter Set

There are several sets of configurable parameters that have been tuned for various environments. When you select this from the *Actions* menu, the tuned parameter sets on your system, such as a database server system, are listed for you and you can select from among these.

Templates   You can select a kernel template to load which is basically a different kernel configuration than you are currently running.

Create a New Kernel After making whatever changes you like to the *Pending Value* of a configurable parameter, you can have SAM create a new kernel for you.

Modify Configurable Parameter

You can change the value of parameter in the *pending* kernel. You simply highlight a parameter and select this from the *Actions* menu.

Modifying a configurable parameter is made much easier by SAM. But although the logistics of changing the parameter are easier, determining the value of the parameter is still the most important part of this process.

Many applications recommend modifying one or more of these parameters for optimal performance of the application. Keep in mind, though, that many of these parameters are related; modifying one may adversely affect another parameter. Many applications will request that you change the *maxuprc* to support more processes. Keep in mind that if you have more processes running, you may end up with more open files and also have to change the *maxfiles* per process. If you have a system primarily used for a single application, you can feel more comfortable in modifying these. But if you run many applications, make sure you don't improve the performance of one application at the expense of another.

When you do decide to modify the value of a configurable parameter, be careful. The range on some of these values is broad. The *maxuprc* (maximum number of user processes) can be reduced as low as three processes. I can't imagine what a system could be used for with this low a value, but SAM ensures the parameter is set to within supported HP-UX ranges for the parameter. "Let the administrator beware" when changing these values. You may find that you'll want to undo some of your changes. Here are some tips. Keep careful notes of the values you change in case you have to undo a change. In addition, change as few values at a time as possible. That way if you're not happy with the results, you know which configurable parameter caused the problem.

Drivers

When you select *Drivers*, the drivers for your current kernel, the template file on which your current kernel is based, and the pending kernel are listed. You'll know that the drivers displayed are for more than your current kernel because you'll see that some of the drivers listed are *Out* of both your current and pending kernels. The following information is listed for you when you enter the *Drivers* subarea:

- Name - Name of the driver.

- Current State - Lists whether the driver is *In* or *Out* of /**stand/ vmunix**.

- Pending State - Lists whether the driver is *In* or *Out* of the pending kernel to be built.

- Description - A few words describing driver.

The Current State indicates whether or not the driver selected is in /**stand/vmunix.**

The Pending State indicates whether or not you have selected this driver to be added to or removed from the kernel. *In* means the driver is part of the kernel or is pending to be part of the kernel. *Out* means the driver is not part of the kernel or is pending to be removed from the kernel.

Using the *Actions* menu, you can select one of the drivers and add or remove it. You can also pick *View Driver Details* from the *Actions* menu after you select one of the drivers. You can select *Create a New Kernel* from the *Actions* menu. If you have indeed modified this screen by adding or removing drivers, you want to re-create the kernel. SAM asks if you're sure you want to rebuild the kernel before it does this for you. The only recommendation I can make here is to be sure you have made your selections carefully before you rebuild the kernel.

Dump Devices

When you enter this subarea, both the *Current Dump Devices* and *Pending Dump Devices* are listed for you. A dump device is used when there is a serious kernel problem with your system and all of main memory is written to disk. This information is a core dump which can later be read from disk and used to help diagnose the kernel problem.

The sizes of the dump areas should be at least as large as main memory in your system. You can specify a disk or logical volume as a dump device (you can also specify a disk section, but I don't recommend you use disk sections at all). The entire disk or logical volume is then reserved as a dump device.

If no dump device is specified, then the core dump is written to primary swap. This has sometimes been a point of confusion; that is, primary swap may indeed be used as a dump device but a dump device is used specifically for core dump purposes whereas primary swap fills this role in the event there is no dump device specified.

Since you probably won't be allocating an entire disk as a dump device, you may be using a logical volume. You must select a logical volume in the root volume group that is unused or is used for non-file-system swap. This is done by selecting *Add* from the *Actions* menu to add a disk or logical volume to the list of dump devices.

Subsystems

Selecting *Subsystems* lists all of your subsystems. For each subsystem the following information is listed:

- Name - Name of the subsystem.

- Current Value - Lists whether the subsystem is *In* or *Out* of **/stand/vmunix**.

- Pending Value -   Lists whether the subsystem is *In* or *Out* of the pending kernel.

- Description - A few words describing parameter.

You can then take a number of *Actions* including the following:

Templates   You can select a kernel template to load which is basically a different kernel configuration than you are currently running.

Create a New Kernel After making whatever changes you like to the *Pending State* of a subsystem, you can have SAM create a new kernel for you.

View Subsystem Details

You get a little more information about the subsystem when you select this.

Add Subsystem to Kernel

When you highlight one of the subsystems and select this from the menu, the *Pending State* is changed to *In* and the subsystem will be added to the kernel when you rebuild the kernel.

Remove Subsystem from Kernel

When you highlight one of the subsystems and select this from the menu, the *Pending State* is changed to *Out* and the subsystem will be removed from the kernel when you rebuild the kernel.

After making selections, you can rebuild the kernel to include your pending changes or back out of this without making the changes.

Networking and Communications

The menu hierarchy for *Networking and Communications* is shown in Figure 4-22.

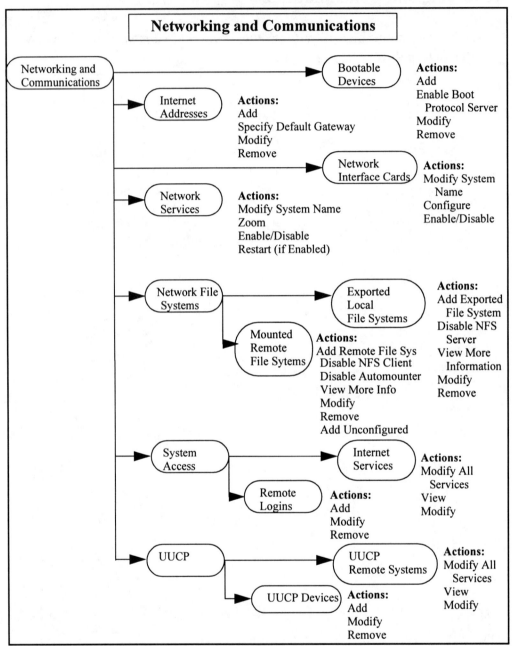

Figure 4-22 Networking and Communications

Bootable Devices

In the *Bootable Devices* subarea you can specify systems which will boot from your system using Bootstrap Protocol (Bootp). Bootp is a means by which a system can discover network information and boot automatically. The Bootp software must be loaded on your system in order for other devices to use it as a boot source. Among the many devices that use Bootp are HP X Stations. In this subarea you can add, modify, or remove a Bootp device. In addition you can enable or disable the Boot Protocol Server.

When you enter the *Bootable Devices* subarea you immediately receive a list of devices which can boot off your system. You can choose *Add* from the *Actions* menu and you'll be asked to enter the following information about the device you are adding:

- Bootp Client Device Name

- Internet Address

- Subnet Mask (this is optional)

- Station Address in hex (this is optional)

- Boot File Name

- Whether you'll be using Ethernet or IEEE 802.3 for booting

You can select *Enable Boot Protocol Server* or *Disable Boot Protocol Server* from the *Actions* menu, depending on whether your system is currently disabled or enabled to support this functionality. When you *Enable Boot Protocol Server,* you also enable Trivial File Transfer Protocol (TFTP) which boot devices use to get boot files. When you enable or disable this, the **/etc/inetd.conf** is edited. This file contains configuration information about the networking services running on your system. If a line in **/etc/inetd.conf** is preceded by a "#," then it is viewed as a comment. The daemon that reads the entries in this file is **/usr/sbin/inetd**. Before enabling or disabling Bootp, you may want to view the **/etc/ inetd.conf** file and see what services are enabled. After you make your change through SAM, you can again view **/etc/inetd.conf** to see what has been modified. See *System Access* for security related to **/etc/inetd.conf.** The following is the *beginning* of the **/etc/inetd.conf** file from a system showing Bootp and TFTP enabled. There is also a brief explanation of the fields in this file at the beginning of the file:

```
## Configured using SAM by root on Sat Aug 25 10:12:51 1997
##
#
# Inetd  reads its configuration information from this file upon ex-
# ecution and at some later time if it is reconfigured.
#
# A line in the configuration file has the following fields separated
# by tabs and/or spaces:
#
#    service name          as in /etc/services
#    socket type           either "stream" or "dgram"
#    protocol              as in /etc/protocols
#    wait/nowait            only applies to datagram sockets, stream
#                          sockets should specify nowait
#    user                  name of user as whom the server should run
#    server program        absolute pathname for the server inetd
#                          will execute
#  server program args.    arguments server program uses as they
#                           normally are starting with argv[0] which
#                          is the name of the server.
#
# See the inetd.conf(4) manual page for more information.
##

##
#
#              ARPA/Berkeley services
#
##
ftp          stream tcp nowait root /usr/lbin/ftpd       ftpd -l
telnet       stream tcp nowait root /usr/lbin/telnetd    telnetd

# Before uncommenting the "tftp" entry below, please make sure
# that you have a "tftp" user in /etc/passwd. If you don't
# have one, please consult the tftpd(1M) manual entry for
# information about setting up this service.

tftp         dgram  udp wait    root  /usr/lbin/tftpd     tftpd
bootps       dgram  udp wait    root  /usr/lbin/bootpd    bootpd
#finger      stream tcp nowait  bin   /usr/lbing/fingerd  fingerd
login        stream tcp nowait  bin   /usr/lbin/rlogind   rlogind
shell        stream tcp nowait  bin   /usr/lbin/remshd    remshd
exec         stream tcp nowait  root  /usr/lbin/rexecd    rexecd
#uucp        stream tcp nowait  bin   /usr/sbin/uucpd     uucpd
```

•
•
•

If you select one of the Bootp client device names, you can then select *Modify* or *Remove* from the *Actions* menu and either change one of the parameters related to the client, such as its address or subnet mask, or completely remove the client.

Internet Addresses

This subarea is for maintaining the default gateway and remote hosts on your system. When you enter this subarea, you receive a list of hosts specified on your system as shown in Figure 4-23.

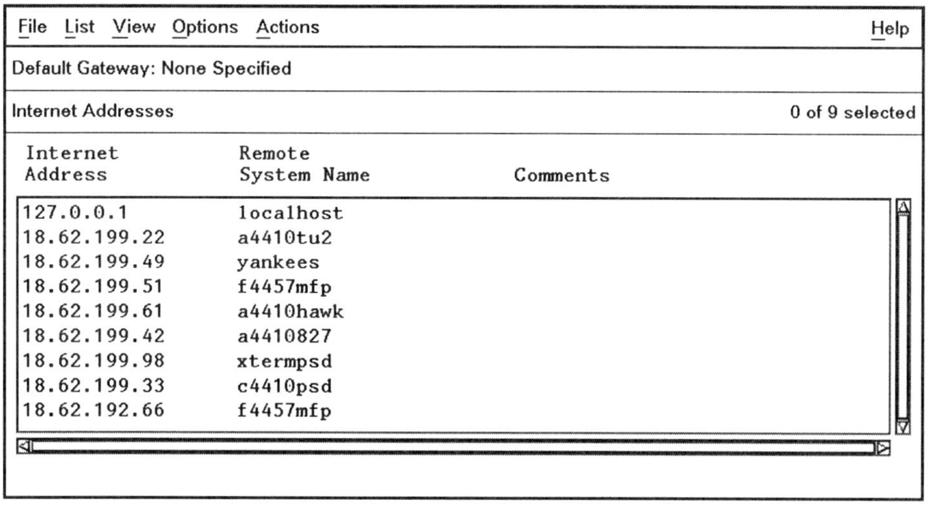

```
 File  List  View  Options  Actions                                  Help

 Default Gateway: None Specified

 Internet Addresses                                         0 of 9 selected

    Internet            Remote
    Address             System Name          Comments
   127.0.0.1            localhost
   18.62.199.22         a4410tu2
   18.62.199.49         yankees
   18.62.199.51         f4457mfp
   18.62.199.61         a4410hawk
   18.62.199.42         a4410827
   18.62.199.98         xtermpsd
   18.62.199.33         c4410psd
   18.62.192.66         f4457mfp
```

Figure 4-23 Internet Addresses

You can then *Add* a new host, *Specify Default Gateway*, *Modify* one of the hosts, or *Remove* one of the hosts, all from the *Actions* menu. When adding a host, you'll be asked for information pertaining to the host including Internet Address; system name; aliases for the system; and comments.

Network Interface Cards

This subarea is used for configuring any networking cards in your system. You can *Enable, Disable*, and *Configure* networking cards as well as *Modify System Name,* all from the *Actions* menu.

The Network Interface Cards screen lists the network cards installed on your system including the following information. You may have to expand the window or scroll over to see all of this information.

- Card Type such as Ethernet, IEEE 802.3, Token Ring, FDDI, and so forth.
- Card Name
- Hardware Path
- Status, such as whether or not the card is enabled
- Internet Address
- Subnet Mask
- Station Address in hex

Included under *Configure* for Ethernet cards is *Advanced Options,* which will modify the Maximum Transfer Unit for this card. Other cards included in your system can also be configured here usch as ISDN, X.25, ATM, and so on.

Network Services

This subarea is used to enable or disable some of the network services on your system. This screen has three columns which are the name, status, and description of the network services. Figure 4-24 from the *Network Services* subarea shows the network services that can be managed.

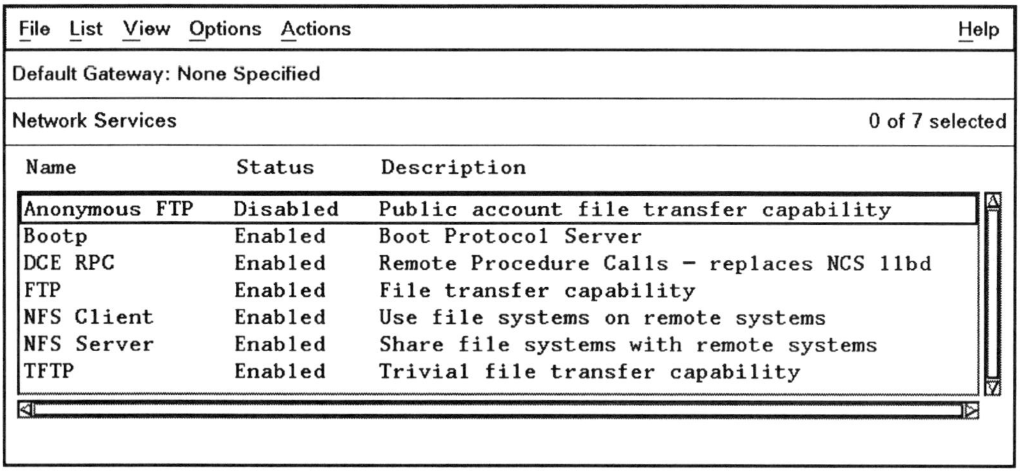

```
File  List  View  Options  Actions                                      Help

Default Gateway: None Specified

Network Services                                              0 of 7 selected

  Name              Status       Description

 Anonymous FTP    Disabled     Public account file transfer capability    ▲
 Bootp            Enabled      Boot Protocol Server
 DCE RPC          Enabled      Remote Procedure Calls - replaces NCS 11bd
 FTP              Enabled      File transfer capability
 NFS Client       Enabled      Use file systems on remote systems
 NFS Server       Enabled      Share file systems with remote systems
 TFTP             Enabled      Trivial file transfer capability           ▼
 ◁                                                                       ▷
```

Figure 4-24 Network Services

After selecting one of the network services shown, you can *Enable* or *Disable* the service depending on its current status, *Restart* the service if it is currently enabled, get more information about the service with *Zoom*, or *Modify System Name,* all from the *Actions* menu.

Network File Systems

This subarea is broken down into *Exported Local File Systems* and *Mounted Remote File Systems*. NFS is broken down into these two areas because you can export a local file system without mounting a remote file system and vice versa. This means you can manage these independently of one another. You may have an NFS server in your environment that won't mount remote file systems, and you may have an NFS client that will mount only remote file systems and never export its local file system.

Under *Exported Local File Systems* you can select the file systems you want exported. The first time you enter this screen you have no exported file systems listed. When you select *Add Exported File System* from the *Actions* menu you enter such information as

- local directory name

- user ID

- whether or not to allow asynchronous writes

- permissions

When this exported file system has been added, you can select it and choose from a number of *Actions* including *Modify* and *Remove*.

Under *Mounted Remote File Systems,* you have listed for you all of the directories and files that are mounted using NFS. These can be either mounted or mounted on demand with automounter. After selecting one of the mounted file systems, you can perform various *Actions*. For every remote file system mounted you have the following columns:

- Mount Directory which displays the name of the local directory name used to mount the remote directory.

- Type which is either *NFS* for standard NFS or *Auto* for auto- mounter (see the paragraph below).

- Remote Server which displays the name of the remote system where the file or directory is mounted.

- Remote Directory which is the name of the directory under which the directory is remotely mounted.

You should think about whether or not you want to use the NFS automounter. With automounter you mount a remote file or directory on demand, that is, when you need it. Using a master map you can specify which files and directories will be mounted when needed. The files and directories are not continuously mounted with automounter, resulting in more efficiency as far as how system resources are being used. There is, however, some overhead time associated with mounting a file or directory on demand as opposed to having it continuously mounted. From a user standpoint this may be slightly more undesirable, but from an administration standpoint, using the automounter offers advantages. Since the automounter is managed through SAM, there is very little additional work you need to perform to enable it.

System Access

This subarea is broken down into *Internet Services* and *Remote Logins.*

When you select *Internet Services,* the screen lists the networking services that are started by the Internet daemon **/usr/sbin/inetd**. I earlier covered **/etc/inetd.conf** which is a configuration file that lists all of the network services supported by a system that is read by **inetd**. There is also a security file **/var/adm/inetd.sec** that serves as a security check for **inetd**. Although there are many other components involved, you can view **inetd**, **/etc/inetd.conf**, and **/var/adm/inetd.sec** as working together to determine what network services are supported and the security level of each.

Listed for you in the *System Access* subarea are *Service Name, Description, Type*, and *System Permission*. In Figure 4-25 the *System Permission* for **shell** is "Denied"; for **ftp** is *Selected-Denied*; for **login** it is *Selected-Allowed*; and for all others is *Allowed*.

```
 File  List  View  Options  Actions                                    Help

 Internet Services                                           0 of 15 selected

  Service                                         System
  Name       Description                  Type    Permission

  printer    Remote spooling line printer  rlp     Allowed
  recserv    HP SharedX receiver service   SharedX Allowed
  spc        User Defined                  N/A     Allowed
  bootps     Bootstrap Protocol requests   ARPA    Allowed
  chargen    Inetd internal server         ARPA    Allowed
  daytime    Inetd internal server         ARPA    Allowed
  discard    Inetd internal server         ARPA    Allowed
  echo       Inetd internal server         ARPA    Allowed
  exec       Remote command execution      ARPA    Allowed
  ftp        Remote file transfer          ARPA    Selected-Denied
  login      Remote user login             ARPA    Selected-Allowed
  shell      Remote command execution, copy ARPA   Denied
  telnet     Remote login                  ARPA    Allowed
  tftp       Trivial remote file transfer  ARPA    Allowed
```

Figure 4-25   System Access - Internet Services

I changed the permission for **shell** by selecting it and using the *Modify* pick from the *Actions* menu and selecting "Denied." The following are three entries from **/var/adm/inetd.sec**. Note that no entry exists for all of the network services that are *Allowed*.

ftp	deny	system1
login	allow	system2
shell	deny	

The four permissions are

- Denied - All systems are denied access to this service.

- Allowed - All systems are allowed access to the service.

- Selected Denied - Only the selected systems are denied access to this service (**system1** under **ftp**).

• Selected Allowed - Only the selected systems are allowed access to this service (**system2** under **login**).

Remote Logins is used to manage security restrictions for remote users who will access the local system. There are two HP-UX files that are used to manage users. The file **/etc/hosts.equiv** handles users and **/.rhosts** handles superusers (root). When you enter this subarea you get a list of users and the restrictions on each. You can then *Add, Remove*, or *Modify* login security.

UUCP

The final subarea under *Networking and Communications* is UUCP. UUCP is a means of transferring files and executing commands on remote systems. UUCP is UNIX-to-UNIX Copy, which means you would use this software when going between UNIX systems. With a modem you can make a direct connection between UNIX systems and perform your system administration tasks.

SAM helps you with UUCP in two ways: by setting up management of remote systems under *UUCP Remote Systems*, and by managing devices to connect to remote systems under *UUCP Devices*.

The first time you enter *UUCP Devices,* you won't have any device files listed. You can select *Add Modem Device* from the *Actions* menu and then select the *Modem Type* and *Modem Device* from the *Add Modem Device* window that appears. If no Modem Devices are present in the list, you can go under *Peripheral Devices* and *Terminals and Modems* and add a modem device.

Under *UUCP Remote Systems* you can *Add, Modify*, or *Remove* a system from the list that appears. The modifications you can make include the following categories of information:

• Set System Information

• Set Calling Out Times

• Set Calling In Configuration

• Set Calling In Directories

- Set Calling Out Configuration

- Set Calling Out Directories

Peripheral Devices

With *Peripheral Devices* you can view any I/O cards installed in your system and peripherals connected to your system. This includes both used and unused. You can also quickly configure any peripheral including printers, plotters, tape drives, terminals, modems, and disks. This is a particularly useful area in SAM because configuring peripherals in HP-UX is tricky. You perform one procedure to connect a printer, a different procedure to connect a disk, and so on when you use the command line. In SAM these procedures are menu driven and therefore much easier.

Two of the six subareas, *Disks and File Systems* and *Printers and Plotters,* have their own dedicated hierarchy within SAM and are covered in this chapter. I won't cover these again in this section. The other four subareas *Cards, Device List, Tape Drives*, and *Terminals and Modems* will be covered in this section.

It's impossible for me to cover every possible device that can be viewed and configured in SAM. What I'll do is give you examples of what you would see on a workstation and a server so you get a feel for what you can do under **Peripheral Devices** with SAM. From what I show here, you should be comfortable that SAM can help you configure peripherals.

Figure 4-26 shows the hierarchy of *Peripheral Devices*.

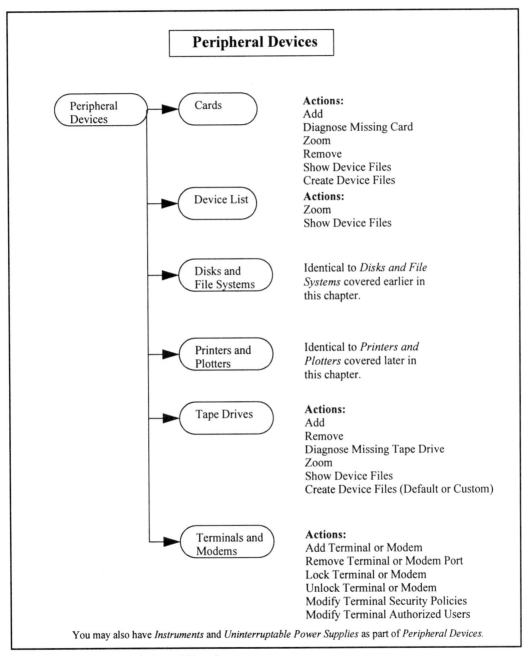

Figure 4-26 Peripheral Devices

Cards

When you select *Cards,* you are provided with a list of I/O cards in your
system. You can also perform such tasks as adding and removing cards.
Having this list of I/O cards is useful. Figures 4-27 and 4-28 show a listing of I/O cards for a workstation and server, respectively.

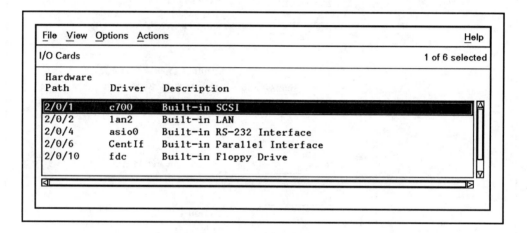

Figure 4-27 *I/O Cards* Window for Workstation

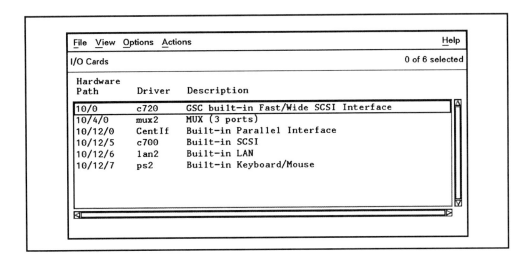

Figure 4-28 *I/O Cards* Window for Server

In *Cards* you can perform the following *Actions*:

Add

You can add a new I/O card in the window that is opened for you.

Diagnose Missing Card

If a card you have installed is not included in the list, you can select this to determine the reason.

Zoom

If you highlight a card and select *Zoom,* you will be provided such information as the hardware path, driver, and description of the card.

Remove   If you highlight a card and select *Remove,* a window will appear which walks you through removing the card from the system.

Show Device Files

If you select this, a window will be opened in which the device files associated with the card will be listed.

Create Device Files

Creates device files for the selected card. This takes place without any user interaction.

Device List

Device List shows all of the peripherals configured into the system. Figures 4-29 and 4-30 show a device list for a workstation and server, respectively.

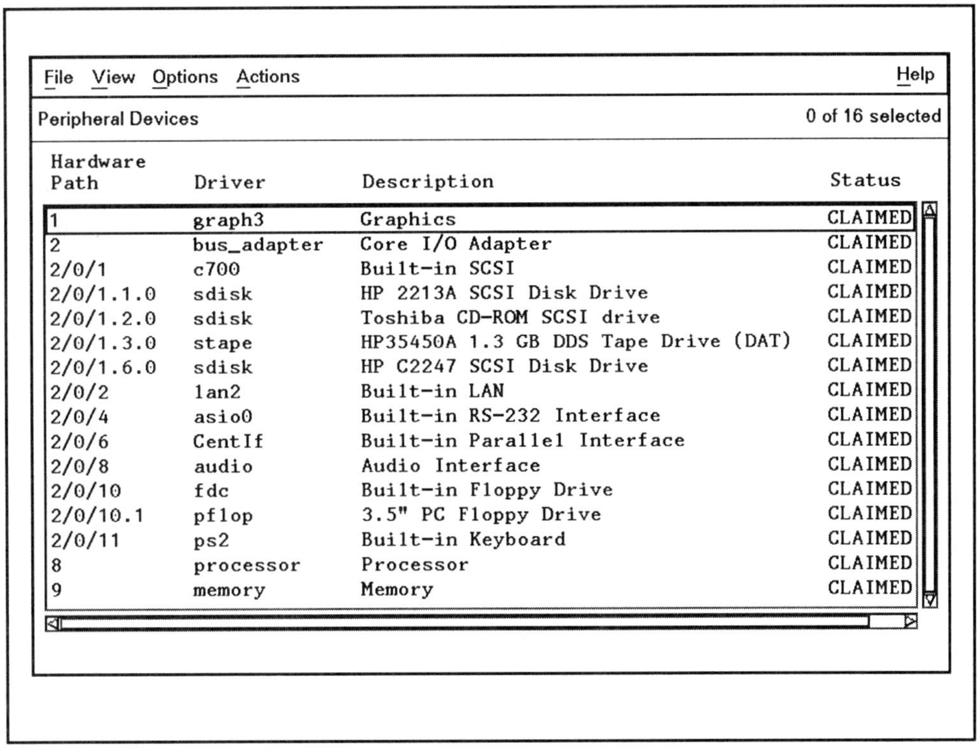

```
 File  View  Options  Actions                                    Help

 Peripheral Devices                                       0 of 16 selected

 Hardware
 Path           Driver        Description                      Status

 1              graph3        Graphics                         CLAIMED
 2              bus_adapter   Core I/O Adapter                 CLAIMED
 2/0/1          c700          Built-in SCSI                    CLAIMED
 2/0/1.1.0      sdisk         HP 2213A SCSI Disk Drive         CLAIMED
 2/0/1.2.0      sdisk         Toshiba CD-ROM SCSI drive        CLAIMED
 2/0/1.3.0      stape         HP35450A 1.3 GB DDS Tape Drive (DAT) CLAIMED
 2/0/1.6.0      sdisk         HP C2247 SCSI Disk Drive         CLAIMED
 2/0/2          lan2          Built-in LAN                     CLAIMED
 2/0/4          asio0         Built-in RS-232 Interface        CLAIMED
 2/0/6          CentIf        Built-in Parallel Interface      CLAIMED
 2/0/8          audio         Audio Interface                  CLAIMED
 2/0/10         fdc           Built-in Floppy Drive            CLAIMED
 2/0/10.1       pflop         3.5" PC Floppy Drive             CLAIMED
 2/0/11         ps2           Built-in Keyboard                CLAIMED
 8              processor     Processor                        CLAIMED
 9              memory        Memory                           CLAIMED
```

Figure 4-29 *Peripheral Devices* Window for Workstation

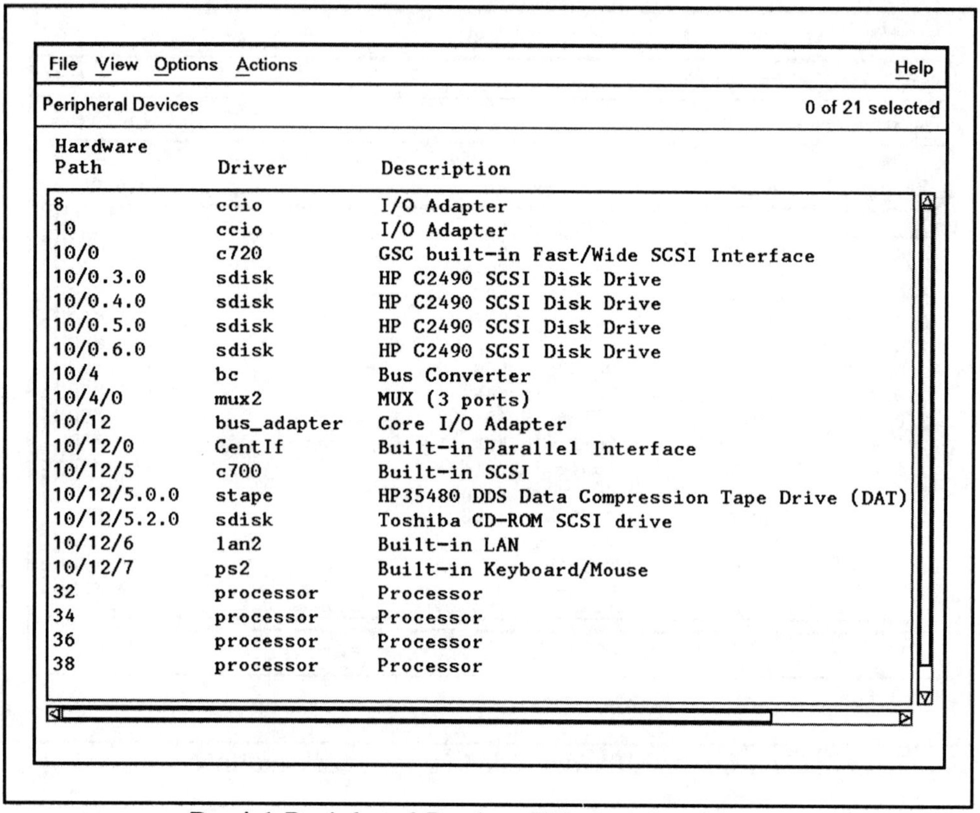

```
┌───────────────────────────────────────────────────────────────────────┐
│ File  View  Options  Actions                                       Help │
├───────────────────────────────────────────────────────────────────────┤
│ Peripheral Devices                                        0 of 21 selected │
├───────────────────────────────────────────────────────────────────────┤
│ Hardware                                                                │
│ Path            Driver        Description                               │
│ ┌──────────────────────────────────────────────────────────────────┐▲ │
│ │8               ccio          I/O Adapter                           │  │
│ │10              ccio          I/O Adapter                           │  │
│ │10/0            c720          GSC built-in Fast/Wide SCSI Interface │  │
│ │10/0.3.0        sdisk         HP C2490 SCSI Disk Drive              │  │
│ │10/0.4.0        sdisk         HP C2490 SCSI Disk Drive              │  │
│ │10/0.5.0        sdisk         HP C2490 SCSI Disk Drive              │  │
│ │10/0.6.0        sdisk         HP C2490 SCSI Disk Drive              │  │
│ │10/4            bc            Bus Converter                         │  │
│ │10/4/0          mux2          MUX (3 ports)                         │  │
│ │10/12           bus_adapter   Core I/O Adapter                      │  │
│ │10/12/0         CentIf        Built-in Parallel Interface           │  │
│ │10/12/5         c700          Built-in SCSI                         │  │
│ │10/12/5.0.0     stape         HP35480 DDS Data Compression Tape Drive (DAT) │  │
│ │10/12/5.2.0     sdisk         Toshiba CD-ROM SCSI drive             │  │
│ │10/12/6         lan2          Built-in LAN                          │  │
│ │10/12/7         ps2           Built-in Keyboard/Mouse               │  │
│ │32              processor     Processor                             │  │
│ │34              processor     Processor                             │  │
│ │36              processor     Processor                             │  │
│ │38              processor     Processor                             │▼ │
│ └◄─────────────────────────────────────────────────────────────────►┘  │
└───────────────────────────────────────────────────────────────────────┘
```

Figure 4-30 Partial *Peripheral Devices* Window for Server

The two *Action* menu picks here are *Zoom* and *Show Device Files*. Selecting *Zoom* produces a window with such information as hardware path, driver, description, and status. The device files associated with the item you have highlighted will be shown if you select *Show Device Files*.

Disks and File Systems was covered earlier in this chapter. *Instruments* may appear if your system supports HP-IB cards. *Printers and Plotters* is covered later in this chapter.

Tape Drives

Tape Drives lists the tape drives connected to your system. You are shown the Hardware Path, Driver, and Description for each tape drive. You can add, remove, diagnose tape drives, list tape drive device files, and add new tape drive device files.

Terminals and Modems

Your system's terminals and modems are listed for you when you enter this subarea. You can perform a variety of tasks from the *Actions* menu including the following:

- Add Terminal

- Add Modem

- Remove Terminal or Modem Port

- Lock Terminal or Modem Port

- Unlock Terminal or Modem Port

- Modify Terminal Security Policies

- Modify Terminal Authorized Users

- Additional Information

Uninterruptable Power Supplies

Your system's uninterruptable power supplies are listed for you when you enter this area including the UPS type, device file of the UPS, hardware path, port number, and whether or not shutdown is enabled. The *Actions* you can select are *Modify Global Configuration*; *Add; Zoom; Remove*; and *Modify*.

Figure 4-31 shows the *Modify Global Configuration* window.

```
┌─────────────────────────────────────────────────────────────┐
│ ┌──────────────────────────────────────────────────────────┐ │
│ │  ┌──────────────────────────────────┐                     │ │
│ │  │ UPS Daemon Status:               │                     │ │
│ │  │                                  │                     │ │
│ │  │  ◇ Activate Daemon               │                     │ │
│ │  │                                  │                     │ │
│ │  │  ◆ Deactivate Daemon             │                     │ │
│ │  └──────────────────────────────────┘                     │ │
│ │                                                            │ │
│ │       Shutdown Delay (minutes):    [ 1 ]                    │ │
│ │                                                            │ │
│ │   Shutdown Timeout (minutes):      [ 5 ]                    │ │
│ │                                                            │ │
│ │       Configuration File Name:   [ /etc/ups_conf ]         │ │
│ │                                                            │ │
│ ├──────────────────────────────────────────────────────────┤ │
│ │  [    OK    ]        [   Cancel   ]        [    Help    ]   │ │
│ └──────────────────────────────────────────────────────────┘ │
└─────────────────────────────────────────────────────────────┘
```

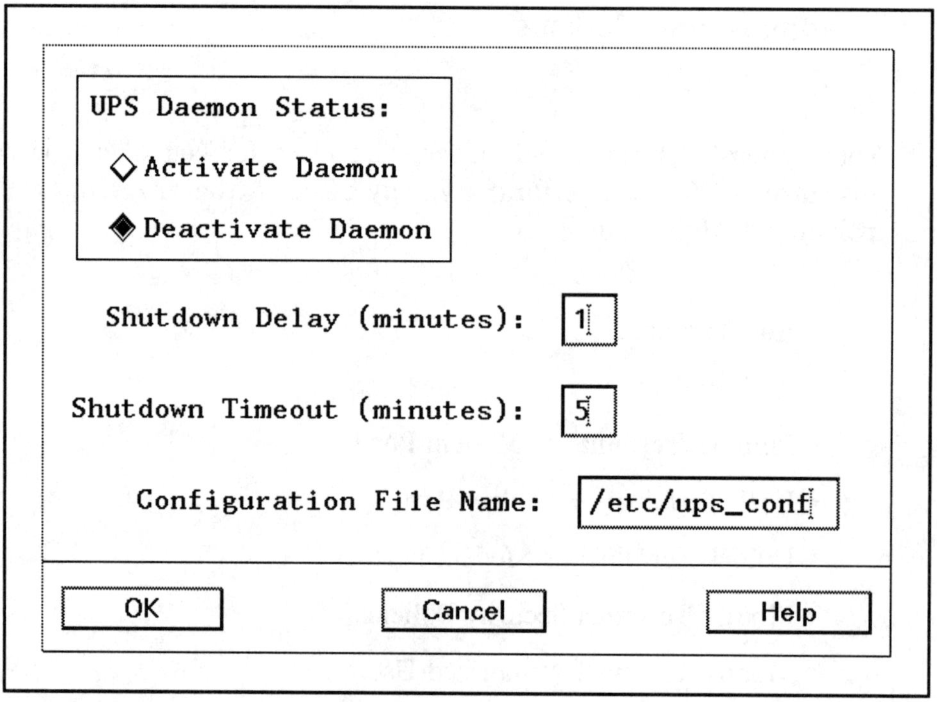

Figure 4-31 *Modify Global Configuration* Window For UPS

Printers and Plotters

Figure 4-32 shows the hierarchy of *Printers and Plotters*.

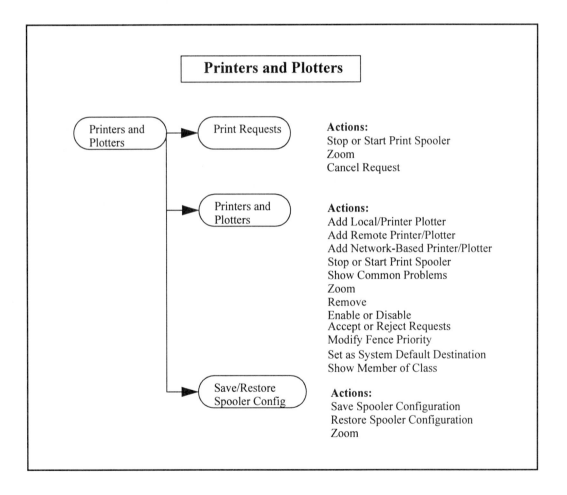

Figure 4-32 Printers and Plotters

Print Requests

Under *Print Requests* you can manage the print spooler and specific print jobs. You can start or stop the print spooler and cancel print jobs. The following information on print requests is listed for you:

Request ID   There is an ID associated with each print job. This is the Printer Name followed by a number.

Owner   Name of the user who requested the print job.

Priority   The priority of a print job is assigned when the job is submitted. The **-p** option of **lp** can be used to assign a priority to a job. Each print destination has a default priority that is assigned to jobs when **-p** is not used on the **lp** command.

File   Name of the file sent to the print queue.

Size   Size of the print job in bytes.

The *Actions* menu allows you to act on print jobs by canceling them. In addition, the print spooler can be stopped and started.

Printers and Plotters

You can configure both local and remote printers in *Printers and Plotters*. When you select *Add Local Printer/Plotter* from the *Actions* menu and then the appropriate type of printer, a window is opened for you in which you can supply the specifics about the printer. Before this window is opened, however, you must specify whether the *type* of printer to be added is: parallel serial; HP-IB; non standard device file; or a printer connected to a TSM terminal as well as which I/O card to add the printer to. One huge advantage to adding the printer using SAM is that this process is entirely menu driven, so you only have to select from among the information that is supplied you.

The window that appears asks you for the following information:

Printer Name   You can pick any name for the printer. I usually like to use a name that is somewhat descriptive, such as ljet4 for a LaserJet 4. The name is limited to 14 alphanumeric characters and underscores.

Printer Model/Interface   SAM supplies a list of all interface models for you when this window is opened. These models are located in the **/usr/lib/lp/model** directory. Each printer has an interface program that is used by the spooler to send a print job to the printer. When an interface model is selected, the model is copied to **/etc/lp/interface/** <printername> where it becomes the printer's interface program. Models can be used without modification or you can create customized interface programs.

Printer Class   You can define a group of printers to be in a class, which means print requests won't go to a specific printer but instead they will go to the first available printer within the class. This is optional.

Default Request Priority   This defines the default priority level of all requests sent to this printer.

Default Destination   Users who do not specify a printer when requesting a print job will have the print request sent to the default printer.

Figure 4-33 is an example *Add Local Printer/Plotter* window.

```
                    Printer Name:     |1jet4|

    Printer Model/Interface...        |laserjet4Si|

          Printer Class...            |laser|        (optional)

    Default Request Priority:         |0  ⊐|

    ■ Make This Printer the Default Destination|

    |   OK   |          |  Cancel  |            |  Help  |
```

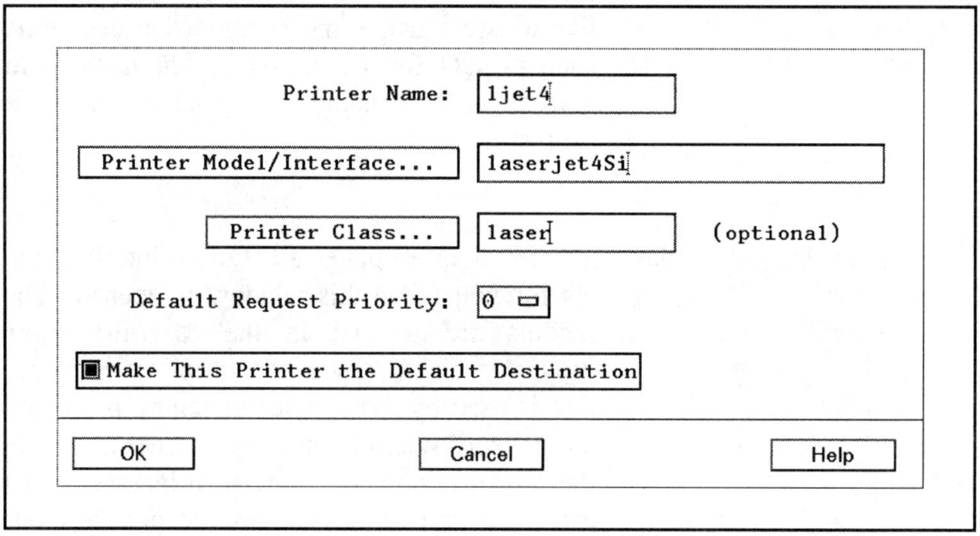

Figure 4-33 *Add Local Printer/Plotter* Window

After this printer has been added, I could use SAM to show me its status or use the **lpstat** command. Here is an example of the **lpstat** command showing ljet4 which was added in the last example.

```
$ /usr/bin/lpstat -t
scheduler is running
system default destination: ljet4
members of class laser:
```

```
        ljet4
device for ljet4: /dev/c1t0d0_lp
ljet4 accepting requests since Nov 21 22:45
printer ljet4 is idle. enabled since Nov 21 22:45
        fence priority : 0
no entries
```

As with all the other tasks SAM helps you with, you can manage printers and plotters manually. Doing this manually, however, is a real pain in the neck and I would strongly recommend you use SAM for managing printers and plotters. Not only does SAM make this easier for you, but I have also had nothing but good results having SAM do this for me. As you go through the SAM Log file you will see a variety of **lp** commands issued. Some of the more common commands, including the **lpstat** command issued earlier, are listed in Table 4-2.

TABLE 4-2 lp COMMANDS

COMMAND	DESCRIPTION
/usr/sbin/accept	Start accepting jobs to be queued
/usr/bin/cancel	Cancel a print job that is queued
/usr/bin/disable	Disable a device for printing
/usr/bin/enable	Enable a device for printing
/usr/sbin/lpfence	Set minimum priority for spooled file to be printed
/usr/bin/lp	Queue a job or jobs for printing
/usr/sbin/lpadmin	Configure the printing system with the options provided
/usr/sbin/lpmove	Move printing jobs from one device to another
/usr/sbin/lpsched	Start the **lp** scheduling daemon
/usr/sbin/lpshut	Stop the **lp** scheduling daemon
/usr/bin/lpstat	Show the status of printing based on the options provided
/usr/sbin/reject	Stop accepting jobs to be queued

Save/Restore Spooler Configuration

Occasionally the spooler can get into an inconsistent state (usually something else has to go wrong with your system that ends up somehow changing or renaming some of the spooler configuration files). SAM keeps a saved version of the spooler's configuration each time SAM is used to make a change (only the most recent one is saved). This saved configuration can be restored by SAM to recover from the spooler's having gotten into an inconsistent state. Your latest configuration is automatically saved by SAM, provided you used SAM to create the configuration as opposed to issuing **lp** commands at the command line and can be restored with *Restore Spooler Configuration* from *Save/Restore Spooler Config*. This screen allows you to save your current spooler configuration or restore previously saved spooler configuration information.

Process Management

Process Management is broken down into three areas which allow you to monitor, control, and schedule processes. Under *Performance Monitors* you can view the performance of your system in several different areas such as disk and virtual memory. *Process Control* allows you to control an individual process by performing such tasks as viewing it, changing its nice priority, killing it, stopping it, or continuing it. You can also view and schedule **cron** jobs under *Scheduled Cron Jobs*. Figure 4-34 shows the menu hierarchy of *Process Management*.

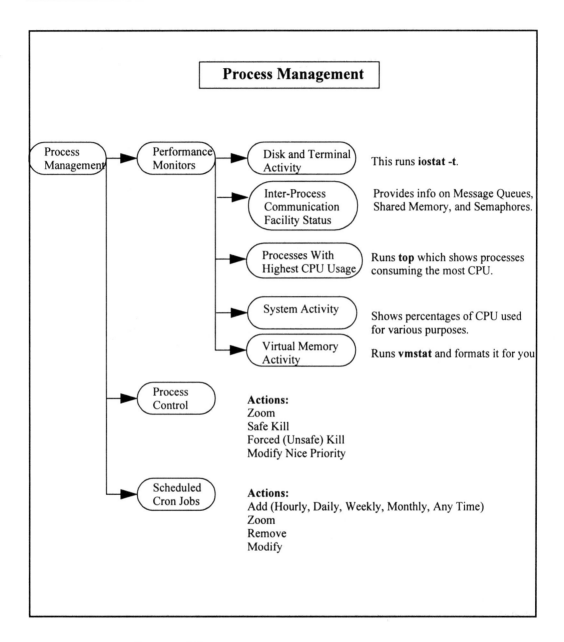

Figure 4-34 Process Management

Performance Monitors

Performance Monitors provides you a window into several areas of your system. If you are serious about becoming familiar with the tools available on your system to help you understand how your system resources are being used, you should take a close look at Chapter 5. Chapter 5 is devoted to getting a handle on how your system resources are being used, including many built-in HP-UX commands. Some of the performance monitors you can select in this subarea are HP-UX commands which you'll need some background in before you can use them. I'll cover these areas only briefly because this material will be covered in more detail in Chapter 4.

Selecting *Disk and Terminal Activity* opens a window which shows the output of **iostat -t**. I have included the description of **iostat** from Chapter 4 to save you the trouble of flipping ahead. When the *Disks and Terminal Activity* window with the output of **iostat** is opened for you, it shows a single **iostat** output. When you hit *return,* the window is automatically closed for you.

The **iostat** command gives you an indication of the level of effort the CPU is putting into I/O and the amount of I/O taking place among your disks and terminals. The following example shows the **iostat -t** command, which will be executed every three seconds, and associated output from an HP-UX 10.x system. The "#" shown is the HP-UX prompt.

```
# iostat -t 3
                        tty                      cpu
                    tin    tout         us     ni     sy    id
                    78     42           2       0     28    70

/dev/dsk/c0t1d0                 /dev/dsk/c0t4d0              /dev/dsk/c0t6d0
bps  sps   msps                 bps   sps  msps              bps  sps  msps
  0    0     0                   33   8.3  25.2                7    1   19.5
                        tty                      cpu
                    tin    tout         us     ni     sy    id
                    66     24           0       0     30    70

/dev/dsk/c0t1d0                 /dev/dsk/c0t4d0              /dev/dsk/c0t6d0
bps  sps   msps                 bps   sps  msps              bps  sps  msps
```

| | 5 | 12 | 15.9 | | 36 | 9.7 | 21 | | 7 | 1.2 | 13.8 |

	tty		cpu		
tin	tout	us	ni	sy	id
90	29	1	0	25	73

/dev/dsk/c0t1d0				/dev/dsk/c0t4d0				/dev/dsk/c0t6d0		
bps	sps	msps		bps	sps	msps		bps	sps	msps
12	1.7	15.5		24	3	19.1		14	2.1	14.6

	tty		cpu		
tin	tout	us	ni	sy	id
48	16	1	0	16	83

/dev/dsk/c0t1d0				/dev/dsk/c0t4d0				/dev/dsk/c0t6d0		
bps	sps	msps		bps	sps	msps		bps	sps	msps
0	0	0		62	9.3	18		12	2	17.2

	tty		cpu		
tin	tout	us	ni	sy	id
32	48	7	0	14	79

/dev/dsk/c0t1d0				/dev/dsk/c0t4d0				/dev/dsk/c0t6d0		
bps	sps	msps		bps	sps	msps		bps	sps	msps
1	0.3	14.4		5	.9	16.2		171	29.4	18.2

	tty		cpu		
tin	tout	us	ni	sy	id
2	40	20	1	42	27

/dev/dsk/c0t1d0				/dev/dsk/c0t4d0				/dev/dsk/c0t6d0		
bps	sps	msps		bps	sps	msps		bps	sps	msps
248	30.9	20.8		203	29.2	18.8		165	30.6	22.1

Descriptions of the reports you receive with **iostat** for terminals, the CPU, and mounted file systems follow.

For every terminal you have connected (tty), you see a "tin" and "tout," which represent the number of characters read from your terminal and the number of characters written to your terminal, respectively. The **-t** option produces this terminal report.

For your CPU, you see the percentage of time spent in user mode ("us"), the percentage of time spent running user processes at a low priority called nice ("ni"), the percentage of time spent in system mode ("sy"), and the percentage of time the CPU is idle ("id").

For every locally mounted file system, you receive information on the kilobytes transferred per second ("bps"), number of seeks per second ("sps"), and number of milliseconds per average seek ("msps"). For disks that are NFS-mounted or disks on client nodes of your server, you will not receive a report; **iostat** reports only on locally mounted file systems.

Inter-Process Communication Facility Status shows categories of information related to communication between processes. You receive status on Message Queues, Shared Memory, and Semaphores. This is a status window only, so again you would hit *return* and the window will close.

Processes with Highest CPU Usage is a useful window that lists the processes consuming the most CPU on your system. Such useful information as the Process ID, its Resident Set Size, and the Percentage of CPU it is consuming are listed.

System Activity provides a report of CPU utilization. You receive the following list:

%usr	Percent of CPU spent in user mode.
%sys	Percent of CPU spent in system mode.
%wio	Percent of CPU idle with some processes waiting for I/O such as virtual memory pages moving in or moving out.
%idle	Percent of CPU completely idle.

Virtual Memory Activity runs the **vmstat** command. This too is covered in Chapter 4, but I have included the **vmstat** description here so you don't have to flip ahead. Some of the columns of **vmstat** are moved around a little when the *Virtual Memory Activity* window is opened for you.

vmstat provides virtual memory statistics. It provides information on the status of processes, virtual memory, paging activity, faults, and the breakdown of the percentage of CPU time. In the following example, the output was produced ten times at five-second intervals. The first argument to the **vmstat** command is the interval; the second is the number of times you would like output produced.

vmstat 5 10:

procs			memory		page						faults			cpu		
r	b	w	avm	free	re	at	pi	po	fr	de	sr	in	sy	cs	us	sy	id
4	0	0	1161	2282	6	22	48	0	0	0	0	429	289	65	44	18	38
9	0	0	1161	1422	4	30	59	0	0	0	0	654	264	181	18	20	62
6	0	0	1409	1247	2	19	37	0	0	0	0	505	316	130	47	10	43
1	0	0	1409	1119	1	10	19	0	0	0	0	508	254	180	69	15	16
2	0	0	1878	786	0	1	6	0	0	0	0	729	294	217	75	17	8
2	0	0	1878	725	0	0	3	0	0	0	0	561	688	435	67	32	1
2	0	0	2166	98	0	0	20	0	0	0	66	728	952	145	8	14	78
1	0	0	2310	90	0	0	20	0	0	0	171	809	571	159	16	21	63
1	0	0	2310	190	0	0	8	1	3	0	335	704	499	176	66	14	20
1	0	0	2316	311	0	0	3	1	5	0	376	607	945	222	4	11	85

You will get more out of the **vmstat** command than you want. Here is a brief description of the categories of information produced by **vmstat**.

Processes are classified into one of three categories: runnable ("r"), blocked on I/O or short-term resources ("b"), or swapped ("w").

Next you will see information about memory. "avm" is the number of virtual memory pages owned by processes that have run within the last 20 seconds. If this number is roughly the size of physical memory minus your kernel, then you are near paging. The "free" column indicates the number of pages on the system's free list. It doesn't mean the process has finished running and these pages won't be accessed again; it just means they have not been accessed recently. I suggest you ignore this column.

Next is paging activity. Only the first field (re) is useful. It shows the pages that were reclaimed. These pages made it to the free list but were later referenced and had to be salvaged. Check to see that "re" is a low number. If you are reclaiming pages which were thought to be free by the system, then you are wasting valuable time salvaging these. Reclaiming pages is also a symptom that you are short on memory.

Next you see the number of faults in three categories: interrupts per second, which usually come from hardware ("in"); system calls per second ("sy"); and context switches per second ("cs").

The final output is CPU usage percentage for user ("us"), system ("sy"), and idle ("id"). This is not as complete as the **iostat** output, which also shows **nice** entries.

Process Control

When you pick *Process Control,* SAM lists the processes on your system and allows you to perform various actions. Using *Process Control* is a much easier way of controlling the processes on your system than executing commands such as **ps**, **nice**, and so forth. Figure 4-35 shows a partial listing of processes.

```
 File  List  View  Options  Actions                                    Help

Process Control                                                  1 of 68 selected

                        Nice
 User         Priority  Priority   Command
┌───────────────────────────────────────────────────────────────────────────┬─┐
│root         154       20         /usr/sbin/biod 4                           │△│
│root         154       20         /usr/sbin/biod 4                           │ │
│root         154       20         /usr/sbin/rpc.statd                        │ │
│root         154       20         /usr/sbin/rpc.lockd                        │ │
│root         154       20         /usr/sbin/inetd                            │▓│
│daemon       154       20         sendmail -bd -q30m -accepting connections  │▓│
│root         154       20         /usr/sbin/snmpd                            │▓│
│root         154       20         /opt/dce/sbin/rpcd                         │▓│
│root         154       20         /opt/ifor/ls/bin/i41md                     │▓│
│root         154       20         /usr/sbin/vtdaemon                         │▓│
│root         154       20         /usr/sbin/cron                             │ │
│root         154       20         /opt/audio/bin/Aserver                     │ │
│root         154       20            /opt/audio/bin/Aserver                  │ │
│root         154       20         /usr/sbin/rpc.mountd                       │ │
│root         154       20         /usr/sbin/nfsd 4                           │ │
│root         154       20            /usr/sbin/nfsd 4                        │ │
│root         154       20            /usr/sbin/nfsd 4                        │ │
│root         154       20            /usr/sbin/nfsd 4                        │ │
│root         156       20         /usr/sbin/getty console console            │ │
│root         154       20         /usr/vue/bin/vuelogin                      │▽│
└───────────────────────────────────────────────────────────────────────────┴─┘
 ◁                                                                            ▷
```

Figure 4-35   Partial *Process Control* Listing.

There are the four following columns of information listed for you.

- *User* - The name of the user who owns the process.

- *Priority* - The priority of the process determines its scheduling by the CPU. The lower the number, the higher the priority. Unless you have modified these priorities, they will be default priorities. Changing the priority is done with the **nice** command which will be covered shortly.

- *Nice Priority* - If you have a process that you wish to run at a lower or higher priority, you could change this value. The lower the value, the higher the CPU scheduling priority.

- *Command* - Lists the names of all the commands executing or running on the system.

In addition to these four columns, there are several others you can specify to be included in the list by selecting *Columns* from the *View* menu. You could include such information as the *Process ID, Parent Process ID, Processor Utilization, Core Image Size*, and so on. Adding *Processor Utilization* as a column, for instance, shows me how much of the processor all processes are consuming including SAM.

You can now select one of the processes and an *Actions* to perform.

When you select a process to kill and pick *Safe Kill* from the *Actions* menu, you get a message which indicates the process number killed and that it may take a few minutes to kill it in order to terminate cleanly. If you select a process to kill and pick *Forced Kill* from the *Actions* menu, you don't get any feedback; SAM just kills the process and you move on.

The **kill** command can be either **/usr/bin/kill** or **kill** that is part of the POSIX shell. The POSIX shell is the default shell for HP-UX. The other shells provide their own **kill** commands as well. We use the phrase "kill a process" in the UNIX world all the time, I think, because it has a powerful connotation associated with it. What we are really saying is we want to terminate a process. This termination is done with a signal. The most common signal to send is "SIGKILL" which terminates the process. There are other signals you can send to the process, but SIGKILL is the most common. As an alternative to sending the signal, you could send the corresponding signal number. A list of signal numbers and corresponding signals is shown below:

Signal Number	Signal
0	SIGNULL
1	SIGHUP
2	SIGINT
3	SIGQUIT
9	SIGKILL
15	SIGTERM

24	SIGSTOP
25	SIGTSTP
26	SIGCONT

I obtained this list of processes from the **kill** manual page.

To **kill** a process with a process ID of 234, you would issue the following command:

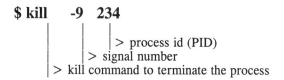

```
$ kill    -9   234
   |       |     |
   |       |     | > process id (PID)
   |       | > signal number
   | > kill command to terminate the process
```

The final selection from the *Actions* menu is to *Modify Nice Priority* of the process you have selected. If you were to read the manual page on **nice,** you would be very happy to see you can modify this with SAM. Modifying the **nice** value in SAM simply requires you to select a process and specify its new **nice** value within the acceptable range.

Scheduling Cron Jobs

The *Scheduled Cron Jobs* menu selection lists all of the **cron** jobs you have scheduled and allows you to *Add, Zoom, Remove*, and *Modify* **cron** jobs through the *Actions* menu. **cron** was described earlier in this chapter under *Backup and Recovery*. I have included some of the **cron** background covered earlier to save you the trouble of flipping back.

The **crontab** file is used to schedule jobs that are automatically executed by **cron. crontab** files are in the **/var/spool/cron/crontabs** directory. **cron** is a program that runs other programs at the specified time. **cron** reads files that specify the operation to be performed and the date and time it is to be performed. Going back to the backup example earlier in this chapter, we want to perform backups on a regular basis. SAM was used to activate **cron** in the backup example using the format described below.

The format of entries in the **crontab** file are as follows:

minute   hour   monthday   month   weekday   user name   command

minute - the minute of the hour, from 0-59
hour - the hour of the day, from 0-23
monthday - the day of the month, from 1-31
month - the month of the year, from 1-12
weekday - the day of the week, from 0 (Sunday) - 6 (Saturday)
user name - the user who will run the command if necessary
              (not used in example)
command - specifies the command line or script file to run

You have many options in the **crontab** file for specifying the *minute, hour, monthday, month,* and *weekday* to perform a task. You could list one entry in a field and then a space, several entries in any field separated by a comma, two entries separated by a dash indicating a range, or an asterisk, which corresponds to all possible entries for the field.

To list the contents of the **crontab** file, you would issue the following command. The output of this command is the **crontab** file created for the user root in the SAM backup example earlier in the chapter:

```
$ crontab -l


00 2 * * 6 /usr/sam/lbin/br_backup DAT FULL Y /dev/rmt/0m /etc/sam/br/
graphDCAa02410 root Y 1 N > /tmp/SAM_br_msgs 2>&1 #sambackup

15 12 * * 1-5 /usr/sam/lbin/br_backup DAT PART Y /dev/rmt/0m /etc/sam/
br/graphDCAa02410 root Y 1 N > /tmp/SAM_br_msgs 2>&1 #sambackup
```

Although these seem to be excruciatingly long lines, they do indeed conform to the format of the **crontab** file. The first entry is the full backup, the second entry is the incremental backup. In the first entry the *minute* is 00; in the second entry the *minute* is 15. In the first entry the *hour* is 2; in the second entry the *hour* is 12. In both entries the *monthday* and *month* are all legal values (*), meaning every *monthday* and *month*. In the first entry the *weekday* is 6 for Saturday (0 is Sunday); in the second entry the *weekdays* are 1-5 or Monday through Friday. The optional *username* is not specified in either example. And finally, the SAM backup command (**/usr/sam/lbin/br_backup**) and its long list of associated information is provided.

minute	hour	monthday	month	weekday	user name	command
00	12	all	all	6	n/a	br_backup
15	12	all	all	1-5	n/a	br_backup

This was done as part of the full and incremental backups that were covered earlier in the chapter. You can, however, schedule **cron** to run any kind of job for you. Using *Add* from the *Actions* menu, you can add *Hourly, Daily, Weekly, Monthly*, or jobs to run *Any Time*. You can also *Remove, Modify*, or *Zoom* in on one of the existing **cron** entries from the *Actions* menu.

Routine Tasks

The following subareas exist under *Routine Tasks* in SAM:

- Backup and Recovery
- Find and Remove Unused Filesets
- Selective File Removal
- System Log Files

• System Shutdown

The hierarchy of *Routine Tasks* is shown in Figure 4-36. Please note that *Backup and Recovery* is identical to the SAM top-level *Backup and Recovery* area discussed earlier in this chapter.

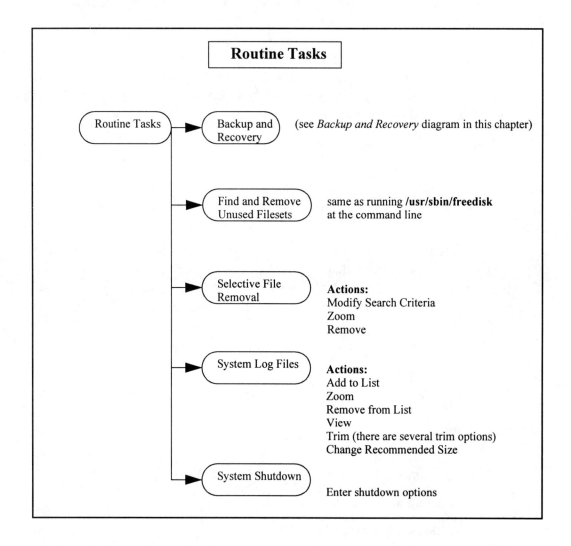

Figure 4-36 Routine Tasks

Backup and Recovery

This is identical to the *Backup and Recovery* area covered earlier in this chapter.

Find and Remove Unused Filesets

Find and Remove Unused Filesets runs the **/usr/sbin/freedisk** utility that is used to recover disk space by locating filesets which can be removed. **freedisk** is a command that identifies filesets that have not been used since they were installed and will remove them for you. The filesets in question would have been installed with **swinstall**.

When you run **freedisk,** it looks for filesets that have not been used since installed. If you use the **-a** option and specify a usage time, then **freedisk** will find the filesets that have not been used since that time. Filesets that have not been used but are depended on by filesets that have been used are treated as though they have been used. Here is an example of the **freedisk** command to identify files that have not been used in 60 days:

$ **/usr/sbin/freedisk -a 60**

freedisk then removes filesets by invoking **swremove,** at which time you can unselect filesets which are slated for removal.

Using SAM, **freedisk** is run for you and reports on what filesets have not been used. This process takes some time. Such activities as collecting filesets, counting filesets, screening files, and checking access times are performed. During the phase where access times are checked, SAM reports on the percent complete of this process. When SAM has completed this phase, it reports the number of filesets which appear to be unused and the total number of filesets. You will also receive a list of filesets which are unused but depended on by other filesets. In an example run I received the following list of filesets which were unused but were not passed to **swremove** because other filesets which were in use depended on these.

AudioSubsystem.AUDIO-SHLIBS
UUCP.UUCP
OS-Core.C-MIN
GraphicsCommon.FAFM-RUN
GraphicsCommon.FAFM-SHLIBS
ProgSupport.PROG-MIN

SAM then allows you to remove any or all of the filesets identified as unused. Then **swremove** is run and you can proceed with removing any filesets you wish.

Selective File Removal

Selective File Removal allows you to search for files to remove. You can specify a variety of criteria for selecting files to remove including the following:

Type of file   There are three different file types you can search for: *Large Files, Unowned Files*, and *Core Files*. A pop-up menu allows you to select which of these to search for. Figure 4-37 shows *Large Files* selected. With *Large Files,* you are searching for files of a minimum size that haven't been modified in the specified time. *Unowned Files* are those files owned by someone other than a valid system user. *Core Files* contain a core image of a terminated process when the process was terminated under certain conditions. Core files are usually related to a problem with a process and contain such information as data, stack, and so forth.

Mount Points   Specify whether or not you want to search across non-NFS mount points. If you select *Yes,* this means the search will include mount points on your system but not extend to NFS mount points. I chose not to include other mount points in the example.

Beginning Path   Your search can begin at any point in the system hierarchy. You can specify the start point of the search in this field. If you want to search only the **/home** directory for files, then change this entry to **/home** and you will search only that directory as I did in the example.

Minimum Size   Specify the smallest size file in bytes that you want searched for. Files smaller than this size will not be reported as part of the search. The minimum size in the example is 500,000 bytes.

Last Modification

If you select *Large Files*, you can make an entry in this field. You enter the minimum number of days since the file was last modified and files that have been modified within that time period will be excluded from the search. This is 30 days in the example.

Figure 4-37 shows an example of specifying which files to search for.

```
+-------------------------------------------------------------------------+
|                                                                         |
|                        Search For: | Large Files   ⌑ |                  |
|                                                                         |
|   Search Across non-NFS Mount Points: | No  ⌑ |                         |
|                                                                         |
|             Beginning of Search Path: | /home         |                 |
|                                                                         |
|               Minimum Size (Bytes): | 500000              |             |
|                                                                         |
|   Time Since Last Modification (Days): | 30  |                          |
|                                                                         |
+-------------------------------------------------------------------------+
|  [    OK    ]              [    Cancel    ]              [    Help    ]   |
+-------------------------------------------------------------------------+
```

Figure 4-37   Searching for Files to Remove

The list of files reported for removal was too long with a minimum size of only 500 KBytes. I increased the minimum size to 5 MBytes and received the list of files in Table 4-3 after my search.

TABLE 4-3   Files Reported For Removal

File Name	Size (Bytes)	Last Modified
/home/denise/demo.mpg	5215336	Jun 19 1995
/home/denise/rock.mpg	17698880	Aug 12 1995
/users/tomd/tst.sasdata2	15666920	Sep 11 1995
/home/joe/testdatabase	23496520	Sep 13 1995

The way to approach removing files is to start with an exceptionally large file size and work your way down in size. It may be that you have a few "unexpected" large files on your system that you can remove and ignore the smaller files.

System Log Files

System Log Files is used to manage the size of your system log files. Log files are generated by HP-UX for a variety of reasons including backup, shutdown, cron, and so forth. Your applications may very well be generating log files as well. Some of these log files can grow in size indefinitely, creating a potential catastrophe on your system by growing and crashing your system. You can be proactive and manage these log files in this subarea.

SAM is aware of many of the log files generated by HP-UX. When you enter the *System Log Files* subarea, information related to log files is listed. You can add to the list of log files SAM knows about and have a complete list of log files presented to you each time you enter this subarea. SAM lists the following information related to log files each time you enter this subarea. (You may have to increase the size of the window to see all this information.)

File Name   Full path name of log file.

Percent Full   SAM has what it thinks should be the maximum size of a log file. You can change this size by selecting *Change Recommended Size* from the *Actions* menu. The percent full is the percentage of the recommended size the log file consumes.

Current Size   The size of the file in bytes is listed for you. You
                    may want to take a look at this. The current size
                    of a log file may be much bigger than you would
                    like. You could then change the recommended
                    size and quickly see which files are greater than
                    100 percent. The converse may also be true. You
                    may think the recommended size for a log file is
                    far too small and change the recommended size
                    to a larger value. In either case you would like to
                    quickly see which files are much bigger than rec-
                    ommended.

Recommended Size

                    This is what you define as the recommended size
                    of the file. Check these to make sure you agree
                    with this value.

Present on System

                    Yes if this file is indeed present on your system;
                    No if it is not present on your system. If a file is
                    not present on your system and it simply does not
                    apply to you, then you can select *Remove from
                    List* from the *Actions* menu. For example, you
                    may not be running UUCP and therefore want to
                    remove all of the UUCP-related log files.

File Type   The only file types listed are *ASCII* and *Non-
                    ASCII*. I found it interesting that **/var/sam/log/
                    samlog** was not one of the log files listed. This is
                    not an ASCII file and must be viewed through
                    View SAM Log from the *Actions* menu, but it is
                    indeed a log file which I thought would appear in
                    the list.

You can trim a log file using the *Trim* pick from the *Actions* menu. You then have several options for trimming the file.

System Shutdown

SAM offers you the following three ways to shut down your system:

- *Halt the System*
- *Reboot (Restart) the System*
- *Go to Single-User State*

In addition, you can specify the number of minutes before shutdown occurs.

Run SAM on Remote Systems

I think SAM is great. If it works well on one system then you, as the system administrator, may as well use it on other systems from a central point of control. *Run SAM on Remote Systems* allows you to set up the system on which you will run SAM remotely from a central point of control.

You can specify any number of remote systems to be controlled by a central system. With the *Actions* menu you can

Add System   A window opens up in which you can specify the name of the remote system you wish to administer locally.

Run SAM   You can select the remote system on which you want to run SAM.

Remove System(s)

Remote systems can be removed from the list of systems on which you will run SAM remotely.

Software Management

Software Management under SAM uses Software Distributor-HP-UX (I'll call this Software Distributor) which was covered in detail in an earlier chapter. I will go over the basics of *Software Management* in SAM so you can see how some of these tasks are performed in SAM. The following subareas exist under *Software Management* in SAM:

- Copy Software to Local Depot
- Install Software to Local Host
- List Software
- Remove Software

The hierarchy of *Software Management* is shown in Figure 4-38.

Figure 4-38 Software Management

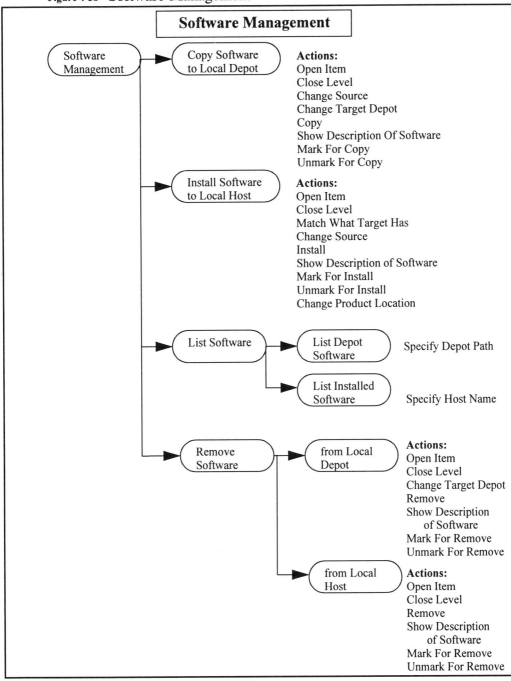

Copy Software to Local Depot

The first task to perform under *Copy Software to Local Depot* is to specify the target depot path. This is the location on your system where software will be stored or managed. Keep in mind that the CD-ROM from which you may be loading software can also be a depot. This is a directory from which your system and other systems can install software. SAM asks if you would like to use **/var/spool/sw** as the directory of the target depot path. I have selected **/var/spool/swdepot** as the target depot path in the upcoming example. You can use this directory or specify another directory name. SAM then asks for the source host name and source depot path. Using the CD-ROM on the system, we would perform the following steps.

The first step when loading software from CD-ROM is to insert the media and mount the CD-ROM. The directory **/SD_CDROM** should already exist on your system. You can use SAM to mount the CD-ROM for you or do this manually. I issued the following command to mount a CD-ROM at SCSI address 2 on a workstation:


```
$ mount /dev/dsk/c0t2d0 /SD_CDROM
```

The dialog box that appears in SAM where you specify the source is shown in Figure 4-39.

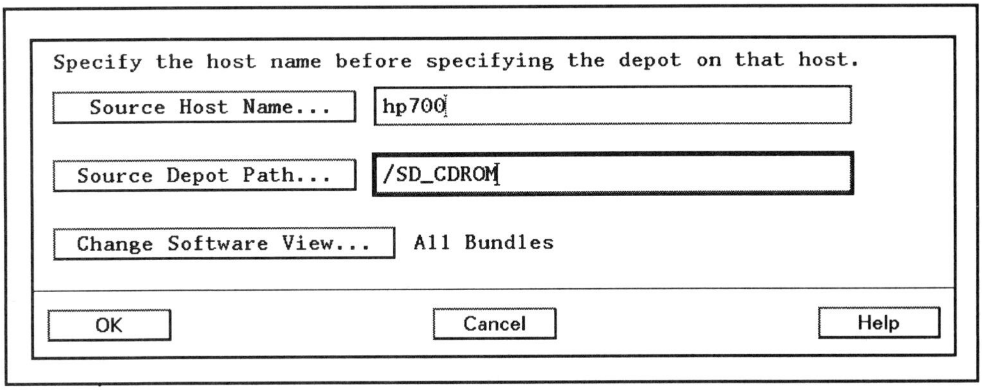

```
┌─────────────────────────────────────────────────────────────────┐
│ ┌───────────────────────────────────────────────────────────┐   │
│ │ Specify the host name before specifying the depot on that host. │
│ │  ┌─────────────────────────┐  ┌──────────────────────────┐ │   │
│ │  │   Source Host Name...   │  │ hp700                    │ │   │
│ │  └─────────────────────────┘  └──────────────────────────┘ │   │
│ │                                                             │   │
│ │  ┌─────────────────────────┐  ┌──────────────────────────┐ │   │
│ │  │   Source Depot Path...  │  │ /SD_CDROM                │ │   │
│ │  └─────────────────────────┘  └──────────────────────────┘ │   │
│ │                                                             │   │
│ │  ┌─────────────────────────────┐                           │   │
│ │  │  Change Software View...    │  All Bundles              │   │
│ │  └─────────────────────────────┘                           │   │
│ │                                                             │   │
│ │  ┌──────────┐        ┌──────────┐        ┌──────────┐      │   │
│ │  │   OK     │        │  Cancel  │        │   Help   │      │   │
│ │  └──────────┘        └──────────┘        └──────────┘      │   │
│ └───────────────────────────────────────────────────────────┘   │
└─────────────────────────────────────────────────────────────────┘
```

Figure 4-39 *Specify Source* Window

At this point you select the software you wish to copy to the software depot from the source. This is done by highlighting the names you wish to be loaded and selecting *Mark For Copy* from the *Actions* menu and then *Copy* from the *Actions* menu. This places the software in the local depot. Figure 4-40 shows the *Software Selection Window* with the *HP C++ Compiler* highlighted with a source of **/SD_CDROM** and target depot directory **/var/spool/swdepot**.

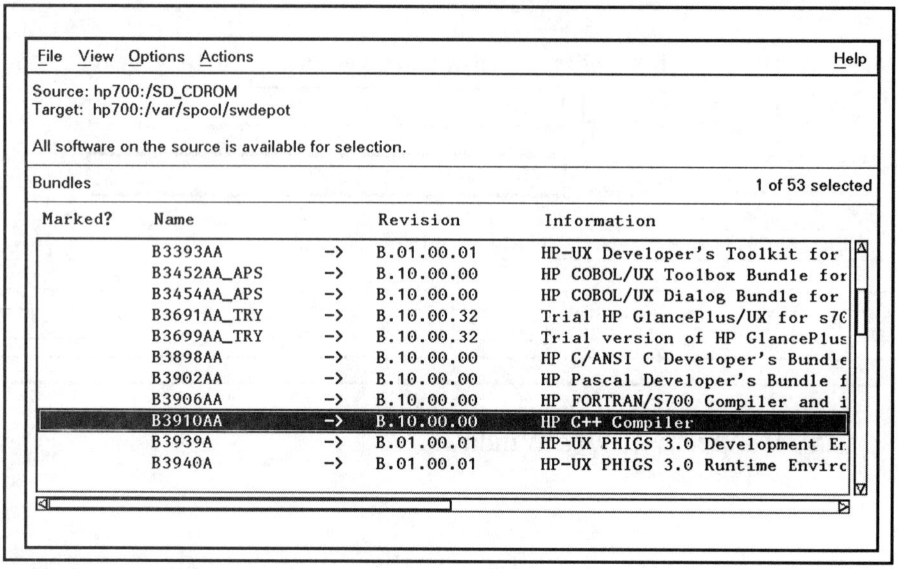

Figure 4-40 *Software Selection* Window

Copy first performs an analysis in which a lot of useful information is produced such as the amount of disk space in the depot directory both before and after the installation takes place, as shown in Figure 4-41.

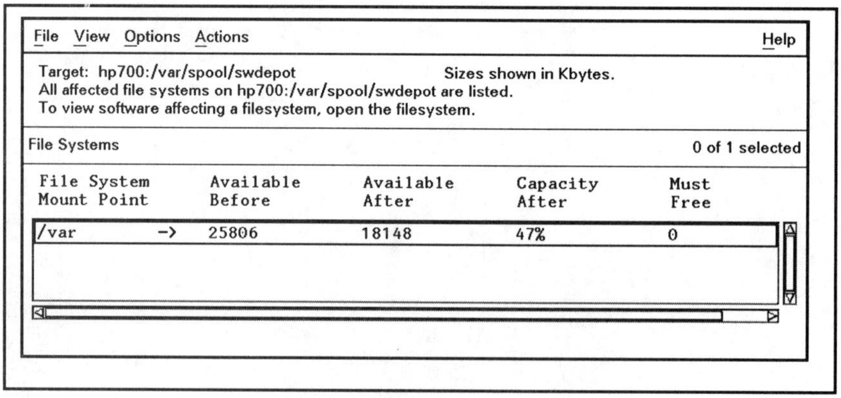

Figure 4-41 *Disk Space Analysis* Window

If you are satisfied with the analysis information, you can load the software. A window showing the status of the installation will appear. It is now in a depot on the hard disk, as opposed to the CD-ROM depot it was loaded from, that this and other systems can access for installing software.

You can select *Save Session As* from the *Actions* menu if you wish to save the list of depots and software.

Install Software to Local Host

Install Software To Local Host is similar to *Copy Software to Local Depot* in that you must specify the Source Host Name and Source Depot Path. The Source Depot Path could be the CD-ROM from which you are loading software, as shown in the previous example, or it could be a directory depot. We just created a directory depot from which software can be copied in the previous example so we could use that directory rather than the CD-ROM. If that directory name is specified as the Source Depot Path, the software in Figure 4-42 is shown in the depot.

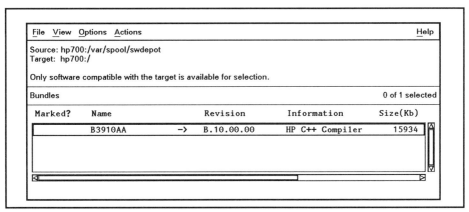

Figure 4-42 Copying From Directory Depot

The *HP C++ Compiler* is the software we loaded into this directory in the previous example. Before loading software you should select *Show Description Of Software* from the *Actions* menu to see if a system reboot is required (you may have to scroll down the window to see the bottom of the description). You want to know this before you load software so you don't load software that requires a reboot at a time that it is inconvenient to reboot. We can now install this software onto the local host by selecting *Mark For Install* and *Install* from the *Actions* menu.

When this installation is complete, after only about four minutes when installing from a local disk on the local host, a system reboot is not required.

List Software

You can select either *List Depot Software* or *List Installed Software*.

Under *List Depot Software*, you specify the host and depot path from which you receive a complete list of software. This can be listed at the bundle, product, subproduct, fileset, or file level. If you have even a small amount of software installed in a depot, the file level is probably going to be too much detail. Listing *HP C++ Compiler* we loaded earlier to the fileset level is both manageable to read and informative. The file level is just too much detail.

List Installed Software allows you to list the software installed on your system to the bundle, product, subproduct, fileset, or file level also. Selecting the bundle level and listing through SAM produces the same output as typing **swlist** at the command line. You can try this on your system to see how the two compare.

Remove Software

You can *Remove Software from Local Depot* or *Remove Software from Local Host*.

We can use the directory depot in **/var/spool/swdepot** we created earlier to delete software. The *HP C++ Compiler* we loaded in this directory can be highlighted, and *Mark For Remove* from the *Actions* menu. Selecting *Remove* from the *Actions* menu will remove the software from the directory depot. You can also *Remove Software From Local Host* using the same procedure.

Time

Not covered.

NFS Diskless Concepts

Rather than cover NFS diskless as an area to be managed, I'm going to deviate from the format found throughout this chapter and instead provide a brief description of NFS diskless.

This is a topic new to HP-UX 10.x. Diskless nodes were implemented with Distributed HP-UX (DUX) in HP-UX 9.x and earlier releases. Distributed HP-UX was first introduced in HP-UX 6.0 in 1986 and was successfully used in many HP installations. The new implementation of diskless nodes in HP-UX 10.x is NFS Diskless. It has many desirable features including the following:

- NFS diskless is the current defacto standard.

- It is not a proprietary solution.

- High-end diskless servers and clients can be symmetric multiprocessing systems.

- Many file system types and features are available such as UNIX File System, Journaled File System, Logical Volume Manager, disk mirroring, and so on.

- The System V Release 4 file system layout described throughout this book is implemented. This file system layout is conducive to extensive file sharing which is used in NFS Diskless.

- Read-only NFS mounts such as **/usr**, **/bin**, and **/opt/** < application > are supported.

- Distributed HP-UX functionality such as context-dependent files have been removed.

- Servers can be both Series 700 and Series 800 units.

- The physical link doesn't matter so servers can use many interfaces such as IEEE 802.3 and FDDI. A server can also assign some diskless systems to one network card, and other systems to other network cards.

- Diskless systems can boot across a gateway, thereby allowing subnets to be used.

- Booting is implemented with standard Boot Protocol (BOOTP) and Trivial File Transfer Protocol (TFTP) protocols.

- Clients can swap to a local disk or swap using NFS to a remote disk.

There are many additional features of NFS diskless; however, since our focus is on management, let's take a closer look at this. Using SAM, all tasks related to NFS diskless administration can be performed. This means you have a single point of administration for the cluster. You have clusterwide resources, such as printers and file systems, that can be managed from any node in the cluster. You can defer some operations until a later point in time if a node is unreachable. And, of course, you can add and delete clients in SAM.

Using SAM you get a single point of administration for several NFS diskless systems. This means that performing an operation in SAM affects all systems in the cluster. The single point of administration areas in SAM include

- Printers/Plotters

- File Systems

- Users/Groups

- Home Directories

- Electronic Mail

- Backups

Although there is a great deal that could be covered on NFS diskless and the many improvements in this area over Distributed HP-UX, the key point from an administrative perspective is that SAM provides a central point of administration for NFS diskless administration. All tasks related to NFS diskless administration can be performed through SAM.

ENWARE X-station Administration (optional)

When you install the ENWARE software on your system, you'll have *ENWARE X-station Administration* as one of your top-level menu picks. This is not a standard area of SAM but makes X-station administration easier. This does not appear unless you install the ENWARE software. You can perform the following X-station related functions from within SAM:

1) Add an X station
2) Remove an X station
3) Printers, plotters
4) Installation testing and version control
5) XDM Administration

Configuring an X-station in SAM is identical to running **/opt/ enware/lbin/xtadm**.

To add an X-station, you would provide the following information in SAM:

Name
IP address
LAN hardware address
Subnet mask
Default Gateway IP address

CHAPTER 5

The Art
of System
Administration

Where Are Your HP-UX System Resources Going?

In this chapter we'll cover some techniques for determining how your HP-UX system resources are being used. Some of the material in this chapter was developed using HP-UX 9.x; however, the same principles and commands apply to later versions of HP-UX.

Everyone likes setting up new systems and the excitement of seeing the system run for the first time. With system setup you get a great deal in return for your investment of time. With an instant ignition system, for instance, you spend a short amount of time in setup and you get a big return - your system is up and running. Similarly, when you perform routine system administration functions with SAM, you spend a short time running SAM and you end up completing a vital task, such as adding a user or performing a system backup.

In Chapter 1, I described a process whereby you spend about two hours unpacking boxes and connecting cables, and then you turn on the power and your system boots. You've done a lot in a short time and it feels great. At this point it's not even lunch time and you can justify taking off the rest of the day!

If a new user were to walk up to your desk and ask you for an account, you say you would be happy to do so but this is a complex process which will take a while. Then you run SAM and in about 30 seconds the new user is added to the system! Again you're quite pleased with yourself for having done so much so quickly.

In this chapter we get into some of the "gray" areas of system administration. System resource utilization and performance monitoring are less straightforward endeavors than others covered, such as system setup and SAM. You play detective some of the time when determining how systems resources are being used and sometimes you guess at what is taking place. That's the reason I think this is where the fun begins.

When determining where system resources are going, I often find system administrators dealing with their computer systems as **SYSTEMS** for the first time. Computer systems are too often thought of as independent components. What may look like the source of a system bottleneck may just be a symptom of some other problem. Keep in mind that components of the system work together; a small problem in one area may manifest itself as a bigger problem in other areas. I'll provide some examples of what to look for throughout this chapter, but keep in mind your system is indeed unique. You have to consider your environment as you use the tools described here.

Understanding where your HP-UX system resources are going is indeed an art. There are great built-in HP-UX commands such as **iostat** and **vmstat**. There are also some fine performance monitoring tools such as HP GlancePlus/UX and HP PerfView to help you. Which tools you use and how you use them are not as clean and orderly as the topics covered earlier.

Why is it so difficult to determine where your system resources are going if there are so many great tools to assist you? To begin with, this is the information age. No one knows better than those of us who deal with information systems that the problem is there is too much information. This can be the problem when you try to determine where your system resources are going. You may end up gathering information about your system in off hours when it is not in use, thereby getting meaningless results. You may end up with long accounting reports with too much data to digest. You may end up with so many network statistics that a fleet of system administrators wouldn't have time to analyze them, let alone one overworked, albeit enthusiastic, administrator.

Since every system and network are different, I can't recommend just one approach for determining where your system resources are going. I can recommend, however, that you understand all of the tools I cover here and then determine which are best suited for your environment. You may decide that you can get all the information you need from the built-in HP-UX commands. You may, on the other hand, determine that you need the best performance tools available. Once you know what each of these techniques does and does not offer, you will be in a much better position to make this decision.

System Components

Now the big question: *What are the components of your system?* At one time we viewed the components of a system as

- **CPU**
- **Memory**
- **I/O**

Well, like all other things in this world, system components have become more complex. All of the components of your system work together, or in some cases against one another. You must, therefore, take an inventory of system components before you can begin to determine how your system resources are being used. Here is a more current list of system components:

1. Applications

- **local** - These applications run locally and don't rely on other systems for either the applications or data.

- **remote** - These are applications that either run remotely or are copied from a remote system to a local system and then run locally. I consider both of these remote applications because an application that has to be copied to the local system before it is run consumes a lot of networking resources, sometimes more than an application which runs remotely would consume.

- **license servers** - Many applications require license servers to be running to ensure that you have a license available for a user who wants to run an application. In a distributed environment you may have an application with several license servers running so that if one or two license servers go down, you still have a third license server running. Because you can have many license servers running for many applications, these may be consuming substantial system resources

2. **Data** - Listing your data as a system resource may be a surprise to you. I think, however, that since most computers and applications are a means to create the data that keeps your company in business, you should indeed consider it as a system resource. In some cases, system and database administrators spend many hours planning how data will be stored in order to achieve the fastest response time. In a distributed engineering application, the location and number of data servers can have a major impact on overall system and network performance. In this respect data is indeed a system resource.

   - **local data** - On local system, consumes primarily system resources.

   - **remote data** - On remote system, consumes resources on local system, remote system, and network.

3. **Windowing environment and user interface**

   - **X, Motif, HP CDE** - You will want to take a close look at the amount of system resources that can be consumed by X, Motif, and HP CDE. Later in this chapter when we look at programs that are consuming system resources, you will see the substantial impact these programs have.

4. **Networking** - Networking is the perceived or real bottleneck in more and more installations. Because of the increasing demand placed on networking resources by client/server applications and other distributed environments, you need to have an understanding of the amount of networking resources your system is consuming and how busy your network is in general. Because I don't cover such advanced network management tools as HP OpenView in this book, we are going to take a look at the commands you can issue to see how busy the network interface is on a particular system and get an idea of the overall amount of traffic on the network.

5. **CPU** - Of course the CPU is a system resource. I just chose not to list it first because until you know how your system is set up in terms of applications, data, user interface, and so on, it is pointless to start looking at the CPU.

6. **Memory** - Memory is the system resource I find most often needs to be increased. What sometimes looks to be a shortage of CPU capacity sometimes turns out to be a lack of memory.

7. **Input/Output (I/O)** - The real question with I/O as a system resource is how long does it take to get my applications or data to and from disk. We'll look at various ways to see what kind of I/O activity you have going on.

Commands and Tools for Determining How System

Resources Are Being Used

There are a variety of approaches you can take to determine how system resources are being used. These choices range from quick snapshots that take but a few seconds to create, to long-range capacity planning programs that you may want to run for weeks or months before you even begin to analyze the data they produce. Figure 5-1 shows the level of data produced by some of the possible approaches to determining how your system resources are being consumed.

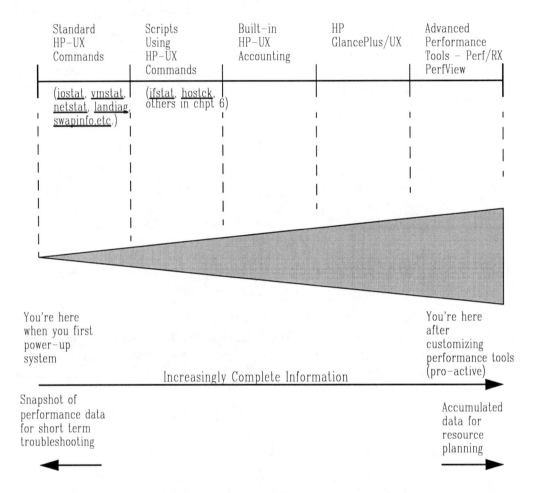

Figure 5-1 Methods Of Determining How System Resources Are Used

This figure shows some commonly used techniques for determining how system resources are being used. We'll cover two of these techniques:

1. Introducing some standard HP-UX commands that give you information about system resources. These are also embedded in some scripts that are included in the shell programming chapter.

2. Using the performance monitoring tool HP GlancePlus/UX.

These two approaches are covered in upcoming sections.

Taking Inventory

In an existing computing environment it is essential to first take an inventory of your computing resources before you begin to determine the level of system resources. The minimum you should include in this inventory are the system resources I listed earlier in this chapter (applications, data, user interface, etc.) so you will know how your network is set up before you begin to determine how your system resources are being used.

I will show examples of systems and portions of networks throughout this chapter. In order to show how system resources are being used, it is essential to know the system components you are dealing with, especially if they are scattered among systems in a distributed environment.

With existing networks this may be a long and painful process, but a process that is well worth the time. A network that has evolved over the course of 20 years will have vast inefficiencies in it that will become apparent immediately upon taking inventory. I have been asked to help improve the performance of such networks and after taking inventory I have developed a list of ways to improve the performance of systems without issuing a single HP-UX command! When you see a user's home directory on one system, her application on another, her data on a third, her application's license server on a fourth, and all of these systems on different subnets, you can quickly develop ways to improve system performance.

You may find some similarities between the examples I use in this chapter and your own computing environment. In any event, I suggest you take an inventory of what you have if you haven't already done so.

There are degrees to which you can take an inventory. You may choose a high-level inventory with little detail that is simply a drawing of your network including systems and major software. A highly detailed inventory, on the other hand, might be a detailed network diagram including all of the hardware components of which each system is comprised and a detailed list of software including what data is located on what disks and so on. The granularity of your inventory depends on what you would like to accomplish. If your goal is to visualize what systems are used for which purpose, then a high-level network diagram may be sufficient. If you need to troubleshoot a disk I/O problem, then you may need to produce a detailed inventory of a system including what files and directories are located on each disk.

Standard HP-UX Commands

To begin, let's look at some commands you can issue from the HP-UX prompt to give you some information about your system. The commands I'll cover are

- **iostat**
- **vmstat**
- **netstat**
- **landiag**
- **ps**
- **swapinfo**
- **showmount and mount**

We'll first look at each of these commands so you get an understanding of the output produced by each and how this output may be used. Later in the chapter we'll then use some of these commands in conjunction with HP GlancePlus/UX to help uncover an interesting performance problem.

I/O and CPU Statistics with iostat

The **iostat** command gives you an indication of the level of effort the CPU is putting into I/O and the amount of I/O taking place among your disks and terminals. The following example shows the **iostat -t** command, which will be executed every three seconds, and associated output from an HP-UX system. The "#" shown is the HP-UX prompt

iostat -t 3

	tty			cpu		
	tin	tout	us	ni	sy	id
	78	42	2	0	28	70
device	bps	sps	msps			
c0t1d0	0	0	0			
c0t4d0	33	.3	25.2			
cot6d0	7	1	19.5			

	tty			cpu		
	tin	tout	us	ni	sy	id
	66	24	0	0	30	70
device	bps	sps	msps			
c0t1d0	15	12	15.9			
c0t4d0	36	9.7	21			
cot6d0	7	1.2	13.8			

	tty			cpu		
	tin	tout	us	ni	sy	id
	90	29	1	0	25	73
device	bps	sps	msps			
c0t1d0	12	1.7	15.5			
c0t4d0	24	3	19.1			
cot6d0	14	2.1	19.6			

	tty			cpu		
	tin	tout	us	ni	sy	id
	48	16	1	0	16	83

device	bps	sps	msps
c0t1d0	0	0	0
c0t4d0	62	9.3	18
cot6d0	12	2	17.2

	tty			cpu		
	tin	tout	us	ni	sy	id
	32	48	7	0	14	79

device	bps	sps	msps
c0t1d0	1	0.3	14.4
c0t4d0	5	0.9	16.2
cot6d0	171	29.4	18.2

	tty			cpu		
	tin	tout	us	ni	sy	id
	2	40	20	1	42	27

device	bps	sps	msps
c0t1d0	248	30.9	20.8
c0t4d0	203	29.2	18.8
cot6d0	165	30.6	22.1

Here are descriptions of the reports you receive with **iostat** for terminals, the CPU, and mounted file systems.

For every terminal you have connected (tty), you see a "tin" and "tout," which represents the number of characters read from your terminal and the number of characters written to your terminal, respectively. The -t option produces this terminal report.

For your CPU, you see the percentage of time spent in user mode ("us"), the percentage of time spent running user processes at a low priority called nice ("ni"), the percentage of time spent in system mode ("sy"), and the percentage of time the CPU is idle ("id").

For every locally mounted file system, you receive information on the kilobytes transferred per second ("bps"), number of seeks per second ("sps"), and number of milliseconds per average seek ("msps"). For disks that are NFS-mounted or disks on client nodes of your server, you will not receive a report; **iostat** reports only on locally mounted file systems.

When viewing the output of **iostat**, there are some parameters to take note of.

First, note the time your CPU is spending in the four categories shown. I have worked on systems with poor performance that the administrator assumed to be a result of a slow CPU when the "id" number was very high indicating the CPU was actually idle most of the time. If the CPU is mostly idle, the chances are the bottleneck is not the CPU but may be I/O, memory, or networking. If the CPU is indeed busy most of the time ("id" is very low), see if any processes are running "nice" (check the "ni" number). It may be that there are some background processes consuming a lot of CPU time that can be changed to run "nice."

Second, compare the milliseconds per average seek ("msps") for all of the disks you have mounted. If you have three identical disks mounted, yet the "msps" for one of the disks is substantially higher than the others, then you may be overworking it while the others remain mostly idle. If so, distribute the work load evenly among your disks so that you get as close to the same number of accesses per disk as possible. Note that a slower disk will always have a higher "msps" than a faster disk, so put your most often accessed information on your faster disks. The "msps" for a disk is usually around 20 milliseconds, as in all three disks (1s0, 4s0, and 6s0) in the last example. A CD-ROM would have a much higher msps of approximately 200 milliseconds.

Virtual Memory Statistics with vmstat

vmstat provides virtual memory statistics. It provides information on the status of processes, virtual memory, paging activity, faults, and the breakdown of the percentage of CPU time. In the following example, the output was produced ten times at five-second intervals. The first argument to the **vmstat** command is the interval; the second is the number of times you would like output produced:

vmstat 5 10:

procs			memory		page						faults			cpu		
r	b	w	avm	free	re	at	pi	po	fr	de	sr	in	sy	cs	us	sy	id
4	0	0	1161	2282	6	22	48	0	0	0	0	429	289	65	44	18	38
9	0	0	1161	1422	4	30	59	0	0	0	0	654	264	181	18	20	62
6	0	0	1409	1247	2	19	37	0	0	0	0	505	316	130	47	10	43
1	0	0	1409	1119	1	10	19	0	0	0	0	508	254	180	69	15	16
2	0	0	1878	786	0	1	6	0	0	0	0	729	294	217	75	17	8
2	0	0	1878	725	0	0	3	0	0	0	0	561	688	435	67	32	1
2	0	0	2166	98	0	0	20	0	0	0	66	728	952	145	8	14	78
1	0	0	2310	90	0	0	20	0	0	0	171	809	571	159	16	21	63
1	0	0	2310	190	0	0	8	1	3	0	335	704	499	176	66	14	20
1	0	0	2316	311	0	0	3	1	5	0	376	607	945	222	4	11	85

You will get more out of the **vmstat** command than you want. Here is a brief description of the categories of information produced by **vmstat**.

Processes are classified into one of three categories: runnable ("r"), blocked on I/O or short-term resources ("b"), or swapped ("w").

Next you will see information about memory. "avm" is the number of virtual memory pages owned by processes that have run within the last 20 seconds. If this number is roughly the size of physical memory minus your kernel, then you are near paging. The "free" column indicates the number of pages on the system's free list. It doesn't mean the process is done running and these pages won't be accessed again; it just means they have not been accessed recently. I suggest you ignore this column.

Next is paging activity. Only the first field ("re") is useful. It shows the pages that were reclaimed. These pages made it to the free list but were later referenced and had to be salvaged. Check to see that "re" is a low number. If you are reclaiming pages which were thought to be free by the system, then you are wasting valuable time salvaging these. Reclaiming pages is also a symptom that you are short on memory.

Next you see the number of faults in three categories: interrupts per second, which usually come from hardware ("in"), system calls per second ("sy"), and context switches per second ("cs").

The final output is CPU usage percentage for user ("us"), system ("sy"), and idle ("id"). This is not as complete as the **iostat** output, which also shows **nice** entries.

You want to verify that the runnable processes ("r") value is higher than the blocked ("b") value and runnable but swapped ("w") processes value. If too many processes are blocked and swapped, your users will get a slower response time. In the example we'll review later in this chapter you'll see many swapped ("w") process and no runnable ("r") or blocked ("b") processes, indicating a great deal of swapping is taking place.

Whenever you see entries in the blocked ("b") or runnable but swapped ("w") columns, you see evidence that processes are standing still. You want to identify the source of the blocked and runnable but swapped processes. The reason will usually be insufficient RAM in your system. Swapped processes are those that have been moved from RAM to disk in an effort to free up RAM for other processes. You may want to look at GlancePlus to do more detailed troubleshooting of memory under the "Memory Detail" screen.

Network Statistics with netstat

netstat provides information related to network statistics. Since network bandwidth has as much to do with performance as the CPU and memory in some networks, you want to get an idea of the level of network traffic you have.

There are two forms of **netstat** that I use to obtain network statistics. The first is **netstat -i** which shows the state of interfaces that are autoconfigured. Since I am most often interested in getting a summary of lan0, I issue this command. Although **netstat -i** gives a good rundown of lan0, such as the network it is on, its name and so on, it does not show useful statistical information.

The following diagram shows the output of **netstat -i**.

```
# netstat -i

Name   Mtu    Network    Address      Ipkts    Ierrs   Opkts    Oerrs   Col

lan0   1497   151.150    a4410.e.h.c   242194   120     107665   23      19884
```

netstat doesn't provide as much extraneous information as **iostat** and **vmstat**. Put another way, most of what you get from **netstat** is useful. Here is a description of the nine fields in the **netstat** example.

Name
: The name of your network interface (Name), in this case "lan0".

Mtu
: The "maximum transmission unit" which is the maximum packet size sent by the interface card.

Network
: The network address of the LAN to which the interface card is connected (151.150).

Address
: The host name of your system. This is the symbolic name of your system as it appears in the **/etc/hosts** file.

Start of statistical information:

Ipkts
: The number of packets received by the interface card, in this case lan0.

Ierrs
: The number of errors detected on incoming packets by the interface card.

Opkts
: The number of packets transmitted by the interface card.

Oerrs The number of errors detected during the transmission of packets by the interface card.

Collis The number of collisions (Collis) that resulted from packet traffic.

netstat provides cumulative data since the node was last powered up; you might have a long elapsed time over which data was accumulated. If you are interested in seeing useful statistical information, you can use **netstat** with different options. You can also specify an interval to report statistics. I usually ignore the first entry since it shows all data since the system was last powered up. This means the data includes non-prime hours when the system was idle. I prefer to view data at the time the system is working its hardest. This second **netstat** example provides network interface information every five seconds.

netstat -I lan0 5

(lan 0)->	input		output		
packets	errs	packets	errs	colls
14600725	14962	962080	0	9239
217	0	202	0	2
324	0	198	0	0
275	0	272	0	3
282	0	204	0	4
297	0	199	0	2
277	0	147	0	1
202	0	304	0	2

With this example you get multiple outputs of what is taking place on the LAN interface. I am showing only half the output. There are another five columns that show the "Total" of all the same information. As I mentioned earlier, you may want to ignore the first output since it includes information over a long time period. This may include a time when your network was idle and therefore the data is not important to you.

You can specify the network interface on which you want statistics reported by using **-I interface**; in the case of the example it was **-I lan0**. An interval of five seconds was also used in this example.

Analyzing **netstat** statistical information is intuitive. You want to verify that the collisions (Coll) are much lower than the packets transmitted (Opkts). Collisions occur on output from your LAN interface. Every collision your LAN interface encounters slows down the network. You will get varying opinions on what is too many collisions. If your collisions are less than 5 percent of "Opkts," you're probably in good shape and better off spending your time analyzing some other system resource. If this number is high, you may want to consider segmenting your network in some way such as by installing networking equipment between portions of the network that don't share a lot of data.

As a rule of thumb, if you reduce the number of packets you are receiving and transmitting ("Ipkts" and "Opkts"), then you will have less overall network traffic and fewer collisions. Keep this in mind as you plan your network or upgrades to your systems. You may want to have two LAN cards in systems that are in constant communication. That way these systems have a "private" LAN over which to communicate and do not adversely affect the performance of other systems on the network. One LAN interface on each system is devoted to intrasystem communication. This provides a "tight" communication path among systems which usually act as servers. The second LAN interface is used to communicate with any systems which are usually clients on a larger network.

You can also obtain information related to routing with **netstat** (see Chapter 3). The **-r** option to **netstat** shows the routing tables, which you usually want to know, and the **-n** option can be used to print network addresses as numbers rather than as names. In the following examples **netstat** is issued with the **-r** option (this will be used when describing the **netstat** output) and the **-rn** options so you can compare the two outputs.

$ netstat -r

Routing tables

Destination	Gateway	Flags	Refs	Use	Interface	Pmtu
hp700	localhost	UH	0	28	lo0	4608
default	router1	UG	0	0	lan0	4608

Routing tables

Destination	Gateway	Flags	Refs	Use	Interface	Pmtu
128.185.61	system1	U	347	28668	lan0	1500

$ netstat -rn

Routing tables

Destination	Gateway	Flags	Refs	Use	Interface	Pmtu
127.0.0.1	127.0.0.1	UH	0	28	lo0	4608
default	128.185.61.1	UG	0	0	lan0	4608
128.185.61	128.185.61.2	U	347	28668	lan0	1500

With **netstat** there is some information provided about the router which is the middle entry. The **-r** option shows information about routing but there are many other useful options to this command. Of particular interest in this output is "Flags," which defines the type of routing that takes place. Here are descriptions of the most common flags from the HP-UX manual pages.

1=U	Route to a *network* via a gateway that is the local host itself.
3=UG	Route to a *network* via a gateway that is the remote host.
5=UH	Route to a *host* via a gateway that is the local host itself.
7=UGH	Route to a *host* via a remote gateway which is a host.

The first line is for the local host or loopback interface called **lo0** at address 127.0.0.1 (you can see this address in the **netstat -rn** example). The UH flags indicate the destination address is the local host itself. This class A address allows a client and server on the same host to communicate with one another with TCP/IP. A datagram sent to the loopback interface won't go out onto the network; it will simply go through the loopback.

The second line is for the default route. This entry says send packets to router1 if a more specific route can't be found. In this case the router has a UG under Flags. Some routers are configured with a U; others, such as the one in this example, with a UG. I've found that I usually end up determining through trial and error whether a U or UG is required. If there is a U in Flags and I am unable to ping a system on the other side of a router, a UG usually fixes the problem.

The third line is for the system's network interface **lan0**. This means to use this network interface for packets to be sent to 128.185.61.

Network Statistics with lanadmin

/usr/sbin/lanadmin provides additional information related to network statistics. When you run **lanadmin,** a menu appears that gives you the option to perform various functions, one of which is display information related to the LAN interface. The following shows the output of **lanadmin** when this option is selected.

```
                        LAN INTERFACE STATUS DISPLAY
                            Tues, 15:47:20
Network Management ID               = 4
Description                         = lan0 Hewlett-Packard LAN Intfc
Type (value)                        = active
MTU Size                            = 1500
Speed                               = 10000000
Station Address                     = 0x80009874511
Administration Status (value)       = up(1)
Operation Status (value)            = up(1)
Last Change                         = 3735
Inbound Octets                      = 912
Inbound Unicast Packets             = 0
Inbound Non-Unicast Packets         = 4518
Inbound Discards                    = 0
Inbound Errors                      = 0
Inbound Unknown Protocols           = 0
Outbound Octets                     = 569144
Outbound Unicast Packets            = 4
Outbound Non-Unicast Packets        = 4518
Outbound Discards                   = 0
Outbound Errors                     = 0
Outbound Queue Length               = 0
Specific                            = 655367
```

```
Ethernet-like Statistics Group

Index                              = 4
Alignment Errors                   = 0
FCS Errors                         = 0
Single Collision Frames            = 0
Multiple Collision Frames          = 0
Deferred Transmissions             = 0
Late Collisions                    = 0
Excessive Collisions               = 0
Internal MAC Transmit Errors       = 0
Carrier Sense Errors               = 0
Frames Too Long                    = 0
Internal MAC Errors                = 0


LAN Interface test mode. LAN Interface Net Mgmt ID = 4
clear                   = Clear statistics registers
display                 = Display LAN intfc status and registers
end                     = End LAN Interface Administration
menu                    = Display this menu
nmid                    = Network Management ID of the LAN intfc
quit                    = Terminate diagnostic, return to shell
reset                   = Reset LAN Interface to execute self-test
Enter Command:
```

lanadmin gives more detailed information about the LAN interface than **netstat**. The type of interface, Maximum Transfer Unit (MTU), speed, administration and operation status (a quick way to see if your interface is up), and the LAN interface address in hex. The hex address is often used when access codes are generated for application software or for generating client kernels.

lanadmin also gives much more detailed error information. Although any error slows down your network, having more detailed information on the type of errors and collisions may be helpful in trouble-shooting a problem.

With **lanadmin** you can also "reset" the network interface which is sometimes helpful when the network interface doesn't seem to be working such as when the LAN interface does not **ping** itself.

Check Processes with ps

To find the answer to "What is my system doing?", use **ps -ef**. This command provides information about every running process on your system. If, for instance, you wanted to know if NFS is running, you would simply type **ps -ef** and look for NFS daemons. Although **ps** tells you every process that is running on your system, it doesn't provide a good summary of the level of system resources being consumed. The other commands we have covered to this point are superior resource assessment commands. On the other hand, I would guess **ps** is the most often issued system administration command. There are a number of options you can use with **ps**. I normally use **e** and **f** which provide information about every ("e") running process and lists this information in full ("f"). The following example is a partial **ps -ef** listing.

ps -ef

UID	PID	PPID	C	STIME	TTY	TIME	COMMAND
root	0	0	0	Jan 2	?	0:00	swapper
root	1	0	0	Jan 2	?	0:01	/etc/init
root	2	0	0	Jan 2	?	0:01	vhand
root	3	0	0	Jan 2	?	0:02	statdaemon
root	8	0	0	Jan 2	?	0:01	unhashdaemon
root	6	0	0	Jan 2	?	0:02	sockregd
root	11	0	0	Jan 2	?	0:01	syncdaemon
root	45	0	0	Jan 2	?	0:02	syncer
lp	49	0	0	Jan 2	?	0:04	lpsched
root	129	1	0	08:07:33	?	0:00	/etc/cron
oracle	2079	2071	0	07:34:22	?	9:22	oracle
daemon	2088	98	0	08:23:11	ttyp0	8:23	/usr/bin/X11
becker	278	57	0	09:22:45	ttyp2	5:21	ANSYS
lori	234	67	0	08:23:43	ttyp3	6:33	ileaf

Here is a brief description of the headings:

UID   The user ID of the process owner.

PID	The process ID. (You can use this number to kill the process.)
PPID	The process ID of the parent process.
C	Process utilization for scheduling.
STIME	Start time of the process.
TTY	The controlling terminal for the process.
TIME	The cumulative execution time for the process.
COMMAND	The command name and arguments.

ps gives a quick profile of the processes running on your system. If you issue the **ps** command and find a process is hung, you can issue the **kill** command. **kill** is a utility that sends a signal to the process you identify. The most common signal to send is "SIGKILL" which terminates the process. There are other signals you can send to the process, but SIGKILL is the most common. As an alternative to sending the signal, you could send the corresponding signal number. The **kill** described here is either **/usr/bin/kill** or **kill** from the default POSIX shell in HP-UX. The other shells also have **kill** commands. A list of signal numbers and corresponding signals is shown next.

Signal number	Signal
0	SIGNULL
1	SIGHUP
2	SIGINT
3	SIGQUIT
9	SIGKILL
15	SIGTERM
24	SIGSTOP
25	SIGTSTP
26	SIGCONT

To kill the last process shown in this **ps** example, you would issue the following command:

```
$ kill -9 234
       |  |  |
       |  |  |> process id (PID)
       |  |> signal number
       |> kill command to terminate the process
```

Show Remote Mounts with showmount

showmount is used to show all remote systems (clients) that have mounted a local file system. **showmount** is useful for determining the file systems that are most often mounted by clients with NFS. The output of **showmount** is particularly easy to read because it lists the host name and the directory which was mounted by the client

NFS servers often end up serving many NFS clients that were not originally intended to be served. This ends up consuming additional HP-UX system resources on the NFS server as well as additional network bandwidth. Keep in mind that any data transferred from an NFS server to an NFS client consumes network bandwith and in some cases may be a substantial amount of bandwith if large files or applications are being transferred from the NFS server to the client. The following example is a partial output of **showmount** taken from a system that is used as an example later in this chapter.

showmount -a

hp100.ct.mp.com:/applic

hp101.ct.mp.com:/applic

hp102.cal.mp.com:/applic

showmount -a

hp103.cal.mp.com:/applic

hp104.cal.mp.com:/applic

hp105.cal.mp.com:/applic

hp106.cal.mp.com:/applic

hp107.cal.mp.com:/applic

hp108.cal.mp.com:/applic

hp109.cal.mp.com:/applic

hp100.cal.mp.com:/usr/users

hp101.cal.mp.com:/usr/users

hp102.cal.mp.com:/usr/users

hp103.cal.mp.com:/usr/users

hp104.cal.mp.com:/usr/users

hp105.cal.mp.com:/usr/users

hp106.cal.mp.com:/usr/users

hp107.cal.mp.com:/usr/users

hp108.cal.mp.com:/usr/users

hp109.cal.mp.com:/usr/users

There are the three following options to the **showmount** command:

-a prints output in the format "name:directory" as shown above.

-d lists all of the local directories that have been remotely mounted by clients.

-e prints a list of exported file systems.

The following are examples of **showmount -d** and **showmount -e**.

```
# showmount -d

/applic

/usr/users

/usr/oracle

/usr/users/emp.data

/network/database

/network/users

/tmp/working


# showmount -e

export list for server101.cal.mp.com

/applic

/usr/users

/cdrom
```

Show Swap with swapinfo

If your system has insufficient main memory for all of the information it needs to work with, it will move pages of information to your swap area or swap entire processes to your swap area. Pages that were most recently used are kept in main memory while those not recently used will be the first moved out of main memory.

I find that many system administrators spend an inordinate amount of time trying to determine what is the right amount of swap space for their system. This is *not* a parameter you want to leave to a rule of thumb. You can get a good estimate of the amount of swap you require by considering the following three factors:

1. How much swap is recommended by the application(s) you run? Use the swap size recommended by your applications. Application vendors tend to be realistic when recommending swap space. There is sometimes competition among application vendors to claim the lowest memory and CPU requirements in order to keep the overall cost of solutions as low as possible, but swap space recommendations are usually realistic.

2. How many applications will you run simultaneously? If you are running several applications, sum the swap space recommended for each application you plan to run simultaneously. If you have a database application that recommends 200 MBytes of swap and a development tool that recommends 100 MBytes of swap, then configure your system with 300 MBytes of swap minimum.

3. Will you be using substantial system resources on periphery functionality such as NFS? The nature of NFS is to provide access to file systems, some of which may be very large, so this may have an impact on your swap space requirements.

You can view the amount of swap being consumed on your system with **swapinfo**. The following is an example output of **swapinfo**.

swapinfo

TYPE	Kb AVAIL	Kb USED	Kb FREE	PCT USED	START/ LIMIT	Kb RESERVE	PRI	NAME
dev	204505	8401	196104	4%	820534	-	1	/dev/vg00/lvol2
reserve	-	30724	-30724					
memory	46344	25136	21208	54%				

Here is a brief overview of what **swapinfo** gives you.

In the previous example the "TYPE" field indicated whether the swap was "dev" for device, "reserve" for paging space on reserve, or "memory" which is RAM that can be used to hold pages if all of the paging areas are in use.

"Kb AVAIL" is the total swap space available in 1024-byte blocks. This includes both used and unused swap. The previous example shows roughly 204 MBytes of device swap.

"Kb USED" is the current number of 1024-byte blocks in use. The previous example shows only about 8.4 MBytes of swap in use.

"Kb FREE" is the difference between "Kb AVAIL" and "Kb USED." In the previous example this is 204 MBytes minus 8 MBytes or roughly 196 MBytes.

"PCT USED" is the "Kb USED" divided by "Kb AVAIL" or 4 percent in the previous example for device and 54 percent for memory.

"START/LIMIT" is the block address of the start of the swap area.

"Kb RESERVE" is "-" for device swap or the number of 1024-byte blocks for file system swap.

"PRI" is the priority of the given to this swap area.

"NAME" is the device name for the swap device.

You can also issue the **swapinfo** command with a series of options. Here are some of the options you can include:

-m to display output of **swapinfo** in MBytes rather than 1024 byte blocks.

-d prints information related to device swap areas only.

-f prints information about file system swap areas only.

sar: The System Activity Reporter

sar is another HP-UX command for gathering information about activities on your system. There are many useful options to **sar**. I'll briefly describe the three that are most often used.

sar -o   Save data in a file specified by "o". After the file name you would usually also enter the time interval for samples and the number of samples. The following example shows saving the binary data in file **/tmp/sar.data** at an interval of 60 seconds 300 times:

```
# sar -o /tmp/sar.data 60 300
```

The data in **/tmp/sar.data** can later be extracted from the file.

sar -f   Specify a file from which you will extract data.

sar -u   Report CPU utilization with headings %usr, %sys, %wio, %idle with some processes waiting for block I/O, %idle. This is similar to the **iostat** and **vmstat** CPU reports. You extract the binary data saved in a file to get CPU information as shown in the following example.

```
# sar -u -f /tmp/sar.data
```

sar -b   Report buffer cache activity. A database application such as Oracle would recommend you use this option to see the effectiveness of buffer cache use. You extract the binary data saved in a file to get CPU information as shown in the following example:

```
# sar -b -f /tmp/sar.data
```

sar -d	Report disk activity. You get the device name, percent that the device was busy, average number of requests outstanding for the device, number of data transfers per second for the device, and other information. You extract the binary data saved in a file to get CPU information as shown in the following example:

```
# sar -b -f /tmp/sar.data
```

sar -q	Report average queue length.
sar -w	Report system swapping activity.

timex to Analyze a Command

If you have a specific command you want to find out more about, you can use **timex**. **timex** reports the elapsed time, user time, and system time spent in the execution of a command you specify.

HP GlancePlus/UX

Using HP-UX commands to get a better understanding of what your system is doing requires you to do a lot of work. In the first case (issuing HP-UX commands) you have the advantage of obtaining data about what is taking place on your system that very second. Unfortunately you can't always issue additional commands to probe deeper into an area, such as a process, that you want to know more about.

Now I'll describe another technique - a tool that can help get useful data in real time, allow you to investigate a specific process, and not bury you in reports. This tool is HP GlancePlus/UX (GlancePlus).

Figure 5-2 shows one of several interactive screens of GlancePlus. There is also a Motif version of GlancePlus. I chose to use the character-based version of GlancePlus because this will run on any display, either graphics or character based, and the many colors used by the Motif version of GlancePlus do not show up well in a book.

Two features of the screen shown in figure 5-2 are worth noticing immediately:

1. Four histograms at the top of the screen give you a graphical representation of your CPU, Disk, Memory, and Swap Utilization in a format much easier to assimilate than a column of numbers.

2. The "Process Summary" has columns similar to **ps -ef** which many system administrators are familiar and comfortable with. GlancePlus, however, gives you the additional capability of filtering out processes that are using very little few resources by specifying thresholds.

Using GlancePlus you can take a close look at your system in many areas including the following:

- Global Summary of Your System (shown in the example)
- CPU
- Memory
- Swap Space
- Disk
- LAN Detail
- NFS by System
- PRM Summary (Process Resource Manager)
- I/O by File System
- I/O by Device
- I/O by Logical Volume
- System Tables

Figure 5-2 is a GlancePlus screen shot.

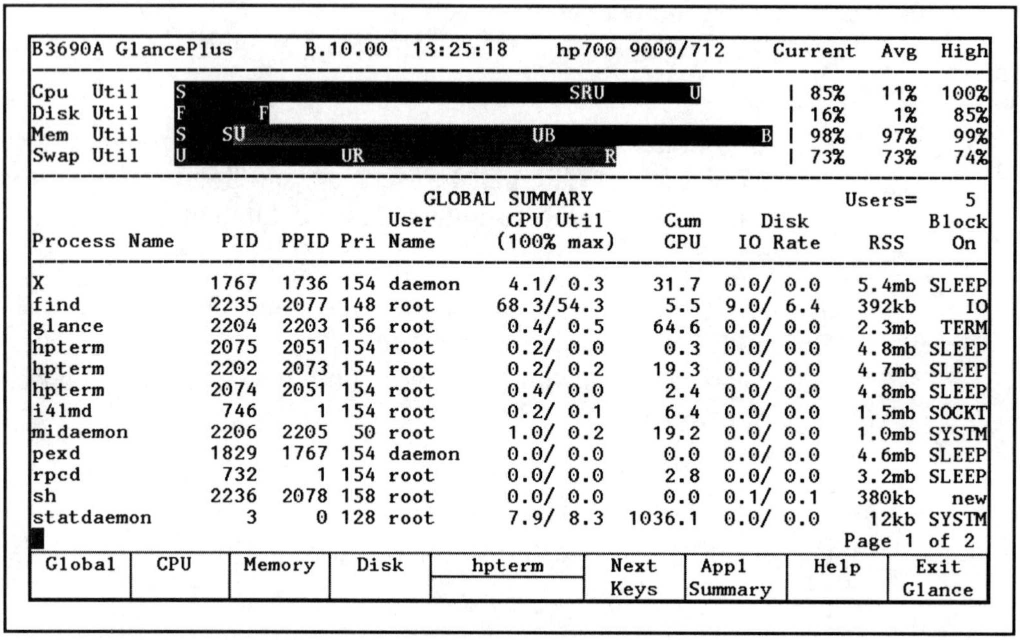

```
B3690A GlancePlus        B.10.00  13:25:18      hp700 9000/712     Current  Avg  High
Cpu  Util  S                               SRU          U       | 85%   11%  100%
Disk Util  F    F                                               | 16%    1%   85%
Mem  Util  S   SU                          UB                 B | 98%   97%   99%
Swap Util  U         UR                    R                    | 73%   73%   74%
                                  GLOBAL SUMMARY                        Users=   5
                                User   CPU Util        Cum     Disk            Block
Process Name    PID  PPID Pri Name    (100% max)      CPU    IO Rate     RSS     On
X              1767  1736 154 daemon   4.1/ 0.3       31.7   0.0/ 0.0   5.4mb  SLEEP
find           2235  2077 148 root    68.3/54.3        5.5   9.0/ 6.4   392kb     IO
glance         2204  2203 156 root     0.4/ 0.5       64.6   0.0/ 0.0   2.3mb   TERM
hpterm         2075  2051 154 root     0.2/ 0.0        0.3   0.0/ 0.0   4.8mb  SLEEP
hpterm         2202  2073 154 root     0.2/ 0.2       19.3   0.0/ 0.0   4.7mb  SLEEP
hpterm         2074  2051 154 root     0.4/ 0.0        2.4   0.0/ 0.0   4.8mb  SLEEP
i41md           746     1 154 root     0.2/ 0.1        6.4   0.0/ 0.0   1.5mb  SOCKT
midaemon       2206  2205  50 root     1.0/ 0.2       19.2   0.0/ 0.0   1.0mb  SYSTM
pexd           1829  1767 154 daemon   0.0/ 0.0        0.0   0.0/ 0.0   4.6mb  SLEEP
rpcd            732     1 154 root     0.0/ 0.0        2.8   0.0/ 0.0   3.2mb  SLEEP
sh             2236  2078 158 root     0.0/ 0.0        0.0   0.1/ 0.1   380kb    new
statdaemon        3     0 128 root     7.9/ 8.3     1036.1   0.0/ 0.0    12kb  SYSTM
                                                                      Page 1 of 2
 Global    CPU    Memory    Disk        hpterm        Next    Appl      Help    Exit
                                                      Keys  Summary           Glance
```

Figure 5-2 HP GlancePlus/UX Global Screen Shot

Since the Global Summary shown in the example tells you where your system resources are going at the highest level, I'll start my description here. Keep in mind that the information shown on this screen can be updated at any interval you choose. If your system is running in a steady-state mode, you may want to have a long interval as you don't expect things to much change. On the other hand, you may have a dynamic environment and want to see the histograms and other information updated every few seconds. In either case, you can change the update interval to suit your needs. Depending on the version of GlancePlus you are using you may see other function keys such as *Process List* and *Application List*.

Global Screen Description

The Global screen provides an overview of the state of system resources and active processes.

The top section of the screen (the histogram section) is common to the many screens of GlancePlus. The bottom section of the screen displays a summary of active processes.

Line 1 provides the product and version number of GlancePlus, the time, name of your system, and system type.

Line 3 provides information about the overall state of the CPU. This tends to be the single most important piece of information administrators want to know about their system - Is my CPU overworked?

The CPU Utilization bar is divided into four parts:

1. "S" indicates the amount of time spent on "system" activities such as context switching and system calls.

2. "N" indicates the amount of time spent running "nice" user processes (those run at a low priority).

3. "U" indicates the amount of time spent running user processes.

4. "R" indicates real-time processes.

The far right of line 3 shows the percentage of CPU utilization. If your system is "CPU-Bound," you will consistently see this number near 100 percent. You get statistics for Current, Average (since analysis was begun), and High.

Line 4 shows Disk Utilization for the busiest mounted disk. This bar indicates the percentage of File System and Virtual Memory disk I/O over the update interval. This bar is divided into two parts:

1. "F" indicates the amount of file system activity of user reads and writes and other non-paging activities.

2. "V" indicates the percentage of disk I/O devoted to paging virtual memory.

The Current, Avg, and High statistics have the same meaning as in the CPU Utilization description.

Line 5 shows the system memory utilization. This bar is divided into three parts:

1. "S" indicates the amount of memory devoted to system use.

2. "U" indicates the amount of memory devoted to user programs and data.

3. "B" indicates the amount of memory devoted to buffer cache.

The Current, Avg, and High statistics have the same meaning as in the CPU Utilization description.

Line 6 shows swap space information, which is divided into two parts:

1. "R" indicates reserved but not in use.

2. "U" indicates swap space in use.

All three of these areas (CPU, Memory, and Disk) may be further analyzed by using the F2, F3, and F4 function keys, respectively. Again, you may see different function keys depending on the version of Glance-Plus you are running. When you select one of these keys, you move from the "Global Summary" screen to a screen that provides more in-depth functions in the selected area. In addition, more detailed screens are available for LAN, NFS, Diskless Server, Swap, and System Table. Since most investigation beyond the Global screen takes place on the CPU, Memory, and Disk screens, I'll describe these in more detail shortly.

The bottom of the Global screen shows the active processes running on your system. Because there are typically many processes running on an HP-UX system, you may want to consider using the "o" command to set a threshold for CPU utilization. If you set a threshold of 5 percent, for instance, then only processes that exceed average CPU utilization over the interval will be displayed. There are other types of thresholds that can be specified such as the amount of RAM used (Resident Size). If you specify thresholds, you see only the processes you're most interested in, that is, those consuming the greatest system resources.

There is a line for each active process that meets the threshold requirements you defined. There may be more than one page of processes to display. The message in the bottom-right corner of the screen indicates which page you are on. You can scroll forward to view the next page with "f" and backwards with "b." Usually only a few processes consume most of your system resources, so I recommend setting the thresholds so that only one page of processes is displayed.

Here is a brief summary of the process headings.

Process Name The name or abbreviation used to load the executable program.

PID   The process identification number.

PPID   The PID of the parent process.

Pri   The priority of the process. The lower the number, the higher the priority. System-level processes usually run between 0 and 127. Other processes usually run between 128 and 255. "Nice" processes are those with the lowest priority and will have the largest number.

User Name   Name of the user who started the process.

CPU Util   The first number is the percentage of CPU utilization this process consumed over the update interval. The second number is the percentage of CPU utilization this process consumed since GlancePlus was invoked. I'm skeptical of using GlancePlus, or any other HP-UX command, to get data over an extended period. I rarely use the second number under this heading. If you have been using GlancePlus for some time but only recently started a process that consumes a great deal of CPU, you may find that the second number is very low. This is because the process you are analyzing has indeed consumed very little of the CPU since GlancePlus was invoked despite being a highly CPU-intensive process.

Cum CPU   The total CPU time used by the process. GlancePlus uses the "midaemon" to gather information. If the **midaemon** started before the process, you will get an accurate measure of cumulative CPU time used by the process. To use this column, start the **midaemon** in the **/etc/rc** script so that you start gathering information on all processes as soon as the system is booted.

Disk IO Rate The first number is the average disk I/O rate per second over the last update interval. The second number is the average disk I/O rate since GlancePlus was started or the process was started. Disk I/O can mean a lot of different things. Disk I/O could mean taking blocks of data off the disk for the first time and putting them in RAM, or it could be entirely paging and swapping. Some processes will simply require a lot more Disk I/O than others. When this number is very high, however, take a close look at whether or not you have enough RAM.

RSS Size   The amount of RAM in KBytes that is consumed by the process. This is called the Resident Size. Everything related to the process that is in RAM is included in this column, such as the process's data, stack, text, and shared memory segments. This is a good column to take a look at. Since slow systems are often erroneously assumed to be CPU-bound, I always make a point of looking at this column to identify the amount of RAM that the primary applications are using. This is often revealing. Some applications use a small amount of RAM but use large data sets, a point often overlooked when RAM calculations are made. This column shows all of the RAM your process is currently using.

Block On   The reason the process was blocked (unable to run). If the process is currently blocked, you will see why. If the process is running, you will see why it was last blocked. There are many reasons a process could be blocked. Here is a list of the most common reasons for the process being blocked.

Abbreviation	Reason for the Blocked Process
CACHE	Waiting for a cache buffer to become available
DISK	Waiting for a disk operation to complete
DUX	Waiting for a diskless transfer to complete
INODE	Waiting for an inode operation to complete

IO	Waiting for a non-disk I/O to complete
IPC	Waiting for shared memory operation to complete
LAN	Waiting for a LAN operation to complete
MBUF	Waiting for a memory buffer
MESG	Waiting for message queue operation to complete
NFS	Waiting for a NFS request to complete
PIPE	Waiting for data from a pipe
PRI	Waiting because a higher-priority process is running
RFA	Waiting for a Remote File Access to complete
SEM	Waiting for a semaphore to become available
SLEEP	Waiting because the process called **sleep** or **wait**
SOCKT	Waiting for a socket operation to complete
SYS	Waiting for system resources
TERM	Waiting for a terminal transfer
VM	Waiting for a virtual memory operation to complete
OTHER	Waiting for a reason GlancePlus can't determine

CPU Detail Screen Description

If the Global screen indicates that the CPU is overworked, you'll want to refer to the CPU detail screen shown in figure 5-3. It can provide useful information about the seven types of states that GlancePlus reports.

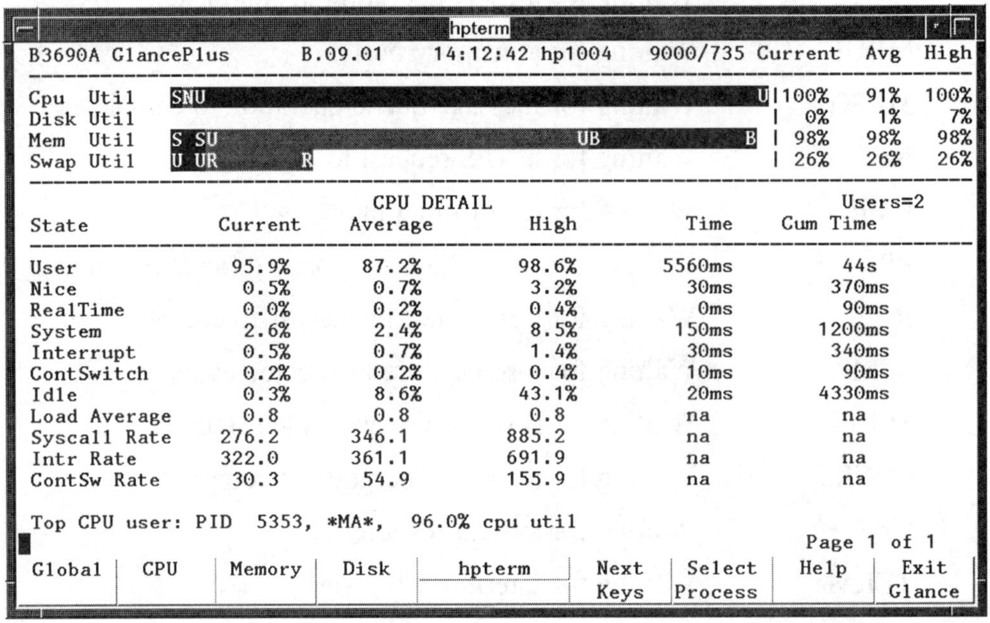

```
┌─┐                                        hpterm                                    ┌─┐
│ B3690A GlancePlus      B.09.01      14:12:42 hp1004    9000/735 Current   Avg   High│
│                                                                                     │
│ Cpu  Util   SNU                                              U│100%    91%    100% │
│ Disk Util                                                      │  0%     1%      7% │
│ Mem  Util   S SU                              UB            B │ 98%    98%     98% │
│ Swap Util   U UR          R                                   │ 26%    26%     26% │
│ ─────────────────────────────────────────────────────────────────────────────────│
│                              CPU DETAIL                               Users=2       │
│ State            Current      Average        High       Time      Cum Time         │
│ ─────────────────────────────────────────────────────────────────────────────────│
│ User              95.9%        87.2%         98.6%      5560ms       44s            │
│ Nice               0.5%         0.7%          3.2%        30ms      370ms           │
│ RealTime           0.0%         0.2%          0.4%         0ms       90ms           │
│ System             2.6%         2.4%          8.5%       150ms     1200ms           │
│ Interrupt          0.5%         0.7%          1.4%        30ms      340ms           │
│ ContSwitch         0.2%         0.2%          0.4%        10ms       90ms           │
│ Idle               0.3%         8.6%         43.1%        20ms     4330ms           │
│ Load Average       0.8          0.8           0.8         na         na             │
│ Syscall Rate     276.2        346.1         885.2         na         na             │
│ Intr Rate        322.0        361.1         691.9         na         na             │
│ ContSw Rate       30.3         54.9         155.9         na         na             │
│                                                                                     │
│ Top CPU user: PID  5353, *MA*,   96.0% cpu util                                     │
│                                                                       Page 1 of 1   │
│ Global │ CPU  │ Memory │ Disk │   hpterm   │ Next  │ Select  │ Help  │ Exit        │
│        │      │        │      │            │ Keys  │ Process │       │ Glance      │
└─────────────────────────────────────────────────────────────────────────────────────┘
```

Figure 5-3 HP GlancePlus/UX CPU Detail Screen Shot

For each of the seven types of states there are columns that provide additional information. Here is a description of the columns.

Current	Displays the percentage of CPU time devoted to this state over the last time interval.
Average	Displays the average percentage of CPU time spent in this state since GlancePlus was started.
High	Displays the highest percentage of CPU time devoted to this state since GlancePlus was started.
Time	Displays the CPU time spent in this state over the last interval.

Cum Time   Displays the total amount of CPU time spent in this state since GlancePlus was started.

Here is a description of the seven states.

User   CPU time spent executing user activities under normal priority.

Nice   CPU time spent running user code in nice mode.

Realtime   CPU time spent executing real-time processes which run at a high priority.

System   CPU time executing system calls and programs.

Interrupt   CPU time spent executing system interrupts. A high value here may indicate of a lot of I/O, such as paging and swapping.

ContSwitch   CPU time spent context switching between processes.

Idle   CPU time spent idle.

The CPU screen also shows your system's run queue length or load average. The current, average, and high values for the number of runnable processes waiting for the CPU are shown. You may want to get a gauge of your system's run queue length when the system is mostly idle and compare these numbers with those you see when your system is in normal use.

The final area reported on the CPU screen is load average, system calls, interrupts, and context switches. I don't inspect these too closely because if one of these is high, it is normally the symptom of a problem and not the cause of a problem. If you correct a problem, you will see these numbers reduced.

You can use GlancePlus to view all of the CPUs in your system as shown in Figure 5-4.

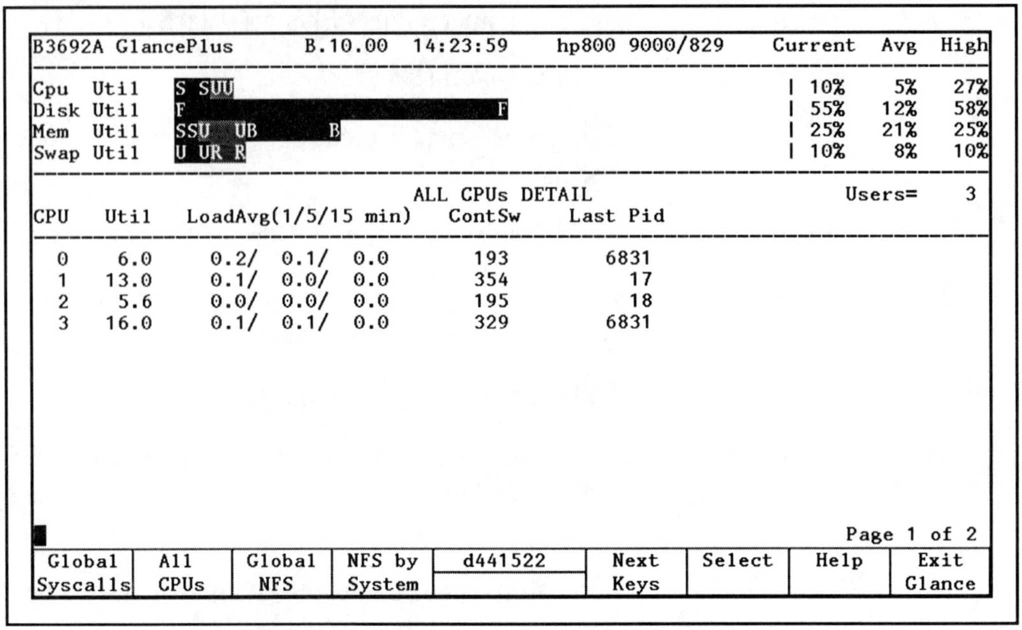

```
B3692A GlancePlus        B.10.00  14:23:59     hp800 9000/829    Current  Avg  High
Cpu  Util  S SUU                                                 | 10%     5%   27%
Disk Util  F                                  F                  | 55%    12%   58%
Mem  Util  SSU  UB       B                                       | 25%    21%   25%
Swap Util  U UR R                                                | 10%     8%   10%
                                    ALL CPUs DETAIL                      Users=    3
CPU    Util   LoadAvg(1/5/15 min)   ContSw    Last Pid

  0     6.0    0.2/  0.1/  0.0       193        6831
  1    13.0    0.1/  0.0/  0.0       354          17
  2     5.6    0.0/  0.0/  0.0       195          18
  3    16.0    0.1/  0.1/  0.0       329        6831




                                                                  Page 1 of 2
  Global   | All   | Global | NFS by  | d441522    | Next   | Select | Help | Exit
  Syscalls | CPUs  | NFS    | System  |            | Keys   |        |      | Glance
```

Figure 5-4 *All CPUs* Screen in GlancePlus HP-UX 10.x

Memory Detail Screen Description

The Memory Detail Screen shown in Figure 5-5 provides information on several types of memory management events. The statistics shown are in the form of counts, not percentages. You may want to look at these counts for a mostly idle system and then observe what takes place as the load on the system is incrementally increased. My experience has been that there are many more memory bottlenecks than CPU bottlenecks, so you may find this screen revealing.

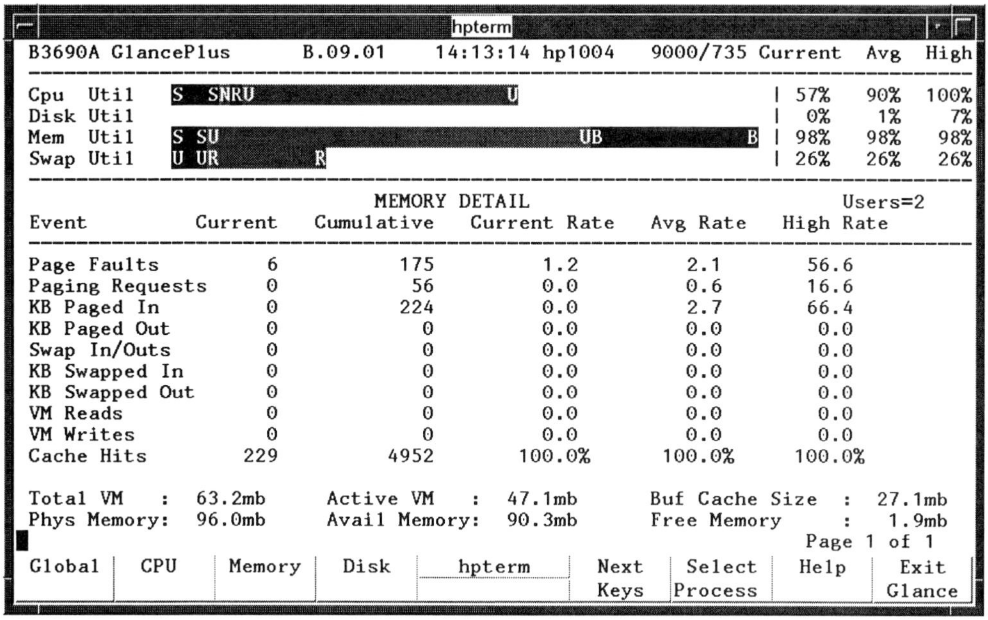

```
┌─┐                              hpterm                        ▾─┐┌─┐
│ B3690A GlancePlus      B.09.01    14:13:14 hp1004    9000/735 Current   Avg   High│
│─────────────────────────────────────────────────────────────────────────────────│
│ Cpu  Util  S  SNRU                            U              │ 57%   90%   100%│
│ Disk Util                                                    │  0%    1%     7%│
│ Mem  Util  S  SU                            UB            B  │ 98%   98%    98%│
│ Swap Util  U  UR        R                                    │ 26%   26%    26%│
│─────────────────────────────────────────────────────────────────────────────────│
│                           MEMORY DETAIL                              Users=2     │
│ Event          Current   Cumulative   Current Rate   Avg Rate   High Rate        │
│─────────────────────────────────────────────────────────────────────────────────│
│ Page Faults         6         175          1.2          2.1        56.6          │
│ Paging Requests     0          56          0.0          0.6        16.6          │
│ KB Paged In         0         224          0.0          2.7        66.4          │
│ KB Paged Out        0           0          0.0          0.0         0.0          │
│ Swap In/Outs        0           0          0.0          0.0         0.0          │
│ KB Swapped In       0           0          0.0          0.0         0.0          │
│ KB Swapped Out      0           0          0.0          0.0         0.0          │
│ VM Reads            0           0          0.0          0.0         0.0          │
│ VM Writes           0           0          0.0          0.0         0.0          │
│ Cache Hits        229        4952        100.0%       100.0%      100.0%         │
│                                                                                   │
│ Total VM   : 63.2mb    Active VM   : 47.1mb    Buf Cache Size  :  27.1mb         │
│ Phys Memory: 96.0mb    Avail Memory: 90.3mb    Free Memory     :   1.9mb         │
│                                                                   Page 1 of 1     │
│ Global │ CPU │ Memory │ Disk │   hpterm   │ Next │ Select │ Help │  Exit          │
│        │     │        │      │            │ Keys │Process │      │  Glance        │
└───────────────────────────────────────────────────────────────────────────────────┘
```

Figure 5-5 HP GlancePlus/UX Memory Detail Screen Shot

The following five statistics are shown for each memory management event:

Current   The number of times an event occurred in the last interval. The count changes if you update the interval, so you may want to select an interval you are comfortable with and stick with it.

Cumulative   The sum of all counts for this event since GlancePlus started.

Current Rate The number of events per second.

Avg Rate   The average of all rates recorded.

High Rate   The highest rate recorded.

Here are brief descriptions of the memory management events for which the statistics are provided.

Page Faults   A fault takes place when a process tries to access a page that is not in RAM. The virtual memory of the system will handle the "page in." Keep in mind the speed of the disk is much slower than RAM, so there is a large performance penalty for the page in.

Paging Requests   The sum of the number of times the routines used to page in and page out information were called.

KB Paged In   The amount of data paged in because of page faults.

KB Paged Out   The amount of data paged out to disk.

Swap In/Outs   The number of processes swapped in and swapped out of memory. A system low on RAM will spend a lot of time swapping processes in and out of RAM. If a lot of this type of swapping is taking place you may see high CPU utilization and see some other statistics go up as well. These may only be symptoms that a lot of swapping is taking place. You may see Reactivations and Deactivations.

KB Swapped In   The amount of information swapped into RAM as a result of processes having been swapped out earlier due to insufficient RAM. You may see KB Reactivated.

KB Swapped Out   The amount of information swapped out when processes are moved to disk. You may see KB Deactiviated.

VM Reads   The total count of the number of physical reads to disk. The higher this number, the more often your system is going to disk.

VM Writes   The total count of the number of physical writes
                 to disk.

Cache Hits   The percentage of hits to cache. A high hit rate
                 reduces the number of disk accesses. This is not
                 a field in HP-UX 10.x.

The following values are also on the Memory screen:

Total VM   The amount of total virtual memory used by all
                 processes.

Active VM   The amount of virtual memory used by all active
                 processes.

Buf Cache Size   The current size of buffer cache.

Phys Memory   The total RAM in your system.

Avail Memory   The amount of RAM available to all user pro-
                 cesses.

Free Memory   The amount of RAM not currently allocated for
                 use.

This screen gives you a lot of information about how your memory subsystem is being used. You may want to view some statistics when your system is mostly idle and when it is heavily used and compare the two. Some good numbers to record are "Avail Memory" (to see if you have any free RAM under either condition) and "Total VM" (to see how much virtual memory has been allocated for all your processes). A system that is RAM rich will have available memory; a system that is RAM poor will allocate a lot of virtual memory.

Disk Detail Screen Description

The disk detail screen is shown in Figure 5-6. You may see groupings of "local" and "remote" information.

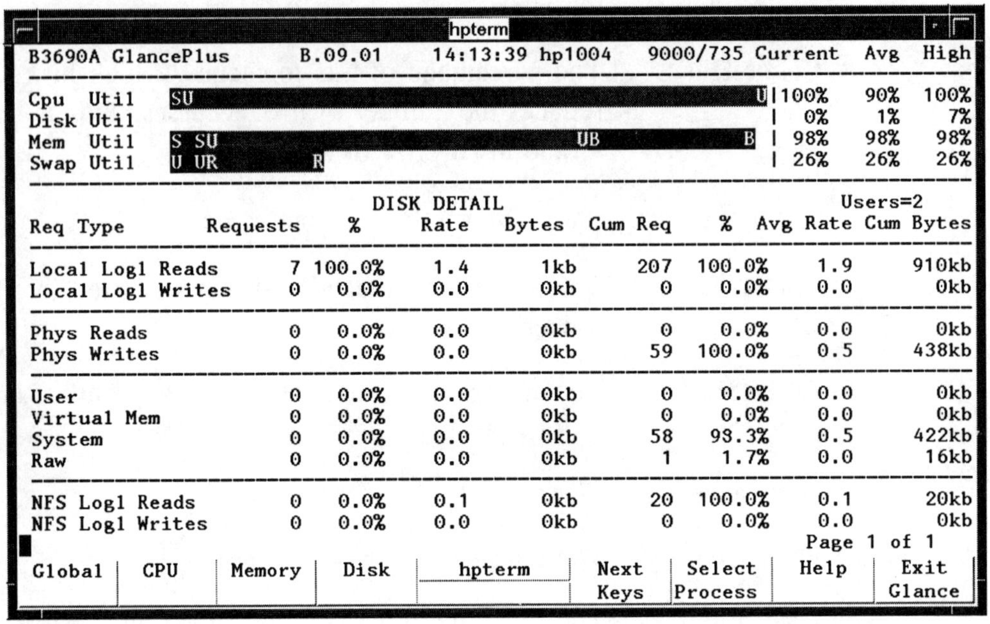

```
┌─                                    hpterm                                    ·┌─┐
│ B3690A GlancePlus      B.09.01      14:13:39 hp1004    9000/735 Current  Avg  High│
│                                                                                   │
│ Cpu  Util  SU                                               U│100%    90%  100%  │
│ Disk Util                                                    │  0%     1%    7%  │
│ Mem  Util  S SU                              UB            B │ 98%    98%   98%  │
│ Swap Util  U UR          R                                   │ 26%    26%   26%  │
│ ──────────────────────────────────────────────────────────────────────────────  │
│                            DISK DETAIL                            Users=2         │
│ Req Type        Requests    %    Rate   Bytes  Cum Req    %    Avg Rate  Cum Bytes│
│ ──────────────────────────────────────────────────────────────────────────────  │
│ Local Logl Reads       7 100.0%   1.4    1kb      207  100.0%    1.9       910kb  │
│ Local Logl Writes      0   0.0%   0.0    0kb        0    0.0%    0.0         0kb  │
│                                                                                   │
│ Phys Reads             0   0.0%   0.0    0kb        0    0.0%    0.0         0kb  │
│ Phys Writes            0   0.0%   0.0    0kb       59  100.0%    0.5       438kb  │
│                                                                                   │
│ User                   0   0.0%   0.0    0kb        0    0.0%    0.0         0kb  │
│ Virtual Mem            0   0.0%   0.0    0kb        0    0.0%    0.0         0kb  │
│ System                 0   0.0%   0.0    0kb       58   93.3%    0.5       422kb  │
│ Raw                    0   0.0%   0.0    0kb        1    1.7%    0.0        16kb  │
│                                                                                   │
│ NFS Logl Reads         0   0.0%   0.1    0kb       20  100.0%    0.1        20kb  │
│ NFS Logl Writes        0   0.0%   0.0    0kb        0    0.0%    0.0         0kb  │
│                                                               Page 1 of 1        │
│ Global │ CPU │ Memory │ Disk │   hpterm   │ Next  │ Select  │ Help │ Exit        │
│                                            │ Keys  │ Process │      │ Glance      │
└─                                                                                  │
```

Figure 5-6 HP GlancePlus/UX Disk Detail Screen Shot

There are eight disk statistics provided for eight events related to logical and physical accesses to all the disks mounted on the local system. These events represent all of the disk activity taking place on the system.

Here are descriptions of the eight disk statistics provided.

Requests	The total number of requests of that type over the last interval.
%	The percentage of this type of disk event relative to other types.
Rate	The average number of requests of this type per second.
Bytes	The total number of bytes transferred for this event over the last interval.

Cum Req   The cumulative number of requests since Glance-
                   Plus started.

%   The relative percentage of this type of disk event
                   since GlancePlus started.

Avg Rate   The average number of requests of this type
                   since GlancePlus started.

Cum Bytes   The total number of bytes transferred for this
                   type of event since GlancePlus started.

Here are descriptions of the disk events for which these statistics are provided which may be listed under "Local" on your system.

Local Logl R&W   The number of logical reads and writes to a
                 disk. Since disks normally use memory buffer
                 cache, a logical read may not require physical
                 access to the disk.

Phys Reads   The number of physical reads to the disk. These
                   physical reads may be due to either file system
                   logical reads or to virtual memory management.

Phys Writes   The number of physical writes to the disk. This
                   may be due to file system activity or virtual
                   memory management.

User   The amount of physical disk I/O as a result of
                   user file I/O operations.

Virtual Mem   The amount of physical disk I/O as a result of
                   virtual memory management activity.

System   The amount of physical disk I/O as a result of
                   system calls.

Raw   The amount of raw mode disk I/O.

NFS Logical R&W   The amount of NFS read and write activity.

A lot of disk activity may also take place as a result of NFS mounted disks. There are statistics provided for both "NFS Inbound" and "NFS Outbound" activity.

Disk access is required on all systems. The question to ask is: What disk activity is unnecessary and slowing down my system? A good place to start is to compare the amount of "User" disk I/O with "Virtual Mem" disk I/O. If your system is performing much more virtual memory I/O than user I/O, you may want to investigate your memory needs.

GlancePlus Summary

In addition to the Global screen and the CPU, Memory, and Disk screens described earlier, there are the following detail screens:

Swap Detail	Shows details on all swap areas. May be called by another name such as *Swap Space* in other releases.
LAN Detail	Gives details about each LAN card configured on your system. This screen may have another name such as *Network by Interface* in other releases.
NFS Detail	Provides details on inbound and outbound NFS mounted file systems. May be called by another name such as *NFS Global* in other releases.
Diskless Server	Provides diskless server information. You might not have this depending on the release you are running.
Individual Process	Allows you to select a single process to investigate. May be called by another name such as *Select Process* in other releases.
I/O By File System	Shows details of I/O for each mounted disk partition.

Queue Lengths   Provides disk queue length details. You might not have this depending on the release you are running.

System Tables   Shows details on internal system tables.

Process Threshold   Defines which processes will be displayed on the Global screen.

As you can see, while I described the four most commonly used screens in detail, there are many others you can use to investigate your system further.

What Should I Look For When Using GlancePlus?

Since GlancePlus provides a graphical representation of the way in which your system resources are being used, the answer is simple: See which bars have a high "Avg" utilization. You can then probe further into the process(es) causing this high utilization. If, for instance, you find your memory is consistently 99 percent utilized, press the F3 function key and have GlancePlus walk you through an investigation of which of your applications and users are memory hogs.

Similarly, you may be surprised to find that GlancePlus shows low utilization of your CPU or other system resources. Many slow systems are assumed to be CPU bound. I have seen GlancePlus used to determine a system is in fact memory bound, resulting in a memory upgrade instead of a CPU upgrade.

The difference between using GlancePlus to determine the level of CPU resources being used and the first two approaches given in this chapter is that GlancePlus takes out a lot of the guess work involved. If you are going to justify a system upgrade of some type to management, it is easier to do this with the hard and fast data GlancePlus provides than the detective work you may need to do with HP-UX commands.

Use the GlancePlus screens I showed you to look for the following bottlenecks:

1. CPU Bottleneck
   Use the "Global Screen" and "CPU Detail Screen" to identify these common CPU bottleneck symptoms:

- Low CPU idle time

- High capacity in User mode

- Many processes blocked on priority (PRI)

2. Memory Bottleneck

   Use the "Global Screen," "Memory Screen," and "Tables Screen" to identify these common Memory bottleneck symptoms:

   - High swapping activity

   - High paging activity

   - Little or no free memory available

   - High CPU usage in System mode

3. Disk Bottleneck

   Use "Global Screen," "Disk I/O Screen," and others to identify these common Disk Bottleneck symptoms:

   - High disk activity

   - High idle CPU time waiting for I/O requests to complete

   - Long disk queues

The best approach to take for understanding where your system resources are going is to become familiar with all three techniques described in this chapter. You can then determine which information is most useful to you.

The most important aspect of this process is to regularly issue commands and review accounting data so that small system utilization problems don't turn into catastrophes and adversely affect all your users.

You may need to go a step further with more sophisticated performance tools. HP can help you identify more sophisticated tools based on your needs.

Using Some of the Performance Tools in a Benchmark

I've worked on a lot of benchmarks over the years. This section contains several examples of system resource utilization from a benchmark. Many of these are useful for characterizing the performance of systems in general, not just during benchmarks.

Before getting any performance information when evaluating a system you need to understand its configuration. I always issue several commands to get a snapshot of a system including **bdf, vgdisplay, lvdisplay, dmesg, ioscan, swapinfo**, and others. Three of the most revealing are **bdf, dmesg** and **ioscan** which follow.

```
$ bdf
Filesystem          kbytes      used    avail %used Mounted on
/dev/vg00/lvol3    1370353     24131  1209186    2% /
/dev/vg00/lvol1      99669     15350    74352   17% /stand
/dev/vg00/lvol7     577144    156584   362845   30% /var
/dev/vg00/lvol6     398869    276426    82556   77% /usr
/dev/vg00/lvol5     398869    266859    92123   74% /opt
/dev/dsk/c4t4d0    4103198   1624039  2068839   44% /opt/oracle
/dev/vg00/lvol4     199381      1086   178356    1% /home
/dev/dsk/c4t3d0    4103198   2722615   970263   74% /backdb


$ dmesg

Feb  6 15:25
vuseg=15a87000
  inet_clts:ok   inet_cots:ok 8 ccio
8/0 c720
8/0.0 tgt
8/0.0.0 sdisk
8/0.0.1 sdisk
8/0.0.2 sdisk
8/0.0.3 sdisk
8/0.0.4 sdisk
8/0.0.5 sdisk
8/0.0.6 sdisk
8/0.7 tgt
8/0.7.0 sctl
8/4 c720
8/4.0 tgt
8/4.0.0 sdisk
8/4.0.1 sdisk
8/4.0.2 sdisk
8/4.0.3 sdisk
8/4.0.4 sdisk
8/4.0.5 sdisk
8/4.0.6 sdisk
8/4.7 tgt
8/4.7.0 sctl
8/8 c720
8/8.0 tgt
8/8.0.0 sdisk
```

```
8/8.0.1 sdisk
8/8.0.2 sdisk
8/8.0.3 sdisk
8/8.0.4 sdisk
8/8.0.5 sdisk
8/8.0.6 sdisk
8/8.7 tgt
8/8.7.0 sctl
8/12 c720
8/12.0 tgt
8/12.0.0 sdisk
8/12.0.1 sdisk
8/12.0.2 sdisk
8/12.0.3 sdisk
8/12.0.4 sdisk
8/12.0.5 sdisk
8/12.0.6 sdisk
8/12.7 tgt
8/12.7.0 sctl
10 ccio
10/0 c720
10/0.3 tgt
10/0.3.0 sdisk
10/0.4 tgt
10/0.4.0 sdisk
10/0.5 tgt
10/0.5.0 sdisk
10/0.6 tgt
10/0.6.0 sdisk
10/0.7 tgt
10/0.7.0 sctl
10/4 bc
10/4/0 mux2
10/8 c720
10/8.0 tgt
10/8.0.0 sdisk
10/8.0.1 sdisk
10/8.0.2 sdisk
10/8.0.3 sdisk
10/8.0.4 sdisk
10/8.0.5 sdisk
10/8.0.6 sdisk
10/8.7 tgt
10/8.7.0 sctl
10/12 bus_adapter
10/12/5 c720
10/12/5.0 tgt
10/12/5.0.0 stape
10/12/5.2 tgt
10/12/5.2.0 sdisk
10/12/5.7 tgt
10/12/5.7.0 sctl
10/12/6 lan2
10/12/0 CentIf
ps2_readbyte_timeout: no byte after 500 uSec
ps2_readbyte_timeout: no byte after 500 uSec
10/12/7 ps2
10/16 bc
```

```
10/16/12 fddi
32 processor
34 processor
36 processor
38 processor
49 memory
Networking memory for fragment reassembly is restricted
to 358293504 bytes
Logical volume 64, 0x3 configured as ROOT
Logical volume 64, 0x2 configured as SWAP
Logical volume 64, 0x2 configured as DUMP
     Swap device table:  (start & size given in 512-byte blocks)
         entry 0 - major is 64, minor is 0x2; start = 0,size = 2097152
WARNING: Insufficient space on dump device to save full
         crashdump.
     Only 1073741824 of 4026532864 bytes will be saved.
     Dump device table:  (start & size given in 1-Kbyte blocks)
         entry 0 - major is 31, minor is 0x46000; start = 105312,size = 1048576
netisr real-time priority reset to 100
Starting the STREAMS daemons.
     9245XB HP-UX (B.10.20) #1: Sun Jun  9 06:31:19 PDT 1996

Memory Information:
     physical page size = 4096 bytes, logical page size =
     4096 bytes
     Physical: 3932160 Kbytes, lockable: 3036260 Kbytes,available: 3481700 Kbytes


$ ioscan

H/W Path    Class                 Description
=================================================
            bc
8           bc                    I/O Adapter
8/0             ext_bus           GSC add-on Fast/Wide SCSI Interface
8/0.0               target
8/0.0.0                 disk      EMC     SYMMETRIX
8/0.0.1                 disk      EMC     SYMMETRIX
8/0.0.2                 disk      EMC     SYMMETRIX
8/0.0.3                 disk      EMC     SYMMETRIX
8/0.0.4                 disk      EMC     SYMMETRIX
8/0.0.5                 disk      EMC     SYMMETRIX
8/0.0.6                 disk      EMC     SYMMETRIX
8/0.7               target
8/0.7.0                 ctl       Initiator
8/4             ext_bus           GSC add-on Fast/Wide SCSI Interface
8/4.0               target
8/4.0.0                 disk      EMC     SYMMETRIX
8/4.0.1                 disk      EMC     SYMMETRIX
8/4.0.2                 disk      EMC     SYMMETRIX
8/4.0.3                 disk      EMC     SYMMETRIX
8/4.0.4                 disk      EMC     SYMMETRIX
8/4.0.5                 disk      EMC     SYMMETRIX
8/4.0.6                 disk      EMC     SYMMETRIX
8/4.7               target
8/4.7.0                 ctl       Initiator
8/8             ext_bus           GSC add-on Fast/Wide SCSI Interface
8/8.0               target
```

```
8/8.0.0              disk         EMC      SYMMETRIX
8/8.0.1              disk         EMC      SYMMETRIX
8/8.0.2              disk         EMC      SYMMETRIX
8/8.0.3              disk         EMC      SYMMETRIX
8/8.0.4              disk         EMC      SYMMETRIX
8/8.0.5              disk         EMC      SYMMETRIX
8/8.0.6              disk         EMC      SYMMETRIX
8/8.7              target
8/8.7.0              ctl          Initiator
8/12     ext_bus                 GSC add-on Fast/Wide SCSI Interface
8/12.0             target
8/12.0.0             disk         EMC      SYMMETRIX
8/12.0.1             disk         EMC      SYMMETRIX
8/12.0.2             disk         EMC      SYMMETRIX
8/12.0.3             disk         EMC      SYMMETRIX
8/12.0.4             disk         EMC      SYMMETRIX
8/12.0.5             disk         EMC      SYMMETRIX
8/12.0.6             disk         EMC      SYMMETRIX
8/12.7             target
8/12.7.0             ctl          Initiator
10       bc                       I/O Adapter
10/0     ext_bus                 GSC built-in Fast/Wide SCSI Interface
10/0.3             target
10/0.3.0             disk         SEAGATE ST15150W
10/0.4             target
10/0.4.0             disk         SEAGATE ST15150W
10/0.5             target
10/0.5.0             disk         SEAGATE ST15150W
10/0.6             target
10/0.6.0             disk         SEAGATE ST15150W
10/0.7             target
10/0.7.0             ctl          Initiator
10/4     bc                       Bus Converter
10/4/0             tty           MUX
10/8     ext_bus                 GSC add-on Fast/Wide SCSI Interface
10/8.0             target
10/8.0.0             disk         EMC      SYMMETRIX
10/8.0.1             disk         EMC      SYMMETRIX
10/8.0.2             disk         EMC      SYMMETRIX
10/8.0.3             disk         EMC      SYMMETRIX
10/8.0.4             disk         EMC      SYMMETRIX
10/8.0.5             disk         EMC      SYMMETRIX
10/8.0.6             disk         EMC      SYMMETRIX
10/8.7             target
10/8.7.0             ctl          Initiator
10/12    ba                       Core I/O Adapter
10/12/0            ext_bus       Built-in Parallel Interface
10/12/5            ext_bus       Built-in SCSI
10/12/5.0            target
10/12/5.0.0            tape       HP       C1533A
10/12/5.2            target
10/12/5.2.0            disk       TOSHIBA CD-ROM XM-5401TA
10/12/5.7            target
10/12/5.7.0            ctl        Initiator
10/12/6            lan           Built-in LAN
10/12/7            ps2           Built-in Keyboard/Mouse
10/16    bc                       Bus Converter
10/16/12           lan           HP J2157A - FDDI Interface
```

```
32          processor           Processor
34          processor           Processor
36          processor           Processor
38          processor           Processor
49          memory              Memory


$ ioscan -funC disk

Class   I  H/W Path    Driver      S/W State H/W Type  Description
=========================================================================
disk    5  8/0.0.0     sdisk       CLAIMED   DEVICE    EMC      SYMMETRIX
                       /dev/dsk/c0t0d0   /dev/rdsk/c0t0d0
disk    6  8/0.0.1     sdisk       CLAIMED   DEVICE    EMC      SYMMETRIX
                       /dev/dsk/c0t0d1   /dev/rdsk/c0t0d1
disk    7  8/0.0.2     sdisk       CLAIMED   DEVICE    EMC      SYMMETRIX
                       /dev/dsk/c0t0d2   /dev/rdsk/c0t0d2
disk    8  8/0.0.3     sdisk       CLAIMED   DEVICE    EMC      SYMMETRIX
                       /dev/dsk/c0t0d3   /dev/rdsk/c0t0d3
disk    9  8/0.0.4     sdisk       CLAIMED   DEVICE    EMC      SYMMETRIX
                       /dev/dsk/c0t0d4   /dev/rdsk/c0t0d4
disk    10 8/0.0.5     sdisk       CLAIMED   DEVICE    EMC      SYMMETRIX
                       /dev/dsk/c0t0d5   /dev/rdsk/c0t0d5
disk    11 8/0.0.6     sdisk       CLAIMED   DEVICE    EMC      SYMMETRIX
                       /dev/dsk/c0t0d6   /dev/rdsk/c0t0d6
disk    12 8/4.0.0     sdisk       CLAIMED   DEVICE    EMC      SYMMETRIX
                       /dev/dsk/c1t0d0   /dev/rdsk/c1t0d0
disk    13 8/4.0.1     sdisk       CLAIMED   DEVICE    EMC      SYMMETRIX
                       /dev/dsk/c1t0d1   /dev/rdsk/c1t0d1
disk    14 8/4.0.2     sdisk       CLAIMED   DEVICE    EMC      SYMMETRIX
                       /dev/dsk/c1t0d2   /dev/rdsk/c1t0d2
disk    15 8/4.0.3     sdisk       CLAIMED   DEVICE    EMC      SYMMETRIX
                       /dev/dsk/c1t0d3   /dev/rdsk/c1t0d3
disk    16 8/4.0.4     sdisk       CLAIMED   DEVICE    EMC      SYMMETRIX
                       /dev/dsk/c1t0d4   /dev/rdsk/c1t0d4
disk    17 8/4.0.5     sdisk       CLAIMED   DEVICE    EMC      SYMMETRIX
                       /dev/dsk/c1t0d5   /dev/rdsk/c1t0d5
disk    18 8/4.0.6     sdisk       CLAIMED   DEVICE    EMC      SYMMETRIX
                       /dev/dsk/c1t0d6   /dev/rdsk/c1t0d6
disk    19 8/8.0.0     sdisk       CLAIMED   DEVICE    EMC      SYMMETRIX
                       /dev/dsk/c2t0d0   /dev/rdsk/c2t0d0
disk    20 8/8.0.1     sdisk       CLAIMED   DEVICE    EMC      SYMMETRIX
                       /dev/dsk/c2t0d1   /dev/rdsk/c2t0d1
disk    21 8/8.0.2     sdisk       CLAIMED   DEVICE    EMC      SYMMETRIX
                       /dev/dsk/c2t0d2   /dev/rdsk/c2t0d2
disk    22 8/8.0.3     sdisk       CLAIMED   DEVICE    EMC      SYMMETRIX
                       /dev/dsk/c2t0d3   /dev/rdsk/c2t0d3
disk    23 8/8.0.4     sdisk       CLAIMED   DEVICE    EMC      SYMMETRIX
                       /dev/dsk/c2t0d4   /dev/rdsk/c2t0d4
disk    24 8/8.0.5     sdisk       CLAIMED   DEVICE    EMC      SYMMETRIX
                       /dev/dsk/c2t0d5   /dev/rdsk/c2t0d5
disk    25 8/8.0.6     sdisk       CLAIMED   DEVICE    EMC      SYMMETRIX
                       /dev/dsk/c2t0d6   /dev/rdsk/c2t0d6
disk    26 8/12.0.0    sdisk       CLAIMED   DEVICE    EMC      SYMMETRIX
                       /dev/dsk/c3t0d0   /dev/rdsk/c3t0d0
disk    27 8/12.0.1    sdisk       CLAIMED   DEVICE    EMC      SYMMETRIX
                       /dev/dsk/c3t0d1   /dev/rdsk/c3t0d1
disk    28 8/12.0.2    sdisk       CLAIMED   DEVICE    EMC      SYMMETRIX
```

```
                          /dev/dsk/c3t0d2   /dev/rdsk/c3t0d2
disk     29  8/12.0.3     sdisk        CLAIMED   DEVICE     EMC      SYMMETRIX
                          /dev/dsk/c3t0d3   /dev/rdsk/c3t0d3
disk     30  8/12.0.4     sdisk        CLAIMED   DEVICE     EMC      SYMMETRIX
                          /dev/dsk/c3t0d4   /dev/rdsk/c3t0d4
disk     31  8/12.0.5     sdisk        CLAIMED   DEVICE     EMC      SYMMETRIX
                          /dev/dsk/c3t0d5   /dev/rdsk/c3t0d5
disk     32  8/12.0.6     sdisk        CLAIMED   DEVICE     EMC      SYMMETRIX
                          /dev/dsk/c3t0d6   /dev/rdsk/c3t0d6
disk      0  10/0.3.0     sdisk        CLAIMED   DEVICE     SEAGATE ST15150W
                          /dev/dsk/c4t3d0   /dev/rdsk/c4t3d0
disk      1  10/0.4.0     sdisk        CLAIMED   DEVICE     SEAGATE ST15150W
                          /dev/dsk/c4t4d0   /dev/rdsk/c4t4d0
disk      2  10/0.5.0     sdisk        CLAIMED   DEVICE     SEAGATE ST15150W
                          /dev/dsk/c4t5d0   /dev/rdsk/c4t5d0
disk      3  10/0.6.0     sdisk        CLAIMED   DEVICE     SEAGATE ST15150W
                          /dev/dsk/c4t6d0   /dev/rdsk/c4t6d0
disk     33  10/8.0.0     sdisk        CLAIMED   DEVICE     EMC      SYMMETRIX
                          /dev/dsk/c5t0d0   /dev/rdsk/c5t0d0
disk     34  10/8.0.1     sdisk        CLAIMED   DEVICE     EMC      SYMMETRIX
                          /dev/dsk/c5t0d1   /dev/rdsk/c5t0d1
disk     35  10/8.0.2     sdisk        CLAIMED   DEVICE     EMC      SYMMETRIX
                          /dev/dsk/c5t0d2   /dev/rdsk/c5t0d2
disk     36  10/8.0.3     sdisk        CLAIMED   DEVICE     EMC      SYMMETRIX
                          /dev/dsk/c5t0d3   /dev/rdsk/c5t0d3
disk     37  10/8.0.4     sdisk        CLAIMED   DEVICE     EMC      SYMMETRIX
                          /dev/dsk/c5t0d4   /dev/rdsk/c5t0d4
disk     38  10/8.0.5     sdisk        CLAIMED   DEVICE     EMC      SYMMETRIX
                          /dev/dsk/c5t0d5   /dev/rdsk/c5t0d5
disk     39  10/8.0.6     sdisk        CLAIMED   DEVICE     EMC      SYMMETRIX
                          /dev/dsk/c5t0d6   /dev/rdsk/c5t0d6
disk      4  10/12/5.2.0 sdisk       CLAIMED   DEVICE     TOSHIBA CD-ROM XM-5401TA
                          /dev/dsk/c6t2d0   /dev/rdsk/c6t2d0
```

You can see from the **ioscan** outputs that this system has a lot of disk capacity. For the first part of this benchmark, from which the data in this section of the book comes, the disk is used minimally. In subsequent parts of the benchmark there is a lot of disk I/O.

Notice that the first **ioscan** shows both a built-in lan and a Fiber Distributed Data Interface (FDDI). The FDDI is used as a high-speed connection between two system used in the benchmark.

After initiating the benchmark I invoked HP GlancePlus/UX to begin characterizing the performance of the system. After a little hopping around in Glance to get a feel for the system, I quickly stumbled across a potential problem. Figure 5-7 shows a GlancePlus screen that clearly identifies that the FDDI is nearly unused at a critical point in the benchmark when it should be heavily used.

```
B3692A GlancePlus B.10.12       11:34:29    Sut26 9000/889   Current   Avg  High
CPU  Util  S    SAU                                    U    | 71%     27%  100%
Disk Util  F  F                                             |  5%      1%   21%
Mem  Util  S    SU                                     UB   | 78%     69%   78%
Swap Util  U                        UR              R       | 88%     76%   88%
Network
                        NETWORK BY INTERFACE                    Users=    3

Interface  Network Type      Packets In    Packets Out    Collisions      Errors

ni0        Serial         0.0/    0.0    0.0/    0.0    0.0/   0.0    0.0/    0.0
ni1        Serial         0.0/    0.0    0.0/    0.0    0.0/   0.0    0.0/    0.0
lo0        Loop           0.0/    5.0    0.0/    5.0    0.0/   0.0    0.0/    0.0
lan1       Lan            0.1/    0.0    0.1/    0.0    0.0/   0.0    0.0/    0.0
lan0       Lan          986.4/  237.0 1009.6/  251.8   11.1/   1.8    0.0/    0.0




                                                           Page 1 of 1
   IO By  | IO By  | IO By  | Swap  |  hpterm   | Next  | Select  |Netwk By| System
 File Sys | Disk   |Logl Vol| Space |           | Keys  | Process |Intrface| Tables
```

Figure 5-7   HP GlancePlus/UX Showing lan Activity

lan1 is the FDDI over which very few packets are being transferred. Since there should be extensive data being transferred over the FDDI at this point in the benchmark, it was clear there was a problem with the benchmark software configuration. I then issued the following **netstat** command to indeed confirm that the interface is unused.

```
$ netstat -I lan1 5

(lan1)-> input         output        (Total)-> input          output
    packets  errs  packets errs colls    packets  errs  packets errs colls
       3880     0     3881    0     0      598018     2   329555    0  1654
          2     0        2    0     0        2736     0     3152    0    12
          0     0        0    0     0        4997     0     5364    0    42
          0     0        0    0     0        4443     0     5263    0    41
          0     0        0    0     0        3822     0     4790    0    37
          0     0        0    0     0        6061     0     6977    0    29
          0     0        0    0     0        5468     0     6483    0    48
          2     0        2    0     0        4718     0     5614    0    45
          0     0        0    0     0        6135     0     6808    0    43
          0     0        0    0     0        6136     0     6887    0    50
          0     0        0    0     0        4872     0     5847    0    33
```

0	0	0	0	0	4673	0	5660	0	30
0	0	0	0	0	6021	0	6831	0	68
2	0	2	0	0	5450	0	6180	0	69
0	0	0	0	0	4208	0	4836	0	35
0	0	0	0	0	3351	0	4083	0	19
0	0	0	0	0	4972	0	5836	0	47
0	0	0	0	0	6381	0	7163	0	52
0	0	0	0	0	5094	0	6146	0	36
2	0	2	0	0	5281	0	6196	0	42

The low input and output packets in this **netstat** output confirm that the FDDI was not used as the source of the extensive data transfer during the benchmark. The problem was easy to fix. The FDDI had not been specified as the interface through which information was to be transferred during the benchmark.

After fixing this problem and the benchmark resumed, I began to view additional performance information. I like to bring up a global Glance screen when I start looking at a system as shown in Figure 5-8.

```
B3692A GlancePlus B.10.12        11:25:50     Sut26 9000/889     Current   Avg  High

Cpu  Util  S        SNNARU                              U  | 93%    20%  100%
Disk Util  F                                               | 1%     1%   21%
Mem  Util  S   SU                              UB          | 78%    68%  78%
Swap Util  U                          UR               R   | 87%    75%  87%
Network
                              PROCESS LIST                   Users=      3
                           User    CPU Util    Cum    Disk          Block
Process Name   PID   PPID Pri Name  ( 400 max)  CPU  IO Rate   RSS     On

oracleFS501   5486   5485 154 oracle  12.2/ 0.0  1.3  0.0/ 0.0  1.5mb SOCKT
oracleFS501   5256   5255 154 oracle  11.4/ 0.0  0.8  0.0/ 0.0  1.5mb SOCKT
oracleFS501   5822   5821 154 oracle  11.2/ 0.0  0.8  0.2/ 0.0  1.5mb SOCKT
oracleFS501   7273   7272 154 oracle  10.8/ 0.1  2.4  0.0/ 0.0  1.6mb SOCKT
oracleFS501   5762   5761 154 oracle  10.4/ 0.1  1.3  0.2/ 0.0  1.6mb SOCKT
oracleFS501   9227   9226 154 oracle  10.2/ 0.1  1.1  0.0/ 0.0  1.5mb SOCKT
oracleFS501   8127   8126 154 oracle  10.2/ 0.1  1.2  0.0/ 0.0  1.5mb SOCKT
oracleFS501   6995   6994 154 oracle  10.2/ 0.1  1.0  0.0/ 0.0  1.5mb SOCKT
oracleFS501   8869   8868 154 oracle  10.2/ 0.1  1.3  0.4/ 0.0  1.5mb SOCKT
oracleFS501   6120   6119 154 oracle  10.2/ 0.1  1.7  0.0/ 0.0  1.5mb SOCKT
oracleFS501   5918   5917 154 oracle  10.0/ 0.0  0.6  0.0/ 0.0  1.5mb SOCKT
oracleFS501   6983   6982 154 oracle  10.0/ 0.1  2.0  0.2/ 0.0  1.5mb SOCKT
                                                          Page 1 of 9

Command  Reset    Print    Adjust     hpterm    Next  Process  Invoke Refresh
 List   to Zero  Toggle  Interval               Keys Threshld  Shell  Screen
```

Figure 5-8 HP GlancePlus/UX Global Screen

The processes shown in the Global screen are sorted by the amount of CPU consumed. The many "oracleFS501" processes shown are being run by the benchmark program.

It seems clear from this figure that the CPU may turn out to be the bottleneck of this portion of the benchmark. The user processes "oracleFS501" are consuming a great deal of system resources. The first of these processes, for instance, is consuming 12.2% out of a total of 400% of CPU resources. There is 400% CPU resources because there are four CPUs in the system times 100% per CPU.

Figure 5-9 shows more detail related to the CPUs of the system.

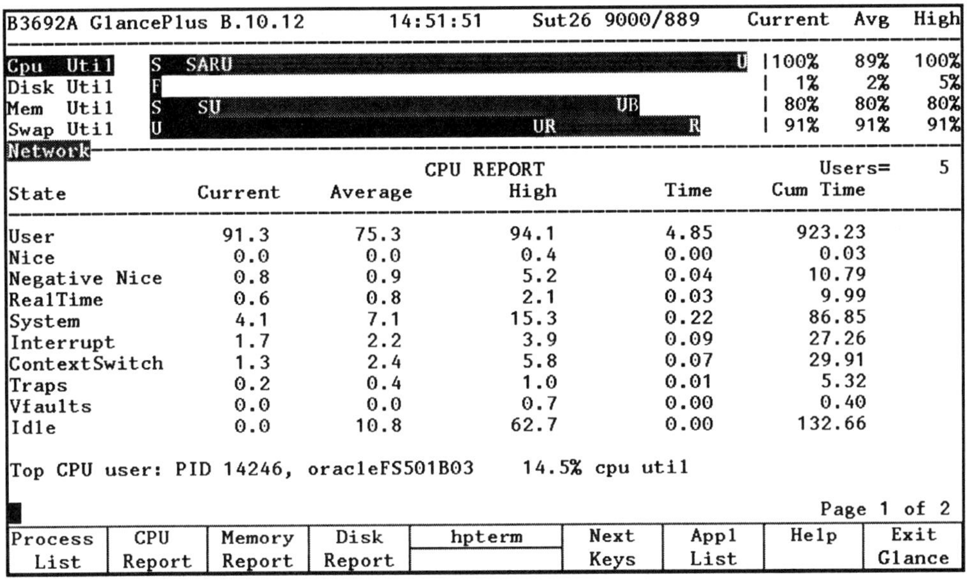

```
B3692A GlancePlus B.10.12        14:51:51     Sut26 9000/889   Current  Avg  High
-------------------------------------------------------------------------------
Cpu  Util  S  SARU                                         U |100%   89%  100%
Disk Util  F                                                 |  1%    2%    5%
Mem  Util  S  SU                              UB            |  80%   80%   80%
Swap Util  U                        UR                   R  |  91%   91%   91%
Network-------------------------------------------------------------------------
                                 CPU REPORT                      Users=     5
State           Current     Average        High        Time    Cum Time
-------------------------------------------------------------------------------
User              91.3        75.3         94.1        4.85      923.23
Nice               0.0         0.0          0.4        0.00        0.03
Negative Nice      0.8         0.9          5.2        0.04       10.79
RealTime           0.6         0.8          2.1        0.03        9.99
System             4.1         7.1         15.3        0.22       86.85
Interrupt          1.7         2.2          3.9        0.09       27.26
ContextSwitch      1.3         2.4          5.8        0.07       29.91
Traps              0.2         0.4          1.0        0.01        5.32
Vfaults            0.0         0.0          0.7        0.00        0.40
Idle               0.0        10.8         62.7        0.00      132.66

Top CPU user: PID 14246, oracleFS501B03      14.5% cpu util

                                                              Page  1 of 2
-------------------------------------------------------------------------------
Process | CPU    | Memory | Disk   | hpterm | Next | Appl | Help | Exit
List    | Report | Report | Report |        | Keys | List |      | Glance
```

Figure 5-9 HP GlancePlus/UX CPU Screen

In this figure it is clear that user processes are consuming the vast majority of CPU resources which is exactly what I expected at this point in the benchmark. In addition, 91.3% of the CPU is consumed by user processes and only 4.1% by system processes. At this point I feel the system is running efficiently.

Prior to starting the benchmark I started **sar** accumulating data at an interval of 60 seconds in the file **sar.data**. This is a binary file from which important performance data can be later extracted. The command used to save the binary performance information in an output file is shown below.

```
# sar -o /tmp/sar.data 60 300
```

We can now view the CPU related information collected by **sar**. **sar** is useful for showing the historical CPU data. In this case the historical data consists of one-minute intervals. In the following example it is clear that the CPU started out mostly idle in this benchmark and then worked its way up to a high level of utilization beginning at 13:39:43.

```
$ sar -b -f sar.data

HP-UX Sut26 B.10.20 U 9000/889    12/05/97

13:01:43    %usr    %sys    %wio    %idle
13:02:43     1       1       0       98
13:03:43     1       1       0       98
13:04:43     1       1       0       98
13:05:43     1       1       0       98
13:06:43     1       1       0       98
13:07:43     1       1       0       98
13:08:43     1       1       0       97
13:09:43    18       3       2       77
13:10:43    16       2       1       81
13:11:43     1       1       0       98
13:12:43     1       1       0       98
13:13:43     1       1       0       98
13:14:43     1       1       0       98
13:15:43     1       1       0       97
13:16:43     1       1       0       98
13:17:43     1       1       0       98
13:18:43     1       1       0       98
13:19:43     1       1       0       98
13:20:43 ·   3       1       0       96
13:21:43     5       1       0       94
13:22:43     1       1       0       98
13:23:43     1       1       0       98
13:24:43     1       1       0       98
```

13:25:43	1	1	0	98
13:26:43	1	1	0	98
13:27:43	1	1	0	98
13:28:43	1	1	0	98
13:29:43	1	1	0	98
13:30:43	1	1	0	97
13:31:43	1	1	0	98
13:32:43	1	1	0	98
13:33:43	1	1	0	98
13:34:43	1	1	0	98
13:35:43	1	1	0	98
13:36:43	1	0	0	99
13:37:43	0	0	0	99
13:38:43	1	0	0	99
13:39:43	35	4	0	61
13:40:43	76	9	0	15
13:41:43	76	9	0	15
13:42:43	71	8	0	21
13:43:43	84	10	0	5
13:44:43	80	13	0	7
13:45:43	60	6	0	34
13:46:43	63	6	0	30
13:47:43	77	8	0	15
13:48:43	85	11	0	4
13:49:43	82	11	0	8
13:50:43	80	9	0	11
13:51:43	60	5	0	34
13:52:43	80	8	0	12
13:53:43	84	10	0	6
13:54:43	72	7	0	21
13:55:43	81	9	0	10
13:56:43	76	8	0	16
13:57:43	70	7	0	23
13:58:43	76	7	0	17
13:59:43	76	8	0	16
14:00:43	74	7	0	19
14:01:43	76	8	0	16
14:02:43	78	8	0	13
14:03:43	77	8	0	15
14:04:43	81	9	0	9
14:05:43	69	7	0	24
14:06:43	76	8	0	16
14:07:43	79	8	0	13
14:08:43	70	7	0	23
14:09:43	80	8	0	11
14:10:43	75	8	0	17
14:11:43	70	7	0	22
14:12:43	77	8	0	15
14:13:43	78	8	0	14
14:14:43	72	7	0	21
14:15:43	79	8	0	12
14:16:43	82	8	0	10
14:17:43	79	8	0	13
14:18:43	78	7	0	15
14:19:43	80	8	0	11
14:20:43	79	8	0	13
14:21:43	73	8	0	18
14:22:43	79	9	0	12

14:23:43	81	9	0	9
14:24:43	78	9	0	13
14:25:43	73	8	0	18
14:26:43	68	8	0	23
14:27:43	67	8	0	25
Average	44	5	0	51

This **sar** output shows the trend of CPU utilization. The earlier Glance screen shot showing very high CPU utilization was taken at a time of peak CPU utilization during the benchmark.

In addition to the CPU, memory was considered a key component in this benchmark run. Figure 5-10 is a GlancePlus memory screen shot.

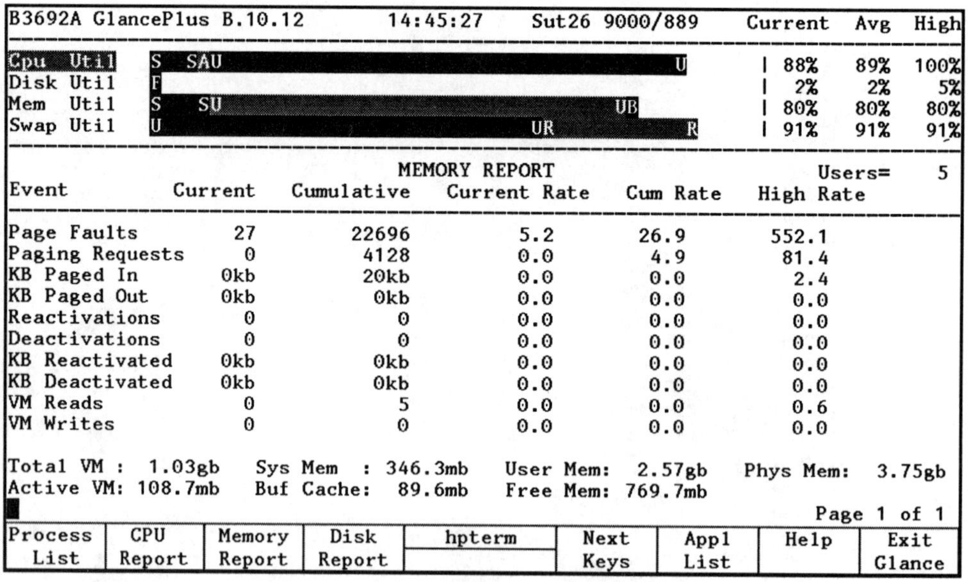

```
B3692A GlancePlus B.10.12        14:45:27    Sut26 9000/889    Current  Avg  High
Cpu  Util  S   SAU                                       U   |  88%   89%  100%
Disk Util  F                                                 |   2%    2%    5%
Mem  Util  S    SU                                     UB    |  80%   80%   80%
Swap Util  U                                    UR        R  |  91%   91%   91%

                                MEMORY REPORT                      Users=    5
Event          Current    Cumulative   Current Rate   Cum Rate   High Rate
Page Faults        27        22696          5.2          26.9       552.1
Paging Requests     0         4128          0.0           4.9        81.4
KB Paged In       0kb         20kb          0.0           0.0         2.4
KB Paged Out      0kb          0kb          0.0           0.0         0.0
Reactivations       0            0          0.0           0.0         0.0
Deactivations       0            0          0.0           0.0         0.0
KB Reactivated    0kb          0kb          0.0           0.0         0.0
KB Deactivated    0kb          0kb          0.0           0.0         0.0
VM Reads            0            5          0.0           0.0         0.6
VM Writes           0            0          0.0           0.0         0.0

Total VM :  1.03gb    Sys Mem :  346.3mb    User Mem:  2.57gb   Phys Mem:  3.75gb
Active VM: 108.7mb    Buf Cache:  89.6mb    Free Mem:  769.7mb
                                                                  Page 1 of 1
Process    CPU      Memory    Disk      hpterm      Next    Appl   Help   Exit
 List     Report    Report    Report                Keys    List          Glance
```

Figure 5-10 HP GlancePlus/UX Memory Screen

This screen shows the memory utilization at a steady 80%. The physical memory in the system is 3.75 GBytes of which roughly 769 MBytes is free. Although 80% is high memory utilization there is still enough free memory at this point in the benchmark to point back to the CPU as the bottleneck.

The disk was not expected to be a factor during the benchmark. Only in the first stage of the benchmark when a database of roughly 100 GBytes was built was there high disk utilization. A large Symmetrix® disk bank was included to hold this 100 GByte database and for a subsequent step in the benchmark when substantially more data and disk activity was to take place. The following figure shows some **uncompress** processes that ran early in the benchmark consuming a lot of CPU and very high disk utilization as the database is created. As soon as the database was created and the benchmark began, the disk utilization dropped back to a very low level.

```
B3692A GlancePlus B.10.12        09:41:18     Sut26 9000/889    Current  Avg   High

Cpu  Util  S            SRU                           U  | 90%    89%   97%
Disk Util  F                                           F | 99%    96%  100%
Mem  Util  S     SUBB                                    | 13%    13%   13%
Swap Util  UR     R                                      | 13%    13%   13%

                                    PROCESS LIST              Users=    3
                                User   CPU Util      Cum    Disk          Block
Process Name   PID  PPID Pri Name    ( 400 max)     CPU   IO Rate    RSS    On

uncompress    1407  1375 149 root    20.8/18.0    211.7  39.6/26.5   732kb CACHE
uncompress    1408  1375 154 root    16.1/18.8    222.0  20.3/29.1   732kb PIPE
uncompress    1416  1375 154 root    15.8/10.0    117.4  12.9/ 2.5   780kb PIPE
uncompress    1412  1375 241 root    15.4/11.6    136.8  17.4/ 7.2   740kb  PRI
uncompress    1410  1375 154 root    15.0/ 8.5    100.2  15.2/ 2.8   740kb PIPE
uncompress    1419  1375 149 root    14.2/11.1    130.8  17.2/ 8.0   756kb CACHE
uncompress    1427  1375 154 root    13.2/11.5    135.7  13.9/10.0   756kb PIPE
uncompress    1421  1375 154 root    12.5/11.2    132.5   5.0/ 3.8   764kb PIPE
midaemon      1489  1488  50 root    10.7/10.4    122.9   0.0/ 0.0   2.1mb SYSTM
uncompress    1420  1375 154 root     9.7/ 8.9    104.4   1.7/ 0.0   772kb PIPE
uncompress    1413  1375 154 root     9.3/ 8.8    103.7   3.5/ 3.1   740kb PIPE
uncompress    1423  1375 241 root     9.3/ 9.3    110.2   9.4/ 4.0   756kb  PRI
                                                                Page 1 of 5

Process  CPU     Memory   Disk     hpterm     Next    Appl    Help    Exit
List     Report  Report   Report              Keys    List            Glance
```

Figure 5-11 HP GlancePlus/UX Showing High Disk Utilization as the Database is built.

The first **uncompress** process is consuming 20% of the CPU (there is 400% CPU available) while the disk is 99% utilized. Since creating the database was preparation for running the benchmark and not the benchmark itself, this high disk utilization was not a concern to me.

The following **sar** output confirms the low disk utilization during the majority of the benchmark. Only a few minutes of data is included in this example because the output is lengthy due to the many disks on the system.

```
$ sar -d -f sar.data

HP-UX Sut26 B.10.20 U 9000/889      12/05/97

10:38:35    device    %busy    avque    r+w/s    blks/s    avwait    avserv
10:39:35    c4t6d0    0.25     2.74      0         5        20.39     13.31
            c0t0d0    0.18     2.98      0         6        21.93      9.64
            c0t0d1    0.20     3.28      0         7        22.99      9.22
            c0t0d2    0.18     3.06      0         7        22.35      8.92
            c0t0d3    0.17     1.56      0         5        13.68      9.97
            c0t0d4    0.18     2.24      0         6        17.69      9.68
            c1t0d0    0.23     3.13      0         7        22.37      9.61
            c1t0d1    0.20     1.46      0         5        12.78      7.50
            c1t0d2    0.22     3.66      0         7        25.62      9.39
            c1t0d3    0.20     2.66      0         7        21.37      9.44
            c1t0d4    0.23     3.09      0         8        24.15      9.23
            c2t0d0    0.27     3.43      0         7        32.70     11.81
            c2t0d1    0.25     2.40      0         5        24.01     14.10
            c2t0d2    0.23     3.41      0         6        31.27     12.48
            c2t0d3    0.23     2.25      0         5        22.13     13.98
            c2t0d4    0.22     1.75      0         4        15.92     13.92
            c3t0d0    0.20     2.80      0         6        19.83      9.51
            c3t0d1    0.20     3.61      0         7        25.34      9.09
            c3t0d2    0.17     2.10      0         4        20.18     10.86
            c3t0d3    0.20     3.39      0         7        23.76      9.11
            c3t0d4    0.17     1.55      0         6        12.27      8.59
            c5t0d0    0.27     2.74      0         7        25.36     12.55
            c5t0d1    0.32     4.67      1         8        39.51     12.01
            c5t0d2    0.28     2.33      0         6        23.27     13.04
            c5t0d3    0.22     2.89      0         5        28.31     13.58
            c5t0d4    0.25     2.93      0         6        28.25     12.62
            c4t4d0    0.32     1.50      0         6        14.46     11.12
10:40:35    c4t6d0    0.13     0.80      0         2         8.44     12.88
            c0t0d0    0.18     2.00      0         7        16.02      8.32
            c0t0d1    0.17     2.55      0         5        18.06      9.88
            c0t0d2    0.15     2.39      0         5        19.05      9.82
            c0t0d3    0.17     3.37      0         6        23.79      8.64
            c0t0d4    0.15     1.67      0         5        14.17      9.78
            c1t0d0    0.17     1.79      0         6        15.08      8.00
            c1t0d1    0.15     2.73      0         6        21.91      8.27
```

	c1t0d2	0.18	1.83	0	6	14.52	6.94
	c1t0d3	0.13	3.00	0	5	21.38	8.72
	c1t0d4	0.12	1.43	0	4	13.37	9.25
	c2t0d0	0.20	1.50	0	5	15.43	10.87
	c2t0d1	0.20	3.05	0	5	29.09	11.74
	c2t0d2	0.20	1.90	0	4	17.37	13.70
	c2t0d3	0.22	2.13	0	5	21.91	12.16
	c2t0d4	0.20	2.79	0	5	29.60	13.22
	c3t0d0	0.17	2.03	0	5	17.48	9.27
	c3t0d1	0.17	2.85	0	5	21.18	9.81
	c3t0d2	0.13	1.74	0	5	14.00	9.17
	c3t0d3	0.15	1.87	0	5	15.87	9.18
	c3t0d4	0.17	1.93	0	6	16.30	8.47
	c5t0d0	0.22	1.80	0	5	19.61	12.06
	c5t0d1	0.17	1.90	0	4	17.66	12.84
	c5t0d2	0.20	1.60	0	5	17.52	11.59
	c5t0d3	0.20	2.18	0	5	20.64	12.26
	c5t0d4	0.13	1.19	0	3	11.34	11.42
	c4t4d0	0.25	0.85	0	5	7.63	11.82
10:41:35	c4t6d0	0.17	0.93	0	4	11.06	12.21
	c1t0d2	0.03	0.50	0	1	5.21	0.83
	c3t0d1	0.02	0.50	0	1	4.74	0.91
	c4t4d0	0.23	0.86	0	5	8.19	11.09
10:42:35	c4t6d0	0.35	1.46	0	7	14.39	16.72
	c0t0d0	0.13	0.94	0	4	9.45	8.67
	c0t0d1	0.17	2.92	0	7	20.85	7.62
	c0t0d2	0.13	2.14	0	4	18.03	9.96
	c0t0d3	0.13	1.44	0	4	12.33	9.42
	c0t0d4	0.15	2.75	0	5	19.55	9.23
	c1t0d0	0.18	2.12	0	6	15.90	7.89
	c1t0d1	0.18	3.12	0	6	22.67	9.11
	c1t0d2	0.13	2.26	0	4	17.11	7.49
	c1t0d3	0.15	1.78	0	5	14.21	9.26
	c1t0d4	0.15	3.13	0	5	22.44	9.00
	c2t0d0	0.17	1.50	0	4	15.58	12.07
	c2t0d1	0.22	1.50	0	5	19.07	13.46
	c2t0d2	0.20	2.21	0	5	22.28	12.85
	c2t0d3	0.18	2.33	0	5	19.62	11.80
	c2t0d4	0.20	2.13	0	5	20.22	12.65
	c3t0d0	0.13	1.12	0	4	12.33	9.02
	c3t0d1	0.10	1.17	0	4	10.22	7.69
	c3t0d2	0.15	2.09	0	6	15.86	7.54
	c3t0d3	0.10	1.50	0	4	12.48	8.43
	c3t0d4	0.12	0.86	0	4	7.80	8.93
	c5t0d0	0.17	1.95	0	5	16.64	10.50
	c5t0d1	0.18	1.81	0	4	15.79	12.00
	c5t0d2	0.20	1.79	0	5	18.02	12.03
	c5t0d3	0.15	2.04	0	3	20.00	13.35
	c5t0d4	0.17	1.25	0	4	13.22	12.45
	c4t4d0	0.25	0.80	0	5	8.13	11.92
10:43:35	c4t6d0	0.40	1.61	1	9	15.81	13.47
	c0t0d0	0.12	1.79	0	4	13.80	9.13
	c0t0d1	0.12	1.86	0	3	15.52	10.17
	c0t0d2	0.13	2.22	0	5	17.55	9.02
	c0t0d3	0.13	1.62	0	5	12.87	8.48
	c0t0d4	0.13	2.34	0	5	17.77	8.50
	c1t0d0	0.17	2.50	0	5	18.74	9.42
	c1t0d1	0.13	1.71	0	4	15.45	10.46

```
c1t0d2    0.17    2.09    0    5    16.18    6.74
c1t0d3    0.13    1.63    0    4    14.21    9.82
c1t0d4    0.15    1.91    0    5    16.92    9.58
c2t0d0    0.22    3.67    0    6    33.16   10.62
c2t0d1    0.17    2.50    0    4    21.72   12.61
c2t0d2    0.20    2.74    0    6    26.35   11.46
c2t0d3    0.17    1.50    0    3    18.71   13.43
c2t0d4    0.18    1.61    0    5    15.70   11.24
c3t0d0    0.15    3.00    0    6    20.56    7.90
c3t0d1    0.10    1.00    0    3     8.48    8.13
c3t0d2    0.13    1.79    0    5    14.48    8.80
c3t0d3    0.13    1.91    0    5    14.55    8.78
c3t0d4    0.15    1.97    0    5    15.41    9.28
c5t0d0    0.23    2.89    0    6    26.02   11.70
c5t0d1    0.17    1.75    0    4    17.14   12.56
c5t0d2    0.18    2.00    0    4    21.24   13.44
c5t0d3    0.22    2.22    0    5    23.23   13.29
c5t0d4    0.20    2.50    0    5    26.82   13.61
c4t4d0    0.48    0.82    1    8     8.48   12.50
```

It was expected as this benchmark progressed that the run queue would grow and later recede. The following **sar** output confirms this.

```
$ sar -q -f sar.data


HP-UX Sut26 B.10.20 U 9000/889     12/05/97


10:38:35 runq-sz %runocc swpq-sz %swpocc
10:39:35     0.0       0     0.0       0
10:40:35     0.0       0     0.0       0
10:41:35     1.0       1     0.0       0
10:42:35     1.0       1     0.0       0
10:43:35     0.0       0     0.0       0
10:44:35     0.0       0     0.0       0
10:45:35     0.0       0     0.0       0
10:46:35     0.0       0     0.0       0
10:47:35     0.0       0     0.0       0
10:48:35     0.0       0     0.0       0
10:49:35     1.0       0     0.0       0
10:50:35     0.0       0     0.0       0
10:51:35     0.0       0     0.0       0
10:52:35     0.0       0     0.0       0
10:53:35     0.0       0     0.0       0
10:54:35     0.0       0     0.0       0
10:55:35     0.0       0     0.0       0
10:56:35     0.0       0     0.0       0
10:57:35     1.0       2     0.0       0
```

10:58:35	0.0	0	0.0	0
10:59:35	1.0	2	0.0	0
11:00:35	0.0	0	0.0	0
11:01:35	1.0	2	0.0	0
11:02:35	0.0	0	0.0	0
11:03:35	1.0	0	0.0	0
11:04:35	0.0	0	0.0	0
11:05:35	1.0	2	0.0	0
11:06:35	1.0	0	0.0	0
11:07:35	1.0	0	0.0	0
11:08:35	1.0	2	0.0	0
11:09:35	1.0	2	0.0	0
11:10:35	1.0	0	0.0	0
11:11:35	1.0	0	0.0	0
11:12:35	1.0	2	0.0	0
11:13:35	0.0	0	0.0	0
11:14:35	0.0	0	0.0	0
11:15:35	1.0	0	0.0	0
11:16:35	8.1	21	0.0	0
11:17:35	7.4	72	0.0	0
11:18:35	3.8	44	0.0	0
11:19:35	6.7	72	0.0	0
11:20:35	8.1	92	0.0	0
11:21:35	10.6	88	0.0	0
11:22:35	13.0	90	0.0	0
11:23:35	6.7	47	0.0	0
11:24:35	7.4	71	0.0	0
11:25:35	6.7	83	0.0	0
11:26:35	8.5	65	0.0	0
11:27:35	8.6	88	0.0	0
11:28:35	5.3	69	0.0	0
11:29:35	5.9	58	0.0	0
11:30:35	4.0	43	0.0	0
11:31:35	7.9	86	0.0	0
11:32:35	7.3	84	0.0	0
11:33:35	5.6	59	0.0	0
11:34:35	6.2	47	0.0	0
11:35:35	7.3	23	0.0	0
11:36:35	0.0	0	0.0	0
11:37:35	0.0	0	0.0	0
11:38:35	0.0	0	0.0	0
Average	7.5	22	0.0	0

The *runq-sz* column shows the average length of the run queue for the one-minute period. The *%runocc* column shows the percentage of time the run queues were occupied by a process. The higher these numbers the more activity that is taking place on the system.

Beginning at 11:13:65 in this file the run queue length begins to increase dramatically. As in the other examples, there is a time period in the benchmark when simulated users are logging on to the system which does not consume much CPU. When the users are finally logged onto the system and simulated updates to the database begin, the CPU load increases and the run queue length increases.

In general, the performance characteristics of this benchmark are what were expected. Because the system is running efficiently, the focus of improving performance was not system related but application related. A substantial amount of database tuning was performed to help reduce the load on the CPU.

A Real-Life Performance Problem

It's true that networks "grow a life of their own" over the years. Many of my customers started out with innocent, self-contained, manageable networks 10 years ago that have now turned into monsters. What happened? Well, first the number of computers grew from 10 to 100. Then the number of applications grew from 2 to 20 when other departments started sharing the same network. Then the data used by the applications grew from 5 MBytes to 200 MBytes. Then more sophisticated technology such as NFS became part of the network.

What if you're asked to improve the performance of an application? The application now takes several hours to complete its run. You are asked to assess the existing system resources (CPU, memory, disk, etc.) and make recommendations of how system resources should be expanded to reduce the completion time of this run. Almost invariably it is assumed that a bigger something (CPU, memory, disk, etc.) is what is required to improve system performance.

Let's walk through the process of improving the performance of a specific computer running a specific application in a distributed environment. All of the activities related to this example were performed on an HP-UX 9.x system. For the most part this is not important since all of the principles and commands used in this example apply to both HP-UX 9.x and HP-UX 10.x.

First Things First - Taking Inventory

If indeed your network has grown or you are unfamiliar with the components of the network, the first step is to take an inventory. To begin you want to know what systems run what applications, where data is stored, and where home directories are located. I like to call this a "functional" inventory. Functional in this case means you don't know every detail of every component but you know the flow of data on the network and where it is located. Figure 5-12 is a greatly simplified version of a real functional network diagram. It is highly simplified because the original just won't fit in this book.

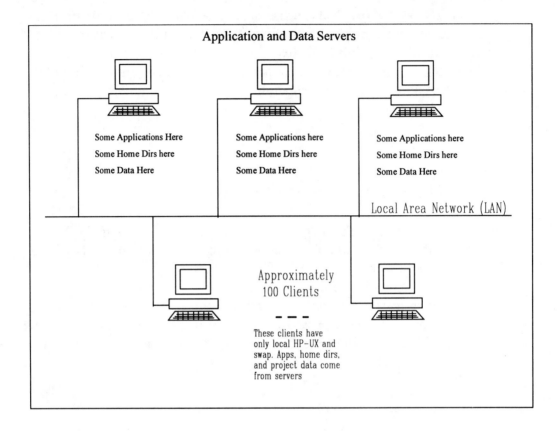

Figure 5-12   A Simplified Network Diagram

This network is set up in such a way that when a user logs in to a client, a home directory is accessed on one of the servers. If a user invokes an application, then the application and project data are copied to the local system. This means that you can expect a lot of network activity initially, but after the application and data are copied to the local system, everything is running on the local system so network activity is low.

This is a simplified network diagram so you can't see the vast number of applications and data spread over these servers. Before we even begin looking at the specific application we want to improve the performance of, you might look at this network diagram and question the amount of redundancy. There are three servers performing basically the same functions. It may make sense to consolidate some of this functionality onto one big server. Having functionality spread over several servers is a characteristic I see when networks have grown over many years. To appreciate the amount of mounting that client systems perform on the server disks, you can use the **showmount** command. The following *partial* **showmount** output (also used earlier in this chapter as an example) on one of the servers gives you an idea of the number of NFS mounted directories on the server:

```
# showmount -a

hp100.ct.mp.com:/applic

hp101.ct.mp.com:/applic

hp102.cal.mp.com:/applic

hp103.cal.mp.com:/applic

hp104.cal.mp.com:/applic

hp105.cal.mp.com:/applic

hp106.cal.mp.com:/applic

hp107.cal.mp.com:/applic

hp108.cal.mp.com:/applic

hp109.cal.mp.com:/applic

hp100.cal.mp.com:/usr/users

hp101.cal.mp.com:/usr/users

hp102.cal.mp.com:/usr/users

hp103.cal.mp.com:/usr/users

hp104.cal.mp.com:/usr/users

hp105.cal.mp.com:/usr/users

hp106.cal.mp.com:/usr/users

hp107.cal.mp.com:/usr/users

hp108.cal.mp.com:/usr/users

hp109.cal.mp.com:/usr/users
```

This is a small fraction of the overall **showmount** output. As described earlier in this chapter showmount has three options:

-a prints output in the format "name:directory" as shown above.

-d lists all of the local directories that have been remotely mounted by clients.

-e prints a list of exported file systems.

Although consolidating information may indeed improve overall efficiency, the original objective is to improve the performance of application runs on client systems. Consolidating home directories and other such improvements might make system administration more efficient, but there is no guarantee this will improve performance. Instead, we want to characterize the application on the client and see how system resources are being used.

Characterize Application

Since the application is taking a long time to run, we need to find the source of the bottleneck. This can be an undersized CPU, lack of memory, or a variety of other problems. We can start by viewing virtual memory with **vmstat**. The following **vmstat** output was produced every five seconds a total of 15 times during an application run:

#vmstat 5 15:

procs			memory		page							faults			cpu		
r	b	w	avm	free	re	at	pi	po	fr	de	sr	in	sy	cs	us	sy	id
0	0	19	9484	91	0	0	0	0	0	0	0	65	84	20	7	0	93
0	0	22	10253	68	0	0	0	0	0	0	0	214	939	127	72	7	21
0	0	25	10288	90	0	0	0	0	0	0	9	289	988	152	73	5	22
0	0	25	10300	89	0	0	0	0	0	0	9	325	820	151	76	3	21
0	0	24	10298	90	0	0	0	0	0	0	2	139	629	94	94	4	2
0	0	21	9889	86	0	0	0	0	0	0	1	189	782	111	72	5	23
0	0	20	9886	77	0	0	0	0	0	0	0	220	998	135	73	5	22
0	0	21	10274	77	0	0	0	0	0	0	0	220	723	124	69	3	28
0	0	22	10285	73	0	0	0	0	0	0	0	265	606	94	90	3	7
0	0	22	10291	69	0	0	0	0	0	0	0	156	872	122	71	5	24
0	0	20	10292	60	0	0	0	0	0	0	0	192	989	139	72	5	23
0	0	21	9913	257	0	0	0	0	0	0	1	282	736	118	81	2	17
0	0	22	9915	257	0	0	0	0	0	0	9	209	596	84	89	5	6
0	0	22	10699	237	0	0	0	0	0	3	7	165	945	117	70	7	23
0	0	21	10211	229	0	0	0	0	0	3	1	331	677	127	71	5	24

From this example you can see that runnable ("r") and blocked ("b") processes are zero, but swapped ("w") processes are roughly 20 for each five-second interval. This is indicative of a system that has a severe memory shortage. Note also that the active virtual memory ("avm") is around 10,000 blocks. 10,000 blocks is roughly 40 MBytes:

$$10,000 \, blocks \times 4,096 \, bytes \, per \, block = 40 \, MBytes$$

With this amount of active virtual memory and swapped processes, you would expect to see a great deal of disk activity. The next logical step would be to run **iostat** and see if indeed there is a great deal of disk activity taking place. **iostat** was run five times at five-second intervals to produce the following output (keep in mind the format of **iostat** output changed slightly from HP-UX 9.x to HP-UX 10.x).

```
# iostat 5 5
                        tty                    cpu
                   tin   tout        us      ni     sy    id
                    0     1          6       0      0    93
/dev/*dsk/c2076d*s*
bps  sps  msps
 2   0.3   0.0

                        tty                    cpu
                   tin   tout        us      ni     sy    id
                    0     73         72      0      5    23
/dev/*dsk/c2076d*s*
bps  sps  msps
17   0.6    0.0

                        tty                    cpu
                   tin   tout        us      ni     sy    id
                    0     97         85      0      4    11
/dev/*dsk/c2076d*s*
bps  sps  msps
 1   0.2    0.0

                        tty                    cpu
                   tin   tout        us      ni     sy    id
                    0     66         87      0      3    10
```

```
/dev/*dsk/c2076d*s*
bps  sps  msps
  0  0.0    0.0
                         tty                    cpu
                     tin   tout        us      ni    sy   id
                       0    55         73       0     5   22
/dev/*dsk/c2076d*s*
bps  sps  msps
  5  1.2    0.0
```

This looks to be very low disk access as indicated by a low number of blocks per second ("bps") and seeks per second ("sps") for a system that has a high number of swapped processes.

The next step is to see how HP GlancePlus/UX characterizes this system. In particular I am interested in the level of disk activity taking place. Figure 5-13 is a GlancePlus Memory Detail screen shot of this system.

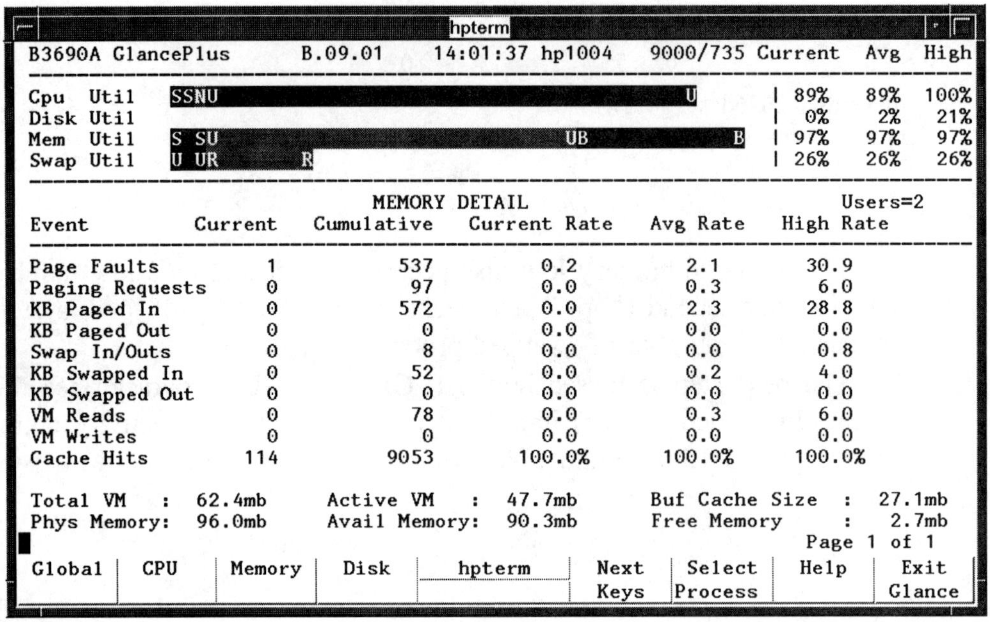

```
┌─                                      ┌──────┐                              ┐ ┌─┐
│                                       │hpterm│                              │ │ │
│  B3690A GlancePlus       B.09.01    14:01:37 hp1004   9000/735 Current  Avg  High│
│ ─────────────────────────────────────────────────────────────────────────────── │
│  Cpu  Util  SSNU                                        U     │ 89%   89%  100% │
│  Disk Util                                                    │  0%    2%   21% │
│  Mem  Util  S SU                          UB               B  │ 97%   97%   97% │
│  Swap Util  U UR            R                                 │ 26%   26%   26% │
│ ─────────────────────────────────────────────────────────────────────────────── │
│                           MEMORY DETAIL                          Users=2        │
│  Event            Current   Cumulative   Current Rate   Avg Rate   High Rate    │
│ ─────────────────────────────────────────────────────────────────────────────── │
│  Page Faults          1          537         0.2          2.1        30.9       │
│  Paging Requests      0           97         0.0          0.3         6.0       │
│  KB Paged In          0          572         0.0          2.3        28.8       │
│  KB Paged Out         0            0         0.0          0.0         0.0       │
│  Swap In/Outs         0            8         0.0          0.0         0.8       │
│  KB Swapped In        0           52         0.0          0.2         4.0       │
│  KB Swapped Out       0            0         0.0          0.0         0.0       │
│  VM Reads             0           78         0.0          0.3         6.0       │
│  VM Writes            0            0         0.0          0.0         0.0       │
│  Cache Hits         114         9053       100.0%       100.0%      100.0%      │
│                                                                                 │
│  Total VM  :  62.4mb    Active VM   :  47.7mb    Buf Cache Size :   27.1mb      │
│  Phys Memory: 96.0mb    Avail Memory:  90.3mb    Free Memory    :    2.7mb      │
│ ▮                                                            Page 1 of 1        │
│ ─────────────────────────────────────────────────────────────────────────────── │
│  Global │ CPU │ Memory │ Disk │   hpterm    │ Next  │ Select  │ Help │ Exit      │
│         │     │        │      │             │ Keys  │ Process │      │ Glance    │
└─                                                                               ─┘
```

Figure 5-13 HP GlancePlus/UX Memory Detail Screen Shot with Over 40 MBytes of Virtual Memory

This GlancePlus screen shot shows data which corresponds to the information **vmstat** and **iostat** provided. Here are some of the pieces of information provided by **vmstat**, **iostat**, and this GlancePlus screen shot:

- The CPU utilization is around 90 percent as reported by **vmstat**, **iostat**, and GlancePlus.

- Memory utilization is 100 percent.

- Active virtual memory is over 40 MBytes as reported by **vmstat** (remember the 10,000 blocks x 4 KByte blocks) and GlancePlus (the GlancePlus results are somewhat higher because I opened up several additional windows in HP CDE).

- Disk activity is 0 percent as reported by both **iostat** and Glance-Plus!

This is becoming somewhat of a puzzle. If there is a high level of active virtual memory and a lot of swapped processes, where is the massive disk activity we expect? As it turns out **netstat** helps solve this problem.

At this point the system should be running its application and not relying on other systems for resources. You may recall that both the application and data have been copied to the local system, so there is no need for other systems to play a part in this application run. As it turns out, however, **netstat** tells us otherwise. The following **netstat** example was obtained while the application was running.

```
# netstat -I lan0 5
```

input		(lan0)	output	
packets	errs	packets	errs	colls
8792739	120618	106184	0	1522
425	5	383	0	3
220	0	191	0	1
352	1	191	0	3
439	1	380	0	1
296	0	193	0	1
274	2	194	0	2
446	1	373	0	6
394	0	216	0	2
329	1	191	0	0
502	5	304	0	5
362	4	268	0	3

netstat -I lan0 5

input		(lan0)	output	
packets	errs	packets	errs	colls
267	1	198	0	1

This output shows that every five seconds there are around 200 input packets and 200 output packets at this network interface. That is a substantial amount of network traffic for a system that should be running in standalone mode at this point. Figure 5-14 is a GlancePlus screen shot showing the "LAN" screen.

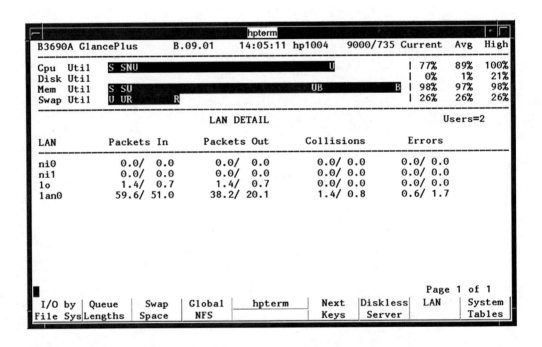

Figure 5-14 HP GlancePlus/UX Network Detail Screen Showing Network Traffic Similar to **netstat**

This screen shot shows the number of packets in and packets out for lan0. Even though the update interval for GlancePlus is five seconds, the same interval as the **netstat** output, GlancePlus updates the packets in and packets out every second. If you take the 200 packets in and out that **netstat** reported every five seconds and divide by five, you get the 40 packets in and out shown by GlancePlus! This can be confusing if you use an interval for **netstat** other than one second and attempt to compare this with the results you get with GlancePlus. The following **netstat** output is for a one-second interval. With this example you can easily see the corresponding numbers both **netstat** and GlancePlus are supplying for packets in and packets out.

```
# netstat -I lan0 1
```

input		(lan0)	output	
packets	errs	packets	errs	colls
8802612	120672	113251	0	1588
35	1	18	0	0
10	0	31	0	1
19	1	22	0	2
76	1	34	0	1
45	0	24	0	1
20	2	35	0	2
34	1	29	0	1
50	0	61	0	2
39	1	21	0	0
39	5	23	0	0
19	4	34	0	2
20	1	32	0	1

These networking figures make clear the vast amount of virtual memory activity taking place across the network. The application uses the user's home directory as the default location for working files as the application run takes place. Since the functional inventory showed the user's home directory on one of the servers and *not* the local system, we have an explanation for the lack of disk access on the local system and the high level of network activity on the local system. The fact that local swap is not being used on the client is further reinforced by the following **swapinfo** example from the client which shows that only 4 percent of the swap space on the client is being used (you may recall this example from earlier in the chapter).

```
# swapinfo
```

TYPE	Kb AVAIL	Kb USED	Kb FREE	PCT USED	START/ LIMIT	Kb RESERVE	PRI	NAME
dev	204505	8401	196104	4%	820534	-	0	/dev/dsk/c201d6s0
hold	0	30724	-30724					

The only remaining piece of the puzzle required to confirm that the server is being used for virtual memory is to run some of the same commands on it. Since it is not an HP system, I chose to run **netstat** on it to see if indeed there was a great deal of network activity on the network interface. I found the numbers to be almost identical to the level of network traffic being generated on the HP client. Since there were no other users on this server system and no other activity in general, all of the data supports the fact that the application was using the remote server system as a swap device. The following is the **netstat** output from the server. Notice that the input packets closely match the output packets from the client.

```
# netstat -I ln0 1
```

	input		(ln0)	output	
packets		errs	packets	errs	colls
8802612		120672	113251	0	1588
35		1	33	0	0
42		0	34	0	1
94		1	444	0	0
38		1	34	0	1
56		0	33	0	1
20		2	45	0	0
34		1	29	0	1
22		0	22	0	0
34		1	24	0	0
29		0	23	0	0
19		4	44	0	0
20		1	21	0	1

After becoming comfortable with the output of commands such as
netstat you could write your own shell programs to modify their output.

If you would like to modify the output of the HP-UX commands,
you can do so with shell programs (covered in Chapter 7). Figure 5-15 is
a shell program called **ifstat** which uses **netstat** and reformats the output.
I have shared this program with a number of people who prefer its output

to that of **netstat**. You may want to refer to Chapter 7 if you are interested in shell programming.

```
#!/bin/sh
# Program: ifstat
# Usage: ifstat interval interface_to_watch

# This program will not stop until you interrupt it
# (using Ctrl-C or Break).
interval=${1:-5}        # set interval to $1 or 5 if $1 is
                        # not given
interface=${2:-lan0}    # set interface to $2 or lan0 if $2 is
                        # not given
echo "Interface statistic information for $interface:\n"
# The parentheses around the while loop returns all its output
# as one command so it can be easily piped to the awk command.
(while true
do
    netstat -i
    sleep $interval
done ) | \

awk 'BEGIN { printf "%10s%10s%10s%10s%10s\n", "ipkts",
                    "ierrs", "opkts", "oerrs", "collis" ;
            printf "%10s%10s%10s%10s%10s\n", "-----",
                    "-----", "-----", "-----", "------" ;
# Initialize the variables that will hold the previous
# historical statistics.
pipkts=0; pierrs=0; popkts=0; poerrs=0; pcollis=0
}
# Find the line we care about. This is the line that starts
# with the specified interface name.
/^'$interface'/ { ipkts = $5 - pipkts; # current - previous
ierrs = $6 - pierrs;
opkts = $7 - popkts;
oerrs = $8 - poerrs;
collis = $9 - pcollis;

printf "%10d%10d%10d%10d%10d\n", ipkts, ierrs,
opkts, oerrs, collis;

pipkts = $5; pierrs = $6; popkts = $7; poerrs = $8;
pcollis = $9
        }
' # End of the awk program.
```

Figure 5-15 **ifstat** Script Example for HP-UX 9.x

The **ifstat** shell program runs **netstat -i** continuously at a specified number of seconds and displays only the *new* information, not the historical information. This program can be run when you suspect problems such as excess traffic or collisions on your network.

Here is an example run of **ifstat** with an interval of five seconds on the system using the remote server for swap:

```
$ ifstat 5 lan0
Interface statistic information for lan0:
ipkts     ierrs    opkts     oerrs    collis
-----     -----    -----     -----    ------
8963197   122657   215233        0      2899
    435        2      396        0         7
    107        5       13        0         0
    210        5      233        0         0
    321        4      341        0         7
    234        2      292        0         5
    198        1      256        0         2
    300        3      289        0         4
```

By using a swap device local to the client, you would expect the run time of this application to be greatly reduced. When this was done, an example run went from six hours to one hour. We have achieved our goal of greatly reducing the time of the application run without changing the system configuration! We may, however, want to continue to analyze the application to see what system resource(s) we want to change to further reduce the application run-time.

This example showed clearly that you may set out to perform a performance analysis in one direction and end up moving in a completely different direction.

CHAPTER 6

Common Desktop Environment

Common Desktop Environment

The Common Desktop Environment (CDE) is the direct lineal descendant of the HP Visual User Environment (HP VUE). CDE represents the effort of major UNIX vendors to unify UNIX at the desktop level. Hewlett-Packard's contribution to this effort is HP VUE, its award winning graphical user environment. HP VUE is the foundation of CDE. This chapter is an introduction to CDE. If you need to fully understand all of the nuances of CDE you'll want to buy *Configuring the Common Desktop Environment* by Charlie Fernandez (Prentice Hall, 1995).

Like HP VUE, the CDE is widely used by X terminal and workstation users. The CDE style manager, which every user has access to, makes it easy to customize CDE on an individual user basis. Sooner or later, however, you may want to provide some common denominator of CDE functionality for your users. If, for instance, you have an application that most users will run, you can set up environment variables, prepare menu picks, provide suitable fonts, and so on, that will make your users more productive. Users can then perform additional customization such as defining file manager characteristics and selecting backgrounds.

To help you thoroughly understand CDE, I'll cover the following topics:

1. Why a Graphical User Interface (GUI)?

2. The Relationship among X, Motif, and CDE

3. X, Motif, and CDE Configuration Files

4. The Sequence of Events When CDE Starts

5. Customizing CDE

6. CDE and Performance

Why a Graphical User Interface (GUI)?

For computers to be used on every desktop, they had to be made easier to use. A new method of accessing computer power was required, one that avoided the command line prompt, that didn't require users to memorize complex commands, and didn't require a working knowledge of technological infrastructures like networking. Not that this information was unimportant; far from it. The information was both too important and too specialized to be of use to the average worker-bee computer user. A knowledge of their applications was all that was important for these users. After all, so the reasoning goes, to drive a car, one doesn't have to be a mechanic, so why should a computer user have to understand computer technology? The Graphical User Interface (GUI) makes computers accessible to the application end user.

The following diagram illustrates the relationship among the computer hardware, the operating system, and the graphical user interface. The computer is the hardware platform on the bottom. The operating system, the next layer up, represents a character-based user interface. To control the computer at this level, users must type commands at the keyboard. The next several layers, beginning with the X Window System, represent the graphical user interface. To control the computer at these levels, users manipulate graphical controls with a mouse.

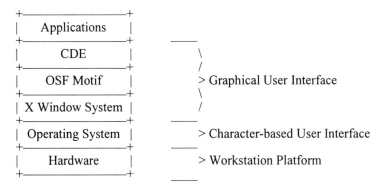

User Interface Components

GUIs replaced memorization with exploration. A user could now use pull-down menus, push buttons, sliding scroll bars, and other direct manipulation to use a computer. Typing operating system commands to perform a function is greatly reduced. With a GUI, it is both easier to learn and easier to use a computer.

While fairly inexpensive in terms of dollars (CDE is bundled "free" with the operating system), GUIs are not without cost in terms of RAM usage and performance. Despite this performance expense, GUIs have become a permanent part of the computing environment. The benefits of their utility are worth the cost.

Beyond the graphical controls that reduce training, make mundane tasks simpler to do, and generally ease the stress of using a computer, there are two other benefits of GUIs worth mentioning: multiple windows per display and client server topology.

The benefit of multiple windows that GUIs provide is that each window (literally a rectangular area surrounded by a window frame) contains a separate application. The user can work with multiple windows open. CDE goes one step further: Its multiple workspaces allow users to separate application windows by task into specific workspaces. For instance, in a workspace named "Mail," users may have application windows showing the list of incoming electronic mail, a mail message they are currently reading, and a message they are composing for later transmission.

In another workspace called "Financials," they could be working on several spreadsheets, each in its own window.

Client/server topology enables the computing resources spread around a network to be accessed efficiently to meet computing needs. In a client/server topology, powerful computers on the network are dedicated to a specific purpose (file management on a file server and running applications on an application server). Users working on less powerful client computers elsewhere on the network access the files or applications remotely. A file server reduces system administration by centralizing file backup, enabling the system administrator to back up only the file server, not each individual client computer. This setup also ensures that files will be backed up at regular intervals. An application server reduces operating costs by reducing the number and size of storage disks required and the size of RAM required on each client computer. A single version of an application resides and runs on the application server and is accessed by multiple users throughout the network.

While this sounds complicated, the CDE GUI makes it easy. To access a file, users "drag and drop" a file icon from the file manager window. To start an application, users double-click the application icon. To print a file, users drag the file to the icon of the appropriate printer in the front panel and drop it there. Users don't have to know where these files and applications are, what directories they are in, what computers they are on, or how they are accessed. It is the underlying infrastructure and control you have put in place along with the power of the GUI that allow users to concentrate on their work and not on the mechanics of their computer.

The Relationship among X, Motif, and CDE

X, OSF/Motif, and CDE are enabling framework technologies. Taken together, X, Motif, and CDE make up the three graphical layers on top of the operating system and the hardware platform.

The GUI layers provide increasingly richer ease-of-use functions in a progressive series of layers that buffer the end user from the "user hostile" character-based interface of the operating system layer.

The X Window System

The X Window System consists of the following:

- Xlib - Low-level library for programming window manipulation, graphics capabilities such as line drawing and text placement, and controlling display output, mouse and keyboard input, and application network transparency.

- Xt Intrinsics - Higher-level library for programming widgets and gadgets (graphical controls components like menus, scroll bars, and push buttons).

- Display servers - Hardware-specific programs, one per display, that manage the graphical input and output.

- Interclient communication conventions (ICCC) - A manual specifying standards for how X client programs should communicate with each other.

- Configuration files - One configuration file that specifies the default session to start (**sys.x11start**) and another specifying values for resources used to shape the X environment (**sys.Xdefaults**).

Through these mechanisms, X provides the standard upon which the graphical part of the network-oriented, client/server, distributed computing paradigm is based. A knowledge of **Xlib** and the **Xt** Intrinsics is important for programming in X and for programming at the Motif level. For system administrators, however, as long as the display servers work and X client applications are ICCC compliant, you shouldn't need to delve into the X layer. CDE enables you to view X pretty much as part of "all that underlying technological infrastructure stuff" and focus on developing appropriate configurations of CDE to meet your users' work context.

Motif

Motif consists of the following:

- mwm window manager - Executable program that provides Motif-based window frames, window management, and a workspace menu in the X environment.

- Motif widget toolkit - Higher-level library of widgets and gadgets, the graphical components used to control the user environment.

- Motif style guide - A manual defining the Motif appearance and behavior for programmers.

- Configuration files - The **system.mwmrc** file containing configuration information for the workspace menu and key and button bindings. Resources for the window manager are in **mwm** in the **/usr/lib/X11/app-defaults** directory.

Motif provides the window manager for the end user, the widget toolkit for application developers, and the style guide to help developers design and build proper Motif-conformant applications. As with X, system administrators can view Motif mostly as "programmer's stuff," part of the underlying infrastructure, and focus on developing appropriate CDE configuration files.

CDE

CDE consists of the following, all of which are based on HP VUE 3.0:

- Workspace manager - Executable program that provides Motif-based window frames, window management, a workspace menu, and the front panel.

- File manager - Program that iconically manages files and directories through direct manipulation.

- Style manager - Container of dialog boxes that control elements of the CDE environment like workspace color and fonts.

- Help manager - Based on the HP Help System, this program provides context-sensitive help text on CDE components.

- Login manager - Daemon-like application that handles login and password verification.

- Session manager - Manager that handles saving and restoring user sessions.

- Application manager - Manager that registers and keeps track of applications in the CDE environment.

- Configuration files - A big bunch, most of which you can avoid dealing with (see below).

Similar to HP VUE, CDE also provides a number of basic, end-user productivity-enhancing applications. In CDE, these include things like a clock showing system time, a calendar showing system date, a datebook/ scheduler program for workgroup coordination, and a MIME mailer for sending multimedia electronic mail messages.

In general, CDE provides a graphical environment into which users, or you, their system administrator, can incorporate the software tools needed to do their work.

X, Motif, and CDE Configuration Files

X, Motif, and CDE all use configuration files to shape their appearance and behavior. Elements of appearance and behavior such as foreground color, keyboard focus policy, or client decoration are resources that can be controlled by values in the appropriate configuration file. In X, Motif, and CDE the word "resource" has a special meaning. It doesn't refer to vague natural resources or generic system resources, but to specific elements of appearance and behavior. Some examples are the **foreground** resource, the **keyboardFocusPolicy** resource, and the **clientDecoration** resource. For example, foreground color could be black, keyboard focus policy could be explicit, and client decoration could be plus-title (title bar only). These would appear in some appropriate configuration file as the following:

```
*foreground:        black

*keyboardFocusPolicy:explicit

*clientDecoration:   +title
```

Which configuration file these resources appear in depends on the scope of the effect desired (systemwide or individual user) and the graphical interface level being used (X, Motif, or CDE).

X Configuration Files

The X Window System has the following configuration files:

sys.x11start

sys.Xdefaults

system.hpwmrc

X*screens

X*devices

X*pointerkey

By convention, these files are located in the **/usr/lib/X11** directory. In addition, each X client application has its own app-defaults configuration file located, also by convention, in the **/usr/lib/X11/app-defaults** directory. Although six files are listed above, unless you're configuring a workstation for multiple display screens (X*screens), multiple input devices (X*devices), or keyboard-only pointer navigation (X*pointerkey), you'll typically need to work with only **sys.x11start**, **sys.Xdefaults**, and **system.hpwmrc**.

The **sys.x11start** file was a script used to start X and X clients before the advent of CDE. System administrators or knowledgeable users modified **sys.x11start** so that the appropriate mix of X clients started "automatically." The **sys.Xdefaults** file was read as X started to obtain values for various appearance and behavior resources. Modifications to **sys.Xdefaults** ensured that the X environment and clients had the proper appearance and behavior. **system.hpwmrc** contained the configuration of the workspace menu and button and key bindings. **system.hpwmrc** has been replaced by the Motif version, **system.mwmrc**.

sys.x11start, **sys.Xdefaults**, and **system.hpwmrc** could be copied to a user's home directory and modified to personalize the user's X environment. These personalized versions, called **.x11start**, **.Xdefaults**, and **.hpwmrc**, overrode the systemwide versions, **sys.x11start**, **sys.Xdefaults**, and **system.hpwmrc**.

For more detailed information on X configuration files, see books such as the classic *Using the X Window System* (HP part number B1171-90067).

Motif Configuration Files

Motif added only one new configuration file to the X list: **system.mwmrc**.

By convention, this file is kept with the X configuration files in **/usr/lib/X11**. Actually, this file isn't new; it is the Motif version of **system.hpwmrc** which simply replaced **system.hpwmrc** in Motif environments.

Where X brought network and interclient communication standards to the graphical user interface, Motif brought a standard for appearance and behavior, the standard originally defined in IBM's System Application Architecture Common User Access (SAACUA), which forms the basis of most PC-based GUIs. Thus, push buttons and scroll bars have a defined look and a defined behavior and double-clicking always causes the default action to happen.

From a programmer's point of view, the Motif widget toolkit represents quite an advance over programming in "raw" X. From a user's or system administrator's point of view, the Motif user environment is about the same as the X environment, except that the **hpwm** window manager is replaced with the Motif window manager. But, because **mwm** is itself a direct lineal descendent of **hpwm**, the way CDE is descended from HP VUE, even this difference is minimal.

CDE Configuration Files

It is possible to point to over 80 files that, in one way or another, contribute to configuring some aspect of CDE. However, if you remove from this list such files as those

• that configure CDE applications as opposed to the environment itself,

- that establish default actions and data-type definitions which, although you will create your own definitions in separate files, you will never modify,

- that are CDE working files and should not be customized,

- that are more appropriately associated with configuring the UNIX, X, and Motif environments underlying CDE, including the various shell environments, then CDE has approximately 19 configuration files as shown in Table 6-1.

TABLE 6-1   CDE CONFIGUATION FILES

* .Xauthority	* sys.font	* Xresources
* .Xdefaults	* sys.resources	* Xservers
* .dtprofile	* sys.sessions	* Xsession
* dtwm.fp	* Xaccess	* Xsetup
* dtwmrc	* Xconfig	* Xstartup
* sys.dtprofile	* Xfailsafe	
* sys.dtwmrc	* Xreset	

Although 19 configuration files is still a lot, don't be alarmed by the number. You won't need to modify many of them, and can ignore; a couple you modify once and then forget about. You need to understand in depth for periodic modification only one or two, perhaps a systemwide *.dt file for custom actions and data types, or maybe **dtwm.fp** if you are required to modify the front panel on a regular basis for some reason.

Still, configuring CDE is not something you want to start hacking with without a little preparation and a good idea of what you want to accomplish. All CDE configuration files are pretty well commented, so a good first step is to print the ones you want to modify.

Table 6-2 organizes CDE configuration files according to content and the breadth of their influence.

The file **sys.dtwmrc**, like **sys.vuewmrc**, **system.hpwmrc**, and **system.mwmrc** before it, controls the configuration of the workspace manager at the system level. This includes all of the following:

Workspace Menu	A menu that displays when mouse button 3 is pressed while the mouse pointer is over the workspace backdrop.
Button Bindings	Definitions of what action happens when a particular mouse button is pressed or released while the mouse pointer is over a particular area (frame, icon, window, or root).
Key Bindings	Definitions of what action happens when a particular key or key sequence is pressed while the mouse pointer is over a particular area (frame, icon, window, or root).

TABLE 6-2 CDE CONFIGURATION FILE INFLUENCE

Nature of Configuration File	Systemwide Influence	User Personal Influence
Environment Variables	sys.dtprofile Xconfig Xsession	.dtprofile
Appearance & Behavior Resources	sys.resources Xconfig Xresources sys.fonts	.Xdefaults
File Types & Action Definitions	misc *.dt files	user-prefs.dt
Client Startup at Login	sys.sessions Xstartup Xsession Xreset Xfailsafe	.xsession sessionetc
Workspace Manager & Front Panel	sys.dtwmrc(/usr/dt/ config/sys.dtprofile) dtwm.fp	dtwmrc (in local .dt dir) user-prefs.fp
Clients/Servers & Access	Xaccess Xservers	.Xauthority

Unlike previous configuration files, **sys.dtwmrc** does not control the following configuration elements:

Front Panel   The box, usually at the bottom of the workspace, that contains commonly referenced indicators and frequently used graphical controls, including a six-button workspace switch.

Slideup Subpanels

Menus that slide up from the front panel at various locations to provide more functionality without consuming more screen space.

Instead, to avoid a massively large and overly complex configuration file, these elements were separated into their own configuration file in CDE, **dtwm.fp**.

Some front panel configuration elements, like the number of workspaces and their arrangement in the workspace switch, are controlled through resources in a **sys.resources**, **dt.resources**, or **.Xdefaults** file. Like other workspace manager configuration files, **sys.dtwmrc** can be copied to a user's home directory, actually to **$HOME/.dt/** as **dtwmrc** and modified to personalize the user's environment beyond the system-wide configuration of **sys.dtwmrc**.

The **sys.resources** file is one of those files you might modify once, then never again. The **dt.resources** file is one of those files you won't ever need to modify and can ignore. The **.Xdefaults** file is one you or your users may modify on occasion. The **sys.resources** file is where you put any non-default resources you want in effect when a brand new user logs in to CDE for the very first time. For example, as system administrator, you may want your users to have a CDE front panel with prenamed workspaces, special colors, particular fonts, or application windows in certain locations. After the first-time login, **sys.resources** is ignored in favor of **dt.resources**. This file, **dt.resources**, resides in **$HOME/.dt/sessions/current** (or **$HOME/.dt/sessions/home** when the home session is restored) and is created automatically by CDE. You can consider it as a CDE working file and forget about it. The **.Xdefaults** file is where you or an end user would list X resources specific to the user's personal CDE environment. **sys.resources**, **dt.resources**, and **.Xdefaults** contain a list of resources and their values.

The **sys.sessions** file controls which clients start the very first time a new user logs in to CDE. The **dt.sessions** file is to **sys.sessions** as **dt.resources** is to **sys.resources**.

It may be efficient to configure CDE to start particular applications for your users. You would specify these applications in **sys.sessions**. When a new user logs in for the first time, the CDE environment includes the specified clients. By logging out, at the end of this first session, the remaining clients would be recorded in **$HOME/.dt/sessions/current** for CDE (**$HOME/.dt/sessions/home** when the home session is restored).

The **sys.dtprofile** file is a template that is automatically copied at first login into each new user's home directory as **.dtprofile**. **sys.dtprofile** replaces **.profile** or **.login** in the CDE environment (although either **.profile** or **.login** can be sourced in **.dtprofile**). The **.dtprofile** file holds the personal environment variables that would, in a character-based environment, be found in **.profile** or **.login**. Use this separate file to avoid the interference terminal I/O commands cause to CDE's graphical environment.

The CDE login manager, **dtlogin**, presets the following environment variables to default values:

DISPLAY	The name of the local display
EDITOR	The default text editor
HOME	The user's home directory as specified in the file **/etc/passwd**
KBD_LANG	The current language of the keyboard
LANG	The current NLS language
LC_ALL	The value of LANG
LC_MESSAGES	The value of LANG
LOGNAME	The user's login name as specified in **/etc/passwd**
MAIL	The default file for mail (usually **/usr/mail/ $USER**)

PATH   The default directories to search for files and appli-
                cations

USER   The user name

SHELL   The default shell as specified in **/etc/passwd**

TERM   The default terminal emulation

TZ   The time zone in effect

Variations to these default values belong in each user's **.dtprofile**. Additional environment variables can be added as needed to shape the user's environment to the needs of the work context. Just beware of using commands that cause any terminal I/O.

Like **.dtprofile**, **Xsession** is a shell script that sets user environment variables. The environment variables in **Xsession** apply systemwide. The environment variables in **.dtprofile** apply only to a user's personal environment. Furthermore, since the login manager runs **Xsession** after the X server has started, the variables in **Xsession** are not available to the X server. Variables typically set in **Xsession** include the following:

EDITOR   The default text editor.

KBD_LANG   The language of the keyboard
                            (usually set to the value of
                            $LANG).

TERM   The default terminal emulation.

MAIL   The default file for mail which is
                            usually **/usr/mail/$USER**.

DTHELPSEARCHPATH   The locations to search for CDE
                            help files.

DTAPPSEARCHPATH   The locations to search for appli-
                            cations registered with the CDE
                            application manager.

DTDATABASESEARCHPATH The locations to search for addi-
                            tional action and data type defini-
                            tions.

XMICONSEARCHPATH   The locations to search for additional icons

XMICONBMSEARCHPATH   Same as above.

As an example, suppose you are the system administrator for several mixed workstation and X terminal clusters located at a single site. Now suppose that different users you administer have grown accustomed to certain text editors. Some like **vi**, others prefer **emacs**, and a couple wouldn't be caught dead without **dmx**. An easy way to provide each user with his or her favored text editor would be to reset their EDITOR variable to the appropriate value in the individual **.dtprofile** files.

Xconfig contains resources that control the behavior of **dtlogin** and it also provides a place to specify the locations for any other **dtlogin** configuration files you create. The **Xconfig** file works on a systemwide basis, so it's one of those files that you modify only once and then forget about. When, during login, **Xconfig** is run, several CDE configuration files get referenced: **Xaccess**, **Xservers**, **Xresources**, **Xstartup**, **Xsession**, **Xreset**, and **Xfailsafe**. Like **Xconfig** itself, most of these files are the type that you modify once when installing CDE and then, unless the network topology changes, you never deal with them again.

Xaccess, as the name implies, is a remote display access control file. **Xaccess** contains a list of the host names allowed or denied XDMCP connection access to the local computer. For example, when an X terminal requests login service, **dtlogin** consults the **Xaccess** file to determine if service should be granted.

The primary use of the **Xservers** file is to list the display screens on the local system which **dtlogin** is responsible for managing. **dtlogin** reads the **Xservers** file and starts an X server for each display listed there. It then starts a child **dtlogin** process to manage the server and display the login screen. Note that **dtlogin** works only locally; **dtlogin** can't start an X server on a remote system or X terminal. For remote display servers, some other mechanism must be used to start the server, which then uses the X Display Management Control Protocol (XDMCP) to request a login screen from **dtlogin**.

The **Xservers** file is another of those files that you may spend some time with initially and then, unless the topography of your network changes, never deal with again. When do you use **Xservers**? When a display doesn't match the default configuration. The default configuration assumes that each system has a single bitmap display and is the system console. X terminals, multiple displays (heads), multiple screens, and Starbase applications all require configuration lines in the **Xservers** file.

The **Xresources** file contains the list of resources that control the appearance and behavior of the login screen. After you substitute your company's logo for the HP logo and change the fonts and colors, you'll probably never have to deal with **Xresources** again (unless your company changes its logo).

Xstartup is a systemwide configuration file executed by the login manager from which it receives several environment variables:

DISPLAY	The name of the local display.
USER	The login name of the user.
HOME	The user's home directory.
PATH	The value of the **systemPath** resource in **Xconfig**.
SHELL	The value of the **systemShell** resource in **Xconfig**.
XAUTHORITY	The file to access for authority permissions.
TZ	The local time zone.

Because it can execute scripts and start clients on a systemwide basis, **Xstartup** is similar to **sys.sessions**. The difference is that **Xstartup** runs as root. Thus, modifications to **Xstartup** should be reserved for actions like mounting file systems.

Xreset is a systemwide companion script to **Xstartup**. It runs as root and essentially undoes what **Xstartup** put in motion.

The **Xfailsafe** file contains customizations to the standard failsafe session. The failsafe session provides a way to correct improper CDE sessions caused by errors in the login and session configuration files. As such, **Xfailsafe** is something your users are never going to use, but you can make your life a little easier with a few judicious customizations.

The **sessionetc** file resides in a user's **.dt/sessions** directory and personalizes that user's CDE session. **sessionetc** handles the starting of additional X clients like **sys.session**, but on a peruser basis, as opposed to systemwide. While **dt.session** also starts clients on a peruser basis, the clients are those of the default or current session. **dt.session** which resides in **.dt/session/current**. sessionetc, which resides in **.dt/session**, should contain only those clients that are not automatically restored. Typically, these are clients that do not set the **WM_COMMAND** property so the session manager can't save or restore them; thus they need to be restarted in **sessionetc**.

The **sys.font** file contains the systemwide default session font configuration. These default fonts were based on usability studies, so **sys.font** is a file you may never change. However, should you encounter a situation that requires a different mix of fonts on a systemwide basis, this is where you'd change them. Note that the font resources and values mentioned in **sys.font** must match exactly the default font resources specified in the file **/usr/dt/app-defaults/C/Dtstyle**.

CDE has a bunch of files that specify CDE action and data type definitions. All these files end with the file extension ***.dt**. An ***.dt** ("dt" for "desk top") contains both data type and action definitions. The default ***.dt** files are in **/usr/dt/appconfig/types/C** and act on a systemwide basis. Similarly, **user-prefs.dt**, the master copy of which is also located in **/usr/dt/appconfig/types/C**, is used at the personal user level.

The **.Xauthority** file is a user-specific configuration file containing authorization information needed by clients that require an authorization mechanism to connect to the server.

CDE Configuration File Locations

Where CDE looks for particular configuration files depends on the nature of the configuration files, principally what the files configure and how wide their influence. Table 6-3 shows the location of system and user configuration files based on the nature of the file content:

TABLE 6-3 CDE SYSTEM AND USER CONFIGURATION FILES

Nature of Configuration File	Systemwide Influence	User Personal Influence
Environment Variables	/usr/dt/config/	$HOME/

TABLE 6-3   CDE SYSTEM AND USER CONFIGURATION FILES (Continued)

Nature of Configuration File	Systemwide Influence	User Personal Influence
Appearance & Behavior Resources	/usr/dt/config/C /usr/dt/app-defaults/C	$HOME/.dt/ $HOME/.dt/sessions/current/ $HOME/.dt/sessions/home/
File Types & Action Definitions	/usr/dt/appconfig/ types/C	$HOME/.dt/types
Client Startup at Login	/usr/dt/config/ /usr/dt/config/C	$HOME/.dt/session/ $HOME/.dt/session/current/ $HOME/.dt/session/home/
Workspace Manager	/usr/vue/config usr/vue/config/panels	$HOME/.dt/

For each of the default systemwide file locations listed in Table 6-3, there is a corresponding location for custom systemwide configuration files. These custom files should be located in the appropriate subdirectory under **/etc/dt**. The basic procedure is to copy the file you need to customize from **/usr/dt/something** to **/etc/dt/something** and then do your modifications there. For example, to change the default logo in **Xresources**, copy **/usr/dt/config/C/Xresources** to **/etc/dt/config/C/Xresources**, open **/etc/dt/config/C/Xresources**, and make your changes.

This is an important point. Files located under **/usr/dt** are considered CDE system files and will be overwritten during updates. Thus any customizations you do there will be lost. Make all modifications to systemwide configuration files in **/etc/dt** and its subdirectories.

How Configuration Files Play Together

From the material covered so far, you've probably concluded correctly that CDE configuration files aren't something to go hacking with without a plan - a well thought out plan. You've probably figured out that the element you want to configure and the breadth of influence you want it to have determine which configuration file you modify.

For instance, if you wanted to set an environment variable, you have a choice of four configuration files: **sys.dtprofile**, **Xconfig**, **Xsession**, and **.dtprofile**. But if you want to set environment variables that affect only a particular user, your choice immediately narrows to a single file, **.dtprofile**.

Now the only remaining piece of the puzzle is to understand the order in which CDE reads its configuration files. When a configuration element (an environment variable, resource, action, or data type) is specified twice but with different values, you obviously want the correct value used and the incorrect value ignored.

The following rules apply:

- For environment variables, the last specified value is used.

- For resources, the last specified value is used. However, this is influenced by specificity. Thus **emacs*foreground** takes precedence over just ***foreground** for emacs clients regardless of the order in which the resources were encountered.

- For actions, the first specified is used.

- For data types, the first specified is used.

Table 6-4 illustrates which specification is used when CDE reads multiple specifications of configuration elements in its configuration files.

TABLE 6-4 WHAT CDE USES FOR CONFIGURATION

Configuration Element	Element Used
resource	last encountered or most specific
environment	last encountered
action	first encountered
file type	first encountered

Put in terms of scope, a user configuration file overrides a system-wide configuration file. Looking at the order of precedence of just systemwide configuration files, the files in **/etc/dt** have precedence over those in **/usr/dt**, so custom configurations have precedence over the CDE default configuration.

For resources, the elements used to specify a GUI's appearance and behavior, CDE sets values according to the following priorities:

1. Command line -   When you start a client from the command line, options listed on the command line have top priority.

2. **Xresources, .Xdefaults, dt.resources, sys.resources** - When CDE starts, it reads these resource configuration files to determine the value of X resources to use for the session.

3. **RESOURCE MANAGER** - Resources already in the property **RESOURCE_MANAGER** may affect an application that is just starting.

4. **app-defaults** - Specifies "default" resource values that differ from built-in resource values.

5. built-in defaults - Default resources that are "hard coded" have the lowest priority.

Specific resource specifications take precedence over general resource specifications. For example, suppose you want a certain font in your text entry areas. You could correctly specify a ***FontList** resource in your personal **.Xdefaults** file only to have it overwritten by an ***XmText*FontList** in an **app-defaults** file. Although **app-defaults** is of lower priority than **.Xdefaults**, the resource specification set there is more specific, so it takes precedence.

For environment variables, CDE sets values according to the following priorities:

1. **$HOME/.dtprofile** - User-specific variables have top priority.

2. **/etc/dt/config/C/Xsession** - Custom systemwide variables not read by X server.

3. **/etc/dt/config/C/Xconfig** - Custom systemwide variables read by X server.

4. **/usr/dt/config/C/Xsession** - Default systemwide variables not read by X server.

5. **/usr/dt/config/C/Xconfig** - Default systemwide variables read by X server.

6. **/usr/dt/bin/dtlogin** - Built-in default variables have the lowest priority.

For datatype and action definitions, CDE looks for **.dt** files according to the following priority:

1. $HOME/.dt/types

2. /etc/dt/appconfig/types/C

3. /usr/dt/appconfig/types/C

Remember, for data types or actions, the first value it finds is the one it uses. So, if you just can't get a file type or action to work, check for a duplicate entry earlier in the file or for an entry in a file with higher priority. Note also that the environment variable DTDATABASESEARCHPATH can be set either in **/etc/dt/config/Xsession** or **$HOME/.dtprofile** to add directories where CDE can search for file type and action definition information.

Specifying Appearance and Behavior

There are only two tricks to specifying appearance and behavior resources in configuration files. The first is to specify the resource and its value correctly. The second is to specify the resource and value in the correct configuration file.

Two caveats involve colors and fonts. The CDE style manager provides a graphical interface for modifying colors and fonts. However, if you specify an application's color or font directly, this specification will override the ability of the style manager to manage that resource for the application.

Typical ways to specify a color or font directly include the following:

- Type the specification on the command line as a startup option.

- Include the specification in the application's app-defaults file.

- Use the **xrdb** utility to add resources for the application to the resource database.

The Sequence of Events When CDE Starts

The following section is a blow-by-blow account of what happens when a user logs in to CDE. In this particular account, assume a distributed topology like a diskless cluster. The account begins with the boot of the hub system and nodes in step 1. By step 4, X servers are running on each node and login screens are being displayed. By step 6, the user is logged in. By step 11, the session manager is busy re-creating the user's session.

1. The **dtlogin** executable is started as part of the **init** process that occurs during the system boot sequence on the hub machine and each cluster node.

2. **dtlogin** reads **/usr/dt/config/Xconfig** to get a list of resources with which to configure the login process. This is where **dtlogin** first learns about files like **Xaccess**, **Xservers**, **Xresources**, **Xstartup**, **Xsession**, and **Xreset** and gets the values of a number of appearance and behavior resources.

3. **dtlogin** reads two files in **/usr/dt/config**:

   - **Xservers**, or the file identified by the **Dtlogin*servers** resource setting in **Xconfig**.

   - **Xresources** or the file identified by the **Dtlogin*resources** resource setting in **Xconfig**.

4. **dtlogin** starts an X server and a child **dtlogin** for each local display.

5. Each child **dtlogin** invokes **dtgreet**, the login screen.

6. When a login and password are validated, a child **dtlogin** sets certain environment variables to default values.

7. The child **dtlogin** runs **/usr/dt/config/Xstartup**.

8. The child **dtlogin** runs **/usr/dt/config/Xsession**.

9. **Xsession** runs **dthello**, the copyright screen.

10. **Xsession** reads **$HOME/.dtprofile**, setting any additional environment variables or overwriting those set previously by **dtlogin**.

11. The child **dtlogin** invokes the session manager, **dtsession**.

12. **dtsession** restores the appropriate session. For example, to restore the current session, **dtsession** reads **dt.resources**, and **dt.session** in **$HOME/.dt/sessions/current**.

At logout, the reverse happens. The session is saved and **dtlogin** runs **/usr/dt/config/Xreset**. When **Xreset** completes, **dtlogin** again displays the login screen as in step 4.

Customizing CDE

Before you modify any CDE configuration files, first develop a strategy. I know I've mentioned this before, but it's important enough to mention again.

The following questions should get you started:

1. What are your user's needs?

2. Which of those needs can be met by reconfiguring CDE?

3. At what level should these changes be made (systemwide, groups of users, individual users only)?

4. Which CDE files do you need to modify (names and locations)?

5. What are the changes and what is their order within the file?

It's also a good idea to have handy a binder containing manual pages for each of the CDE components (for looking up resources and their values) and a copy of each of the CDE configuration files.

The following sections assume you're making systemwide modifications. To make modifications for individual users, follow the same procedure on the equivalent user's personal file.

Adding Objects to or Removing Objects from the Front Panel

There are two ways to add objects to the CDE front panel:

- •Drag and drop them into a slideup subpanel and then make them the default for that subpanel.

- •Modify the **/etc/dt/appconfig/types/C/dtwm.fp** configuration file.

To add a control button through drag and drop,

1. Drag the application icon you want as a front panel button from an application manager view and drop the icon onto the installation section (the top section) of the appropriate subpanel.

2. Place the mouse pointer over the icon and press mouse button 3 to display the subpanel menu.

3. Select Copy to Main Panel.

To add a control button by editing the dtwm.fp file,

1. If you haven't already done so, copy **dtwm.fp** from **/usr/dt/app-config/types/C** to **/etc/dt/appconfig/types/C**.

2. Add the new control definition using the format:

```
CONTROL NewControl
{
TYPE         icon
CONTAINER_NAME Top
CONTAINER_TYPE BOX
ICON         NewControlBitmap
PUSH_ACTION   NewControlExecutable
}
```

Note that all control definitions have the following general syntax:

KEYWORD value

To avoid a lot of typing, it's easiest just to copy an existing definition and insert it where you want your new control to be and then modify it. As you move down the list of control definitions, you're moving from left to right across the front panel. (Notice the POSITION_HINTS value increases in each definition.) So, if you want your new control to be to the right of the date on the front panel, you'd insert the control on the line below "date" and add a POSITION_HINTS 3 line to your definition; if you wanted your new control to be to the left of "date," insert the control on the line above "date" with a POSITION_HINTS of 1.

The new control definition can be located anywhere in the list of control definitions. The POSITION_HINTS line keeps it from getting inadvertently bumped to a new position. It's still a good idea to copy an existing definition and avoid extra typing - it reduces the chance of typing mistakes. Don't forget to include the curly braces.

The basic control definition has six parts:

- **CONTROL name** - The definition name. This is the only part of the definition outside the curly braces.

- **TYPE** - The type of control. Several types exist. The most useful for customizing the front panel are probably blank and an icon. A blank is useful as a space holder. An icon can start an action or application or be a drop zone.

- **ICON** - The bitmap to display on the front panel. Front panel bitmaps are located in the **/usr/dt/appconfig/icons** directory.

- **CONTAINER_NAME** - The name of the container that holds the control. This must correspond to the name of an actual container listed in **dtwm.fp**.

- **CONTAINER_TYPE** - The type of container that holds the control. This can be **BOX**, **SWITCH**, or **SUBPANEL**, but it must agree with the type of the container name.

- **PUSH_ACTION** - This is what happens when the control button is pushed. **PUSH_ACTION** is just one of several possible actions. For more information see the **dtwm** manual page.

To remove a control button from the front panel, type a pound sign (#) in the leftmost column of the **CONTROL** definition line. The (#) turns the control specification into a comment line.

Changing the Front Panel in Other Ways

In addition to adding or removing buttons, you can shape the front panel in other ways. These other ways use workspace manager resources to modify default values. The following resources relate to the front panel:

- **clientTimeoutInterval** - Length of time the busy light blinks and the pointer remains an hourglass when a client is started from the front panel.

- **geometry** - x and y coordinate locations of the front panel.

- **highResFontList** - Font to use on a high-resolution display.

- **lowResFontList** - Font to use on a low-resolution display.

- **mediumResFontList** - Font to use on a medium-resolution display.

- **name** - Name of the front panel to use when there are multiple front panels in **dtwm.fp**.

- **pushButtonClickTime** - Time interval distinguishing two single mouse clicks from a double-click (to avoid double launching an application accidently).

- **waitingBlinkRate** - Blink rate of the front panel busy light.

- **workspaceList** - List of workspace names.

- **title** - Title to appear on a workspace button.

Like all other workspace manager resources, these front panel resources have the following syntax:

Dtwm*screen*resource: value

For example, suppose instead of the four default workspaces, your users need a front panel with six workspaces named Mail, Reports, Travel, Financials, Projects, and Studio. Further, they prefer a large font and have decided upon New Century Schoolbook 10-point bold. As system administrator, you'd make everyone happy with the following resource specifications:

Dtwm*0*workspaceList: One Two Three Four Five Six
Dtwm*0*One*title: Mail
Dtwm*0*Two*title: Reports
Dtwm*0*Three*title: Travel
Dtwm*0*Four*title: Financials
Dtwm*0*Five*title: Projects
Dtwm*0*Six*title: Studio
Dtwm*0*highResFontList:
                -adobe-new century schoolbook-bold-r-normal\
                --10-100-75-75-p-66-iso8859-1

The screen designation is usually 0, except for displays capable of both image and overlay planes. The order of screens in the **X*screens** file is what determines the screen number; the first screen, typically the image plane, is designated as 0. Note also the inclusion of workspace names (One, Two, Three, Four, Five, and Six) in the six title resource specifications.

If none of your users have ever logged in, you're in luck. You can add the above lines to **sys.resources**. But, since you're probably not that lucky (almost no one is), the easiest way to effect the changes is to use the **EditResources** action to insert the new resource lines into each user's **RESOURCE_MANAGER** property and then restart the workspace manager.

The obvious disadvantage is that you have to physically go to each user's work area and take over the machine for a few minutes. However, on the plus side, the changes are immediate and are automatically saved in the correct **dt.resources** for users who restore their current session. You also avoid having your changes overwritten, which could happen if you modify the right **dt.resources** file at the wrong time, while the user is still logged in.

Have Some Fun Yourself

It's unfortunate, but often true, that users benefit from GUIs mostly because their system administrator has slogged through a **vi** or **emacs** session editing some configuration file to get things to work as desired. However, any time you need to edit resources, you can use CDE's drag-and-drop facility to your advantage, enjoy some of the fruits of your labor, and avoid some of the drudgery.

If **dtpad** is the default editor, you can create a file with the resource modifications in it, start the **EditResources** action, and then drop the resource modifications into the resource list that appears in the **EditResources dtpad** window.

If you haven't already played around with **dtpad**, try it. In most cases, you'll probably find it suitable for your users who need a small, fast text editor they can master without learning. **dtpad** has a menu bar with pull-down menus that contain some basic functionality. More important, **dtpad** supports cut-and-paste and drag-and-drop; users don't have to memorize commands but can simply select and manipulate text directly with the mouse.

Adding Things to Slideup Subpanels

Subpanels are defined in **dtwm.fp** after the front panel and front panel control definitions. To associate a subpanel with a front panel control button, the front panel control name is listed as the container name in the subpanel definition.

To add a slideup subpanel to the front panel:

1. Copy the file **/usr/dt/appconfig/types/C/dtwm.fp** to **/etc/dt/app-config/types/Cdtwm.fp** if you haven't already done so.

2. Decide which control button the slideup is to be associated with.

3. Create the subpanel definition file in **/etc/dt/appconfig/types/C/ dtwm.fp**. This will take the following form:

```
SUBPANEL   SubPanelName
{
CONTAINER_NAME   AssociatedFrontPanelControlButton
TITLE  SubPanelTitle
}
```

4. Create subpanel control definitions for the subpanel. These will take the following form:

```
CONTROL   ControlName
{
TYPE  icon
CONTAINER_NAME   SubPanelName
CONTAINER_TYPE   SUBPANEL
ICON  BitmapName
PUSH_ACTION   ActionName
}
```

As with front panel control buttons, it's easier to copy and modify an existing subpanel file than to start from scratch.

Front Panel Animation

Animation for front panel or slideup subpanel drop zones is created by displaying a progressive series of bitmaps. By convention, the bitmaps are in **/usr/dt/appconfig/icons**. The list of bitmaps to display is contained in animation definitions at the end of **dtwm.fp**.

To create an animation sequence for a drop zone:

1. Create a progressive series of bitmaps.

2. Add a list of these bitmap files to the appropriate configuration file using the following syntax:

```
ANIMATION AnimationName
{
bitmap0
bitmap1
bitmap2
bitmap3
bitmap4
bitmap5
}
```

3. Add a line to the appropriate control definition using the syntax:

```
DROP_ANIMATION AnimationName
```

Adding Things to the Workspace Menu

The workspace menu is defined in **sys.dtwmrc**. For one or two changes, you can modify the existing workspace menu. For major changes, it's probably easier to insert an entirely new menu definition in **sys.dtwmrc**.

A menu definition has the following syntax:

```
Menu MenuName
{
  "Menu Name"          f.title
  "Frame"              f.exec /nfs/system1/usr/frame/bin/maker
  "Second Item"        action
  "Third Item"         action
}
```

The first line specifies the menu name, following the keyword **Menu**. The lines between the curly braces list the items that appear in the menu in their order of appearance; thus the first line is the title as designated by the function **f.title**. The second line is an example of a definition that would start **FrameMaker** on a remote application server in a distrib-uted environment. Numerous other functions exist, approximately 45 in all. For a complete list, see the **dtwmrc** (4) man page.

For users to display the menu, you need to bind the menu definition to a mouse button and a screen location using the action **f.menu MenuName**. For example, if your users want to post the menu by press-ing mouse button 3 when the pointer is on the workspace background, you would insert the following line in the Mouse Button Bindings Description section at the end of **sys.dtwmrc**:

<Btn3Down> root f.menu MenuName

(Actually, it would be easier to modify the line that's already there by exchanging **MenuName** for **DtRootMenu** on the second line.)

Creating Actions and File Types

An action starts a process such as a shell script or an application. An action can be connected to a front panel button to start when the button is pushed. An action can be connected to a front panel drop zone to be per-formed when a data file is dropped on the drop zone. An action can be associated with an icon in a file manager window so the action can be started by double-clicking the icon. An action can be associated with a particular data type so that double-clicking the data file icon starts the action and opens the data file.

In addition to setting up a front panel and default session to meet your user's needs, the single most important thing you can do to make computing life easier for the people who depend on you is to create actions and data types.

CDE actions and data types are defined in files that end in **.dt** (for desk top). Similar to most other CDE configuration files, *.**dt** files have a systemwide version which can be copied into a user's personal directory and customized for personal use. Most systemwide *.**dt** files are found in **/usr/dt/appconfig/types/C**; personal *.**dt** files are created by copying **user-prefs.dt** from **/usr/dt/appconfig/types/C** to **$HOME/.dt/types**.

The default search path CDE uses to look for actions and file types includes the following main directories in the order listed:

- $HOME/.dt/types

- /etc/dt/appconfig/types

- /usr/dt/appconfig/types

You can add further directories to the search path using the **DTDA-TABASESEARCHPATH** environment variable. Insert this environment variable and the new search path in **/usr/dt/config/Xsession** for a system-wide influence. Insert the environment variable and search path in **$HOME/.dtprofile** for individual users.

The following are the recommended locations in which to create an action or file type definition:

- Create a completely new file in the **/etc/dt/appconfig/types** directory. This file will have a systemwide influence. Remember, the file must end with the **.dt** extension.

- Copy **user-prefs.dt** from **/usr/dt/appconfig/types** to the **/etc/dt/appconfig/types** directory and insert the definition there for systemwide use.

- Copy **user-prefs.vf** to **$HOME/.dt/types** and insert the definition there for individual users.

A typical action has the following syntax:

```
ACTION     ActionName
{
TYPE     type
keyword   value
keyword   value
}
```

For example, here's a FrameMaker action:

```
ACTION     FRAME
{
TYPE    COMMAND
WINDOW-TYPE NO-STDIO
EXEC-STRING /nfs/hpcvxmk6/usr/frame/bin/maker
}
```

A typical data type has the following syntax:

```
DATA_ATTRIBUTES        AttributesName

{
 keyword      value
 keyword      value
 ACTIONS      action, action
}
DATA_CRITERIA

{

DATA_ATTRIBUTES AttributesName

keyword      value

keyword      value

}
```

Notice that a data type definition is actually in two parts: an attribute part and a criteria part. The attribute portion of the data type definition specifies the look of the data type; the criteria portion specifies the behavior of the data type.

For example, here's a file type for FrameMaker files that uses the FRAME action:

```
DATA_ATTRIBUTES    FRAME_Docs

{
 DESCRIPTION     This file type is for frameMaker documents.
 ICON            makerIcon
 ACTIONS         FRAME
}
DATA_CRITERIA

{

DATA_ATTRIBUTES_NAME FRAME_Docs

NAME_PATTERN *.fm

MODE  f

}
```

You can create actions and file types from scratch using these formats. However, the easiest way to create an action is to use the **Create-Action** tool. **CreateAction** is located in the Desktop Applications folder of the Applications Manager and presents you with a fill-in-the-blank dialog box that guides you through creating an **action.dt** file containing the action definition. You can then move this file to the appropriate directory for the range of influence you want the action to have: **/etc/dt/appconfig/ types** for a systemwide influence; **$HOME/.dt/types** for individual users.

Using Different Fonts

Although CDE fonts have been carefully selected for readability, you may have valid reasons to prefer other fonts. To make your fonts available systemwide throughout the CDE environment, put them in **/etc/dt/ app-defaults/Dtstyle** so they will appear in the style manager's font dialog box. To make fonts available only for a particular X client application, specify the font in the **app-defaults** file for the application; by convention this file is located in **/usr/lib/X11/app-defaults**. Just remember, this overrides the fonts in the style manager.

The font dialog box can contain a maximum of seven font sizes. You can adjust this number downward by resetting the value of **Dtstyle*Num-Fonts** in **/etc/dt/app-defaults/Dtstyle**; however, you can't increase the number higher than seven.

The Font Dialog section of the **Dtstyle** configuration file has seven **SystemFont** resources and seven **UserFont** resources. Again, you can have fewer than seven system and seven user fonts, but you can't have more.

To specify fonts for a particular application, use the ***FontList** resource in the **app-defaults** file for the application.

To modify font resources on an individual-user basis, you can use the **EditResources** action as described in the section *Changing the Front Panel in Other Ways*.

CDE and Performance

CDE isn't a monolithic application; it's a set of components layered on top of the operating system, the X Window System, and Motif. Each underlying layer takes its share of RAM before CDE or any other client even starts. Because of the low-level nature of these layers, the RAM they use is hardly ever regained through swapping to disk.

In some cases, operating system overhead and user application requirements restrict the amount of RAM available for a graphical user interface to little more than enough to run a window manager such as Motif. Since the CDE workspace manager and the Motif window manager take roughly the same amount of RAM, users can enjoy an enriched graphical environment with the added value of the CDE's multiple workspaces at essentially no extra RAM cost over running the Motif window manager.

Sample RAM Sizes

Table 6-5 illustrates some sample RAM sizes for HP VUE 3.0. Official numbers for CDE are not yet available, but should be similar, though a little bigger, than those contained in table 6-5. The numbers represent working environment RAM and the RAM required after login; during login, a spike in RAM usage occurs as applications and other processes start up. This spike would include, in the case of CDE, starting **dtlogin**, **Xsession**, and **dtsession**. Immediately after login, these clients become inactive and are swapped out, so they don't appear in the working environment numbers.

A word of warning: Don't read too much into the numbers. RAM usage numbers vary with the system, the application set, and especially with how the application set is used by each user.

Additionally, kernel size, daemon size, and X server size can vary widely depending on the configuration and the user. An X server hack may be running an X server stripped down to just 1/2 MByte, the supposed X server ThrashPoint, and get excellent performance. Alternatively, a user with a penchant for large root window bitmaps can quickly swell their X server size to 12 MBytes and still not have reached the RMaxPoint shown below.

TABLE 6-5 SAMPLE HYPOTHETICAL RAM SIZES

Process	ThrashPoint	MTRAM	RMaxPoint
misc daemons	2 MBytes	3 MBytes	5 MBytes
file buffers	1-1/2 MBytes	3-1/4 MBytes	6-1/2 MBytes
kernel	2 MBytes	3 MBytes	5 MBytes
Xserver	1/2 MBytes	2 MBytes	7 MBytes
workspace manager	3/4 MBytes	1 MBytes	1-1/4 MBytes
file manager	1/2 MBytes	3/4 MBytes	2 MBytes
help manager	1/2 MBytes	3/4 MBytes	1 MBytes
style manager	1/2 MBytes	1 MBytes	1 MBytes
hpterm console	1/2 MBytes	3/4 MBytes	1-1/4 MBytes
message server	1/4 MBytes	1/3 MBytes	1/2 MBytes
Total	9 MBytes	16+ MBytes	30-1/2MBytes

The ThrashPoint column shows the typical absolute minimum RAM required to "run" the default HP VUE components, including operating system and X server overhead; however, "run" is a misnomer. The ThrashPoint is when the system just sits there and thrashes, swapping pages in and out of RAM, unable to get enough of an application's code into RAM to execute it before having to swap it out.

The RMaxPoint column shows the other extreme, a reasonable maximum amount of RAM for running the default HP VUE including operating system and X server overhead. The RMaxPoint is when all code for every process is in RAM so nothing gets swapped out. The sizes for some items in this column can vary considerably; the kernel hack's kernel size would be smaller; the user with a penchant for big root window bitmaps would have an X server considerably larger.

The MTRAM column shows a typical amount of RAM required to run the default CDE including operating system and X server overhead.

The MTRAM is when a typical user experiences acceptable performance. Acceptable means real-time response to visual controls and drag-and-drop. Again, a caveat: If the user is doing a local compile or working remotely on a heavily loaded network, performance will be worse. If the user is mostly reading Email and word processing, performance will be better.

From the table, the typical size of HP VUE (without operating system or X server overhead) is 6^+ MBytes. HP VUE includes the HP VUE managers (the Motif window manager is included in the workspace manager), a console hpterm, and the message server.

For best results with CDE, better figure a minimum of 24 Mbytes of RAM with 32 Mbytes or better being preferred.

Tactics for Better Performance

Unless all your users have RAM-loaded powerhouses for systems, you will need to spend some time developing a performance strategy. If you conceive of performance as a bell-shaped curve, satisfaction lies on the leading edge. Your performance strategy should do everything it can to keep your users on the leading edge.

Probably the most logical approach is to start small and grow. In other words, start out with minimal user environments on all the systems on your network. Gradually add software components until you or your users begin to notice performance degradation. Then back off a little. Such an approach might take several weeks or more to evaluate as you add components and as your users spend several days actually working in the environment to determine the effect of your changes on system performance and their frustration levels.

The most RAM-expensive pieces of CDE are the workspace manager, the session manager, and the file manager. The workspace manager is expensive because portions of it are always in RAM (assuming you are moving windows around and switching workspaces). The CDE workspace manager is no more expensive than the Motif window manager; if you want a GUI, it's just a price you have to pay. The session manager is expensive only during logout and login as it saves and restores sessions. The rest of the time, the session manager is dormant and gets swapped out of RAM. Saving your current work session is nice at the end of the day, but it's something to consider giving up if you want to improve your login and logout performance. The file manager is expensive because it wakes up periodically and jumps into RAM to check the status of the file system and update its file manager windows. When it jumps into RAM, it pushes something else out, for example, maybe the desktop publishing program you're using.

Here are some other ideas that you may find useful:

Terminal Emulators	**xterms** are a little less RAM-expensive than **dtterms**. Unless you need the block mode functionality of an **dtterm**, **xterm** might be a better choice for terminal emulation.
Automatic Saves	Some applications automatically save data at periodic intervals. While this feature can be beneficial, you need to evaluate its effect in light of performance. If the application is central to your users' work, fine, but if not, it might be a good idea to disable the automatic save feature.
Scroll Buffers	Large scroll buffers in terminal emulators can be a real convenience, but they can also take up a lot of RAM. Even modestly sized scroll buffers, when multiplied by three or four terminal emulators, consume a lot of RAM.

Background Bitmaps | Avoid large bitmaps; they increase the X server size. Especially avoid switching large bitmaps frequently within a session. If you are hunting for a new background, be sure to restart the X server after you've found the one you want and have included it in the proper **sessionetc** file. The most efficient bitmaps are small ones that can be repeated to tile the background.

Front Panel | Reconfigure the front panel to minimize the number of buttons. Keep just enough to meet user needs. This decreases the workspace manager size in RAM and speeds login and logout.

Pathnames | Whenever possible, use absolute pathnames for bitmap specifications. While this decreases the flexibility of the system, it speeds access time

Conclusion

Graphical user interfaces are here to stay. While they offer users an easy-to-learn, easy-to-use computing environment, they can make life a little uneasy for system administrators. The default CDE is ready to use, but given its power and flexibility, you will inevitably want to customize the CDE environment for your users' work context and optimum performance. Take the time to develop a good idea of what changes you need to make, the order in which to make them, and exactly where to make them. In so doing, all the power and flexibility of CDE will be open to you.

CHAPTER 7

Shell Programming for System Administrators

Shell Programming

There is much more to a shell than meets the eye. The shell is much more than the command line interpreter everyone is used to using. UNIX shells actually provide a powerful interpretive programming language as well.

You may be asking yourself, "Why do I need to know about shell programming?" As a system administrator you will find that there are many things in your system that are controlled using shell programs.

Using shell programs (sometimes called shell scripts), you can build many tools to make your life as an administrator easier. Using shell scripts, you can automate mundane tasks that require several commands to be executed sequentially. You can build new commands to generate reports on system activities or configurations. You could also build scripts that provide shortcuts for executing long or complex command lines.

The shell is one of the most powerful features on any UNIX system. If you can't find the right command to accomplish a task, you can probably build it quite easily using a shell script.

In this chapter I will show you the basic things you need to know to start programming in the Bourne and C shells. We will be first covering the Bourne shell (as opposed to the Korn or C shells) because it is the simplest to program and it is a subset of the default HP-UX 10.x shell - the POSIX shell .Once you can program in the Bourne shell, it is easy to adapt to the other available shells and all Bourne shell programs will run in the POSIX shell. The C shell will then be covered because it is used so widely.

The best way to learn shell programming is by example. There are many examples given in this chapter. Some serve no purpose other than to demonstrate the current topic. Most, however, are useful tools or parts of tools that you can easily expand and adapt into your environment. The examples provide easy to understand prompts and output messages. Most examples show what is needed to provide the functionality we are after. They do not do a great deal of error checking. From my experience, however, it only takes a few minutes to get a shell program to do what you want; it can take hours to handle every situation and every error condition. Therefore, these programs are not very dressed up (maybe a sport coat versus a tuxedo). I'm giving you what you need to know to build some useful tools for your environment. I hope you will have enough knowledge and interest by the time we get to the end of this chapter to learn and do more. You should assume any shell program that uses HP-UX commands works with HP-UX 9.x and may have to be modified to work with HP-UX 10.x. This is because the output of many HP-UX commands such as **iostat** have changed going from HP-UX 9.x to HP-UX 10.x. Modifying existing shell scripts is easier than writing them from scratch so you may find changing the scripts in this chapter to be a worthwhile learning experience.

Bourne Shell Programming for System Administrators

A shell program is simply a file containing a set of commands you wish to execute sequentially. The file needs to be set with execute permissions so you can execute it just by typing the name of the script.

There are two basic forms of shell programs:

1. Simple command files - When you have a command line or set of command lines that you use over and over, you can use one simple command to execute them all.

2. Structured programs - The shell provides much more than the ability to "batch" together a series of commands. It has many of the features that any higher-level programming language contains:

   - Variables for storing data

   - Decision-making controls (the **if** and **case** commands)

   - Looping abilities (the **for** and **while** loops)

   - Function calls for modularity

Given these two basic forms you can build everything from simple command replacements to much larger and more complex data manipulation and system administration tools.

Here is a simple shell script example:

```
#!/bin/sh
# This is a simple shell program that displays today's date
# in a short message.
echo "Today's date is"
date +%x
```

Before we go on let's take a look at what each line does.

```
#!/bin/sh
```

The different shells (Bourne, Korn, and C) do not use all the same commands. Each has some commands that work differently or don't work at all in other shells. Simple commands like those in this script will work in all shells, but there are many cases where that is not true.

Normally, when you run a shell program, the system tries to execute commands using the same shell you are using for your interactive command lines. The first line makes sure the system knows that this is a Bourne shell (**/bin/sh**) script so it can start a Bourne shell to execute the commands. Note that the **#!** must be the very first two characters in the file.

If we don't include this line, someone running a shell other than the Bourne shell might have unexpected results when trying to run one of our programs.

As a good practice you should include **#!shellname** as the first line of every shell program you write. This, however, is an area where there is a change between HP-UX 10.x and HP-UX 9.x. Keep in mind that the default shell in HP-UX 10.x is the POSIX shell. Table 7-1 shows the locations of the most commonly used shells in HP-UX 10.x.

TABLE 7-1   Shell Locations

Shell Name	Location
POSIX shell	/usr/bin/sh
C shell	/usr/bin/csh
Bourne shell	/usr/old/bin/sh
Korn shell	/usr/bin/ksh

Note that I claimed I was giving you an example of a Bourne shell program yet I used **#!/bin/sh** and this does not appear in the table for any shell! **/bin/sh** is the HP-UX 9.x location for the Bourne shell. If indeed you are writing a Bourne shell program, you should use the new location of the Bourne shell (**/usr/old/bin/sh**) in your Bourne shell programs. I would, however, recommend you use the new POSIX shell for your shell programs and since the POSIX shell is a superset of the Bourne shell, then all of the information in this section applies to both the Bourne and POSIX shells. My program that begins with a **#!/bin/sh** does, however, work. This is because the HP-UX 10.x designers provided a link from the old Bourne shell path to the new path. Because this is a potentially confusing area and there is a lot of HP-UX 10.x and 9.x compatibility built-in, it's worth taking a quick look at the characteristics of these shell programs.

```
$ ll -i /usr/bin/sh

  603 -r-xr-xr-x 2 bin bin 405504 Dec 12 03:00 /usr/bin/sh

$ ll -i /bin/sh

  603 -r-xr-xr-x 2 bin bin 405504 Dec 12 03:00 /bin/sh
```

This long listing, with the "-i" option to give me the inode number of the file, proves to be quite revealing. The POSIX shell **/usr/bin/sh** and the Bourne shell **/bin/sh** have the same inode number. Even though I think I am running the Bourne shell when I type **#!/bin/sh** I am actually runing the POSIX shell **/usr/bin/sh**! Because I hate to be behind the times, I think I'll continue typing **#!/bin/sh** and therefore be running the POSIX shell. You can take this analysis one step further and look at the Bourne shell:

```
$ ll -i /usr/old/bin/sh

 16518 -r-xr-xr-x 1 bin bin 200704 Dec 12 03:00/bin/old/bin/sh
```

Here we can see that the old Bourne shell is indeed a different program, with a different inode number, and a different size. I would not recommend you use this shell.

There is also an **/sbin/sh** that my system uses when it boots because **/usr/bin/sh** may not be mounted at the time of boot.

Now, getting back to Bourne shell programming lets look at an example.

```
# This is a simple shell program that displays today's date
# in a short message.
```

These are comments. Everything after a # in a command line is considered a comment. (**#!** on the first line is the one very big exception.)

```
echo "Today's date is"
```

The **echo** command generates prompts and messages in shell programs. See the echo(1) manual entry to see all of the options available with echo for formatting your output. We commonly enclose the string to be displayed in double quotes. In this case we did it because we needed to let the shell know that the apostrophe was part of the string and not a single quote that needs a match.

```
date
```

Executes the **date** command.

After we have the commands in the file we need to make the file executable:

```
$ chmod +x today
```

(The "$" is the default Bourne shell command line prompt.) Changing the permissions this way makes the file executable by anyone. You will only need to do this once after creating the file. See chmod(1) if you need more information on setting permissions.

To execute our new script, we type its name, as shown below:

```
$ today
Today's date is
01/27/93
$
```

Here is a more complex example:

```
#!/bin/sh
# This is a simple shell program that displays the current
# directory name before a long file listing (ll) of that
# directory.
# The script name is myll
echo "Long listing of directory:"
pwd
echo
```

```
ll
```

This is what **myll** looks like when it runs:

```
$ myll
Long listing of directory:
/tmp
total 14398
-rw------- 1 gerry  users   47104  Jan 27 21:09 Ex01816
-rw-rw-rw- 1 root   root        0  Jan 27 09:17 test
-rw-r--r-- 1 ralph  users   14336  Jan 21 15:05 poetry
-rw-r--r-- 1 root   other   66272  Jan 27 10:51 up.log
```

Before we can do more complex shell programs we need to learn more about some of the programming features built into the shell.

Shell Variables

A shell variable is similar to a variable in any programming language. A variable is simply a name you give to a storage location. Unlike most languages, however, you never have to declare or initialize your variables; you just use them.

Shell variables can have just about any name that starts with a letter (uppercase or lowercase). To avoid confusion with special shell characters (like file name generation characters), keep the names simple and use just letters, numbers and underscore (_).

To assign values to shell variables you simply type

```
name=value
```

Note that there are no spaces before and after the = character.

Here are some examples of setting shell variables from the command line. These examples work correctly.

```
$ myname=ralph
```

```
$ HerName=mary
```

This one does not work because of the space after "his."

```
$ his name=norton
his: not found
```

The shell assumes that "his" is a command and tries to execute it. The rest of the line is ignored.

This example contains an illegal character (+) in the name:

```
$ one+one=two
one+one=two: not found
```

A variable must start with a letter:

```
$ 3word=hi
3word=hi: not found
```

Now that we can store values in our variables we need to know how to use those values. The dollar sign ($) is used to get the value of a variable. Any time the shell sees a $ in the command line, it assumes that the characters immediately following it are a variable name. It replaces the $variable with its value. Here are some simple examples using variables at the command line:

```
$ myname=ralph
$ echo myname
myname
$ echo $myname
ralph
$ echo $abc123
```

In the first **echo** command there is no $, so the shell ignores **myname** and **echo** gets **myname** as an argument to be echoed. In the second **echo**, however, the shell sees the $, looks up the value of **myname,** and puts it on the command line. Now **echo** sees **ralph** as its argument (not **myname** or **$myname**). The final **echo** statement is similar except that we have not given a value to **abc123** so the shell assumes it has no value and replaces **$abc123** with nothing. Therefore echo has no arguments and echos a blank line.

There may be times when you want to concatenate variables and strings. This is very easy to do in the shell:

```
$ myname=ralph
$ echo "My name is $myname"
My name is ralph
```

There may be times when the shell can become confused if the variable name is not easily identified in the command line:

```
$ string=dobeedobee
$ echo "$stringdoo"
```

We wanted to display "dobeedobee," but the shell thought the variable name was stringdoo, which had no value. To accomplish this we can use curly braces around the variable name to separate it from surrounding characters:

```
$ echo "${string}doo"
dobeedobeedoo
```

You can set variables in shell programs in the same way, but you would also like to do things such as save the output of a command in a variable so we can use it later. You may want to ask users a question and read their response into a variable so you can examine it.

Command Substitution

Command substitution allows us to save the output from a command (**stdout**) into a shell variable. To demonstrate this, let's take another look at how our "today" example can be done using command substitution.

```
#!/bin/sh
d=`date +%x`
echo "Today's date is $d"
```

The back quotes (`) around the **date** command tell the shell to execute date and place its output on the command line. The output will then be assigned to the variable **d**.

```
$ today
Today's date is 01/27/93
```

We could also have done this without using the variable **d**. We could have just included the **date** command in the echo string:

```
#!/bin/sh
echo "Today's date is `date +%x`"
```

Reading User Input

The most common way to get information from the user is to prompt him or her and then read their response. The **echo** command is most commonly used to display the prompt; then the **read** command is used to read a line of input from the user (**stdin**). Words from the input line can be assigned to one or several shell variables.

Here is an example with comments to show you how **read** can be used:

```
#!/bin/sh
# program: readtest
echo "Please enter your name: \c" # the \c leaves cursor on
                                  # this line.
read name # there is no $ because we are doing an assignment
          # of whatever the user enters into name.
```

```
echo "Hello, $name"
echo "Please enter your two favorite colors: \c"
read color1 color2 # first word entered goes into color1
                   # remainder of line goes into color2
echo "You entered $color2 and $color1"
```

If we ran this program it would look something like this:

```
$ readtest
Please enter your name: gerry
Hello, gerry
Please enter your two favorite colors: blue green
You entered green and blue
$
```

Notice how the **read** command assigned the two words entered for colors into the two respective color variables. If the user entered fewer words than the read command was expecting, the remaining variables would be set to null. If the user enters too many words, all extra words entered are assigned into the last variable. This is how you can get a whole line of input into one variable. Here's an example of what would happen if you entered more than two colors:

```
$ readtest
Please enter your name: gerry
Hello, gerry
Please enter your two favorite colors: chartreuse orchid blue
You entered orchid blue and chartreuse
$
```

Arguments to Shell Programs

Shell programs can have command line arguments just like any regular command. Command line arguments you use when you invoke your shell program are stored in a special set of variables. These are called the positional parameters.

The first ten words on the command line are directly accessible in the shell program using the special variables **$0-$9**. This is how they work:

$0	The command name
$1	The first argument
$2	The second argument
$3	.
	.
	.
$9	The ninth argument

If you are not sure how many command line arguments you may get when your program is run, there are two other variables that can help:

$#	The number of command line arguments
$*	A space-separated list of all of the command line arguments (which does not include the command name).

The variable **$*** is commonly used with the **for** loop (soon to be explained) to process shell script command lines with any number of arguments.

Figure 7-1 illustrates some simple examples of using arguments in our shell programs:

```
#!/bin/sh
# This is a simple shell program that takes one command line
# argument (a directory name) then displays the full pathname
# of that directory before doing a long file listing (ll) on
# it.
#
# The script name is myll
cd $1
echo "Long listing of the `pwd` directory:"
echo
ll
```

Figure 7-1 **myll** Shell Program

If we run **myll** with a directory name, the script changes directory, echoes the message containing the full path name (notice the command substitution), then executes the **ll** command.

Note that the **cd** in the **myll** program will change only the working directory of the script; it does not affect the working directory of the shell we run **myll** from.

```
$ myll /tmp
Long listing of the /tmp directory:
total 380
drwxrwxrwx 2 bin     sys     1024 Feb 1 15:01 files
-rw-rw-rw- 1 root    root       0 Feb 1 13:07 ktl_log
-rw-rw-rw- 1 root    root       0 Feb 1 13:07 ntl_lib.log
-rw-rw-rw- 1 root    root     115 Feb 1 13:07 ntl.read
-rw-r--r-- 1 root    other 108008 Feb 2 08:42 database.log
-r-xr--r-- 1 root    other    466 Feb 1 15:29 updist.scr
```

In this case we could give **myll** no argument and it would still work properly. If we don't provide any command line arguments, then **$1** will be null so nothing goes on the command line after **cd**. This will make **cd** take us to our home directory and perform the **ll** there.

If we provide more than one argument, only the first is used and any others are ignored.

If we use a command line argument it *must* be a directory name; otherwise the **cd** command fails and the script terminates with a "bad directory" error message. Later I will show how to test for valid directory and file names so you can work around potential errors.

A more complex example can be used to build new versions of the **ps** command. Below are two examples that use command line arguments and command substitution to help you with your process management.

The **psg** shell program in Figure 7-2 is handy for searching through what is typically a long process status listing to find only certain commands or user processes. These examples use **grep**. **grep** finds all lines that contain the pattern you are searching for.

```
#!/bin/sh
# Program name: psg
# Usage: psg some_pattern
#
# This program searches through a process status (ps -ef)
# listing for a pattern given as the first command line
# argument.
procs=`ps -ef`                    # Get the process listing
head=`echo "$procs" | line`       # Take off the first line (the
                                  # headings)
echo "$head"                      # Write out the headings
echo "$procs" | grep -i $1 | grep -v $0 # Write out lines
     # containing $1 but not this program's command line

# Note that $procs MUST be quoted or the newlines in the ps
# -ef listing will be turned into spaces when echoed. $head
# must also be quoted to preserve any extra white space.
```

Figure 7-2 **psg** shell Program

Here's what **psg** looks like when it runs. In this example we want to look at all of the Korn shells running on the system.

```
$ psg ksh
  UID    PID  PPID  C  STIME        TTY   TIME  COMMAND
  root  1258  1252  0  18:00:34  ttyp1  0:00  ksh
  root  1347  1346  0  18:03:15  ttyp2  0:01  ksh
 ralph  1733  1732  0  20:06:11  ttys0  0:00  -ksh
```

In this example we want to see all the processes that **ralph** is running:

```
$ psg ralph
  UID    PID  PPID  C  STIME        TTY   TIME  COMMAND
```

```
ralph  1733  1732  0  20:06:11  ttys0  0:00  -ksh
ralph  1775  1733  0  20:07:43  ttys0  0:00  vi afile
```

This program also works to find terminal, process ID, parent process ID, start date, and any other information from **ps**.

The **gkill** shell program in Figure 7-3 searches through a **ps -ef** listing for a pattern (just like **psg**); then it kills all listed processes. The examples use the **cut** command, which allows you to specify a range of columns to retain.

```
#!/bin/sh
# Program name: gkill
# Usage: gkill some_pattern
# This program will find all processes that contain the
# pattern specified as the first command line argument then
# kills those processes.
# get the process listing
procs=`ps -ef`
echo "The following processes will be killed:"
# Here we list the processes to kill. We don't kill this
# process
echo "$procs" | grep -i $1 | grep -v $0
# Allow the user a chance to cancel.
echo "\nPress Return to continue Ctrl-C to exit"
# If the user presses Ctrl-C the program will exit.
# Otherwise this read waits for the next return character and
# continue.
read junk
# find the pattern and cut out the pid field
pids=`echo "$procs" | grep -i $1 | grep -v $0 | cut -c9-15`
# kill the processes
kill $pids
```

Figure 7-3 **gkill** Shell Program

If we don't provide any command line arguments, **grep** issues an error and the program continues. In the next section we will learn how to check if **$1** is set and how to gracefully clean up if it's not.

Here is an example of running **gkill**:

```
$ gkill xclock

The following processes will be killed:
  marty 3145 3016 4 15:06:59 ttyp5 0:00 xclock
```

```
Press return to continue Ctrl-C to exit

[1] + Terminated                        xclock &
```

Testing and Branching

Decision making is one of the shell's most powerful features. There are two ways to check conditions and branch to a piece of code that can handle that condition.

For example, you may want to ask the user a question and then check if the answer was yes or no. You may also want to check if a file exists before you operate on it. In either case you can use the **if** command to accomplish the task. Here are a few shell script segments that explain each part of the **if** command:

```
echo "Continue? \c"
read ans
if [ "$ans" = "n" ]
then
      echo "Goodbye"
      exit
fi
```

The **echo** and **read** provide a prompt and response as usual. The **if** statement executes the next command and if it succeeds, it executes any commands between the **then** and the **fi** (if spelled backwards).

Note that the \c in the **echo** command suppresses the new line that **echo** normally generates. This leaves the cursor on the line immediately after the "Continue? " prompt. This is commonly used when prompting for user input.

The **test** command is the most common command to use with the **if** command. The ["$ans" = "n"] is the **test** command. It performs many types of file, string, and numeric logical tests and if the condition is true, the test succeeds.

The syntax of the **test** command requires spaces around the **[ ]** or you will get a syntax error when the program runs. Also notice the double quotes around the response variable **$ans**. This is a strange anomaly with the **test** command. If the user presses only [[RETURN]] at the prompt without typing any other character, the value of **$ans** will be null. If we didn't have the quote marks around **$ans** in the **test** command, it would look like this when the value of **$ans** was substituted into the test command:

[= "n"]

This would generate a "test: argument expected" error when you run the program. This is a very common mistake and if you ever get this error, you should look for variables in your **test** commands with null values.

There is another form of the **if** command that is very common. It allows you to do one thing if a condition is met or do something else if not:

```
if [    ]          # if some condition is true
then
                   # do something
else
                   # otherwise do this
fi
```

There are many conditions that the **test** command can test as shown in Table 7-2.

TABLE 7-2 test Command Conditions

String tests:

["$a" = "string"]	True if $a is equal to "string"
["$a" != "string"]	True if $a is NOT equal to "string"
[-z "$a"]	True if $a is null (zero characters)
[-n "$a"]	True if $a is NOT null

TABLE 7-2 **test** Command Conditions

String tests:

Numeric tests:

[$x -eq 1]	True if $x is equal to 1
[$x -ne 1]	True if $x is NOT equal to 1
[$x -lt 1]	True if $x is less than 1
[$x -gt 1]	True if $x is greater than 1
[$x -le 1]	True if $x is less than or equal to 1
[$x -ge 1]	True if $x is greater than or equal to 1

File tests:

[-d $file]	True if $file is a directory
[-f $file]	True if $file is a file
[-s $file]	True if $file is a file with > 0 bytes
[-r $file]	True if $file is readable
[-w $file]	True if $file is writable
[-x $file]	True if $file is executable

Tests can be combined using **-a** to logically "AND" the tests together, **-o** to logically "OR" two tests and **!** to "negate" a test. For example, this test statement is true only if the **$interactive** variable is set to true or **$file** is a directory:

```
[ "$interactive" = "TRUE" -o -d $file ]
```

This will be used in some upcoming example programs.

Here is a useful extension to the **gkill** program earlier shown. It checks to see that we have exactly one command line argument before the program will attempt to do the processing. It uses a numeric test and the $# variable, which represents the number of command line arguments. It should be inserted before any other lines of code in the **gkill** example given above.

```
# If we don't have exactly one command line argument write an
# error and exit.
if [ $# -ne 1 ]
then
    echo "Usage: $0 pattern"
    echo "Some pattern matching the processes to kill must
    echo "be specified"
    exit 1 # Exit 1 terminates the program and tells the
           # calling shell that we had an error.
fi
```

Some other possible extensions to the **gkill** program might be to

- Allow the user to specify a signal to use with the **kill** command. For example
  gkill -9 ralph
  would find all of Ralph's processes and then kill them with **kill -9**.

- Make sure that a valid message is printed if we can't find any processes to kill using the specified pattern.

This same type of command line check is easily applied to the **psg** program to make sure you have just exactly one argument representing the pattern to search for.

When you are reading user input, you may want to check if the user entered a value at all. If they didn't, you would provide a reasonable default value. This is easily done with a variable modifier.

This example reads answer ("ans") from the user and then checks its value using an **if** command:

```
echo "Do you really want to remove all of your files? \c"
read ans
if [ ${ans:-n} = y ]
then
    rm -rf *
fi
```

The **${ans:-n}** statement checks the value of **$ans**. If there is a value in **$ans,** use it in the command line. If the user simply pressed [[RETURN]] at the prompt, **$ans** will be null. In this case **${ans:-n}** will evaluate to n when we do the comparison. Basically, in one small statement it says, "if the user did not provide an answer, assume he meant n."

There is another modifier that is often used:

```
${var:=default}
```

It returns the value of **var** if it is set; it returns the default if **var** is not set and it will also assign the default as the value of **var** for future use.

All of the modifiers available in the Bourne shell are in the **sh** manual entry.

Making Decisions with the case Statement

The **case** statement is another way to make decisions and test conditions in shell programs. It is most commonly used to check for certain patterns in command line arguments. For example, if you wanted to determine if the first command line argument is an option (starts with a -), the **case** statement is the easiest way to do that. The **case** statement is also used to respond to different user input (such as asking the user to select a choice from a menu).

The **case** statement is probably one of the most complicated shell commands because of its syntax:

```
case pattern_to_match in
        pattern1)   cmdA
                    cmdB
                ;;
        pattern2)  cmdC
                ;;
                . . .
        *)  cmdZ
                ;;
esac
```

pattern_to_match is usually a shell variable that your are testing (like a command line argument or a user response). If **pattern_to_match** matches **pattern1,** then commands **cmdA** and **cmdB** are executed. The **;;**

separates this pattern's command list from the next pattern. In all cases, when **;;** is reached, the program jumps to the **esac** (**case** spelled backwards).

If **pattern_to_match** matches **pattern2,** then **cmdC** is executed and we jump to **esac**, the end of the **case** statement.

The ***** is provided so if **pattern_to_match** did not match anything else, it will execute **cmdZ**. It's important to have a default action to handle the case where the user types an invalid entry.

For more robust pattern matching any file name generation characters (*, [ ], ?) can be used to do special pattern matches. There is also a very useful way to check for multiple patterns in one line using the | symbol which means logical "OR". Here's an example:

```
echo "Do you want to continue? (y/n) \c"
read ans
case $ans in
        y|Y) echo "Continuing"
             . . .
             ;;
        n|N) echo "Done, Goodbye"
             exit
             ;;
        *) echo "Invalid input"
             ;;
esac
```

Here is another example where we are testing to see if **$1** (the first command line argument) is a valid option (a character we recognize that begins with a -).

```
case $1 in
        -l | -d) # Perform a listing
                echo "All files in $HOME:\n"
                ll -R $HOME | more
                ;;
        -i) # -i means set an interactive flag to true
            interactive="TRUE"
                ;;
        *)  # Invalid input
            echo "$0: $1 is an invalid option"
            exit 1
                ;;
```

```
esac
```

A **case** statement similar to this is used in the **trash** program at the end of this chapter.

Looping

There are many times when you want to perform an action repeatedly. In the shell there are two ways to do this:

1. The **for** loop takes a list of items and performs the commands in the loop once for each item in the list.

2. The **while** loop executes some commands (usually the **test** command) if that command executes successfully. (If the test condition is true, then the commands in the loop are executed and then the command is again executed to see if we should loop again.)

The basic format of the **for** loop is

```
for var in list_of_items
do
        cmdA
        cmdB
        cmdC
done
```

When the loop starts, the variable **var** has its value set to the first word in the **list_of_items** to loop through. Then the three commands between the **do** and the **done** statements are executed. After the program reaches the **done** statement, it goes back to the top of the loop and assigns **var** to the next item in the list, executes the commands, etc. The last time through the loop, the program continues with the next executable statement after the **done** statement.

The **list_of_items** can be any list of words separated by white space. You can type the words or use variables or command substitution to build the list. For example, let's say we want to copy a new **.kshrc** file into the home directory of several users. A **for** loop is the easiest way to do this:

```
for name in ralph norton alice edith archie
do
        echo $name
        cp /tmp/.kshrc.new /users/$name/.kshrc
done
```

This example can be extended to copy certain files to several machines using the **rcp** command and verify that they got there using the **remsh** command:

```
for host in neptune jupiter mars earth sun
do
        echo $host
        rcp /etc/passwd /etc/hosts $host:/etc
        rcp /.profile $host:/.profile
        remsh $host ll /etc/passwd /etc/hosts /.profile
done
```

You can also process lists of files in the current directory using command substitution to generate the **list_of_items**:

```
for file in 'ls'
do
      if [ -r $file ]
      then
              echo "$file is readable"
      fi
done
```

Note that **for file in *** would have done the same thing.

If you have a large list of things you would like to loop through and you don't want to type them on the command line, you can enter them in a file instead. Then, using the **cat** command and command substitution, you can generate the **list_of_items**:

```
for i in 'cat important_files'
do
```

```
        # do something with each of the files listed in the
        # important_files file.
done
```

The **for** loop, however, is most commonly used to process the list of command line arguments (**$***):

```
for name in $*
do
     if [ ! -f $name -a ! -d $name ]
     then
        echo "$name is not a valid file or directory name"
     else
       # do something with the file or directory
     fi
done
```

The **trash** program contains a **for** loop that processes command line arguments in a similar way.

Figure 7-4 is an example of a program that can be used to customize how SAM adds a user to the system for HP-UX 9.x. It uses a **for** loop and a **case** statement to parse the command line that SAM used to invoke it. This example was adapted from the file **/usr/sam/config/ct_adduser.ex**. It copies a **.kshrc** file and a **.logout** file to the new user's home directory after SAM has added the user to the system. The name of this program should be entered in the "Program to run after adding a user" field of SAM's User Task Customization screen.

```
#! /bin/sh
#
# This script illustrates how to process the parameter string
# from SAM for the "Add a New User Account to the System"
# task.
#
# Iterate through the parameter string and extract the
# arguments.
#

# SAM passes all necessary information to us as command line
# arguments. This chunk of code is provided for you.
for param in $*
do
      case $param in
            -l) login_name=$2; shift 2;;
            -h) home_dir=$2; shift 2;;
            -v) uid=$2; shift 2;;
            -g) group=$2; shift 2;;
            -s) shell=$2; shift 2;;
            -p) password=$2; shift 2;;
            -R) real_name=$2; shift 2;;
            -L) office_loc=$2; shift 2;;
            -H) home_phone=$2; shift 2;;
            -O) office_phone=$2; shift 2;;
      esac
done
#
#
# These are the commands we have to add to copy in a .kshrc
# and a .logout file into the new user's home directory.

# standard.kshrc and standard.logout are just the names of the
# default shell files previously created for every new user.

cp /etc/standard.kshrc $home_dir/.kshrc
cp /etc/standard.logout $home_dir/.logout

exit 0
```

Figure 7-4 **newadduser.ex** Shell Program

The While Loop

The **while** loop has the following format:

```
while cmd1
do
        cmdA
        cmdB
        cmdC
done
```

    cmd1 is executed first. If it executes successfully, then the commands between the **do** and the **done** statements are executed. **cmd1** is then executed again; if successful, the commands in the loop are executed again, etc. When **cmd1** fails, the program jumps past the **done** statement and resumes execution with the next executable statement.

    Most of the time the command executed in place of **cmd1** is the **test** command. You can then perform logical tests as described in the **if** section. If the test succeeds (is true), the commands in the loop are executed and the script tests the condition again. The **while** loop is useful if you have a fixed number of times you want the loop to run or if you want something to happen until some condition is met.

    This program displays the primary LAN interface (lan0) statistics using **netstat** ten times, once every 30 seconds:

```
i=1
while [ $i -le 10 ]
do
        netstat -i | grep lan0
        sleep 30
        i=`expr $i + 1`
done
```

    The **expr** command is the only way we can do math in the Bourne shell. (The Korn and C shells have some math functions builtin). The line

```
expr $i + 1
```

takes the current value of the variable **i** (which must be an integer or the **expr** command will complain) and adds 1 to it, writing the result to standard output (stdout). By using the **expr** command with command substitution, we can capture the result and assign it back into **i**. This is how we increment variables in the shell. The **expr** command can also perform integer subtraction, multiplication, division, remainder, and matching functions. See the **expr** manual entry for all of the details.

The **while** loop can also be used to process command line arguments one at a time, using the number of command line arguments and the **shift** command:

```
while [ $# -ne 0 ]
do
    case $1 in
    -*) # $1 must be an option because it starts with -
        # Add it to the list of options:
        opts="$opts $1"
        ;;
     *) # $1 must be an argument. Add it to the list of
        # command line arguments:
        args="$args $1"
        ;;
  esac
  shift
done
```

The **shift** command shifts the remaining arguments in **$*** to the left by one position and decrements **$#**. What was the first argument (**$1**) is now gone forever; what was in **$2** is now in **$1**, etc. In the process of shifting command line arguments, **$#** is also decremented to accurately reflect the number of arguments left in **$***.

You may want some commands to run until the user stops the program or until some stop condition is met. An infinite **while** loop is the best way to do this. For example, let's say we are prompting users for some input and we will continue to prompt them until they give us valid input:

```
while true
do
    # prompt users and get their response
    echo "Enter yes or no: \c"
```

```
    read ans

    # Check if the response is valid
    if [ "$ans" = "yes" -o "$ans" = "no" ]
    then
    # If it is valid, stop the looping
    break
  else
    # Otherwise print an error message and try it again
    # from the top of the loop
    echo "Invalid input, try again!\n"
    fi
done
# Now that we have valid input we can process the user's
# request
    .
    .
    .
```

true is a special command that always executes successfully. The loop does not terminate unless the user stops the program by killing it or until a **break** command is executed in the loop. The **break** command will stop the loop.

Shell Functions

As you write shell programs, you will notice that there are certain sets of commands that appear in many places within a program. For example, several times in a script you may check user input and issue an appropriate message if input is invalid. It can be tedious to type the same lines of code in your program numerous times. It can be a nuisance if you later want to change these lines.

Instead, you can you can put these commands into a shell function. Functions look and act like a new command that can be used inside the script. Here's an example of a basic shell function:

```
# This is a function that may be called from anywhere within
# the program. It displays a standard usage error message
# then exits the program.

print_usage()
{
```

```
        echo "Usage:"
        echo "To trash files: $0 [-i] files_to_trash..."
        echo "Display trashed files: $0 -d"
        echo "Remove all trashed files: $0 -rm"
        echo "Print this message: $0 -help"
        exit 1
}
```

print_usage is now a new command in your shell program. You can use it anywhere in this script.

Shell functions also have their own set of positional parameters (**$1-$9, $#,** and **$***) so you can pass them arguments just like any other command. The only nuance is that **$0** represents the name of the shell program, not the name of the function.

This shell function is used several times in the **trash** program example.

The system startup program **/etc/rc** in HP-UX 9.x is made up of shell functions that are invoked from one of three places in the program, depending on your system configuration. **/etc/rc** is a good example of an advanced shell program. **/sbin/rc** is the startup program in HP-UX 10.x.

Figure 7-5 is a fairly complex program that exercises all of the concepts we have covered so far. It is a **trash** program that removes files from their original locations. Instead of removing them permanently, it places them in a trash can in your home directory. This is a fairly robust program, but I'm sure you can think of many extensions as you read through it.

```
#!/bin/sh
# Program name: trash
# Usage:
#   To trash files:      trash [-i] file_names_to_trash ...
#   Display trashed files:     trash -d
#   Remove all trashed files: trash -rm
#   Print a help message:      trash -help

# This program takes any number of directory or file name
# arguments. If the argument is a file it will be removed
# from its current place in the file system and placed in the
# user's trash directory ($HOME/.trash). If the argument is a
# directory name the program will ask if the user really
# wants to trash the whole directory.
#
# This program also takes a -i (interactive) option. Like
# the rm command, if the -i is the first argument on the
# command line, the program stops and asks if each file
# named in the remaining arguments should be trashed.

#
# The -d (display) option shows the contents of the
# user's trashed files.
#
# The -help option displays a usage message for the user.
```

Figure 7-5 **trash** Shell Program

```
# The -rm (remove) option interactively
# asks the user if each file or directory in the trash
# directory should be removed permanently.
#
# The -h, -d and -rm options may not be used with
# any other command line arguments.

# Possible extensions:
# - Enhance the -rm option to remove a list of files
# from the trash directory from the command line.
# - Create a program to be run by cron once nightly to empty
# everyone's trash directory.

# This is a function that may be called from anywhere within
# the program. It displays a standard usage error message
# then exits the program.
print_usage()
{
   echo "Usage:"
   echo "To trash files: $0 [-i] file_names_to_trash ..."
   echo "Display trashed files:   $0 -d"
   echo "Remove all trashed files: $0 -rm"
   echo "Print this message:      $0 -help"
exit 1
}
# Make sure we have at least one command line argument before
# we start.
if [ $# -lt 1 ]
then
    print_usage
fi

# If this flag is true then we need to do interactive
# processing.
interactive="FALSE"

# This is the name of the trash can.
trash_dir="$HOME/.trash"

# Make sure the trash directory exists before we go any
# further.
if [ ! -d $trash_dir ]
then
    mkdir $trash_dir
fi
# Sort out the command line arguments.
case $1 in
   -help) # Print a help message.
      print_usage
      ;;
```

Figure 7-5 **trash** Shell Program (Continued)

```
-d | -rm) # a -d or -rm were given
      # If it was not the only command line argument
      # then display a usage message and then exit.
      if [ $# -ne 1 ]
      then
           print_usage
      fi

      # Otherwise do the task requested.
      if [ $1 = "-d" ]
      then
           echo "The contents of $trash_dir:\n"
           ll -R $trash_dir | more
      else
           # remove all files from the trash directory
           rm -rf $trash_dir/*
           # get any dotfiles too
           rm -rf $trash_dir/.[!.]*
      fi

      # Now we can exit successfully.
      exit 0
      ;;
-i) # If the first argument is -i ask about each file as it
    # is processed.
    interactive="TRUE"
    # Take -i off the command line so we know that the
    # rest of the arguments are file or directory names.

    shift
    ;;

 -*)# Check for an option we don't understand.
    echo "$1 is not a recognized option."
    print_usage
    ;;
    esac

# Just for fun we'll keep a count of the files that were
# trashed.
count=0

for file in $*
do
 # First make sure the file or directory to be renamed exists.
 # If it doesn't, add it to a list of bad files to be written
 # out later. Otherwise process it.
 if [ ! -f $file -a ! -d $file ]
 then
     bad_files="$bad_files $file"
 else
# If we are in interactive mode ask for confirmation
# on each file. Otherwise ask about directories.
```

Figure 7-5 **trash** Shell Program (Continued)

```
if [ "$interactive" = "TRUE" -o -d $file ]
then
    # Ask the user for confirmation (default answer is no).
    if [ -d $file ]
    then
        echo "Do you want to trash the dir $file ? (y/n) n\b\c"
    else
        echo "Do you really want to trash $file ? (y/n) n\b\c"
    fi
    read doit

    # If they answered y then do the move.
    # Otherwise print a message that the file was not touched.
    if [ "${doit:-n}" = y ]
    then
        mv -i $file $trash_dir
        echo "$file was trashed to $trash_dir"
        count=`expr $count + 1`
    else
        echo "$file was not trashed"
    fi

  else # We are not in interactive mode, so just do it.
      mv -i $file $trash_dir count=`expr
      $count + 1`
  fi
fi
done

echo "$0: trashed $count item(s)"

if [ -n "$bad_files" ]
then
    echo "The following name(s) do not exist and \c"
    echo "could not be trashed:"
    echo "$bad_files"
fi

exit 0
```

Figure 7-5 **trash** Shell Program (Continued)

awk in Shell Programs

awk is a very powerful symbolic programming language. A *what*?

Simply stated, **awk** searches for patterns in lines of input (from **stdin** or from a file) For each line that matches the specified pattern, it can perform some very complex processing on that line. The code to actually process matching lines of input is a cross between a shell script and a C program.

Data manipulation tasks that would be very complex with combinations of **grep, cut,** and **paste** are very easily done with **awk**. Since **awk** is a programming language, it can also perform mathematical operations or check the input very easily. (Shells don't do math very well.) It can even do floating-point math. (Shells deal only with integers and strings.)

The basic form of an **awk** program looks like this:

```
awk '/pattern_to_match/ { program to run }' input_file_names
```

Notice that the whole program is enclosed in single quotes. If no input file names are specified, **awk** reads from **stdin** (as from a pipe).

The **pattern_to_match** must appear between the / characters. The pattern is actually called a regular expression. Some common regular expression examples are shown in the examples.

The program to execute is written in **awk** code, which looks something like C. The program is executed whenever a line of input matches the **pattern_to_match**. If **/pattern_to_match/** does not precede the program in **{ }**, then the program is executed for every line of input.

awk works with fields of the input lines. Fields are words separated by white space. The fields in **awk** patterns and programs are referenced with **$**, followed by the field number. For example the second field of an input line is **$2**. If you are using an **awk** command in your shell programs, the fields (**$1, $2,** etc.) are not confused with the shell script's positional parameters because the **awk** variables are enclosed in single quotes so the shell ignores them.

But let's not talk about it! Let's see some examples.

This simple example lists just the terminals that are active on your system (the terminal name is the second field of a **who** listing

```
who | awk '{ print $2 }'
```

Note that **cut** could have done this also, but you would have had to know exactly which columns the terminal name occupied in the **who** output as shown below:

```
who | cut -c12-20
```

If the user or terminal name is longer than normal in any line, this command will not work. The **awk** example will work because it looks at fields not columns.

In our **gkill** example, we used **grep** and **cut** to find the process IDs of the processes to kill:

```
procs=`ps -ef`
procs_to_kill=`echo "$procs" | grep -i $1`
pids=`echo "$procs_to_kill" | cut -c9-15`
```

These three complex commands can be replaced with one **awk** command:

```
pids=`ps -ef | awk '/'$1'/ { print $2 } ' `
```

The $1 is actually outside the single quotes, so it is interpreted by the shell as the first command line argument.

The **llsum** program shown in Figure 7-6 is a more complex example. A few things to note:

- **BEGIN** is a special pattern that means execute the **awk** program in {} before the first line of input. It is usually used for initializing variables and printing headers on the output.
- **END** is used after the last line of input, generally for summarizing the input.
- **printf** is a formatted print statement, as in C. The first argument is a format string containing what you want to print. It contains special characters for printing different things such as %s means we are printing a string.

%**d** means we are printing an integer.

%**f** means we are printing a floating-point number.

- The **$1 ~ /pattern/** says: IF the first field matches the pattern, then do the program in **{}**.

```
#!/bin/sh
# Program: llsum
# Usage: llsum files_or_directories_to_summarize
#
# Displays a truncated long listing (ll) and displays size
# statistics of the files in the listing.
# A sample long listing for reference. Notice that the first
# line of output is less than 8 fields long and is not
# processed.
# ll
# total 46
# drwxrwxrwx 2  gerry aec 24           Mar 21 18:25  awk_ex
# crw--w--w- 1  root  sys 0 0x000000   Mar 22 15:32  /dev/con
#
# awk field numbers:
#     $1       $2 $3    $4   $5              $6   $7  $8     $9
ll $*  | \
awk ' BEGIN { x=i=0; printf "%-16s%-10s%8s%8s\n",\
                "FILENAME","OWNER","SIZE","TYPE" }

# Print out the owner, size, and type. Then sum the size.
$1 ~ /^[-dlps]/  { # line format for normal files
          printf "%-16s%-10s%8d",$9,$3,$5
          x = x + $5
          i++
          }
# If the line starts with a - it's a regular file; d is
# directory, etc.
  $1 ~ /^-/ { printf "%8s\n","file" } # standard file types
  $1 ~ /^d/ { printf "%8s\n","dir" }
  $1 ~ /^l/ { printf "%8s\n","link" }
  $1 ~ /^p/ { printf "%8s\n","pipe" }
  $1 ~ /^s/ { printf "%8s\n","socket" }
  $1 ~ /^[bc]/ {        # line format for device files
          printf "%-16s%-10s%8s%8s\n",$10,$3,"","dev"
          }
END
{ printf "\nThese files occupy %d bytes (%.4f Mbytes)\n",\
 x, x / (1024*1024)
    printf "Average file size is %d bytes\n", x/i
}' | \
more # Pipe the output through the more command so it will
     # page.
```

Figure 7-6 **llsum** Shell Program

The following is an example of running **llsum**:

```
$ llsum /users/tomd
FILENAME            OWNER        SIZE    TYPE

.Xauthority         tomd           49    file
.cshrc              tomd          818    file
.exrc               tomd          347    file
.login              tomd          377    file
.mosaic-global      tomd         6988    file
.mosaic-hotlist     tomd           38    file
.mosaic-personal    tomd         1024    dir
.mosaicpid          tomd            5    file
.profile            tomd          382    file
.sh_history         tomd          426    file
.vue                tomd         1024    dir
.vueprofile         tomd         3971    file
700install          tomd       368640    file
Install.mosaic      tomd         6762    file
README.mosaic       tomd         7441    file
README.ninstall     tomd        24354    file
krsort              tomd        34592    file
krsort.c            tomd         3234    file
krsort.dos          tomd        32756    file
krsort.q            tomd         9922    file
krsortorig.c        tomd         3085    file
print.xwd           tomd        44786    file
qsort               tomd        33596    file
qsort.c             tomd         4093    file
qsort.test          tomd         5503    file
qsorttest.q         tomd         4097    file
qsorttest.q         tomd         9081    file
test.xwd            tomd       589291    file

The files listed occupy 1196682 bytes (1.1412 Mbytes)
Average file size is 4738 bytes

$
```

awk can also be very useful for summarizing data from standard monitoring commands like **netstat** and **vmstat** as in the program in figure 7-7.

```
#!/bin/sh
# Program: ifstat
# Usage: ifstat interval interface_to_watch

# This program will not stop until you interrupt it
# (using Ctrl-C or Break).
interval=${1:-5}       # set interval to $1 or 5 if $1 is
                       # not given
interface=${2:-lan0}   # set interface to $2 or lan0 if $2 is
                       # not given

echo "Interface statistic information for $interface:\n"
# The parentheses around the while loop returns all its output
# as one command so it can be easily piped to the awk command.
(while true
do
    netstat -i
    sleep $interval
done ) | \

awk 'BEGIN { printf "%10s%10s%10s%10s%10s\n", "ipkts",
                    "ierrs", "opkts", "oerrs", "collis" ;
            printf "%10s%10s%10s%10s%10s\n", "-----",
                    "-----", "-----", "-----", "------" ;
# Initialize the variables that will hold the previous
# historical statistics.
pipkts=0; pierrs=0; popkts=0; poerrs=0; pcollis=0
}

# Find the line we care about. This is the line that starts
# with the specified interface name.
/^'$interface'/ { ipkts = $5 - pipkts; # current - previous
ierrs = $6 - pierrs;
opkts = $7 - popkts;
oerrs = $8 - poerrs;
collis = $9 - pcollis;

printf "%10d%10d%10d%10d%10d\n", ipkts, ierrs,
opkts, oerrs, collis;

pipkts = $5; pierrs = $6; popkts = $7; poerrs = $8;
pcollis = $9
        }
' # End of the awk program.
```

Figure 7-7 **ifstat** Shell Program

netstat -i shows input and output packet statistics since the system was last booted or since the LAN interface was last reset. Unfortunately the numbers can be very large after the system runs for a few days. The **ifstat** shell program runs **netstat -i** continuously for a specified number of seconds and displays only the NEW information, not the historical information. This program can be run when you suspect problems such as excess traffic or collisions on your network.

Here is an example run of **ifstat** with an interval of five seconds:

```
$ ifstat 5
Interface statistic information for lan0:

ipkts ierrs opkts oerrs collis
----- ----- ----- ----- ------
 2234    15  2112    12     65
 1560    18  1480    11     44
```

These values reflect the current activity. They do not contain the history of packets since the system booted.

Some trivia to wow your friends with at your next cocktail party: **awk** is the first letter of the last names of its authors: Alfred Aho, Peter Weinberger, and Brian Kernighan.

C Shell Programming for System Administrators

(Much of the material in this section is from *The Unix C Shell Field Guide* by Gail Anderson and Paul Anderson, Prentice Hall, ISBN 013937468X.)

The C shell is similar to the Bourne shell covered earlier in that it provides a user interface to HP-UX. You can use the C shell in the following three ways:

- Interactively type commands on the command line.

- Group commonly executed sets of commands into command files you can execute by typing the name of the file.

- Create C shell programs (usually called shell scripts) using the structured programming techniques of the C shell.

These three techniques are listed in the order in which you'll probably use them. First, you log in and use interactive commands. Then you group together commonly used commands and execute them with a single command. Finally, you may want to create sophisticated shell scripts.

For this reason I'll describe these aspects of the C shell in the order in which they are listed. Under the interactive description I'll also cover the C shell environment and startup programs associated with the C shell.

Before we get into the C shell itself, I would like to take a look at the C shell program. In HP-UX 9.x the path for the C shell was **/bin/csh**. In HP-UX 10.x the path is **/usr/bin/csh**. Here is a long listing with the "-i" option to provide the inode number of the file:

```
$ ll -i /usr/bin/csh

  456 -r-xr-xr-x 1 bin bin 135168 Dec 12 03:00 /usr/bin/csh

$ ll -i /bin/csh

  456 -r-xr-xr-x 1 bin bin 135168 Dec 12 03:00/bin/csh
```

These are one and the same program because they have the same inode number. The designers of HP-UX 10.x provided many such transitional features in the operating system. When **/bin/csh** is used in this chapter, you can view it as being identical to the HP-UX 10.x path of / **usr/bin/csh**.

Issuing Commands

The first activity you perform after you log in to the system is to issue commands at the prompt. A command you may want to issue immediately is **ll**. Here is what I see on my system after executing this:

```
sys1 5: ll -a
total 22
drwxr-xr-x  3 cshtest users 1024 Nov 1 11:02 .
dr-xr-xr-x 12 bin      bin   1024 Nov 1 11:01 ..
-rw-r--r--  1 cshtest users  818 Nov 1 11:01 .cshrc
-rw-r--r--  1 cshtest users  347 Nov 1 11:01 .exrc
-rw-r--r--  1 cshtest users  377 Nov 1 11:01 .login
-rw-r--r--  1 cshtest users  382 Nov 1 11:01 .profile
drwxr-xr-x  4 cshtest users 1024 Nov 1 11:43 .vue
-rwxr-xr-x  1 cshtest users 3971 Nov 1 11:02 .vueprofile
sys1  6:
```

The C shell prompt consists of system name (sys1) followed by the command number and a colon. I'll cover the prompt shortly.

ll shows two files related to the C shell in this user area:

.cshrc and **.login**

Figure 7-8 is the contents of **.cshrc**.

```
# .cshrc for C shell
#
# Default user .cshrc file (/bin/csh initialization).

# Usage:  Copy this file to a user's home directory
# then customize it and test.  It is run by csh each
# time it starts up.

# Set up default command search path:
#
# (For security, this default is a minimal set.)

    Set path=( /bin /usr/bin )

# Set up C shell environment:
    if   ( $?prompt ) then # shell is interactive.
      set history  = 20    # previous commands to remember.
      set savehist = 20    # number to save across sessions.
      set system = `hostname`        # name of this system.
      set prompt = "$system \!: "   # command prompt.

      # Sample alias:

      alias    h     history

      # More sample aliases, commented out by default:

      #alias   d     dirs
      #alias   pd    pushd
      #alias   pd2   pushd +2
      #alias   po    popd
      #alias   m     more
endif
```

Figure 7-8 Sample .cshrc

Figure 7-9 shows the contents of **.login**:

```
# .login for C shell

# @(#) $Revision:  64.2  $

# Default user .login file ( /bin/csh initialization)

# Set up the default search paths:
set path=(/bin /usr/bin /usr/contrib/bin /usr/local/bin.)

#set up the terminal
eval `tset -s -Q -m ' :?hp' `
stty erase "^H" kill "^U" intr "^C" eof "^D" susp "^Z"  hupcl
    ixon ixoff tostop
tabs

# Set up shell environment:
set noclobber
set history=20
```

Figure 7-9 Sample **.login**

The .cshrc File

The **.cshrc** is first read and executed by the C shell. You can modify the **.cshrc** file to specify the command line prompt you wish to use, initialize the history list, and define aliases. The following are descriptions of the way the **.cshrc** file shown in Figure 7-8 defines these.

Initialize History List in .cshrc

The C shell can keep a history list of the commands you have issued. If you wish to reissue a command or view a command you earlier issued, you can use the history list.

The commands issued are referred to by number so it is helpful to have a number appear at the command prompt. The following line in **.cshrc** provides a number following the system name:

```
set prompt = "$system \!: "

sys1 1:
```

We will get into shell and environment variables shortly, but for now it is sufficient to know that **$system** corresponds to system name "sys1."

You can specify any number of commands you want to keep a history of. The following line in **.cshrc** sets the history list to 20:

set history = 20

If you were to now issue a series of commands, you could view these. If we had issued five commands since login, we could view these with **history** as shown:

```
sys1 6: history
        1    ll
        2    whoami
        3    cd /tmp
        4    pwd
        5    cat database.log
```

All of these commands (**ll, whoami, cd /tmp, pwd, cat data-base.log**) are in the history list with their corresponding numbers. You can repeat the last command with **!!**, the second command with **!2**, and the last command that started with "c" with **!c**. After issuing the commands you could do the following:

```
sys1    7:!!
             cat database.log

sys1    8:!2
              whoami

sys1    9:!c
             cat database.log
```

Table 7-3 includes some of the more commonly used history list recall commands.

TABLE 7-3   Recalling from History List

Command	Description	Example
!N	Issue command **N**	**!2**
!!	Issue last command	**!!**
!-N	Issue **Nth** command from last command issued	**!-N**
!str	Issue last command starting with **str**	**!c**
!?str?	Issue last command that had **str** anyplace in command line	**!?cat?**
!{str}str2	Append **str2** to last command with **str1**	**!{cd} /tmp**
^str1^str2^	Substitute **str2** for **str1** in last command	**^cat^more^**

Aliases in .cshrc

An alias is a name that you select for a frequently used command or series of commands. You can use the **.cshrc** file as a place where your aliases are stored and read every time you log in. You can also define aliases at the command line prompt, but these will be cleared when you log out.

Here is an example of a useful alias.

```
sys1 1: alias h history
sys1 2: h
        history
```

Every time you type **h** the history command is executed. You can obtain a list of aliases you currently have active by issuing the alias command. You can also alias a set of commands as shown:

```
sys1 3:alias procs 'echo "Number of processes are: \c";
ps -ef | wc -l'
                        # single quote on outside
                        # double quote on inside
```

When you run **procs** you see the following:

```
sys1 4: procs
        Number of processes are: 44
```

There is a lot of quoting taking place in this command line. To understand what is taking place on this line Table 7-4 will help.

TABLE 7-4 Shell Quoting

Character(s)	Description
'cmd'	Single quote means take string character literally
"str"	Double quote means allow command and variable substitution

Character(s)	Description
\c	Escape character that prevents everything following it from printing including new line
'str'	Grave means execute command and substitute output

Applying Table 7-4 to the earlier **procs** alias, we can see what this alias is comprised of. The alias begins with a single quote which means execute the command(s) within the single quotes. The first command is the **echo** command which uses double quotes to specify the characters to **echo**. Embedded in the double quotes is the escape character \c which prevents a new line from being printed. The semicolons separate commands. **ps** is then run to produce a list of processes and the output is piped (|) to word count (**wc**) which produces a count of the number of lines.

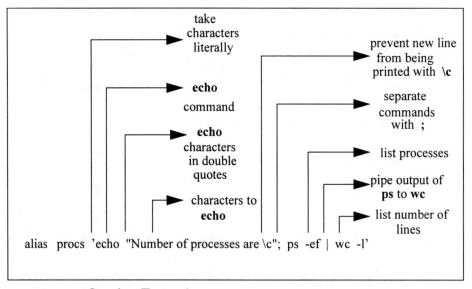

Figure 7-10 Quoting Example

As you can see in Figure 7-10, some of the quoting becomes tricky. An understanding of quoting is important if you wish to modify and reuse existing shell scripts or craft your own. A few other aliases you may want to try out are

```
alias psf 'ps -ef | more'
alias psg 'ps -ef | grep -i'
alias lsf 'lsf -aq'
```

The .login File

The **.login** file is read after the **.cshrc** file. There are only two issues related to setup present in the example shown. The first is the **tset** command which sets the **TERM** environment variable. The **eval** preceding **tset** means the C shell will execute **tset** and its arguments without creating a child process. This allows **tset** to set environment variables in the current shell instead of a subshell which would be useless. The **stty** command is used to set terminal I/O options. The two set commands are used to define shell variables which I'll describe shortly. The **noclobber** does not permit redirection to write over an existing file. If you try to write over an existing file, such as **/tmp/processes** below, you will receive a message that the file exists:

```
sys1   1:  ps  -ef  > /tmp/processes
            /tmp/processes:  File exists
```

The " > " means to take the output of **ps** and rather than write it to your screen, it will be written to **/tmp/processes**. The file **/tmp/processes** will not be written over, however, with the output of **ps -ef** because **/tmp/processes** already exists and an environment variable called **noclobber** has been set. If **noclobber** is set, then redirecting output to this file will not take place. This is a useful technique for preventing existing files from being accidently overwritten. There are many forms of redirection that you'll find useful. Table 7-5 shows some commonly used forms of redirection.

TABLE 7-5   COMMONLY USED REDIRECTION FORMS

Command	Example	Description
<	wc -l < .login	Standard input redirection: execute **wc** (word count) and list number of lines (**-l**) in **.login**
>	ps -ef > /tmp/processes	Standard output redirection: execute ps and send output to file **/tmp/processes**
>>	ps -ef >> /tmp/processes	Append standard output: execute **ps** and append output to the end of file **/tmp/processes**
>!	ps -ef >! /tmp/processes	Append output redirection and override **noclobber**: write over **/tmp/processes** even if it exists
>>!	ps -ef >>! /tmp/processes	Append standard output and override **noclobber**: append to the end of **/tmp/processes**

Shell and Environment Variables

You are indeed special to your HP-UX system. Information about your user environment in the C shell is stored in shell variables and environment variables. You can view shell variables with the **set** command and environment variables with the **env** command as shown below.

```
sys1 1:  set
argv          ()
autologout    60
cwd           /users/cshtest
history       20
home          /users/cshtest
path          (/bin /usr/bin)
prompt        sys1 !:
savehist      20
shell         /bin/csh
```

```
status      0
system      sys1
term        hpterm
user        cshtest
sys1        2


sys1  6:  env
DEMO_HOME=/demo7100
PATH=/bin/usr/bin
EDITOR=/usr/vue/bin/vuepad
LOGNAME=cshtest
MAIL=/usr/mail/cshtest
USER=cshtest
DISPLAY=sys1:0.0
SHELL=/bin/csh
HOME=/users/cshtest
TERM=hpterm
TZ=EST5EDT
PWD=/users/cshtest
WINDOWID=8388625
COMUMNS=81
LINES=37
sys1  7:
```

Shell variables are defined using **set**. We saw in the **.cshrc** file earlier that the **history** shell variable is set with

set history = 20

Environment variables are defined with **setenv** as shown below:

setenv EDITOR vi

Applications will often use environment variables for their operation.

File Name Expansion

Before we can cover shell programming it is worth taking a look at file name expansion. As the system administrator (or a system user manipulating files), you will surely be preparing shell scripts that deal with file names. An overview of file name expansion is useful to ensure you're comfortable with this topic before you start writing shell scripts.

Table 7-6 lists some common filename expansion and pattern matching.

TABLE 7-6   File Name Expansion and Pattern Matching

Character(s)	Example	Description
*	1) ls *.c	Match zero or more characters
?	2) ls conf.?	Match any single character
[list]	3) ls conf.[co]	Match any character in list
[lower-upper]	4) ls libdd.9873[5-6].sl	Match any character in range
str{str1,str2,str3,...}	5) ls ux*.{700,300}	Expand str with contents of {}
~	6) ls -a ~	Home directory
~username	7) ls -a ~gene	Home directory of username

The following descriptions of the examples shown in Table 7-6 are more detailed.

1. To list all files in a directory that end in ".c," you could do the following:

```
sys1 30:  ls *.c
          conf. SAM.c  conf.c
```

2. To find all of the files in a directory named "conf" with an extension of one character, you could do the following:

```
sys1 31:   ls conf.?
           conf.c  conf.o  conf.1
```

3. To list all of the files in a directory named "conf" with only the extension "c" or "o," you could do the following:

```
sys1 32:   ls conf.{co}
           conf.c  conf.o
```

4. To list files with similar names but a field that covers a range, you could do the following:

```
sys1 46:   ls libdd9873[5-6].sl
           libdd98735.sl  libdd98736.sl
```

5. To list files that start with "ux," and have the extension "300" or "700," you could do the following:

```
sys1 59:   ls ux*.{700,300}
           uxbootlf.700  uxinstfs.300  unistkern.300
           unistkern.700 unistlf.700
```

6. To list the files in your home directory you could use ~ :

```
sys1 62:   ls -a ~
           .              .cshrc.org  .login      .shrc.org
           ..             .exrc       .login.org  .vue
           .chsrc  .history      .profile    .vueprofile
```

7. To list the files in the home directory of a user you can do the following:

```
sys1 65:   ls -a ~gene
                       .history    .vue        splinedat
                       .login      .vueprofile trail.txt
           .chsrc      .login.org  ESP-File    under.des
           .cshrc.org  .profile    Mail        xtra.part
           .exrc       .shrc.org   opt
```

Many of these techniques are useful when writing shell scripts so it is a good idea to become familiar with file name expansion.

umask and Permissions

An additional topic to cover before shell programming techniques is file permissions and the way they relate to **umask**. This is important because you will write some shell programs anyone can use and others that you will want only a limited number of users, possibly just the system administrator, to use. **umask** is used to specify permission settings for new files and directories.

Let's start with an example of a long listing of a file:

```
sys1 1: ll script1
-rwxr-xr-x  1  marty  users  120 Jul 26 10:20 script1
```

The access rights for this file are defined by the position of read (r), write (w), and execute (x) when the **ll** command is issued. Figure 7-11 shows the three groups of three access rights for this file.

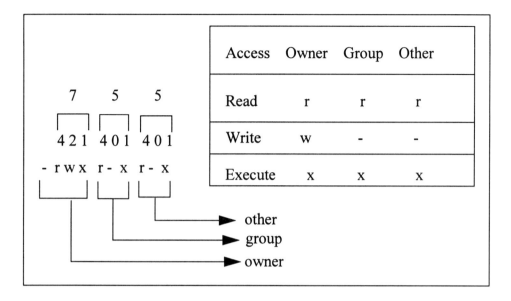

Figure 7-11 Example of File Permissions

The owner of this file has read, write, and execute permissions on the file. The group to which the user belongs has read and execute permissions, and others also have read and execute permissions. The permissions on this file can be specified by the octal sum of each field which is 755.

What happens if you craft a new shell script or any new file? What permission settings will exist? You will want to execute the shell script so you will need execute permission for the file. You can use **umask** to define the defaults for all your new files and directories.

You can view your umask with the following command:

```
sys1 2: umask
```

You can set the **umask** in **.cshrc** to define permission settings for new files and directories. The **umask** is used to *disable* access. You start with a **umask** and use the fields to disable some level of access. The **umask** command uses three octal fields. The fields are the sum of the access codes for user, group, and other as shown in Figure 7-12.

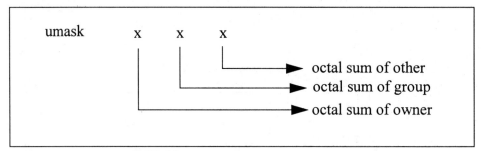

Figure 7-12   **umask** Fields

The *complement* of the umask field is "*anded*" with the default setting to change the **umask**. If you wanted to remove write permissions of files in Figure 7-13 for "group" and "other," you would assign a **umask** of 022 as shown.

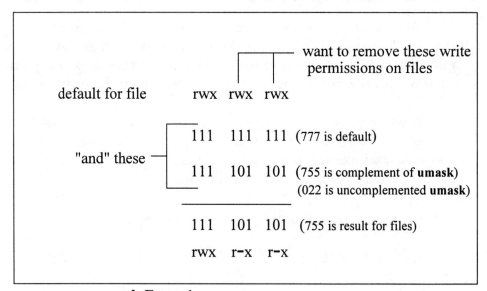

Figure 7-13   **umask** Example

umask 022 changes the file permissions to 755 in this example.

If you create a new file (**script2**) for your shell script you may need to make it executable with the **chmod** command. If a file has permissions of 666 (rw-rw-rw-) and you wish to give the owner execute permission, you would issue the following command:

```
sys1 3: chmod 766 script2
```

C Shell Programming

Now that I have covered many of the basics of the C shell, I'll go into some techniques that can be used to write shell programs. I'll cover each shell programming technique briefly and use basic examples to help reinforce each technique. Eventually I'll provide some sophisticated shell programs which you can modify and build on to meet your specific requirements. In all of the following shell programs any line beginning with a "#" is a comment. This is true except for the very first line of a shell program in which the shell the script is written for is executed. In all of the following programs the C shell is executed with **#!/bin/csh**.

Command Substitution

The shell variables earlier covered can be used to save the output from a command. You can then use these variables when issuing other commands. The following shell program executes the **date** command and saves the results in the variable **d**. The variable **d** is then used within the **echo** command:

```
# program "today" which provides the date
set d `date +%x`
echo "Today's date is $d"
```

When we run **today** the following is produced:

```
sys1 1: today
        Today's date is 02/15/95
```

The " + %x" in the above example produces the current date. Command substitution of this type is used in several upcoming shell scripts.

Reading User Input

There are two commonly used ways to read user input to shell programs. The first is to prompt the user for information and the second is to provide arguments to shell programs.

To begin I'll cover prompting a user for information. Either a character, word, or sentence can be read into a variable. The following example first shows prompting the user for a word, and then a sentence:

```
#!/bin/csh
echo "Please inter your name: \c"
set name = $<
echo "hello, $name"
echo "Please enter your favorite quote: \c"
set quote = $<
echo "Your favorite quote is:"
echo $quote
```

Here is a example of running this program:

```
sys1 1: userinput
        Please enter your name: marty
        Hello, marty
        Please enter your favorite quote: Creating is
        the essence of life.
        Your favorite quote is:
        Creating is the essence of life.
```

Using this technique you can prompt a user for information in a shell program. This technique will be used in an upcoming program.

You can also enter command line arguments. When you type the name of the shell script, you can supply arguments that are saved in the variables **$1** through **$9**. The first ten words on the command line are directly accessible in the shell program using the special variables **$0-$9**. This is how they work:

$0	The command name
$1	The first argument
$2	The second argument
$3	.
	.
	.
$9	The ninth argument

If you are not sure how many command line arguments you may get when your program is run, there are two other variables that can help:

$#	The number of command line arguments
$*	A space-separated list of all of the command line arguments (which does *not* include the command name).

The variable **$*** is commonly used with **for** loop (soon to be explained) to process shell script command lines with any number of arguments.

The following script changes to the specified directory (**$1**) and searches for the specified pattern (**$2**) in the specified file (**$3**):

```
#!/bin/csh
# search
# Usage: search directory pattern file
        echo " "
        cd $1# change to search dir and
        grep -n "$2" $3# search for $2 in $3
```

```
            echo " " # print line
endif
```

grep is used to search a file for a pattern and print the line in which the pattern was found. **awk** (which will be used later) can be used to pick out a specific field within a line.

Here is an example run of the **search** program.

```
sys1 1: search  /users/cshtest  path  .login

        7:# Set up the default search paths:
        8:set path=(/bin /usr/bin /usr/contrib/bin
           /usr/local/bin)
```

Testing and Branching

There are many kinds of decision making your shell programs can per-form. **if** provides the flexibility to make decisions and take the appropri-ate action. Let's expand the search script to verify that the minimum number of arguments (3) is provided.

```
#!/bin/csh
# search
# Usage: search directory pattern files

if ($#argv < 3) then          # if < 3 args provided

    echo "Usage: search directory pattern files"
                              # then print Usage
else
    echo " "                  # else print line and
    cd $1                     # change to search dir and
    grep -n "$2" $3           # search for $2 in $3
    echo " "                  # print line
endif
```

Here are four commonly used forms of **if**:

1)   if (expression) command

2)   if (expression) then
                              command(s)
                        endif

3)   if (expression) then
                              command(s)
                          else
                              command(s)
                        endif

4)   if (expression) then
                              command(s)
                        [else if expression) then
                              command(s)]

                        .
                        .
                        .

                    [else
                              command(s)]
                        endif

There are many operators that can be used in the C shell to compare integer values, such as the < used in the previous example. Here is a list of operators:

>	greater than
<	less than
>=	greater than or equal to
<=	less than or equal to
==	equal to
!=	not equal to

Looping

The C shell supports a number of techniques to support looping including:

   1) The **foreach** loop which takes a list of items and performs the commands in the loop once for each item in the list.

   2) The **while** loop which executes a command (such as the **test** command) if the command executes successfully.

   The format of the **foreach** loop is

```
foreach name (list)
          command(s)
end
```

   The following example uses a **foreach** loop to test whether or not the systems in the **/etc/hosts** file are connected to the local host.

```
#!/bin/csh
#Program name: csh_hostck

#This program will test connectivity to all other hosts in
#your network listed in your /etc/hosts file.

# It uses the awk command to get the names from the hosts file
#and the ping command to check connectivity.

#Note that we use /bin/echo because csh echo doesn't support
#escape chars like \t or \c which are used in  the  #foreach
#loop.

#Any line in /etc/hosts that starts with a number represents
#a host entry. Anything else is a comment or a blank line.

#Find all lines in /etc/hosts that start with a number and
#print the second field (the hostname).

set hosts=`awk '/^[1-9]/ { print $2 }' /etc/hosts`
                 # grave on outside, single quote on inside

   /bin/echo "Remote host connection status:"
```

```
foreach sys ($hosts)
    /bin/echo "$sys - \c"
                    # send one 64 byte packet and look for
                    # the"1 packets received" message in
                    # the output that indicates success.

    ping $sys 64 1 | grep "1 packets received" > /dev/null
    if ( $status == 0 ) then
            echo "OK"
    else
            echo "DID NOT RESPOND"
    endif
end
```

The crazy looking line with **awk** is used to obtain the name of remote hosts from the **/etc/hosts** file. The **foreach** loop takes all of the items in the list (the hosts in this case) and checks the status of each.

You could use the **while** loop to execute commands for some number of iterations. The **while** loop is in the following format:

```
while (expression)
            command(s)
end
```

The following example executes the HP-UX 9.x version of **netstat**, prints out the heading once, and the status of lan0 nine times:

```
#!/bin/csh
# program to run netstat every at specified interval
# Usage: netcheck interval

set limit=9                 # set limit on number times
                            # to run netstat

echo " "
netstat -i | grep Name      # print netstat line with headings
set count=0
while ($count<$limit)        # if limit hasn't reached
                            # limit run netstat
        netstat -i | grep lan0
        sleep $1            # sleep for interval
                            # specified on command line
        @ count++           # increment limit
end
```

```
echo "count has reached $limit, run netcheck again to see lan0
status"
```

Here is an example run of the program:

```
sys1 1: netcheck 2
Name   Mtu  Network   Address Ipkts Ierrs Opkts Oerrs Coll
lan0*  1500 none      none    0     0     0     0     0
lan0*  1500 none      none    0     0     0     0     0
lan0*  1500 none      none    0     0     0     0     0
lan0*  1500 none      none    0     0     0     0     0
lan0*  1500 none      none    0     0     0     0     0
lan0*  1500 none      none    0     0     0     0     0
lan0*  1500 none      none    0     0     0     0     0
lan0*  1500 none      none    0     0     0     0     0
lan0*  1500 none      none    0     0     0     0     0
count has reached 9, run netcheck again to see lan0 status
```

This program increments the expression with

@ count+ +

If the expression is true, then the command(s) will execute. The @count+ + is an assignment operator in the form of

@ variable_name operator expression

In this case the variable is first assigned with " = " and is later auto incremented (+ +). There are a number of operations that can be performed on the variable as described in Table 7-7.

TABLE 7-7   Assignment Operators

Operation	Symbol	Example with count = 100	Result
store value	=	@count=100	100
auto increment	++	@count++	101

Operation	Symbol	Example with count = 100	Result
auto decrement	--	@count--	99
add value	+=	@count+=50	150
subtract value	-=	@count-=50	50
multiply by value	*=	@count*=2	200
divide by value	/=	@count/2	50

There are also comparison operators, such as the " < " used in the example, as well as arithmetic, bitwise, and logical operators. As you craft more and more shell scripts, you will want to use all of these operators.

There are a set of test conditions related to files that are useful when writing shell scripts that use files. Using the format - **operator filename** you can use the tests in Table 7-8.

TABLE 7-8   Operator Filename Tests

Operator	Meaning
r	read access
w	write access
x	execute access
o	ownership
z	zero length
f	file, not a directory
d	directory, not a file

The following program (**filetest**) uses these operators to test the file **.login**. Since **.login** is not executable, of zero length, or a directory, I would expect **filetest** to find these false.

Here is long listing of **.login**:

```
sys1 1:  ll .login
-rw-r--r-- 1 cshtest  users 382 Nov 30 18:24 .login
```

Here is a listing of the shell script **filetest**:

```
#  Program to test file $1

if (-e $1) then
    echo "$1 exists"
    else
    echo "$1 does not exist"
endif

if (-z $1) then
    echo "$1 is zero length"
    else
    echo "$1 is not zero length"
endif

if (-f $1) then
    echo "$1 is a file"
    else
    echo "$1 is not a file"
endif

if (-d $1) then
    echo "$1 is a directory"
    else
    echo "$1 is not a directory"
endif

if (-o $1) then
    echo "you own $1 "
    else
```

```
            echo "you don't own $1 "
endif

if (-r $1) then
      echo "$1 is readable"
      else
      echo "$1 is not readable"
endif

if (-w $1) then
      echo "$1 is writable"
      else
      echo "$1 is not writable"
endif

if (-x $1) then
      echo "$1 is executable"
      else
      echo "$1 is not executable"
endif
```

Here is the output of filetest using **.login** as input:

```
sys1 2: filetest .login
      .login exists
      .login is not of zero length
      .login is a file
      .login is not a directory
      you own .login
      .login is readable
      .login is writable
      .login is not executable
```

Decision Making with switch

You can use **switch** to make decisions within a shell program. You can use **switch** to test command line arguments or interactive input to shell programs (as in the upcoming example). If, for example, you wanted to create a menu in a shell program and you needed to determine which option a user selected when running this shell program, you could use **switch**.

The syntax of switch looks like the following:

switch (pattern_to_match)

       case pattern1
           commands
           breaksw

       case pattern2
           commands
           breaksw

       case pattern 3
           commands
           breaksw

      default
           commands
           breaksw

endsw

pattern_to_match is the user input that you are testing and if it is equal to **pattern1,** then the commands under **pattern1** are executed. If **pattern_to_match** and **pattern2** are the same, then the commands under **pattern2** will be executed, and so on. If there is no match between **pattern_to_match** and one of the case statement patterns, then the default is executed. The following example uses **switch**.

```
#!/bin/csh
# Program pickscript to run some of
# the C shell scripts we've created
# Usage: pickscript
```

```
echo " ------------------------------------------"
echo "              Sys Admin Menu              "
echo "------------------------------------------"
echo " "
echo " 1           netcheck for network interface  "
echo " "
echo " 2           hostck to check connection   "
echo "             to hosts in /etc/hosts        "
echo " "
echo " ------------------------------------------"
echo " "
echo " Please enter your selection -> \c"

set pick = $<      # read input which is number of script
echo " "
switch ($pick)     # and assign to variable pick

    case 1          # if 1 was selected execute this
        $HOME/cshscripts/netcheck 5
        breaksw

    case 2          # if 2 was selected execute this
        $HOME/cshscripts/hostck
        breaksw
    default
        echo "Please select 1 or 2 next time"
    breaksw

endsw
```

Debugging C Shell Programs

When you begin C shell programming, you'll probably make a lot of simple syntax-related errors. You can have the C shell check the syntax of your program without executing it using the **-n** option to **csh**. I also use the **-v** to option to produce a verbose output. This can sometimes lead to too much information so I start with -v and if there is too much feedback, I eliminate it.

The following example is the earlier **search** program expanded to include a check that three arguments have been provided. When checking to see that **$#argv** is equal to 3, I left off the left parentheses. Here is the listing of the program and a syntax check showing the error:

```
sys 1 1: cat search
#!/bin/csh
# search
# Usage: search directory pattern files

if ($#argv != 3 then        # if < 3 args provided
        echo "Usage: search directory pattern files"
                            # then print Usage
else
        echo " "            # else print line and
        cd $1               # change to search dir and
        grep -n "$2" $3     # search for $2 in $3
        echo " "            # print line
endif


sys 1 2: csh -nv search
        if ( $#argv != 3 then
        Too many ('s
```

The **csh -nv** has done a syntax check with verbose output. First the line in question is printed and then an error message that tells you what is wrong with the line. In this case it is clear that I have left off the left parenthesis.

After fixing the problem, I can run the program with the **-x** which causes all commands to be echoed immediately before execution. The following example shows a run of the search program:

```
sys1 1: csh -xv ./search cwd grep hostck

if ( $#argv != 3 ) then
if ( 3 != 3 ) then

echo " "
echo

cd $1
cd cwd
~/cshscripts
grep -n "$2" $3
grep -n grep hostck
22:/etc/ping $sys 64 1 | grep "1 packets received" >
    /dev/null
echo " "
echo

endif
endif
```

You can follow what is taking place on a line by line basis. The line beginning with 22 is the line in the file **hostck** that has **grep** in it, that is, the output you would receive if the program had been run without the **-xv** options.

I would recommend performing the syntax check (**-n**) with a new shell program and then echo all commands with the **-x** option only if you get unexpected results when you run the program. The debugging options will surely help you at some point when you run into problems with the shell programs you craft.

How Long Does It Take?

You can use the **time** command to see a report of the amount of **time** your shell program takes to run. When you issue the time command you get a report in the format shown in Figure 7-14.

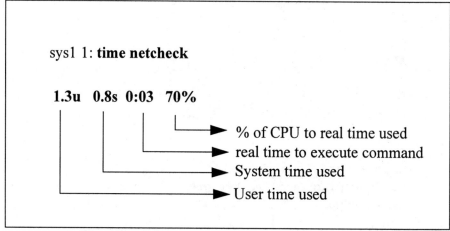

sys1 1: **time netcheck**

1.3u 0.8s 0:03 70%

→ % of CPU to real time used
→ real time to execute command
→ System time used
→ User time used

Figure 7-14 **time** Example

Because some of the scripts you write may consume a substantial amount of system resources, you may want to consider investigating some of the job control capabilities of the C shell. The simplest job control you can use is to run scripts in the background so the priority of the script is low. By issuing the script name followed by the **&,** you will run the script in the background. If you run several scripts in the background, you can get the status of these by issuing the **jobs** command. This is a more advanced C shell topic but depending on the level of complexity of scripts you write, you may want to look into job control.

CHAPTER 8

HP-UX System Auditing

What Should You Audit?

In this chapter I'm first going define the aspects of systems that I audit and then give some example scripts you can use as the basis for your own audit program. I have prefaced pretty much every system administration topic I've covered by saying "every installation is unique." Having given my standard disclaimer, let me list some areas to audit that apply to virtually every installation. You surely have others that are peculiar to your installation that should be included in an audit of your system(s).

Important Files The first thing any audit program should do is save the most important files on your system. You need to determine what files are important. When I cover this topic I give a listing of some important files you should consider saving on a regular basis.

Security   Who can shut down your HP-UX system? Who
                        has switched to superuser in the last 24 hours.
                        Have there been any failed attempts to login as
                        root in the last 24 hours? Are there old users in
                        the **/etc/password** file? Most system administra-
                        tors can't answer these questions (I know I can't
                        answer them about the system in my office).
                        There are simple security checks you can per-
                        form to answer these questions.

Logical Volume Review   One Logical Volume Manager change
                        can have a big impact on your system. I have
                        worked at installations that had several unused
                        disks on their system and the system administra-
                        tor didn't know it! An audit program should doc-
                        ument your existing Logical Volume Manager
                        configuration and perform some checks.

Performance   How is swap set up? If you put two swap sec-
                        tions on one disk, this will provide lower perfor-
                        mance. Have you run **sar**, **vmstat**, or **iostat**
                        recently? An audit should include a performance
                        snapshot.

Disk Usage   Who are the disk hogs on your system? There is
                        a command to help you quickly determine this.
                        You don't want old files, especially core files,
                        floating around your system. An audit program
                        should look for these.

Kernel   Was your HP-UX kernel built with your existing
                        /stand/system file? A different **system** file may
                        have been used. Can you use all of your hard-

ware? You may have hardware attached to your system for which you do not have a driver built into your kernel.

System Boot   Does your system boot smoothly? Run **dmesg** to see information produced at the last system boot.

System Crash   See if the directory exists where core files would be placed and if so, see if there are core files in it.

Printers   Get printer status. Should you encounter a system disaster it will be easier to rebuild your system printers configurations if you have documented your printers.

Patches   Report all patches currently installed on the system.

Networking   Run all networking commands to get a snapshot of what is configured.

These are all worthwhile areas to document and audit. Even if you do not find a single problem with your system, the audit will produce a document providing a snapshot of your system.

Let's take a closer look at some of these areas.

Important Files

In the event of a system catastrophe it would be helpful to have saved all of your important system files. Here is a listing of some files that I have copied from their original locations to **/tmp/IMPORTANT**:

```
-rw-------  1  root  syts     502  Apr  24  19:19  /tmp/IMPORTANT/PATCHES_ONLY

-rw-------  1  root  syts   52561  Apr  24  19:19  /tmp/IMPORTANT/archive.imp

-rw-------  1  root  syts   14317  Apr  24  19:19  /tmp/IMPORTANT/bootptab

-rw-------  1  root  syts    1617  Apr  24  19:19  /tmp/IMPORTANT/hosts

-rw-------  1  root  syts    3653  Apr  24  19:19  /tmp/IMPORTANT/inetd.conf

-rw-------  1  root  syts    1347  Apr  24  19:19  /tmp/IMPORTANT/inittab

-rw-------  1  root  syts    1462  Apr  24  19:19  /tmp/IMPORTANT/lvmrc

-rw-------  1  root  syts   59667  Apr  24  19:19  /tmp/IMPORTANT/lvdisplay.out

-rw-------  1  root  syts    2947  Apr  24  19:19  /tmp/IMPORTANT/netconf

-rw-------  1  root  syts    5707  Apr  24  19:19  /tmp/IMPORTANT/passwd

-rw-------  1  root  syts    2642  Apr  24  19:19  /tmp/IMPORTANT/profile

-rw-------  1  root  syts   75759  Apr  24  19:19  /tmp/IMPORTANT/rc.log

-rw-------  1  root  syts    7779  Apr  24  19:19  /tmp/IMPORTANT/services

-rw-------  1  root  syts     257  Apr  24  19:19  /tmp/IMPORTANT/syslog.conf

-rw-------  1  root  syts     615  Apr  24  19:19  /tmp/IMPORTANT/system

-rw-------  1  root  syts    4996  Apr  24  19:19  /tmp/IMPORTANT/vgdisplay.out

-rw-------  1  root  syts    2061  Apr  24  19:19  /tmp/IMPORTANT/vue

-rw-------  1  root  syts    2061  Apr  24  19:19  /tmp/IMPORTANT/cde
```

Some of these files, like **lvdisplay.out** and **vgdisplay.out**, contain a full listing of the logical volume information for this system. You never know when you will have to rebuild a volume group and having this information in a file can be handy. Notice also there are several files which contain patch-related information.

Security

Who can shut down system? The **/etc/shutdown.allow** file has in it a list of those who have permission to shut down a system. Verify only the users you want to shut down a system have entries in this file.

When has the system been shutdown and by whom is in **shutdown-log**. Part of **shutdownlog** with a panic is shown below:

```
16:58 Mon Feb  12,  1996.  Reboot:  (by system1!root)

21:49 Mon Feb  12,  1996.  Reboot:  (by system1!root)

16:46 Tue Feb  13,  1996.  Reboot after panic:  steven:
invalid relocation status

16:28 Sun Mar  24,  1996.  Reboot:  (by system1!root)

17:08 Thu Mar  28,  1996.  Reboot:  (by system1!root)
```

Very few users should be switching to superuser. You may have users that need to make system adjustments in a development environment. In a production environment, however, you should very seldom see a switch to superuser. The **/var/adm/sulog** file has in it all **su** commands issued. All of the following entries have switched from a user name to root.

```
SU 04/22 19:57 - ttyp2 mike-root

SU 04/22 19:57 - ttyp2 mike-root

SU 04/22 19:57 + ttyp2 mike-root

SU 04/23 11:00 + ttyu1 chang-root

SU 04/23 11:12 + ttyu2 denise-root
```

Review of bad login attempts in quick succession, or as root, can be viewed with the **lastb** command. The following example shows several bad login attempts as root.

```
root ttyp6    Tue Apr 16 13:00-13:00 (00:00)

root ttyp6    Tue Apr 16 13:01-13:01 (00:00)

root ttyp6    Tue Apr 16 13:01-13:01 (00:00)

root ttyp6    Tue Apr 16 13:02-13:02 (00:00)

root ttyp6    Tue Apr 16 13:02-13:02 (00:00)

root ttyp6    Tue Apr 16 13:03-13:03 (00:00)

root ttyp6    Tue Apr 16 13:03-13:03 (00:00)

                   .

                   .

                   .
```

Use **pwck** to check the **/etc/passwd** file looking for all types of problems. This command performs a sanity check on the **passwd** file that, although it is not a log file, is an important file that should be monitored closely. The following are two errors in the **passwd** file that were found by running the **pwck** command. The first is a user with a **passwd** entry but with no files on the system. The second is a user with an incorrect home directory name:

```
denise - Login name not found on system

jlance:Hhadsf4353hadsfae:110:20:Joe  Lance,,,:/net/sys1/net/
sys1/home/jlance:/usr/bin/sh
Login directory not found
```

Use **grpck** to check the **/etc/group** file looking for all types of problems.

This command performs a check of the **group** file which must also be carefully monitored. The following example shows a **group** entry in which there are no users present and a group which contains a user for which there is no entry in the **passwd** file:

```
database:10:
        No users in this group

development1:*:200:nadmin,charles,william
        william - Login name not found in password file
```

Logical Volume Review

Check integrity of the **/etc/lvmtab** file. One way of doing this is to compare **strings lvmtab** with **vgscan -v -p**. In the following example, the output of **strings lvmtab** is used as input to **vgscan** and this yields an unused volume group.

```
# vgscan -v -p

/dev/vgsys
/dev/dsk/c2d0s2
/dev/dsk/c3d0s2


/dev/vgtext
/dev/dsk/c4d0s2
```

```
/dev/dsk/c5d0s2


/dev/vgroot
/dev/dsk/c4d0s2
/dev/dsk/c7d0s2


The volume group /dev/vg00 was not matched with any
Physical Volumes.

Scan of the Physical Volumes complete.


# ll -d /dev/vg*


drwxrwxrwx  2 root     root    1024 Nov 7  1997 /dev/vg00
drwxrwxrwx  2 root     sys     1024 Jan 20 1997 /dev/vgroot
drwxrwxrwx  2 root     root    1024 Nov 7  1997 /dev/vgsys
drwxrwxrwx  2 root     root    1024 Nov 7  1997 /dev/vgtext
```

The command **ll /dev/vg*** shows four volume groups, only three of which are used. **/dev/vg00** exists but is not in use.

A common problem with a mirrored root volume is that the data is mirrored but there is no boot area on the mirror. This means if the primary root volume becomes unbootable then you won't be able to boot off the mirror. Identify boot lif areas with **lifls -Clv /dev/rdsk/***. You can also run the **lvlnboot** command to see all disks that are bootable. The following example shows a root disk (c0t6d0) as bootable as well as its mirror (c1t3d0).

```
# lvlnboot -v

Boot Definitions for Volume Group /dev/vg00:
Physical Volumes belonging in Root Volume Group:

        /dev/dsk/c0t6d0 (10/0.6.0)    -- Boot Disk
        /dev/dsk/c1t3d0 (10/4/4.3.0)  -- Boot Disk
```

.
.
.

I am surprised at the number of times that unused disks are found on a system. The following subroutine of an audit program identifies unused disks with the output of **ioscan** providing input to **pvdisplay**.

```
pvtest ()
{
for me in `ioscan -fkC disk | awk '{print $3}' `
do
     if [ "$me" != "H/W" ]
     then
     echo "\n$PROG>>>>> from ioscan -fkC , check PV info" | tee -a $DESTF
     diskn=`lssf /dev/dsk/* | grep $me | grep 'section 0' | awk '{print $16}'`
       echo "$PROG>>>>> the disk is $diskn" | tee -a $DESTF
       echo "$PROG>>>>> listing first 25 lines by: pvdisplay -v $diskn |\ head -25" |
tee -a $DESTF

     pvdisplay -v $diskn 2>&1 | head -25 | tee -a $DESTF
     fi
done
}
```

Here is the result for a disk that was not identified as part of a volume group:

```
pvdisplay: Couldn't query physical volume "/dev/dsk/c0d0s2":
```

The specified path does not correspond to a physical volume attached to any volume group. This means that the disk is physically attached to the system but is not in a volume group.

Performance

Performance is a discipline unto itself. You are not going to perform a detailed performance analysis as part of a system audit. You can get a snapshot of your system that you can later sit down and review, however, which may provide some interesting results.

As part of the audit you should run the following performance-related commands; **vmstat**, **iostat**, **uptime**, **sar -u** and **sar -b**. The following are examples of running **sar -u** and **sar -b**.

```
# sar -u 5 5


HP-UX system1 B.10.20 A 9000/819    12/24/96


19:08:02    %usr    %sys    %wio    %idle

19:08:07     1       2       1       96
19:08:12     1       1       0       99
19:08:17     0       1       0       99
19:08:22     1       1       0       98
19:08:27     0       1       0       99

Average      1       1       0       98

# sar -b 5 10


HP-UX system1 B.10.20 A 9000/819    12/24/96


19:08:27 bread/s lread/s %rcache bwrit/s lwrit/s %wcache pread/s pwrit/s

19:08:32     0      46     100      0       5     100      0       0
19:08:37     0      28     100      1       4      80      0       0
19:08:42     0      13     100      0       0       0      0       0
19:08:47     0       0       0      0       0       0      0       0
19:08:52     0      37     100      0       0       0      0       0
19:08:57     0       6     100      1       2      50      0       0
19:09:02     0      29     100      0       0       0      0       0
19:09:07     0      27     100      2       4      59      0       0
19:09:12     0      13     100      0       0       0      0       0
19:09:17     0       0       0      0       0       0      0       0

Average      0      20     100      0       2      77      0       0
```

An area that is often overlooked when it comes to performance is swap space. If swap is properly configured you can get much better performance out of it than if it is inefficiently configured.

Run **swapinfo -at** and **swapinfo -m**. Swap is sometimes added to systems in a random fashion. The following example shows two swap sections on **/dev/dsk/c0t6d0**, which is a bad practice:

```
# swapinfo -at

           Kb      Kb      Kb  PCT  START/      Kb
TYPE     AVAIL    USED    FREE USED  LIMIT RESERVE PRI   NAME        ( disk )

dev      512000    0     512000  0%     0     -    1   /dev/vg00/lvol2   c0t6d0

dev      274432    0     274432  0%     0     -    0   /dev/vg00/lvol8   c0t6d0

dev      262144    0     262144  0%     0     -    0   /dev/vg03/lvol20  c1t4d0

dev      524288    0     524288  0%     0     -    0   /dev/vg02/lvol21  c1t2d0
```

It is not a good practice to put two swap sections on the same disk as has been done with **c0t6d0** in this example. It is better is distribute the load among multiple disks and to have the sections the same size to enhance interleaving swap. This size should also be big enough to hold a core dump.

Disk and File System Information

The first thing you need to know about how your disks are being used is which users are consuming the most space. The following subroutine from an audit program uses the **diskusg** command to determine the disk hogs.

```
#!/usr/bin/ksh
# 1st print stats concerning the disk's file systems
echo "This program produces logical volume statistics and the amount of disk"
echo "space consumed by users on each logical volume. \n"
for fs in `bdf| grep '^/' | awk '{print $1}'`
do
fsys=`fstyp $fs`
echo "\n $printing logical volume stats for $fs using fstyp -v \n"
fstyp -v $fs 2>&1
if [ $fsys = vxfs ]
then
echo "\n finding space consumed per user for logical volume "
echo " $fs with vxdiskusg $fs \n"
/usr/sbin/acct/vxdiskusg $fs 2>&1 | tee -a $DESTF
else
# assume hfs type
echo "\n finding space consumed per user for logical volume "
echo " $fs with diskusg $fs \n"
echo "\nUserID login number of blocks "
echo "------ -------------------- \n"
        /usr/sbin/acct/diskusg $fs 2>&1
fi
done
```

Here is an example of finding hogs for filesystem **/dev/vg00/lvol6** mounted as **/usr**. In this example *mike* is consuming substantially more space than *jclairmo*.

diskusg /dev/vg00/lvol6

0	root	105254
1	daemon	304
2	bin	375704
5	uucp	882
9	lp	386
101	jclairmo	36
102	mike	43580

Use **find** to search for old and large files, core files, and so on. **find** can be used to uncover such information as large old files such as those greater than 1MB and older than 120 days as in the following example.

```
# find / \( -fsonly hfs -o -fsonly vxfs \) -a \( -atime +120 -a -size +1000000c \) -
print |    xargs -nl 11


-rw-------   1 jhowell  users     2150400 Nov  1 00:44 /home/jjersey/acrobat/READ.TAR
-rw-------   1 jhowell  users     3921920 Nov  1 00:44 /home/jjersey/acrobat/HPUXR.TAR
```

The following command can be used to find all core files on your system.

```
find / \( -fsonly hfs -o -fsonly vxfs \) -name core -exec what {} \ ;
```

Kernel, Boot, and Printer Information

This section could almost be called miscellaneous because it checks several different areas.

Run **ioscan -fk** to check the kernel. You may find errors such as hardware for which there is no driver installed as in the following example.

```
Class      I  H/W Path   Driver     S/W State H/W Type Description

=========================================================================


              .

              .

              .


disk       4  10/4/4.1.0  disc3     CLAIMED   DEVICE   HP C2490WD
unknown    -  9           ?         No_Driver

              .

              .

              .
```

The two lines left in this **ioscan** output shows that there is an "unknown" device at hardware path 9 for which there is no driver installed. Although you don't know what this is and it is probably not serious, this is the purpose of the audit program - to identify any potential problems on your system.

I very seldom watch a system boot yet there can be some revealing information produced at boot time. Running **dmesg** can show problems uncovered at boot such as the following message showing the **/var** logical volume as full.

```
/var
file: table is full
file: table is full
file: table is full
file: table is full
file: table is full
file: table is full
file: table is full
file: table is full
file: table is full
file: table is full
```

```
file: table is full
file: table is full
file: table is full
```

You can determine if the existing kernel was built with **/stand/sys-tem**. Run **system_prep -s** and compare it to **/stand/system**. The following routine performs this check.

```
#!/bin/ksh
DESTF="$home/audit.ker.out"
export DESTF
{
 /usr/lbin/sysadm/system_prep -s system.tmp
diffs=`diff system.tmp /stand/system`
if [ ! -z "$diffs" ]
then
echo "the system file is different: $diffs"
echo "/stand/vmunix WAS NOT built with /stand/system"
else
echo "/stand/vmunix was built with /stand/system"
fi
}
```

One area of your system that you might have a difficult time rebuilding is printer-related setup. Run the following commands and save the output for future reference.

lpstat -s
lpstat -d
lpstat -t

If you should encounter a system crash, **/var/adm/crash** is used to save the core dump to your file system. The following routine checks if this directory exists.

```
#!/usr/bin/ksh
echo "\n\n"
echo "The /var/adm/crash directory is needed by savecore in order to save the status"
echo "if a system crash occurs. The coredump can then be copied to a file and"
echo "sent to HP for analysis."
echo "See the savecore manual page to get more information about saving a core dump."

REMEMBERCORE=0
if [ -d /var/adm/crash ]
     then
                    echo "\n\t/var/adm/crash exists \c"
                    if [ -r /var/adm/crash/core.? ]
                    then
                    echo "and contains a dump."
                    echo "\n\tPlease copy the dump in /var/adm/crash to tape."
                    echo "\n\nHere is a listing of the core dump(s) on `hostname`. \n"
                    ll /var/adm/crash/core.?
                    REMEMBERCORE=1
     else
                    echo "and contains NO dump."
fi

else
                    echo "\n\n WARNING: /var/adm/crash did not exist."
                    echo " use mkdir -p /var/adm/crash "
fi
```

Patches

Whether or not the appropriate patches are on your system, you need to include an inventory of patches as part of the audit. Patches are difficult to keep up with but are essential to the proper operation of your system. The first few lines of each patch you have installed give a description of the patch including its number. A good audit program will read this information and save it in a file so you have this in the directory with your other important files.

Networking

System administrators spend a lot of time setting up networking. If you encountered a system disaster of some type, it would be helpful to have a section that thoroughly documented your networking setup. The following bullet items describe some of the more common areas of networking to check.

- See if your system is an NFS server and check **/etc/exports** for exported file systems.

- Check **syslog** for errors with the following command:

```
# grep err /var/adm/syslog/syslog.log
```

- Check rpc registration with

```
# rpcinfo -p
```

- Check your system information with DNS.

```
# nslookup $HOSTNAME
```

- Check for the existence of **/etc/resolv.conf** which would indicate that your system uses DNS.

```
# ll /etc/resolv.conf
```

- View lan devices with

```
# ll /dev/lan*
```

- Check LAN cards by running **lanscan** for all interfaces.

- Check kernel for LAN card configuration with

```
# ioscan -funC lan
```

- Show routes with

```
# netstat -r
```

- Check for SNA with

```
# snapshownet
```

- Check for uucp with

```
# /usr/lbin/uucp/uucheck -v
```

Auditing your system becomes increasingly more important as you make changes to it. The auditing I have covered in this section does not even address the applications you are running. Having a well-documented system and putting effort into reviewing the audit results will pay dividends in the long run. Fixing the small problems you find as a result of the audit may prevent much bigger problems down the road.

Some Example Scripts

You would ultimately like to have a full audit program that you could run on all of your HP-UX systems on a regular basis. The topics I have suggested in this chapter are a good place to start. You may also have additional aspects of your systems that should also be audited periodically.

The following sections contain several short scripts that could be run to get a feel for the type of output you could produce with your audit script. Many such short scripts could then be combined to produce a larger, more comprehensive audit program. The short scripts you craft could be used as subroutines called by a main program.

The following sections show example scripts and the result of having run the scripts. The earlier discussions in this chapter cover the topics of auditing your system so I do not include much additional explanation in the upcoming sections.

Kernel

The following script, called **audker.sh**, determines if the existing kernel was built with **/stand/system**. The program runs **system_prep -s** and compares it to the file **/stand/system**.

```ksh
#!/bin/ksh
DESTF="$home/audit.ker.out"
export DESTF
{
 /usr/lbin/sysadm/system_prep -s system.tmp
diffs=`diff system.tmp /stand/system`
if [ ! -z "$diffs" ]
then
echo "the system file is different: $diffs"
echo "/stand/vmunix WAS NOT built with /stand/system"
else
echo "/stand/vmunix was built with /stand/system"
fi
}
```

The following output was received from having run **audker.sh**.

```
# audker.sh

the system file is different: 51a52
> spt0
/stand/vmunix WAS NOT built with /stand/system
```

This output indicates that the original **system** file is different than the **system** file just generated from the currently running kernel. The following listings show both **system** files. The first listing is the original **system** file that includes the *spt0* driver.

The second listing does not include the *spt0* driver which means it is not part of the current HP-UX kernel.

First listing: original system file

```
* Drivers and Subsystems

CentIf
CharDrv
asp
c720
ccio
cdfs
cio_ca0
clone
core
diag0
diag2
disc3
dlpi
dmem
echo
ffs
hpstreams
inet
inet_clts
inet_cots
klog
lan2
lasi
ldterm
lv
lvm
mux2
netdiag1
netman
nfs
ni
pa
pckt
pfail
pipedev
pipemod
ps2
ptem
ptm
pts
sad
sc
scsi1
scsi2
scsi3
sctl
sdisk
sio
spt
spt0                        <---- spt0 driver in old system file
stape
strlog
strpty_included
tape2
```

```
tape2_included
target
timod
tirdwr
tpiso
uipc
vxbase
wsio


* Kernel Device info

dump lvol


* Tunable parameters

dbc_max_pct       10
dbc_min_pct       10
maxswapchunks     1024
maxuprc           100
maxusers          250
msgmax            32768
msgmnb            32768
msgmni            100
msgseg            7168
msgtql            256
nfile             (24*(NPROC+16+MAXUSERS)/10+32+2*(NPTY+NSTRPTY))
npty              250
nstrpty           60
semmni            96
semmns            192
swapmem_on        0
```

Second listing: new system file

```
* Drivers and Subsystems

CentIf
CharDrv
asp
c720
ccio
cdfs
cio_ca0
clone
core
diag0
diag2
disc3
dlpi
dmem
echo
ffs
hpstreams
inet
inet_clts
inet_cots
klog
lan2
lasi
```

```
ldterm
lv
lvm
mux2
netdiag1
netman
nfs
ni
pa
pckt
pfail
pipedev
pipemod
ps2
ptem
ptm
pts
sad
sc
scsi1
scsi2
scsi3
sctl
sdisk
sio
spt                              <--- spt0 driver not in current kernel
stape
strlog
strpty_included
tape2
tape2_included
target
timod
tirdwr
tpiso
uipc
vxbase
wsio


* Kernel Device info

dump lvol


* Tunable parameters

dbc_max_pct      10
dbc_min_pct      10
maxswapchunks    1024
maxuprc          100
maxusers         250
msgmax           32768
msgmnb           32768
msgmni           100
msgseg           7168
msgtql           256
nfile            (24*(NPROC+16+MAXUSERS)/10+32+2*(NPTY+NSTRPTY))
npty             250
nstrpty          60
semmni           96
semmns           192
swapmem_on       0
```

Disk Information

The following script, called **auddisk.sh,** lists all disks on the system and then provides a detailed description of each disk.

```
#!/bin/ksh

{
echo "The following is a description of disks by ioscan -fkC disk\n"
ioscan -fkC disk
echo "\n\n"
echo "The following is a detailed description of the disks earlier"
        echo "identified by ioscan."

echo "\n\nHardware disk information:\n"
for DEV in `ioscan -funC disk | awk '{print $2}' | \
              grep '\/dev\/rdsk'`
do
IS_THERE=$(/etc/diskinfo $DEV 2>&1)
                     if [ ${IS_THERE%% *} != "diskinfo:" ]
                         then
                                    /etc/diskinfo -v $DEV 2>&1
                    fi
echo "   - - - - - - - - - - - - - -"
echo ""
done
        }
```

The following output was received from running **auddisk.sh.**

auddisk.sh

The following is a description of disks by ioscan -fkC disk

Class	I	H/W Path	Driver	S/W State	H/W Type	Description	
disk	3	10/0.1.0	sdisk	CLAIMED	DEVICE	SEAGATE	ST32550W
disk	4	10/0.2.0	sdisk	CLAIMED	DEVICE	HP	C2490WD
disk	0	10/0.5.0	sdisk	CLAIMED	DEVICE	SEAGATE	ST32550W
disk	1	10/0.6.0	sdisk	CLAIMED	DEVICE	SEAGATE	ST32550W
disk	9	10/4/12.5.0	disc3	CLAIMED	DEVICE	DGC	C2300WDR5
disk	10	10/4/12.5.1	disc3	CLAIMED	DEVICE	DGC	C2300WDR5
disk	11	10/4/12.6.0	disc3	CLAIMED	DEVICE	DGC	C2300WDR5
disk	12	10/4/12.6.1	disc3	CLAIMED	DEVICE	DGC	C2300WDR5
disk	13	10/8.0.0	sdisk	CLAIMED	DEVICE	HP	C3586A
disk	14	10/8.0.1	sdisk	CLAIMED	DEVICE	HP	C3586A
disk	15	10/8.1.0	sdisk	CLAIMED	DEVICE	HP	C3586A
disk	16	10/8.1.1	sdisk	CLAIMED	DEVICE	HP	C3586A
disk	2	10/12/5.2.0	sdisk	CLAIMED	DEVICE	TOSHIBA	CD-ROM

The following is a detailed description of the disks earlier
identified by ioscan.

Hardware disk information:

SCSI describe of /dev/rdsk/c0t1d0:
               vendor: SEAGATE
           product id: ST32550W
                 type: direct access
                 size: 2082636 Kbytes
      bytes per sector: 512
            rev level: HP07
      blocks per disk: 4165272
          ISO version: 0
         ECMA version: 0
         ANSI version: 2
      removable media: no
      response format: 2
      (Additional inquiry bytes: (32)31 (33)34 (34)34 (35)37 (36)31 (37)30 (38)32
(39)0 (40)0 (41)0 (42)0 (43)0 (44)0 (45)0 (46)0 (47)0 (48)0 (49)0 (50)0 (51)0 (52)0
(53)0 (54)0 (55)0 (56)0 (57)0 (58)0 (59)0 (60)0 (61)0 (62)0 (63)0 (64)0 (65)0 (66)0
(67)0 (68)0 (69)0 (70)0 (71)0 (72)0 (73)0 (74)0 (75)0 (76)0 (77)0 (78)0 (79)0 (80)0
(81)0 (82)0 (83)0 (84)0 (85)0 (86)0 (87)0 (88)0 (89)0 (90)0 (91)0 (92)43 (93)6f (94)70
(95)79 (96)72 (97)69 (98)67 (99)68 (100)74 (101)20 (102)28 (103)63 (104)29 (105)20
(106)31 (107)39 (108)39 (109)35 (110)20 (111)53 (112)65 (113)61 (114)67 (115)61
(116)74 (117)65 (118)20 (119)41 (120)6c (121)6c (122)20 (123)0 (124)3f (125)8e (126)98
(127)0 (128)0 (129)2 (130)0 (131)0 (132)0 (133)0 (134)0 (135)0 (136)0 (137)0 (138)0
(139)0 (140)0 (141)0 (142)0)
      - - - - - - - - - - - - -

SCSI describe of /dev/rdsk/c0t2d0:
               vendor: HP
           product id: C2490WD
                 type: direct access
                 size: 2082636 Kbytes
      bytes per sector: 512
            rev level: 4250
      blocks per disk: 4165272
          ISO version: 0
         ECMA version: 0
         ANSI version: 2
      removable media: no
      response format: 2
      - - - - - - - - - - - - -

SCSI describe of /dev/rdsk/c0t5d0:
               vendor: SEAGATE
           product id: ST32550W
                 type: direct access
                 size: 2082636 Kbytes
      bytes per sector: 512
            rev level: HP06
      blocks per disk: 4165272
          ISO version: 0
         ECMA version: 0
         ANSI version: 2
      removable media: no
      response format: 2
      (Additional inquiry bytes: (32)30 (33)37 (34)32 (35)35 (36)30 (37)36 (38)30
(39)0 (40)0 (41)0 (42)0 (43)0 (44)0 (45)0 (46)0 (47)0 (48)0 (49)0 (50)0 (51)0 (52)0
(53)0 (54)0 (55)0 (56)0 (57)0 (58)0 (59)0 (60)0 (61)0 (62)0 (63)0 (64)0 (65)0 (66)0
(67)0 (68)0 (69)0 (70)0 (71)0 (72)0 (73)0 (74)0 (75)0 (76)0 (77)0 (78)0 (79)0 (80)0
(81)0 (82)0 (83)0 (84)0 (85)0 (86)0 (87)0 (88)0 (89)0 (90)0 (91)0 (92)43 (93)6f (94)70
(95)79 (96)72 (97)69 (98)67 (99)68 (100)74 (101)20 (102)28 (103)63 (104)29 (105)20

```
(106)31   (107)39   (108)39   (109)35   (110)20   (111)53   (112)65   (113)61   (114)67   (115)61
(116)74   (117)65   (118)20   (119)41   (120)6c   (121)6c   (122)20   (123)0   (124)3f   (125)8e   (126)98
(127)0   (128)0   (129)2   (130)0   (131)0   (132)0   (133)0   (134)0   (135)0   (136)0   (137)0   (138)0
(139)0   (140)0   (141)0   (142)0 )
        - - - - - - - - - - - - - -

        SCSI describe of /dev/rdsk/c0t6d0:
                vendor: SEAGATE
            product id: ST32550W
                  type: direct access
                  size: 2082636 Kbytes
      bytes per sector: 512
             rev level: HP06
        blocks per disk: 4165272
           ISO version: 0
          ECMA version: 0
          ANSI version: 2
        removable media: no
        response format: 2
        (Additional inquiry bytes: (32)31   (33)34   (34)33   (35)33   (36)38   (37)37   (38)32
(39)0   (40)0   (41)0   (42)0   (43)0   (44)0   (45)0   (46)0   (47)0   (48)0   (49)0   (50)0   (51)0   (52)0
(53)0   (54)0   (55)0   (56)0   (57)0   (58)0   (59)0   (60)0   (61)0   (62)0   (63)0   (64)0   (65)0   (66)0
(67)0   (68)0   (69)0   (70)0   (71)0   (72)0   (73)0   (74)0   (75)0   (76)0   (77)0   (78)0   (79)0   (80)0
(81)0   (82)0   (83)0   (84)0   (85)0   (86)0   (87)0   (88)0   (89)0   (90)0   (91)0   (92)43   (93)6f   (94)70
(95)79   (96)72   (97)69   (98)67   (99)68   (100)74   (101)20   (102)28   (103)63   (104)29   (105)20
(106)31   (107)39   (108)39   (109)35   (110)20   (111)53   (112)65   (113)61   (114)67   (115)61
(116)74   (117)65   (118)20   (119)41   (120)6c   (121)6c   (122)20   (123)0   (124)3f   (125)8e   (126)98
(127)0   (128)0   (129)2   (130)0   (131)0   (132)0   (133)0   (134)0   (135)0   (136)0   (137)0   (138)0
(139)0   (140)0   (141)0   (142)0 )
        - - - - - - - - - - - - - -

        SCSI describe of /dev/rdsk/c4t5d0:
                vendor: DGC
            product id: C2300WDR5
                  type: direct access
                  size: 8146176 Kbytes
      bytes per sector: 512
             rev level: HP02
        blocks per disk: 16292352
           ISO version: 0
          ECMA version: 0
          ANSI version: 2
        removable media: no
        response format: 2
        (Additional inquiry bytes: (32)41   (33)55   (34)4e   (35)41   (36)20   (37)43   (38)4f
(39)4e   (40)54   (41)52   (42)4f   (43)4c   (44)4c   (45)45   (46)52   (47)20   (48)20   (49)20   (50)20
(51)0   (52)0   (53)0   (54)0   (55)0   (56)0   (57)0   (58)0   (59)0   (60)0   (61)0   (62)0   (63)0   (64)0
(65)0   (66)0   (67)0   (68)0   (69)0   (70)0   (71)0   (72)0   (73)0   (74)0   (75)0   (76)0   (77)0   (78)0
(79)0   (80)0   (81)0   (82)0   (83)0   (84)0   (85)0   (86)0   (87)0   (88)0   (89)0   (90)0   (91)2   (92)1
(93)6   (94)0   (95)39   (96)34   (97)2d   (98)33   (99)31   (100)36   (101)35   (102)2d   (103)31   (104)31
(105)30   (106)0   (107)a   (108)f5   (109)17   (110)0   (111)35   (112)7   (113)10   (114)0   (115)0
(116)0   (117)0   (118)0   (119)0   (120)0   (121)0   (122)0 )
        - - - - - - - - - - - - - -

        SCSI describe of /dev/rdsk/c4t5d1:
                vendor: DGC
            product id: C2300WDR5
                  type: direct access
                  size: 8146176 Kbytes
      bytes per sector: 512
             rev level: HP02
        blocks per disk: 16292352
           ISO version: 0
          ECMA version: 0
          ANSI version: 2
        removable media: no
```

```
                response format: 2
                (Additional inquiry bytes: (32)41 (33)55 (34)4e (35)41 (36)20 (37)43 (38)4f
(39)4e (40)54 (41)52 (42)4f (43)4c (44)4c (45)45 (46)52 (47)20 (48)20 (49)20 (50)20
(51)0 (52)0 (53)0 (54)0 (55)0 (56)0 (57)0 (58)0 (59)0 (60)0 (61)0 (62)0 (63)0 (64)0
(65)0 (66)0 (67)0 (68)0 (69)0 (70)0 (71)0 (72)0 (73)0 (74)0 (75)0 (76)0 (77)0 (78)0
(79)0 (80)0 (81)0 (82)0 (83)0 (84)0 (85)0 (86)0 (87)0 (88)0 (89)0 (90)0 (91)2 (92)1
(93)6 (94)0 (95)39 (96)34 (97)2d (98)33 (99)31 (100)36 (101)35 (102)2d (103)31 (104)31
(105)30 (106)0 (107)a (108)f5 (109)17 (110)0 (111)35 (112)7 (113)10 (114)0 (115)0
(116)0 (117)0 (118)0 (119)0 (120)0 (121)0 (122)0 )
                - - - - - - - - - - - - -

        SCSI describe of /dev/rdsk/c4t6d0:
                  vendor: DGC
              product id: C2300WDR5
                    type: direct access
                    size: 8146176 Kbytes
        bytes per sector: 512
               rev level: HP02
          blocks per disk: 16292352
             ISO version: 0
            ECMA version: 0
            ANSI version: 2
          removable media: no
          response format: 2
                (Additional inquiry bytes: (32)41 (33)55 (34)4e (35)41 (36)20 (37)43 (38)4f
(39)4e (40)54 (41)52 (42)4f (43)4c (44)4c (45)45 (46)52 (47)20 (48)20 (49)20 (50)20
(51)0 (52)0 (53)0 (54)0 (55)0 (56)0 (57)0 (58)0 (59)0 (60)0 (61)0 (62)0 (63)0 (64)0
(65)0 (66)0 (67)0 (68)0 (69)0 (70)0 (71)0 (72)0 (73)0 (74)0 (75)0 (76)0 (77)0 (78)0
(79)0 (80)0 (81)0 (82)0 (83)0 (84)0 (85)0 (86)0 (87)0 (88)0 (89)0 (90)0 (91)1 (92)0
(93)5 (94)0 (95)39 (96)34 (97)2d (98)33 (99)31 (100)36 (101)35 (102)2d (103)31 (104)31
(105)30 (106)0 (107)35 (108)7 (109)10 (110)0 (111)a (112)f5 (113)17 (114)0 (115)0
(116)0 (117)0 (118)0 (119)0 (120)0 (121)0 (122)0 )
                - - - - - - - - - - - - -

        SCSI describe of /dev/rdsk/c4t6d1:
                  vendor: DGC
              product id: C2300WDR5
                    type: direct access
                    size: 8146176 Kbytes
        bytes per sector: 512
               rev level: HP02
          blocks per disk: 16292352
             ISO version: 0
            ECMA version: 0
            ANSI version: 2
          removable media: no
          response format: 2
                (Additional inquiry bytes: (32)41 (33)55 (34)4e (35)41 (36)20 (37)43 (38)4f
(39)4e (40)54 (41)52 (42)4f (43)4c (44)4c (45)45 (46)52 (47)20 (48)20 (49)20 (50)20
(51)0 (52)0 (53)0 (54)0 (55)0 (56)0 (57)0 (58)0 (59)0 (60)0 (61)0 (62)0 (63)0 (64)0
(65)0 (66)0 (67)0 (68)0 (69)0 (70)0 (71)0 (72)0 (73)0 (74)0 (75)0 (76)0 (77)0 (78)0
(79)0 (80)0 (81)0 (82)0 (83)0 (84)0 (85)0 (86)0 (87)0 (88)0 (89)0 (90)0 (91)1 (92)0
(93)5 (94)0 (95)39 (96)34 (97)2d (98)33 (99)31 (100)36 (101)35 (102)2d (103)31 (104)31
(105)30 (106)0 (107)35 (108)7 (109)10 (110)0 (111)a (112)f5 (113)17 (114)0 (115)0
(116)0 (117)0 (118)0 (119)0 (120)0 (121)0 (122)0 )
                - - - - - - - - - - - - -

        SCSI describe of /dev/rdsk/c5t0d0:
                  vendor: HP
              product id: C3586A
                    type: direct access
                    size: 2097152 Kbytes
        bytes per sector: 512
               rev level: HP02
          blocks per disk: 4194304
             ISO version: 0
```

```
                        ECMA version: 0
                        ANSI version: 2
                     removable media: no
                     response format: 2
                 - - - - - - - - - - - - - -


        SCSI describe of /dev/rdsk/c5t0d1:
                              vendor: HP
                          product id: C3586A
                                type: direct access
                                size: 10485760 Kbytes
                    bytes per sector: 512
                           rev level: HP02
                      blocks per disk: 20971520
                         ISO version: 0
                        ECMA version: 0
                        ANSI version: 2
                     removable media: no
                     response format: 2
                 - - - - - - - - - - - - - -


        SCSI describe of /dev/rdsk/c5t1d0:
                              vendor: HP
                          product id: C3586A
                                type: direct access
                                size: 2097152 Kbytes
                    bytes per sector: 512
                           rev level: HP02
                      blocks per disk: 4194304
                         ISO version: 0
                        ECMA version: 0
                        ANSI version: 2
                     removable media: no
                     response format: 2
                 - - - - - - - - - - - - - -


        SCSI describe of /dev/rdsk/c5t1d1:
                              vendor: HP
                          product id: C3586A
                                type: direct access
                                size: 10485760 Kbytes
                    bytes per sector: 512
                           rev level: HP02
                      blocks per disk: 20971520
                         ISO version: 0
                        ECMA version: 0
                        ANSI version: 2
                     removable media: no
                     response format: 2
                 - - - - - - - - - - - - - -


        SCSI describe of /dev/rdsk/c1t2d0:
                              vendor: TOSHIBA
                          product id: CD-ROM XM-4101TA
                                type: CD-ROM
                                size: 347936 Kbytes
                    bytes per sector: 2048
                           rev level: 1084
                      blocks per disk: 173968
                         ISO version: 0
                        ECMA version: 0
                        ANSI version: 2
                     removable media: yes
                     response format: 2
                     (Additional inquiry bytes: (32)34 (33)2f (34)31 (35)38 (36)2f (37)39 (38)34
   (39)0 (40)0 (41)0 (42)0 (43)0 (44)0 (45)0 (46)0 (47)0 (48)0 (49)0 (50)0 (51)0 (52)0
```

```
(53)0  (54)0  (55)0  (56)0  (57)0  (58)0  (59)0  (60)0  (61)0  (62)0  (63)0  (64)0  (65)0  (66)0
(67)0  (68)0  (69)0  (70)0  (71)0  (72)0  (73)0  (74)0  (75)0  (76)0  (77)0  (78)0  (79)0  (80)0
(81)0  (82)0  (83)0  (84)0  (85)0  (86)0  (87)0  (88)0  (89)0  (90)0  )
         - - - - - - - - - - - - -
```

Logical Volume Summary

After viewing the physical disks connected to the system, it would be helpful to see some summary information on logical volumes including the physical disks to which the logical volumes have been assigned. The following script, called **audlvsum.sh**, provides a concise summary of the logical volumes on a system.

```
#!/usr/bin/ksh

USAGE="Usage: $0 [-d]"

VOLORDER='y'    #default - sort by logical volume
             #           n = sort by disk

while (( $# > 0 ))
do
  case "$1" in
    -d ) VOLORDER='n'
      ;;
    * ) echo unrecognized option: "$1"
        echo $USAGE
      exit 1
  ;;
  esac
  shift
done

if [ "$VOLORDER" = "y" ]    #determine sorting order based on cmdline option
then
  FINISH=sort
else
  FINISH=cat
fi

# width specifiers to make the output align better
#
# LVMINFO = LV + USE + 6
# DISKINFO = HW + ID + 8
#
typeset -L28 LVMINFO
typeset -L18 LV
typeset -L30 DISKINFO
typeset -L10 ID
typeset -L12 HW
typeset -R9  SZ
typeset -R4  USE FRE

ioscan -f|grep -e disk -e ext_bus|awk '{print $1" "$2" "$3}'|while read LINE
do set $LINE
  TY="$1"
```

```
if [ "$TY" = "ext_bus" ]
then
  C="$2"
else
  HW="$3"
  T="`echo $HW | cut -f 2 -d .`"
  D="`echo $HW | cut -f 3 -d .`"
  INFO="`diskinfo /dev/rdsk/c${C}t${T}d${D}`"
  ID=`echo $INFO | sed -e 's/^.*product id: //' -e 's/ .*$//'`
  PVD="`pvdisplay -v /dev/dsk/c${C}t${T}d${D} 2>&1|sed '/Physical ext/,$d'`"


  DISKINFO="HW $HW  ID $ID"
  if echo $PVD |grep "find the volume group" > /dev/null
  then
    SZ=`echo $INFO | sed -e 's/^.*size: //' -e 's/ .*$//'`
    LVMINFO="Non-LVM disk $SZ KB"
    DEVFILE=" /dev/rdsk/c${C}t${T}d${D}"
    echo "$LVMINFO$DISKINFO$DEVFILE"
    if [ "$VOLORDER" = "n" ]
    then
        echo
    fi
  else
    PE=`echo $PVD | sed -e 's/^.*PE Size[^0-9]*//' -e 's/ .*$//'`
    TOT=`echo $PVD | sed -e 's/^.*Total PE[^0-9]*//' -e 's/ .*$//'`
    FRE=`echo $PVD | sed -e 's/^.*Free PE[^0-9]*//' -e 's/ .*$//'`
    VG=`echo $PVD | sed -e 's/^.*VG Name *//' -e 's/ .*$//'`
    VG=`basename $VG`

    echo "$PVD" | sed '1,/^   LV Name/d' | while read LVINFO
    do
      set $LVINFO
      LV="$VG/`basename $1`"
      FULLLV="/dev/$VG/`basename $1`"   #Version without spaces
      USE="$3"
      LVMINFO="$LV${USE}x${PE}MB"
      SYSUSE=`sed 's/#.*//' < /etc/fstab |
                     grep "$FULLLV[     ]" | awk '{ print $2 }'`
      echo "$LVMINFO$DISKINFO$SYSUSE"
    done
    LV="$VG/UNUSED"
    LVMINFO="$LV${FRE}x${PE}MB"
    echo "$LVMINFO$DISKINFO"
    if [ "$VOLORDER" = "n" ]
    then
        echo
    fi
  fi
 fi
done | $FINISH
```

I redirected the output of this script to **audlvsum.out**, shown in the following listing. This output produces a lot of useful information including unused areas of physical volume groups.

```
Non-LVM disk      347936 KB   HW 10/12/5.2.0   ID CD-ROM     /dev/rdsk/c1t2d0
Non-LVM disk     2097152 KB   HW 10/8.1.0      ID C3586A     /dev/rdsk/c5t1d0
Non-LVM disk    10485760 KB   HW 10/8.1.1      ID C3586A     /dev/rdsk/c5t1d1
vg00/UNUSED         0x4MB     HW 10/0.5.0      ID ST32550W
vg00/UNUSED         0x4MB     HW 10/0.6.0      ID ST32550W
vg00/lvol1         12x4MB     HW 10/0.6.0      ID ST32550W   /stand
vg00/lvol2        128x4MB     HW 10/0.6.0      ID ST32550W
vg00/lvol3         25x4MB     HW 10/0.6.0      ID ST32550W   /
vg00/lvol4        256x4MB     HW 10/0.6.0      ID ST32550W   /opt
vg00/lvol5         50x4MB     HW 10/0.6.0      ID ST32550W   /tmp
vg00/lvol6         36x4MB     HW 10/0.6.0      ID ST32550W   /usr
vg00/lvol6        220x4MB     HW 10/0.5.0      ID ST32550W   /usr
vg00/lvol7        188x4MB     HW 10/0.5.0      ID ST32550W   /var
vg00/lvol8        100x4MB     HW 10/0.5.0      ID ST32550W   ...
vg01/UNUSED       256x4MB     HW 10/4/12.5.0   ID C2300WDR5
vg01/UNUSED       256x4MB     HW 10/4/12.6.0   ID C2300WDR5
vg01/UNUSED       327x4MB     HW 10/8.0.0      ID C3586A
vg01/add          125x4MB     HW 10/8.0.0      ID C3586A     /add
vg01/lvol10      1023x4MB     HW 10/4/12.5.0   ID C2300WDR5  /dev01
vg01/lvol10      1023x4MB     HW 10/4/12.6.0   ID C2300WDR5  /dev01
vg01/lvol12       256x4MB     HW 10/4/12.5.0   ID C2300WDR5  /mdd
vg01/lvol12       256x4MB     HW 10/4/12.6.0   ID C2300WDR5  /mdd
vg01/lvol14        59x4MB     HW 10/8.0.0      ID C3586A     /npscm
vg01/lvol14       453x4MB     HW 10/4/12.5.0   ID C2300WDR5  /npscm
vg01/lvol14       453x4MB     HW 10/4/12.6.0   ID C2300WDR5  /npscm
vg03/UNUSED        90x4MB     HW 10/4/12.5.1   ID C2300WDR5
vg03/UNUSED        90x4MB     HW 10/4/12.6.1   ID C2300WDR5
vg03/lvol11      1023x4MB     HW 10/4/12.5.1   ID C2300WDR5  /dev02
vg03/lvol11      1023x4MB     HW 10/4/12.6.1   ID C2300WDR5  /dev02
vg03/lvol31       375x4MB     HW 10/4/12.5.1   ID C2300WDR5  /ccur
vg03/lvol31       375x4MB     HW 10/4/12.6.1   ID C2300WDR5  /ccur
vg03/lvol41       500x4MB     HW 10/4/12.5.1   ID C2300WDR5  /usr/wind
vg03/lvol41       500x4MB     HW 10/4/12.6.1   ID C2300WDR5  /usr/wind
vg04/UNUSED         0x4MB     HW 10/0.1.0      ID ST32550W
vg04/UNUSED         0x4MB     HW 10/0.2.0      ID C2490WD
vg04/lvol1         25x4MB     HW 10/0.2.0      ID C2490WD    /OLDROOT
vg04/lvol2        125x4MB     HW 10/0.2.0      ID C2490WD
vg04/lvol4         88x4MB     HW 10/0.1.0      ID ST32550W   /OLDOPT
vg04/lvol4        125x4MB     HW 10/0.2.0      ID C2490WD    /OLDOPT
vg04/lvol5          6x4MB     HW 10/0.2.0      ID C2490WD    /OLDTMP
vg04/lvol5         19x4MB     HW 10/0.1.0      ID ST32550W   /OLDTMP
vg04/lvol6        215x4MB     HW 10/0.1.0      ID ST32550W   /OLDUSR
vg04/lvol7          2x4MB     HW 10/0.2.0      ID C2490WD    /OLDVAR
vg04/lvol7        186x4MB     HW 10/0.1.0      ID ST32550W   /OLDVAR
vg04/lvol8         67x4MB     HW 10/0.2.0      ID C2490WD
vg04/lvol9        157x4MB     HW 10/0.2.0      ID C2490WD
vg05/UNUSED         0x4MB     HW 10/8.0.1      ID C3586A
vg05/lvol10      2431x4MB     HW 10/8.0.1      ID C3586A     /home
vg05/lvol21       128x4MB     HW 10/8.0.1      ID C3586A     ...
```

Logical Volume Detail

The previous script provided a useful summary of logical volumes. The
next useful information to have would be detailed information on the logi-

cal volumes of the system. The following script, called **audlvdis.sh**, provides detailed information on the logical volumes connected to a system.

```ksh
#!/usr/bin/ksh
echo "a listing by: lvdisplay -v " >$ARCHDIR/lvdisplay_v.txt
for lv in `vgdisplay -v | grep 'LV Name' | awk '{print $3}'`
do
entry=`bdf | grep $lv`
if [ ! -z "$entry" ]
then
echo "\n$PROG>>>>> $lv IS mounted, line from bdf is:\n$entry"
else
echo "\n$PROG>>>>> $lv IS NOT mounted"
fi
echo "$PROG>>>>> documenting first 30 lines of lvm information \
by: lvdisplay -v $lv | head -30
echo "the logical volume is:$lv"
lvdisplay -v $lv | head -30
lvdisplay -v $lv >>$ARCHDIR/lvdisplay_v.txt
done
echo "PROG>>>>> archived by lvdisplay -v >$ARCHDIR/lvdisplay_v.txt"
```

I redirected the output of this script to **audlvdis.out**, shown in the following listing. Only the first few logical volumes are listed.

```
>>>>> /dev/vg00/lvol3 IS mounted, line from bdf is:
/dev/vg00/lvol3      99669   33110   56592   37% /
>>>>> documenting first 30 lines of lvm information by: lvdisplay -v /dev/vg00/
lvol3 | head -30
        the logical volume is:/dev/vg00/lvol3
        --- Logical volumes ---
        LV Name                     /dev/vg00/lvol3
        VG Name                     /dev/vg00
        LV Permission               read/write
        LV Status                   available/syncd
        Mirror copies               0
        Consistency Recovery        MWC
        Schedule                    parallel
        LV Size (Mbytes)            100
        Current LE                  25
        Allocated PE                25
        Stripes                     0
        Stripe Size (Kbytes)        0
        Bad block                   off
        Allocation                  strict/contiguous

        --- Distribution of logical volume ---
        PV Name             LE on PV  PE on PV
        /dev/dsk/c0t6d0     25        25

        --- Logical extents ---
        LE    PV1                   PE1  Status 1
        0000  /dev/dsk/c0t6d0       0140 current
        0001  /dev/dsk/c0t6d0       0141 current
```

```
          0002 /dev/dsk/c0t6d0    0142 current
          0003 /dev/dsk/c0t6d0    0143 current
          0004 /dev/dsk/c0t6d0    0144 current
          0005 /dev/dsk/c0t6d0    0145 current
          0006 /dev/dsk/c0t6d0    0146 current
          0007 /dev/dsk/c0t6d0    0147 current

     >>>>> /dev/vg00/lvol2 IS NOT mounted
     >>>>> documenting first 30 lines of lvm information by: lvdisplay -v /dev/vg00/
lvol2 | head -30
     the logical volume is:/dev/vg00/lvol2
     --- Logical volumes ---
     LV Name                     /dev/vg00/lvol2
     VG Name                     /dev/vg00
     LV Permission               read/write
     LV Status                   available/syncd
     Mirror copies               0
     Consistency Recovery        MWC
     Schedule                    parallel
     LV Size (Mbytes)            512
     Current LE                  128
     Allocated PE                128
     Stripes                     0
     Stripe Size (Kbytes)        0
     Bad block                   off
     Allocation                  strict/contiguous

          --- Distribution of logical volume ---
          PV Name           LE on PV  PE on PV
          /dev/dsk/c0t6d0   128       128

          --- Logical extents ---
          LE    PV1           PE1  Status 1
          0000 /dev/dsk/c0t6d0    0012 current
          0001 /dev/dsk/c0t6d0    0013 current
          0002 /dev/dsk/c0t6d0    0014 current
          0003 /dev/dsk/c0t6d0    0015 current
          0004 /dev/dsk/c0t6d0    0016 current
          0005 /dev/dsk/c0t6d0    0017 current
          0006 /dev/dsk/c0t6d0    0018 current
          0007 /dev/dsk/c0t6d0    0019 current

     >>>>> /dev/vg00/lvol1 IS mounted, line from bdf is:
     /dev/vg00/lvol1    47829    29893    13153    69% /stand
     >>>>> documenting first 30 lines of lvm information by: lvdisplay -v /dev/vg00/
lvol1 | head -30
     the logical volume is:/dev/vg00/lvol1
     --- Logical volumes ---
     LV Name                     /dev/vg00/lvol1
     VG Name                     /dev/vg00
     LV Permission               read/write
     LV Status                   available/syncd
     Mirror copies               0
     Consistency Recovery        MWC
     Schedule                    parallel
     LV Size (Mbytes)            48
     Current LE                  12
     Allocated PE                12
     Stripes                     0
     Stripe Size (Kbytes)        0
     Bad block                   off
     Allocation                  strict/contiguous

          --- Distribution of logical volume ---
          PV Name           LE on PV  PE on PV
          /dev/dsk/c0t6d0   12        12
```

```
      --- Logical extents ---
      LE    PV1                PE1   Status 1
      0000  /dev/dsk/c0t6d0    0000  current
      0001  /dev/dsk/c0t6d0    0001  current
      0002  /dev/dsk/c0t6d0    0002  current
      0003  /dev/dsk/c0t6d0    0003  current
      0004  /dev/dsk/c0t6d0    0004  current
      0005  /dev/dsk/c0t6d0    0005  current
      0006  /dev/dsk/c0t6d0    0006  current
      0007  /dev/dsk/c0t6d0    0007  current

   >>>>> /dev/vg00/lvol6 IS mounted, line from bdf is:
   /dev/vg00/lvol6    1025617  605780  317275   66%  /usr
   >>>>> documenting first 30 lines of lvm information by: lvdisplay -v /dev/vg00/
lvol6 | head -30
   the logical volume is:/dev/vg00/lvol6
   --- Logical volumes ---
   LV Name                      /dev/vg00/lvol6
   VG Name                      /dev/vg00
   LV Permission                read/write
   LV Status                    available/syncd
   Mirror copies                0
   Consistency Recovery         MWC
   Schedule                     parallel
   LV Size (Mbytes)             1024
   Current LE                   256
   Allocated PE                 256
   Stripes                      0
   Stripe Size (Kbytes)         0
   Bad block                    on
   Allocation                   strict

      --- Distribution of logical volume ---
      PV Name            LE on PV  PE on PV
      /dev/dsk/c0t6d0    36        36
      /dev/dsk/c0t5d0    220       220

      --- Logical extents ---
      LE    PV1                PE1   Status 1
      0000  /dev/dsk/c0t6d0    0471  current
      0001  /dev/dsk/c0t6d0    0472  current
      0002  /dev/dsk/c0t6d0    0473  current
      0003  /dev/dsk/c0t6d0    0474  current
      0004  /dev/dsk/c0t6d0    0475  current
      0005  /dev/dsk/c0t6d0    0476  current
      0006  /dev/dsk/c0t6d0    0477  current

   >>>>> /dev/vg00/lvol4 IS mounted, line from bdf is:
   /dev/vg00/lvol4    1025617  667722  255333   72%  /opt
   >>>>> documenting first 30 lines of lvm information by: lvdisplay -v /dev/vg00/
lvol4 | head -30
   the logical volume is:/dev/vg00/lvol4
   --- Logical volumes ---
   LV Name                      /dev/vg00/lvol4
   VG Name                      /dev/vg00
   LV Permission                read/write
   LV Status                    available/syncd
   Mirror copies                0
   Consistency Recovery         MWC
   Schedule                     parallel
   LV Size (Mbytes)             1024
   Current LE                   256
   Allocated PE                 256
   Stripes                      0
   Stripe Size (Kbytes)         0
```

```
Bad block                    on
Allocation                   strict

   --- Distribution of logical volume ---
   PV Name              LE on PV  PE on PV
   /dev/dsk/c0t6d0       256       256

   --- Logical extents ---
   LE    PV1                 PE1  Status 1
   0000 /dev/dsk/c0t6d0      0165 current
   0001 /dev/dsk/c0t6d0      0166 current
   0002 /dev/dsk/c0t6d0      0167 current
   0003 /dev/dsk/c0t6d0      0168 current
   0004 /dev/dsk/c0t6d0      0169 current
   0005 /dev/dsk/c0t6d0      0170 current
   0006 /dev/dsk/c0t6d0      0171 current
   0007 /dev/dsk/c0t6d0      0172 current
```

Patches

The following script, called **audpatch.sh,** is used to produce a list of patches installed on your system. The program categorizies the patches as well as listing them.

```
#!/bin/ksh

echo "\nThis is a list of patches installed on system 'hostname'\n"

swlist > swlist.out

        WORD_COUNT=$(cat swlist.out | grep PHKL | wc -1)
        echo "\n\nNumber of kernel patches on 'hostname' is $WORD_COUNT."
echo "\nKernel patches : \n"
        echo " Patch Number \t\t\t\t Revision \t Description"
        cat swlist.out | grep PHKL

        WORD_COUNT=$(cat swlist.out | grep PHCO | wc -1)
        echo "\n\nNumber of command patches on 'hostname' is $WORD_COUNT."
echo "\nCommand patches : \n"
        echo " Patch Number \t\t\t\t Revision \t Description"
        cat swlist.out | grep PHCO

        WORD_COUNT=$(cat swlist.out | grep PHNE | wc -1)
        echo "\n\nNumber of network patches on 'hostname' is $WORD_COUNT."
echo "\nNetwork patches : \n"
        echo " Patch Number \t\t\t\t Revision \t Description"
        cat swlist.out | grep PHNE

        WORD_COUNT=$(cat swlist.out | grep PHSS | wc -1)
        echo "\n\nNumber of subsystem patches on 'hostname' is $WORD_COUNT."
echo "\nSubsystem patches : \n"
        echo " Patch Number \t\t\t\t Revision \t Description"
        cat swlist.out | grep PHSS
```

The following output was received from running **audpatch.sh**.

```
# audpatch.sh

This is a list of patches installed on system hpux1


Number of kernel patches on hpux1 is 25.

Kernel patches :

   Patch Number   Revision            Description
      PHKL_10258   B.10.00.00.AA   exec, ptrace, MMF, large shmem, large buf cache
      PHKL_10443   B.10.00.00.AA   SCSI Passthru driver cumulative patch
      PHKL_10453   B.10.00.00.AA   LVM kernel and pstat cumulative patch
      PHKL_10459   B.10.00.00.AA   cumulative patch for SystemV semaphores, semop()
      PHKL_10464   B.10.00.00.AA   HP-PB SCSI cumulative patch (scsi1/scsi3)
      PHKL_10670   B.10.00.00.AA   disc3/disc30 cumulative patch
      PHKL_7764    B.10.00.00.AA   Data loss when truncating VxFS (JFS) files
      PHKL_7765    B.10.00.00.AA   hpux(1M) for kernels larger than 13 MBytes
      PHKL_7900    B.10.00.00.AA   JFS KI, page fault, deadlock, & setuid fixes
      PHKL_8188    B.10.00.00.AA   B_NDELAY and Zalon chip hang workaround.
      PHKL_8204    B.10.00.00.AA   Fix for system hang during panic
      PHKL_8377    B.10.00.00.AA   Fix vmtrace bug. Release malloc memory.
      PHKL_8656    B.10.00.00.AA   panic with autochanger connected to FW interface
      PHKL_8684    B.10.00.00.AA   Two panics page fault on ICS - sysmemunreserve.
      PHKL_8780    B.10.00.00.AA   panic on GSC/HSC MP machines on kernel semaphore
      PHKL_9076    B.10.00.00.AA   MMF performance, large SHMEM, large buffer cache
      PHKL_9152    B.10.00.00.AA   Performance enhancements for PA-8000 systems.
      PHKL_9156    B.10.00.00.AA   NFS Kernel Cumulative Megapatch
      PHKL_9362    B.10.00.00.AA   Fix panic caused by MP race
      PHKL_9366    B.10.00.00.AA   Data corruption on PA-8000 based systems.
      PHKL_9371    B.10.00.00.AA   Various fixes for unmountable VxFS file systems
      PHKL_9570    B.10.00.00.AA   NFS and VxFS (JFS) cumulative patch
      PHKL_9712    B.10.00.00.AA   VxFS (JFS) patch for "edquota -t"
      PHKL_9724    B.10.00.00.AA   select() system call performance improvement
      PHKL_SP20    B.10.00.00.AA   Unofficial_test_patch

Number of command patches on hpux1 is 11.

Command patches :

   Patch Number   Revision            Description
      PHCO_10016   A.01.20         HP Disk Array Utilities w/AutoRAID Manager
      PHCO_10027   B.10.00.00.AA   libc cumulative patch
      PHCO_10048   B.10.00.00.AA   LVM commands cumulative patch
      PHCO_10175   B.10.00.00.AA   libc year2000 white paper
      PHCO_10295   B.10.00.00.AA   Allows umounting a disabled vxfs snapshot FS
      PHCO_7817    B.10.00.00.AA   fixes LVM maintenance mode HFS fsck error
      PHCO_8549    B.10.00.00.AA   extendfs_hfs fix for large file systems
      PHCO_9228    B.10.00.00.AA   Fbackup(1M) Long User or Group Name Patch
      PHCO_9396    B.10.00.00.AA   Fix for umountable VxFS file systems
```

```
            PHCO_9543      B.10.00.00.AA  Allows umount to unmount a Stale NFS FS
            PHCO_9895      B.10.00.00.AA  Cumulative SAM Patch 4.


    Number of network patches on hpux1 is 6.

    Network patches :

        Patch Number  Revision            Description
         PHNE_10512    B.10.00.00.AA  LAN products cumulative Patch
         PHNE_6190     B.10.00.00.AA  cumulative ocd(1M) patch
         PHNE_8328     B.10.00.00.AA  cumulative telnetd(1M) patch
         PHNE_9060     B.10.00.00.AA  Fix a panic in STREAMS
         PHNE_9107     B.10.00.00.AA  cumulative ARPA Transport patch
         PHNE_9438     B.10.00.00.AA  Cumulative Mux and Pty Patch


    Number of subsystem patches on hpux1 is 12.

    Subsystem patches :

        Patch Number  Revision            Description
         PHSS_7789     C.10.20.02     Predictive Support: SCSISCAN-Switch Log
         PHSS_8490     B.10.00.00.AA  cumulative pxdb patch.
         PHSS_8590     B.10.00.00.AA  third diagnostic patch
         PHSS_8709     B.10.00.00.AA  X11R5/Motif1.2 Development Nov96 Patch
         PHSS_8711     B.10.00.00.AA  X11R6/Motif1.2 Development Nov96 Patch
         PHSS_9096     B.10.00.00.AA  HP C++ core library components (A.10.24)
         PHSS_9356     B.10.00.00.AA  X11R5/Xt/Motif Nov-D Point patch
         PHSS_9400     B.10.00.00.AA  ld(1) cumulative patch
         PHSS_9778     B.10.00.00.AA  X11R6/Xt/Motif Nov96-D Point patch
         PHSS_9803     B.10.00.00.AA  CDE Runtime Mar97 Patch
         PHSS_9855     B.10.00.00.AA  HP C++ (A.10.24) with a correct eh/lib++.a
         PHSS_9977     B.10.00.00.AA  HP aC++ (A.01.02) to fix numerous defects
```

The following is the file **swlist.out** that was produced in the script by running the **swlist** command. You can see that the summary list of patches produced by **audpatch.sh** is much easier to read than this **swlist** output.

```
    # Initializing...
    # Contacting target "hpux1"...
    #
    # Target:  hpux1:/
    #

    #
    # Bundle(s):
    #

        2UserDegradeB.10.20         HP-UX 2-User License (For degrading user license
level)
        A3516A_APZA.01.16       HP Disk Array Utilities for Unix (S800)
        B2491A_APZB.10.20       MirrorDisk/UX
        B3191A_APZB.10.20         DCE/9000 Core Services Media and Manuals, Interna-
tional version
```

```
        B3193A_APZB.10.20          DCE/9000 Application Development Tools Media and Man-
uals
        B3395AA_APZB.10.20.02      HP-UX Developer's Toolkit for 10.0 Series 800
        B3519AA_APZB.10.20          DCE/9000 Quickstart Bundle, International version,
Media and Manuals
        B3701AA_APZ_TRYB.10.20.89     Trial HP GlancePlus/UX Pak for s800 10.20
        B3900AA_APZB.10.20.02      HP C/ANSI C Developer's Bundle for HP-UX 10.20 (S800)
        B3912AA_APZB.10.20.02      HP C++ Compiler S800
        B3912BA_APZA.01.00         HP aC++ Compiler S800
        B3919CA_AGLB.10.20         HP-UX 8-User License
        B3920CAB.10.20          HP-UX Media Kit (Reference Only. See Description)
        B4085CBEngC.05.25          English C SoftBench S800 10.x
        B4087CBEngC.05.25          English C++ SoftBench S800 10.x
        B4474EA_APZ7.09            ENWARE X Station Software
        B5050BBEngC.05.25          English SoftBench CM S800 10.x
        DCEProgB.10.20          DCE Programming and Archive Libraries
        DCESystemAdminB.10.20        DCE System Administration Utilities
        GSLDevEnvB.10.20          GSL Starbase/PEX Development Environment
        HPUXEngGS800B.10.20         English HP-UX VUE Runtime Environment
        Integ-LogonB.10.20        Integrated Logon Bundle
        J2559CD.01.08        Hewlett-Packard JetAdmin for Unix Utility
        MiscDiagB.10.20.02        HPUX 10.0 Support Tools Bundle
        OnlineDiagB.10.20.02       HPUX 10.0 Support Tools Bundle
        SoftBenchRefC.05.25        SoftBench 5.0 (Reference Only.  See Description)
        VUE-to-CDE-ToolsB.10.20       VUE to CDE Migration Tools (for all languages)
        #
        # Product(s) not contained in a Bundle:
        #

        LROMB.02.01        HP LaserROM/UX
        OVOPC-UX10-NODA.03.01        OpC Mgd Node SW running on HP-UX 10.0
        PHCO_10016A.01.20        HP Disk Array Utilities w/AutoRAID Manager
        PHCO_10027B.10.00.00.AA  libc cumulative patch
        PHCO_10048B.10.00.00.AA  LVM commands cumulative patch
        PHCO_10175B.10.00.00.AA  libc year2000 white paper
        PHCO_10295B.10.00.00.AA  Allows umounting a disabled vxfs snapshot FS
        PHCO_7817B.10.00.00.AA   fixes LVM maintenance mode HFS fsck error
        PHCO_8549B.10.00.00.AA   extendfs_hfs fix for large file systems
        PHCO_9228B.10.00.00.AA   Fbackup(1M) Long User or Group Name Patch
        PHCO_9396B.10.00.00.AA   Fix for umountable VxFS file systems
        PHCO_9543B.10.00.00.AA   Allows umount to unmount a Stale NFS FS
        PHCO_9895B.10.00.00.AA   Cumulative SAM Patch 4.
        PHKL_10258B.10.00.00.AA  exec, ptrace, MMF, large shmem, large buf cache
        PHKL_10443B.10.00.00.AA  SCSI Passthru driver cumulative patch
        PHKL_10453B.10.00.00.AA  LVM kernel and pstat cumulative patch
        PHKL_10459B.10.00.00.AA  cumulative patch for SystemV semaphores, semop()
        PHKL_10464B.10.00.00.AA  HP-PB SCSI cumulative patch (scsi1/scsi3)
        PHKL_10670B.10.00.00.AA  disc3/disc30 cumulative patch
        PHKL_7764B.10.00.00.AA   Data loss when truncating VxFS (JFS) files
        PHKL_7765B.10.00.00.AA   hpux(1M) for kernels larger than 13 MBytes
        PHKL_7900B.10.00.00.AA   JFS KI, page fault, deadlock, & setuid fixes
        PHKL_8188B.10.00.00.AA   B_NDELAY and Zalon chip hang workaround.
        PHKL_8204B.10.00.00.AA   Fix for system hang during panic
        PHKL_8377B.10.00.00.AA   Fix vmtrace bug. Release malloc memory.
        PHKL_8656B.10.00.00.AA   panic with autochanger connected to FW interface
        PHKL_8684B.10.00.00.AA   Two panics page fault on ICS - sysmemunreserve.
        PHKL_8780B.10.00.00.AA   panic on GSC/HSC MP machines on kernel semaphore
        PHKL_9076B.10.00.00.AA   MMF performance, large SHMEM, large buffer cache
        PHKL_9152B.10.00.00.AA   Performance enhancements for PA-8000 systems.
        PHKL_9156B.10.00.00.AA   NFS Kernel Cumulative Megapatch
        PHKL_9362B.10.00.00.AA   Fix panic caused by MP race
        PHKL_9366B.10.00.00.AA   Data corruption on PA-8000 based systems.
        PHKL_9371B.10.00.00.AA   Various fixes for unmountable VxFS file systems
        PHKL_9570B.10.00.00.AA   NFS and VxFS (JFS) cumulative patch
        PHKL_9712B.10.00.00.AA   VxFS (JFS) patch for "edquota -t"
        PHKL_9724B.10.00.00.AA   select() system call performance improvement
```

```
PHKL_SP20B.10.00.00.AA  Unofficial_test_patch
PHNE_10512B.10.00.00.AA  LAN products cumulative Patch
PHNE_6190B.10.00.00.AA  cumulative ocd(1M) patch
PHNE_8328B.10.00.00.AA  cumulative telnetd(1M) patch
PHNE_9060B.10.00.00.AA  Fix a panic in STREAMS
PHNE_9107B.10.00.00.AA  cumulative ARPA Transport patch
PHNE_9438B.10.00.00.AA  Cumulative Mux and Pty Patch
PHSS_7789C.10.20.02     Predictive Support: SCSISCAN-Switch Log
PHSS_8490B.10.00.00.AA  cumulative pxdb patch.
PHSS_8590B.10.00.00.AA  third diagnostic patch
PHSS_8709B.10.00.00.AA  X11R5/Motif1.2 Development Nov96 Patch
PHSS_8711B.10.00.00.AA  X11R6/Motif1.2 Development Nov96 Patch
PHSS_9096B.10.00.00.AA  HP C++ core library components (A.10.24)
PHSS_9356B.10.00.00.AA  X11R5/Xt/Motif Nov-D Point patch
PHSS_9400B.10.00.00.AA  ld(1) cumulative patch
PHSS_9778B.10.00.00.AA  X11R6/Xt/Motif Nov96-D Point patch
PHSS_9803B.10.00.00.AA  CDE Runtime Mar97 Patch
PHSS_9855B.10.00.00.AA  HP C++ (A.10.24) with a correct eh/lib++.a
PHSS_9977B.10.00.00.AA  HP aC++ (A.01.02) to fix numerous defects
```

Software Check

The following script, called **audswchk.sh**, runs the **swverify** command to verify the software installed on your system.

```
#!/usr/bin/ksh
# testing of swverify command
echo " About to verify installed software using swverify"
echo " Please be patient, this can take 10-20 minutes"
swverify -x allow_incompatible=true -x autoselect_dependencies=false \* 1>/dev/
null 2>&1
begnum=`grep -n 'BEGIN verify AGENT SESSION' /var/adm/sw/swagent.log | \
tail -1 | cut -d: -f1`
endnum=`cat /var/adm/sw/swagent.log | wc -l`
let tailnum='endnum-begnum'
if [ "$tailnum" -gt 0 ]; then
echo "Writing swverify data to file audswchk.out"
tail -n $tailnum /var/adm/sw/swagent.log >audswchk.out 2>&1
fi
```

The following output was created from running **audswchk.sh**. In addition to this output file there is also a message written to the screen indicating that it may take some time for this script to complete. The system on which this **audswchk.sh** was run is a smooth running system with no known errors, yet this output is very long and shows some warnings and errors that could result in serious problems.

```
WARNING: Fileset "VUEHelpDevKit.VUE-HELP-PRG,l=/,r=B.10.20.01" had file
         warnings.
WARNING: Directory "/" should have mode "1363" but the actual mode is
         "755".
WARNING: Directory "/" should have owner,uid "xbuild,3395" but the
         actual owner,uid is "root,0".
WARNING: Directory "/" should have group,gid "users,20" but the actual
         group,gid is "root,0".
WARNING: Fileset "VUEHelpDevKit.VUE-PRG-MAN,l=/,r=B.10.20.01" had file
         warnings.
WARNING: Directory "/" should have mode "555" but the actual mode is
         "755".
WARNING: Directory "/" should have owner,uid "xbuild,3395" but the
         actual owner,uid is "root,0".
WARNING: Directory "/" should have group,gid "users,20" but the actual
         group,gid is "root,0".
WARNING: Directory "/usr" should have owner,uid "root,0" but the actual
         owner,uid is "bin,2".
WARNING: Directory "/usr" should have group,gid "other,1" but the
         actual group,gid is "bin,2".
WARNING: Directory "/usr/lib" should have owner,uid "root,0" but the
         actual owner,uid is "bin,2".
WARNING: Directory "/usr/lib" should have group,gid "other,1" but the
         actual group,gid is "bin,2".
WARNING: Directory "/usr/lib/X11" should have owner,uid "xbuild,3395"
         but the actual owner,uid is "bin,2".
WARNING: Directory "/usr/lib/X11" should have group,gid "users,20" but
         the actual group,gid is "bin,2".
WARNING: Fileset "X11MotifDevKit.IMAKE,l=/,r=B.10.20.02" had file
         warnings.
WARNING: Directory "/" should have mode "555" but the actual mode is
         "755".
WARNING: Directory "/" should have group,gid "other,1" but the actual
         group,gid is "root,0".
ERROR:   File "/usr/lib/libXm.a" missing.
ERROR:   Fileset "X11MotifDevKit.MOTIF12-PRG,l=/,r=B.10.20.02" had file
         errors.
WARNING: Directory "/" should have mode "555" but the actual mode is
         "755".
WARNING: Directory "/" should have owner,uid "xbuild,3395" but the
         actual owner,uid is "root,0".
WARNING: Directory "/" should have group,gid "users,20" but the actual
         group,gid is "root,0".
WARNING: Directory "/usr/dt" should have owner,uid "root,0" but the
         actual owner,uid is "bin,2".
WARNING: Directory "/usr/dt" should have group,gid "other,1" but the
         actual group,gid is "bin,2".
WARNING: Directory "/usr/dt/share" should have owner,uid "root,0" but
         the actual owner,uid is "bin,2".
WARNING: Directory "/usr/dt/share" should have group,gid "other,1" but
         the actual group,gid is "bin,2".
WARNING: Directory "/usr/dt/share/man" should have owner,uid "root,0"
         but the actual owner,uid is "bin,2".
WARNING: Directory "/usr/dt/share/man" should have group,gid "other,1"
         but the actual group,gid is "bin,2".
WARNING: Directory "/usr/share" should have owner,uid "xbuild,3395" but
         the actual owner,uid is "bin,2".
WARNING: Directory "/usr/share" should have group,gid "users,20" but
         the actual group,gid is "bin,2".
WARNING: Directory "/usr/share/man/man3.Z" should have owner,uid
         "xbuild,3395" but the actual owner,uid is "bin,2".
WARNING: Directory "/usr/share/man/man3.Z" should have group,gid
         "users,20" but the actual group,gid is "bin,2".
WARNING: Fileset "X11MotifDevKit.MOTIF12-PRGMAN,l=/,r=B.10.20.02" had
         file warnings.
WARNING: Directory "/" should have mode "555" but the actual mode is
```

```
                "755".
WARNING: Directory "/" should have group,gid "other,1" but the actual
                group,gid is "root,0".
WARNING: Fileset "X11MotifDevKit.X11R5-PRG,l=/,r=B.10.20.02" had file
                warnings.
WARNING: Directory "/" should have mode "555" but the actual mode is
                "755".
WARNING: Directory "/" should have group,gid "other,1" but the actual
                group,gid is "root,0".
WARNING: Directory "/usr/newconfig" should have owner,uid "root,0" but
                the actual owner,uid is "bin,2".
WARNING: Directory "/usr/newconfig" should have group,gid "other,1" but
                the actual group,gid is "bin,2".
WARNING: Fileset "X11MotifDevKit.X11R6-PRG,l=/,r=B.10.20.02" had file
                warnings.
WARNING: Directory "/" should have mode "555" but the actual mode is
                "755".
WARNING: Directory "/" should have group,gid "other,1" but the actual
                group,gid is "root,0".
WARNING: Directory "/usr/contrib/lib" should have owner,uid
                "xbuild,3395" but the actual owner,uid is "bin,2".
WARNING: Directory "/usr/contrib/lib" should have group,gid "users,20"
                but the actual group,gid is "bin,2".
WARNING: Fileset "X11MotifDevKit.X11R6-PRG-CTRB,l=/,r=B.10.20.02" had
                file warnings.
WARNING: Directory "/" should have mode "555" but the actual mode is
                "755".
WARNING: Directory "/" should have group,gid "other,1" but the actual
                group,gid is "root,0".
ERROR:   File "/usr/share/man/man3.Z/XHPSSChange.3x" had a different
                mtime than expected.
ERROR:   Fileset "X11MotifDevKit.X11R6-PRG-MAN,l=/,r=B.10.20.02" had
                file errors.

       * Summary of Analysis Phase:
ERROR:         Verify failed Diag-Sys-800.SUP-CORE-800,l=/,r=B.10.20.02
ERROR:         Verify failed OS-Core.CORE-KRN,l=/,r=B.10.20
ERROR:         Verify failed OS-Core.C2400-UTIL,l=/,r=B.10.20
ERROR:         Verify failed OS-Core.Q4,l=/,r=B.10.20
ERROR:         Verify failed LVM.LVM-RUN,l=/,r=B.10.20
ERROR:         Verify failed LVM.LVM-MIRROR-RUN,l=/,r=B.10.20
ERROR:         Verify failed PHKL_10258.PHKL_10258,l=/,r=B.10.00.00.AA
ERROR:         Verify failed PHKL_10464.PHKL_10464,l=/,r=B.10.00.00.AA
ERROR:         Verify failed PHKL_10670.PHKL_10670,l=/,r=B.10.00.00.AA
ERROR:         Verify failed PHKL_SP20.PHKL_SP20,l=/,r=B.10.00.00.AA
ERROR:         Verify failed
         Sup-Tool-Mgr-800.STM-UUT-800-RUN,l=/,r=B.10.20.02
ERROR:         Verify failed UserLicense.08-USER,l=/,r=B.10.20
WARNING:       Verified with warnings ACXX.ACXX,l=/opt/aCC,r=A.01.00
WARNING:       Verified with warnings ACXX.ACXX-HELP,l=/opt/aCC,r=A.01.00
WARNING:       Verified with warnings
         ACXX.ACXX-JPN-E-MAN,l=/opt/aCC,r=A.01.00
WARNING:       Verified with warnings
         ACXX.ACXX-JPN-S-MAN,l=/opt/aCC,r=A.01.00
WARNING:       Verified with warnings ACXX.ACXX-MAN,l=/opt/aCC,r=A.01.00
WARNING:       Verified with warnings ACXX.ACXX-SC,l=/opt/aCC,r=A.01.00
WARNING:       Verified with warnings
         ACXX.ACXX-STDLIB,l=/opt/aCC,r=A.01.00
WARNING:       Verified with warnings
         AudioDevKit.AUDIO-PGMAN,l=/opt/audio,r=B.10.10.00
WARNING:       Verified with warnings
         AudioDevKit.AUDIO-PRG,l=/opt/audio,r=B.10.10.00
WARNING:       Verified with warnings
         C-ANSI-C.C,l=/opt/ansic,r=B.10.20.00
ERROR:         Verify failed C-Plus-Plus.HPCXX,l=/opt/CC,r=B.10.20.00
ERROR:         Verify failed C-Plus-Plus.HPCXX-MAN,l=/opt/CC,r=B.10.20.00
```

```
ERROR:       Verify failed CDE.CDE-RUN,l=/,r=B.10.20
WARNING:        Verified with warnings
             CDEDevKit.CDE-DEMOS,l=/,r=B.10.20.02
WARNING:        Verified with warnings
             CDEDevKit.CDE-HELP-PRG,l=/,r=B.10.20.02
WARNING:        Verified with warnings CDEDevKit.CDE-INC,l=/,r=B.10.20.02
WARNING:        Verified with warnings
             CDEDevKit.CDE-MAN-DEV,l=/,r=B.10.20.02
WARNING:        Verified with warnings CDEDevKit.CDE-PRG,l=/,r=B.10.20.02
WARNING:        Verified with warnings
             COBOLRT.COBRT,l=/opt/cobol,r=B.11.25
WARNING:        Verified with warnings
             COBOLCRT.COBCRT,l=/opt/cobol,r=B.11.25
WARNING:        Verified with warnings
             COBOLDEV.COBDEV,l=/opt/cobol,r=B.11.25
WARNING:        Verified with warnings
             COBOLTBOX.COBTBOX,l=/opt/cobol,r=B.11.25
WARNING:        Verified with warnings
             CustomerServ.CUST-SERV,l=/opt/secustserv,r=C.05.25
WARNING:        Verified with warnings
             CustomerServ.CUST-SERV-J,l=/opt/secustserv,r=C.05.25
ERROR:          Verify failed
             DCE-CoreAdmin.DCE-CORE-DIAG,l=/opt/dce,r=B.10.20
WARNING:        Verified with warnings
             DigitalVideoDK.DVC-PRG,l=/,r=B.10.20.01
WARNING:        Verified with warnings
             DigitalVideoDK.DVC-PRGMAN,l=/,r=B.10.20.01
WARNING:        Verified with warnings
             DigitalVideoDK.DVC-SHLIBS,l=/,r=B.10.20.01
WARNING:        Verified with warnings
             DigitalVideoDK.DVC-SRV,l=/,r=B.10.20.01
WARNING:        Verified with warnings
             DigitalVideoDK.DVIDEO-FILES,l=/,r=B.10.20.01
WARNING:        Verified with warnings
             DigitalVideoDK.DVIDEO-PGMAN,l=/,r=B.10.20.01
WARNING:        Verified with warnings
             DigitalVideoDK.DVIDEO-PRG,l=/,r=B.10.20.01
WARNING:        Verified with warnings
             DigitalVideoDK.VIDEOOUT-PGMAN,l=/,r=B.10.20.01
WARNING:        Verified with warnings
             DigitalVideoDK.VIDEOOUT-PRG,l=/,r=B.10.20.01
WARNING:        Verified with warnings
             DigitalVideoDK.VIDEOOUT-SHLIBS,l=/,r=B.10.20.01
ERROR:       Verify failed ENWARE.HPXT-SUPPL,l=/opt/hpxt/enware,r=7.09
ERROR:       Verify failed ENWARE.HPXT-700RX,l=/opt/hpxt/enware,r=7.09
ERROR:       Verify failed ENWARE.HPXT-AUDIO,l=/opt/hpxt/enware,r=7.09
ERROR:       Verify failed ENWARE.HPXT-CDE,l=/opt/hpxt/enware,r=7.09
ERROR:          Verify failed
             ENWARE.HPXT-CLIENTS,l=/opt/hpxt/enware,r=7.09
ERROR:       Verify failed ENWARE.HPXT-ENVIZE,l=/opt/hpxt/enware,r=7.09
ERROR:       Verify failed ENWARE.HPXT-NFS,l=/opt/hpxt/enware,r=7.09
ERROR:       Verify failed ENWARE.HPXT-FLOPPY,l=/opt/hpxt/enware,r=7.09
ERROR:          Verify failed
             ENWARE.HPXT-HP8FONTS,l=/opt/hpxt/enware,r=7.09
ERROR:          Verify failed
             ENWARE.HPXT-ISOFONTS,l=/opt/hpxt/enware,r=7.09
ERROR:          Verify failed
             ENWARE.HPXT-MISCFONT,l=/opt/hpxt/enware,r=7.09
ERROR:       Verify failed ENWARE.HPXT-MPEG,l=/opt/hpxt/enware,r=7.09
ERROR:          Verify failed
             ENWARE.HPXT-PRINTER,l=/opt/hpxt/enware,r=7.09
ERROR:          Verify failed
             ENWARE.HPXT-SCANNER,l=/opt/hpxt/enware,r=7.09
ERROR:       Verify failed ENWARE.HPXT-TOKN,l=/opt/hpxt/enware,r=7.09
ERROR:       Verify failed ENWARE.HPXT-VT320,l=/opt/hpxt/enware,r=7.09
ERROR:       Verify failed ENWARE.HPXT-XLOCK,l=/opt/hpxt/enware,r=7.09
```

```
ERROR:        Verify failed ENWARE.HPXT-XTOUCH,l=/opt/hpxt/enware,r=7.09
WARNING:      Verified with warnings
              MeasureWare.MWA,l=/opt/perf,r=B.10.20.89
WARNING:      Verified with warnings
              GraphicsPEX5DK.PEX5-EXAMPLES,l=/opt/graphics/PEX5,r=B.10.20
WARNING:      Verified with warnings
              GraphicsPEX5DK.PEX5-HELP,l=/opt/graphics/PEX5,r=B.10.20
WARNING:      Verified with warnings
              GraphicsPEX5DK.PEX5-PRG,l=/opt/graphics/PEX5,r=B.10.20
WARNING:      Verified with warnings
              GraphicsSBaseDK.FAFM-MAN,l=/opt/graphics/starbase,r=B.10.20
WARNING:      Verified with warnings
              GraphicsSBaseDK.FAFM-PRG,l=/opt/graphics/starbase,r=B.10.20
WARNING:      Verified with warnings
              GraphicsSBaseDK.SBDL-DEMO,l=/opt/graphics/starbase,r=B.10.20
WARNING:      Verified with warnings
              GraphicsSBaseDK.SBDL-MAN,l=/opt/graphics/starbase,r=B.10.20
WARNING:      Verified with warnings
              GraphicsSBaseDK.SBDL-PRG,l=/opt/graphics/starbase,r=B.10.20
WARNING:      Verified with warnings
              GraphicsSBaseDK.STAR-DEMO,l=/opt/graphics/starbase,r=B.10.20
WARNING:      Verified with warnings
              GraphicsSBaseDK.STAR-HARDCOPY,l=/opt/graphics/starbase,r=B.10.20

WARNING:      Verified with warnings
              GraphicsSBaseDK.STAR-MAN,l=/opt/graphics/starbase,r=B.10.20
WARNING:      Verified with warnings
              GraphicsSBaseDK.STAR-PRG,l=/opt/graphics/starbase,r=B.10.20
WARNING:      Verified with warnings
              GraphicsSBaseDK.STAR-WEBDOC,l=/opt/graphics/starbase,r=B.10.20
ERROR:        Verify failed
              HPAutoRAID.HPAutoRAID-MAN,l=/opt/hparray,r=A.01.16
ERROR:        Verify failed
              HPAutoRAID.HPAutoRAID-RUN,l=/opt/hparray,r=A.01.16
ERROR:        Verify failed HPNP.HPNP-RUN,l=/opt/hpnp,r=D.01.08
WARNING:      Verified with warnings
              ImagingDevKit.IMAGE-FILES,l=/,r=B.10.20.02
WARNING:      Verified with warnings
              ImagingDevKit.IMAGE-PGMAN,l=/,r=B.10.20.02
WARNING:      Verified with warnings
              ImagingDevKit.IMAGE-PRG,l=/,r=B.10.20.02
ERROR:        Verify failed LSSERV.LSSERV-ADMIN,l=/opt/ifor,r=B.10.20
WARNING:      Verified with warnings
              LSSERV.LSSERV-SERVER,l=/opt/ifor,r=B.10.20
ERROR:        Verify failed OVOPC-UX10-NOD.OVOPC-UX10,l=/,r=A.03.01
ERROR:        Verify failed PHCO_10048.PHCO_10048,l=/,r=B.10.00.00.AA
WARNING:      Verified with warnings SystemAdmin.SAM-HELP,l=/,r=B.10.20
WARNING:      Verified with warnings SystemAdmin.SAM,l=/,r=B.10.20
ERROR:        Verify failed PHSS_8709.PHSS_8709,l=/,r=B.10.00.00.AA
ERROR:        Verify failed PHSS_9855.PHSS_9855,l=/,r=B.10.00.00.AA
WARNING:      Verified with warnings
              SB-BMSFramework.BMS-ENG-A-MAN,l=/opt/softbench,r=C.05.25
WARNING:      Verified with warnings
              SB-BMSFramework.BMS-JPN-E-MAN,l=/opt/softbench,r=C.05.25
WARNING:      Verified with warnings
              SB-BMSFramework.BMS-JPN-E-MSG,l=/opt/softbench,r=C.05.25
WARNING:      Verified with warnings
              SB-BMSFramework.BMS-JPN-S-MAN,l=/opt/softbench,r=C.05.25
WARNING:      Verified with warnings
              SB-BMSFramework.BMS-JPN-S-MSG,l=/opt/softbench,r=C.05.25
WARNING:      Verified with warnings
              SB-BMSFramework.SB-BMS,l=/opt/softbench,r=C.05.25
WARNING:      Verified with warnings
              SB-BMSFramework.SB-BMSFW,l=/opt/softbench,r=C.05.25
ERROR:        Verify failed
              SB-BMSFramework.SB-FONTS,l=/opt/softbench,r=C.05.25
```

```
WARNING:      Verified with warnings
              SB-BMSFramework.SB-MSGCONN,l=/opt/softbench,r=C.05.25
WARNING:      Verified with warnings
              SB-BMSFramework.SBM-ENG-A-MAN,l=/opt/softbench,r=C.05.25
WARNING:      Verified with warnings
              SB-CM.SBCM-CLT,l=/opt/softbench,r=B.01.55
WARNING:      Verified with warnings
              SB-CM.SBCM-ENG-A-HLP,l=/opt/softbench,r=B.01.55
WARNING:      Verified with warnings
              SB-CM.SBCM-ENG-A-MAN,l=/opt/softbench,r=B.01.55
WARNING:      Verified with warnings
              SB-CM.SBCM-GUI,l=/opt/softbench,r=B.01.55
WARNING:      Verified with warnings
              SB-CM.SBCM-J,l=/opt/softbench,r=B.01.55
WARNING:      Verified with warnings
              SB-CM.SBCM-JPN-E-HLP,l=/opt/softbench,r=B.01.55
WARNING:      Verified with warnings
              SB-CM.SBCM-JPN-E-MAN,l=/opt/softbench,r=B.01.55
WARNING:      Verified with warnings
              SB-CM.SBCM-JPN-E-MSG,l=/opt/softbench,r=B.01.55
WARNING:      Verified with warnings
              SB-CM.SBCM-JPN-S-HLP,l=/opt/softbench,r=B.01.55
WARNING:      Verified with warnings
              SB-CM.SBCM-JPN-S-MAN,l=/opt/softbench,r=B.01.55
WARNING:      Verified with warnings
              SB-CM.SBCM-JPN-S-MSG,l=/opt/softbench,r=B.01.55
WARNING:      Verified with warnings
              SB-CM.SBCM-SRV,l=/opt/softbench,r=B.01.55
WARNING:      Verified with warnings
              SB-SoftBenchCore.SB40-LIBS,l=/opt/softbench,r=C.05.25
WARNING:      Verified with warnings
              SB-SoftBenchCore.SB-LSMGR,l=/opt/softbench,r=C.05.25
WARNING:      Verified with warnings
              SB-SoftBenchCore.SB-GNUBIN,l=/opt/softbench,r=C.05.25
ERROR:        Verify failed
              SB-SoftBenchCore.SB-CORE,l=/opt/softbench,r=C.05.25
WARNING:      Verified with warnings
              SB-SoftBenchCore.SB-COMMON,l=/opt/softbench,r=C.05.25
WARNING:      Verified with warnings
              SB-SoftBenchCore.SB-DT,l=/opt/softbench,r=C.05.25
WARNING:      Verified with warnings
              SB-SoftBenchCore.SB-DEMO,l=/opt/softbench,r=C.05.25
WARNING:      Verified with warnings
              SB-SoftBenchCore.SB-ENG-A-MAN,l=/opt/softbench,r=C.05.25
WARNING:      Verified with warnings
              SB-SoftBenchCore.SB-GNUBIN-MAN,l=/opt/softbench,r=C.05.25
WARNING:      Verified with warnings
              SB-SoftBenchCore.SB-GNUSRC,l=/opt/softbench,r=C.05.25
WARNING:      Verified with warnings
              SB-SoftBenchCore.SB-JPN-E-MAN,l=/opt/softbench,r=C.05.25
WARNING:      Verified with warnings
              SB-SoftBenchCore.SB-JPN-E-MSG,l=/opt/softbench,r=C.05.25
WARNING:      Verified with warnings
              SB-SoftBenchCore.SB-JPN-S-MAN,l=/opt/softbench,r=C.05.25
WARNING:      Verified with warnings
              SB-SoftBenchCore.SB-JPN-S-MSG,l=/opt/softbench,r=C.05.25
WARNING:      Verified with warnings
              SB-SoftBenchCore.SB40-EDL,l=/opt/softbench,r=C.05.25
WARNING:      Verified with warnings
              SB-SoftBenchCore.SBL-ENG-A-MAN,l=/opt/softbench,r=C.05.25
WARNING:      Verified with warnings
              SB-CPersonality.SB-ADA,l=/opt/softbench,r=C.05.25
WARNING:      Verified with warnings
              SB-CPersonality.SB-C,l=/opt/softbench,r=C.05.25
WARNING:      Verified with warnings
              SB-CPersonality.SB-CBTC,l=/opt/softbench,r=C.05.25
```

```
WARNING:     Verified with warnings
         SB-CPersonality.SB-DDE,l=/opt/softbench,r=C.05.25
WARNING:     Verified with warnings
         SB-CPersonality.SBC-ENG-A-HLP,l=/opt/softbench,r=C.05.25
WARNING:     Verified with warnings
         SB-CPersonality.SBC-ENG-A-MAN,l=/opt/softbench,r=C.05.25
WARNING:     Verified with warnings
         SB-CPersonality.SBC-JPN-E-HLP,l=/opt/softbench,r=C.05.25
WARNING:     Verified with warnings
         SB-CPersonality.SBC-JPN-E-MAN,l=/opt/softbench,r=C.05.25
WARNING:     Verified with warnings
         SB-CPersonality.SBC-JPN-E-MSG,l=/opt/softbench,r=C.05.25
WARNING:     Verified with warnings
         SB-CPersonality.SBC-JPN-S-HLP,l=/opt/softbench,r=C.05.25
WARNING:     Verified with warnings
         SB-CPersonality.SBC-JPN-S-MAN,l=/opt/softbench,r=C.05.25
WARNING:     Verified with warnings
         SB-CPersonality.SBC-JPN-S-MSG,l=/opt/softbench,r=C.05.25
WARNING:     Verified with warnings
         SB-CXXAdvisor.SB-RLCK,l=/opt/softbench,r=C.05.25
WARNING:     Verified with warnings
         SB-CXXAdvisor.SBA-ENG-A-HLP,l=/opt/softbench,r=C.05.25
WARNING:     Verified with warnings
         SB-CXXAdvisor.SBA-ENG-A-MAN,l=/opt/softbench,r=C.05.25
WARNING:     Verified with warnings
         SB-CXXPersnlty.SB-CBTCXX,l=/opt/softbench,r=C.05.25
WARNING:     Verified with warnings
         SB-CXXPersnlty.SB-CXX,l=/opt/softbench,r=C.05.25
WARNING:     Verified with warnings
         SB-CXXPersnlty.SBX-JPN-E-MSG,l=/opt/softbench,r=C.05.25
WARNING:     Verified with warnings
         SB-CXXPersnlty.SBX-JPN-S-MSG,l=/opt/softbench,r=C.05.25
WARNING:     Verified with warnings
         SB-CobolPersnlty.SB-CBTCOBOL,l=/opt/softbench,r=C.05.25
WARNING:     Verified with warnings
         SB-CobolPersnlty.SB-COBOL,l=/opt/softbench,r=C.05.25
WARNING:     Verified with warnings
         SB-CobolPersnlty.SB-COBOL-J,l=/opt/softbench,r=C.05.25
WARNING:     Verified with warnings
         SB-CobolPersnlty.SBO-ENG-A-HELP,l=/opt/softbench,r=C.05.25
WARNING:     Verified with warnings
         SB-CobolPersnlty.SBO-JPN-E-HELP,l=/opt/softbench,r=C.05.25
WARNING:     Verified with warnings
         SB-CobolPersnlty.SBO-JPN-E-MAN,l=/opt/softbench,r=C.05.25
WARNING:     Verified with warnings
         SB-CobolPersnlty.SBO-JPN-E-MSG,l=/opt/softbench,r=C.05.25
WARNING:     Verified with warnings
         SB-CobolPersnlty.SBO-JPN-S-HELP,l=/opt/softbench,r=C.05.25
WARNING:     Verified with warnings
         SB-CobolPersnlty.SBO-JPN-S-MAN,l=/opt/softbench,r=C.05.25
WARNING:     Verified with warnings
         SB-CobolPersnlty.SBO-JPN-S-MSG,l=/opt/softbench,r=C.05.25
WARNING:     Verified with warnings SW-DIST.SD-FAL,l=/,r=B.10.20
ERROR:       Verify failed VUE.VUE-RUN,l=/,r=B.10.20
WARNING:     Verified with warnings
         VUEHelpDevKit.VUE-HELP-PRG,l=/,r=B.10.20.01
WARNING:     Verified with warnings
         VUEHelpDevKit.VUE-PRG-MAN,l=/,r=B.10.20.01
WARNING:     Verified with warnings
         X11MotifDevKit.IMAKE,l=/,r=B.10.20.02
ERROR:       Verify failed X11MotifDevKit.MOTIF12-PRG,l=/,r=B.10.20.02
WARNING:     Verified with warnings
         X11MotifDevKit.MOTIF12-PRGMAN,l=/,r=B.10.20.02
WARNING:     Verified with warnings
         X11MotifDevKit.X11R5-PRG,l=/,r=B.10.20.02
WARNING:     Verified with warnings
```

```
                  X11MotifDevKit.X11R6-PRG,l=/,r=B.10.20.02
         WARNING:     Verified with warnings
                  X11MotifDevKit.X11R6-PRG-CTRB,l=/,r=B.10.20.02
         ERROR:       Verify failed
                  X11MotifDevKit.X11R6-PRG-MAN,l=/,r=B.10.20.02
         ERROR:    47 of 952 filesets had Errors.
         WARNING: 124 of 952 filesets had Warnings.
                * 781 of 952 filesets had no Errors or Warnings.
         ERROR:    The Analysis Phase had errors and warnings.  See the above
                   output for details.


         =======  19:18:13 EDT  END verify AGENT SESSION (pid=21385)
                  (jobid=hpux1-0144)
```

Password and Group Check

The following script, called **audpassw.sh**, checks the **/etc/passwd** and **/etc/group** files looking for potential problems.

```
      #!/usr/bin/ksh

    echo    "*****************************************************************"    >
audpasswd.out
    echo " This program performs password and group checks on system 'hostname'."
>> audpasswd.out
    echo
"*****************************************************************\n\n\n"    >>  aud-
passwd.out
    echo   "Check for multiple root users by using awk on /etc/passwd." >> aud-
passwd.out
    echo  "The following users have a user ID of 0.\n" >> audpasswd.out
    awk -F: '{ if ( $3 == 0 ) print $1 }' /etc/passwd >> audpasswd.out

    echo "\n\nThe following users do not have a password assigned. " >> audpasswd.out
    echo "This could be a serious security problem on the system.\n" >> audpasswd.out
    awk -F: '{ if ( $2 == "" ) print $1 }' /etc/passwd >> audpasswd.out

    echo  "\n\n\nRunning password consistency check using pwck program." >> aud-
passwd.out
    echo "This program prints the password entry and corresponding" >> audpasswd.out
    echo "problem such as login directory not found or bad character" >> aud-
passwd.out
    echo "in login name.\n" >> audpasswd.out
    pwck 2>> audpasswd.out

    echo  "\n\n\nRunning group consistency check using grpck program." >> aud-
passwd.out
    echo "This program prints the group entry and corresponding" >> audpasswd.out
    echo "problem such as invalid GID, login name not in password" >> audpasswd.out
    echo "file, and groups in which there are no users.\n" >> audpasswd.out
    grpck 2>>audpasswd.out
```

This script produces the file **audpasswd.out**. This file has in it several potential user and group related problems, such as a user without a password.

```
**********************************************************************
   This program performs password and group checks on system hpux1.
**********************************************************************


   Check for multiple root users by using awk on /etc/passwd.
   The following users have a user ID of 0.

   root
   sam_exec


   The following users do not have a password assigned.
   This could be a serious security problem on the system.

   tburns



   Running password consistency check using pwck program.
   This program prints the password entry and corresponding
   problem such as login directory not found or bad character
   in login name.

   mcohn:2c4hWtfYlRwks:148:101:Mike,Cohn,,:/home/mcohn:/usr/local/bin/tcsh
   Login directory not found

   sam_exec:*:0:1::/home/sam_exec:/usr/bin/sh
   1 Bad character(s) in logname

   opc_op:*:777:77:OpC default operator:/home/opc_op:/usr/bin/ksh
   1 Bad character(s) in logname



   Running group consistency check using grpck program.
   This program prints the group entry and corresponding
   problem such as invalid GID, login name not in password
   file, and groups in which there are no users.



   tty::10:
   Null login name


   users::20:root,testhp,addadm,mflahert,tdolan,clloyd,eschwartz,jperwinc,denise
   denise - Logname not found in password file


   nogroup:*:-2:
   Invalid GID
   Null login name
```

Check for Disk Hogs

With the shell program in this section you can regularly check both the characteristics of each logical volume as well as the amount of disk space consumed by each user. The following script, called **audhogs.sh**, uses the **fstyp**, **diskusg**, and **vxdiskusg** programs to produce reports.

```
#!/usr/bin/ksh
# 1st print stats concerning the disk's file systems
echo "This program produces logical volume statistics and the amount of disk"
echo "space consumed by users on each logical volume. \n"
for fs in `bdf| grep '^/' | awk '{print $1}'`
do
fsys=`fstyp $fs`
echo "\n $printing logical volume stats for $fs using fstyp -v \n"
fstyp -v $fs 2>&1
if [ $fsys = vxfs ]
then
echo "\n finding space consumed per user for logical volume "
echo " $fs with vxdiskusg $fs \n"
/usr/sbin/acct/vxdiskusg $fs 2>&1 | tee -a $DESTF
else
# assume hfs type
echo "\n finding space consumed per user for logical volume "
echo " $fs with diskusg $fs \n"
echo "\nUserID login number of blocks "
echo "------ -------------------- \n"
        /usr/sbin/acct/diskusg $fs 2>&1
fi
done
```

I redirected the output of this script to **audhogs.out**. This file contains a summary of each logical volume and the amount of disk space on each logical volume consumed by each user. Only the first few logical volumes are shown.

```
This program produces logical volume statistics and the amount of disk
space consumed by users on each logical volume.

   logical volume stats for /dev/vg00/lvol3 using fstyp -v

hfs
f_bsize: 8192
f_frsize: 1024
f_blocks: 99669
f_bfree: 66562
f_bavail: 56595
f_files: 16128
f_ffree: 12525
f_favail: 12525
f_fsid: 1073741827
f_basetype: hfs
```

```
f_namemax: 255
f_magic: 95014
f_featurebits: 1
f_flag: 0
f_fsindex: 0
f_size: 102400

 finding space consumed per user for logical volume
 /dev/vg00/lvol3 with diskusg /dev/vg00/lvol3


UserID login number of blocks
------ ----- --------------

0       root        35014
1001    softcm      2
2       bin         30782
5       uucp        2
9       lp          410
100     adduser     4

  logical volume stats for /dev/vg00/lvol1 using fstyp -v

hfs
f_bsize: 8192
f_frsize: 1024
f_blocks: 47829
f_bfree: 17936
f_bavail: 13153
f_files: 7680
f_ffree: 7654
f_favail: 7654
f_fsid: 1073741825
f_basetype: hfs
f_namemax: 255
f_magic: 95014
f_featurebits: 1
f_flag: 0
f_fsindex: 0
f_size: 49152

 finding space consumed per user for logical volume
 /dev/vg00/lvol1 with diskusg /dev/vg00/lvol1


UserID login number of blocks
------ ----- --------------

0       root        59784
2       bin         2

  logical volume stats for /dev/vg00/lvol7 using fstyp -v

hfs
f_bsize: 8192
f_frsize: 1024
f_blocks: 723288
f_bfree: 431130
f_bavail: 358801
f_files: 351168
f_ffree: 340324
f_favail: 340324
f_fsid: 1073741831
f_basetype: hfs
f_namemax: 255
f_magic: 95014
```

```
f_featurebits: 1
f_flag: 0
f_fsindex: 0
f_size: 770048

finding space consumed per user for logical volume
/dev/vg00/lvol7 with diskusg /dev/vg00/lvol7


UserID login number of blocks
------ ----- --------------

0       root    318706
1       daemon  344
1001    softcm  4696
2       bin     197450
4       adm     1754
5       uucp    38
9       lp      328
100     adduser 2
102     user1   164
103     user2   6
104     user3   2
105     user4   68
107     user5   84
109     user6   288
113     user7   192
115     user8   416
116     user9   112
119     user10  110
```

.
.
.

Check Crash Directory

It is important to have the directory **/var/adm/crash** on your system.
Should your system crash, a core directory is produced that has in it a core
dump that includes the contents of RAM at the time of system boot. The
following script, called **audcrash.sh**, checks to see if the **/var/adm/crash**
directory exists, if it has a core dump in it, and if so, lists the contents of the
core dump directory.

```
#!/usr/bin/ksh
echo "\n\n"
echo "The /var/adm/crash directory is needed by savecore in order to save the status"
echo "if a system crash occurs. The coredump can then be copied to a file and"
echo "sent to HP for analysis."
echo "See the savecore manual page to get more information about saving a core dump."

REMEMBERCORE=0
if [ -d /var/adm/crash ]
    then
```

```
                    echo "\n\t/var/adm/crash exists \c"
                    if [ -r /var/adm/crash/core.? ]
                    then
                    echo "and contains a dump."
                    echo "\n\tPlease copy the dump in /var/adm/crash to tape."
                    echo "\n\nHere is a listing of the core dump(s) on `hostname`. \n"
                    ll /var/adm/crash/core.?
                    REMEMBERCORE=1
        else
                    echo "and contains NO dump."
fi

else

                    echo "\n\n WARNING: /var/adm/crash did not exist."
                    echo " use mkdir -p /var/adm/crash "
fi
```

I redirected the output of this script to **audcrash.out**. This file indicates that **/var/adm/crash** exists, that it has in it core dumps, and lists the
contents of the core dump directories.

```
The /var/adm/crash directory is needed by savecore in order to save the status
if a system crash occurs. The coredump can then be copied to a file and
sent to HP for analysis.
See the savecore manual page to get more information about saving a core dump.

/var/adm/crash exists and contains a dump.

Please copy the dump in /var/adm/crash to tape.


Here is a listing of the core dump(s) on hpux1.


/var/adm/crash/core.0:
total 40152
-rw-r--r--  1 root      root           560 Oct 23  12.22 INDEX
-rw-r--r--  1 root      root      13477963 Oct 23  12.22 core.0.1.gz
-rw-rw-rw-  1 root      sys           3007 Oct 23  12.22 dmesg.out
-rw-r--r--  1 root      root       7045532 Oct 23  12.22 vmunix

/var/adm/crash/core.1:
total 40152
-rw-r--r--  1 root      sys            560 Jun  5 16:48 INDEX
-rw-r--r--  1 root      sys       13477963 Jun  5 16:48 core.0.1.gz
-rw-rw-rw-  1 root      sys           3007 Jun  5 16:48 dmesg.out
-rw-r--r--  1 root      sys        7045532 Jun  5 16:48 vmunix
```

CHAPTER 9

Windows NT and HP-UX
Interoperability Topics

Interoperability Topics

I could spend another 500 pages covering just Windows NT and HP-UX interoperability. There are hundreds of technologies and products that enhance Windows NT and HP-UX interoperability. Since it would not be feasible for me to cover even a small fraction of these technologies and products in this book, I decided to devote this chapter to technologies that bridge the gap between some fundamental Windows NT and HP-UX differences in operation. The following is a list of what I consider to be the top interoperability topics which are covered in this chapter

- **HP-UX Application Server That Displays on HP-UX Using the X Window System** - X Windows is a networked windowing environment that is the standard on HP-UX systems. If you install X Windows on your Windows NT system, you can run applications on your HP-UX system and use X Windows on your Windows NT to manage those applications. The HP-UX system is acting as the application server but the applications are controlled from X Windows running on the Windows NT system.

• **Network File System (NFS) Used to Share Data** - The next section covers using NFS to share data between Windows NT and HP-UX systems. NFS comes with HP-UX and by loading NFS on a Windows NT system you can freely access HP-UX file systems on the Windows NT systems and vice versa. I focus only on accessing HP-UX file systems on the Windows NT systems because, as I earlier mentioned, I think it is more likely the HP-UX system will act as a data and application server and the Windows NT system will act as a client. There is, however, no reason that NFS could not be used to access Windows NT file systems while on an HP-UX system.

• **Windows NT Functionality on HP-UX** - Putting the X Window System and NFS on Windows NT brings important HP-UX functionality to the Windows NT operating system. It is equally useful to bring Windows NT functionality to HP-UX. Advanced Server 9000 is a software product that runs on HP-UX and brings important Windows NT functionality such as file and print services to HP-UX.

• **Common Set of Commands** - The Windows NT Resource Kit provides countless useful utilities including a set of POSIX commands that are familiar to HP-UX system administrators. Commands such as **chmod**, **ls**, and **mv** run on Windows NT.

• **Common Software Development Environment** - With a mixed Windows NT and HP-UX-based software development environment there come a lot of challenges. Any time you mix two or more operating systems in software development you end up with different development tools, compilers, and other functionality. HP SoftBench OpenStudio is a development environment that provides common development functionality in a mixed Windows NT and HP-UX software development environment.

Although the system administration topics are pretty much the same going from operating system to operating system, the peculiarities of each operating system define how you will perform a given function. For this reason system administration is seldom covered as a general topic; rather, it is covered for a particular operating system. In this book, however, the assumption is that you have both Windows NT and HP-UX in your environment. You need to manage both and manage them separately for the most part; however, there are advantages to implementing technology that can enhance interoperability between the two operating systems.

What I'll cover in this interoperability chapter are some of the most basic, and at the same time some of the most useful, technologies you can put in place to help with interoperability between Windows NT and HP-UX.

You could certainly go beyond the interoperability topics I cover to much more advanced functionality; however, what I cover in the interoperability chapter is a big interoperability gain for very little cost and effort.

Why the X Window System?

Windows NT and HP-UX have their user environments that work great in supporting their respective operating systems. If, however, you want to go beyond logging into a Windows NT system to perform Windows NT system administration and logging into an HP-UX system to perform HP-UX system administration, then you need some way of getting access to one of these systems from the other. The X Window System is an ideal way to get remote access to an HP-UX system while sitting on your Windows NT system.

X Window System Background

X Windows is a *network*-based windowing environment, not a system-based windowing environment. For this reason it is ideal for giving you a window into your HP-UX system from your Windows NT system.

X Windows is an industry standard for supporting windowed user interfaces across a computer network. Because it is an industry standard, many companies offer X server products for operating systems such as Windows NT (we'll get into the "server" and "client" terminology of X Windows shortly.) X Windows is not just a windowing system on your computer but a windowing system across the network.

X Windows is independent of the hardware or operating system on which it runs. All it needs are a server and a client. The server and client may be two different systems or the same system; it doesn't matter. The server is a program which provides input devices such as your display, keyboard, and mouse. The client is the program that takes commands from the server such as an application.

The client and server roles are much different than those we normally associate with these terms. The X Windows server is on your local system; in this chapter it will be your Windows NT system, and the X Windows client is the application that responds to the server; in this chapter it will be the HP-UX system running a program such as the System Administration Manager (SAM) or HP SoftBench. We normally think of the small desktop system as the client and the larger, more powerful system as the server. With X Windows, however, it is the system that controls X Windows that is the server and the system that responds to the commands is the client. I often refer to a powerful client as the "host" to minimize confusion over this.

Sitting on one of the Windows NT systems on a network, you could open an X Window into several HP-UX hosts. You could therefore have one window open to HP-UX_System1 and another window open to HP-UX_System2, and so on.

X Server Software

There are many fine X Server products on the market. I loaded Exceed 5 from Hummingbird Communications LTD. on my system for demonstrating how X Windows can be used in a Windows NT and HP-UX environment. Figure 9-1 shows the full menu structure from having loaded both Hummingbird's X Windows product Exceed as well as its NFS product, which I'll be using in the next section, called Maestro.

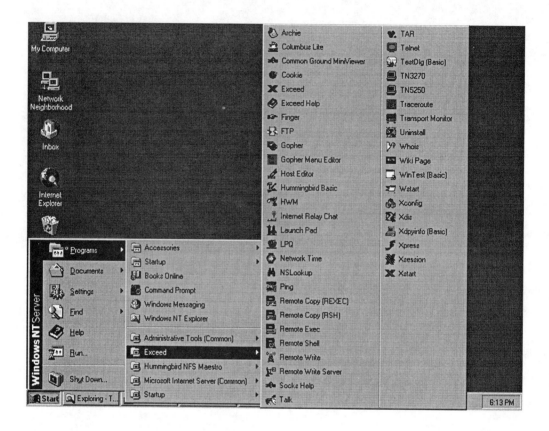

Figure 9-1   *Programs-Exceed* Menu

Not all of the items shown in the *Programs-Exceed* menu are related to X Windows. Many are for the networking products I'll get into in the next section.

The last menu pick under *Exceed* is *Xstart*. This menu pick allows you to establish an X Windows connection between your Windows NT system and HP-UX system. You can specify the host to which you want to connect, the HP-UX system in this case, the user you want to be connected as on the host, and the command to run on the HP-UX system. Figure 9-2 shows the *Xstart* window.

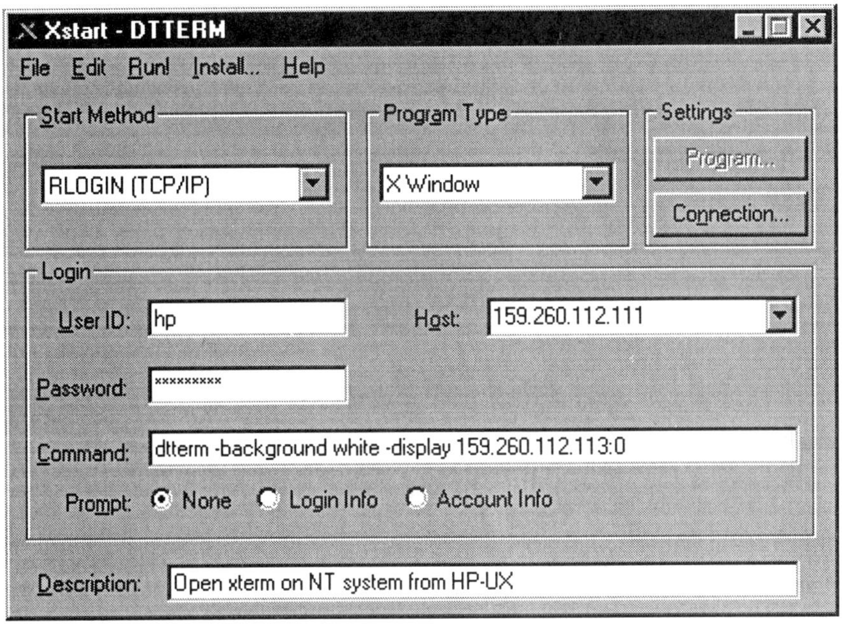

Figure 9-2 Establishing an X Windows Connection

The window in Figure 9-2 is labeled "dtterm." After you set up the *Xstart* window with the information you want, you can save the configuration. In this case I am issuing the **dtterm** command so I saved the window under this name. The complete **dtterm** command is

dtterm -background white -display 159.260.112.113:0

This command will start a **dtterm** window, which is a standard window program on HP-UX with a white background, and display the window on the system at the IP address 159.260.112.113. The IP address in this case is the Windows NT system on which you are issuing the command which is the X Windows server. The ":0" indicates that the first display on the Windows NT system will be used for **dtterm** because in the X Windows world it is possible to have several displays connected to a system.

The system on which the command runs is 159.260.112.111. This is the HP-UX system which acts as the X Windows client.

When you hit *Run!* from the pull-down menu, the **dtterm** command will be run on the host you have specified in the dialog box. Although you are typing this information on your Windows NT system, this command is being transferred to the HP-UX you specified in the *Xstart* box. This will have the same result as typing the **dtterm** command shown on the HP-UX system directly.

When you hit *Run!* a **dtterm** window appears on your Windows NT system which is a window into your HP-UX system. Figure 9-3 shows the **dtterm** window open on the Windows NT system.

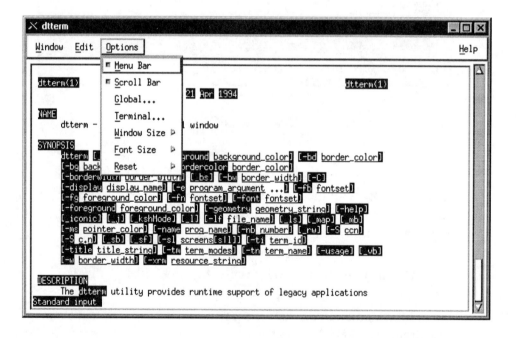

Figure 9-3   **dtterm** Running on HP-UX and Displayed on Windows NT

Figure 9-3 is a **dtterm** window displayed on the Windows NT system but running on the HP-UX system. The window has open the HP-UX manual page for **dtterm** and one of the pull-down menus of **dtterm**. You could issue any commands in this **dtterm** window that you could issue if you were sitting on the HP-UX system directly. Keep in mind, though, that your access to the HP-UX system is based on the user you specified in the *Xstart* window.

You could use *Xstart* to run any program for which you have appropriate permissions on the HP-UX system. Figure 9-4 shows an **xterm** window which is displayed on the Windows NT system but is running on the HP-UX system.

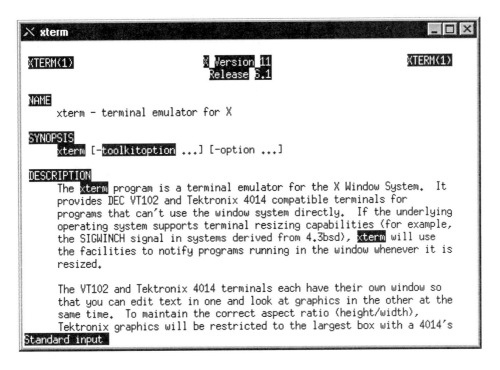

Figure 9-4   **xterm** Running on HP-UX and Displayed on Windows NT

You are by no means limited to running only terminal windows such as **dtterm** and **xterm** under X Windows in this environment. You could perform system management functions as well. Figure 9-5 shows the System Administration Manager (SAM), which was covered in an earlier chapter, running on the HP-UX system and displayed on the Windows NT system with *DCE Cell Management* selected.

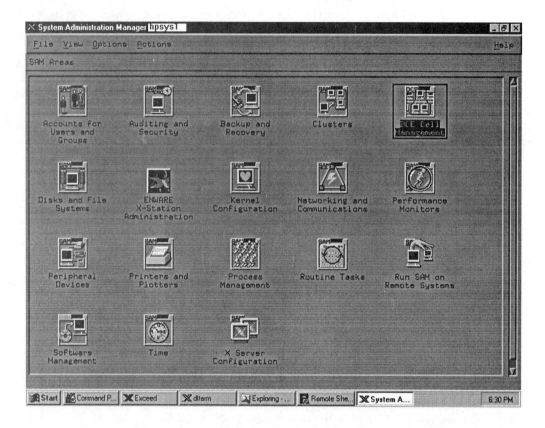

Figure 9-5   SAM Running on HP-UX and Displayed on Windows NT

In this case I have maximized the SAM window to take up the entire Windows NT environment. You still have access to the *Task Bar* at the bottom of the screen.

Another common use of X Windows software in this environment is for program development. Many users on the Windows NT system could get access to HP-UX servers using X Windows. Figure 9-6 shows the HP SoftBench development tool running on the HP-UX system and displayed on the Windows NT system. An application like SoftBench opens up many X Windows on the Windows NT system which is handled for you by the X server software.

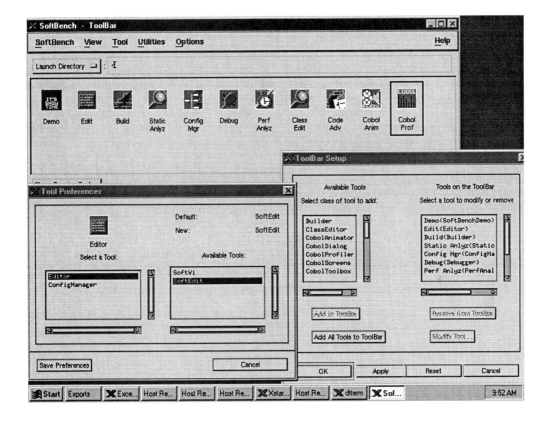

Figure 9-6 HP SoftBench Running on HP-UX and Displayed on Windows NT

This technique, using X Windows on the Windows NT system to display applications running on the HP-UX system, is powerful in this heterogenous environment. It is also inexpensive and simple to install.

We can also take this interoperability one step further by introducing data sharing into this mixed environment. This is covered in the next section.

Windows NT and HP-UX Networking

You can't really cover networking between any two operating systems without covering networking. Intersystem communication requires networking functionality that is a common denominator between two different operating systems. Since NFS is standard functionality on HP-UX and widely available on Windows NT, let's start by looking at NFS.

NFS Background

The earlier networking chapter covered TCP/IP in some detail. I suggest you read this chapter if you have not done so already. I am going to jump right into NFS background in this chapter and won't go over the TCP/IP material covered in earlier chapters. I am not going to limit the discussion and examples in this chapter to NFS. There are other services used to share files that are also useful such as File Transfer Protocol (FTP) which I'll show examples of as well. Because NFS is so widely used in the HP-UX user community, it is one of my goals to expose you to how NFS can be used in a Windows NT and HP-UX environment.

NFS allows you to mount disks on remote systems so they appear as though they are local to your system. Similarly, NFS allows remote systems to mount your local disk so it looks as though it is local to the remote system.

NFS, like X Windows, has a unique set of terminology. Here are definitions of some of the more important NFS terms.

Node	A computer system that is attached to or is part of a computer network.
Client	A node that requests data or services from other nodes (servers).
Server	A node that provides data or services to other nodes (clients) on the network.
File System	A disk partition or logical volume, or in the case of a workstation, this might be the entire disk.
Export	To make a file system available for mounting on remote nodes using NFS.
Mount	To access a remote file system using NFS.
Mount Point	The name of a directory on which the NFS file system is mounted.
Import	To mount a remote file system.

Before any data can be shared using NFS, the HP-UX system must be set up with exported file systems. The **/etc/exports** file in HP-UX defines what file systems are exported.

This file has in it the directories exported and options such as "ro" for read only, and "anon" which handles requests from anonymous users. If "anon" is equal to 65535, then anonymous users are denied access.

The following is an example **/etc/exports** file in which **/opt/app1** is exported to everyone but anonymous users, and **/opt/app1** is exported only to the system named system2:

```
/opt/app1    -anon=65534
/opt/app2    -access=system2
```

You may need to run **/usr/sbin/exportfs -a** if you add a file system to export.

Although we are going to focus on exporting HP-UX file systems to be mounted by Windows NT systems in this chapter, there is no reason we could not do the converse as well. Windows NT file systems could be mounted on an HP-UX system just as HP-UX file systems are mounted in Windows NT. Remote file systems to be mounted locally on an HP-UX system are put in **/etc/fstab**. Here is an example of an entry in **/etc/fstab** of a remote file system that is mounted locally. The remote directory **/opt/app3** on system2 is mounted locally under **/opt/opt3**:

```
system2:/opt/app3   /opt/app3   nfs   rw,suid   0   0
```

You can use the **showmount** command on HP-UX systems to show all remote systems (clients) that have mounted a local file system. **showmount** is useful for determining the file systems that are most often mounted by clients with NFS. The output of **showmount** is particularly easy to read because it lists the host name and the directory which was mounted by the client. There are the three following options to the **showmount** command:

-a prints output in the format "name:directory" as shown above.

-d lists all of the local directories that have been remotely mounted by clients.

-e prints a list of exported file systems.

Using Windows NT and HP-UX Networking

I will use the NFS Maestro product from Hummingbird Communications LTD. on Windows NT to demonstrate the networking interoperability in this chapter. Figure 9-7 shows the menu for the Maestro product after I installed it.

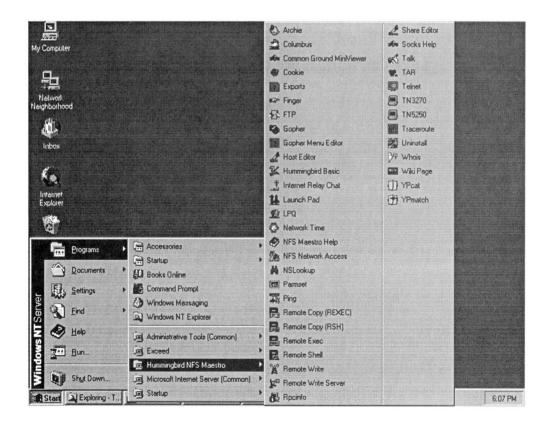

Figure 9-7 Hummingbird Maestro Menu in Windows NT

As you can see in Figure 9-7 there is much more than NFS functionality that is part of Maestro. I will cover some additional functionality later in this chapter; however, my specific objectives are to cover the most important Windows NT and HP-UX interoperability topics related to networking.

Before we use NFS with our Windows NT and HP-UX systems, let's first see what file systems we have available to us.

Using the **dtterm** from the previous section, we can sit at the Windows NT system and open a window into the HP-UX system. Figure 9-8 shows opening a **dtterm** and viewing the **/etc/exports** file.

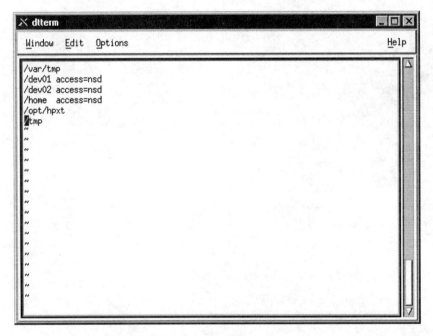

Figure 9-8 **dtterm** Window Showing **/etc/exports** on HP-UX System

There are several file systems exported on this HP-UX system. Some, such as **/opt/hpxt** and **/tmp,** have no restrictions on them; others do have restrictions. We don't, however, have to open a **dtterm** in order to see this file. We can use the Maestro menu pick *Exports* to bring up the window shown in Figure 9-9.

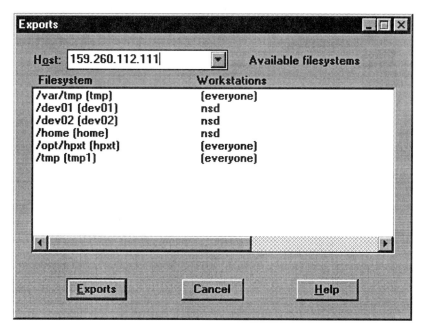

Figure 9-9 *Exports* Window Showing Exported File Systems

You can use the IP address as shown in the figure or the host name to specify the host on which you wish to view the exported file systems. You can see that this window takes the **/etc/exports** file and clarifies some of the entries. The entries for which there are no restrictions now have an "(everyone)" associated with them.

Now we can specify one or more of these exported file systems on the HP-UX system that we wish to mount on the Windows NT system. Using the *NFS Network Access* from the Maestro menu, we can specify one of these file systems to mount. Figure 9-10 shows mounting **/home** on the HP-UX system on the **G:** drive of the Windows NT system.

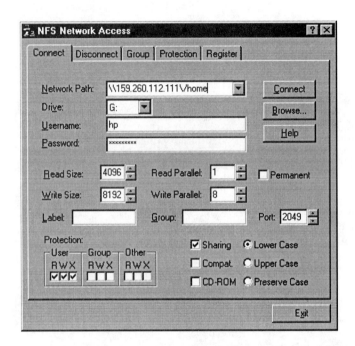

Figure 9-10   *NFS Network Access* Window Mounting **/home** as **G:**

After you hit the *Connect* button in the window, you will have **/home** mounted as **G:**. The means by which you specify the system and file system you wish to mount with Maestro is two slashes preceding the IP address or system name, another slash following the IP address or system name, and then the name of the file system you wish to mount. Note that the forward slash is part of the file system name. I used the IP address of the system. To view all of the mounted file systems on the Windows NT system you could invoke Windows NT *Explorer*. Figure 9-11 shows several file systems mounted in an *Explorer* window including **/home** on **G:**.

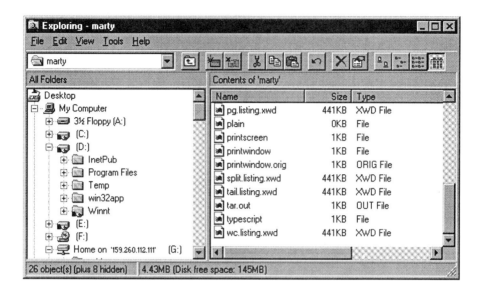

Figure 9-11   Windows NT *Explorer* Showing **/home** as **G:**

This window shows **/home** on drive **G:**. On the right side of the window is a listing of files in **/home/marty** on the HP-UX system. These files are now fully accessible on the Windows NT system (provided the appropriate access rights have been provided). You could now manipulate these HP-UX files in *Explorer* on the Windows NT system just as if they were local to the system. This is a powerful concept - to go beyond the barrier of only the Windows NT file system to freely manipulate HP-UX files.

An example of how you might go about using *Explorer* is to copy a Windows NT directory to HP-UX. Figure 9-12 shows two *Explorer* windows. The top window has an **exceed** directory on the Windows NT system which is being copied to a directory of the same name on the HP-UX system in the bottom window. As the copy from the Windows NT system to the HP-UX system takes place, a status window appears which shows the name of the file within the **exceed** directory (**exstart1.bmp**) being copied.

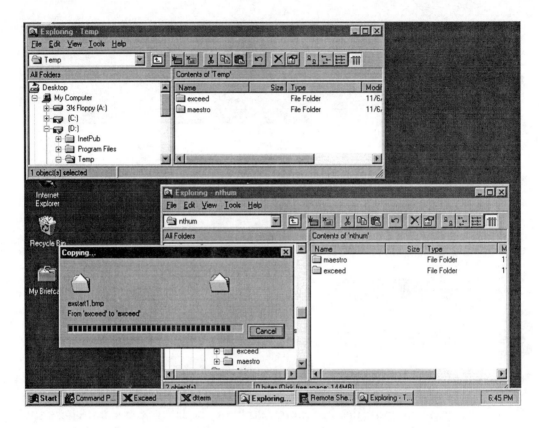

Figure 9-12   Copy a Windows NT Directory to HP-UX Using *Explorer*

This copy from Windows NT to HP-UX using *Explorer* demonstrates the ease with which files can be shared between these two operating systems.

File Transfer Protocol (FTP)

I started this section covering NFS on Windows NT and HP-UX for interoperability because NFS is the predominate means of sharing files in the HP-UX world. NFS is used almost universally to share data among networked HP-UX systems. NFS allows you to share data in real time, meaning that you can work on an HP-UX file while sitting at your Windows NT system. This is file sharing. You can also copy data between your Windows NT and HP-UX systems using FTP. This is not file sharing, however; the FTP functionality of Maestro makes it easy to transfer files between Windows NT and HP-UX.

Figure 9-13 shows the window that you would use to establish a connection to an HP-UX system from Windows NT.

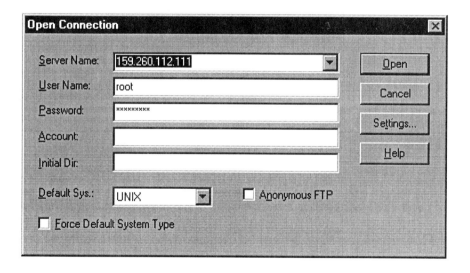

Figure 9-13   Establishing a Connection to HP-UX from Windows NT

After having established the connection, a window appears in which you can traverse the HP-UX file systems while working at your Windows NT system. Figure 9-14 shows viewing the **/opt/softbench** directory on an HP-UX system through the FTP window.

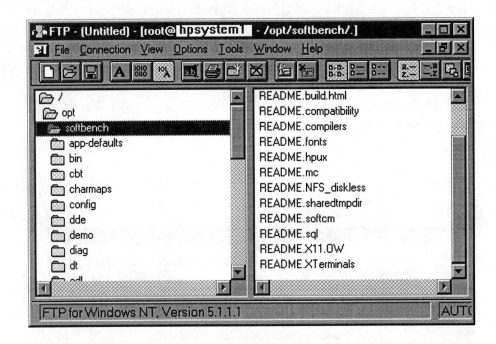

Figure 9-14 Viewing the **/opt/softbench** Directory Using *FTP* Window

You can also copy files graphically using FTP. You can open two *FTP* windows and copy files and directories from one system to the other. Figure 9-15 shows copying the directory **d:\temp\maestro** on the Windows NT system to **/home/marty/nthum/maestro** on the HP-UX system. This was performed using the icons in the two windows. The **maestro** directory did not exist on the HP-UX and was created as part of the copy.

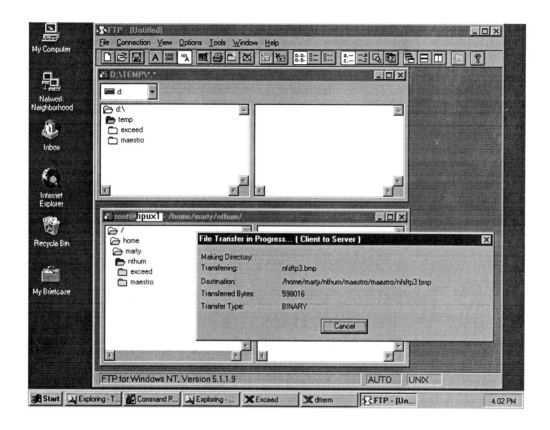

Figure 9-15 Using FTP to Copy Directory from Windows NT to HP-UX

There are a variety of options you can select when running FTP. Notice in Figure 9-15 that the "Transfer Type:" is binary. This is one of the options I selected prior to initiating the transfer.

Although this functionality is not as extensive as the file sharing of NFS, it is widely used to copy files from system to system and therefore can play a role in Windows NT and HP-UX interoperability.

I used icons to specify the information to be copied in this example. You could also have used the FTP command. The following is an overview of FTP including an example of running it from the command line and a command summary.

File Transfer Protocol (FTP) Transfer a file, or multiple files, from one system to another such as Windows NT to HP-UX. The following example shows copying the file **/tmp/krsort.c** from system2 (remote host) to the local directory on system1 (local host).

	comments
$ ftp system2	Issue ftp command
Connected to system2.	
system2 FTP server (Version 16.2) ready.	
Name (system2:root): root	Login to system2
Password required for root.	
Password:	Enter password
User root logged in.	
Remote system type is UNIX.	
Using binary mode to transfer files.	
ftp> **cd /tmp**	**cd** to **/tmp** on system2
CWD command successful	
ftp> **get krsort.c**	Get **krsort.c** file
PORT command successful	
Opening BINARY mode data connection for **krsort.c**	
Transfer complete.	
2896 bytes received in 0.08 seconds	
ftp> **bye**	Exit ftp
Goodbye.	
$	

In this example both systems are running HP-UX; however, the commands you issue through **FTP** are operating system independent. The **cd** for change directory and **get** commands used above work for any operating system on which **FTP** is running. If you become familiar with just a few **FTP** commands, you may find that transferring information in a heterogeneous networking environment is not difficult.

Since **FTP** is so widely used, I'll describe some of the more commonly used **FTP** commands.

ftp - File Transfer Program for copying files across a network.

The following list includes some commonly used **ftp** commands. This list is not complete.

ascii   Set the type of file transferred to ASCII. This means you will be transferring an ASCII file from one system to another. This is the default so you don't have to set it.

   Example: **ascii**

binary   Set the type of file transferred to binary. This means you'll be transferring a binary file from one system to another. If, for instance, you want to have a directory on your HP-UX system which will hold applications that you will copy to non-HP-UX systems, then you will want to use binary transfer.

   Example: **binary**

cd   Change to the specified directory on the remote host.

   Example: **cd /tmp**

dir   List the contents of a directory on the remote system to the screen or to a file on the local system if you specify a local file name.

get   Copy the specified remote file to the specified local file. If you don't specify a local file name, then the remote file name will be used.

lcd   Change to the specified directory on the local host.

Example: **lcd /tmp**

ls   List the contents of a directory on the remote system to the screen or to a file on the local system if you specify a local file name.

mget   Copy multiple files from the remote host to the local host.

Example: **mget *.c**

put   Copy the specified local file to the specified remote file. If you don't specify a remote file name, then the local file name will be used.

Example: **put test.c**

mput   Copy multiple files from the local host to the remote host.

Example: **mput *.c**

system   Show the type of operating system running on the remote host.

bye/quit   Close the connection to the remote host.

Example: **bye**

There are other **FTP** commands in addition to those I have covered here.

Other Connection Topics

There are other means by which you can connect to the HP-UX system.
Two popular techniques for connecting to other systems are FTP, which was
just covered, and TELNET. Maestro supplies the capability for both of
these. I could sit on the Windows NT system using TELNET with a window open on the HP-UX system and issue commands.

Figure 9-16 shows the *Connect* window used to specify whether you
want to use RLOGIN or TELNET to establish the connection.

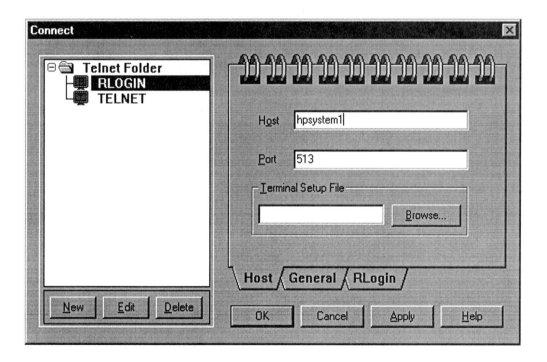

Figure 9-16 Selecting RLOGIN or TELNET

I selected TELNET in the Connect window and was able to log in to the HP-UX system as shown in Figure 9-17.

Figure 9-17   TELNET Window

In this window we could issue HP-UX commands just as if we were sitting on a terminal connected directly to the HP-UX system. I prefer the **dtterm** window used earlier with X Windows to opening a TELNET session, but TELNET is widely used in heterogenous environments. With X Windows you get graphical functionality that is not part of TELNET.

Whenever you work with a networking product you will have to deal with the way in which hosts are managed. You can have as many hosts defined in Maestro as you like. Rather than type in the host you wish to connect to every time, you can manage a lists of hosts from which you select when you perform one of the functions in this section. In the *Xstart* and *Open Connection* windows shown earlier, for instance, there is a pull down menu that allows you to select from a list of hosts. Figure 9-18 shows the Host Name Maintenance window in which you define the IP address and name of a system that will get added to the file defining hosts on your system.

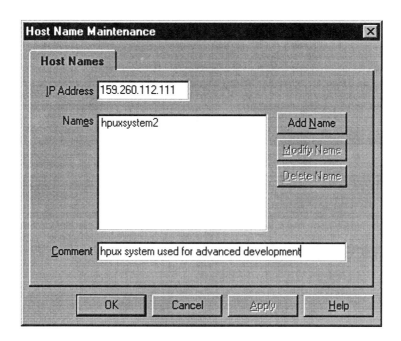

Figure 9-18 *Host Name Maintenance* Window

The host related information you specify in this window will update the file on your Windows NT used to keep track of hosts.

Another configuration issue you have to be concerned with are the programs running on your host, in this case the HP-UX system, that are required to support the networking functionality such as NFS. The *Rpcinfo* menu pick under Maestro will query the HP-UX host and list the services it is running. Figure 9-19 shows this window.

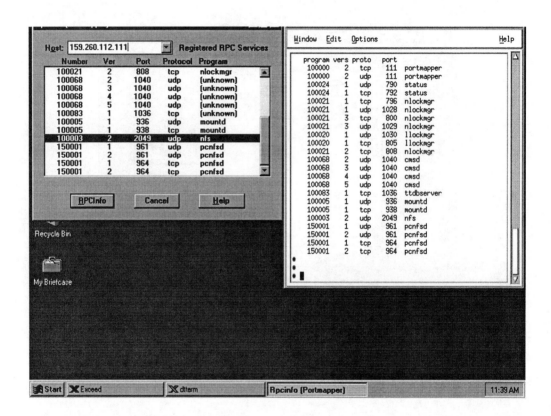

Figure 9-19 *Rpcinfo* Window (left) on Windows NT and Output of **rpcinfo** Command in HP-UX (right)

The left window is the Maestro *Rpcinfo* window. The right window is a **dtterm** window on the HP-UX system showing the result of having run the **rpcinfo** command in HP-UX.

RPC stands for Remote Procedure Call. There are a variety of programs for which there is RPC-related information. Several programs are required to achieve the Windows NT and HP-UX interoperability.

You can see that the contents of these windows are identical. The first number shown is the program number. There are widely accepted RPC numbers for various programs. For NFS the program number is 100003. The next number is the version of the protocol. In this case NFS is version 2. The next number is the port. The port number is used by both the client, which is the Windows NT system in our case, and the server, which is the HP-UX system in our case, to communicate using NFS. The next field is the protocol used which is usually UDP or TCP. The final field is the program name.

In the case of NFS I had to ensure that NFS, **portmapper**, **mountd**, and **pcnfsd** were running on my HP-UX system before I could use the Maestro NFS product.

Rpcinfo is a useful tool for viewing all of the information on the host to which your Windows NT system will connect.

Windows NT Functionality on HP-UX - Advanced Server 9000

To this point we have been discussing moving HP-UX functionality such as X Windows and NFS onto Windows NT in order to achieve interoperability. Why not do the converse? Having some Windows NT functionality on HP-UX would certainly be helpful in some cases. HP-UX resources such as printers and disks could then be shared with several Windows NT systems on the network.

HP Advanced Server 9000 is just such an HP product that runs on your HP-UX system. It provides Windows NT functionality that facilitates Windows NT and HP-UX interoperability. With Advanced Server 9000 your HP-UX system can act as a Primary or Backup Domain Controller, a file server, a print server, or other Windows NT functional component.

This chapter makes use of some of the **net** commands of Windows NT, especially the **net share** command. When I am working on the HP-UX system (*dloaner*) in this chapter, I use the command line including some net commands. When I am working on the Windows NT system (*hpsystem1*) in this section, I will use graphical Windows NT functionality which is preferable to issuing commands on the command line. I use both the command line and graphical methods so you can see the difference in the two approaches. You may want to explore some of these **net** commands using the on-line help of your Windows NT system as you progress through this chapter. Here is a list of some widely used **net** commands and a brief explanation of each:

net accounts   Used to maintain the user accounts database.

net computer   Used to add or delete computers from the domain database.

net config server

Display or change settings for a server service on which the command is executed.

net config workstation

Display or change settings for the workstation service on which the command is executed.

net continue   Reactivate a Windows NT service that has been suspended with the **net pause** command.

net file   Used for network file manipulation such as listing ID numbers, closing a shared file, removing file locks, and so on.

net group   Used to add, display, or modify global groups on servers.

net help	Display a listing of help options for any net commands.
net helpmsg	Displays explanations of Windows NT network messages such as errors, warnings, and alerts.
net localgroup	Used to modify local groups on computers.
net name	Used to add or delete a "messaging name" at a computer which is the name to which messages are sent.
net print	Used to list print jobs and shared queues.
net send	Send messages to other users, computers, and "messaging names" on the network.
net session	Used to list or disconnect sessions between the computer and other computers on the network.
net share	Share a server's resources with other computers on the network.
net start	Used to start services such as *server*.
net statistics	Displays the statistics log for the local Workstation or Server service.
net stop	Used to stop services such as *server*.

net time	Synchronize the computer's clock with another computer on the domain.
net use	Displays, connects, or disconnects a computer with shared resources.
net user	Creates or modifies user accounts.
net view	Lists resources being shared on a computer.

Let's take a closer look at how you configure and use Advanced Server 9000 in a networked environment.

Installing Advanced Server 9000 on HP-UX

It's easy to install and configure Advanced Server 9000 on your HP-UX system. Advanced Server 9000 is installed using Software Distributor on your HP-UX system just as you would load any other software. After installing Advanced Server 9000, you would run the configuration script called **asu_inst**. The following text shows running **asu_inst** to configure the HP-UX system *dloaner* to be a Backup Domain Controller (BDC) for the Windows NT system *hpsystem1*.

```
# /opt/asu/lanman/bin/asu_inst

This request script will prompt you for information which is necessary
to install and configure your Advanced Server for UNIX Systems.
```

There are two installation modes:

Express Setup - the installation scripts use default settings so
installation is quick and easy. You may change these settings
after installation completes. The server is installed as a
primary domain controller in its own domain.

Custom Setup - this mode allows you to specify the settings at the
beginning of installation. If you select this mode, you must
specify the server's name, the domain it will participate in,
and the role in that domain.

NOTE: The installation requires a password for the administrative account.
A default password of 'password' will be used, although you may elect to
be prompted for a different password at the end of the installation.

If you are installing many servers it is strongly recommended that you use
the default password for all installations. Be sure to change these
passwords after determining that your network is operating correctly.

Do you want Express Setup [y/n]? y

Advanced Server for UNIX provides a NETLOGON service which simplifies the
administration of multiple servers. A single user accounts database can be
shared by multiple servers grouped together into an administrative
collection called a domain. Within a domain, each server has a designated
role. A single server, called the primary domain controller, manages all
changes to the user accounts database and automatically distributes those
changes to other servers, called backup domain controllers, within the same
domain. You may now supply a server name (the name which this server
will be known on the network), the role that this server will perform
in that domain (primary or backup), and a domain name.

Enter the name of the server
or press Enter to select 'dloaner':

Each server must be given a role in a domain. The possible roles are:

primary domain controller:
     Administration server. Distributes user accounts information
          to backup domain controllers. Validates network logon requests.
     There can be only one primary domain controller per domain.

backup domain controller:
             Receives user account information from the primary domain
             controller. Validates network logon requests and can be promoted
     to primary if the primary domain controller is not accessible.

Enter role (primary or backup): backup

This installation will configure the server as a backup domain controller.
You will be prompted to enter the name of the primary domain controller,
and an administrative account name on the primary along with its password.
In order for this installation to complete successfully, the primary domain
controller must be running and connected to the network.

Enter the name of the primary domain controller (eg, abc_asu): hpsystem1

Confirm choices for server dloaner:
                         role   : backup
                         primary: hpsystem1
Is this correct [y/n]? y

```
_&a0y0C_J
Enter the name of an administrative account on the primary
domain controller 'hpsystem1' or press Enter to select 'administrator':

This procedure requires the password for the administrative account on
'hpsystem1'.  If the password is the default ('password') created
during installation, you will not need to be prompted for a password.
If you have changed the password, you should allow this program  to prompt
for a password after the files have been installed.

Do you want to use the default password [y/n]? y

Advanced Server/9000
Copyright (c) 1988, 1991-1996 AT&T and Microsoft
Copyright (c) 1992-1996 Hewlett-Packard
All rights reserved

Adding Advanced Server for UNIX Systems administrative users and groups
Add
Comment <Advanced Server account>
Home Dir </opt/asu/lanman>
UID <100>
GID <99>
Shell </sbin/false>
Name <lanman>
pw_name: lanman
pw_passwd: *
pw_uid: 100
pw_gid: 99
pw_age: ?
pw_comment:
pw_gecos: Advanced Server account
pw_dir: /opt/asu/lanman
pw_shell: /sbin/false
enter addusr
pw_name = lanman
pw_passwd = *
pw_uid = 100
pw_gid = 99
pw_gecos = Advanced Server account
pw_dir = /opt/asu/lanman
pw_shell = /sbin/false
enter_quiet_zone()
exit_quiet_zone()
exiting addusr, error = 0
Add
Comment <Advanced Server Administrator>
Home Dir </var/opt/asu/lanman/lmxadmin>
GID <99>
Name <lmxadmin>
pw_name: lmxadmin
pw_passwd: *
pw_uid: 0
pw_gid: 99
pw_age: ?
pw_comment:
pw_gecos: Advanced Server Administrator
pw_dir: /var/opt/asu/lanman/lmxadmin
pw_shell:
enter addusr
pw_name = lmxadmin
pw_passwd = *
pw_uid = 0
pw_gid = 99
pw_gecos = Advanced Server Administrator
pw_dir = /var/opt/asu/lanman/lmxadmin
```

```
pw_shell =
enter_quiet_zone()
exit_quiet_zone()
exiting addusr, error = 0
Add
Comment <Advanced Server GUEST Login>
Shell </sbin/false>
GID <99>
Name <lmxguest>
pw_name: lmxguest
pw_passwd: *
pw_uid: 0
pw_gid: 99
pw_age: ?
pw_comment:
pw_gecos: Advanced Server GUEST Login
pw_dir:
pw_shell: /sbin/false
enter addusr
pw_name = lmxguest
pw_passwd = *
pw_uid = 0
pw_gid = 99
pw_gecos = Advanced Server GUEST Login
pw_dir = /usr/lmxguest
pw_shell = /sbin/false
enter_quiet_zone()
exit_quiet_zone()
exiting addusr, error = 0
Add
Comment <Advanced Server World Login>
Shell </sbin/false>
GID <99>
Name <lmworld>
pw_name: lmworld
pw_passwd: *
pw_uid: 0
pw_gid: 99
pw_age: ?
pw_comment:
pw_gecos: Advanced Server World Login
pw_dir:
pw_shell: /sbin/false
enter addusr
pw_name = lmworld
pw_passwd = *
pw_uid = 0
pw_gid = 99
pw_gecos = Advanced Server World Login
pw_dir = /usr/lmworld
pw_shell = /sbin/false
enter_quiet_zone()
exit_quiet_zone()
exiting addusr, error = 0

Creating Directory: /home/lanman
Setting owner, group, and permissions for installed files....

Enter the password for administrator on hpsystem1:
Re-enter password:

Contacting the server 'hpsystem1' ... Success

Creating Advanced Server for UNIX Systems accounts database.

Starting the Advanced Server for UNIX Systems...
```

```
The Advanced Server for UNIX Systems is now operational.
#
```

After the installation and configuration is complete, you have **netde-mon** running, which is an essential component of Advanced Server 9000, as shown in the following **ps** command:

```
# ps -ef | grep netdemon
    root  1100     1  0 10:18:38 ?         0:00 /opt/lmu/netbios/bin/netdemon
#
```

In addition to netdemon, NetBIOS must also be running.

Advanced Server 9000 starts several processes on your HP-UX sys-tem in addition to **netdemon**. You can also verify that the Advanced Server 9000 server is running by viewing its processes with the **ps** command.

```
# ps -ef | grep lm
    root  3285     1  0 10:37:19 ?       0:00 lmx.dmn
    root  3200     1  0 10:36:57 ?       0:00 lmx.ctrl
    root  3262  3200  0 10:37:07 ?       0:00 lmx.srv -s 1
    root  3295     1  0 10:37:20 ?       0:00 lmx.sched
    root  3289     1  0 10:37:19 ?       0:00 lmx.browser
    root  1100     1  0 10:18:38 ?       0:00 /opt/lmu/netbios/bin/netdemon
#
```

Many process are shown here such as the *lmx.dmn* which is the dae-mon, *lmx.ctrl* which is the control process; *lmx.sched* which is the sched-uler; *lmx.browser* which is the browser; and *lmx.srv* which is a client session. If Advanced Server 9000 were not running, you would use the **net start server** command to start the server. Similarly, you stop the server with **net stop server**.

In addition, you have several users and groups that have been created on your HP-UX system to facilitate using Advanced Server 9000 with your Windows NT systems. The new users are shown in the upcoming **/etc/ passwd** file and the new groups are shown in the upcoming **/etc/group** file.

```
# cat /etc/passwd
root:jThTuY9OhNxGY:0:3::/:/sbin/sh
daemon:*:1:5::/:/sbin/sh
bin:*:2:2::/usr/bin:/sbin/sh
sys:*:3:3::/:
adm:*:4:4::/var/adm:/sbin/sh
```

```
uucp:*:5:3::/var/spool/uucppublic:/usr/lbin/uucp/uucico

lp:*:9:7::/var/spool/lp:/sbin/sh

nuucp:*:11:11::/var/spool/uucppublic:/usr/lbin/uucp/uucico

hpdb:*:27:1:ALLBASE:/:/sbin/sh

nobody:*:-2:-2147483648::/:

lanman:*:100:99:Advanced Server account:/opt/asu/lanman:/sbin/false

lmxadmin:*:202:99:Advanced Server Administrator:/var/opt/asu/lanman/lmxadmin:

lmxguest:*:203:99:Advanced Server GUEST Login:/usr/lmxguest:/sbin/false

lmworld:*:204:99:Advanced Server World Login:/usr/lmworld:/sbin/false

# cat /etc/group

root::0:root

other::1:root,hpdb

bin::2:root,bin

sys::3:root,uucp

adm::4:root,adm

daemon::5:root,daemon

mail::6:root

lp::7:root,lp

tty::10:

nuucp::11:nuucp

users::20:root

nogroup:*:-2:

DOS----::99:lanman

DOS-a--::98:lanman

DOS--s-::97:lanman

DOS---h::96:lanman

DOS-as-::95:lanman

DOS-a-h::94:lanman

DOS--sh::93:lanman

DOS-ash::92:lanman

#
```

In addition to the HP-UX system modifications that have automatically taken place, the Windows NT Primary Domain Controller (PDC) now recognizes the HP-UX system as the backup domain controller. Figure 9-20 shows a screen shot from the Windows NT system *hpsystem1*, which is the primary domain controller. The screen shot shows *dloaner* acting as the backup domain controller and the default shared directories on the HP-UX system *dloaner*. The share properties for one of the shares, **C:\opt\asu\lanman**, is also shown.

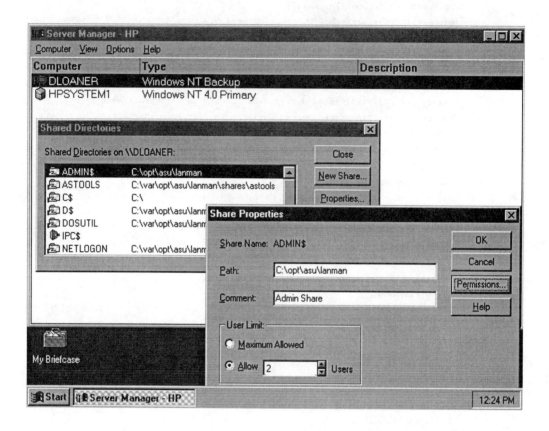

Figure 9-20 Default Shares after Loading and Configuring Advanced Server 9000

These shares can also be viewed on the command line of the HP-UX system using the net command as shown in the following output.

```
# /opt/asu/lanman/bin/net share

Sharename    Resource                          Remark
----------------------------------------------------------------------------------
ADMIN$       C:\OPT\ASU\LANMAN                 Admin Share
IPC$                                           IPC Share
C$           C:\                               Root Share
D$           C:\VAR\OPT\ASU\LANMAN\SHARES      SystemRoot Share
ASTOOLS      C:\VAR\OPT\ASU\LANMAN\SHARES...   Advanced Server Tools
```

```
DOSUTIL       C:\VAR\OPT\ASU\LANMAN\SHARES... DOS Utilities
NETLOGON      C:\VAR\OPT\ASU\LANMAN\SHARES... Logon Scripts Directory
PATCHES       C:\VAR\OPT\ASU\LANMAN\SHARES... Client Patches
PRINTLOG      C:\VAR\OPT\ASU\LANMAN\SHARES... LP printer messages
USERS         C:\HOME\LANMAN                  Users Directory
The command completed successfully.
#
```

These are the default shares that have been set up by Advanced Server 9000. Those followed by a $ are hidden shares used only for administrative purposes. When you run *Windows NT Explorer,* you won't see these hidden directories.

You can set up additional shares such as the printer and disk. We will set up in upcoming sections.

Sharing a Printer

In addition to the default sharing that takes place with Advanced Server 9000, there may be additional resources you want to share between Windows NT and HP-UX systems.

For example, you may have a printer used in your HP-UX environment to which you want Windows NT systems to have access. The following commands show adding a shared printer and viewing it in HP-UX.

The first command is **lpstat** on HP-UX that shows the status of the existing printer *laser*.

```
# lpstat -t
scheduler is running
system default destination: laser
device for laser: /dev/c2t0d0_lp
laser accepting requests since Feb 11 17:23
printer laser is idle.  enabled since Feb 11 17:23
fence priority : 0
no entries
#
```

Next we run the **net** command and specify the printer *laser* as a shared printer device.

```
# /opt/asu/lanman/bin/net net share laser=laser /print
laser was successfully shared
```

To see the configuration of the printer we can issue the net print command as shown below:

```
# net print laser /options
Printing options for LASER

Status              Queue Active
Remark
Print Devices       laser
Driver              HP-UX LM/X Print Manager
Separator file
Priority            5
Print after         12:00 AM
Print until         12:00 AM
Print processor
Parameters          COPIES=1 EJECT=AUTO BANNER=YES
The command completed successfully.
#
```

After printing a text file from the Windows NT system onto the device *laser* connected to the HP-UX system running Advanced Server 9000, I got a bunch of unintelligible information on the printed sheet. The Advanced Server 9000 printer was not configured raw. I issued the following command to make the printer raw:

```
# net print laser /parms:types=-oraw
The command completed successfully.
```

The new configuration, with the *TYPES=-oraw*, is shown in the following output. This device successfully printed from the Windows NT system to the HP-UX system running Advanced Server 9000 on which *laser* is connected.

```
# net print laser /options
Printing options for LASER

Status              Queue Active
Remark
Print Devices       laser
Driver              HP-UX LM/X Print Manager
Separator file
Priority            5
Print after         12:00 AM
Print until         12:00 AM
Print processor
Parameters          COPIES=1 TYPES=-oraw EJECT=AUTO BANNER=YES
The command completed successfully.
#
```

We can now view all of the shared devices with the **net** command.

```
# /opt/asu/lanman/bin/net share

Sharename   Resource                          Remark
-------------------------------------------------------------------------
ADMIN$      C:\OPT\ASU\LANMAN                  Admin Share
IPC$                                          IPC Share
C$          C:\                               Root Share
D$          C:\VAR\OPT\ASU\LANMAN\SHARES      SystemRoot Share
ASTOOLS     C:\VAR\OPT\ASU\LANMAN\SHARES...   Advanced Server Tools
DOSUTIL     C:\VAR\OPT\ASU\LANMAN\SHARES...   DOS Utilities
NETLOGON    C:\VAR\OPT\ASU\LANMAN\SHARES...   Logon Scripts Directory
PATCHES     C:\VAR\OPT\ASU\LANMAN\SHARES...   Client Patches
PRINTLOG    C:\VAR\OPT\ASU\LANMAN\SHARES...   LP printer messages
USERS       C:\HOME\LANMAN                    Users Directory
LASER       laser                             Spooled
The command completed successfully.
#
```

The last item in this listing is the printer *laser* that was added with the **net** command. All of the previous commands were issued on the HP-UX system running Advanced Server 9000. We can now view the shared devices of *dloaner* on the Windows NT system using *Explorer* to confirm the printer *laser* is a shared device as shown in Figure 9-21.

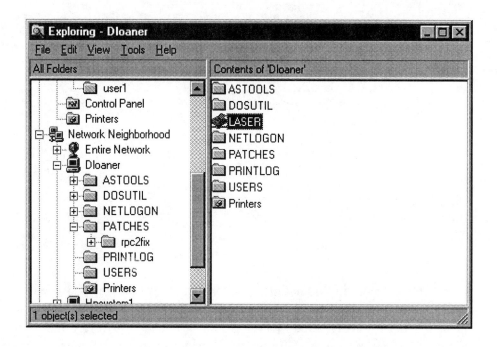

Figure 9-21   Windows NT Explorer Showing Printer *Laser*

The details of this shared printer can be viewed in *Printers* under *Control Panel*.

Sharing a File System

With the printer having been added the shares that are now set up on the HP-UX system running Advanced Server 9000 look like the following:

```
# /opt/asu/lanman/bin/net share

Sharename    Resource                        Remark
--------------------------------------------------------------------------------
ADMIN$       C:\OPT\ASU\LANMAN               Admin Share
```

```
IPC$                                              IPC Share
C$          C:\                                   Root Share
D$          C:\VAR\OPT\ASU\LANMAN\SHARES          SystemRoot Share
ASTOOLS     C:\VAR\OPT\ASU\LANMAN\SHARES...       Advanced Server Tools
DOSUTIL     C:\VAR\OPT\ASU\LANMAN\SHARES...       DOS Utilities
NETLOGON    C:\VAR\OPT\ASU\LANMAN\SHARES...       Logon Scripts Directory
PATCHES     C:\VAR\OPT\ASU\LANMAN\SHARES...       Client Patches
PRINTLOG    C:\VAR\OPT\ASU\LANMAN\SHARES...       LP printer messages
USERS       C:\HOME\LANMAN                        Users Directory
LASER       laser                                 Spooled
The command completed successfully.
#
```

The shares shown include the printer that was added. We could now issue the **net share** command and add an HP-UX file system to be shared. To share the **/home** directory on the HP-UX system *dloaner,* we would issue the following command:

```
# /opt/asu/lanman/bin/net share home=c:/home
home was shared successfully
```

Note that the HP-UX notation for the directory was issued with the slash (/) rather than backslash (\) as you would on a Windows NT system. We can now view the shares on *dloaner*, including the new *HOME* share, with the **net** command.

```
# /opt/asu/lanman/bin/net share

Sharename   Resource                              Remark
-------------------------------------------------------------------------------
ADMIN$      C:\OPT\ASU\LANMAN                     Admin Share
IPC$                                              IPC Share
C$          C:\                                   Root Share
D$          C:\VAR\OPT\ASU\LANMAN\SHARES          SystemRoot Share
ASTOOLS     C:\VAR\OPT\ASU\LANMAN\SHARES...       Advanced Server Tools
DOSUTIL     C:\VAR\OPT\ASU\LANMAN\SHARES...       DOS Utilities
HOME        C:\HOME
NETLOGON    C:\VAR\OPT\ASU\LANMAN\SHARES...       Logon Scripts Directory
PATCHES     C:\VAR\OPT\ASU\LANMAN\SHARES...       Client Patches
PRINTLOG    C:\VAR\OPT\ASU\LANMAN\SHARES...       LP printer messages
USERS       C:\HOME\LANMAN                        Users Directory
LASER       laser                                 Spooled
The command completed successfully.
#
```

You could now view this share on the Windows NT system and map it to a drive as shown in Figure 9-22.

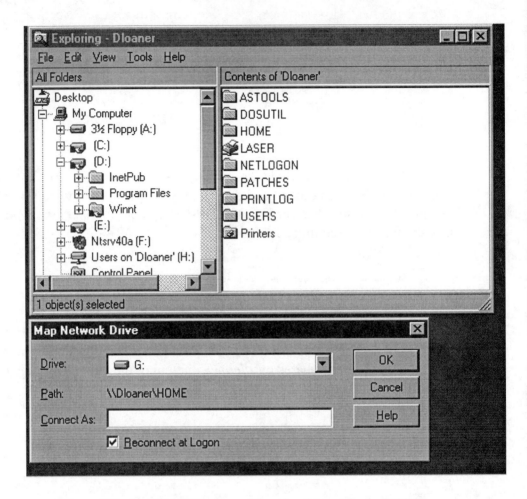

Figure 9-22   Windows NT *Explorer* Showing New Share *HOME*

Only a small subset of Advanced Server 9000 functionality was covered in this section. We covered using an HP-UX system running
Advanced Server 9000 as a backup domain controller, sharing an HP-UX
connected printer with a Windows NT network, and sharing an HP-UX
connected disk with a Windows NT network. These are some of the more
common uses for Advanced Server 9000. Nearly everything you can do

with a Windows NT system can be done with Advanced Server 9000 so don't limit yourself to only the functionality covered in this section.

POSIX Utilities

The Microsoft Windows NT Server Resource Kit (referred to as Resource Kit throughout this section) has on it several POSIX utilities that HP-UX system administrators will find useful when using Windows NT. The Resource Kit in general is a fantastic system administration resource. Although I will focus on only POSIX utilities in this book, it has on it a wealth of information. The Resource Kit is available from Microsoft Press, Redmond, WA. The POSIX utilities include such useful commands as **cat, chmod, find, ls, mv,** and others. The commands that are available on the Resource Kit vary somewhat from architecture to architecture. I will focus on only the "I386" utilities and not the utilities for other architectures in this section.

The Resource Kit has on it the file **POSIX.WRI** that describes the POSIX utilities in detail. In this section I'll just provide a brief overview of the utilities and examples of using some of the utilities. Most HP-UX system administrators are familiar with these utilities in HP-UX but may find differences in the options to these utilities when using the Resource Kit version.

I have made every effort to limit the number of "add-on" products to Windows NT and HP-UX covered in this book. The Resource Kit, however, is so useful to Windows NT system administrators that not covering at least some part of it, such as the POSIX utilities, would leave a void in the discussion of Windows NT interoperability. You can find out more information about the Resource Kit on the Microsoft Web site. You can buy it at many computer, electronic, and book stores. Be sure to buy the Resource Kit for the version of Windows NT you are running. There is also a Resource Kit for both the Server and Workstation versions of Windows NT. I used the Server Resource Kit for the POSIX commands covered in this section.

Both the source code and executables for the POSIX utilities are on the Resource Kit. The following is a listing of the POSIX executables for

I386 on the Resource Kit CD-ROM. I used the POSIX utility **ls -l** to produce this listing.

```
F:\I386\GNU\POSIX> ls -l

-rwxrwxrwx    1 Everyone Everyone    101748 Sep  6 12:39 CAT.EXE
-rwxrwxrwx    1 Everyone Everyone    116188 Sep  6 12:39 CHMOD.EXE
-rwxrwxrwx    1 Everyone Everyone    110920 Sep  6 12:39 CHOWN.EXE
-rwxrwxrwx    1 Everyone Everyone    111208 Sep  6 12:39 CP.EXE
-rwxrwxrwx    1 Everyone Everyone    173580 Sep  6 12:39 FIND.EXE
-rwxrwxrwx    1 Everyone Everyone    144256 Sep  6 12:39 GREP.EXE
-rwxrwxrwx    1 Everyone Everyone     90960 Sep  6 12:39 LN.EXE
-rwxrwxrwx    1 Everyone Everyone    128532 Sep  6 12:39 LS.EXE
-rwxrwxrwx    1 Everyone Everyone     88984 Sep  6 12:39 MKDIR.EXE
-rwxrwxrwx    1 Everyone Everyone     99096 Sep  6 12:39 MV.EXE
-rwxrwxrwx    1 Everyone Everyone    114564 Sep  6 12:39 RM.EXE
-rwxrwxrwx    1 Everyone Everyone     85004 Sep  6 12:39 RMDIR.EXE
-rwxrwxrwx    1 Everyone Everyone    362528 Sep  6 12:39 SH.EXE
-rwxrwxrwx    1 Everyone Everyone     91244 Sep  6 12:39 TOUCH.EXE
-rwxrwxrwx    1 Everyone Everyone    287628 Sep  6 12:39 VI.EXE
-rwxrwxrwx    1 Everyone Everyone     95392 Sep  6 12:39 WC.EXE
```

The directory in which these utilities are located is the **F:** drive, which is my CD-ROM, in **I386\GNU\POSIX**, which is the I386 version of these utilities. The following are command summaries of the POSIX utilities. A brief description of some the utilities as well some of the more commonly used options to the utilities are included. In some cases there is also an example of having run the utility. The **POSIX.WRI** file on the Resource Kit provides an exhaustive description of each utility.

cat

cat - Display, combine, append, copy, or create files.

Some commonly used options

-n   Line numbers are displayed along with output lines.

-u   Output is unbuffered, which means it is handled character by character.

-v   Print most nonprinting characters visibly.

The following example shows using the -n option with **cat**.

```
D:\WINNT\system> cat -n setup.inf

   1   [setup]
   2       help = setup.hlp
   3
   4   ;   Place any programs here that should be run at the end of setup.
   5   ;   These apps will be run in order of their appearance here.
   6   [run]
   7
   8   [dialog]
   9       caption   = "Windows Setup"
  10       exit      = "Exit Windows Setup"
  11       title     = "Installing Windows 3.1"
  12       options   = "In addition to installing Windows 3.1, you can:"
  13       printwait = "Please wait while Setup configures your printer(s)..."

                              .
                              .
                              .

  20   [data]
```

```
21  ; Disk space required
22  ; <type of setup>= <Full install space>, <Min install space>
23
24       upd2x386full = 10000000,6144000 ; 10.0 Mb, 6.144 Mb
25       upd2x286full = 9000000,6144000  ;  9.0 Mb, 6.144 Mb
26       upd3x386full = 5500000,5000000  ;  5.5 Mb, 5.0 Mb
27       upd3x286full = 5500000,5000000  ;  5.5 Mb, 5.0 Mb
28
29       new386full   = 10000000,6144000 ; 10.0 Mb, 6.144 Mb
30       new286full   = 9000000,6144000  ;  9.0 Mb, 6.144 Mb
31
32       netadmin     = 16000000         ; 16.0 Mb
33       netadminupd  = 16000000         ; 16.0 Mb
34       upd2x386net  = 300000           ;    .3 Mb
35       upd3x386net  = 300000           ;    .3 Mb
36       upd2x286net  = 300000           ;    .3 Mb
37       upd3x286net  = 300000           ;    .3 Mb
38       new386net    = 300000,300000    ;    .3 Mb,   .3 Mb
39       new286net    = 300000,300000    ;    .3 Mb,   .3 Mb
40
41
42
43  ; Defaults used in setting up and names of a few files
44       startup      = WIN.COM
```

chmod

chmod - Change permissions of specified files using symbolic or absolute (sometimes called numeric) modes. Symbolic mode is described below.

Symbol of whom is affected:

u	User is affected.
g	Group is affected.
o	Other is affected.
a	All users are affected.

Operation to perform:

+	Add permission.
-	Remove permission.
=	Replace permission.

Permission specified:

r	Read permission.
w	Write permission.
x	Execute permission.
u	Copy user permissions.
g	Copy group permissions.
o	Copy other permissions.

The following example uses both modes. Using absolute or numeric mode, the permissions on the file **cat1.exe** are changed from 666 to 777. Using symbolic mode, the execute permissions are then removed for all users.

```
D:\> ls -l cat1.exe
-rw-rw-rw-    1 Administ Administ    71323 Feb 20 11:34 cat1.exe
D:\> chmod 777 cat1.exe
D:\> ls -l cat1.exe

-rwxrwxrwx    1 Administ Administ    71323 Feb 20 11:34 cat1.exe
D:\> chmod a-x cat1.exe
D:\> ls -l cat1.exe
-rw-rw-rw-    1 Administ Administ    71323 Feb 20 11:34 cat1.exe
```

cp

cp - Copy files and directories.

Some commonly used options

-i   Interactive copy whereby you are prompted to confirm whether or not you wish to overwrite an existing file.

-f   Force existing files to be overwritten by files being copied if there is a conflict in file names.

-p   Preserve permissions when copying.

-R   Copy recursively which includes subtrees.

The following example shows using the **cp** command to copy **cat1.exe** to **cat2.exe** and then a listing of all files beginning with **cat** is produced.

```
D:\> cp cat1.exe cat2.exe

D:\> ls -l cat*

-rw-rw-rw-    1 Administ Administ     71323 Feb 20 11:34 cat1.exe
-rw-rw-rw-    1 Administ Administ     71323 Feb 20 11:47 cat2.exe
```

find

find - Recursively descend a directory structure looking for the file(s) listed.

Some commonly used options

-f   Specify a file hierarchy for **find** to traverse.

-s   When symbolic links are encountered, the file referenced
            by the link and not the link itself will be used.

-x   Don't descend into directories that have a device number
            different than that of the file from which the decent
            began.

-print   Prints path name to standard output.

-size n   True if the file's size is n.

grep

grep - Searches for text and displays result.

The following example shows using grep to find the expression "shell" everywhere it appears inside the file **setup.inf**.

```
D:\> grep shell setup.inf

[shell]
00000000="shell versions below 3.01",,unsupported_net
00030100="shell versions below 3.21",,novell301
00032100="shell versions 3.21 and above",,novell321
00032600="shell versions 3.26 and above",,novell326
    #win.shell, 0:
    #win.shell, 0:
[win.shell]
    shell.dll
  system.ini, Boot,     "oldshell"        ,"shell"
```

ls

ls - List the contents of a directory.

Some commonly used options

-a	List all entries.
-c	Use time file was last modified for producing order in which files are listed.
-d	List only the directory name, not its contents.
-g	Include the group in the output.
-i	Print the inode number in the first column of the report.
-q	Nonprinting characters are represented by a "?".
-r	Reverse the order in which files are printed.
-s	Show the size in blocks instead of bytes.
-t	List in order of time saved with most recent first.
-u	Use time of last access instead of last modification for determining order in which files are printed.
-A	Same as -a except current and parent directories aren't listed.
-C	Multicolumn output produced.
-F	Directory followed by a "/", executable by an "*", symbolic link by an "@".
-L	List file or directory to which link points.
-R	Recursively list subdirectories.

Several examples are included.

```
D:\> ls -a

Blue Monday 16.bmp
Blue Monday.bmp
Coffee Bean 16.bmp
Coffee Bean.bmp
Config
Cursors
FORMS
FeatherTexture.bmp
Fiddle Head.bmp
Fonts
Furry Dog 16.bmp
Furry Dog.bmp
Geometrix.bmp
Gone Fishing.bmp
Greenstone.bmp
Hazy Autumn 16.bmp
Help
Hiking Boot.bmp
Leaf Fossils 16.bmp
Leather 16.bmp
Maple Trails.bmp
Media
NETLOGON.CHG
NOTEPAD.EXE
Petroglyph 16.bmp
Prairie Wind.bmp
Profiles
REGEDIT.EXE
Rhododendron.bmp
River Sumida.bmp
Santa Fe Stucco.bmp
Seaside 16.bmp
Seaside.bmp
ShellNew
Snakeskin.bmp
Soap Bubbles.bmp
Solstice.bmp
Swimming Pool.bmp
TASKMAN.EXE
TEMP
Upstream 16.bmp
WIN.INI
WINFILE.INI
WINHELP.EXE
Zapotec 16.bmp
Zapotec.bmp
_DEFAULT.PIF
black16.scr
clock.avi
control.ini
explorer.exe
inetsrv.mif
inf
lanma256.bmp
lanmannt.bmp
network.wri
poledit.exe
printer.wri
repair
setup.old
setuplog.txt
system
system.ini
system32
vmmreg32.dll
welcome.exe
winhlp32.exe
```

```
D:\ls -l

-rwxrwxrwx   1 Administ NETWORK      8310 Aug  9  1996 Blue Monday 16.bmp
-rwxrwxrwx   1 Administ NETWORK     37940 Aug  9  1996 Blue Monday.bmp
-rwxrwxrwx   1 Administ NETWORK      8312 Aug  9  1996 Coffee Bean 16.bmp
-rwxrwxrwx   1 Administ NETWORK     17062 Aug  9  1996 Coffee Bean.bmp
drwx---rwx   1 Administ Administ        0 Feb 10 10:39 Config
drwx---rwx   1 Administ Administ        0 Feb 10 16:22 Cursors
drwxrwxrwx   1 Administ NETWORK         0 Feb 10 16:23 FORMS
-rwxrwxrwx   1 Administ NETWORK     16730 Aug  9  1996 FeatherTexture.bmp
-rwxrwxrwx   1 Administ NETWORK     65922 Aug  9  1996 Fiddle Head.bmp
drwx---rwx   1 Administ Administ     8192 Feb 10 10:39 Fonts
-rwxrwxrwx   1 Administ NETWORK     18552 Aug  9  1996 Furry Dog 16.bmp
-rwxrwxrwx   1 Administ NETWORK     37940 Aug  9  1996 Furry Dog.bmp
-rwxrwxrwx   1 Administ NETWORK      4328 Aug  9  1996 Geometrix.bmp
-rwxrwxrwx   1 Administ NETWORK     17336 Aug  9  1996 Gone Fishing.bmp
-rwxrwxrwx   1 Administ NETWORK     26582 Aug  9  1996 Greenstone.bmp
-rwxrwxrwx   1 Administ NETWORK     32888 Aug  9  1996 Hazy Autumn 16.bmp
drwx---rwx   1 Administ Administ        0 Feb 19 15:10 Help
-rwxrwxrwx   1 Administ NETWORK     37854 Aug  9  1996 Hiking Boot.bmp
-rwxrwxrwx   1 Administ NETWORK     12920 Aug  9  1996 Leaf Fossils 16.bmp
-rwxrwxrwx   1 Administ NETWORK      6392 Aug  9  1996 Leather 16.bmp
-rwxrwxrwx   1 Administ NETWORK     26566 Aug  9  1996 Maple Trails.bmp
drwx---rwx   1 Administ Administ        0 Feb 10 16:23 Media
-rwxrwxrwx   1 Administ NETWORK     65536 Feb 11 10:35 NETLOGON.CHG
-rwxrwxrwx   1 Administ NETWORK     45328 Aug  8  1996 NOTEPAD.EXE
-rwxrwxrwx   1 Administ NETWORK     16504 Aug  9  1996 Petroglyph 16.bmp
-rwxrwxrwx   1 Administ NETWORK     65954 Aug  9  1996 Prairie Wind.bmp
drwxrwxrwx   1 Administ NETWORK      4096 Feb 10 16:32 Profiles
-rwxrwxr-x   1 Administ NETWORK     71952 Aug  8  1996 REGEDIT.EXE
-rwxrwxrwx   1 Administ NETWORK     17362 Aug  9  1996 Rhododendron.bmp
-rwxrwxrwx   1 Administ NETWORK     26208 Aug  9  1996 River Sumida.bmp
-rwxrwxrwx   1 Administ NETWORK     65832 Aug  9  1996 Santa Fe Stucco.bmp
-rwxrwxrwx   1 Administ NETWORK      8312 Aug  9  1996 Seaside 16.bmp
-rwxrwxr-x   1 Administ NETWORK     17334 Aug  9  1996 Seaside.bmp
drwxrwxrwx   1 Administ NETWORK         0 Feb 10 16:22 ShellNew
-rwxrwxrwx   1 Administ NETWORK     10292 Aug  9  1996 Snakeskin.bmp
-rwxrwxrwx   1 Administ NETWORK     65978 Aug  9  1996 Soap Bubbles.bmp
-rwxrwxr-x   1 Administ NETWORK     17334 Aug  9  1996 Solstice.bmp
-rwxrwxrwx   1 Administ NETWORK     26202 Aug  9  1996 Swimming Pool.bmp
-rwxrwxrwx   1 Administ NETWORK     32016 Aug  8  1996 TASKMAN.EXE
drwxrwxrwx   1 Administ NETWORK         0 Feb 20 09:59 TEMP
-rwxrwxrwx   1 Administ NETWORK     32888 Aug  9  1996 Upstream 16.bmp
-rwxrwxrwx   1 Administ NETWORK       239 Feb 10 16:23 WIN.INI
-rwxrwxr-x   1 Administ NETWORK         3 Aug  8  1996 WINFILE.INI
-rwxrwxr-x   1 Administ NETWORK    256192 Aug  8  1996 WINHELP.EXE
-rwxrwxrwx   1 Administ NETWORK      8312 Aug  9  1996 Zapotec 16.bmp
-rwxrwxr-x   1 Administ NETWORK      9522 Aug  9  1996 Zapotec.bmp
-rwxrwxr-x   1 Administ NETWORK       707 Aug  8  1996 _DEFAULT.PIF
-rwx---r-x   1 Administ Administ     5328 Aug  8  1996 black16.scr
-rwx---r-x   1 Administ Administ    82944 Aug  8  1996 clock.avi
-rwxrwxrwx   1 Administ NETWORK         0 Feb 10 11:18 control.ini
-rwx---r-x   1 Administ Administ   234256 Aug  8  1996 explorer.exe
-rwxrwxrwx   1 Administ NETWORK      1628 Feb 10 11:20 inetsrv.mif
drwx---rwx   1 Administ Administ    47104 Feb 10 10:56 inf
-rwx---r-x   1 Administ Administ   157044 Aug  8  1996 lanma256.bmp
-rwx---r-x   1 Administ Administ   157044 Aug  8  1996 lanmannt.bmp
-rwx---r-x   1 Administ Administ    67328 Aug  8  1996 network.wri
-rwx---r-x   1 Administ Administ   123152 Aug  8  1996 poledit.exe
-rwx---r-x   1 Administ Administ    34816 Aug  8  1996 printer.wri
drwx---rwx   1 Administ Administ        0 Feb 10 16:24 repair
-rwxrwxrwx   1 Administ NETWORK      2499 Feb 10 16:23 setup.old
-rwxrwxrwx   1 Administ NETWORK       138 Feb 10 16:22 setuplog.txt
drwx---rwx   1 Administ Administ     4096 Feb 20 10:07 system
-rwx---r-x   1 Administ Administ       219 Aug  8  1996 system.ini
drwx---rwx   1 Administ Administ   167936 Feb 20 09:50 system32
-rwx---r-x   1 Administ Administ    24336 Aug  8  1996 vmmreg32.dll
-rwx---r-x   1 Administ Administ    22288 Aug  8  1996 welcome.exe
-rwx---r-x   1 Administ Administ   310032 Aug  8  1996 winhlp32.exe
```

```
D:\> ls -C

Blue Monday 16.bmpGreenstone.bmpRhododendron.bmpWINFILE.INI      poledit.exe
Blue Monday.bmp Hazy Autumn 16.bmpRiver Sumida.bmpWINHELP.EXE    printer.wri
Coffee Bean 16.bmpHelp          Santa Fe Stucco.bmpZapotec 16.bmprepair
Coffee Bean.bmp Hiking Boot.bmp Seaside 16.bmp  Zapotec.bmp      setup.old
Config          Leaf Fossils 16.bmpSeaside.bmp  _DEFAULT.PIF     setuplog.txt
Cursors         Leather 16.bmp  ShellNew        black16.scr      system
FORMS           Maple Trails.bmpSnakeskin.bmp   clock.avi        system.ini
FeatherTexture.bmpMedia         Soap Bubbles.bmpcontrol.ini      system32
Fiddle Head.bmp NETLOGON.CHG    Solstice.bmp    explorer.exe     vmmreg32.dll
Fonts           NOTEPAD.EXE     Swimming Pool.bmpinetsrv.mif     welcome.exe
Furry Dog 16.bmpPetroglyph 16.bmpTASKMAN.EXE    inf              winhlp32.exe
Furry Dog.bmp   Prairie Wind.bmpTEMP            lanma256.bmp
Geometrix.bmp   Profiles        Upstream 16.bmp lanmannt.bmp
Gone Fishing.bmpREGEDIT.EXE     WIN.INI         network.wri
```

mkdir

mkdir - Create specified directories.

A commonly used option

-p   Create intermediate directories to achieve the full path. If
            you want to create several layers of directories down,
            you would use **-p**.

mv

mv - Rename files and directories.

Some commonly used options

-i   Interactive move whereby you are prompted to confirm whether or not you wish to overwrite an existing file.

-f   Force existing files to be overwritten by files being moved if there is a conflict in file names.

rm

rm - Remove files and directories.

Some commonly used options

-d   Remove directories as well as other file types.

-i   Interactive remove whereby you are prompted to confirm
          whether or not you wish to remove an existing file.

-f   Force files to be removed.

-r (-R)   Recursively remove the contents of the directory and
          then the directory itself.

touch

touch - Change the modification and or last access times of a file or create a file.

Some commonly used options

       -c   Does not create a specified file if it does not exist.

       -f   Force a touch of a file regardless of permissions.

The following example creates **file1** with **touch**.

```
D:\> ls -l file1
ls:file1: No such file or directory

D:\> touch file1

D:\> ls -l file1

-rw-rw-rw-    1 Administ Administ        0 Feb 20 11:45 file1
```

WC

wc - Produce a count of words, lines, and characters.

Options

           -l   Print the number of lines in a file.

           -w   Print the number of words in a file.

           -c   Print the number of characters in a file.

The first example lists the contents of a directory and pipes the output to wc. The second example provides wc information about the file system.ini.

```
D:\> ls

CAT.EXE
CHMOD.EXE
CHOWN.EXE
CP.EXE
FIND.EXE
GREP.EXE
LN.EXE
LS.EXE
MKDIR.EXE
MV.EXE
RM.EXE
RMDIR.EXE
SH.EXE
TOUCH.EXE
VI.EXE
WC.EXE

D:\> ls | wc -wlc

      16      16      132

D:\> wc -wlc system.ini

      13      17      219 system.ini
```

HP SoftBench OpenStudio

SoftBench OpenStudio is a product designed to empower C++ developers writing distributed applications for a mixed Windows and HP-UX environment. It combines Microsoft's Developer Studio (Visual C++) with state-of-the-art distributed computing technology to provide a single environment from which to develop applications for Windows NT, Windows 95, and HP-UX.

SoftBench Openstudio provides these capabilities through a unique client/server architecture. Hewlett Packard has taken the critical components of C++ application development - the C++ compiler, the linker, and the debugger - and transformed them into CORBA object servers. In addition, HP has taken these servers and integrated them into Microsoft's Developer Studio. This means that a programmer can use Developer Studio to manipulate C++ source code on a PC and compile and debug this code on an HP-UX system using the same Developer Studio front end.

Three Key Features of OpenStudio

There are three key features of SoftBench OpenStudio:

1) The remote build capability allows HP-UX object code and executables to be generated from source created on the Windows platform.

2) The remote debug capability enables the developer to debug HP-UX executables from a Windows GUI.

3) An extended project mechanism allows the developer to easily change HP-UX specific compile and link options. This mechanism is similar to the existing project mechanism available in Developer Studio.

SoftBench OpenStudio is tightly integrated into Microsoft's Developer Studio, so in order to understand the capabilities of OpenStudio, one must have some familiarity with Developer Studio. Developer Studio's mechanism for managing collections of files and compiler settings is particularly relevant. In general, when Developer Studio starts up, it starts up on a workspace. A workspace consists of a collection of projects. A project consists of a single set of files and a set of one or more project configurations. Users can easily add or remove files from a project using the GUI features of Developer Studio. A configuration specifies the settings for the compiler, linker, and debugger which determine the final output for a project build. These settings include the optimization or debug level for the compiler, libraries to be searched by the linker, startup options for the program when it is debugged, and many others. The user must specify a single configuration for any particular build. Changing a configuration is a simple matter of selecting a new configuration from a pull-down list of available configurations, and creating a new configuration is similarly easy.

Manipulating HP-UX Source Code

SoftBench OpenStudio was designed to enable the developer to have four main ways to manipulate HP-UX source code. These are called use cases, and they are

1) Legacy HP-UX Code. This use case allows a developer who has code in an existing HP-UX build mechanism to manipulate the code via

Visual C++. This will allow initiation of a build, browsing error messages, and debugging of the code. This use case, however, will not allow for the use of the extended project mechanism.

2) New HP-UX Code. This use case allows a developer to generate a project for an HP-UX application or library from scratch. Compiles and links can be initiated from Developer Studio, any errors browsed, and the target debugged. In addition, the extended project options allow the developer to set the HP-UX-specific compile and link options from a single interface.

3) Portable code. This use case allows the developer to quickly and easily compile, link, and debug code on both HP-UX and Windows platforms. Specifically, the target platform is specified using the Developer Studio configuration mechanism. When the source is to be compiled on HP-UX, the developer chooses an HP-UX specific configuration. For Windows, a Windows-specific configuration is used. Switching between the two is as easy as switching between any other configurations.

4) Client/Server code. The final use case is for a developer who needs a single workspace to manage separate subprojects which correspond to code which needs to be compiled on both HP-UX and Windows. This use case is valuable when, for instance, a developer is writing the client side of an application for Windows and the server side of the same application for HP-UX. In this case, each subproject has its own configuration. Switching between the two allows the developer to "focus" on the particular component using Developer Studio.

Careful selection of class libraries can greatly improve the productivity of developers in a heterogeneous environment. A primary selection criterion should be whether the library exists on both Windows and HP-UX. Good examples of such libraries are the iostream library and the Standard Template Library available as standard C++ libraries. In addition, there are many third-party software vendors who supply multiplatform libraries.

One in particular is Rogue Wave Software, that supplies class libraries for basic data structures, GUI development, networking, and more.

Using such a class library is complementary to OpenStudio because it provides a portable API which the developer can count on to be available on both HP-UX and Windows. The code written to this portable API can be compiled and debugged on the desired platform using the OpenStudio cross-development capabilities.

SoftBench OpenStudio Control Panel

The SoftBench OpenStudio Control Panel is the primary point of control for OpenStudio. It serves the following purposes:

Main integration point into SoftBench OpenStudio

Allows you to maintain default settings

Allows you to setup Settings for the current configuration

Allows you to set network drive mappings

Gives user help with setting build options

Access to on-line help

The SoftBench OpenStudio Control Panel is shown in Figure 9-23.

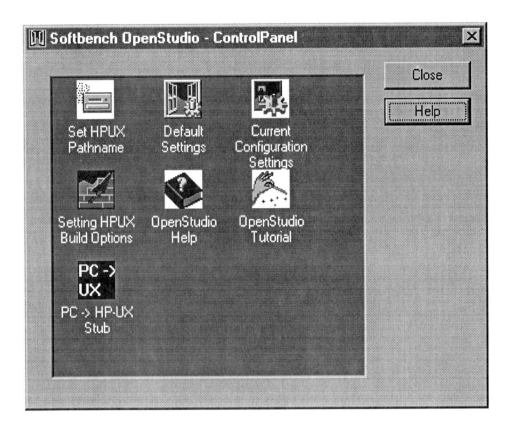

Figure 9-23 SoftBench OpenStudio Control Panel

The SoftBench OpenStudio Control Panel is a modal dialog box. When you select a particular icon in the Control Panel, the new dialog box comes up and the Control Panel removes itself. If you want the Control Panel back up, you must restart it from the *Tools* menu, by choosing *SoftBench OpenStudio*. The only exception pertains to the SoftBench OpenStudio Tutorial and Help files, which once launched are independent of the Control Panel and remain active until they are directly closed.

The following are descriptions of the functionality provided by some of the SoftBench OpenStudio Control Panel icons.

Set HP-UX Pathname: Selecting this icon brings up the Set HP-UX Pathname dialog box indicating the HP-UX machine name and path for network drive mappings.

Default Settings: Selecting this icon brings up the *Property Pages* for setting your global settings for environment variables and servers.

Current Configuration: Selecting this icon brings up the *Property Pages* for setting your current settings based upon your configuration.

Setting HP-UX Build Options: The Setting HP-UX Build Options dialog box gives assistance with setting build options. It must be used in conjunction with the Microsoft Developer Studio Build Settings dialog box. Your actual input for the HP-UX build settings takes place in the Microsoft Developer Studio Build Settings dialog box, but the convention and syntax are based upon the Setting HP-UX Build Options dialog box. Without this assistance it might be difficult entering the correct data into the Microsoft Developer Studio Build Settings dialog box.

SoftBench OpenStudio Tutorial and Help: The Tutorial gets you started using SoftBench OpenStudio based upon tasks provided with sample code. The SoftBench OpenStudio Help is the general reference and user's guide that covers all the topics involved in using SoftBench Open-Studio.

Conclusion

SoftBench OpenStudio is a powerful tool for any organization involved in developing software in a mixed NT/HP-UX environment. It provides integration into Microsoft's Developer Studio, the most widely used C++ development environment available on the Windows platform. Using state-of-the-art distributed computing technologies, it makes HP-UX compiler, link, and debug servers available to Developer Studio. Finally, HP and its partners offer a suite of complimentary products and services, including class libraries and consulting, which make a complete development environment for software development in a heterogeneous installation.

OpenStudio addresses the key issue of increased cost associated with development in a complex, heterogeneous environment.

OpenStudio reduces hardware costs because developers can use a single desktop machine for both software development tasks and office automation tasks.

OpenStudio decreases overall support costs because it reduces the total number of different types of machines an organization must support.

OpenStudio reduces training costs because developers need only to be trained in a single development environment - Microsoft Developer Studio - with which they may already have some experience.

CHAPTER 10

The vi Editor

The vi Editor

As you already know from the HP Common Desktop Environment (HP CDE) chapter, there is a graphical editor supplied with HP CDE. We are now going to take a step back and cover the visual editor, **vi**, which is used to edit text files. With a fine graphics-based editor as a standard part of the HP-UX operating system and a plethora of editors available as part of personal computer windowing environments, why are we covering **vi**? The answer is twofold. First, not everyone using HP-UX has access to a graphics display and may therefore need to know and use **vi**. Since **vi** comes with HP-UX and is a powerful editor, many new HP-UX users end up using and liking it. Second, **vi** has traditionally been thought of as *the* UNIX editor. There are few UNIX users who have not used **vi**. This does not mean it is everyone's primary editor; however, virtually all UNIX users have had some experience with **vi**.

I'll cover the basics of using **vi** in this chapter. You can experiment with what is covered here, and if you really like it, you can investigate some of the more advanced features of **vi**.

Starting a vi Session

Let's jump right in and edit a file. From the command line we type **vi** and the name of the file we wish to edit, in this case **wisdom**.

```
$ vi wisdom
```

We are then editing the file **wisdom** as shown in Figure 10-1. **wisdom** contains a passage from *Tao Te Ching* or *Book of the Way*. We will use this file throughout this chapter.

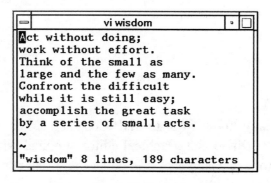

```
                        vi wisdom                    ▫ ☐
Act without doing;
work without effort.
Think of the small as
large and the few as many.
Confront the difficult
while it is still easy;
accomplish the great task
by a series of small acts.
~
~
"wisdom" 8 lines, 189 characters
```

Figure 10-1 Editing the File **wisdom**

The bottom line in Figure 10-1 is the message line in **vi**. After invoking **vi,** the message line indicates the name of the file, the number of lines, and the number of characters in the file. Different messages appear on the message line depending on the command you issue, as we will see in upcoming examples. If a tilde (~) appears on any lines in the file, as it does in the two lines above the message line in **wisdom**, it means there are not enough lines to fill up the screen. The cursor is the dark box that appears at line 1 in Figure 10-1.

We can specify several file names and after saving the first file move on to the second file by entering **:n**, and continue going through the list of files in this way. Or, we can specify a file and position the cursor on the last line in the file. The default is for the cursor to appear over the first character in the file as shown in Figure 10-1.

Table 10-1 shows some of the ways we can start a **vi** session.

Table 10-1 Starting a **vi** Session

Command	Description
vi file	Edit **file.**
vi -r file	Edit last saved version of **file** after a crash.
vi -R file	Edit the file in read only mode.
vi + file	Edit **file** and place cursor on last line.
vi file1 file2 file3 ...	Edit **file1** through **file3** and after saving changes in **file1** you can move to **file2** by entering **:n**.

A feature of **vi** that often confuses new users is that there are modes to **vi**. When you are in *command mode*, everything you type is interpreted as a command. In *command mode* you can specify such actions as the location to which you want the cursor to move. When you are in *input mode,* everything you type is information to be added to the file. *Command mode* is the default when you start **vi**. You can move into *command mode* from *input mode* at any time by hitting the *escape* key. You move into *insert mode* from *command mode* by typing one of the *input mode* commands covered shortly.

Cursor Control Commands

A key skill to develop in **vi** is getting the cursor to the desired position. You do this in *command mode*. There are a variety of ways to move the cursor around the screen. Table 10-2 summarizes some of the more commonly used cursor movements.

Table 10-2 Cursor Control Commands in **vi**

Command	Cursor Movement
h	Move left one character.
j	Move down one line.
k	Move up one line.
l or space	Move right one character.
G	Go to the last line of the file.
nG	Go to line number **n**.
G$	Go to the last character in the file.
w	Go to the beginning of the next word.
b	Go to the beginning of the previous word.
L	Go to the last line of the screen.
M	Go to the middle line of the screen.
H	Go to the first line of the screen.
e	Move to the end word.
(	Go to the beginning of the sentence.
)	Go to the end of the sentence.
{	Go to the beginning of the paragraph.
}	Go to the beginning of the next paragraph.

I know it seems a little strange at first that you have to remember these commands in order to get the cursor to the desired position, but this is the way **vi** works. Let's use **wisdom** to show how some of these cursor movements work. Figures 10-2 and 10-3 show some cursor movements. Like all of the upcoming figures, Figures 10-2 and 10-3 show **wisdom** before a command is entered on the left and the result after the command is entered on the right. The command issued appears in the middle. Some of the commands in upcoming figures use the *enter* and *escape* keys.

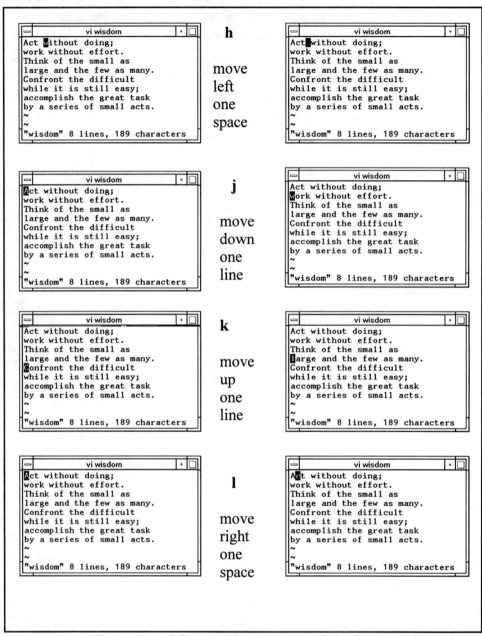

Figure 10-2 Examples of Cursor Movement in **vi** (**h**, **j**, **k**, and **l**)

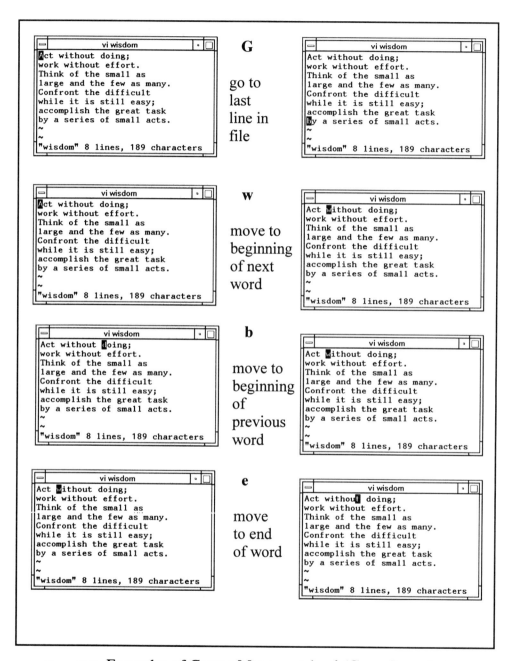

Figure 10-3 Examples of Cursor Movement in **vi** (**G**, **w**, **b**, and **e**)

Adding Text in vi

Now that we know how to move the cursor around, let's do something with it. It is important to first learn about cursor movement since the commands for adding text take place relative to the position of the cursor. Table 10-3 summarizes some commands for adding text.

Table 10-3 Adding Text in **vi**

Command	Insertion Action
a	Append new text after the cursor.
i	Insert new text before the cursor.
o	Open a line below the current line.
O	Open a line above the current line.
:r file	Read file and insert after current line.
escape	Get back to command mode.

Let's now look at some examples for adding text into **wisdom** in Figure 10-4.

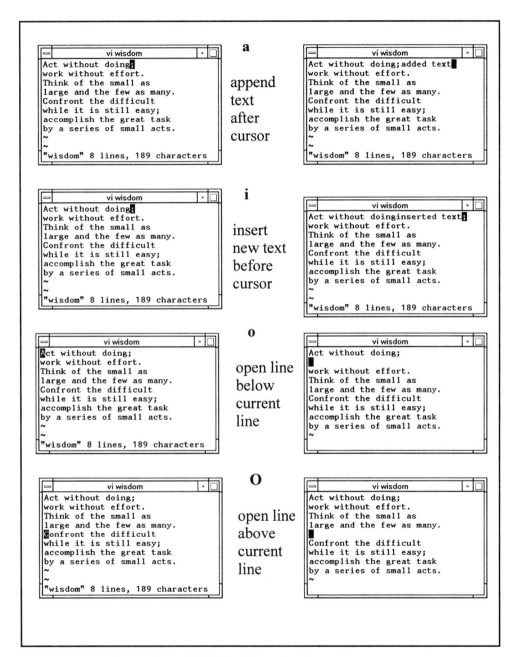

Figure 10-4   Examples of Adding Text in **vi**

Deleting Text in vi

We also needed to learn about cursor movement before learning how to delete text, since the commands for deleting text take place relative to the position of the cursor. Table 10-4 summarizes some commands for deleting text.

Table 10-4 Deleting Text in **vi**

Command	Deletion Action
x	Delete the character at the cursor. You can also put a number in front of x to specify the number of characters to delete.
X	Delete the previous character. You can also put a number in front of X to specify the number of previous characters to delete.
dw	Delete to the beginning of the next word.
dG	Delete lines to the end of the file.
dd	Delete the entire line.
db	Delete the previous word. You can also put a number in front of db to specify the number of previous words to delete.

Let's now look at some examples for deleting text from **wisdom** in Figures 10-5 and 10-6.

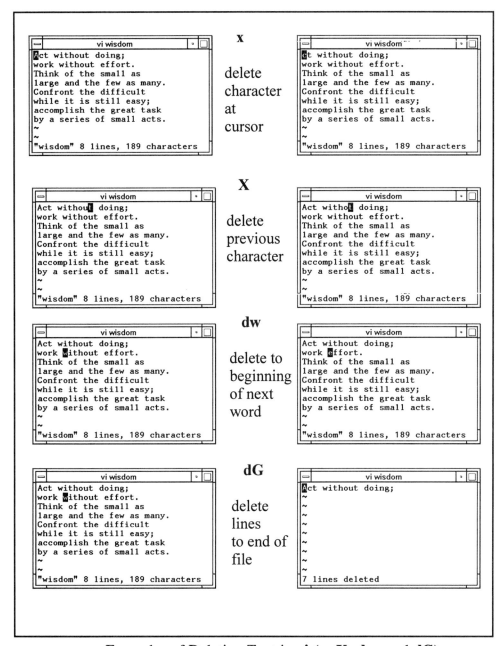

x

delete
character
at
cursor

X

delete
previous
character

dw

delete to
beginning
of next
word

dG

delete
lines
to end of
file

Figure 10-5 Examples of Deleting Text in **vi** (**x**, **X**, **dw**, and **dG**)

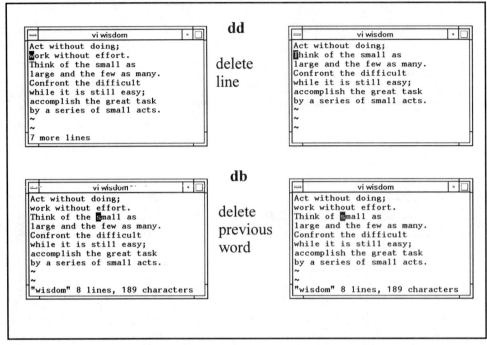

Figure 10-6   Examples of Deleting Text in **vi** (**dd** and **db**)

Changing Text in vi

Okay, you've added text, deleted text, now you want to change text. **vi** isn't so bad so far, is it? Table 10-5 summarizes some commands for changing text.

Table 10-5 Changing Text in **vi**

Command (Preceding these commands with a number repeats the commands any number of times.)	Replacement Action
rX	Replace the current character with **X**.
R	Replace the current characters until *escape* is entered.
cw	Change to the beginning of the next word.
cG	Change to the end of the file.
cc	Change the entire line.

Let's now look at some examples of replacing text from **wisdom** in Figures 10-7 and 10-8.

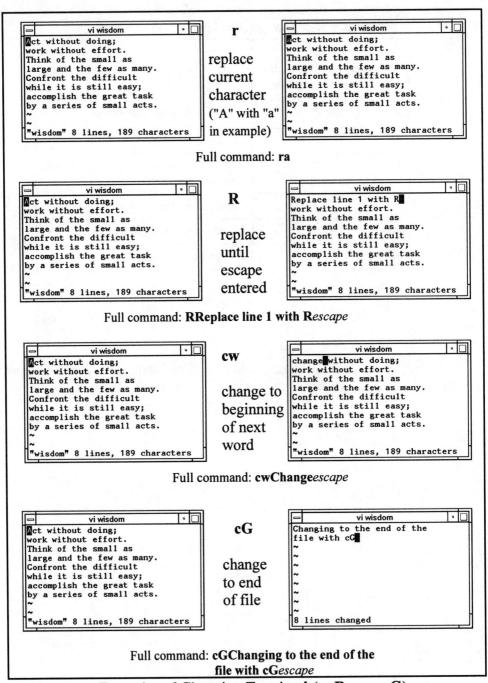

Full command: **ra**

Full command: **RReplace line 1 with R**escape

Full command: **cwChange**escape

Full command: **cGChanging to the end of the**
file with cGescape

Figure 10-7 Examples of Changing Text in **vi** (**r**, **R**, **cw**, **cG**)

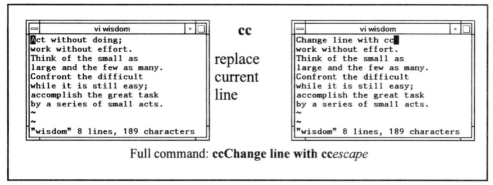

Figure 10-8   Example of Changing Text in vi with cc

Search and Replace in vi

You have a lot of search and replace functionality in **vi**. Table 10-6 summarizes some of the more common search and replace functionality in **vi**.

Table 10-6 Search and Replace in **vi**

Command	Search and Replace Action
/text	Search for **text** going forward into the file.
?text	Search for **text** going backward into the file.
n	Repeat search in the same direction as the original search.
N	Repeat the search in the opposite direction as the original search.
:s/oldtext/newtext/	Substitute **newtext** for **oldtext**.
:m,ns/oldtext/newtext/	Substitute **newtext** for **oldtext** in lines **m** through **n**.

Let's now look at some examples of searching and replacing text in **wisdom** in Figure 10-9.

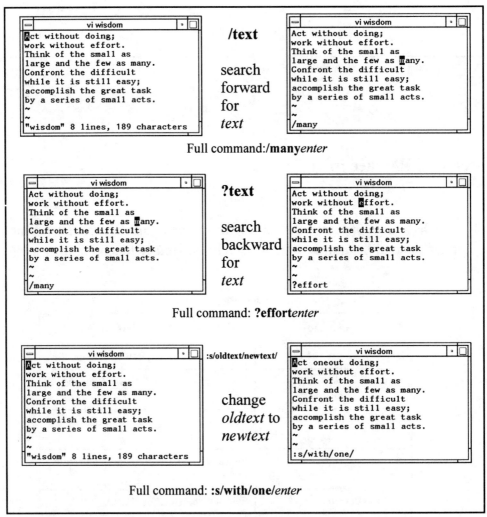

Figure 10-9 Examples of Search and Replace in **vi**

Copying Text in vi

You can copy text in **vi**. Some commands for copying are shown in Table 10-7.

Table 10-7 Copying in **vi**

Command	Copy Action
yy	Yank the current line.
nyy	Yank **n** lines.
p (lower case)	Put yanked text after cursor.
p (upper case)	Put yanked text before cursor.

Let's now look at some examples of copying text in **wisdom** in Figure 10-10.

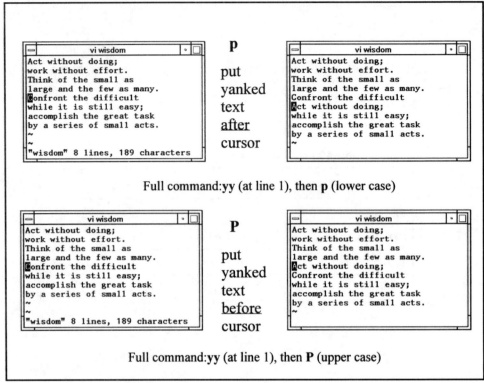

Figure 10-10 Copying in **vi**

Undo in vi

You can easily undo changes in **vi** with the commands shown in Table 10-8.

Table 10-8 Undo in **vi**

Command	Undo Action
u	Undo the last change.

Table 10-8 Undo in **vi**

Command	Undo Action
U	Undo all changes to the current line.
. (period)	Repeat the last change.

Save Text and Exit vi

There are a number of different ways to save files and exit **vi**, some of which are summarized in Table 10-9.

Table 10-9 Saving Text and Exiting **vi**

Command	Save and/or Quit Action
:w	Save the file but don't exit **vi**.
:w filename	Save changes in the file **filename** but don't quit **vi**.
:wq	Save the file and quit **vi**.
:q!	Quit **vi** without saving the file.

Options in vi

There are many options you can set and unset in **vi**. To set an option you type **:set** *option*. To unset an option you type **:set no***option***.** Table 10-10 summarizes some of the more commonly used options.

Table 10-10 vi Options

Option	Action
:set all	Print all options.
:set no*option*	Turn off *option*.
:set nu	Prefix lines with line number.
:set ro	Set file to read only.
:set showmode	Show whether input or replace mode.
:set warn	Print a warning message if there has not been a write since the last change to the file.

Let's now look at some examples of replacing text from **wisdom** in Figure 10-11.

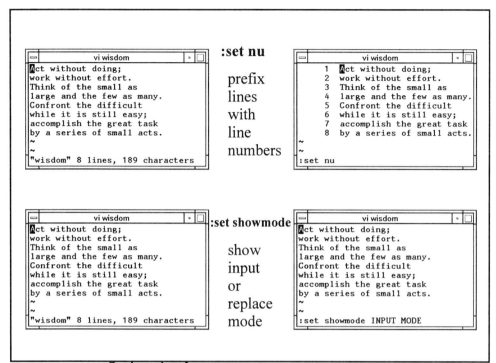

Figure 10-11   Options in **vi**

INDEX

X

HUMMINGBIRD COMMUNICATIONS LTD. SOFTWARE LICENSE AGREEMENT

<u>WARNING:</u> READ CAREFULLY BEFORE ATTEMPTING TO USE A COPY OF THE SOFTWARE. This License Agreement is a legal agreement between you (either an individual or a single entity) and Hummingbird Communications Ltd. (HCL) for this Hummingbird software which includes computer software and associated printed materials (if any), and may include online or electronic documentation. By downloading, installing, copying or otherwise using the software you agree to be bound by the terms of this License Agreement.

DEFINITIONS:

HCL. Hummingbird Communications Ltd.

SOFTWARE. Enclosed HCL software product and its manuals and documentation.

COMPUTER. The single computer unit, regardless of platform or operating environment, on which you will load and use the SOFTWARE.

CLIENT. A single user with a single access address, which may include, but not limited to, an Account, a Mailbox, or an IP address.

1. GRANT OF LICENSE. HCL grants you this non-exclusive license to use the enclosed SOFTWARE. The SOFTWARE is licensed to a single user on a single COMPUTER. You may use the SOFTWARE and any related updates on the COMPUTER while you possess and operate the COMPUTER only. A separate License Agreement and fee is required for additional COMPUTERS on which the SOFTWARE is used. You may physically transfer the SOFTWARE from one COMPUTER to another provided that you remove any copy(ies) of the SOFTWARE from the COMPUTER from which the SOFTWARE is being transferred. Its component parts may not be separated for use on more than one COMPUTER or by more than one user at any time. If this SOFTWARE is a licensed Pack or a Site License providing multiple licenses, you may make and use as many copies of the SOFTWARE as you have "Proof of License" certificates. If this product contains "Client Access License" certificates, HCL grants the right for a number of CLIENTS to access this SOFTWARE equal to the total number of "Client Access License" certificates you have purchased for this SOFTWARE. If the enclosed Software is permanently installed on a single computer and one person uses that computer more than 80% of the time it is in use, then that person may also install the Software on a portable or home computer.

2. TITLE AND COPYRIGHT. The SOFTWARE (including any images, "applets", photographs, animations, video, audio, music and text incorporated into the SOFTWARE) is owned by HCL or its suppliers and is protected by Canadian copyright laws and international treaty provisions. HCL Licenses you to make one copy only of the software for backup purposes. Part of this SOFTWARE may have been developed by a third party software supplier, which holds copyright and other proprietary rights to the SOFTWARE.

3. DUAL MEDIA. You may receive the SOFTWARE in more than one media. Regardless of the type or size of media you receive, you may use only the media appropriate for the number of COMPUTERS as expressly permitted by this License Agreement.

4. RESTRICTIONS ON USE. This License Agreement is your proof-of-license to exercise the rights granted herein and must be retained by you. You may not transfer, sublicense, rent, network, distribute or grant your rights in the SOFTWARE, or in the License Agreement, to others. You may not attempt in any way to determine the source or the object code for the SOFTWARE, modify, disassemble, reverse assemble, or create derivative works based on the SOFTWARE. You agree to allow HCL or its agent to inspect or conduct an independent audit from time to time on your use of the SOFTWARE to verify your compliance to this agreement.

5. TERMINATION. You may terminate this License Agreement at any time. HCL reserves the ht to terminate this License Agreement upon breach of these terms and conditions. In the event of termi- ion, you will either return all copies of the SOFTWARE to HCL or, with HCL's prior consent, provide L with a certificate of destruction of all copies of the SOFTWARE.

6. LIMITED WARRANTY. HCL warrants for a period of NINETY (90) DAYS from the date purchase that the SOFTWARE will execute its programming instructions when properly installed on the MPUTER. Due to the complex nature of computer software, HCL does not warrant that the operation of SOFTWARE will be uninterrupted or error free.

7. MEDIA. HCL warrants the media upon which this SOFTWARE is recorded to be free of fects in materials and workmanship under normal use for a period of NINETY (90) DAYS from the date purchase.

8. REMEDIES. In the event that this SOFTWARE fails to execute its programming instruc- ns, or if any media proves to be defective during the warranty period, your remedy shall be to return the edia to HCL for replacement. Should HCL be unable to replace the media within a reasonable time, your ternate remedy shall be a refund of the purchase price upon return of the product and all copies.

9. NOTICE OF WARRANTY CLAIMS. You must notify HCL in writing of any warranty aim not later that thirty (30) days after the expiration of the warranty period.

10. NO OTHER WARRANTIES. To the maximum extent permitted by applicable law, HCL isclaims all other warranties, either express or implied, including but not limited to implied warranties of erchantability and fitness for a particular purpose, with respect to the SOFTWARE. This limited warranty ives you specific legal rights. Some jurisdictions do not allow limitations on how long an implied warranty sts, so the above limitation or exclusion may not apply to you.

11 . NO LIABILITY FOR CONSEQUENTIAL DAMAGES. To the maximum extent permit- d by applicable law, in no event shall HCL be liable for any lost revenues or profits, loss of data or other pecial, indirect, incidental or consequential damages, even if HCL has been advised of the possibility of uch damages. Because some jurisdictions do not allow the exclusion or limitations of liability for conse- uential or incidental damages, the above limitation may not apply.

12. JURISDICTION. This License is governed by the Laws of the Province of Ontario, or by he Laws of the country in which the product was acquired.

13. U.S. GOVERNMENT RESTRICTED RIGHTS. The SOFTWARE is provided with estricted rights. Use, duplications or disclosure by the U.S. Government, is subject to restrictions as set orth in subparagraph (c) (1) (ii) of The Rights in Technical Data and Computer Software clause at DFARS 252.227-7013, or subparagraphs (c) (1) and (2) (a) (15) of the Commercial Computer Software-Restricted Rights at 48 CFR 52.227-19, as applicable, similar clauses in the FAR and NASA FAR Supplement, any uccessor or similar regulation.

LICENSE AGREEMENT AND LIMITED WARRANTY

READ THE FOLLOWING TERMS AND CONDITIONS CAREFULLY BEFORE OPENIN
THIS DISK PACKAGE. THIS LEGAL DOCUMENT IS AN AGREEMENT BETWEEN YOU AN
PRENTICE-HALL, INC. (THE "COMPANY"). BY OPENING THIS SEALED DISK PACKAGE, YO
ARE AGREEING TO BE BOUND BY THESE TERMS AND CONDITIONS. IF YOU DO NOT AGRE
WITH THESE TERMS AND CONDITIONS, DO NOT OPEN THE DISK PACKAGE. PROMPTL
RETURN THE UNOPENED DISK PACKAGE AND ALL ACCOMPANYING ITEMS TO THE PLAC
YOU OBTAINED THEM FOR A FULL REFUND OF ANY SUMS YOU HAVE PAID.

1.		**GRANT OF LICENSE:** In consideration of your payment of the license fee, which is part c
the price you paid for this product, and your agreement to abide by the terms and conditions of this Agree
ment, the Company grants to you a nonexclusive right to use and display the copy of the enclosed softwar
program (hereinafter the "SOFTWARE") on a single computer (i.e., with a single CPU) at a single locatio
so long as you comply with the terms of this Agreement. The Company reserves all rights not expressl
granted to you under this Agreement.

2.		**OWNERSHIP OF SOFTWARE:** You own only the magnetic or physical media (the enclose
disks) on which the SOFTWARE is recorded or fixed, but the Company retains all the rights, title, and own
ership to the SOFTWARE recorded on the original disk copy(ies) and all subsequent copies of the SOFT
WARE, regardless of the form or media on which the original or other copies may exist. This license is not ;
sale of the original SOFTWARE or any copy to you.

3.		**COPY RESTRICTIONS:** This SOFTWARE and the accompanying printed materials and use
manual (the "Documentation") are the subject of copyright. You may <u>not</u> copy the Documentation or the
SOFTWARE, except that you may make a single copy of the SOFTWARE for backup or archival purposes
only. You may be held legally responsible for any copying or copyright infringement which is caused o
encouraged by your failure to abide by the terms of this restriction.

4.		**USE RESTRICTIONS:** You may <u>not</u> network the SOFTWARE or otherwise use it on more
than one computer or computer terminal at the same time. You may physically transfer the SOFTWARE
from one computer to another provided that the SOFTWARE is used on only one computer at a time. You
may <u>not</u> distribute copies of the SOFTWARE or Documentation to others. You may <u>not</u> reverse engineer,
disassemble, decompile, modify, adapt, translate, or create derivative works based on the SOFTWARE or the
Documentation without the prior written consent of the Company.

5.		**TRANSFER RESTRICTIONS:** The enclosed SOFTWARE is licensed only to you and may
<u>not</u> be transferred to any one else without the prior written consent of the Company. Any unauthorized trans-
fer of the SOFTWARE shall result in the immediate termination of this Agreement.

6.		**TERMINATION:** This license is effective until terminated. This license will terminate auto-
matically without notice from the Company and become null and void if you fail to comply with any provisions or limitations of this license. Upon termination, you shall destroy the Documentation and all copies of
the SOFTWARE. All provisions of this Agreement as to warranties, limitation of liability, remedies or damages, and our ownership rights shall survive termination.

7.		**MISCELLANEOUS:** This Agreement shall be construed in accordance with the laws of the
United States of America and the State of New York and shall benefit the Company, its affiliates, and assign-
ees.

8.		**LIMITED WARRANTY AND DISCLAIMER OF WARRANTY:** The Company warrants
that the SOFTWARE, when properly used in accordance with the Documentation, will operate in substantial
conformity with the description of the SOFTWARE set forth in the Documentation. The Company does not
warrant that the SOFTWARE will meet your requirements or that the operation of the SOFTWARE will be

interrupted or error-free. The Company warrants that the media on which the SOFTWARE is delivered all be free from defects in materials and workmanship under normal use for a period of thirty (30) days)m the date of your purchase. Your only remedy and the Company's only obligation under these limited rranties is, at the Company's option, return of the warranted item for a refund of any amounts paid by you replacement of the item. Any replacement of SOFTWARE or media under the warranties shall not extend e original warranty period. The limited warranty set forth above shall not apply to any SOFTWARE which e Company determines in good faith has been subject to misuse, neglect, improper installation, repair, teration, or damage by you. EXCEPT FOR THE EXPRESSED WARRANTIES SET FORTH ABOVE, HE COMPANY DISCLAIMS ALL WARRANTIES, EXPRESS OR IMPLIED, INCLUDING WITHOUT IMITATION, THE IMPLIED WARRANTIES OF MERCHANTABILITY AND FITNESS FOR A PAR-ICULAR PURPOSE. EXCEPT FOR THE EXPRESS WARRANTY SET FORTH ABOVE, THE COM-NY DOES NOT WARRANT, GUARANTEE, OR MAKE ANY REPRESENTATION REGARDING HE USE OR THE RESULTS OF THE USE OF THE SOFTWARE IN TERMS OF ITS CORRECTNESS, CCURACY, RELIABILITY, CURRENTNESS, OR OTHERWISE.

IN NO EVENT, SHALL THE COMPANY OR ITS EMPLOYEES, AGENTS, SUPPLIERS, OR ONTRACTORS BE LIABLE FOR ANY INCIDENTAL, INDIRECT, SPECIAL, OR CONSEQUEN-IAL DAMAGES ARISING OUT OF OR IN CONNECTION WITH THE LICENSE GRANTED UNDER HIS AGREEMENT, OR FOR LOSS OF USE, LOSS OF DATA, LOSS OF INCOME OR PROFIT, OR THER LOSSES, SUSTAINED AS A RESULT OF INJURY TO ANY PERSON, OR LOSS OF OR DAM-GE TO PROPERTY, OR CLAIMS OF THIRD PARTIES, EVEN IF THE COMPANY OR AN AUTHO-IZED REPRESENTATIVE OF THE COMPANY HAS BEEN ADVISED OF THE POSSIBILITY OF UCH DAMAGES. IN NO EVENT SHALL LIABILITY OF THE COMPANY FOR DAMAGES WITH ESPECT TO THE SOFTWARE EXCEED THE AMOUNTS ACTUALLY PAID BY YOU, IF ANY, FOR HE SOFTWARE.

SOME JURISDICTIONS DO NOT ALLOW THE LIMITATION OF IMPLIED WARRAN-TIES OR LIABILITY FOR INCIDENTAL, INDIRECT, SPECIAL, OR CONSEQUENTIAL DAMAGES, O THE ABOVE LIMITATIONS MAY NOT ALWAYS APPLY. THE WARRANTIES IN THIS AGREE-MENT GIVE YOU SPECIFIC LEGAL RIGHTS AND YOU MAY ALSO HAVE OTHER RIGHTS WHICH VARY IN ACCORDANCE WITH LOCAL LAW.

ACKNOWLEDGMENT

YOU ACKNOWLEDGE THAT YOU HAVE READ THIS AGREEMENT, UNDERSTAND IT, AND AGREE TO BE BOUND BY ITS TERMS AND CONDITIONS. YOU ALSO AGREE THAT THIS AGREEMENT IS THE COMPLETE AND EXCLUSIVE STATEMENT OF THE AGREEMENT BETWEEN YOU AND THE COMPANY AND SUPERSEDES ALL PROPOSALS OR PRIOR AGREE-MENTS, ORAL, OR WRITTEN, AND ANY OTHER COMMUNICATIONS BETWEEN YOU AND THE COMPANY OR ANY REPRESENTATIVE OF THE COMPANY RELATING TO THE SUBJECT MAT-TER OF THIS AGREEMENT.

Should you have any questions concerning this Agreement or if you wish to contact the Company for any reason, please contact in writing at the address below.

Robin Short
Prentice Hall PTR
One Lake Street
Upper Saddle River, New Jersey 07458

About the CD-ROM

There are two CD-ROMs included with this book. The CD-ROMs can be viewed on the platforms listed on the CD-ROM labels.

To load one of the applications on a CD-ROM, you would simply traverse the hierarchy of the desired application, select the platform on which you wish to load the application, and then perform the installation process.

Many of the applications, such as those from Hummingbird, come with a manual set on-line. You can review the manuals to get an understanding of the products and read the installation instructions as well.

If, for instance, you are interested in loading the Exceed product from Hummingbird, I would recommend you do the following.

1) Place CD-ROM number 2 in your CD-ROM drive.

2) Traverse the hierarcy to get to the Exceed manual set. On my Windows NT system the Explorer path to the manual is the following.

```
L:\poniatowski\hummbird\Exceed\Nt_intel\Manuals\Gsexeed
```

3) Selecting this path displays the manual for Exceed for Windows, Windows NT, and Windows 95. Included in this document are the complete installation and uninstallation instructions for the Exceed product. Follow these instructions for a smooth installation of Exceed.

All of the directories on this CD-ROM are equally easy to use. By identifying the documentation included in each directory you can easily view and load files on your system.

Many of the files on the CD-ROM require a viewer. These are fully formatted files such as manuals and marketing material. You can load the acrobat viewer by going to the acrobat directory on the CD-ROM and selecting the platform on which you wish to load the viewer. The viewer is on the CD-ROM for several platforms including HP-UX. If you should experience any difficulties installing a viewer from the CD-ROM, the files are also downloadable from the Web at: http://www.adobe.com